Commentary
on
ROMANS

Commentary
on
ROMANS

by

ERNST KÄSEMANN

Translated and edited by
Geoffrey W. Bromiley

WILLIAM B. EERDMANS PUBLISHING COMPANY
GRAND RAPIDS, MICHIGAN

Copyright © 1980 by Wm. B. Eerdmans Publishing Co.
255 Jefferson Ave., SE, Grand Rapids, Mich. 49503
All rights reserved
Printed in the United States of America

Reprinted, March 1982

Translated from the fourth German edition of *An Die Römer*, © Ernst Käsemann,
J. C. B. Mohr (Paul Siebeck) Tübingen 1980.

The Publishers wish to thank Duane Priebe for his assistance in editing this translation.

Library of Congress Cataloging in Publication Data

Käsemann, Ernst.
Commentary on Romans.

Commentary with text of Paul's epistle to the Romans.
Translation of An die Römer.
1. Bible. N.T. Romans—Commentaries.
I. Bromiley, Geoffrey William. II. Bible.
N.T. Romans. English. 1980. III. Title.
BS2665.3.K3313   277'.1077   79-27866
ISBN 0-8028-3499-X

To
Charles Kingsley and Margaret Barrett
in gratitude for
three decades of constant friendship

Preface

When on the third day of my first semester in May, 1925, full of curiosity, I attended Erik Peterson's lecture on the Epistle to the Romans, the course of my study and in some sense, as befits a theologian, my life was decided. The basic problem was posed. In the following semesters I then listened to the expositions of H. von Soden and R. Bultmann. I then turned successively to the work of K. Barth, A. Schlatter, Luther, and Calvin, studied them critically, and was led by them into interpretation ancient and modern. No literary document has been more important for me. Thus the circle of my theological work closes logically as I now seek to show in my own commentary what the apostle says to me and what is the result of my preoccupation with the towering mountains of scholarly production.

This preliminary observation will perhaps explain why I could not carry out the original assignment: to revise Lietzmann's *Handbuch*. Within the limits of its aim and premises I still regard the work of my predecessor as unsurpassable, but I could not follow his footsteps without denying myself and what for me are present-day realities and needs. His work challenges me to be as brief and yet as scholarly as possible. Beyond that, I must go my own way, even in the translation. Nothing from historical scholarship that seems essential is to be withheld. But the emphasis will lie on what Paul meant theologically. This criterion will decide what must be taken into account in detailed exegesis and what is dispensable to our understanding. Among his readers Lietzmann could presuppose philological and historical knowledge which today is missing. Today, however, new lexicons of several kinds, which are standard tools of exegesis, have largely outdated and broadened the helps he offered, and we may refer to these. To the extent that concepts and connections in the history of religions need not be analyzed afresh, references to them will be given sparingly and only for the sake of illustration. To give readers some idea of the state of research, and to help them to make up their own minds through considering varied and opposing interpretations, I have made lavish use of the literature of the past fifty years. Since no provision was made for footnotes in the *Handbuch*, I have used, not without some misgivings, parentheses in the text, as Lietzmann did, to indicate at least the points of debate. After considerable thought and some experiments, I have decided against the use of the excursus. When an excursus is not merely a survey of material that can be found elsewhere, it necessarily leads to generalizing systematics or becomes a small monograph. I think it best to follow the text step by step until the wider horizon appears of itself, even though this method also has its disadvantages, does not rule out mistakes, and demands strict vigilance from the partner in discussion. Finally, I do not regard myself as competent to deal in a basic way with textual problems as Lietzmann did, and when necessary simply give my personal judgment.

Until I have proof to the contrary I proceed on the assumption that the text has a central concern and a remarkable inner logic that may no longer be entirely comprehensible to us. Hence the major sections of the epistle are not only marked off from one another but are also broken down again into relatively complete sections, at the head of which I give lists of the relevant literature available to me. If these bibliographies are at all complete, I owe this to all my former assistants at Tübingen, who have kept up with the flood of publications and directed them to me. My work has thus been shaped by two concerns. As I have sought for systematic clarity in general, so the many details and the information are meant to make critical testing possible and to stimulate open discussion. Only thus will it be seen whether the whole is correct or at least leads to fruitful antitheses. In true theology there is no place for global judgments, and concreteness is always required. Awareness of the provisional nature of the solutions offered at any time and expected from theology does not release it from, but obligates it to, unceasing labor. Each of its statements is to be thought through by the reader either in assent or rejection, and it thus remains a question instead of lulling to sleep or granting secure possession. The impatient, who are concerned only about results or practical application, should leave their hands off exegesis. They are of no value for it, nor, when rightly done, is exegesis of any value for them.

In the third edition, which became necessary after only one year, I tried to make my expressions more precise, to continue my interaction with the literature, and to correct numerous mistakes. Since 1974 the discussion of the Epistle to the Romans has become so intensive and enriched in such an interesting way, especially through significant new commentaries, that this fourth edition would seem to require a thorough revision. The state of research is no longer fully evident from my references, but a further expansion of the data within the text, which already are an inconvenience for reading, is not possible. In fact, reducing them to a minimum appears appropriate, and this would make room for presentation of pertinent new material. Unfortunately I have neither time nor energy for that. I can only correct some untenable assertions and typographical errors, with the continuing help of friends and students. Having arrived at the limits set for me, I accept the provisional nature of my own thought and deeds, and willingly leave the way clear for others.

Tübingen, 15 December 1979   ERNST KÄSEMANN

Contents

CONTENTS

Commentaries

(cited at the respective passage only by author's name)

P. Althaus, *Der Brief an die Römer* (Das Neue Testament Deutsch, VI; 10th ed. 1966)

H. Asmussen, *Der Römerbrief* (1952)

O. Bardenhewer, *Der Römerbrief des Heiligen Paulus* (1926)

C. K. Barrett, *A Commentary on the Epistle to the Romans* (HNTC; 1957)

K. Barth, *The Epistle to the Romans* (Eng. tr. 1933)

R. Baulès, *L'Évangile Puissance de Dieu* (Lectio Divina 53; 1968)

J. A. Bengel, *Gnomon Novi Testamenti* (Ed. III, 1773, ed. P. Steudel; 8th ed. 1915)

E. Best, *The Letter of Paul to the Romans* (The Cambridge Bible Commentary; 1967)

P. Billerbeck, *Kommentar zum Neuen Testament aus Talmud und Midrasch*, III (1926)

F. F. Bruce, *The Epistle of Paul to the Romans* (5th ed. 1969)

E. Brunner, *The Letter to the Romans* (Eng. tr. 1959)

J. Calvin, *In omnes Novi Testamenti Epistolas Commentarii*, I (ed. A. Tholuck, 2nd ed. 1834; Corpus Reformatorum 77, 1892)

C. H. Dodd, *The Epistle of Paul to the Romans* (MNTC; 8th ed. 1941)

H. Franzmann, *Romans* (Concordia Commentary; 1968)

E. Gaugler, *Der Römerbrief* (Prophezei) (2 vols., 1945-52)

F. S. Gutjahr, *Der Brief an die Römer* (2 vols., 1923-27)

J. Huby, *Saint Paul, Épître aux Romains* (Verbum Salutis, X; 2nd ed. by S. Lyonnet; 1957)

A. Jülicher, *Der Brief an die Römer* (Die Schriften des Neuen Testamentes 2; 3rd ed. 1917)

K. E. Kirk, *The Epistle to the Romans* (The Clarendon Bible; 1955)

J. Knox, in *The Interpreter's Bible*, IX (1954)

E. Kühl, *Der Brief des Paulus an die Römer* (1913)

O. Kuss, *Der Römerbrief* (unfinished; 2 vols.; 1957-59)

M. J. Lagrange, *Saint Paul, Épître aux Romains* (Études bibliques; 6th ed. 1950)

F. J. Leenhardt, *L'Épître de St. Paul aux Romains* (Commentaires du Nouveau Testament 6; 1957; Eng. tr. *The Epistle to the Romans: A Commentary*, 1961)

H. Lietzmann, *An die Römer* (HNT, VIII; 4th ed. 1933)

COMMENTARIES

M. Luther, *Vorlesung über den Römerbrief* 1515/1516 (ed. J. Ficker, *Anfänge reformatorischer Bibelauslegung,* I, 3rd ed. 1925; German translation by E. Ellwein, 4th ed. 1957; Eng. tr. *Luther's Works,* XXV, 1972)

O. Michel, *Der Brief an die Römer* (Kritisch-exegetischer Kommentar über das Neue Testament, Neubearbeitung; 4th ed. 1966)

H. C. G. Moule, *The Epistle to the Romans* (1893; 2nd ed. n.d.)

J. Murray, *The Epistle to the Romans* (The New International Commentary on the New Testament; 2 vols., 1959-65; repr. 1973)

A. Nygren, *Commentary on Romans* (Eng. tr. 1949)

A. Pallis, *To the Romans* (1920)

H. Ridderbos, *Aan de Romeinen* (Commentaar op het Nieuwe Testament; 1959)

W. Sanday and A. C. Headlam, *The Epistle to the Romans* (The International Critical Commentary; 5th ed. 1902, repr. 1962)

K. H. Schelkle, *Paulus, Lehrer der Väter. Die altkirchliche Auslegung von Röm 1–11* (1956)

A. Schlatter, *Gottes Gerechtigkeit* (1935; 2nd ed. 1952)

H. W. Schmidt, *Der Brief des Paulus an die Römer* (Theologischer Handkommentar zum Neuen Testament, VI; 1963)

J. Sickenberger, *Die Briefe des Heiligen Paulus an die Korinther und Römer* (Die Heiligen Schriften des Neuen Testaments, ed. F. Tillmann, VI; 4th ed. 1932)

V. Taylor, *The Epistle to the Romans* (Epworth Preacher's Commentaries; 1955)

T. Zahn, *Der Brief des Paulus an die Römer* (1910; 3rd ed. 1925)

Short Titles of Literature Cited Frequently

Amiot, *Key Concepts*
    F. Amiot, *The Key Concepts of St. Paul* (Eng. tr. 1962)
Asting, *Verkündigung*
    R. Asting, *Die Verkündigung des Wortes im Urchristentum* (1939)
Balz, *Heilsvertrauen*
    H. R. Balz, *Heilsvertrauen und Welterfahrung. Strukturen der paulinischen Eschatologie nach Römer 8,18-39* (1971)
Barrett, *First Adam*
    C. K. Barrett, *From First Adam to Last* (1962)
K. A. Bauer, *Leiblichkeit*
    K. A. Bauer, *Leiblichkeit, das Ende aller Werke Gottes* (SNT 4; 1971)
F. C. Baur, *Paul*
    F. C. Baur, *Paul, the Apostle of Jesus Christ: His Life and Works, His Epistles and Teachings* (2nd ed., Eng. tr. 1876)
Becker, *Heil Gottes*
    J. Becker, *Das Heil Gottes. Heils- und Sündenbegriffe in den Qumrantexten und im Neuen Testament* (SUNT 3; 1964)
Benoit, *Exégèse*
    P. Benoit, *Exégèse et Théologie* (2 vols.; 1961)
Berger, "Abraham"
    K. Berger, "Abraham in den paulinischen Hauptbriefen," *MTZ* 17 (1966) 47-89
Beyschlag, *Theodicee*
    W. Beyschlag, *Die paulinische Theodicee, Römer IX-XI. Ein Beitrag zur biblischen Theologie* (1868)
Bjerkelund, *Parakalô*
    C. J. Bjerkelund, *Parakalô. Form, Funktion und Sinn der parakalô-Sätze in den paulinischen Briefen* (1967)
Blank, *Paulus*
    J. Blank, *Paulus und Jesus; eine theologische Grundlegung* (SANT 18; 1968)
Bläser, *Gesetz*
    P. Bläser, *Das Gesetz bei Paulus* (NTAbh 19/1-2; 1941)
Bonsirven, *Exégèse*
    J. Bonsirven, *Exégèse rabbinique et exégèse Paulinienne* (1939)
Bornkamm, *Early Christian Experience*
    G. Bornkamm, *Early Christian Experience* (1969; Eng. tr. of articles from *Das Ende des Gesetzes* [5th ed. 1966])

Bornkamm, *Ende des Gesetzes*
  G. Bornkamm, *Das Ende des Gesetzes. Gesammelte Aufsätze* (1952)
Bornkamm, *Geschichte und Glaube,* II
  G. Bornkamm, *Geschichte und Glaube II. Gesammelte Aufsätze IV* (1971)
Bornkamm, *Paul*
  G. Bornkamm, *Paul* (Eng. tr. 1971)
Bornkamm, *Studien*
  G. Bornkamm, *Studien zu Antike und Christentum. Gesammelte Aufsätze II* (2nd ed. 1963)
Bousset, *Kyrios Christos*
  W. Bousset, *Kyrios Christos* (Eng. tr. 1970)
Bousset-Gressmann, *Religion*
  W. Bousset and H. Gressmann, *Die Religion des Judentums im späthellenistischen Zeitalter* (HNT 21; 4th ed. 1966)
Bouttier, *En Christ*
  M. Bouttier, *En Christ. Étude d'exégèse et de théologie Pauliniennes* (1962)
Brandenburger, *Adam*
  E. Brandenburger, *Adam und Christus. Exegetisch-religionsgeschichtliche Untersuchung zu Röm. 5:12-21 (1. Kor. 15)* (WMANT 7; 1962)
Brandenburger, *Fleisch*
  E. Brandenburger, *Fleisch und Geist* (WMANT 29; 1968)
Braun, *Gerichtsgedanke*
  H. Braun, *Gerichtsgedanke und Rechtfertigungslehre bei Paulus* (UNT 19; 1930)
Braun, *Gesammelte Studien*
  H. Braun, *Gesammelte Studien zum Neuen Testament und seiner Umwelt* (2nd ed. 1967)
Braun, *Qumran*
  H. Braun, *Qumran und das Neue Testament* (2 vols.; 1966)
Bultmann, "Glossen"
  R. Bultmann, "Glossen im Römerbrief," *TLZ* 72 (1947) 197-202
Bultman, *History and Eschatology*
  R. Bultmann, *The Presence of Eternity: History and Eschatology* (1957)
Bultmann, *Stil*
  R. Bultmann, *Der Stil der paulinischen Predigt und die kynisch-stoische Diatribe* (FRLANT 13; 1910)
Bultmann, *Theology*
  R. Bultmann, *Theology of the New Testament* (2 vols.; Eng. tr. 1951)
Cambier, *L'Évangile*
  J. Cambier, *L'Évangile de Dieu selon l'Épître aux Romains* (Vol. I; 1967)
Cerfaux, *Christ*
  L. Cerfaux, *Christ in the Theology of St. Paul* (Eng. tr. 1959)
Cerfaux, *Christian*
  L. Cerfaux, *The Christian in the Theology of St. Paul* (Eng. tr. 1967)
Cerfaux, *Church*
  L. Cerfaux, *The Church in the Theology of St. Paul* (Eng. tr. 2nd ed. 1959)
Champion, "Benedictions"
  L. G. Champion, "Benedictions and Doxologies in the Epistles of Paul" (Dissertation, Heidelberg, 1934)

Conzelmann, *Outline*
  H. Conzelmann, *An Outline of the Theology of the New Testament* (Eng. tr. 1969)
Cranfield, *Commentary*
  C. E. B. Cranfield, *A Commentary on Romans 12–13* (SJT Occasional Papers 12; 1965)
Cranfield, "Law"
  C. E. B. Cranfield, "St. Paul and the Law," *New Testament Issues* (ed. R. A. Batey; 1970) 148-172
Cullmann, *Christology*
  O. Cullmann, *The Christology of the New Testament* (Eng. tr. 2nd ed. 1963)
Cullmann, *Salvation*
  O. Cullmann, *Salvation in History* (Eng. tr. 1967)
Dahl, *Volk Gottes*
  N. A. Dahl, *Das Volk Gottes. Eine Untersuchung zum Kirchenbewusstsein des Urchristentums* (1941; reprint 1963)
Daube, *Rabbinic Judaism*
  D. Daube, *The New Testament and Rabbinic Judaism* (1956)
Davies, "Paul"
  W. D. Davies, "Paul and the Dead Sea Scrolls: Flesh and Spirit," *The Scrolls and the New Testament* (ed. K. Stendahl; 1957) 157-182
Davies, *Rabbinic Judaism*
  W. D. Davies, *Paul and Rabbinic Judaism: Some Rabbinic Elements in Pauline Theology* (2nd ed. 1955)
Deichgräber, *Gotteshymnus*
  R. Deichgräber, *Gotteshymnus und Christushymnus in der frühen Christenheit. Untersuchungen zur Form, Sprache und Stil der frühchristlichen Hymnen* (SUNT 5; 1967)
Deissmann, *Light*
  A. Deissmann, *Light from the Ancient East* (Eng. tr. 2nd ed. 1927)
Deissmann, *Paul*
  A. Deissmann, *Paul: A Study in Social and Religious History* (Eng. tr. 2nd ed. 1927)
Delling, "Paulusverständnis"
  G. Delling, "Zum neueren Paulusverständnis," *NovT* 4 (1960) 95-121
Delling, *Worship*
  G. Delling, *Worship in the New Testament* (Eng. tr. 1962)
Dibelius, "Vier Worte"
  M. Dibelius, "Vier Worte des Römerbriefs, 5,5; 5,12; 8,10; 11,30s," *Symbolae biblicae upsalienses* 3 (1944) 3-17
Dodd, *Gospel*
  C. H. Dodd, *Gospel and Law; The Relation of Faith and Ethics in Early Christianity* (1951)
Dodd, *Meaning*
  C. H. Dodd, *The Meaning of Paul for Today* (1958)
Duchrow, *Weltverantwortung*
  U. Duchrow, *Christenheit und Weltverantwortung. Traditionsgeschichte und systematische Struktur der Zweireichlehre* (1970)
van Dülmen, *Theologie*
  A. van Dülmen, *Die Theologie des Gesetzes bei Paulus* (Stuttgarter biblische Monographien 5; 1968)

xvii

Dupont, *Gnosis*
    J. Dupont, *Gnosis, La connaissance religieuse dans les épîtres de Saint Paul* (1949)
Dupont, "Structure"
    J. Dupont, "Le Problème de la structure littéraire de l'épître aux Romains," *RB* 62 (1955) 365-397
Eichholz, *Paulus*
    G. Eichholz, *Die Theologie des Paulus im Umriss* (1972)
Ellis, *Use*
    E. E. Ellis, *Paul's Use of the Old Testament* (1957)
Eltester, *Eikon*
    F. W. Eltester, *Eikon im Neuen Testament* (BZNW 23; 1958)
Enslin, *Ethics*
    M. S. Enslin, *The Ethics of Paul* (2nd ed. 1962)
Fascher, Προφήτης
    E. Fascher, Προφήτης, *eine sprach- und religionsgeschichtliche Untersuchung* (1927)
Feuillet, "Citation"
    A. Feuillet, "La citation d'Habacuc ii 4 et les huit premiers Chapîtres de l'Épître aux Romains," *NTS* 6 (1959/60) 52-80
Filson, *Recompense*
    F. V. Filson, *St. Paul's Conception of Recompense* (1931)
Fuchs, *Freiheit*
    E. Fuchs, *Die Freiheit des Glaubens. Römer 5-8 ausgelegt* (BEvT 14; 1949)
Fuchs, *Natural Law*
    J. Fuchs, *Natural Law, A Theological Investigation* (Eng. tr. 1965)
Furnish, *Ethics*
    V. P. Furnish, *Theology and Ethics in Paul* (1968)
Gale, *Analogy*
    H. M. Gale, *The Use of Analogy in the Letters of Paul* (1964)
Galley, *Heilsgeschehen*
    K. Galley, *Altes und neues Heilsgeschehen bei Paulus* (1965)
Gäumann, *Ethik*
    N. Gäumann, *Taufe und Ethik. Studien zu Römer 6* (BEvT 47; 1967)
Gibbs, *Creation*
    J. G. Gibbs, *Creation and Redemption* (1971)
Goppelt, *Christentum*
    L. Goppelt, *Christentum und Judentum im ersten und zweiten Jahrhundert. Ein Aufriss der Urgeschichte der Kirche* (1954)
Goppelt, *Typos*
    L. Goppelt, *Typos* (1939; reprint 1966)
Grabner-Haider, *Paraklese*
    A. Grabner-Haider, *Paraklese und Eschatologie bei Paulus* (NTAbh N.F. 4; 1968)
Greeven, *Gebet*
    H. Greeven, *Gebet und Eschatologie in Neuen Testament* (NTF 3/1; 1931)
Grundmann, *Kraft*
    W. Grundmann, *Der Begriff der Kraft in der neutestamentlichen Gedankenwelt* (BWANT 60; 1932)

Gunkel, *Wirkungen*

    H. Gunkel, *Die Wirkungen des heiligen Geistes, nach der populären Anschauung der apostolischen Zeit und nach der Lehre des Apostels Paulus* (1888)

Hahn, *Titles of Jesus*

    F. Hahn, *The Titles of Jesus in Christology: Their History in Early Christianity* (Eng. tr. 1969)

Hanson, *Unity*

    S. Hanson, *The Unity of the Church in the New Testament: Colossians and Ephesians* (1946; reprint 1963)

Harder, *Gebet*

    G. Harder, *Paulus und das Gebet* (1936)

Harnisch, *Verhängnis*

    W. Harnisch, *Verhängnis und Verheissung der Geschichte* (FRLANT 97; 1969)

Hegermann, *Schöpfungsmittler*

    H. Hegermann, *Die Vorstellung vom Schöpfungsmittler im hellenistischen Judentum und Urchristentum* (TU 82; 1961)

Heidland, *Anrechnung*

    H.-W. Heidland, *Die Anrechnung des Glaubens zur Gerechtigkeit. Untersuchungen zur Begriffsgeschichte von* חשב *und* λογίζεσθαι (BWANT 71; 1936)

Hengel, *Judaism*

    M. Hengel, *Judaism and Hellenism: Studies in their Encounter in Palestine During the Early Hellenistic Period* (Eng. tr. 1974)

Hommel, *Schöpfer*

    H. Hommel, *Schöpfer und Erhalter. Studien zum Problem Christentum und Antike* (1956)

Hoppe, *Heilsgeschichte*

    T. Hoppe, *Die Idee der Heilsgeschichte bei Paulus mit besonderer Berücksichtigung des Römerbriefes* (BFCT I.30.2; 1926)

Jeremias, *Abba*

    J. Jeremias, *Abba. Studien zur neutestamentlichen Theologie und Zeitgeschichte* (1966)

G. Jeremias, *Lehrer*

    G. Jeremias, *Der Lehrer der Gerechtigkeit* (SUNT 2; 1963)

Jervell, *Imago*

    J. Jervell, *Imago Dei. Gen. 1,26f. im Spätjudentum, in der Gnosis und in den paulinischen Briefen* (FRLANT 76; 1960)

Joest, *Gesetz und Freiheit*

    W. Joest, *Gesetz und Freiheit. Das Problem des Tertius usus legis bei Luther und die neutestamentliche (Parainese* (1951, 3rd ed. 1961)

Jülicher, *Introduction*

    A. Jülicher, *An Introduction to the New Testament* (Eng. tr. 1904)

Jüngel, *Paulus und Jesus*

    E. Jüngel, *Paulus und Jesus* (1962)

Käsemann, *Essays*

    E. Käsemann, *Essays on New Testament Themes* (SBT 41; 1964 Eng. tr. of articles from *Exegetische Versuche und Besinnungen*, I [2nd ed. 1960])

Käsemann, *New Testament Questions*

    E. Käsemann, *New Testament Questions for Today* (1969 Eng. tr. of articles from *Exegetische Versuche und Besinnungen*, II [2nd ed. 1965])

Käsemann, *Perspectives*
    E. Käsemann, *Perspectives on Paul* (Eng. tr. 1971)
Kertelge, *Rechtfertigung*
    K. Kertelge, *Rechtfertigung bei Paulus. Studien zur Struktur und zum Bedeutungsgehalt des paulinischen Rechtfertigungsbegriffs* (NTAbh N.F. 3; 1967)
H. Kittel, *Herrlichkeit Gottes*
    H. Kittel, *Die Herrlichkeit Gottes. Studien zu Geschichte und Wesen eines neutestamentlichen Begriffs* (BZNW 16; 1934)
Klein, *Rekonstruktion*
    G. Klein, *Rekonstruktion und Interpretation. Gesammelte Aufsätze zum Neuen Testament* (BEvT 50; 1969)
Klein, *Zwölf Apostel*
    G. Klein, *Die zwölf Apostel. Ursprung und Gehalt einer Idee* (FRLANT 77; 1961)
J. Knox, *Life*
    J. Knox, *Life in Christ Jesus; Reflections on Romans 5–8* (1961)
W. L. Knox, *Church*
    W. L. Knox, *St. Paul and the Church of the Gentiles* (2nd ed. 1961)
Kramer, *Christ*
    W. R. Kramer, *Christ, Lord, Son of God* (Eng. tr. 1966)
Kuhn, "πειρασμός"
    K. G. Kuhn, "πειρασμός–ἁμαρτία–σάρξ im Neuen Testament und die damit zusammenhängenden Vorstellungen," *ZTK* 49 (1952) 200-222
Kümmel, *Introduction*
    W. G. Kümmel, *Introduction to the New Testament* (Eng. tr. 2nd ed. 1975)
Kümmel, *Man*
    W. G. Kümmel, *Man in the New Testament* (Eng. tr. 1963)
Kümmel, *Theology*
    W. G. Kümmel, *The Theology of the New Testament* (Eng. tr. 1973)
Kuss, *Auslegung, I*
    O. Kuss, *Auslegung und Verkündigung,* I (1963)
Kuss, *Paulus*
    O. Kuss, *Paulus. Die Rolle des Apostels in der theologischen Entwicklung der Urkirche* (1971)
Lackmann, *Geheimnis*
    M. Lackmann, *Vom Geheimnis der Schöpfung* (1952)
Larsson, *Vorbild*
    E. Larsson, *Christus als Vorbild* (ASNU 23; 1962)
Ligier, *Péché*
    L. Ligier, *Péché d'Adam et Péché du Monde,* II (1961)
Limbeck, *Ordnung*
    M. Limbeck, *Die Ordnung des Heils. Untersuchungen zum Gesetzesverständnis des Frühjudentums* (1971)
Ljungman, *Pistis*
    H. Ljungman, *Pistis; A Study of its Presuppositions and its Meaning in Pauline Use* (Eng. tr. 1964)
Lohse, *Einheit*
    E. Lohse, *Die Einheit des Neuen Testaments. Exegetische Studien zur Theologie des Neuen Testaments* (1973)

Lüdemann, *Anthropologie*
    H. Lüdemann, *Die Anthropologie des Apostels Paulus und ihre Stellung innerhalb seiner Heilslehre* (1872)
Lütgert, *Römerbrief*
    W. Lütgert, *Der Römerbrief als historisches Problem* (BFCT 17/2; 1913)
Luz, "Aufbau"
    U. Luz, "Zum Aufbau von Röm 1–8," *TZ* 25 (1969) 161-181
Luz, *Geschichtsverständnis*
    U. Luz, *Das Geschichtsverständnis des Paulus* (BEvT 49; 1968)
Lyonnet, *Étapes*
    S. Lyonnet, *Les Étapes de l'histoire du Salut selon l'épître aux Romains* (1969)
Lyonnet, *Quaestiones*
    S. Lyonnet, *Quaestiones in Epistolam ad Romanos* (2 vols.; 1955-56)
Maier, *Israel*
    F. W. Maier, *Israel in der Heilsgeschichte nach Römer 9–11* (Biblische Zeitfragen 12/11-12; 1929)
Manson, *Studies*
    T. W. Manson, *Studies in the Gospels and Epistles* (ed. M. Black; 1962)
Marxsen, *Introduction*
    W. Marxsen, *Introduction to the New Testament* (Eng. tr. 1968)
Mattern, *Gericht*
    L. Mattern, *Das Verständnis des Gerichtes bei Paulus* (ATANT 47; 1966)
Maurer, *Gesetzeslehre*
    C. Maurer, *Die Gesetzeslehre des Paulus nach ihrem Ursprung und in ihrer Entfaltung dargelegt* (1941)
Mauser, *Gottesbild*
    U. Mauser, *Gottesbild und Menschenwerdung. Eine Untersuchung zur Einheit des Alten und Neuen Testaments* (BHT 43; 1971)
Merk, *Handeln*
    O. Merk, *Handeln aus Glauben. Die Motivierungen der Paulinischen Ethik* (Marburger theologische Studien 5; 1968)
Meuzelaar, *Leib*
    J. J. Meuzelaar, *Der Leib des Messias* (1961)
Michaelis, *Einleitung*
    W. Michaelis, *Einleitung in das Neue Testament* (2nd ed. 1954)
Michaelis, *Versöhnung*
    W. Michaelis, *Versöhnung des Alls. Die frohe Botschaft von der Gnade Gottes* (1950)
Michel, *Bibel*
    O. Michel, *Paulus und seine Bibel* (BFCT 2/18; 1929; reprint 1972)
Minear, *Images*
    P. S. Minear, *Images of the Church in the New Testament* (1960)
Minear, *Obedience*
    P. S. Minear, *The Obedience of Faith. The Purposes of Paul in the Epistle to the Romans* (SBT 2/19; 1971)
Molland, *Euangelion*
    E. Molland, *Das paulinische Euangelion. Das Wort und die Sache* (1934)
Moltmann, *Hope*
    J. Moltmann, *Theology of Hope* (Eng. tr. 1967)

Moore, *Judaism*
    G. F. Moore, *Judaism in the First Centuries of the Christian Era* (vols. I-II, 6th ed. 1950; vol. III, 3rd ed. 1948)
C. Müller, *Gottes Volk*
    C. Müller, *Gottes Gerechtigkeit und Gottes Volk. Eine Untersuchung zu Römer 9–11* (FRLANT 86; 1964)
H. Müller, "Auslegung"
    "Die Auslegung alttestamentlichen Geschichtsstoffes bei Paulus" (Dissertation, Halle, 1960)
Munck, *Christ*
    J. Munck, *Christ and Israel: An Interpretation of Romans 9–11* (Eng. tr. 1967)
Munck, *Salvation*
    J. Munck, *Paul and the Salvation of Mankind* (Eng. tr. 1959)
Mundle, *Glaubensbegriff*
    W. Mundle, *Der Glaubensbegriff des Paulus* (1932)
Nababan, "Bekenntnis"
    A. E. S. Nababan, "Bekenntnis und Mission in Römer 14 und 15" (Dissertation, Heidelberg, 1963)
Neugebauer, *In Christus*
    F. Neugebauer, *In Christus. EN ΧΡΙΣΤΩΙ. Eine Untersuchung zum paulinischen Glaubensverständnis* (1961)
Niederwimmer, *Freiheit*
    K. Niederwimmer, *Der Begriff der Freiheit im Neuen Testament* (1966)
Nielen, *Gebet*
    J. M. Nielen, *Gebet und Gottesdienst im Neuen Testament* (1937)
Norden, *Agnostos Theos*
    E. Norden, *Agnostos Theos. Untersuchung zur Formengeschichte religiöser Rede* (4th ed. 1956)
NT Essays, Manson
    New Testament Essays: Studies in Memory of Thomas Walter Manson, 1893-1958 (ed. A. J. B. Higgins; 1959)
Oepke, *Gottesvolk*
    A. Oepke, *Das neue Gottesvolk in Schrifttum, Schauspiel, bildender Kunst und Weltgestaltung* (1950)
Paulsen, *Überlieferung*
    H. Paulsen, *Überlieferung und Auslegung in Römer 8* (WMANT 43; 1974)
Peterson, "Kirche"
    E. Peterson, "Die Kirche aus Juden und Heiden," *Theologische Traktate* (1951) 239-292; previously published as *Die Kirche aus Juden und Heiden* (1933), 72 pages.
Pfister, *Leben*
    W. Pfister, *Das Leben im Geist nach Paulus* (1963)
Plag, *Wege*
    C. Plag, *Israels Wege zum Heil. Eine Untersuchung zu Römer 9 bis 11* (1969)
Prat, *Theology*
    F. Prat, *The Theology of St. Paul* (2 vols.; Eng. tr. 1933-34)
Rauer, *Schwachen*
    M. Rauer, *Die Schwachen in Korinth und Rom* (Biblische Studien [Freiburg] 21; 1923)
Richardson, *Theology*
    A. Richardson, *An Introduction to the Theology of the New Testament* (1958)

Richter, *Untersuchungen*
    G. Richter, *Kritisch-polemische Untersuchungen über den Römerbrief* (BFCT 12/6; 1908)
Ridderbos, *Paul*
    H. Ridderbos, *Paul: An Outline of His Theology* (Eng. tr. 1975)
Robinson, *Body*
    J. A. T. Robinson, *The Body: A Study in Pauline Theology* (SBT 5; 1952)
Roetzel, *Judgement*
    C. J. Roetzel, *Judgement in the Community* (1972)
Roller, *Formular*
    O. Roller, *Das Formular der paulinischen Briefe. Ein Beitrag zur Lehre vom antiken Briefe* (1933)
Roloff, *Apostolat*
    J. Roloff, *Apostolat–Verkündigung–Kirche* (1965)
Romans Debate
    The Romans Debate (ed. K. P. Donfried; 1977)
Rössler, *Gesetz*
    D. Rössler, *Gesetz und Geschichte, Untersuchungen zur Theologie der jüdischen Apokalyptik und der pharisäischen Orthodoxie* (WMANT 3; 1960)
Sand, *Fleisch*
    A. Sand, *Der Begriff „Fleisch" in den paulinischen Hauptbriefen* (1967)
Sass, *Apostelamt*
    G. Sass, *Apostelamt und Kirche* (1939)
Schlatter, *Glaube*
    A. Schlatter, *Der Glaube im Neuen Testament* (4th ed. 1927)
Schlatter, *Theologie*
    A. Schlatter, *Die Theologie der Apostel* (2nd ed. 1922)
Schlier, *Die Zeit der Kirche*
    H. Schlier, *Die Zeit der Kirche. Exegetische Aufsätze und Vorträge* (2nd ed. 1958)
Schmithals, *Office of Apostle*
    W. Schmithals, *The Office of Apostle in the Early Church* (Eng. tr. 1969)
K. L. Schmidt, *Judenfrage*
    K. L. Schmidt, *Die Judenfrage im Lichte der Kapitel 9–11 des Römerbriefes* (Theologische Studien 13; 2nd ed. 1947)
O. Schmitz, *Christusgemeinschaft*
    O. Schmitz, *Die Christusgemeinschaft des Paulus im Lichte seines Genetivgebrauchs* (NTF 1/2; 1924)
Schnackenburg, *Baptism*
    R. Schnackenburg, *Baptism in the Thought of St. Paul: A Study in Pauline Theology* (Eng. tr. 1964)
Schniewind, *Euangelion*
    J. Schniewind, *Euangelion. Ursprung und erste Gestalt des Begriffs Evangelium* (2 vols.; BFCT 2/13, 25; 1927, 1931; reprint 1970)
Schniewind, *Wort*
    J. Schniewind, *Die Begriffe Wort und Evangelium bei Paulus* (1910)
Schoeps, *Paul*
    H. J. Schoeps, *Paul: The Theology of the Apostle in the Light of Jewish Religious History* (Eng. tr. 1961)
Schrage, *Einzelgebote*
    W. Schrage, *Die konkreten Einzelgebote in der paulinischen Paränese* (1961)

Schrenk, "Missionsdokument"
    G. Schrenk, "Der Römerbrief als Missionsdokument," *Studien zu Paulus* (ATANT 26; 1954) 81-106
Schrenk, *Weissagung*
    G. Schrenk, *Die Weissagung über Israel im Neuen Testament* (1951)
Schulz, "Rechtfertigung"
    S. Schulz, "Zur Rechtfertigung aus Gnade in Qumran und bei Paulus," *ZTK* 56 (1959) 155-185
Schumacher, *Letzte Kapitel*
    R. Schumacher, *Die beiden letzten Kapitel des Römerbriefes. Ein Beitrag zu ihrer Geschichte und Erklärung* (NTAbh 14/4; 1929)
Schunack, *Problem*
    G. Schunack, *Das hermeneutische Problem des Todes im Horizont von Römer 5 untersucht* (1967)
Schwanz, *Imago Dei*
    P. Schwanz, *Imago Dei als christologisch-anthropologisches Problem in der Geschichte der Alten Kirche von Paulus bis Clemens von Alexandrien* (1970)
A. Schweitzer, *Mysticism*
    A. Schweitzer, *The Mysticism of Paul the Apostle* (Eng. tr. 1931)
Schweizer, *Erniedrigung*
    E. Schweizer, *Erniedrigung und Erhöhung bei Jesus und seinen Nachfolgern* (ATANT 28; 2nd [rev.] ed. 1962)
Schweizer, *Lordship*
    E. Schweizer, *Lordship and Discipleship* (SBT 28; 1960 Eng. tr. of 1st German ed. of *Erniedrigung*)
E. Schweizer, "Mystik"
    E. Schweizer, "Die 'Mystik' des Sterbens und Auferstehens mit Christus bei Paulus," *Beiträge zur Theologie. Neutestamentliche Aufsätze, 1955-1970* (1970) 183-203
Schweizer, *Neotestamentica*
    E. Schweizer, *Neotestamentica. Aufsätze* (1963)
Seidensticker, *Opfer*
    P. Seidensticker, *Lebendiges Opfer. Ein Beitrag zur Theologie des Apostels Paulus* (NTAbh 20/1-3; 1954)
Siber, *Mit Christus*
    P. Siber, *Mit Christus leben. Eine Studie zur paulinischen Auferstehungshoffnung* (ATANT 61; 1971)
Smits, *Citaten*
    C. Smits, *Oud-testamentische citaten in het Nieuwe Testament, III: De brieven van Paulus* (Collectanea Franciscana Neerlandica 8/3; 1957)
Spicq, *Agape*
    C. Spicq, *Agape in the New Testament, II* (Eng. tr. 1965)
Stählin, *Skandalon*
    G. Stählin, *Skandalon* (BFCT 2/24; 1930)
Stadler, *Werk*
    K. Stadler, *Das Werk des Geistes in der Heiligung bei Paulus* (1962)
von Stromberg, *Studien*
    A. von Stromberg, *Studien zur Theorie und Praxis der Taufe in der christlichen Kirche der ersten zwei Jahrhunderte* (1913)

Stuhlmacher, *Evangelium*
P. Stuhlmacher, *Das paulinische Evangelium I. Vorgeschichte* (FRLANT 95; 1968)
Stuhlmacher, *Gerechtigkeit*
P. Stuhlmacher, *Gerechtigkeit Gottes bei Paulus* (FRLANT 87; 2nd ed. 1966)
Tachau, *Einst*
P. Tachau, *"Einst" und "Jetzt" im Neuen Testament* (FRLANT 105; 1972)
Tannehill, *Dying*
R. C. Tannehill, *Dying and Rising with Christ: A Study in Pauline Theology* (BZNW 32; 1967)
Taylor, *Forgiveness*
V. Taylor, *Forgiveness and Reconciliation: A Study in New Testament Theology* (1941)
Thüsing, *Per Christum*
W. Thüsing, *Per Christum in Deum. Studien zum Verhältnis von Christozentrik und Theozentrik in den paulinischen Hauptbriefen* (NTAbh N.F. 1; 1965)
Thyen, *Stil*
H. Thyen, *Der Stil der jüdisch-hellenistischen Homilie* (FRLANT 65; 1955)
Thyen, *Studien*
H. Thyen, *Studien zur Sündenvergebung im Neuen Testament und seinen alttestamentlichen und jüdischen Voraussetzungen* (FRLANT 96; 1970)
Ulonska, *Paulus*
H. Ulonska, *Paulus und das Alte Testament* (1964)
Vischer, "Geheimnis"
W. Vischer, "Das Geheimnis Israels. Eine Erklärung der Kapitel 9–11 des Römerbriefes," *Judaica* 6 (1950) 81-132
Vögtle, *Zukunft*
A. Vögtle, *Das Neue Testament und die Zukunft des Kosmos* (1970)
Vollmer, *Zitate*
H. Vollmer, *Die alttestamentlichen Zitate bei Paulus* (1895)
Weber, *Problem*
H. E. Weber, *Das Problem der Heilsgeschichte nach Römer 9–11* (1911)
Wegenast, *Tradition*
K. Wegenast, *Das Verständnis der Tradition bei Paulus und in den Deuteropaulinen* (WMANT 8; 1962)
Weinel, *Paulus*
H. Weinel, *Paulus, der Mensch und sein Werk* (2nd ed. 1915)
Weinel, *St. Paul*
H. Weinel, *St. Paul, The Man and his Work* (1906 Eng. tr. of 1st German ed. of *Paulus*)
Weiss, "Beiträge"
J. Weiss, "Beiträge zur Paulinischen Rhetorik," *Theologische Studien, Herrn Wirkl. Oberkonsistorialrath. Professor D. Bernhard Weiss zu seinen 70. Geburtstag dargebracht* (1897) 165-247
H. F. Weiss, *Untersuchungen*
H. F. Weiss, *Untersuchungen zur Kosmologie des hellenistischen und palästinischen Judentums* (TU 97; 1966)
Wendland, *Ethik*
H.-D. Wendland, *Ethik des Neuen Testaments* (Grundriss zum Neuen Testament 4; 1970)

Wendland, *Mitte*
> H.-D. Wendland, *Die Mitte der paulinischen Botschaft. Die Rechtfertigungslehre des Paulus in Zusammenhang seiner Theologie* (1935)

Wengst, *Formeln*
> K. Wengst, *Christologische Formeln und Lieder des Urchristentums* (SNT 7; 1972)

Wetter, *Charis*
> G. P. Wetter, *Charis. Ein Beitrag zur Geschichte des ältesten Christentums* (UNT 5; 1913)

Wetter, *Vergeltungsgedanke*
> G. P. Wetter, *Der Vergeltungsgedanke bei Paulus. Eine Studie zur Religion des Apostels* (1912)

Windisch, *Judentum*
> H. Windisch, *Paulus und das Judentum* (1935)

Wobbe, *Charis-Gedanke*
> J. Wobbe, *Der Charis-Gedanke bei Paulus* (NTAbh 13/3; 1932)

Wolff, *Jesaja 53*
> H. W. Wolff, *Jesaja 53 im Urchristentum* (3rd ed. 1952)

Wrede, *Paul*
> W. Wrede, *Paul* (Eng. tr. 1907)

Zeller, *Juden*
> D. Zeller, *Juden und Heiden in der Mission des Paulus. Studien zum Römerbrief* (1973)

Ziesler, *Meaning*
> J. A. Ziesler, *The Meaning of Righteousness in Paul* (1972)

Other Important Literature

F. C. Bauer, "Über Zweck und Veranlassung des Römerbriefs und der damit zusammenhängenden Verhältnisse der römischen Gemeinde," *Tübinger Zeitschrift für Theologie* (1836) 59-178

W. A. Beardslee, *Human Achievement and Divine Vocation in the Message of Paul* (1961)

G. Bertram, "Die Himmelfahrt Jesu vom Kreuz aus und der Glaube an seine Auferstehung," *Festgabe für Adolf Deissmann zum 60. Geburtstag 7. November 1926* (1927) 187-217

G. B. Caird, *Principalities and Powers; A Study in Pauline Theology* (1956)

A. Deissmann, *Die neutestamentliche Formel, „in Christo Jesu" untersucht* (1892)

M. Dibelius and W. G. Kümmel, *Paul* (Eng. tr. 1953)

C. H. Dodd, *The Apostolic Preaching and its Developments* (7th ed. 1951)

E. Fuchs, *Christus und der Geist bei Paulus* (UNT 23; 1932)

W. Gutbrod, *Die paulinische Anthropologie* (WMANT 67; 1934)

I. Hermann, *Kyrios und Pneuma. Studien zur Christologie der paulinischen Hauptbriefe* (SANT 2; 1961)

E. Käsemann, *Leib und Leib Christi. Eine Untersuchung zur paulinischen Begrifflichkeit* (BHT 9; 1933)

G. Lindeskog, *Studien zum neutestamentlichen Schöpfungsgedanken* (1952)

E. Lohmeyer, *Grundlagen paulinischer Theologie* (BHT 1; 1929)

A. D. Nock, *St. Paul* (1938)

Paul and Qumran: Studies in New Testament Exegesis (ed. J. Murphy-O'Conner; 1968)

E. Percy, *Der Leib Christi* (Σῶμα Χριστοῦ) *in den paulinischen Homologumena und Antilegomena* (Lunds universitets årsskrift N.F. 1/38/1; 1942)

A. Schweitzer, *Paul and His Interpreters; A Critical History* (Eng. tr. 1912)

A. Wikenhauser, *Die Kirche als der mystische Leib Christi nach dem Apostel Paulus* (2nd ed. 1940)

H. Windisch, *Paulus und Christus. Ein biblisch-religionsgeschichtlicher Vergleich* (UNT 24; 1934)

Abbreviations

Reference Works, Journals, and Series

ASNU	Acta seminarii neotestamentica upsaliensis
ATANT	Abhandlungen zur Theologie des Alten und Neuen Testaments
BAGD	W. Bauer, W. F. Arndt, F. W. Gingrich, and F. W. Danker, *A Greek-English Lexicon of the New Testament* (2nd ed., 1979)
BDF	F. Blass, A. Debrunner, and R. W. Funk, *A Greek Grammar of the New Testament*
BEvT	Beiträge zur evangelischen Theologie
BFCT	Beiträge zur Förderung christlicher Theologie
BHH	Biblisch-Historisches Handwörterbuch (ed. B. Reicke and L. Rost)
BHT	Beiträge zur historischen Theologie
Bib	*Biblica*
BZ	*Biblische Zeitschrift*
BWANT	Beiträge zur Wissenschaft vom Alten und Neuen Testament
BZNW	Beihefte zur *ZNW*
CBQ	*Catholic Biblical Quarterly*
ConNT	*Coniectanea neotestamentica*
EKK	Evangelisch-katholischer Kommentar
ETL	*Ephemerides theologicae lovanienses*
EvT	*Evangelische Theologie*
ExpT	*Expository Times*
FRLANT	Forschungen zur Religion und Literatur des Alten und Neuen Testaments
HNT	Handbuch zum Neuen Testament
HTR	*Harvard Theological Review*
JBL	*Journal of Biblical Literature*
JTS	*Journal of Theological Studies*
KuD	*Kerygma und Dogma*
LCL	Loeb Classical Library
Liddell-Scott	H. G. Liddell, R. Scott, and H. S. Jones, *A Greek-English Lexicon*
MTZ	*Münchener theologische Zeitschrift*
NovT	*Novum Testamentum*
NovT Sup	Novum Testamentum Supplements

NRT	*La nouvelle revue théologique*
N.S. (N.F., N.R.)	New series (Neue Folge, Neue Reihe)
NTAbh	Neutestamentliche Abhandlungen
NTF	Neutestamentliche Forschungen
NTS	*New Testament Studies*
RAC	*Reallexikon für Antike und Christentum*
RB	*Revue biblique*
RGG	*Die Religion in Geschichte und Gegenwart*, 3rd ed. (1957-1965) unless otherwise noted
RHPR	*Revue d'histoire et de philosophie religieuses*
RSPT	*Revue des sciences philosophiques et théologiques*
RSR	*Recherches de science religieuse*
SANT	Studien zum Alten und Neuen Testament
SBT	Studies in Biblical Theology
SE	*Studia Evangelica*
SEÅ	*Svensk exegetisk årsbok*
SJT	*Scottish Journal of Theology*
SNT	Studien zum Neuen Testament
ST	*Studia theologica*
Studia Paulina	*Studia Paulina in honorem Johannis de Zwaan septuagenarii* (1953)
Stud.Paul.Congr.	*Studiorum Paulinorum Congressus Internationalis Catholicus 1961* (Analecta Biblica 17-18, 1963)
SUNT	Studien zur Umwelt des Neuen Testaments
TDNT	*Theological Dictionary of the New Testament* (ed. G. Kittel and G. Friedrich)
ThBl	*Theologische Blätter*
ThStKr	*Theologische Studien und Kritiken*
TLZ	*Theologische Literaturzeitung*
TQ	*Theologische Quartalschrift*
TU	Texte und Untersuchungen
TZ	*Theologische Zeitschrift*
UNT	Untersuchungen zum Neuen Testament
VD	*Verbum Domini*
WMANT	Wissenschaftliche Monographien zum Alten und Neuen Testament
ZNW	*Zeitschrift für die neutestamentliche Wissenschaft*
ZST	*Zeitschrift für systematische Theologie*
ZTK	*Zeitschrift für Theologie und Kirche*

Abbreviations of ancient documents are those used by the *Journal of Biblical Literature*.

Commentary
on
ROMANS

I. Introduction (1:1-17)

The introduction of the epistle consists of the prescript in vv. 1-7, the proem in vv. 8-15, and the theme in vv. 16-17. Formally the last is part of the proem, but it is here separated in virtue of the importance of its contents. Paul modifies the structure of the Hellenistic epistle (Roller, *Formular,* 54ff., 81ff., 213ff.) not only by loosening up the introduction but also by giving it an individuality through personal observations and theological statements. In no other letter does he do this at such length, with such feeling, or with so many significant themes as here. There are three reasons for this.

1) Although the epistles of Paul are all occasional writings, they are not private letters in our sense. We cannot make a sharp distinction between epistle and letter (as did Deissmann, *Light,* 228-230) since the Pauline epistles are not artificial letters. We should also remember that, for the most part, these writings are meant to be read in the congregation and hence to bring proclamation and instruction, and that the apostle as well as the individual congregation which represents Christ's whole body exist from the very first within the eschatological parameter. Thus the nature of the purely private letter is no longer pertinent.

2) In the eyes of the rest of the Christian world the Roman congregation shared the renown of the imperial capital. This undoubtedly influenced Paul's style.

3) As will be seen, this congregation was also very important for the apostle's future missionary plans. So far, however, he was unknown to it personally and had to introduce himself officially. Although the theological presentation has an explicitness and emphasis which mark it off from Paul's other epistles, the letter is by no means to be regarded as a theological tractate. That may be true of the content, but the epistolary form is preserved in the introduction and conclusion (Roller, *Formular,* 23ff.), and the apostle's impulsive temperament constantly leaps over both conventions and strict logic. This makes it difficult to find a neat formula for his literary legacy (Michel).

This points to a problem which arises especially in this epistle through the very marked mixture of received tradition, distinctive deviation from that tradition, and independent development of it. As the founder of a community does not work in a vacuum, so Paul as letter writer has to reckon not merely with the lively reaction of the churches to his teaching. There are rivals and opponents in his sphere of mission, which itself is in different stages of development and is

3

affected by constantly changing currents. The result is a presentation which both demands and permits appeal to the common tradition and simultaneously necessitates theological debate and correction. All the New Testament writers are concerned to take up and set in order the existing, and sometimes very contradictory, positions in primitive Christianity. Paul, who remained a controversial figure since his conversion, can be understood only when we see him, now offensively and now defensively, under the pressure of this need for theological clarification.

A. Prescript (1:1-7) [2

¹Paul, a servant of Christ Jesus, (as) a called apostle set apart (for service) to the gospel of God, ²which he promised before through his prophets in holy scriptures, ³(treating) of his Son, born of David's seed according to the flesh, ⁴instituted the Son of God in power according to the spirit of holiness, since the Resurrection from the dead, Jesus Christ, our Lord. ⁵Through him we have received grace and apostleship, to the glory of his name to establish obedience of faith among all nations, ⁶to which you also belong (as) the called of Jesus Christ, ⁷to all the beloved of God at Rome (and) called saints. Grace be to you and peace from God, our Father, and the Lord Jesus Christ.

Bibliography: P. Stuhlmacher, "Theologische Probleme des Römerbrief-präskripts," *EvT* 27 (1967) 374-389. **1:** G. A. Harrer, "Saul who also is called Paul," *HTR* 33 (1940) 19-34; G. Sass, "Zur Bedeutung von δοῦλος bei Paulus," *ZNW* 40 (1941) 24-32; S. V. McCasland, "Christ Jesus," *JBL* 65 (1946) 377-383; N. A. Dahl, "Die Messianität Jesu bei Paulus," *Studia Paulina*, 83-95; K. Berger, "Zum traditionsgeschichtlichen Hintergrund christologischer Hoheitstitel," *NTS* 17 (1970/71) 391-425. On the term **"apostle,"** besides the monographs of G. Klein, W. Schmithals, J. Roloff, and the survey in E. Güttgemanns, "Literatur zur Neutestamentlichen Theologie," *Verkündigung und Forschung* 12 (1967) 61-79, cf.: K. Lake in *The Beginning of Christianity* (ed. F. J. F. Jackson and K. Lake) I, Vol. V (1933) 46-52; A. Fridrichsen, *The Apostle and His Message* (1947); H. von Campenhausen, "Der urchristliche Apostelbegriff," *ST* 1 (1947) 96-130; E. Lohse, "Ursprung und Prägung des christlichen Apostolates," *TZ* 9 (1953) 259-275; E. M. Kredel, "Der Apostelbegriff in der neueren Exegese," *Zeitschrift für Katholische Theologie* 78 (1956) 169-193; B. Gerhardsson, "Die Boten Gottes und die Apostel Christi," *SEÅ* 27 (1962) 89-131; T. Holtz, "Zum Selbstverständnis des Apostels Paulus," *TLZ* 91 (1966) 321-330; A. Satake, "Apostolat und Gnade bei Paulus," *NTS* 15 (1968/69) 96-107. **"Gospel":** J. W. Bowman, "The Term Gospel and its Cognates in the Palestinian Syriac," *New Testament Essays: Studies in Memory of Thomas Walter Manson, 1893-1958* (ed. A. J. B. Higgins; 1959) 54-67; H. Schlier, "Εὐαγγέλιον im Römerbrief," *Wort Gottes in der Zeit. Festschrift Karl Hermann Schelkle zum 65. Geburtstag* (ed. H. Feld and J. Nolte; 1973) 127-142. **3-4:** E. Schweizer, "Röm 1, 3f. und der Gegensatz von Fleisch und Geist vor und bei Paulus," *Neotestamentica*, 180-89; E. Linnemann, "Tradition und Interpretation in Röm 1, 3f.," *EvT* 31 (1971) 264-276; H. Schlier, "Zu Röm 1, 3f.," *Neues Testament und Geschichte* (Cullmann Festschrift, ed. H. Baltensweiler and Bo Reicke; 1972) 207-218; M. E. Boismard, "Constitué Fils de Dieu," *RB* 60 (1953) 5-17; L. C. Allen, "The Old Testament Background of (προ-)ὁρίζειν in the New Testament," *NTS* 17 (1970/71) 104-108; W. Foerster, *Herr ist Jesus. Herkunft und Bedeutung des urchristlichen Kyrios-Bekenntnisses* (1924); P. Vielhauer, "Ein Weg zur neutestamentlichen Christologie?" *Aufsätze zum Neuen Testament* (Theologische Bücherei 31; 1965) 141-199. **5:** W. Wiefel, "Glaubensgehorsam? Erwägungen zu Römer 1, 5," *Wort und Gemeinde. Festschrift für Erdmann Schott zum 65. Geburtstag* (1967) 137-144; R. Gyllenberg, "Glaube und Gehorsam," *ZST* 14 (1937) 547-566. **7:** E. Lohmeyer, "Probleme paulinischer

Theologie, I. Briefliche Grussüberschriften," *ZNW* 26 (1927) 158-173; A. Pujol, "De salutatione Apostolica Gratia vobis et pax," *VD* 12 (1932) 38-40, 76-82; G. Friedrich, "Lohmeyers These über das paulinische Briefpräscript kritisch beleuchtet," *TLZ* 81 (1956) 343-46; D. J. Doughty, "The Priority of χάρις," *NTS* 19 (1972/73) 163-180.

After the model of the Greek epistle (Roller, *Formular*), the Pauline prescript follows the sequence superscription–adscription–salutation, but after the oriental and Jewish pattern (though cf. Sickenberger) it separates the salutation from the first two in a sentence of its own (cf. the examples in Lietzmann and Michel and the typical Greek prescripts in Acts 15:23; 23:26; Jas 1:1). Also, the greeting (salutation) is replaced by a blessing. Here, as compared with other Pauline letters, the superscription is very long. It comprises the apostle's self-designation in v. 1, the gospel in vv. 2-3a, the title of God's Son with elucidations in vv. 3b-4, and then the apostolic task in its full range in vv. 5-6.

In all his epistles the apostle calls himself Paul. This corresponds to the practice of the Diaspora Jew accommodating himself to the world around him. Thus a name sounding like the Hebrew one was chosen. The idea that the reason for the change of name lay in the apostle's humility, or in his encounter with the proconsul Sergius Paulus (Acts 13:6-12), is absurd. In calling himself δοῦλος Χριστοῦ Paul does not humbly (*contra* Leenhardt) put himself on a par with other Christians (*contra* Zahn, Lagrange, Barrett). Rather, he is using the honorific title of the OT men of God which had also been adopted at Qumran (cf. Michel). This title expresses (as in Revelation) election as well as the submission of an instrument to the will of God. Jesus here represents God, since his divine sonship in the metaphysical sense, which is presupposed throughout the NT, characterizes the uniqueness of the Revealer.

In spite of the textual problem, "Christ" should be read before "Jesus," even though "Christ" is already used as a proper name by Paul (Kramer, *Christ*, 42f.). As the frequent occurrence of the combination "Christ Jesus" in liturgical texts shows, this order recalls the original messianic significance, of which Paul is certainly aware even though he does not emphasize it (cf. the excursus in Lietzmann; Dahl, "Messianität," 84ff.) and indeed allows it to be overshadowed by the Kyrios title. An analogy exists in the eschatologically grounded double name Simon Peter (Berger, "Hintergrund," 391ff.). Whether the Jewish tradition of the anointed prophet stands behind the title Christ as thus used (Berger) is at least questionable and cannot be proved in Paul's case.

The origin and significance of the Christian apostolate have been hotly debated, and the issues surrounding the pre-Pauline apostolate can hardly be settled now. It seems fairly certain that the Semitic idea of sending with an authoritative commission determined the NT understanding of the apostle. The Twelve were identified with the apostolate only after Paul. Paul himself coined the expression "apostle of Christ" with its variations and contrasted it with the function both of innumerable missionaries and also of "community apostles" (cf. Phil 2:25). The influence of the Jewish institution *šālî(a)ḥ* (esp. Rengstorf in *TDNT*, I, 407ff.; Gerhardsson, "Boten," 105ff.; but cf. Klein, *Zwölf Apostel*, 26f.) may be present when the NT refers to the sending out of the apostles two by two. Elsewhere, however, it is to be rejected, because the legal character of this institution finds no counterpart in primitive Christianity and, conversely, the eschatological character of the NT apostle, who is called to proclaim the gospel, is absent from the Jewish institution. Only with Paul's understanding of his apostleship do we touch somewhat solid ground (Kramer, *Christ*, 55ff.).

The broader problem comes into view when Galatians 1 is compared with the Lucan writings, so it need not be discussed here. One should be careful, however, not to make Paul's understanding of the apostle of Christ the crux of the whole problem, as is usually done today when the Church's traditional view [4 is subjected to criticism. It is probable that Paul's view has its roots in earlier tradition (1 Cor 9:1; 15:8f.), especially in the concept of "witnesses to the Resurrection" (Acts 1:22). Yet we must take into account that Paul's self-understanding underwent a development, which, in spite of many points of contact with pre- and non-Pauline views, makes comparison with them difficult. If it is true that until the Apostolic Council and the dispute with Peter at Antioch Paul had been the junior partner of Barnabas and as such a delegate of the church at Antioch, then this can hardly be reconciled with his later view of himself as the last witness of the Resurrection and as the one chosen to fulfill the apocalyptic function of the apostle to the nations. The attacks on Paul's apostleship make it clear that he did not fit the traditional idea and that, for all the points of similarity with other apostles, he has to be treated as unique, as he obviously regarded himself. While his epistles allow inferences about other views, it is the best course exegetically simply to work out his own understanding of himself as an apostle and to discuss the traditional elements only as they arise in given cases.

Every Christian, with his calling to salvation, is also called to service. Yet the divine κλῆσις does not confer endowment and responsibility in general. It confers them in the form of a specific charisma (cf. my article "Ministry and Community in the New Testament," *Essays*, 65ff.). The κλητὸς ἀπόστολος is, according to 1 Cor 12:28, a charismatic before and alongside others (*contra*, e.g., Satake, "Apostolat," 102f.), but in his concrete calling and task he is distinct from all others. This comes to expression in the predication ἀφωρισμένος, taken from the OT (cf. Lev 20:26; Isa 29:22; Ezek 45:1), which does not (*contra* Zahn, Schlatter, Franzmann, Nygren, Michel) refer to the contrast with Paul's Pharisaic past. Instead, like Gal 1:15 (Gaugler; Schlier, "Εὐαγγέλιον," 131; but cf. Schmithals, *Office of Apostle*, 27), this predication reminds us of Jer 1:5, namely, the election which precedes a concrete commission. The prophetic calling appears now, of course, in an apocalyptic perspective, as in *As. Mos.* 1:14: "For this reason God has selected and distinguished [*excogitavit et invenit*] me and prepared me to be the mediator of his covenant from the beginning of the world." The apostle has a special relationship to the gospel, which is manifested on earth through, him and even embodied in him. Yet the gospel retains precedence over the apostolate. It posits the apostolate from within itself. εἰς, as in 1:5; 15:26, 31; 16:5f.; 2 Cor 11:10, means "for" (Lietzmann). In the *koine* the article after the preposition often is omitted when the expression that follows has a technical character (BAGD, 165b).

In spite of much solid research in the last generation, the derivation and concrete meaning of the singular τὸ εὐαγγέλιον used absolutely have still not been

6

satisfactorily explained. The Greek word (cf. E. Klostermann, *Das Markus-evangelium* [HNT 3; 2nd ed. 1926] on Mark 1:1) only gradually took on the sense of "good news," and this was by no means the rule. In the LXX, which is familiar with the verb but not the singular noun, and also in Philo, the sense is simply "news," "message." The situation seems to be different in the language of the emperor cult, from which many interpreters used to explain the NT word (Deissmann, *Light*, 366f.; Klostermann on Mark 1:1; W. Schneemelcher in E. Hennecke and W. Schneemelcher, *New Testament Apocrypha* [2 vols.; Eng. tr. 1963-65] I, 71ff.). A key passage here is the well-known Calendar Inscription from Priene,

5] ἦρξεν δὲ τῶι κόσμωι τῶν δι' αὐτὸν εὐαγγελί[ων ἡ γενέθλιος] τοῦ θεοῦ, which may be translated, "The birthday of the emperor god opened up for the world a series of good tidings in his favor." Yet it is not satisfactory to derive the NT term in its absolute and technical use from this source even if the sacral significance in the inscription is not contested (as it is in Bultmann, *Theology*, I, 87f.). The antithesis between the worship of Christ and emperor worship does not play in the primitive Church the role presupposed for such a derivation (even by Friedrich, *TDNT*, II, 725). Indeed, the mutilation of the inscription allows us to replace the usual translation by "joyous sacrifices," and in any case the existence of the plural does not directly lead to a singular, which is what Paul uses exclusively (on this whole subject cf. Stuhlmacher, *Evangelium*, 11ff., 199ff.).

Yet some important objections to the growing modern derivation of εὐαγγέλιον from the proclamation in Deutero-Isaiah (Schniewind, *Euangelion*; Friedrich, *TDNT*, II, 707-736; Stuhlmacher, *Evangelium*, esp. 109ff.; Michel, *RAC*, VI, 1107-1160) have not been fully met. Whereas the verb and participle do indeed mean "bring good tidings" and "bearer of good tidings," with an eschatological orientation, the decisive noun is missing in Deutero-Isaiah. The OT usage adopted by the LXX is made concrete in Deutero-Isaiah. What simply meant good or bad news in the rest of the OT, sometimes even given prominence by a determinative adjective, now receives, within an eschatological context, the meaning message of salvation. Rabbinic exegesis deals comparatively rarely (Billerbeck; Friedrich, *TDNT*, II, 714f.) with the proclamation of Deutero-Isaiah and mostly only in the form of citation rather than reflection. We find the latter clearly, however, in Qumran, when the bearer of good tidings in 1QH 18:14 and 11QMelch is probably equated with the Teacher of Righteousness or with Melchizedek (Stuhlmacher, *Evangelium*, 142ff.). The LXX already shows acquaintance with the expository tradition that comes to expression here (Stuhlmacher, 159ff.). In postbiblical Judaism, for which especially the interchangeability of בשורה and שמועה is significant, examples of this strand of the tradition increase and we find that both noun and verb refer not only to concrete historical news, the prophetic message of salvation and disaster, its acceptance by the community, but also to the message of angels, or the divine announcement of blessing and comfort (Stuhlmacher, 129ff., 137ff.). It may also be allowed that the phrase "eternal gospel to proclaim" in Rev 14:6 and the reference to it in Rev 10:7 belong to this tradition and indicate its acceptance in Jewish Christianity. This proclamation is related apocalyptically to divine judgment as victory over the world.

Nevertheless, when all this is added up, the following still must be considered. First, this tradition is not widely used in the NT period. Second, in spite of Matt

11:5 and parallels, one can hardly maintain (*contra* Molland, *Euangelion,* 33 and *passim*) that Jesus understood his own mission from the message of Deutero-Isaiah. Third, the sparing use of the word-group by the Synoptists, and especially the absence of the verb in Mark, do not support the view that Palestinian Christians made an early and comprehensive use of this tradition. Adoption of a technical use of the verb in Christian-Palestinian Syriac (Bowman, "Gospel," 60f.) would prove only its use by the missionary community. Fourth, in Rev 14:6; 10:7 the marked ambivalence of judgment and salvation has not yet been overcome. Fifth, no direct analogy to the absolute use of the noun in Paul can be found (Stuhlmacher, *Evangelium,* 135). What all this amounts to is that the Deutero-Isaiah tradition was relatively unimportant and that one cannot speak of its unbroken continuity. This tradition did not attain a dominant place in earliest Jewish Christianity. There was simply a possibility of using it, no more and no less. Its recognition and adoption took place within the missionary community on Hellenistic soil (cf. Bultmann, *Theology,* I, 87f.; Bornkamm, *RGG,* II, 749f.; Stuhlmacher, *Evangelium,* 58ff., 218ff.), which might also have been aware of the etymology of the Greek word.

This last statement is supported by Paul's characteristic use of the noun in the absolute, which is usually regarded as his own creation. The meaning, however, is no less debated than the derivation. Certainly the word-group first of all denotes the oral proclamation of missionary work, so that the verb is connected with an object, as in Acts 8:4; 15:35 or Rom 10:15. It can even denote the message of judgment, as in Luke 3:18; Acts 14:15; Rev 14:6. From here it is only a short step to equate gospel and kerygma and to treat the former consistently as a *nomen actionis* (Bultmann, *Theology,* I, 87f.). Yet this applies neither here nor in 1 Cor 15:1f., where, in remarkable conjunction with typical verbs for passing on teaching (παραλαμβάνειν παραδιδόναι κατέχειν), it denotes the *didaché,* which is then developed in the verses that follow (Stuhlmacher, *Evangelium,* 266ff.). In a similar way gospel is defined here by the confession in vv. 3b-4. Since none of this corresponds to Paul's normal usage, one may see in these two passages evidence of a pre-Pauline use of the noun in the absolute. In analogy to the distinctive τὸ εὐαγγέλιον τῆς βασιλείας in Matt 4:23; 9:35; 24:14, missionary proclamation as salvation message is viewed in 1 Cor 15:1-5 and Rom 1:1ff. in terms of its central content, that is, by referring to the resurrection of Jesus and the lordship initiated therewith.

This means that the transfer out of the Jewish and Jewish-Christian tradition based on Deutero-Isaiah into Christian preaching in the Gentile-Christian territory becomes visible. If this tradition is adopted in the proclamation of good news relating to a definite event, and characterized here as a divine message by the subjective genitive θεοῦ denoting authorship, then the noun which now comes to the forefront, and which is used in the absolute in 1 Cor 15:1f., no longer embraces ambiguously both salvation and judgment, and is no longer oriented to the end of the world as in Rev 14:6, but is defined by the exaltation of Christ connected with his resurrection. The verb, which generally retains the sense "proclaim," can be used emphatically to denote eschatological proclamation. If this reconstruction holds up, Paul does not initiate this development but refines it. He could follow it, and even go back to its roots here and in 1 Cor 15:1f., because his central concern, too, was with the saving message about the exalted Lord. As will be shown, he had to sharpen it in terms of his doctrine of justification. He had thus to highlight more radically the noun used absolutely.

No more than a sketch of the complicated history of the word-group has been attempted. Yet in the light of it two demarcations are necessary with reference to the modern debate. First, the identification of gospel and kerygma, which cannot be ruled out in every case, weakens the apostle's point. The two are indissolubly related, but must be distinguished. The distinction appears when Paul in 1:16 and especially 1 Cor 9:16 (indirectly also in 1 Cor 1:18ff.; 2 Cor 2:14ff.) understands the gospel as power that determines life and destiny, just as the λόγος τοῦ θεοῦ is personified as an independent entity (Schniewind, *Wort*, 112; Molland, *Euangelion*, 46; Friedrich, *TDNT*, II, 732; Stuhlmacher, *Evangelium*, 70ff.). This understanding of the gospel as power may be seen in 11:28; 15:16, 19, in proclamation which brings about the inauguration of the eschatological order of salvation of the καινὴ διαθήκη (2 Cor 3:6ff.). In this covenant God himself intervenes in the world with power as Lord, Creator, and Judge. He does so by establishing the present Christian message (Asting, *Verkündigung*, 366) without, however, merging into it (Asmussen). The Christ event both precedes the message (Schlier, "Εὐαγγέλιον," 129) and continues itself in the message, so that it is not the content of an idea or of one doctrine among others.

The second demarcation is necessary because of a possible misunderstanding of v. 2. It cannot be denied that this verse anchors the gospel in salvation history (Schlier, "Εὐαγγέλιον," 135). God made known his will for the gospel in the past through the Old Testament prophets. Their task is seen here, not in the explication and application of the gospel through preaching as performed by NT prophets according to 1 Corinthians 14, but in the proclamation of the future eschatological event. The holy Scriptures—an expression which Paul borrowed from the Diaspora (Lietzmann; Schrenk, *TDNT*, I, 751)—preserved in writing the announcements of a plan of salvation which has more than momentary and local significance because it leads world history to its goal. Thus the Scriptures have more than a historical context because as ἐπαγγελία they participate in the εὐαγγέλιον. The dialectical relation between promise and gospel is theologically relevant. For Paul (Romans 4; Galatians 3) ἐπαγγελία is a prototype of the gospel even as the law is its antithesis. The standard pattern of promise and fulfilment rationalizes this function. The apostle's concern, however, is not to let the contingency of the eschatological gospel appear to be an unpredictable miraculous portent. If Israel is not shown here as the recipient and guardian of the promise, although this is naturally implied, we can see that what Paul has in view is not earthly continuity but the interconnection of God's work in the first time and the last time. It should not be overlooked, however, that in some sense the gospel, too, retains the character of promise. It is a poor formulation, however, when the gospel is called God's proleptic self-declaration and this is explained in terms of the hiddenness of his declaration in the word (*contra* Stuhlmacher, "Probleme," 377; *Evangelium, passim*, e.g., 82). It is true that Paul calls the gospel a mystery. His own proclamation is oriented to the eschatological world-dominion of Christ, which is present already and already witnessed to. The hiddenness of Christ's lordship in the word wards off the idea that Christ's lordship becomes our possession. It

9

must be continually received anew by us, and bring us into its powerful influence, because we are still journeying and have not yet reached the destination. Use of the term prolepsis leaves the unintentional impression that the gospel is not the final word which embraces the whole of salvation, which is already fully given in the present, the final word beyond which there is no more to be said or experienced. The dialectic of promise and gospel, or of gospel and God's apocalyptic self-declaration, is not the dialectic of a historical process of growth. Rather, it arises from the fact that in world history the promise is known only from the gospel as its prototype, and that the gospel can be maintained as God's promise for the world only in conflict and peril and hence only by proclaiming it ever anew.

Christ is not the author of the gospel (*contra* Schniewind, *Wort,* 107, 111); he [8 is its decisive content. This may be seen from the forced prepositional expression περὶ τοῦ υἱοῦ αὐτοῦ in v. 3, which refers back to the εὐαγγέλιον θεοῦ and replaces an objective genitive εὐαγγέλιον τοῦ Χριστοῦ (cf. 1:9; Gal 1:7). This reference and variation are necessary because the gospel has already been defined in v. 1 and the relative clause in v. 2 acts as a digression. The title "Son of God" is introduced solemnly. According to Paul it indicates the true content of the gospel, although a more precise statement will be given in v. 16. There can be no contesting the fact that the title, except as it refers to Israel or is conferred at enthronement (Ps 2:7), is as rare in Judaism as it is common in Hellenism (Jeremias, *The Prayers of Jesus* [SBT 2/6; 1967] 11-29 [=*Abba,* 15-33]). Its Christian use can hardly be traced back to an experience of Jesus (*contra* Cullmann, *Christology,* 275ff.). Even if "Abba" should denote the specific relation of Jesus to God (Jeremias, *Prayers of Jesus,* 29-65 [=*Abba,* 33-67]), still the post-Easter title Son of God would not necessarily derive from it, especially if Jesus drew his disciples into this relationship to God. But we shall have to deal with the early history of this title in a moment. Provisionally one might state that no NT author understood the unique divine sonship of Jesus otherwise than in a metaphysical sense. Jesus is God's Son as the one who was of the divine nature and like God (Phil 2:6) and who was God (John 1:1). The NT interest focuses on the function of the *eikón* of God, whether generally as the incomparable revealer or specially as the mediator of the first or of the eschatological creation. Only when this is clearly perceived can the problem of vv. 3b-4 be properly seen too.

The view has increasingly gained ground that we have in vv. 3b-4 a pre-Pauline liturgical fragment. The verses are composed with even more care than the rest of the prescript, as may be seen especially from the antithetical parallelism, the use of the participle, and the typically Semitic placing of the verb first, as, e.g., in 1 Tim 3:16, etc. (Norden, *Agnostos Theos,* 254ff.). Open to debate are the beginning of the formula and the hypothesis of Pauline additions to it. While it is quite conceivable that Paul anticipates with the title "Son of God" what is important for him and what is characteristic of the gospel, it is hard to think (*contra* Bultmann, *Theology,* I, 49) that the title Son of God, deduced from v. 3a, formed the original introduction of the pre-Pauline tradition. If it did, v. 4 would lose its significance through anticipation. If both κατά expressions are regarded as Pauline constructions (Bultmann, *Theology,* I, 49; Dahl, "Messianität," 90; Wengst, *Formeln,* 112ff.; Linnemann, "Tradition," 273f.), then the problem is simplified—but at the expense of a weakening of the antithesis. Semitic texts do not support the scholarly tendency to discover scanable and very symmetrical cola. Removing problems through textual criticism is highly dubious. No one has taken the trouble to specify why κατὰ σάρκα is disruptive in v. 3b. The antithesis in v. 4 makes good sense. That this contrast of flesh and spirit cannot be ascribed to Paul alone can be seen, for example, from John 6:63. Furthermore, it is not formulated in a specifically Pauline way here. Finally, its orientation is christological rather than (as in Paul) anthropological. In good OT and Jewish fashion σάρξ refers here to the weak and corruptible flesh, not the flesh entangled in sin as in 8:3.

The word ἁγιωσύνη occurs in exhortation in 1 Thess 3:13; 2 Cor 7:1, but the expression πνεῦμα ἁγιωσύνης corresponds to "Spirit of holiness" in Isa 63:10f.; Ps 51:11, even though the LXX (50:13) has πνεῦμα ἅγιον, notwithstanding its use of ἁγιωσύνη elsewhere. It is hard to see why Paul himself would not have used the adjective ἅγιον or the familiar noun ἁγιασμός. On the other hand, the phrase also appears in T. Levi 18:11 with reference to the saints of the end-time: καὶ πνεῦμα ἁγιωσύνης ἔσται ἐπ'αὐτοῖς. The exact Greek equivalent in the Qumran passages 1QS 4:21; 8:16; 9:3; 1QH 7:6f.; 9:32; CD 2:12 (Michel) cannot be determined. What is meant is not moral holiness (Kuss) but originally cultic, and then (as often) holiness transposed into the eschatological sphere (Schlier, "Zu Röm 1, 3f.," 212), which finally overcomes what is profane and secular and opens up access to God. In this sense the expression fits in well with the context, whose second line, which is decisive for interpretation of the whole, begins with τοῦ ὁρισθέντος. The traditional doctrine of the two natures of Christ has always hampered interpretation at this point, as the textual variants already show (cf. L. C. Allen, "Background," 104ff.) with their reference to divine predestination. Luther notes in the scholia to his lecture that it is doubtful whether there has ever been any correct exposition. Yet ὁρίζειν τινά τι, as in Acts 10:42; 17:31; Ign. Eph. 3:2, can mean merely "define someone as something, appoint as something" (still against the consensus of more recent commentaries is Ridderbos, Paulus, 66: "gerehabiliteerd" [rehabilitated], although the Eng. tr. has "vindicated" [Paul, 67]). The reference here is to the enthronement of Christ as Son of God, and the Spirit of holiness was the power which accomplished this. This view may correspond fully to the passage in Testament of Levi, but it is unusual in Paul. For the apostle the Spirit proceeds from Christ or represents him, but the Spirit does not act upon him. It seems, then, that the statement is pre-Pauline and must be part of the original formula.

We are thus granted a perspective by which to understand these verses. As in Mark 12:35; 2 Tim 2:8 and the infancy stories, the title "Son of David" is ascribed to the earthly Jesus, as befits the messianic king according to Ps. Sol. 17:21ff. (cf. also 4QFlor on 2 Sam 7:11ff.). There can thus be no question of a theology of humiliation in v. 3b (Kramer, Christ, 109; Wengst, Formeln, 115). The one described in earthly terms as the messianic king is destined for appointment and enthronement as Son of God and thus follows a course which is divided into two stages by the Resurrection (but cf. Schlier, "Zu Röm 1, 3f.," 212ff.). It can be seen that this understanding has been constantly obscured by the influence of the doctrine of the two natures and the consequent reference to Jesus' two modes

11

of existence (Lietzmann; Kühl; Lagrange; Kuss; Althaus; Black). Unlike Paul himself the formula does not presuppose the preexistence and divine sonship of the earthly Jesus (contra Lietzmann). The antithesis of the two lines and the use of the term "appoint" make it clear that Jesus receives the dignity of divine sonship only with his exaltation and enthronement. Hence the two participles speak expressly of becoming rather than being. As in Acts 2:36; 13:33 one detects the adoptionist christology of primitive Christianity (Dodd; Knox; Eichholz, Paulus, 128ff.; Schweizer, TDNT, VI, 417; Hahn, Titles of Jesus, 248f.; Stuhlmacher, "Probleme," 382; Wengst, Formeln, 114). ἐξ ἀναστάσεως νεκρῶν, in the temporal sense, marks the decisive turning point (Lietzmann; Hahn, Titles of Jesus, 250 contra the grammatically possible causal view of Schweizer, Erniedrigung, 91; Gaugler; Murray; Ridderbos). If the expression is regarded as a Pauline addition [1 (Barrett), then the pre-Pauline formula loses both precision and also the concluding emphasis, which is by no means accidental. This concluding emphasis gives the participle ὁρισθέντος its unequivocal sense. Nor should one regard ἐξ ἀναστάσεως νεκρῶν as an abbreviation, made for the sake of sound and brevity, of the fuller phrase one might expect: "since his resurrection from the dead" (Lietzmann; Kuss). The hymnic tradition does not isolate Christ's resurrection, but views it in its cosmic function as the beginning of general resurrection (Schlatter; Nygren; Franzmann).

It is understandable that ἐν δυνάμει should cause difficulty and that recourse should constantly be had to the idea of a gloss or a Pauline addition, which as a panacea eventually leads to absurdity (Barrett; Schweizer, Erniedrigung, 91; Wegenast, Tradition, 71; Kramer, Christ, 110; Wengst, Formeln, 114; differently Schlier, "Zu Röm 1, 3f.," 209f.). Nothing is in fact gained by this theory, since the apostle would only strengthen and not weaken the adoptionism of the formula thereby. Nor should it be left in doubt (as does Lietzmann) whether the expression should be related to the verb (Sanday and Headlam; Schlatter; Hahn, Titles of Jesus, 249) or, as most exegetes agree, to the noun. In the former case it would clash with the κατά construction. ἐν δυνάμει is parallel to ἐν δόξῃ in 1 Tim 3:16 and ἐν δεξιᾷ τῆς μεγαλωσύνης ἐν ὑψηλοῖς in Heb 1:3, and is thus typical of the christological hymn rather than Paul. In the religious vocabulary of Hellenism δύναμις, δόξα, φῶς, and πνεῦμα are more or less synonymous. Christ is enthroned as Son of God in the heavenly sphere of power.

We can now at last discuss the meaning of the two κατά phrases. The two stages of Christ's way are rightly connected with the two spheres of earth and heaven; and πνεῦμα, which in pre-Pauline Christianity is not so strictly related to christology as in Paul, can have a dynamistic, animistic, or spatial orientation. Hellenism cannot think of the divine energy apart from a substratum of substance and streaming forth into a field of force (cf. my article on the Spirit in the NT in RGG, II, 1272ff.). Nevertheless (contra Schweizer, Erniedrigung, 91ff. [Lordship, 59f.]; "Röm 1, 3f.," 160ff.; TDNT, VI, 416f.; Barrett; Michel; Wegenast, Tradition, 74; Hahn, Titles of Jesus, 247) the interpretation given does not necessarily suggest relating κατὰ πνεῦμα to the heavenly sphere. This is done already by ἐν δυνάμει and is excluded by the genitive construction. The Spirit of holiness is the power in virtue of which Jesus is appointed the Son of God, just as the oral tradition of Jesus' baptism spoke of his messianic appointment by the Holy Spirit. One can see from 4:25 and elsewhere that the same preposition can have a slightly different meaning when used in rhetorical parallelism in two consecutive lines. If the second κατά is not taken instrumentally, one is forced to give a causal sense to the ἐξ at the end, and this shows that there can be no avoiding the idea of effective force in the context.

If the above explanation is correct, we have in the formula the trace of a very early christology. One may place it in Hellenistic-Jewish Christianity (e.g., Kramer, *Christ*, 121f.; Wengst, *Formeln*, 116). At least Palestinian influence cannot be denied in view of the motif of the messianic king and his enthronement and in view of the singular function of the Spirit. It is credible that the formula is related to the baptismal message (Wengst, *Formeln*, 116), because the title "Son of God" seems to have its earliest locus there. The reception of the Spirit and adoption are connected with baptism for the Christian; thus Christ's baptism is a model for Christian baptism. An important point is that the formula summarizes the essence of the gospel insofar as the gospel can present as its object the way of the earthly Jesus to his exaltation and enthronement, as Mark did in his own manner with his concept of the messianic secret. The path is thus prepared here for the writing of the gospels (Stuhlmacher, "Probleme," 383ff.; *Evangelium*, 288; Wengst, *Formeln*, 118ff.). On the other hand, it should be remembered that what Paul takes from the formula as the decisive thing for him and, according to 1:9, as characteristic of the gospel, is only the title "Son of God," which for Paul belongs to the preexistent one. By putting v. 3a first and closing with the Kyrios title in v. 4, he corrected the formula's view (Schweizer, *TDNT*, VI, 416f.; Wengst, *Formeln*, 112; less decisively Kramer, *Christ*, 185). One can leave undecided whether he did it intentionally or not. The formula performed the service of showing that he shared the same basis of faith as the Christians at Rome. To assume, however, that the church actually knew the formula (e.g., Kuss) exceeds the limits of permissible conjecture (Zeller, *Juden*, 47).

A solemn plerophoric title which combines "Jesus" with "Christ" as a proper name closes the statement on the criterion of the gospel and opens another statement on the task of the apostle. The origin of the title "Kyrios" has been continually debated since Bousset's famous book *Kyrios Christos* and the criticism of it by W. Foerster (*Herr ist Jesus*). It can hardly be contested (though cf. Bultmann, *Theology*, I, 51) that Bousset's total derivation of the title from the Hellenistic mystery cults must at least be modified. From the very first the "Maranatha" of the primitive community has rightly been adduced against Bousset's conclusion. On the other hand, the opposing view (e.g., Hahn, *Titles of Jesus*, 73ff.; Kümmel, *Theology*, 111ff.) goes too far when it places the roots of the title in the absolute in the Palestinian tradition (cf. on this Vielhauer, "Ein Weg," 147ff.). It is best to distinguish the Palestinian Mare-Kyrios as the returning Son of Man and world judge from the Kyrios who is addressed and worshiped in the acclamation κύριος Ἰησοῦς as the oldest form of the confession to the cultically present Lord (Vielhauer, "Ein Weg," 167; Kramer, *Christ*, 99ff., 154ff.; Schweizer, *Erniedrigung*, 165; Conzelmann, *Outline*, 82ff.). Whether or how strongly the Maranatha formed a bridge to the Kyrios acclamation (Cullmann, *Christology*, 205ff.) can scarcely be determined with certainty. Finally, the exegesis of the LXX

13

allowed the Lord of the Christian community, who is opposed to the lords of the Gentile world as in 1 Cor 8:5f., to be set forth in his dignity as cosmocrator. Bousset's thesis may be right, then, to the extent that it was only on Gentile soil, and in antithesis to the deities of the mystery cults, that Kyrios became the dominant christological title, and that it is this for Paul too (Wengst, *Formeln,* 131ff.). Although the relation of the Lord to the community bears the main stress for the apostle, Paul does not regard him as the cult God of Christians, as seems to have been the case to a large extent in Hellenistic Christianity. For Paul the Kyrios is the representative of the God who claims the world and who with the church brings the new creation into the midst of the old world that is perishing.

Christ's Lordship is the basis of the task of the apostle according to v. 5 and of his right to address the Roman church according to v. 6. The first person plural is undoubtedly literary and gives an official emphasis. Hence it does not include [1: all the apostles (*contra* Zahn; Schlatter; Roller, *Formular,* 172); this would not fit in with v. 5b. One of the remarkable features of this epistle is that fellow workers are not mentioned in it as in the other epistles, although the traffic between Rome and Corinth, the probable place of writing, must have brought Christians in the two cities together. Paul approaches the Roman community as an individual, and he does this consciously, since he intends to give an account of his own message. What he is he has become through grace, which both uses him as its instrument and also gives him authority.

χάριν καὶ ἀποστολήν, linked explicatively (though cf. Schlier, "Εὐαγγέλιον," 136f.), are almost a hendiadys. The apostolate is the specific grace granted to Paul. Against a still common view it must be stated that in Paul χάρις does not mean primarily a divine attribute (Wobbe, *Charis-Gedanke,* 32). It does not mean, in good Greek fashion, God's graciousness, nor concretely his free love (Taylor). It almost always means the power of salvation which finds expression in specific gifts, acts, and spheres and which is even individualized in the charismata. The long ecclesiastical tradition that has distinguished office and charisma has resulted in removing the apostolate in general from the charismata and in opposing it to them. In the light of 1 Cor 12:28, and of ἡ χάρις ἡ δοθεῖσα μοι, which is used in almost stereotyped fashion in 12:3; 15:15; 1 Cor 3:10; Gal 2:9, the legitimacy of this view must be contested in the case of Paul, unique though his charisma is.

As a power grace does not establish human qualities but service. The combination of terms does not mean that we are to think first of being a Christian and then of the apostolate (*contra* Zahn; Lietzmann). The apostle's specific task is to create "obedience of faith" among all the Gentiles. The genitive πίστεως here cannot be an objective genitive (*contra* Lietzmann; Kuss; Michel; Black), since the object, as in v. 3a, is indicated by the prepositional phrase ὑπὲρ τοῦ ὀνόματος αὐτοῦ. The latter cannot then mean (as in BAGD, 838b) "to spread his name"; the name, as elsewhere in antiquity, is the nature of its bearer becoming manifest, and it can thus be personified. Hence the genitive construction is again explicative. This is supported by the fact that faith and obedience are interchangeable in 1:8, 1 Thess 1:8 and Rom 15:18; 16:19; or in 2 Cor 10:5, 15. Faith is described as obedience to the gospel in 10:16 (Bultmann, *Theology,* I, 314f.; *TDNT,* VI, 205f.; Furnish, *Ethics,* 184f.). These passages also show that the obedience of faith relates to the revelation of Christ, as is particularly evident in 2 Cor 9:13. Within this context the meaning of our passage is clear. The danger naturally arises of drawing the consequence that sanctification in active obedience is the true point of faith. This danger cannot be avoided if the parallels are ignored and the genitive constructions here and elsewhere are declared to be *ad hoc* combinations (Wiefel, "Glaubensgehorsam," 137ff., in criticism more applicable to Schlatter than to Bultmann). The context, the sequence in 10:14ff., and an expression like ἀκοὴ πίστεως in Gal 3:2 make it perfectly plain that the obedience of faith means acceptance of the message of salvation (Bultmann, *Theology,* I, 89f.). The missionary situation has given both noun and verb their predominant meaning, and the characteristic linking of faith and obedience in Paul has a meaning which is not primarily ethical but, as is especially clear in 2 Cor 10:4-6, eschatological: When the revelation of Christ is accepted, the rebellious world submits again to its Lord. This understanding of faith corresponds to the apostle's Kyrios christology.

13]   It is in this light that we are to understand the mission of Paul to all the Gentiles, which undoubtedly is the meaning of ἔθνη here (although cf. Michel; Zahn; Schlatter). The God who reveals himself in Christ wills to subject the world, not just human existence, to himself. Paul's specific service is to realize this among the Gentiles, while others are sent to the Jews. Stress falls on ἐν πᾶσιν, which indicates the cosmic scope and also makes possible the transition to v. 6. The Romans belong to this world outside Judaism. We may gather from this that at least a majority of the community there (although cf. Zahn) were Gentile-Christians.

In v. 6 the recipients of the epistle are addressed with the same plerophoric solemnity as the writer uses in relation to himself. The absence of the term ἐκκλησία is surprising here as in the rest of Romans (ch. 16 excluded) and admits of no plausible explanation (*contra* Minear, *Obedience,* 7ff., 41f., even feuding groups would still form a community). Instead, primitive Christian self-predications are used. Like Paul himself, the Christians in Rome are called by Jesus Christ, namely, called out of the Gentile world in order to belong to the one Kyrios from now on.

Verse 7a finally brings the long-awaited adscription with remarkable brevity, compared with the characterization of the apostolate, although in a very official tone. We again find the distinctive πᾶσιν, which embraces all the members of the community. The much-debated omission of ἐν Ῥώμῃ in later readings (cf. the excursuses in Zahn; Lietzmann) is inexplicable after τοῖς οὖσιν unless one assumes that it was for the purpose of changing this epistle into a general one (Knox, 363f.). This omission produced the textual emendation ἐν ἀγάπῃ θεοῦ, which is obviously a secondary refinement. ἀγαπητοῖς θεοῦ is not in primary apposition but relates to τοῖς οὖσιν and in content can hardly be differentiated from κλητοῖς ἁγίοις. In OT terminology the beloved of God are the elect who are sure of this in their calling. Gentile-Christians would hardly have been aware that in the LXX formula (Exod 12:16, etc.) κλητὴ ἁγία, the sacred assembly is hidden behind the phrase about the elect saints (Asting, *Verkündigung,* 141ff.; Procksch, *TDNT,* I, 106; Schlier, "Εὐαγγέλιον," 141). The title "saints" transfers the honor

15

of the OT people of God to Christianity. In part, at least, the original cultic sense is retained when the concept is transposed into eschatology: He who is admitted to the place of the divine presence is holy. The reference is to heavenly being. Hence one should not see here the ethicizing of cultic terms, although this did in fact take place. Christians are holy, not because of their conduct, but because they stand before the face of their Lord and therewith of God.

The salutation in v. 7b is divided rhythmically into three lines with four words in each, and apart from 1 Thessalonians and Galatians, which has no greeting, it is common to the authentic letters of Paul. The attractive thesis that we have here a liturgical formula for the opening of divine worship (Lohmeyer, "Grussüberschriften," 162) cannot be sustained. 1 Thess 1:1 must be considered the point of origin for this salutation (Schrenk, *TDNT*, V, 1007) which was not, except by Ephesians, retained in the post-Pauline community. In this light the lack of any article in the salutation can easily be explained (Friedrich, "These," 345f.). That does not exclude the possibility that the apostle expected his epistle to be read at worship and thus took special pains to construct a "liturgical" greeting (Kramer, *Christ*, 90ff., 151ff.). The combination at the end, which, as in 1 Thess 1:1; 3:11; 2 Thess 1:12; 2:16, speaks of God as our Father and then (*contra* Schrenk, *TDNT*, V, 1007f.) independently sets Jesus Christ alongside him as Lord, may be pre-Pauline (Lohmeyer, "Grussüberschriften," 164; Michel; *contra* Kramer, *Christ*, [1◄ 152f.). At any rate, this is a blessing, not just a greeting. The earlier common view that Paul deepened χαίρειν by using χάρις, and thus combined the Greek and Hebrew greetings (cf. Sanday and Headlam; Bruce; Knox), is now outmoded (Lohmeyer, "Grussüberschriften," 159; Friedrich, "These," 345f.; Michel). Paul is, rather, modifying an oriental-Jewish formula which remains intact in *2 Apoc. Bar.* 78:2 and Gal 6:16: "Mercy and peace be with you." What is meant is the eschatological saving treasure of the power of grace which does not merely give people spiritual peace but embraces them totally. With access to God it establishes even on earth the divine order of peace as the sphere of a life which is open-ended and without fear. All this, of course, is dependent on the fact that God truly became our Father and Jesus Christ our Lord.

B. Proem (1:8-15)

⁸*First, I give thanks to my God through Jesus Christ for you all, because your faith is proclaimed in the whole world.* ⁹*For my witness is God, whom I serve with my spirit in the gospel of his Son, that unceasingly I remember you, always in my prayers,* ¹⁰*praying that one day at last I might succeed in coming to you by God's will.* ¹¹*For I long to see you, that I may impart to you something of spiritual grace to strengthen you,* ¹²*that is, that I might be comforted together with you by the mutual faith (common to) you and me.* ¹³*Nor will I conceal from you, brethren, that (already) I have often intended to come to you—but have been prevented up to the present time—in order that I may gather some fruits among you as among the rest of the Gentiles.* ¹⁴*I am under obligation to Greeks and barbarians, wise and foolish.* ¹⁵*For this reason, so*

far as I am concerned, there is a readiness to preach the gospel to you in Rome also.

Bibliography: P. Schubert, *Form and Function of the Pauline Thanksgivings* (BZNW 20; 1939); G. Eichholz, "Der ökumenische und missionarische Horizont der Kirche. Eine exegetische Studie zu Röm 1, 8-15," *EvT* 21 (1961) 15-27. 8: A. Schettler, *Die paulinische Formel "durch Christus"* (1907); O. Kuss, "Die Formel 'durch Christus' in den paulinischen Hauptbriefen," *Trierer Theologische Zeitschrift* 65 (1956) 193-204; Greeven, *Gebet.* 9: G. Stählin, "Zum Gebrauch von Beteurungsformeln im Neuen Testament," *Donum Gratulatorium. Ethelbert Stauffer* (1962) 115-143. 11ff.: Schrenk, "Missionsdokument"; H. Preisker, "Das historische Problem des Römerbriefs," *Wissenschaftliche Zeitschrift der Friedrich-Schiller-Universität Jena,* Ges. und sprachw. Reihe (1952/53) Heft 1, 25-30; J. Knox, "A Note on the Text of Romans," *NTS* 2 (1955/56) 191-93; K. H. Rengstorf, "Paulus und die älteste römische Christenheit," *SE* II (1964) 447-464; G. Klein, "Paul's Purpose in Writing the Epistle to the Romans," *Romans Debate,* 32-49. 14: P. Minear, "Gratitude and Mission in the Epistle to the Romans," *Basileia. Walter Freytag zum 60. Geburtstag* (ed. J. Hermelink and H. J. Margull; 1959) 42-48.

In vv. 8a, 9-10a Paul follows even in detail (though cf. Roller, *Formular,* 65) the structure of the pagan-Hellenistic epistle which was adopted in the Jewish Diaspora in 2 Macc 1:11f. and in Philo (cf. Schubert's analysis). This structure, which introduces religious thanksgiving and intercession as a direct concern of the writing, is never applied purely conventionally. In spite of a certain formality it presupposes a common religious bond and a relationship of trust between author and recipient, and in every way serves a concrete concern. Among typical features found in our text are: the reason for the thanksgiving after the stereotyped introductory εὐχαριστῶ τῷ θεῷ; the final clause after the intercession; the περί = "with regard to," with respect to the recipients; the ἀδιαλείπτως μνείαν ποιοῦμαι and the ἐπὶ τῶν προσευχῶν μου indicating time and circumstances. In the light of the structure, πάντοτε, which seems superfluous alongside ἀδιαλείπτως, is to be related to this indication of time and circumstance (*contra* Pallis; Lagrange; Murray; Barrett; H. W. Schmidt), and should thus be separated from δεόμενος (Michel). In view of the long prescript it is understandable that the customary πρὸ μὲν πάντων is replaced by πρῶτον μέν with no ἔπειτα δέ following.

Paul himself has filled out and christianized the formula. In the style of a person praying in the OT he speaks of "my" God as in Phil 1:3; 4:19, etc. The phrase διὰ 'Ιησοῦ Χριστοῦ should not be given too strong a christological emphasis in the sense of the mediator concept (*contra* patristic tradition, many commentaries, and, e.g., Wobbe, *Charis-Gedanke,* 92f.; Stuiber, *RAC,* IV, 214). The reference is to the exalted Lord (Schettler, *Formel,* 6) and not primarily (Kuss, "Formel," 193ff.) to the act of salvation, though (*contra* Schettler, 43) διὰ 'Ιησοῦ Χριστοῦ is not meant to explain psychologically Paul's feelings of gratitude. As in 12:1 διά has the sense "in virtue of," as in common prayer today; appeal is thus made to the basis and validation of prayer (Schettler, 14; Kramer, *Christ,* 88).

The ὅτι clause of v. 8b introduces a *captatio benevolentiae.* In it πίστις does not mean coming to faith (Lietzmann; Bultmann, *TDNT,* VI, 212) but the state of faith (Schlatter; Michel; Kuss). This faith is universally known because it is that of the church in the imperial capital. For the hyperbole there is a fine parallel in

17

an Egyptian funerary inscription: ὧν ἡ σωφροσύνη κατὰ τὸν κόσμον λελάληται (cited in BAGD, 446a). One may also compare 1 Thess 1:8. Similar hyperbole governs the whole passage. It is expressed also in πάντες, ἀδιαλείπτως, πάντοτε, in καταγγέλλειν (which outdoes the simple "reported"), and finally in the oath in v. 9a. From it, and from the following context, we learn little about the personal relation or "deep inner fellowship" of the apostle with the community (contra Rengstorf, "Paulus," 450ff.). Paul is concerned to assure the Romans of his high regard and lively remembrance. The oath, which occurs in 1 Sam 12:6 LXX and which is a common formula in Paul, has pagan parallels (BAGD, 494a; Klauser, RAC, II, 220f.; with reservations Stählin, "Beteuerungsformeln," 132). It probably indicates that Paul did not know that Jesus prohibited oaths. God can be invoked as witness because Paul's service is totally dedicated to him.

In this context λατρεύειν can have a cultic sense (Michel). But the life of prayer is not made parallel with proclamation (contra Zahn; Strathmann, TDNT, IV, 64f.). τὸ πνεῦμα μου does not mean God's Spirit (contra Schlatter; E. Schweizer, TDNT, VI, 435), but is identical with ψυχή here and means the inner core that governs man (Michel; Leenhardt). ἐν means "with," as in 1 Cor 4:21. The tenor of Phil 3:3 is different, so that it offers no real parallel, nor does the reference to the fact that among the Rabbis prayer is called "service in the heart" help clarify the scope of the statement (Billerbeck; Michel). With his whole being Paul serves the gospel, which is defined christologically by the objective genitive, as in v. 3.

Only at the end of v. 9 does the text speak of the apostle's prayer, and the concrete wish expressed thereby, introduced by δεόμενος, comes only in v. 10. εἴ πως expresses uncertainty. ἤδη ποτέ, as in Phil 4:10, means "some day at last" [16 (Lietzmann; Michaelis, TDNT, V, 113) and suggests impatience. The passive of the verb εὐοδόω, which probably is taken from the LXX, could refer to God's action (Lagrange) and then have the meaning "to receive the prepared way," as in Tob 5:17. But, for the sake of the infinitive which follows, the figurative sense "to succeed," found in 2 Chr 32:30; Sir 41:1, is to be preferred. The "God willing," which we also find in a similar way among pious Jews and pagans (cf. Billerbeck; Deissmann, Light, 181 n. 16), and which occurs in the NT at 15:32; 1 Cor 4:19; 16:7; Acts 18:21; Jas 4:15, shows why, in the apostle's opinion, his wish has not been fulfilled thus far. Without abandoning it, he does not here assert his intention definitely in the form of a fixed program, as in the parallel statements in 15:22-29 (Black). This is very surprising and will need to be explained later.

Surprising too (pointed out by Klein, "Purpose," esp. 45) is the alternation in Paul's claim to authority, which is steadily diminished until it comes to the fore again undisguised at the end of vv. 11-15. To explain this in terms of tact on Paul's part (A. Fridrichsen, The Apostle and his Message [1947] 7f.) is too simple. Yet the difficulty in the verse is overplayed if one introduces the completely un-Pauline view, found, however, in Acts 7:5ff.; 9:27f. and especially in the story of Cornelius, that a church needs to be established, or at least sanctioned, by an apostle (Klein, "Purpose," 45-49; cf., in sharp criticism, Kuss, Paulus, 198f.). If this had had to be made clear to the Romans and thereby Paul's responsibility toward them had to be set forth, then this would have had to be done directly and plainly. But precisely this does not happen at all in our section, in which Paul has increasing difficulty in formulating precisely the reasons for his projected journey and his expectations. This allows only the conclusion that Paul feels very insecure in relation to the unmet recipients of his letter and is thus forced into an apologetic defensive. He obviously fears the mistrust and the suspicions of both his person and his work which are circulating in Rome (Preisker, "Problem"; Michel). This leads him to vague remarks about his intentions and to constant qualifications of his hopes. The visit is not even definitely announced. The odd τί in v. 11b leaves the possibilities open. Most unusual is the combination χάρισμα πνευματικόν, which is used only here. According to 1 Cor 12:3ff. all charismata are πνευματικά. In his stance against enthusiasm Paul scrupulously avoids the latter term whenever he can and replaces it by the former. The strange use in the present passage does not permit us, of course, to deny the charisma motif in favor of the general sense of "gift" (G. P. Wetter, Charis. Ein Beitrag zur Geschichte des ältesten Christentums [1913] 169; Lagrange). Probably, along the lines of 15:27, the adjective restricts the scope of charismatic effects to the blessing which comes with preaching.

The series of qualifications continues in the infinitive clause. Paul cannot be the first to bring the gospel to the Romans, he can only "strengthen" them in it—probably a use of missionary language (Zeller, Juden, 53). Yet even this statement might be misunderstood and so requires fresh correction. In his correction (v. 12) the apostle even omits the next link in the chain of thought. He does not speak of the paraclesis which he might bring as consolation and admonition, since preaching evangelically always gives power and obligation simultaneously. Paul anxiously avoids any claim that might sound authoritative and is thus prepared to let the logic of the structure of the sentence suffer (Lietzmann; Lagrange; Barrett). The mutual consolation of the brethren, from which he himself will profit, now appears to be his expectation. The pronouns ὑμῶν τε καὶ ἐμοῦ, which are rather superfluous alongside ἐν ἀλλήλοις, underscore this impression.

The planned visit is thus definitely divested of any official character, in obvious contradiction of the real plans of the apostle and of the claim raised in v. 5. In no sense can this be edifyingly covered over by reference to Paul's modesty (Zahn; Kühl; Gutjahr; Lietzmann; H. W. Schmidt; Kuss), humility (Gaugler; Brunner; Murray), tact and sensitivity (Althaus; Nygren), or (Michel) the caution induced by opposition (for a correct analysis cf. Klein, "Purpose," 45; Zeller, Juden, 53f.). The sudden change from the stylized certainty of the prescript and the dignity of the thanksgiving to the uncertainty and embarrassment which comes to light here (Schubert, Thanksgivings, 5, 33) is hard to explain. It is inadequate to say that in the visit to Rome Paul is clashing with the basic principle solemnly enunciated in 15:20; 2 Cor 10:15f., namely, that he will not enter the missionary territory of others (contra Lagrange; Dodd; Barrett). For he could simply have pointed out, as he does in 15:24, that Rome is a necessary stage on a journey elsewhere. Why, then, is the apostle here not clear and to the point? Why does he see himself required to justify even his writing to the Romans? Why does this letter, conversely, have the character of a summary of his teaching? Why does the threefold assurance of the long-planned visit sound like an apology or even a defense against the suspicion that he was not serious or in no hurry?

When these questions are asked, and contrasted with the real yet concealed plans of the apostle and also with his tremendous claim in v. 5, we come face to face with the problem of Paul's apostolate which influences almost all his epistles and is often their crucial point. The authority which he asserts does not accord with what is conceded to him in fact. Even at the end of his course he stands in the twilight of unclear situations and in conflict with opposing opinions about him. He has to reckon with the fact that doors which he passionately wishes to open are closed to him. The most important theological epistle in Christian history is undoubtedly also the record of an existence struggling for recognition and of an apostolicity called into question. Apart from this insight Romans cannot be interpreted correctly.

As though feeling that he has gone too far, Paul begins afresh in v. 13. In so doing he uses an expression found also in 11:25; 1 Cor 10:1; 12:1; 2 Cor 1:8; 1 Thess 4:13. This expression, which is always followed by an address, corresponds to the γινώσκειν σε θέλω of Hellenistic letters (BAGD, 355) and can also be employed in paraenesis, in distinction from its present use. Taking up v. 10b, the cherished intention of a Roman visit is again asserted along with the unspecified hindrance to it. The careless sentence structure becomes clear when v. 13c is construed as a parenthesis and the introductory καί (BDF, §465[1]) is taken adversatively (J. Weiss, "Beiträge," 212; Kühl; H. W. Schmidt). According to v. 10 ἐκωλύθην is to be related to divine direction. ἄχρι τοῦ δεῦρο is common (BAGD, 176). ἀδελφός is a primitive Christian term for a member of the community which has both Jewish and pagan analogies (Lietzmann). καρπὸν ἔχειν, as in Phil 1:22, comes from the missionary vocabulary of edification. τινά, like τί in v. 11, is a qualifier. The final clause marks a fresh reversal in the train of thought; with καθώς Paul returns to the claim of v. 5.

In v. 14 all uncertainty of tone disappears. Since it is placed under the ἀνάγκη of 1 Cor 9:16, the apostle's mandate is clear and unshakable. He always speaks of it with definite feeling. Even if ὀφειλέτης εἰμί is not said with emphasis as in 8:12; 15:27; Gal 5:3, it does not denote a general duty (contra Minear, "Gratitude," 42ff., following Schlatter) but the special apostolic obligation. Its only boundary is that posed by the Lord, and it embraces (cf. Sass, Apostelamt, 30f.) the whole Gentile world. By it all earthly barriers are relativized, such as the antitheses which from the Greek standpoint differentiate the civilized from the barbarians (Windisch, TDNT, I, 546f.; cf. II, 515). Paul does not deny the reality of the antitheses. But as a messenger of the gospel he can uninhibitedly stride across the conventions and prejudices of the divided cosmos. The wise do not frighten him, and he is equally at home with the foolish. The whole world stands open to him, insofar as he is a servant of the Kyrios (1 Cor 3:21f.).

As though he cannot let the matter drop, he again returns to the subject of the journey in v. 15. If τὸ πρόθυμον is to be regarded as the subject (Sanday and Headlam; Ridderbos), κατ᾽ ἐμέ is a common periphrasis for the genitive in the koine, as in Acts 18:15; 26:3; Eph 1:15 (BDF, §224). But a limiting sense for κατ᾽ ἐμέ cannot be flatly rejected in view of the hindrances already mentioned (Kühl; Lagrange; Gutjahr; Barrett contra Lietzmann; Bardenhewer). The adjective πρόθυμον, used as a noun, needs to be supplemented by an ἐγένετο. The omission of the reference to Rome in G is obviously secondary. If Paul is speaking emphatically of "evangelizing," all the reservations in vv. 10-12 seem to be pointless. But the catchword εὐαγγελίσασθαι is needed here to make the transition to what

20

follows. This also shows that materially vv. 16-17 still belong to the proem, which (Schubert, *Thanksgivings*) in its present form always culminates in a specific concern. They are separated in exposition, then, only in order to give them clear prominence as the theme of the whole epistle. In this letter Paul summarizes the content of the gospel, and in this verse and the following he summarizes the content of this letter (Bengel).

C. Theme (1:16-17)

[16]*For I am not ashamed of the gospel. For it is the power of God to salvation to every one who believes, to the Jew first and also to the Greek.* [17]*For in it the righteousness of God is revealed from faith to faith, as it is written: He who is righteous by faith will live.*

Bibliography: O. Michel, "Zum Sprachgebrauch von ἐπαισχύνομαι in Röm 1, 16," *Glaube und Ethos. Festschrift für Georg Wehrung* (ed. R. Paulus; 1940) 36-53; C. K. Barrett, "I am not ashamed of the Gospel," *Analecta Biblica* 42 (1970) 19-50; Grundmann, *Kraft;* O. Glombitza, "Von der Scham der Gläubigen. Zu Röm 1, 14-17," *NovT* 4 (1960) 74-80; W. Michaelis, "Rechtfertigung aus Glauben bei Paulus," *Festgabe für Adolf Deissmann zum 60. Geburtstag 7. November 1926* (ed. K. L. Schmidt; 1927) 116-138; R. Gyllenberg, "Glaube bei Paulus," *ZST* 13 (1936) 613-626; A. Fridrichsen, "Aus Glauben zu Glauben, Röm 1, 17," *ConNT* 12 (1948) 54; T. Häring, Δικαιοσύνη θεοῦ *bei Paulus* (1896); H. Cremer, *Die paulinische Rechtfertigungslehre im Zusammenhange ihrer geschichtlichen Voraussetzungen* (2nd ed. 1900); K. Müller, "Beobachtungen zur paulinischen Rechtfertigungslehre," *Theologische Studien M. Kähler* (1905) 87-110; A. Schmitt, "Δικαιοσύνη θεοῦ," *Natalicium Johannes Geffcken zum 70. Geburtstag* (ed. R. Helm; 1931) 111-131; O. Zänker, "Δικαιοσύνη θεοῦ bei Paulus," *ZST* 9 (1932) 398-420; R. Gyllenberg, "Die paulinische Rechtfertigungslehre und das Alte Testament," *Studia Theologica* (Riga) 1 (1935) 35-52; H.-D. Wendland, *Mitte;* F. R. Hellegers, "Die Gerechtigkeit Gottes im Römerbrief" (Diss., Tübingen, 1939); H. Hofer, *Die Rechtfertigungsverkündigung des Paulus nach neuerer Forschung. 37 Thesen* (1940); S. Lyonnet, "De Justitia Dei in Epistola ad Romanos," *VD* 25 (1947) 23-34, 118-121, 129-144, 193-203, 257-263; *idem*, "La justice de Dieu," *Étapes*, 25-53; V. Taylor, *Forgiveness and Reconciliation* (1948); H. Riesenfeld, "Accouplements de termes contradictoires dans le Nouveau Testament," *ConNT* 9 (1944) 1-21; A. Oepke, "Δικαιοσύνη θεοῦ bei Paulus in neuer Beleuchtung," *TLZ* 78 (1953) 257-264; E. Käsemann, "The Righteousness of God' in Paul," *New Testament Questions*, 168-182; R. Bultmann, "Δικαιοσύνη θεοῦ," *JBL* 83 (1964) 12-16; G. Klein, "Gottes Gerechtigkeit als Thema der neuesten Paulus-Forschung," *Verkündigung und Forschung* 12 (1967) 1-11; H. Conzelmann, "Paul's Doctrine of Justification, Theology or Anthropology?" *Theology of the Liberating Word* (ed. F. Herzog; 1971) 108-123; E. Käsemann, "Justification and Salvation History in the Epistle to the Romans," *Perspectives*, 60-78; E. Lohse, "Die Gerechtigkeit Gottes in der paulinischen Theologie," *Einheit*, 209-227; A. Feuillet, "La citation d'Habakuk II, 4 et les huit premiers chapitres de l'épître aux Romains," *NTS* 6 (1959/60) 52-80; A. Strobel, *Untersuchungen zum eschatologischen Verzögerungsproblem auf Grund der spätjüdisch-urchristlichen Geschichte von Habakuk 2, 2ff.* (NovTSup 2; 1961); J. A. Fitzmyer, "The Use of Explicit Old Testament Quotations in Qumran Literature and in the New Testament," *NTS* 7 (1960/61) 297-333; G. Jeremias, *Der Lehrer der Gerechtigkeit* (1963); E. Güttgemanns, "Gottesgerechtigkeit und strukturale Semantik," *Studia Linguistica Neotestamentica* (1971) 59-98; G. Herold, *Zorn und Gerechtigkeit bei Paulus. Eine Untersuchung zu Röm 1, 16-18* (1973). For Schlier, "Εὐαγγέλιον," see bibliography for 1:1-7.

Verse 16a refers back to v. 14. οὐ γὰρ ἐπαισχύνομαι should not be understood psychologically, i.e., that Paul need not fear the imperial capital since he is obligated to the whole cosmos (contra Gutjahr; Bardenhewer; Gaugler; J. Knox; Glombitza, "Scham," 74ff.). Rather, we have here a fixed confessional formula which, in emphatic negation, replaces a ὁμολογεῖν (Michel; Barrett, "Not ashamed"; Stuhlmacher, Gerechtigkeit, 78f.), but no longer stresses the original context of the eschatological lawsuit (contra Herold, Zorn, 28-141, 229ff.). It is again clear that gospel and preaching should not simply be equated. What is confessed is neither the action of preaching nor its content. The gospel is more than the message actualized in the church. It is God's declaration of salvation to the world, which is outside human control, which is independent even of the church and its ministers, and which constantly becomes a reality itself in proclamation in the power of the Spirit. It can thus be called δύναμις θεοῦ.

If in Hellenism this would denote miraculous power, under OT/Jewish influence the basic idea shifts to God's activity which directs history (Grundmann, Kraft, 20, 84ff.) and, as here, is torn away from the realm of individual acts of power. The gospel is not one miracle among others. It is the epiphany of God's eschatological power pure and simple. In the same way Mekilta Exodus 15:13, 26, among others, identifies the Torah with the "strength of God" in its exposition of Ps 29:11. From this parallel we should not deduce (contra Grundmann, TDNT, II, 309; Fascher, RAC, IV, 436f.) that Paul is formulating his view in antithesis to the Jewish one. The parallel, however, is probably characteristic for the historical setting of the present statement.

The operation of God's power corresponds to its eschatological nature. It creates salvation in a manner which determines the whole person in time and eternity. This was the expectation of Hellenistic religion as such, and also was promised in the message of the Osiris mysteries; cf. Firmicus Maternus, De errore profanarum religionum, 22: θαρρεῖτε μύσται τοῦ θεοῦ σεσωσμένου ἔσται γὰρ ἡμῖν ἐκ πόνων σωτηρία. The early Christian mission was presented with the term σωτηρία from the LXX as a Hellenizing designation of divine help (Harder, Gebet, 114f.). Its early apocalyptic intensification on Jewish soil is shown by many Qumran texts which speak of the end-time salvation and its attestations (cf. Michel). For Paul and his sources in the tradition, according to 13:11; 5:9; 1 Cor 3:15; 5:5; Phil 1:19, σωτηρία denotes deliverance in the final judgment. Yet the translation "deliverance" does not quite do justice to the fact that, according to 8:24, 2 Cor 6:2, and this passage, the redemption for the new aeon, connected with σωτηρία, already has become a present reality through Christ in the midst of the world and not just an anticipation "in principle" (Lietzmann). Thus παντὶ τῷ πιστεύοντι is sharply opposed here to the consistent limitation to god-fearing members of the covenant people at Qumran. It expresses both the presence of salvation and also its universal scope. Where faith is, there is the place of salvation, and this implies not only assurance of future deliverance from the judgment, but, beyond that, also present peace and joy as a state of openness before God and man. The reference to "every" believer shows that the interpretation by early history-of-religions research, that Paul never has the individual in mind (Wrede, Paul, 113f., 132), is wrong. Universalism and the most radical individuation are here two sides of the same coin.

The subject of faith will be dealt with fully in ch. 4. Hence some preliminary

22

observations demanded by the text must suffice for the moment. In this verse "believe" clearly has the original sense characteristic of the missionary situation, "receive the gospel." The Greek sense, "regard something as true," plays no role for Paul, just as the OT sense, "trust," or, derived from it (Gyllenberg, "Glaube," 626), "become part of a new relationship with God," is still not decisive. The verse speaks of faith only as a decision, so that its character as a gift is not yet in the foreground, but the very dubious speculation about a "supra-individual phenomenon" must be strenuously resisted (contra Stuhlmacher, Gerechtigkeit, 81ff.). Also inadequate is the definition of faith, overplaying the relation to the word, as "disposition of spirit toward God which answers to God's loving disposition toward us" (J. Knox) or as a humble and liberating resignation of oneself to the hidden epiphany of the Kyrios who comes in the word (Stuhlmacher, Gerechtigkeit, 81f.). The gospel is not an epiphany hidden in the word nor is faith a resignation of oneself to it. Rather faith is an appropriation of the eschatological public proclamation made to the whole world and to each individual. Each person is placed in a situation of personal responsibility. That happens at the same time in a worldwide context. We see this both from παντί and also from the elucidatory expression at the end: to the Jew first and also to the Greek.

As previously Greeks and barbarians represented the Gentile world (Windisch, TDNT, I, 546-553), now Jews and Greeks represent the whole cosmos. Paul views the cosmos as historically determined by mankind and not therefore as the ordered nexus of gods and men and things created for their sakes, as Chrysippus formulated it along Stoic lines in Frag. 527. Thus for the apostle the world before and outside Christ divides over the nomos. Therefore it belongs to the gospel, as it enters into earthly realities, to deal with the nomos from the very outset. A later age no longer understood this. Hence Marcion, followed by textual variants, cut out πρῶτον. Its offensiveness may still be seen when reference is made to a factually worthless concession (Lietzmann), or when an interpolation from 2:1f. is conjectured (J. Weiss, "Beiträge," 212f.), or (Zahn; Kühl; H. W. Schmidt) when the term is applied to both Jew and Greek as those who share a common privilege and a common need. We find the same construction, however, in 2 Cor 8:5: "First to the Lord and then to us," and we should not weaken the phrase by speaking of advantage rather than precedence (contra Barth; Michel; correctly Zeller, Juden, 141ff.). Paul gives Judaism precedence for the sake of the continuity of the plan of salvation. If he did not do so, his doctrine of justification would have only the historical interest of a polemical teaching and the doctrine of the incarnation would have to replace it.

God's self-manifestation is decisive for all history. As the Gentiles are not left without a knowledge of his will, so the nomos, as a record of the divine claim, is a power which divides history. The apostle's theology involves a definite salvation-historical perspective. The interpreter who radically denies this is forced to reduce the Lord of history to the creator of the particular moment and hence to do violence to the Pauline doctrine of God. Naturally the precedence of Israel is not understood with the exclusivism we find in Judaism. Who God really is for Paul does not finally derive from the law but from the gospel. Derivation of the δικαιοσύνη θεοῦ from the law is rejected; rather, this righteousness is proclaimed as the righteousness of faith. This catchword not only gives precision to, but is a constitutive interpretation of, what was earlier called present σωτηρία, and therefore of the gospel which Paul first defined in the pre-Pauline christological formula of vv. 3-4 (cf. Bornkamm, *RGG*, V, 177; *Paul*, 117). The doctrine of justification is the specifically Pauline understanding of christology just as the latter is the basis of the former (cf. my essay "Justification and Salvation History," 73ff.; Eichholz, *Paulus*, 38).

That is a thesis which will have to be substantiated in the exegesis of the epistle as a whole, since it is strongly contested even in the Protestantism that derives from the Reformation. Today, to be sure, it is no longer said with the astonishing lucidity of critical Liberalism that the totality of Paul's religion can be set forth without even mentioning the doctrine of justification since it deals with past polemics (Wrede, *Paul*, 123), and constitutes only a "subsidiary crater" in the mysticism of the apostle (A. Schweitzer, *Mysticism*, 225). This doctrine is today recognized even across confessional boundaries as an inalienable constituent of Paul's theology. But the old conflict still arises when justification is regarded as the consequence rather than the content of the gospel (Molland, *Euangelion*, 62f.), or when it is set in the shadow of salvation history and accepted merely as a specific explanation and application of eschatology (Ridderbos, *Paul*, 162), or when it is placed in antithesis (Schweitzer) to the receiving of the Spirit (Ridderbos, *Paul*, 29ff.). Not justification but christology is supposed to be the theme of the epistle, which otherwise might end with 5:1-11 (Friedrich, *RGG*, V, 1139; cf. Ridderbos, *Paul*, *loc. cit.*). These voices undoubtedly represent the dominant position in modern Pauline interpretation and indicate the unsolved basic problem with or without critical reflections. We have here a point of division, which appeared in similar form already in the NT, even in Paul's own mission field, and which continued throughout the history of dogma.

The analysis and interpretation of v. 17 is all the more important since this verse, no less debated than the subject matter as a whole, is the fork in the road for all subsequent exposition. At least in the course of the last century we have freed ourselves from the Greek understanding of δικαιοσύνη as a norm of what is right for God and man (cf. on this Stuhlmacher, *Gerechtigkeit*, 102ff.). The setting in the history of religions of the Pauline theologoumenon is provided by the OT and Judaism. In a way that is, at first glance, confusingly similar to our text Wis 12:16 says of the divine power and dominion: ἡ γὰρ ἰσχύς σου δικαιοσύνης ἀρχή. In a way that is also similar to the present verse, CD 20:20 in Qumran expresses the eschatological hope as follows: "Until salvation and righteousness are revealed for those that fear God."

Unfortunately little is gained concretely by this fixing of the historical background. Further progress is made with the insight (already Cremer, *Rechtfertigungslehre*, 335; K. Müller, "Beobachtungen," 90f.; very clearly Bultmann, *Theology*, I, 270ff.; and in almost complete agreement with this Wendland, *Mitte*) that in biblical usage righteousness, which is essentially forensic, denotes a relation in which one is set, namely, the "recognition" in which one, for example, is acknowledged to be innocent. In Jewish apocalyptic this understanding is applied to the verdict of justification at the last judgment. Justification, at first the presupposition and condition of salvation, as a gift already conferred *in nuce* includes eternal life, and thus becomes itself the benefit of salvation. This is at

24

least true for Paul, especially in the key passage Phil 3:9, in which God's righteousness, reminiscent of צִדְקָתָם מֵאִתִּי. in Isa 54:17, seems to be directly defined by δικαιοσύνη ἐκ θεοῦ.

This must appear all the more as an "authentic interpretation" (Zahn; Billerbeck, following Cremer; Häring; finally, e.g., Bultmann; Nygren; Ridderbos; and Lohse, "Gerechtigkeit," 226f.; but cf. Schrenk, TDNT, II, 206; Lyonnet, "Justitia," 23-34) since it runs parallel to the formula δικαιοσύνη ἐκ/διὰ πίστεως. The Pauline view (according to Bultmann and, e.g., Ridderbos, Paul, 163) is supposed to differ from the Jewish view in that what in Judaism remained an object of hope, and hence of final uncertainty, is regarded by Paul as eschatologically present.

Through its eschatological approach this interpretation from the beginning escapes a difficulty that has always seriously plagued exposition. Previously it was not clear whether the righteousness of God is a divine quality or the gift given to mankind, possibly even (BAGD, 197a; Lietzmann, Lagrange) an ethical quality transferred, in some process, from God to mankind (e.g., Sanday and Headlam; Zänker, "Δικαιοσύνη," 418). In good Reformation tradition, this interpretation did not need to verify the eschatologically understood act of justification either psychologically, ethically, or anthropologically in terms of human development. It had no need to reflect, therefore, on the experience in the consciousness of the believer (K. Müller, "Beobachtungen," 98ff.), or to differentiate the righteousness of faith from the righteousness of life (Hellegers, "Gerechtigkeit," 36ff.), the two stages of the beginning and end of Christian existence (Hofer, Rechtfertigungsverkündigung, 54ff.). To the extent that this interpretation is oriented to the OT motif of covenant faithfulness, it can plausibly explain why δικαιοσύνη never means penal righteousness in Paul even though it retains its forensic character (Bornkamm, Paul, 138), and why not a purely formal verdict but the liberating claim and address of grace becomes a reality in justification (Wendland, Mitte, 26ff.). This approach avoids the foolish debate whether the presence or absence of the article distinguishes the divine righteousness from that received by men (Oepke, "Neue Beleuchtung," 259ff.) or from a righteousness that stands in contrast with penal righteousness (Zahn; Hellegers, "Gerechtigkeit," 45).

A complete history of the interpretation of δικαιοσύνη θεοῦ in Paul can scarcely be given here since it would embrace many volumes. Yet the range of interpretation must be seen paradigmatically in order to avoid escaping the problems of exegeting this passage through shortcuts, as has happened up to the present. Even the interpretation presented above has its weaknesses. Since the discovery of the Dead Sea Scrolls the eschatological presence of the salvation received with God's righteousness can no longer be regarded as an approach peculiar to Paul (in a limited way, Roetzel, Judgement, 74ff.). Many statements, especially in the Hodayoth, disprove this. Some examples may be given to show the extent of the parallels to Paul's proclamation. Thus in 1QH 15:14f.; 16:10 God is the creator of the righteous, whom he has ordained from the womb for the time of good pleasure. Hence 13:16f. confesses, "Only through your goodness is man justified." According to 11:17f. this takes place through the righteousness which is with God and, identical with salvation, expresses itself in God's bestowal of grace. It is said of its effect in 4:37, "You forgive the unjust and purify man from guilt by your righteousness." The standing in new obedience made possible in this way is given a basis in 7:19: "In your righteousness you have raised me up." Parallel to this is 7:14: "In your truth you have guided my steps on the path of righteousness." Now there are those who "are ready for righteousness" (5:21f.), for service to righteousness (6:19), thus who are the "elect of righteousness" (2:13) or simply the righteous (1:36). That this always involves an alien righteousness for which new prayer must continually be made is shown by 11:30f.: "Purify me through your righteousness, as I have waited for your goodness and set my hope upon your grace."

In an age of general Jewish intensification of the Torah this justification can naturally lead only to a radicalized life in the law. This is apparently the decisive difference from Paul's theology, and indeed an unbridgeable gulf between the two. This gulf arises just as clearly from the side of the apostle in virtue of his christology, which rules out the Qumran understanding of the law. Here, then, the true criterion of his doctrine of justification must be sought, not in his present eschatology and everything connected with it, such as his doctrine of the Spirit. The adversaries agree on *sola gratia*. They agree so closely that it has been possible to try to derive Paul's doctrine of grace from that of Qumran (Schulz, "Rechtfertigung," 182ff.; but cf. Zeller, *Juden,* 175ff.).

Although this last conclusion remains highly doubtful, and different strands at Qumran warn us against totally explaining the texts quoted as absolutely binding, the problem of Paul's conception has thereby been brought to a new stage. Interpretation can no longer be content to take Phil 3:9 as the normative key to Paul's doctrine of justification with no awareness at all of the broad agreement here between Paul and Qumran. Obviously it is also not enough to regard Paul's *sine lege* and *sola fide* and Qumran's orientation to the intensified Torah as characteristic ways of radicalizing a common basic outlook, which in the history of religions may be designated apocalyptic. This would lead to a historical conclusion which leaves the theological validity of Paul's argument up in the air.

Even reference to Paul's christology as the reason for the difference remains within the sphere of a purely historical explanation and does not answer the material theological question. This question runs as follows: Why and to what extent does Paul view the righteousness of God *sine lege* and *sola fide* as the content of the gospel and the end-time gift pure and simple? That it has to be regarded as God's gift is not derived only from Phil 3:9 but is apparent everywhere, and allows the righteousness of God and the righteousness of faith to be equated. Greek grammar and its distinction between an objective and a subjective genitive, between a genitive of relation and a genitive of author, can help to clarify interpretation to some extent. But grammatical distinctions merely label and abridge what is perceived to be a material problem without finally clarifying it. Why does Paul fundamentally reject the Jewish doctrine of justification by using the catchword ἰδία δικαιοσύνη even though this Jewish doctrine, at least in some Qumran strata, appeals to *sola gratia* no less than he himself does (cf. further J. Becker, *Heil Gottes,* 120ff., 149ff., 257f.; Stuhlmacher, *Gerechtigkeit,* 159ff.)? The appeal to *sola gratia* finds classical expression, probably drawn from heretical views (cf. Harnisch, *Verhängnis,* 235ff.), in 4 Ezra 8:31-36: "For we and our fathers have

26

done works of death, but thou, for the sake of us sinners, art called the merciful one. For if thou wilt have mercy on us who have done no (good) works, then thou wilt be called the merciful one. . . . For in this thy goodness [secondarily added, thy righteousness], Lord, will show itself, when thou hast mercy on those who have no treasure of works." Here, even if Jewish orthodoxy sharply rejected it, the justification of the ungodly is believed and proclaimed in Judaism, and thus the most extreme intensification of Paul's doctrine of grace is recognized. This means that a new beginning is probably called for if we are to see correctly what is peculiar to the apostle and to grasp properly the "polemical teaching," which is for him constitutive of the gospel.

That has been attempted, doubtless in dependence on the older, and as such superseded, understanding of the righteousness of God as a divine quality which lays hold of mankind. Subjected to sharp criticism was a presumed "Reformation" interpretation which paid attention only to the gift the believer receives and thus weakened the parallelism of the genitive construction δικαιοσύνη θεοῦ with the constructions δύναμις θεοῦ and ὀργή θεοῦ occurring in the context (Schlatter). This position argued that δικαιοσύνη θεοῦ is a subjective genitive that from the beginning expresses an action of God (Schrenk, *TDNT*, II, 203f.), and rejected an understanding which relates only to the individual (ibid.; already in Müller, "Beo-bachtungen," 92ff.; also Wendland, *Mitte*, 44f.; Nygren). Just as, in view of the OT equivalent (Gyllenberg, "Glaube"), incorporation into the covenant fellowship was presented as the work of God's righteousness, so emphasis should now fall on integration into a universal event of salvation (Schrenk, *TDNT*, II, 206f.). It could even be maintained (Schmitt, "Δικαιοσύνη θεοῦ"; Hellegers, "Gerechtig-keit," 68) that righteousness of God in a weakened form means simply salvation or (Baulès) divine love. The mark of this understanding, which is a variation of the older idea of righteousness as a divine quality, is the presupposition that Paul's genitive construction denotes a *nomen actionis* and designates the eschatological action of salvation (Dodd; Huby; Taylor; Barrett; in inclination also Althaus; Michel; Kuss; most strongly Lyonnet, "Justitia," 31ff.: The attribute of God is the saving activity of God; *Étapes*, 32ff.). Against this line of interpretation, which now seems to be predominant, the following objections arise: it unduly neglects the Pauline characteristic that the righteousness granted to faith is a gift; it frequently overlooks the forensic and apocalyptic horizon of the Pauline expression; it simply makes righteousness an alternative term for the mercy, kindness, and love of God (Zeller, *Juden*, 178).

The older battle lines still exist, fundamentally the same although in modern form. They have been brought closer together only insofar as history-of-religions work on the OT and Judaism can no longer be ignored and this work raises the question of how far Paul still stood under the leading idea of covenant faithfulness, with which indeed a relationship is posited, an action as well as a state is denoted, and the idea of penal righteousness is excluded (Furnish, *Ethics*, 144ff.). At least this religio-historical dependence, which explains the closeness of Paul's statements to the Qumran texts quoted above, should no longer be contested. Rom 3:5, 25 show irrefutably that the apostle was acquainted with it. If in connection with the antithesis of the two covenants he speaks in 2 Cor 3:9 of the διακονία τῆς δικαιοσύνης, he likewise presupposes this historical context in his theology, makes use of an expression for which 1QH 6:19 could have been a model, and understands God's righteousness primarily as power rather than as gift. He understands it primarily as power when he speaks of subjection to this righteousness in Rom 10:3, or when he sets the whole of the Christian life under this sign of submission in Rom 6:13ff., or when he even identifies δικαιοσύνη and θεός by placing them in parallel in 6:18, 22 (almost always underplayed, or ignored as, e.g., by Lohse, "Gerechtigkeit"!). When Christ in 1 Cor 1:30 and the Christian community in 2 Cor 5:21 are designated as God's righteousness (cf. on all these passages Stuhlmacher, *Gerechtigkeit*, 74-99), one may speak of a typical Semitic abstraction, but this contributes little to interpretation. In any case the probable original reading of *T. Dan* 6:10, ἀπόστητε οὖν ἀπὸ πάσης ἀδικίας καὶ κολλήθητε τῇ δικαιοσύνῃ τοῦ θεοῦ, could have made clear that in Judaism God's righteousness has a field of radiation and a place of manifestation, which fits well with both Pauline texts. It will become clear in 3:21 that δικαιοσύνη θεοῦ and δόξα θεοῦ are used synonymously and that in 8:30 and 2 Cor 3:18 Paul speaks analogously of the present glorification of Christians. Finally, in 2 Cor 3:8f. he uses "ministry of righteousness" and "ministry of the Spirit" alternately. Must we not infer from this that in some respect righteousness, glory, and Spirit are identical for him? If we make this inference against the dominant trend, however, we inevitably run up against the problem that Spirit is for the apostle both the divine power which encounters us in Christ and also the gift which is eschatologically granted to the Christian. This fact cannot be resolved nor even be understood by debating the suitable classification of such genitive constructions in the code of a Greek grammar, as O. Schmitz (*Christusgemeinschaft*) has quite appropriately pointed out in his book on the Christian fellowship with its rather comical-sounding title. What is even more comical is that when the δικαιοσύνη θεοῦ is discussed there is virtual consensus today in speaking of a genitive of author, yet everyone conceals his own opinion behind this grammatical cipher. In a technical age, rules of language often wrap material problems in a thick fog and make it possible for opposing views to achieve an easy peace.

Paul himself permits us to reconcile the apparent contradiction, for power and gift are not true antitheses in his eyes (cf. my essay "Righteousness," 169ff.). The context of the present verse demonstrates this when Paul designates the gospel which is revealed and given to Christians simultaneously as the power of God. The apostle's christology treats nothing other than Christ as in the full sense God's gift for us—"given for us"—and yet no less our Lord. In Paul χάρις is primarily the power of grace and yet it comes to individually concretized expression in charisma. Through the gift of Christ's body we are also incorporated into the sphere of the lordship of Christ's body, according to 1 Cor 10:16. All this not only has a broad inner context in Paul's theology; it is also constitutive for it. For the apostle knows of no gift which does not also challenge us to responsibility, thereby showing itself as a power over us and creating a place of service for us. Conversely, he knows no God who can be isolated from his creation, only the God who is manifest in his creation in judgment and grace, and who acts in relation to it as Lord. The apostle's genitive constructions which speak of the eschatological gifts fit without exception in this basic view, and do so in such a

28

way that the stress falls on the genitive: it is in reality God himself who enters the earthly sphere in what he grants to us.

If this is so, however, the interpretation of the phrase "righteousness of God" in Paul is no longer a problem. It speaks of the God who brings back the fallen world into the sphere of his legitimate claim (*contra* the polemic of Lohse, "Gerechtigkeit," 225f.), whether in promise or demand, in new creation or forgiveness, or in the making possible of our service, and—what must be no less considered according to Gal 5:5—who sets us in the state of confident hope and, according to Phil 3:12, constant earthly change. With recourse to the Kyrios acclamation we may summarize the whole message of the epistle in the brief and paradoxical statement that the Son of God is as our Kyrios the one eschatological gift of God to us and that herein is revealed simultaneously both God's legitimate claim on us and also our salvation.

The Qumran texts which speak of present justification share the same power–gift structure. Since christology does not determine these texts they can speak only of a renewal of the old covenant, accomplished through forgiveness, purification, and active sanctification in the service of the law, although sometimes they introduce the concept of a new creation. Because of his christological connection and basis Paul must identify the righteousness of God with the righteousness of faith and let the stress fall on the conferred gift of salvation. On this account, however, standing in salvation is both here and everywhere standing in obedience, that is, in the presence and under the power of Christ. To this extent Paul's doctrine of justification is simply a precise theological variation of the primitive Christian proclamation of the kingdom of God as eschatological salvation. By no means accidentally it to that extent takes up the previously given message of the enacted change in aeons and extends this message anthropologically to the proclamation of a change in existence. Since the christological connection is absent in Qumran, the identification of the righteousness of God with the righteousness of faith is also absent, the change in aeons is restricted to the sphere of the covenant, and anthropologically it is impossible to advance beyond the ethical dualism of the conflict between flesh and spirit. In this light the similarity and the difference of the two approaches are understandable.

Since already at Qumran the renewal of the covenant is apocalyptically related to the concept of the divine righteousness, the question arises whether Paul did not find this concept already established in a fixed formula. It is striking that he does not speak only of justification. His antithesis between one's own righteousness and that which God gives, and his personification of God's righteousness, would be most easily explained by an already given formula of this sort, especially since it also seems to be present, although in another sense (*contra* Stuhlmacher, *Gerechtigkeit*, 188ff.), in *T. Dan* 6:10 and also in Matt 6:33; Jas 1:20. The Jewish references to it are not overwhelming. Deut 33:21, the only passage in the Hebrew OT, speaks in the singular of the righteousness of God (cf. Oepke, "Neue Beleuchtung," 260ff.), but it is probable (cf. Stuhlmacher, *Gerechtigkeit*, 142ff.) that this is a Masoretic alteration from an original plural, "demonstrations of salvation." Since the LXX and Hellenistic Judaism drop out (Stuhlmacher, 106-112), apart from *T. Dan* 6:10 only a few Qumran passages can withstand strict standards of evaluation. Remarkably, they are not found in the *Hodayoth*, but in

29

the confession of 1QS 10:25; 11:12 and particularly in the inscription "righteousness of God" on standards for the holy war, 1QM 4:6. In context (*contra* Thyen, *Studien*, and his criticism of Stuhlmacher, cf. 56ff.) this inscription is absolutely not to be reinterpreted as "vengeance of God." To what degree further traces of a fixed formula may be found (cf. Stuhlmacher, 154ff.; Zeller, *Juden*, 171) depends very largely on the interpreter's approach. Even with extreme caution we may hold that it is not only possible but probable that Paul did take over this characteristic catchword as a fixed formula from Jewish apocalyptic (rejected by Lohse, "Gerechtigkeit," 216ff.) and that he impressed on this tradition the stamp of his own theology. If this is so, we should begin with the genitive construction and its original reference to God's covenant faithfulness. This blocks from the beginning the temptation to treat δικαιοσύνη initially by itself and to reach a purely juridical meaning, or even, in the light of Greek usage, to come up where possible with the sense of a legal norm. Our further analysis need concern itself only with how the apostle develops this catchword for his epistle and orients it in various ways.

If v. 17 contains the theme of the epistle, due weight must be given to each word in it. Even if ἀποκαλύπτειν does not necessarily have an "apocalyptic" sense, in this context that seems most natural. The gospel is the power of God because in it the divine righteousness breaks into the world as eschatological revelation. Two mutually opposing views are both refuted herewith. One cannot maintain (*contra* Bornkamm, *Paul*, 114f.) that the presence of salvation does not fit into any apocalyptic concept. Nor can one argue on the other side (*contra* Stuhlmacher, *Gerechtigkeit*, 79ff., 238f., and *passim*) that the reference here is, in anticipation of the ultimate revelation, to the still hidden epiphany which is veiled in the word. If the texts quoted from the *Hodayoth* and the idea of the new covenant at Qumran have not already reduced the first thesis to absurdity, the epistle itself will do so continually. Otherwise, as is now claimed in many places, talk of the eschatological character of the primitive Christian message would be without meaning. Admittedly it is an illegitimate exaggeration to import the slogan about the end of history into Paul's writings (probably first done by Bultmann, *History and Eschatology*, 36, 43). Nevertheless, from John the Baptist to the Revelation of John the dawn of the end-time, and thus salvation as apocalyptically present, is proclaimed.

The second thesis not only runs contrary to the wording of this verse but also illegitimately transfers what is true of faith to the word, which neither in Paul nor in Reformation theology could be regarded as a "veil," and which in contrast to the Torah has no cover over it according to 2 Corinthians 3. According to 1 Cor 1:18ff. the revelation of the Son of God is a stumbling block and foolishness because it is publicly proclaimed to Jew and Greek (i.e., to all the world, as in 1 Tim 3:16). As the message of the lordship of Christ it can never be surpassed in content, even though according to Paul its universal acceptance has yet to come. The bridge from the message of justification to an ontology can be built only by speculation. But this necessarily pushes the word of the cross into the background, and faith, instead of being acceptance of this word and nothing more, becomes a stage in an apocalyptic process of development. Such a view of faith is ruled out by the end of v. 17a, which has often been a subject of puzzlement. If ἐκ πίστεως εἰς πίστιν is not simply declared to be meaningless (Pallis), it is usually referred to a movement either in the life of the individual Christian or in salvation history (cf. the survey in Kuss). That it has the character of Semitic rhetoric (J. Weiss, "Beiträge," 213; Lietzmann; Ridderbos; but cf. Oepke, *TDNT*, II, 430 and, e.g., H. W. Schmidt) may be seen from several parallels: ἐκ κακῶν εἰς κακά, Jer 9:2; ἐκ δύναμεως εἰς δύναμιν, Ps 83:8; ἐκ θανάτου εἰς θάνατον, 2 Cor 2:16; ἀπὸ δόξης εἰς δόξαν, 2 Cor 3:18; καθ' ὑπερβολὴν εἰς ὑπερβολήν, 2 Cor 4:17; to which one may add χάριν ἀντὶ χάριτος, John 1:16 and the burial inscription ἐκ γῆς εἰς γῆν ὁ βίος οὗτος (cited in BAGD, 663). On the basis of its position the expression can scarcely belong to the subject, and on the basis of the subject matter it cannot belong to the verb (*contra* Murray). Logically, then, it is related only loosely to the preceding statement. In the sense of *sola fide* it emphatically sets forth "unbroken continuity" (Fridrichsen, "Aus Glauben," 54) or, better, the "dimension of the new world" (Stuhlmacher, *Gerechtigkeit*, 83; similarly Michel; Gaugler): The revelation of God's righteousness, because it is bound to the gospel, takes place always only in the sphere of faith.

Using a common formula for a quotation, Paul proves his point from Hab 2:4. The δέ in the quotation supports the literal adoption of an existing text but not (*contra* Lagrange; Kuss) in a modification of the LXX, since the LXX speaks, not of faith, but of God's faithfulness: ὁ δὲ δίκαιός μου ἐκ πίστεώς μου ζήσεται. The exact parallel in Gal 3:11, and even more so the form in Heb 10:38, ὁ δὲ δίκαιός μου ἐκ πίστεως ζήσεται, which corresponds materially but does not derive from Paul, suggests that we have here an exposition of the original text which understands באמונתו in terms of the situation of the Christian community. Since we are acquainted with an analogous interpretation in terms of the situation of the Qumran community (1QpHab 8:2f.) occasioned by the meditation on the *kairos* in Hab 2:3 (Strobel, *Untersuchungen*, 173ff.), we can no longer trace back the Christian version to the apostle himself (as Michel, *Bibel*, 73f., 90 still does). He took it over from the Jewish-Christian mission, which found in Hab 2:4 a prophecy of salvation by faith in the Messiah just as Qumran found salvation in commitment to the Teacher of Righteousness.

Full discussion of this Qumran text cannot be undertaken here (cf. Herold, *Zorn*, 152ff.). It is of interest for our purpose only insofar as it helps us to see the possibility of the Christian exposition on the basis of existing Jewish speculations and meditations, and the contrast with this exposition. The Jewish text tells us that "God will save all doers of the law of the house of Judah from the house of judgment because of their toil and their faithfulness to the Teacher of Righteousness." Against a messianological interpretation of the passage, and an understanding of the relationship to the Teacher which sees a reference to personal, saving faith, conclusive objections have been raised: In 1QpHab 10:12 toil means labor over the Torah. The reference to the Teacher follows because he guarantees the correct exposition and proclamation (G. Jeremias, *Lehrer*, 144f.). One may question whether it talks of faith instead of faithfulness (Braun, *Qumran*, I, 170; II, 172), but this is less likely. In any case the Teacher is himself the object of personal attachment (Braun, II, 169), even if this is caused by his teaching and not his person (G. Jeremias, *Lehrer*, 145). The relationship to him, however, stands under the sign of observance of the law. The material difference from the Christian interpretation is thus unmistakable.

31

On the other hand, some notable steps have been taken toward the Christian interpretation. Nowhere else in Judaism is Hab 2:4 seen in terms of attachment to a person. Again, the construction of the noun with the preposition ב, which does not occur in the OT, corresponds to a πίστις ἐν, as is found in Gal 3:26, etc. (G. Jeremias, *Lehrer*, 145f.), even if ἐν does not here denote the object of faith. Naturally this does not mean that primitive Christianity knew and developed this tradition. The all-important object is missing in Paul's quotations and their parallels, and faith has here a different sense from that in the OT and Judaism. What is demonstrated is simply that there had been meditation on Hab 2:4 and that this might have attracted the attention of the primitive church.

This community gathered from the verse that eschatological life is promised to faith. Possibly in the early days of the Gentile mission this could have had a polemical edge—to faith alone. This, anyway, is the point in Paul. Perhaps he went a step further. In Heb 10:38 and even Gal 3:11, as in the original Hebrew text and the LXX, the phrase ἐκ πίστεως belongs with the verb. Here, however, the context and the apostle's doctrine of justification suggest—although this is strongly contested—that it is to be related to the subject (J. Knox; Black; Schlier, "Εὐαγγέλιον," 140; Herold, *Zorn*, 180f.; differently Feuillet, "Citation," 52f., 62f., 76). The prophetic future promises permanence. To make the quotation govern the structure of chs. 1–4 and 5–8 (Nygren; modified by Feuillet, e.g., 54ff.) is artificial and does not take the second half of the epistle into account. Paul's interpretation of Hab 2:4 neither does justice to the OT text nor finds any support in Jewish exegesis (cf. Billerbeck; Moore, *Judaism*, II, 237f.). At this point this differs greatly from Paul. It refers to the faith of the patriarchs, or to the minimal demand of the monotheistic confession, or to trust in God as the sum of all the commandments, or to the fulfilment of the commandments. Qumran also finds a reference to faithfulness to the Teacher of Righteousness. In any case, πίστις is always understood as a work. Hence the problem of the primitive Christian proof from Scripture arises already in this verse. In Paul it reveals the dialectical relation to the OT which is necessarily bound up with his understanding of the law.

II. The Need for the Revelation of the Righteousness of God (1:18–3:20)

This section of the epistle speaks of human guilt and divine judgment in relation to Gentiles and Jews, who are viewed as representatives of humanity and together define the nature of the cosmos. This is why the two subsections 1:18-32 and 2:1–3:20 overlap. In the first part the spotlight undoubtedly falls on the Gentile world, but the total emphasis increasingly involves criticism of religious humanity, specifically represented by Judaism. This is the reason for our present arrangement.

Bibliography: E. Grafe, "Das Verhältnis der paulinischen Schriften zur Sapienta Salomonis," *Festschrift C. v. Weizsäcker* (1892) 251-286; E. Weber, *Die Beziehungen von Röm 1–3 zur Missionspraxis des Paulus* (BFCT 9/2; 1905); A. Daxer, "Römer 1,18-2,10 im Verhältnis zur spätjüdischen Lehrauffassung" (Diss., Rostock, 1914); A. Oepke, *Die Missionspredigt des Apostels Paulus* (1920); K. Oltmanns, "Das Verhältnis von Röm 1,18-3, 20 zu 3, 21ff." *ThBl* 8 (1929) 110-16; G. Kuhlmann, *Theologia naturalis bei Philon und Paulus* (1930); M. Pohlenz, "Paulus und die Stoa," *ZNW* 42 (1949) 69-104; W. L. Knox, *Some Hellenistic Elements in Primitive Christianity* (Schweich Lectures, 1942; 1944); J. Jeremias, "Zur Gedankenführung in den paulinischen Briefen," *Studia Paulina*, 146-154; P. Dalbert, *Die Theologie der hellenistisch-jüdischen Missionsliteratur unter Ausschluss von Philo und Josephus* (1954); G. Bornkamm, "The Revelation of God's Wrath (Romans 1–3)," *Early Christian Experience*, 47-70; R. C. M. Ruijs, *De strukter van de brief aan de Romeinen. Een stilistische, vormhistorische en thematische analyse van Rom 1,16–3,23* (1964); H. M. Schenke, "Aporien im Römerbrief," *TLZ* 92 (1967) 881-88. For Strobel, *Untersuchungen,* and Herold, *Zorn,* see bibliography for 1:16-17.

The tension between cosmology and anthropology characterizes the whole of Paul's theology. The typically Jewish distinction between Gentile and Jew, which is evident especially in Eph 2:11ff., sets forth the worldwide scope of his theology and also indicates the nature of humanity in its exemplary possibilities and realities. This section of the epistle deals with the totality of the cosmos and not just with an aggregate of individuals; hence, it deals with humanity as such and not just with representatives of religious groupings. This is the basic presupposition of the argument, but it also stands in the way of a logically clear reproduction of it. However, in the light of the indisputable temperament of the apostle and the doubtless considerable difficulties in dictating such a long epistle, may one expect anything like systematic logic at all? In particular, do not the many digressions and the leaps in the train of thought show that what we have here is not a self-contained treatise but the deposit of many debates which, because of its conver-

33

sational character, which shines through everywhere, should be given the title "Dialogue with the Jews" (Jeremias, "Gedankenführung," 149)?

Particularly in this section of the epistle such questions relate to the older thesis (e.g., Michel) that the vivid experience and preaching of Paul the missionary is reflected here in a special way. There is some truth in this thesis, but it probably applies to all the Pauline epistles. It is only the strength of this influence that is problematic. The use of stylistic devices which had already been developed by the diatribe (cf. Bultmann, *Stil, passim*), and especially the discussion of objections raised by real or fictitious opponents, can hardly be overlooked.

It is another matter, however, when the inner consistency in the structure of the epistle, which is directed toward a concrete goal, is destroyed by the assertion that Paul has merely assembled fragments from earlier disputations and sermons. In contrast to many speeches in Acts, these chapters do not so much offer stylized examples or summaries of missionary proclamation as reflections which take up the motifs of such proclamation (Kuss).

The epistle is clearly addressed to a community whose firm status as Christians is not in doubt, and from whom a high degree of theological understanding is required in view of the dogmatic concentration of this letter (cf. Oepke, *Missionspredigt*, 70, 82ff.; with some exaggeration Jervell, *Imago*, 313). The accusations made by the apostle are not directed against them and are not meant to stir them to repentance. A religio-historical explanation of our text, which places it ultimately within the context of apologetics and polemics, as they were pursued by the Diaspora synagogue (Dupont, *Gnosis*, 21ff.), fails to perceive its true scope. The theme, argument, and outcome of the whole letter point instead to the sphere of a uniquely modified Jewish-Christian apocalyptic. There is modification to the extent that the Jewish doctrine of the two aeons is assumed as known and yet (*contra* Nygren; Stählin, *TDNT*, V, 433) with good reason is not adopted explicitly. From apocalyptic one can grasp the blackness of the picture which leaves hardly any place for a consideration of authentic religiosity, presents the general depravity of humanity without differentiation, and demonstrates it by the most abhorrent perversions. Into this framework elements of a different provenance and even of a missionary tendency might also fit easily. But whereas, for example, in the Jewish parts of the *Sibylline Oracles* apocalyptic serves the propaganda which calls for repentance, the situation is the direct opposite in Paul. Paul uses other traditions in the service of his concern to depict the world under the wrath of God.

Only in light of this insight can one appropriately define the theological relevance of this portion of the letter and its relation to what follows. If one characterizes it as preliminary (Dodd), as the basis of the positive presentation (Michel), or more dubiously as propaedeutic (Oepke, *Missionspredigt*, 104), in any case one cannot speak of its "pre-evangelical" (Oepke, *TDNT*, III, 586f.) or even (Lietzmann on 2:26) "hypothetical" character. In fact the presupposition of all that is to come is given here. But it is not a matter of making psychological "contact" as in preaching, a contact which would prepare the hearers for the true message— if only by emphasizing the contrast between what men deserve and what God does instead. Equally it does not merely establish that the world does not possess the righteousness which Paul proclaims (*contra* Lagrange). In all these interpretations the overemphasis on missionary motifs avenges itself. In view of the contact of this section with Wisdom of Solomon 12–14, missionary motifs cannot be contested. This proves the use of common tradition (Michel, *Bibel*, 14-18), not the direct dependence of the apostle (*contra* Grafe, "Verhaltnis"; Norden, *Agnostos Theos*, 128ff.; Herold, *Zorn*, 189f.). Nevertheless, the tradition is put to use here from a different perspective.

This may be seen if, in anticipation of the exposition of the next section, the connection of 1:18ff. with the theme in v. 16 is considered. Verses 17 and 18 are deliberate antithetical parallels. The γάρ, which introduces the basis, in v. 18 corresponds to the threefold repetition in vv. 16f., and is not therefore a mere transitional particle (*contra* Lietzmann; Kuss). The need for the righteousness of God comes to light simultaneously with its actualization (Eichholz, *Paulus*, 64f.; Zeller, *Juden*, 146f.). For ἀποκαλύπτεται does not denote the urgent announcement of the wrath of the last day (Kühl), or of God's wrath ensuing from now on (Zahn), or, without reference to time, the retribution of God (Lietzmann; Lagrange), or his nemesis (Dodd). The present tense has the same force as in v. 17. It relates to something which is already present although not yet recognized, to something which only now comes to light along with the gospel and in the realm of the gospel (though cf. Ridderbos, *Paul*, 109f.). For in this salvation-historical context Paul is not speaking of the divine ἀνοχή before Christ (*contra* Oepke, *TDNT*, III, 583; Bornkamm, "Revelation," 62f.; Herold, *Zorn*, 267ff., 335, who relates the revelation of the wrath to the cross and therefore finds the basis of the revelation of righteousness in the revelation of the wrath), as he does in 2:4 or Acts 14:16; 17:30. As in 5:12ff.; 7:7ff.; 8:18f.; chs. 9–11, the nature of the world before Christ and outside him is to stand under the wrath of God, namely, in lostness, bondage, and rejection (Stählin, *TDNT*, V, 431). This is disclosed, not by two different revelations, but in one and the same act of revelation.

Prior to the gospel man does not really know what sin is even though he lives in it. Similarly he does not know about the wrath to which he has fallen victim. Wrath is not (correctly Bornkamm, "Revelation," 48) the content of the gospel, nor (*contra* Gaugler; Black; Roetzel, *Judgement*, 79f.) part of the divine righteousness, nor its function (Herold, *Zorn*, 302, 329). Justifying righteousness and condemning righteousness do not run parallel (*contra* Kühl; Lietzmann). Yet the eschatological present implicitly illuminates the past (cf. Schenke, "Aporien," 888), which was previously concealed (Bornkamm, "Revelation," 61ff.). This is not the result nor is it the true point of the gospel, but its reverse side. It is not merely something of which man now becomes conscious from within but an event which encounters him from without and which is therefore characterized as eschatological revelation.

Here also everything depends on stressing the character of divine righteousness as power. God has always exercised his claim to dominion over creation by meeting the disobedient with retribution. As justification, the gospel always means deliverance from wrath, the justification of the ungodly, eschatological *creatio ex nihilo*, and anticipation of the resurrection of the dead, as 4:17 clearly says. These verses are not pedagogical preparation for the message of salvation (*contra* Leenhardt), but characterize its cosmic breadth and depth. Its reality and necessity coincide. To bring out its world-embracing reality, the apostle first proclaims its necessity. He does this for Christians who no longer need propaedeutics or a missionary point of contact. The righteousness of God in its universal character can be grasped only when the world before and apart from Christ is seen under the wrath of God, although missionary preaching should not and must not make God's wrath its starting point. It is no accident that vv. 16ff. precede this section. Here, then, the Gentiles are not addressed directly on the subject of the reality which determines them.

A. The Revelation of God's Wrath on the Gentiles (1:18-32)

[2

¹⁸For God's wrath is revealed from heaven on every ungodliness and unrighteousness of men, who with unrighteousness suppress the truth. ¹⁹For what can be known of God is manifest to them. God himself has made it known to them. ²⁰For from the creation of the world he is perceived in his invisibility and known in what is made, (which means:) his eternal power and deity, so that they are without excuse. ²¹For although they knew God, they did not give (him) honor or thanks as God, but they became empty in their thoughts, and their foolish heart was darkened. ²²While they claimed to be wise they became foolish. ²³They exchanged the glory of the incorruptible God for the likeness of the image of mortal humanity and of birds and animals and reptiles. ²⁴Therefore God gave them up in the lusts of their hearts to uncleanness, to the dishonoring of their own bodies by themselves. ²⁵They have changed the truth of God into a lie and offered worship and service to the creature instead of the Creator—blessed be he for ever, Amen. ²⁶Therefore God has given them up to shameful passions. Their women have exchanged natural intercourse for unnatural. ²⁷Men similarly have given up natural intercourse with women, being consumed with passion for one another. Men committed shameless acts with men and received in their own persons due retribution for their error. ²⁸Because they did not see fit to acknowledge God, God gave them up to an empty mind and to illicit conduct: ²⁹Filled with every kind of unrighteousness, wickedness, covetousness, malice; full of envy, murder, strife, deceit, malignity. (They are) gossips, ³⁰slanderers, haters of God, violent, insolent, boasters, inventors of evil, rebellious against parents; ³¹foolish, inconstant, without love, without mercy. ³²They knew God's just decree that those who do such things deserve to die; (nevertheless) they not only do them but even approve when others do them.

Bibliography: 18: H. Schulte, *Der Begriff der Offenbarung im NT* (BEvT 13; 1949); R. Bultmann, "Der Begriff der Offenbarung im NT," *Glauben und Verstehen*, III, 1-34; D. Lührmann, *Das Offenbarungsverständnis bei Paulus und in Paulinischen Gemeinden* (WMANT 16; 1965); A. Ritschl, *Die christliche Lehre von der Rechtfertigung und Versöhnung*, II (2nd ed. 1882) 119-148; M. Pohlenz, *Vom Zorne Gottes. Eine Studie über den Einfluss der griechischen Philosophie auf das alte Christentum* (FRLANT 12; 1909); A. T. Hanson, *The Wrath of the Lamb* (1957); G. H. C. Macgregor, "The Concept of the Wrath of God in the NT," *NTS* 6 (1960/61) 101-109. **19ff.:** A. Fridrichsen, "Zur Auslegung von Röm 1, 19f.," *ZNW* 17 (1916) 159-168; H. Schlier, "Von den Heiden," *Die Zeit der Kirche*, 29-37; F. Flückiger, "Zur Unterscheidung von Heiden und Juden in Röm. 1,18–2,3," *TZ* 10 (1954) 154-58; A. Feuillet, "La connaissance naturelle de Dieu par les hommes, d'après *Rom.* 1,

18-32," *Lumière et Vie* 14 (1954) 63-80; M. Barth, "Speaking of Sin (Some Interpretative Notes on Romans 1.18–3.20)," *SJT* 8 (1955) 288-296; H. Bietenhard, "Natürliche Gottes-erkenntnis bei den Heiden?" *TZ* 12 (1956) 275-288; S. Schulz, "Die Anklage in Röm. 1, 18-32," *TZ* 14 (1958) 161-173; H. Ott, "Röm. 1, 19ff. als dogmatisches Problem," *TZ* 15 (1959) 40-50. **22ff.:** E. Klostermann, "Die adäquate Vergeltung in Rm 1₂₂₋₃₁," *ZNW* 32 (1933) 1-6; J. Jeremias, "Zu Rm 1₂₂₋₃₂," *ZNW* 45 (1954) 119-123; K. Koch, "Gibt es ein Vergel-tungsdogma im AT?" *ZTK* 52 (1955) 1-42; J. Schneider, *Doxa. Eine bedeutungsgeschichtliche Studie* (1932); C. Mohrmann, "Note zur δόξα," *Sprachgeschichte und Wortbedeutung. Festschrift, Albert Debrunner gewidmet* (1954) 321-28; H. Schlier, "Doxa bei Paulus als heilsgeschichtlicher Begriff," *Stud.Paul.Congr.,* I, 45-56; N. Hyldahl, "A Reminiscence of the OT at Romans i. 23," *NTS* 6 (1959/60) 297-306. **28ff.:** A. Bonhöffer, *Epiktet und das NT* (1911); B. S. Easton, "NT Ethical Lists," *JBL* 51 (1932) 1-12; E. de los Rios, "Ad catalogos peccatorum apud S. Paulum animadversiones," *VD* 12 (1932) 364-370; A. Vögtle, *Die Tugend- und Laster-kataloge im NT exegetisch, religions- und formgeschichtlich untersucht* (1936); S. Wibbing, *Die Tugend- und Lasterkataloge im NT und ihre Traditionsgeschichte unter besonderer Be-rücksichtigung der Qumran-Texte* (BZNW 25; 1959); E. Kamlah, *Die Form der katalogischen Paränese im NT* (1964). **31:** A. Fridrichsen, "᾽ΑΣΥΝΘΕΤΟΣ," *ConNT* 9 (1944) 47f. See also the bibliography for 1:18–3:20.

Verse 18 gives the theme of the section, vv. 19-21 characterize the guilt of the Gentiles, and vv. 22-32 portray God's judgment. The concept of the wrath of God, which is common in Paul, does not derive from Greek tradition but from OT-Jewish apocalyptic. Hence it is not to be viewed as an emotion nor set within the framework of a moral world view. Otherwise we should have to agree with Ritschl (*Rechtfertigung*, II, 153f.) that what comes to expression here is an anthropo-morphic approach that obscures the love of God. Marcion already perceived it this way, and excised θεοῦ. Our starting point should be that the manifestation of this wrath is described in vv. 24ff. Then psychologizing language about holy indignation (Nygren; Gaugler; Murray; Fichtner, *TDNT*, V, 407f.; Feuillet, "Con-naissance," 66) is impossible. Remaining in the foreground, however, is the characteristic which psychology would like to avoid by establishing a purely im-manent causal connection between guilt and retribution (Dodd; Hanson, *Wrath,* 69, 81ff., 110; Macgregor, "Concept," 105ff.; already Wetter, *Vergeltungsgedanke,* 21ff.; but cf. Barrett; J. Knox). The thrice-repeated παρέδωκεν αὐτούς shows incontestably (cf. Mauser, *Gottesbild,* 148ff.) that in the apparently purely im-manent causal connection God himself is at work in a hidden way, so that his ὀργή does not become an impersonal nemesis nor even (*contra* Hanson, *Wrath,* 110) a human condition. Unlike the Rabbinate (cf. Billerbeck), Paul does not even bother with angels of destruction in an attempt to keep the evil remote from God.

Phenomenonologically wrath is the power of the curse. The decisive per-spective is the eschatological one, which already in Zeph 1:18; Dan 8:19 allows the last judgment to be called technically the day of wrath (Bultmann, *Theology,* I, 288f.; cf. already Ritschl, *Rechtfertigung,* II, 140ff.). Among the many Jewish parallels (cf. Michel; Sjöberg/Stählin, *TDNT,* V, 413f.), *1 Enoch* 91:7 comes closest to our verse: "If, however, sin, unrighteousness, blasphemy, and violence increase in all conduct, and backsliding, iniquity, and uncleanness grow, then there comes on all a great judgment from heaven, and the Lord comes forth with wrath and chastisement to hold judgment on the earth." The parallelism between

1:18ff. and 2:1ff. (Bornkamm, "Revelation," 59) and the antithesis between the righteousness which reveals itself in the gospel and the wrath which discloses itself ἀπ' οὐρανοῦ in the stereotyped phraseology of Judaism and primitive Christianity (as in the Enoch quotation cited) show that the apocalyptic view is also held by Paul (Roetzel, *Judgement*, 81ff.; Herold, *Zorn*, 306ff.). World history has always stood under the sign of the last judgment and destruction. This is not true only from the time of the preaching of the gospel (*contra* Pallis; Schenke, "Aporien," 888), although it is revealed simultaneously with it. The reference of ἀπ' οὐρανοῦ is not to God's inaccessible dwelling (Kuss; Leenhardt) nor to the heavenly nature of the wrath (Michel) but to the unmediated (Barrett) and unavoidable (Schlier, "Heiden," 30) fate which afflicts humanity. ἐπί contains a hostile element while πᾶσαν rules out any exceptions. To the intensity of the judgment corresponds the totality of the world which stands under it, so that the statement about Gentiles applies to the heathen nature of mankind as such, and hence implies the guilty Jew as well.

This heathen nature is characterized by ἀσέβεια and ἀδικία. These two terms do not denote irreligion and immorality (Zahn; Billerbeck; Leenhardt), nor breaches of the first and second tables of the law (Schlatter; H. W. Schmidt), nor religious and moral offenses (Schlier, "Heiden," 30; Ridderbos). According to the context immorality is the punishment, not the guilt (Kühl; Gutjahr; Nygren; Michel; Foerster, *TDNT*, VII, 190). Both are comprised, as a kind of hendiadys, in ἀδικία, which as in 3:5 obviously stands opposed to the righteousness of God and for this reason can be associated with ἀσέβεια (Schrenk, *TDNT*, I, 149-163; Lyonnet, *Quaestiones*, I, 76). Conversely, ἀδικία also protects against understanding ἀσέβεια in a purely cultic sense.

The whole world even in its secularity belongs to the Creator. This is its ἀλήθεια (truth), namely (as in v. 19), the opening up of the divine world and its claim (Bultmann, *TDNT*, I, 243), not correct religious and moral knowledge (Bardenhewer), nor right conduct (Michel). The reality of the world and the basic sin of mankind consist in not recognizing God in his reality that opens itself to us. Instead the latter is suppressed in rebellious opposition to the right established therewith. Possibly κατέχειν ἐν does not have here the usual sense of holding captive or oppressing but the meaning found in magical texts, i.e., binding with a spell (cf. Liddell-Scott, 926, I.d; Deissmann, *Light*, 306 n. 4; Schlier, "Heiden," 30). Certainly the sense is not "to restrain" as in 2 Thess 2:6 (*contra* Strobel, *Untersuchungen*, 194ff.). Paul perceives the assault on divine truth as demonic and he characterizes it with horror as sacrilege.

Verse 19 establishes v. 18b: One cannot excuse this event, as happens in Acts 3:17; 17:30, with ignorance. Mankind can be addressed on the basis of the experience of the divine reality. φανεροῦν, which is a term in the vocabulary of revelation, takes up ἀποκαλύπτειν in order to maintain a revelation received (Lührmann, *Offenbarungsverständnis*, 21f., 148). ἐν αὐτοῖς naturally does not refer to what is inward (Zahn; Gutjahr; Huby) but means "among them" or, better, a paraphrase of the dative (BDF, §220[1]; Pallis). The next statement adds emphasis. God's free will graciously created such a possibility. According to vv.

21, 28, 32 everything depends on the fact that this possibility was and is truly present, and τὸ γνωστὸν τοῦ θεοῦ is to be understood in the light of this. Since the stress is on φανερόν, and if not we should have tautology, the sense "knowable," which occurs in Sir 21:7 LXX, is to be preferred to the usual "known" (contra the Reformers; Bengel; Schlatter; Sanday and Headlam). It remains questionable, however, whether it is to be translated partitively, "what is knowable of God" (the common view) or—in analogy to τὰ ἀόρατα αὐτοῦ in v. 20, cf. 2:4; 1 Cor 4:5; 2 Cor 4:17—"God in his knowability" (Fridrichsen, "Auslegung," 160; Bultmann, TDNT, I, 719; Ligier, Péché, 174).

In any case this catchword raises the hotly contested issue of a natural theology in Paul. At least one may not treat it in isolation on the basis of the context and intention of the passage, but should realize from the beginning that the apostle is building here on a complex tradition. Undoubtedly the abstract expressions τὰ ἀόρατα αὐτοῦ, ἀΐδιος δύναμις, θειότης, and the phrase νοούμενα καθορᾶται suggest a connection with popular Hellenistic philosophy. The question, also raised in 12:1, of rational worship of God stands behind it as its sustaining basis. Stoic theology, in opposition to the national cults, their sacrifices, and their anthropomorphic ideas, is driven by this question to the assertion in Pseudo-Aristotle De mundo 399a-b (ed. W. L. Larrimer, pp. 88, 90) that God is ὁ πάντων ἡγεμών τε καὶ γενέτωρ, ἀόρατος ὢν ἄλλῳ πλὴν λογισμῷ. . . . ταῦτα χρὴ καὶ περὶ θεοῦ διανοεῖσθαι δυνάμει μὲν ὄντος ἰσχυροτάτου, κάλλει δὲ εὐπρεπεστάτου, ζωῇ δὲ ἀθανάτου, ἀρετῇ δὲ κρατίστου, διότι πάσῃ θνητῇ φύσει γενόμενος ἀθεώρητος ἀπ' αὐτῶν τῶν ἔργων θεωρεῖται, "the leader and author of all things, unseen except to the eye of reason. . . . This is what we must also believe about God, who is mightiest in power, outstanding in beauty, immortal in life, and supreme in excellence, because though he is invisible to every mortal thing he is seen through his deeds" (tr. D. J. Furley, LCL). To the unity of the world experienced as an οἰκουμένη corresponds that God who may be known only in the meaningful 36] διοίκησις of the cosmos. This leads to the paradoxical formulation that God is simultaneously ὁ ἀφανής and ὁ φανερώτατος in Corpus Hermeticum V, or effugit oculos, cogitatione visendus est, "he has escaped our sight; he has to be perceived in thought," in Seneca Naturales quaestiones vii.30.3 (tr. T. H. Corcoran, LCL). In Cicero Tusculanarum i.69 true worship is rendered to God by mankind as contemplatorem caeli ac deorum cultorem, "to observe the heavens and cultivate the gods." Epictetus Discourses i.6.19 says of God: τὸν δ' ἄνθρωπον θεατὴν εἰσήγαγεν αυτοῦ τε καὶ τῶν ἔργων τῶν αὐτοῦ, "he brought man into the world to be a spectator of himself and of his works." Philo shows in typical fashion, as already Sirach (cf. Hengel, Judentum, 265ff.), that the Diaspora synagogue had taken up this argumentation when in De praemiis et poenis 43 he delcares: κάτωθε ἄνω προῆλθον οἷα διά τινος οὐρανίου κλίμακος ἀπὸ τῶν ἔργων εἰκότι λογισμῷ στοχασάμενοι τὸν δημιουργόν, "they have advanced from down to up by a sort of heavenly ladder and by a probable (reasonable) calculation inferred the creator from his works." In Wis. 13:5 we read: ἐκ γὰρ μεγέθους καὶ καλλονῆς κτισμάτων ἀναλόγως ὁ γενεσιουργὸς αὐτῶν θεωρεῖται, "For from the greatness and beauty of created things comes a corresponding perception of their Creator" (RSV). Ep. Arist. 132 sums up as follows: μόνος ὁ θεός ἐστι καὶ διὰ πάντων ἡ δύναμις αὐτοῦ φανερὰ γίνεται, "there is only one God and his power is evident through

39

everything." (For further material cf. the works quoted and Michaelis, *TDNT*, V, 321ff., 334ff., 368f., 379.)

Acts 14:15-17; 17:22-29 draws on the same tradition, and here one surely can and must speak of natural theology. In Paul, however, things are not quite so simple (though cf. Daxer, "Lehrauffassung," 6ff.; Hommel, *Schöpfer*; Dupont, *Gnosis*, 21f.; Moule; Murray; Bruce; et al.). Characteristic of Paul is what he does not adopt and the great restraint shown in what he does adopt. In contrast to Acts, for example, creation is not an independent doctrine in the authentic Pauline epistles even though they are constantly influenced by the focus on God's creative work and the creatureliness of mankind (cf. on this G. Bornkamm, "Paulus," *RGG*, V, 177ff.). This focus is eschatologically oriented. Therefore discussions dealing with the beginning of the world theoretically and in isolation are omitted. Reality prior to the fall cannot be reconstructed, so it cannot be regarded as the ideal of existing life. Even God is spoken of only in his relation to humanity and the world after the fall. There is no reflection on his attributes and nature as such (*contra* Hommel, *Schöpfer*, 8; Ligier, *Péché*, 173).

Paul makes no reference to the διοίκησις and τάξις of the cosmos, in order to base the knowledge of God thereon, as is done in *Ep. Arist.* 254; Aristobulus ii.17f.; Acts 17:26, or, with a view to the all-uniting *nomos*, to interrelate the understanding of God, the world, and self (cf. Cleanthes' "Hymn to Zeus," translated in C. K. Barrett, *The New Testament Background: Selected Documents* [1963] 63f.). Metaphysical questions are so alien to the apostle that the general possibility of knowledge of God is not perceived as a problem. It is presupposed as self-evident for everyone. Hence, unlike Wis 13:1, 61; 14:14, 22, he does not seek to enlighten those who are in ἀγνωσία τοῦ θεοῦ, nor, unlike Acts 17:27, does he in pedagogic-missionary fashion describe the seeking and finding of God as our task (cf. Pohlenz, "Paulus," 95ff.; Dupont, *Gnosis*, 24), nor, finally, does he accusingly or with tragic pathos depict the misery of the Gentiles. The rhetoric that actually determines our text (J. Weiss, "Beiträge," 213) serves the merciless accusation and the prophetic depiction of a comprehensive curse. The sphere of Hellenistic discussion concerning true service of God is thus abandoned and the path of OT preaching about obdurate hearers is entered (though cf. Michel; S. Schulz, "Anklage," 170f., who argue for Hellenization!).

It is in this light that we are to understand the OT allusions, and the talk about the wrath of God, about κτίσας instead of the τεχνίτης of Wis 13:1, and about the ἀσύνετος καρδία in vv. 21, 23 (Bornkamm, "Revelation," 67 n. 38). *2 Apoc. Bar.* 54:17ff. is an example of the way in which Jewish apocalyptic combines OT traditions with motifs from Hellenistic theology and thus prepares the [way for what Paul says: "Turn only to destruction, you who are already evildoers; for you will be sternly visited, seeing that you of old disregarded the understanding of the Most High. For his works have not taught you, nor has the skilful construction of his creation, which lasts forever, convinced you." *T. Naph.* 3:2-5 in its condemnation even uses the Pauline idea of exchanging the divine for the earthly.

When all this is borne in mind, it seems very unlikely that in v. 20 the apostle has in mind the paradoxical oxymoron τὰ ἀόρατα . . . καθορᾶται (*contra* Zahn; Gutjahr; Bardenhewer; Lagrange; Leenhardt; Fridrichsen, "Auslegung," 160f.).

In this case one would have expected a simpler construction of the sentence. According to 2 Cor 4:18; 5:7 Paul's theology expressly opposes present "sight." νοούμενα relates to ἀόρατα. Hence (contra Fridrichsen, 164) we are not to see in τοῖς ποιήμασιν νοούμενα a parenthetic parallel to the rest of the sentence. We cannot even find the stipulated paradox of seeing the invisible by taking the modal verb in the active sense (Michaelis, TDNT, V, 380) and equating it with a νῷ καθορῶμεν. One cannot appeal for support to the most instructive text, Corpus Hermeticum V:2: νόησις γὰρ μόνον ὁρᾷ τὸ ἀφανές (contra Fridrichsen, 165ff.; similarly Lietzmann; Kuss; Leenhardt; Behm, TDNT, IV, 950). For νοῦς is not for Paul "the eye of the understanding" (BAGD, 540b) in the Stoic or mystical sense of a divinely given perceptive capacity which as such is adequate to deal with transcendent reality (contra Daxer, "Lehrauffassung," 6, 15f.; similarly Kühl; Feuillet, "Connaissance," 68). Instead it is the critical, evaluative understanding, which recognizes the claim of a situation or of a demanding will (Bultmann, Theology, I, 211ff.).

To translate τὰ ἀόρατα by "sum of the divine nature" (Fridrichsen, "Auslegung," 160; Murray) or "multiplicity of the divine attributes" (Zahn; Gutjahr; Bardenhewer) certainly corresponds to the Hellenistic tradition. But it does not do justice to the apposition in v. 20b, which does not limit ἀόρατα (Kühl) or make it actual in eminent attributes (Zahn), but (Lagrange; Barrett) offers an interpretation: God in his invisibility, and in the θειότης that distinguishes him from cosmic being and is eternal, perpetual power. With astonishing freedom from bias, Paul here employs Hellenistic terminology, and thereby uses a term which occurs elsewhere in biblical literature only in Wis 18:9 (BAGD, 354a). By doing so he follows the trail of the polemic against anthropomorphism which Philo had already undertaken by the way of negation (cf. Kuhlmann, Theologia naturalis, 12ff.). Philo makes it plain, of course, that Hellenistic Judaism was trying to safeguard the transcendence of God hereby. In De migratione Abrahami 183 we thus read that "he is before, and excels, all things created and is not contained in any." According to De posteritate Caini 15 everything hinges on our seeing that he is invisible. Naturally this transcendence can be asserted only as a metaphysical statement, thus not with ultimate radicality, if an attempt is made at the same time to gather or derive the concrete nature of God from his immanence. Here God remains a present object about whom general statements can be made and who can be comprehended as the cause of the world.

The decisive question to our text is whether Paul wanted to say no more than Hellenistic Judaism. If so, he would in fact be advocating a natural theology which could scarcely be reconciled with his eschatology and christology. It should be noted that he does not here explain, prove, defend, or seek a point of contact. 38] He accuses, reduces Hellenistic motifs to a minimum, characterizes God's deity as a power that encounters us, concentrates it in lordship, and perceives human guilt, not in ignorance, but in revolt against the known Lord. An interpretation is thus demanded which radicalizes the trend found in Philo.

In rabbinic fashion (Billerbeck), especially in view of the work of creation, retaining OT usage (e.g., Ps 103:22), ποιήματα is mentioned. Thus 1QH 5:36 says: "They change the works of God through their guilt." To the person who critically understands these works in their claim and summons they are, as Paul sees it, a pointer to his Lord and therefore to his own creatureliness. They have been this from the very beginning and for everyone to the extent that, in face of them, one can become aware of his dependence on his Creator and limitation by his Lord, not by rational deduction but existentially and immediately (correctly, Hooker, "Adam," 299). True service of God according to Paul is marked by the ability to stand outside oneself before God even before the "through Christ" is added. The very reality of the "works," which include historical experiences (Ligier, *Péché*, 271), sets us in this standing before God's majesty which, with some exaggeration but correctly in principle, Luther calls naked deity or God's naked self. Their mere occurrence makes it clear to us that we are not our own lords (Bultmann, *Theology,* I, 228f.; Barth; Bornkamm, *RGG,* V, 178f.; Oltmanns, "Verhältnis," 115; Schlatter; Ott, "Problem," 43ff.; Michaelis, *TDNT,* V, 381).

God remains "invisible" here to the extent that we cannot get power over him or calculate him metaphysically; rather, he "has" us. Corruption of the worship of God according to v. 23 consists in trying to lay hold of God in the creature (Eichholz, *Paulus,* 70ff.). Already we find here a rejection of the enthusiasm which (in Stoic fashion) sees itself hidden in the world order or mystically thinks it can elevate itself above the world. It is no accident that, in opposition to enthusiasm, 8:19 refers back to this verse with the catchword ἀποκαραδοκία τῆς κτίσεως.

A solution is also offered herewith to the apparent contradiction with 1 Cor 1:21, which says that the world in its wisdom did not know God, whereas here God is said to be known. Precisely when God reveals himself as the Lord and mankind is thus pointed to its human limits, rebels do not acknowledge God, and hence knowledge of God is not retained in practice (Bultmann, *TDNT,* I, 705ff.; Schlier, "Heiden," 31). The truth is thus demonically conjured away by the attack on God's right, and the result is that only the mighty revelation of righteousness, which establishes God's just claim, can reverse the spell.

In v. 20c rebellion is seen as the signature of human reality before and apart from Christ. The infinitive εἰς τὸ εἶναι is not to be taken as final (Zahn; Kühl; Schlatter; Nygren; Michel; H. W. Schmidt) and related to the last judgment. The declarative sense of the accusation can be maintained only if it is understood as consecutive (e.g., Oepke, *TDNT,* II, 430).

This is given greater precision in v. 21. διότι summarizes vv. 19-20. For the fourth time in our verses Paul states the reality and not just the possibility of knowledge of God. The whole argument rests on this. If stress falls herewith on οὐχ ὡς θεόν, this confirms the interpretation suggested. What follows shows that Paul does not overlook Gentile religion. But he does not grant that it satisfies the majesty of God, which is the point of the honoring and thanking, whose omission is sin in 4 Ezra 8:60. When this honoring and thanking really occurs, God is worshiped for God's sake (Schlatter), namely, as Creator, Lord, and Judge.   [39

The text says that God's wrath falls as a curse from heaven on despisers of the first commandment. This applies not merely with reference to a "primal revelation" (Gaugler, clearly following Althaus), but continually, if people have to do with the true God, even though this becomes apocalyptically clear only with the gospel. The Gentile, too, as Paul sees it, has already had continued dealings with the true God. For his reality is incessantly experienced creatureliness and to that extent it is reality before God. Unless people deny their humanity, they continually confront the omnipotence of the invisible God, namely, the perceptible basis and boundary of their own existence (Oltmanns, "Verhältnis," 115; but cf. Schlier, "Doxa," 48). This is, of course, only the premise for the theme of the passage, according to which man in his historical reality constantly assaults God's omnipotence, because in flight or aggression he tries to escape his own creatureliness. In and after the fall he remains human and a creature. Wanting to escape God's deity, but unable to do so, he experiences it as a curse (*contra* Herold, *Zorn*, 312ff.: wrath of fidelity and forbearance) before he experiences it, with the gospel, as the wrath of the final Judge directed against him. Obviously this line of argument is not natural theology in the Hellenistic or the modern sense (cf. Nygren). It is an eschatological illumination of existence and the world.

By changing the verb from the active to the passive, and indicating the results of sin, v. 21bc marks the transition to the next and much longer section on the divine retribution. Two presuppositions of the train of thought need to be clearly emphasized. Bengel correctly observes that it refers to a change in existence but does not formulate this precisely enough, speaking only of the conformity of the mind with its object. In Paul's theology change of existence always takes place as a change of lordship, thus with the relation to another lord, and is nothing other than entry into a new relation. A person's reality is decided by what lord he has. As this applies to becoming a Christian and to the resurrection, so here it applies to the event of the fall that continues universally. The servant becomes like his master and shows this by his behavior. For Paul no man is ever really without a master or on his own. He who evades the Creator runs into his Judge.

Secondly, the apostle speaks about the Judge and his wrath after the style of apocalyptic, namely, with reference to the last day as his essential manifestation. For Jew and Gentile, world history already stands in the storm clouds of final judgment. Like primitive Christian prophecy before him, Paul with the eschatological law of retribution proclaims the fact that God's retributive action is already at work on all human sin. To be sure, this provisionally happens with remarkable indirectness, corresponding to the knowledge of God from the works of creation. It consists in the handing over of the guilty to the reality which results from his guilt. God's wrath occurs in the present according to the principle of Wis 11:16 (δι' ὧν τις ἁμαρτάνει, διὰ τούτων κολάζεται, "one is punished by the very things by which he sins" [RSV]), which is adopted in *T. Gad* 5:10 and with variations in *Jub.* 4:32 and 1QS 4:11f. In this regard Paul takes up the OT view that a human act establishes a "destiny" and that God sets up and maintains this connection both for the individual and for society. The wicked act smites him who does it and at the same time creates a sphere of disaster. In modified form this view was linked with legal categories and brought under the schema of retribution (K. Koch, "Vergeltungsdogma"). This is undoubtedly the case in Paul. Sometimes the connection between guilt and destiny as the reality of God's wrath is correctly perceived but wrongly explained in terms of immanent causality (Dodd and his pupils). For Paul everything depends on the fact that in this apparently immanent event God himself is secretly at work to exact retribution (Taylor; differently Herold, *Zorn*, 315ff.). He exercises judgment by delivering up the guilty to the

40]

43

separation from God which they want. Their wish becomes their fate and therefore the power which rules them. Conversely this power lets them once again become what they wish and do, namely, creatures in the corruption of creatureliness.

Verse 21b is already to be construed in the light of these presuppositions. It probably contains an allusion to Jer 2:5: ἀπέστησαν μακρὰν ἀπ' ἐμοῦ καὶ ἐπορεύθησαν ὀπίσω τῶν ματαίων καὶ ἐματαιώθησαν, with which a reminiscence of Ps 94:11 seems to be linked: "The Lord knows the thoughts of men, that they are vain." This is developed further already in Wis 13:1: μάταιοι μὲν γὰρ πάντες ἄνθρωποι φύσει, οἷς παρῆν θεοῦ ἀγνωσία. Paul himself, borrowing the LXX catchword from this tradition, establishes ματαιότης as the characteristic of the world which breaks free from its creatureliness and which God in his wrath delivers up to itself. Since mention had just been made of idolatry, the verb probably reflected the OT characterizing of idols as vain. He who disregards the truth falls into the slavery mentioned also in 8:19f., into the futility caused thereby, and into the related darkness. He becomes incapable of discriminating perception, loses any grasp of reality, and falls victim to illusion. ἐν τοῖς διαλογισμοῖς denotes man's inner life and καρδία his personality. ἀσύνετος probably already designates the result, not the presupposition, of the process. The false god and the false person belong together and mutually condition one another (Baulès).

In distinction from the usual division, v. 22 is to be regarded as the beginning of the next section. In the three concentric circles 22-24, 25-27, and 28-31, with the artistic parallels δόξα / ἀτιμάζεσθαι in 22-24, μετήλλαξαν / μετήλλαξαν in 25-27, and οὐκ ἐδοκίμασαν / εἰς ἀδόκιμον νοῦν in 28-31, the fall into specifically Gentile sins is depicted as a suitable retribution for the guilt of idolatry presented in 22f., 25, and 28a (cf. Klostermann, "Vergeltung," and J. Jeremias, "Zu Rm 1₂₂₋₃₂"). Verse 32 summarizes the whole.

The threefold παρέδωκεν αὐτοὺς ὁ θεός, introduced by διό in v. 24, διὰ τοῦτο in 26, and καθώς in 28, marks the changing from guilt to fate. No progression in thought is to be seen (Lietzmann; Sanday and Headlam; Klostermann, "Vergeltung," 2f.; but cf. Schlier, "Heiden," 34f.; Leenhardt; H. W. Schmidt). Guilt and punishment remain materially the same. There is, however, stylistic intensification. Portrayal of guilt is increasingly shorter and that of corruption increasingly extensive, culminating in the list of vices in vv. 29-31. Possibly the first two trains of thought, with their emphasis on sexual deviation, are more closely related as compared with the third (Jeremias, "Zu Rm 1₂₂₋₃₂," 120). In Paul rhetoric always serves a material purpose and strengthens a definite intention. The cosmos which will not recognize God's deity in service becomes a chaos of unfettered perversion. A flood of vices, so to speak, pours over it. The manifestation of God's wrath, like the manifestation of his righteousness, does not remain in the purely private or (contra Murray) moral sphere. It leads from the inner darkening of existence to the objectifying of folly in idolatry. In its cosmic scope it anticipates the eschatologically public character of the last judgment (Ligier, Péché, 208).

Folly can no longer diagnose its own situation. Even under ὀργή it does not [4] cease to boast about itself. As in Acts 24:5; 25:19, φάσκειν, originally iterative, means the boastful, ardent assertion, which in addition is here objectively false

44

(Bertram, *TDNT*, IV, 846). In the apostle's Hellenistic environment, religion is the integrative part of wisdom, so that Col 2:8 can speak of it as "philosophy." The transition to v. 23 arises from that. Paul quotes Ps 105[106]:20 LXX: καὶ ἠλλάξαντο τὴν δόξαν αὐτῶν ἐν ὁμοιώματι μόσχου ἔσθοντος χόρτον, and possibly he also has Jer 2:11 in mind: εἰ ἀλλάξονται ἔθνη θεοὺς αὐτῶν; καὶ οὗτοι οὐκ εἰσιν θεοί. ὁ δὲ λαός μου ἠλλάξατο τὴν δόξαν αὐτοῦ. The reference to worship of the golden calf at the end of Ps 105:20 was too specific for the apostle's argumentation. Gentile idolatry was to be attacked in general, as happens in the prohibition in Deut 4:15-19. Nevertheless, to complete the quotation in accord with his purpose, Paul did not use the language of Deut 4:15-19, but of the creation story in Gen 1:20-27 (Hyldahl, "Reminiscence," 285ff.; Ligier, *Péché*, 172f.). The construction ὁμοίωμα εἰκόνος derives from the Psalm.

The meaning "glory" for δόξα is not derived from classical usage. The LXX seems first to have used it for כבוד in the sense of "honor" and then employed it schematically for the Hebrew word in the full range of its meaning (H. Kittel, *Herrlichkeit Gottes, contra* J. Schneider, *Doxa*). Perhaps this could be done the more easily because the profane sense of "honor" was connected with what the courtly speech of the orient called "radiance" (Mohrmann, "Note," 321ff.). At any rate the genitive construction which follows rules out what would otherwise be the possibility (*contra* J. Jeremias, "Beobachtungen zu neutestamentlichen Stellen an Hand des neugefundenen griechischen Henoch-Textes," *ZNW* 38 [1939] 115-124, esp. p. 121) that δόξα is a substitute for God's name. This would destroy the exact correspondence in v. 23a. The thought is clear. Only perversion sets idols in the place of the divine glory. This was already established in *T. Naph.* 3:2ff., quoted earlier.

The formulation, however, is very awkward, linking the pleonasm ὁμοίωμα εἰκόνος with the antithesis of the statement (Ridderbos). Both these terms mean "image," as the former does in the Psalm. To suggest an epexegetical genitive is no help (Zahn; H. W. Schmidt). Nor is the daring thesis that εἰκών is meant to remind us of humanity's divine likeness in Gen 1:26 (Jervell, *Imago*, 325ff. and *passim*). εἰκών governs also the animals mentioned. The association certainly may be derived from the creation story. However, the singular ἄνθρωπος, used generally, alongside the succeeding plurals offers no sure support (*contra* Hyldahl, "Reminiscence" and Hooker, "Adam"). φθαρτὸς ἄνθρωπος does not mean (*contra* Jervell, *Imago*) the primal man; there can be no reference to making an image of this man. It is arbitrary to relate vv. 19ff. exclusively to Adam (*contra* Hooker, "Adam"). The pleonasm is best understood intensively (Barrett: "the inferior, shadowy character"). This is supported by the fact that in Judaism the κατ' εἰκόνα καὶ καθ' ὁμοίωσιν of Gen 1:26f. is understood as a hendiadys and could be resolved into a genitive construction (Jervell, *Imago*, 321). Otherwise one must assume that εἰκών means "shape," which is unusual, at least in Paul, or, in pedantic distinction from ὁμοίωμα, the "archetype" from which a copy has been made (Kittel, *TDNT*, II, 392f., 395). Most exegetes favor the former.

[42] Obviously expressed here, in traditional Jewish polemic (cf. Billerbeck), is abhorrence of Gentile idolatry. The list in v. 23b is directed specifically against Egyptian religion, which already incensed Wis 11:15; 12:24. It should not be objected that such a polemic ignores the Hellenistic theology of the enlightenment

and its spiritual character, so that it does not do justice to Gentile religion as a whole. This objection misses the apostle's point. According to v. 25 Paul is objecting to the fact that the creature replaces the Creator, and he adduces in support the idolatry which may be seen everywhere in the Gentile world. One certainly cannot deduce from the quotation from the Psalm that Paul's first target is Jewish guilt (contra Jervell, Imago, 318ff.; M. Barth, "Speaking," 291). This contradicts not only the context and the thrust of the Jewish tradition used, but also the first interpretation of this passage, or at least the view underlying it, in Eph 4:17ff. Precisely the point of the verse is that Paul extends to the whole human race what Jer 2:11 restricted to the people of God.

This can be done meaningfully only under two very important presuppositions. First, for Paul the history of Israel documented in Scripture has exemplary significance for the world. He thus breaks the framework of a mere covenant history and establishes the eschatological interpretation which is expressly demanded in 1 Cor 10:11. The hermeneutic of Judaism, which orients the OT to the time of salvation and expounds it accordingly, is thus radicalized. In the light of the age of salvation that has now come, Israel's history is relevant for world history to the extent that it universally illuminates the relation of God and mankind, and therefore must be expounded anthropologically.

Second, if this history cannot be understood merely as a historical record, then decisive events of the past, like the incident of the golden calf, cannot just be put in the past and treated chronologically. They stand in a nexus of events reaching forward and backward, a nexus that is characterized by a continuity such as that of guilt and destiny in the present chapter, and which gives precision to Paul's view of salvation history. The history of salvation and destruction runs together in such a way that its spheres can interlace and overlap and thus have a continuity which is not subject to immanent control. Instead, particular situations of ultimate significance, which Paul undoubtedly views as historical, mark recurrent basic relations and thus have typologically the character of prototypes.

This does not mean that the apostle simply sees in them models of recurrent anthropological decisions. Instead, they point to a fateful nexus of events within the given reality of which the individual always already finds himself. For this reason Gentile reality can be related here to the worship of the golden calf by the wilderness generation and in this light it can be interpreted within its eschatological horizon. Therefore, there is also a connection of this reality and this report with the creation story, to which the wording of v. 23b points.

Judaism had already linked the traditions of creation and exodus, and of the fall and Israel's guilt, and had seen the loss of the divinely given δόξα as the result (cf. Jervell, Imago, 321). Paul presupposes this tradition. In distinction from the Psalm but in line with rabbinic exegesis and LXX readings, he speaks of the glory of God, not that of Israel (Billerbeck). This δόξα is granted by God to Israel, as to the first man, as a share of God's glory, and therefore it could be exchanged for the sake of the creature by Adam and by God's people in repetition of the fall into sin. That the history of the fall continues into the present may be [43] seen from v. 25, which describes Gentile guilt as a fall from the state of creatureliness. It may be seen also in the change from the present to the aorist from v. 21a on, which is not (as for Michel) to be evaluated as purely rhetorical.

46

Neither a purely historical nor a mythical approach does justice to the contents. Paul related what he regarded as actual history, even of the primal past, to that of his own day. Modern man could regard this only as mythologizing. His point is obviously to show that the contingency of present decision is not isolated from the nexus of guilt and doom which goes back to the beginning of the world, and also, conversely, that the present is not absolved of responsibility by this nexus (cf. Bultmann, *Theology,* I, 249ff.). He would agree with *2 Bar.* 54:19, "Each of us has become his own Adam." Yet we are always in the continuity of the history initiated by Adam, which from Paul's standpoint does not atomize into moments, but also cannot be calculated speculatively. These statements are taken up in ch. 4; 5:12ff.; 7:7ff.; 8:19ff. and will have to be discussed further when we reach these passages. They also govern chs. 9–11 and are thus of fundamental importance for the whole epistle.

Finally, it may be pointed out that this passage is indispensable to an understanding of the righteousness of God. It confirms antithetically a point yet to be developed further, namely, that Paul expands God's covenant faithfulness to the faithfulness of the Creator to his creation, differing from earlier Jewish Christianity in this regard. It corresponds exactly to this when Israel's worship of the golden calf is viewed in our text as a prototype also of Gentile aberration and, in relation to the creation story, is interpreted as a mark of that fall from creatureliness. In both respects we have a universal extension of that which in Judaism applied only within the Sinaitic covenant.

For the apostle, history is governed by the primal sin of rebellion against the Creator, which finds repeated and universal expression. It is thus governed by the wrath of God, which throws the creature back on itself, corresponding to its own will, and abandons it to the world. Paul is adopting here an existing tradition (Daxer, "Lehrauffassung," 25ff.; Jeremias, "Zu Rm 1₂₂₋₃₂," 119f.; though cf. Feuillet, "Connaissance," 75f.). This is shown in Acts 7:42, where God's retribution punishes Israel's sin through a παρέδωκεν, namely, abandonment to worship of the stars. Here, of course, the judicial element associated with παραδιδόναι (K. A. Bauer, *Leiblichkeit,* 140ff.) leaves no place for apocalyptic, and there is no recollection of this when the same tradition (Jervell, *Imago,* 289ff., 314) is given the form of self-abandonment to immorality in consequence of sin. Paul's thinking, however, stands out sharply against the background of such modifications. He seems to be in agreement with Philo *De decalogo* 91: πηγὴ δὲ πάντων ἀδικημάτων ἀθεότης, "the source of all wrongs is godlessness." But Paul paradoxically reverses the cause and consequence: Moral perversion is the result of God's wrath, not the reason for it (Stählin, *TDNT,* V, 444; Baulès). Again, this wrath does not manifest itself directly as a judicial function (*contra* Schlatter), nor, as *tradere* can also mean (Hommel, *Schöpfer,* 10), as protection of God's sovereign right, let alone as abstention from interference (Dodd). On the contrary, it brings about the surrender of existence to determination by the world, which will later be called σάρξ. This means its abandonment to chaos.

44]   The Creator divests himself of his directly perceptible sovereign right and becomes the hidden Judge, striking with corruption those who can live neither without him nor against him (K. A. Bauer, *Leiblichkeit,* 143f.). Men have to endure what they wanted to attain—they are themselves their guilt and its cost (Bengel).

Despisers of God bring down God's curse on themselves. In this judgment one may see plainly what the reality of mankind and the world is when it breaks free from God and is given up by him to immanence. Its characteristic is will and not, in Greek fashion, reason. It now finds expression in ἐπιθυμία as selfish desire and objectifies itself in ἀκαθαρσία, which, as in 6:19; Gal 5:19, blocks access to the sacred and characterizes Gentile life as licentiousness for the Jew. The ἐν is a Semitic way of marking the nature and sphere which can no longer reflect creatureliness (cf. the examples in K. A. Bauer, *Leiblichkeit*, 141f.). The infinitive, which is to be taken as a passive, is consecutive (result). ἐν αὐτοῖς is probably instrumental (L. Radermacher, *Neutestamentliche Grammatik* [2nd ed. 1925] 227) and hence is not equal to ἐν ἀλλήλοις (Sanday and Headlam). Judgment affects the bodily sphere in the same way as redemption in 1 Cor 5:5; 11:30. The realism of the next verse makes this clear and therewith marks an important perspective for the whole epistle.

The relative clauses in vv. 25 and 32 emphasize and substantiate what has already been said (Michel; BAGD, 587a). καί in v. 25b is epexegetical. ἀλήθεια again means the self-disclosing reality of God, not an attribute of God nor his "true nature." Hence τὸ ψεῦδος is not the false conduct of man, nor abstractly the false god, but the deception which objectively conceals the truth, especially in Gentile religion. σεβάζεσθαι, a *koine* term for σέβεσθαι, means religious veneration, and λατρεύειν cultic worship. παρά with accusative, originally comparative "more than" (Lietzmann; Riesenfield, *TDNT*, V, 733f.), takes on the exclusive sense "instead of" (BDF, §236[3]). Whereas in *Ep. Arist.* 139 Judaism says of itself θεὸν σεβόμενοι παρ᾽ ὅλην τὴν κτίσιν, "worshiping God rather than the whole creation," in the Gentile world the creature is deified. This horrifies Paul so much that according to Jewish custom (Billerbeck), he not only sanctifies God's name doxologically but apotropaically (Schlier, "Heiden," 35) sets himself at a distance from this abomination and interrupts the statement with an acclamation. He uses here a common Jewish blessing. εἰς τοὺς αἰῶνας, which was popularized by the LXX, replaces the normal Hellenistic singular. Eternity also seems to be Semitic—an unending course of time. The doxology is followed, as in 9:5, by the traditional acclamation Amen, which properly is spoken in confirmation by the hearer (P. Glaue, *RAC*, I, 378-380).

πάθη ἀτιμίας as a qualitative genitive, used in a thoroughly non-Stoic fashion (Pohlenz, *Zorn*, 82) as in *T. Jos.* 7:8, sums up the description in v. 24 and announces the theme of vv. 26b-27. Not without reason homosexuality seemed to the Jews to be typically Gentile even though the Jews' own relations were viewed critically in the Rabbinate and marriage had at any rate to be protected (Billerbeck; Lietzmann; Lagrange). χρῆσις in the sexual sense is common (BAGD, 886a). Paul does not share the ideal underlying the Stoic slogans φυσικός and παρὰ φύσιν, because there is for him no nature either detached from God or identifiable with God (Koester, *TDNT*, IX, 267). For him these words, which characteristically occur now for the first time and only in an adverbial use of the substantive, demonstrate degeneration: People refuse to be bound by the order immanent in the world and humanity (Eichholz, *Paulus*, 76f.). One-sidedly emphasizing sex, he speaks of women and men with scorn. One cannot (*contra* Michel) attribute the sequence here to the fall story. The original τε . . . τε   [4.

48

strengthens ὁμοίως καί. If ὄρεξις means animal desire, then τὴν ἀσχημοσύνην κατεργάζεσθαι is a euphemism (cf. Lietzmann) for sexual intercourse. τὴν ἀντιμισθίαν ἀπολαμβάνειν probably comes from legal language. πλάνη is hardly backsliding from God (Kuss) but dissoluteness, and ἀντιμισθία is its ruinous result (Braun, *TDNT*, VI, 243). It has often been stressed that Paul here in the strictest Jewish tradition (cf. Wis 14:12-24f.) does not mean to accuse or suspect every Gentile, but also overlooks imperial attempts at reform, so that his picture appears distorted. In good apocalyptic fashion, however, the individual is for him inseparable from his world, which is characterized as such.

The third variation, vv. 28ff., makes it fully clear that there is no longer any protective dike in this cosmos. As often, καθώς is causal. δοκιμάζειν means to test and then make up one's mind; here, as in 1 Cor 16:3; 2 Cor 8:22, to learn to value (Grundmann, *TDNT*, II, 259). ἐν ἐπιγνώσει ἔχειν (parallels in BAGD, 333b; Lietzmann) does not intensify (*contra* Kuss), since there was not previously any question of bare recognition. It designates, however, the constantly renewed possibility of perceiving the unextinguished reality of God (Bornkamm, "Revelation," 58). ἔχειν, then, is not to be taken with τὸν θεόν (H. Hanse, *"Gott haben" in der Antike und im frühen Christentum* [1939] 104, *contra* Schlatter). ἀδόκιμος denotes that which fails (the test). The play on words with the introductory verb emphasizes the divine retribution. He who leaves his Lord loses control over himself together with his sense of the order of being, and can no longer be summoned to responsibility. His conduct demonstrates that he is no longer restrained by the conventional limit of what is "seemly," and even the humanity that Gentiles honor means nothing for him (Schlier, "Heiden," 35).

The plural, the negative form, and the intention of the apostle show that τὰ μὴ καθήκοντα is not borrowed directly from the Stoic doctrine of duties (*contra* Michel; Kirk; Black), whose catchword is τὸ παρὰ τὸ καθῆκον (Bonhöffer, *Epiktet*, 157f.; Schlier, *TDNT*, III, 439f.; Enslin, *Ethics*, 93ff.). Yet Paul does use a modification of this catchword which occurs in 2 Macc 6:4; 3 Macc 4:16, and with variations in Philo *De mutatione nominum* 241. The very harmless and substantially indefinite summing up of the following vices in the theme "the unseemly" shows that the apostle at least borrows from the vocabulary of popular philosophy.

In vv. 29-31 the accusatives refer back to αὐτούς in v. 28. We find similar lists in Paul at 13:13; 1 Cor 5:10f.; 2 Cor 12:20f.; Gal 5:19-21. They are never structured in content. The meaning here is unmistakable: Idolatry opens the floodgates for vices which destroy society and turn creation back into terrible chaos. In this way the curse of God's wrath accomplishes its purpose (Kamlah, *Katalogische Paränese*, 18f.).

The final word has not yet been said on the origin of such lists of vices in the history of religions. Paul is obviously not gathering information from personal experience nor from the situation at Rome (so Feuillet, from "Connaissance," 65; de los Rios, "Animadversiones," 368; Minear, *Obedience*, 51). It is the abiding merit of Lietzmann, in his well-documented excursus, to have pointed to the lists of vices and virtues in popular philosophy as the source of such lists in the NT, and to have based the connection with the present passage above all on the emphasis on sins of the mind. Nevertheless, direct Stoic influence cannot be maintained, since the NT lists are not oriented to the four cardinal virtues and the

corresponding vices. There are thus important conceptual differences. The asyn-   [
detic sequence of the lists is a feature of the diatribe of popular philosophy (so
especially Vögtle, *Kataloge*; Kamlah, *Katalogische Paränese*, 139ff.)

No more satisfying is derivation of Paul's list from the Hellenistic Jewish
tradition in Philo, 4 Maccabees, and Wisdom of Solomon, since this does not
explain the dualistic-eschatological element, which cannot be explained in terms
of a doctrine of virtue. It is thus a step forward, and at the same time a return
to the older view of A. Seeberg in *Der Katechismus der Urchristenheit* (1903),
that a connection with the Jewish doctrine of the Two Ways has now been reconstructed (Daxer, "Lehrauffassung," 35ff.) and that support for this reconstruction
is found in Qumran, e.g., 1QS 4:2-14 (Wibbing, *Traditionsgeschichte*, 43ff. and
even earlier Vögtle, *Kataloge*, 204ff., then especially Kamlah, *Katalogische Paränese*, 40ff.). This tradition, which is widespread in Judaism, helps to explain
many things: the eschatological dualism of spirit and flesh, which is metaphysical
as well as ethical, as the background and theme in Gal 5:17ff.; the similar dualism
of light and darkness in Rom 13:12f.; Eph 5:3-13; the understanding of ostensible
virtues as a manifestation of obedience and of the vices as a basis or proof of
judgment.

Even this, however, offers no completely satisfying explanation of our passage
(Vögtle, *Kataloge*, 192ff.). For Paul does not take the heading of his list from
the context of the Way of Death but borrows it from popular philosophy. Nor
does he fill his list with the characteristic abstract terms of Qumran but with the
basic principles and common indications of wrongdoing. Finally, social rather
than religious offenses stand in the foreground (cf. Braun, *Qumran*, II, 294, 297f.,
301). Stylistic differences of this kind are at least as important as material agree-
ments in form-critical study.

One may conclude from all this that various streams unite here which flowed
together even before Paul in Hellenistic Judaism. On any other view forced solutions become necessary (e.g., Wibbing, *Traditionsgeschichte*, 93f., 97f.). The
material center may thus shift. In the present passage it probably lies closer to
popular philosophy.

Naturally, in so long a list one may expect scribal errors and additions. Thus
Western variants (cf. Lietzmann) substitute πορνεία for πονηρία, which is hard
to distinguish from κακία, and the sequence of vices 2 to 4 is changed, which is
especially interesting. There is a clear tendency not to let the more specialized
word "covetousness" come between "evil" and "malice," and to put κακία first.
The more difficult text B Or has thus to be considered original. After ἀστόργους
in v. 31 C א ἀσπόνδους, familiar from 2 Tim 3:3. In v. 32 a very ancient error
(Lietzmann) omits the finite form of the verb.

The structure of the list is rhetorical, not logical (cf. Michel). πεπληρωμένους
introduces the first group of four members, which (*contra* Lagrange; Schlier,
"Heiden," 36; Vögtle, *Kataloge*, 17) can hardly be general dispositions if πλεο-
νεξία retains its concrete sense. μεστούς opens a second group with five members.
In what follows no word predominates; the vices just spring out in rapid succession as from Pandora's box. It is not clear whether all twelve are related (Vögtle;
Schlier) or whether the two-membered expressions in v. 30 divide the first eight
from the last four (Michel; Kuss). The view that the beginning of the third group

47] is made up of pairs of words is not impossible, although improbable (Zahn; Michel; Schulz, "Anklage," 167f.; Wibbing, *Traditionsgeschichte,* 82). The coupling of θεοστυγεῖς and καταλάλους (Pallis; Barrett) would be odd. The former word, found only in the sense "hated by God," would not fit in with active words. Yet the context and θεοστυγία, "hatred of God," in 1 Clem 35:5 support the active sense (cf. further BAGD, 358b).

The rhetoric of the whole may be plainly seen in the similarity of φθόνου to φόνου and ἀσυνέτους to ἀσυνθέτους, in the chiasmus of the two-membered expressions, in the similar-sounding endings of the first group and the constructions with the alpha-privative in the last group, and in the skilful insertion of double expressions in v. 30. The whole context shows that it is hardly accidental that ἀδικία stands at the head (Vögtle, *Kataloge,* 213f.; Schrenk, *TDNT,* I, 155), although it is not a "comprehensive term" (Daxer, "Lehrauffassung," 48), since πάσῃ relates to all that follows. κατάλαλος is used only here in the Bible, while καταλαλία occurs in Wis 1:11 as well as in Paul. κακοήθεια denotes craftiness rather than malicious disparagement (BAGD, 397a), and ἀσύνθετος means "self-willed" or "difficult" (Fridrichsen, "'ΑΣΥΝΘΕΤΟΣ," 47f.). In ἐφευρετὰς κακῶν it is difficult to say whether the emphasis is on the planning and inventing of evil (Barrett) or on its detection by "snoopers" (Schlier, "Heiden," 36).

Verse 32 has a threefold function. First, it summarizes, as may be seen from ἐπιγνόντες, which is reminiscent of vv. 19, 21, 28, and also from τὰ τοιαῦτα πράσσοντες. Secondly, it brings to a climax everything that has been said from v. 24 on with the sentence of judgment and the final clause. Finally, by means of the final clause and the legal terms δικαίωμα and ἄξιοι θανάτου the verse forms a transition to ch. 2 (Daxer, "Lehrauffassung," 64f.; Barrett).

The typically Pauline use of the singular of principle δικαίωμα τοῦ θεοῦ (Schrenk, *TDNT,* II, 221) means the law's demand or statute, as in 2:26; 8:4. This confirms yet again our earlier interpretation. Knowledge of God does not relate speculatively to his nature but to his claim to lordship and the creatureliness that we experience therewith. All the misunderstandings that arise here, and in 1:19-32 in general, are finally dependent on an understanding of revelation to the Gentiles as objectively present and rationally deductible, whether in a "primal revelation," in natural law (Vögtle, *Kataloge,* 191; similarly Daxer, "Lehrauffassung," 62), or in the relation of δικαίωμα to the Torah or at least to the so-called Adamic and Noachic commandments (Pallis; Jervell, *Imago,* 319; Flückiger, "Unterscheidung," 156ff.; M. Barth, "Speaking," 291; Davies, *Rabbinic Judaism,* 115f.). Unlike Judaism (cf. Billerbeck; Moore, *Judaism,* I, 227ff., 453), Paul does not have to presuppose a Gentile knowledge and rejection of the Torah to establish man's guilt. A characteristic of this passage is that neither in Jewish nor Stoic fashion does he find the knowledge of God a problem of mission (Bornkamm, "Revelation," 56ff.). With his existence in the world a person stands before God even before religion discloses that to him and before he reflects on it in his attempts at theology. Already required of him is reverence, thankfulness, and a humanity which is not arrogant and does not flee responsibility. For that reason it can be shown that in fact he lives in a perverted creatureliness.

Paul does not have to consider, like his expositors, what in his list is really worthy of death according to Gentile or Jewish law, nor does he have to look ahead (*contra* Michel; Daxer, "Lehrauffassung," 62f.; Wibbing, *Traditionsge-schichte*, 117) to the final judgment which will execute the death sentence. According to 8:19 the lost creation cries for freedom because it is already aware of the sentence of death hanging over it. In δικαίωμα, then, one does not know a legal decree in the secular sense (Dupont, *Gnosis*, 27f.) and this knowledge does not stand in contradiction to v. 28 as lost through guilt (Flückiger, "Unterscheidung"). Instead it is constantly set aside as knowledge of the judgment which has been passed on our existence and which we suffer already in the perversion of creation (Schlatter). It does not keep us either from doing wrong or from the applause that enjoyably accompanies all vice.

There are astonishing parallels to the final clause in *T. Ash.* 6:2 (πράσσουσι τὸ κακὸν καὶ συνευδοκοῦσι τοῖς πράσσουσιν τὸ κακόν, "they do evil and approve evil") and in Seneca *Epistulae morales* 39:6 (*turpia non solum delectant, sed etiam placent*, "men are not only attracted, but even pleased, by shameful things" [LCL]). Paul has in mind either graphic depictions in the ancient novel (Lagrange) or more probably (Bultmann, "Glossen," 200 n. 3) scenes from comedy and mime. Hence v. 32 does not go with what follows (Schrage, *Einzelgebote*, 193, correctly *contra* Flückiger, "Unterscheidung," 154ff.). Nevertheless, Jewish criticism of the Gentile world forms such an excellent connecting point that it marks the beginning of a new section well.

B. Judgment on the Jews (2:1–3:20)

The theme and structure of this section are wrongly debated. What is needed is to bring out the specific understanding of the apostle. According to this, the world and the individual are directly related to one another and the signature of cosmology may be perceived in anthropology. Since even as a Christian Paul sees the world before and apart from Christ as divided by the *nomos*, he retains for it the historical depth which is set forth by the antithesis of Jew and Gentile. For him man exists only concretely, that is, in view of the particular world that determines him, and hence in status as Jew and Gentile, which is relevant in terms of the history of salvation or perdition. Only with Christ as the end of the law does that humanization occur in which the distinction between Jew and Gentile exists only in memory (Gal 3:28). Anthropological interest in the totality of the world constantly intersects that of salvation history, and the two offer mutual safeguards against psychological or mythological misunderstanding. The result is a dialectic with fluid transitions. In either Jew or Gentile the reality of mankind in its religious alternatives is disclosed in exemplary fashion.

Nevertheless, mankind as such must continually be addressed to the extent that this distinction concerns his exemplary possibilities and not a purely historical problem. From the perspective of the apostle's antinomian front one can understand that the new section is particularly comprehensive and that the conclusion summarizes with regard to the Jew the judgment that falls on every man. Paradoxically, the expression "to the Jew first and also the Gentile" is maintained here in precisely the reverse order of the presentation. When the justification of the ungodly is to be declared, the point of contact will necessarily be religious man. God's wrath on the Gentiles is equally the prelude to judgment on the Jews, which is repeated with completely reversed premises in the relation of chs. 1–8 to chs. 9–11. The need for the gospel of God's righteousness does not seem so compelling in relation to the Jew. Hence his illusions must be eradicated. This yields a structure based on the subject matter. The basic principle is enunciated in vv. 1-11. Before the Judge there is no respect of persons. We then find a threefold development in vv. 12-29: first, justification only on the basis of possession of the Torah is rejected in vv. 12-16; then Jewish transgression of the law is demonstrated in vv. 17-24; and circumcision as a privilege is devalued in vv. 25-29. In 3:1-8 Jewish objections to Paul's proclamation are then dealt with. Finally, in 3:9-20 it is shown that the common guilt rules out the law as a way of salvation.

1. The Criterion of Eschatological Judgment (2:1-11)

¹*Therefore you are without excuse, O man, whenever you judge. For in judging another you condemn yourself. You do the very same thing even though you judge.* ²*But we know that God's judgment suitably falls on those who do such things.* ³*Do you imagine, O man, that you who judge those who do such things, and (yet) do them yourself, will escape God's judgment?* ⁴*Or do you despise the riches of his kindness, patience, and longsuffering, not noting that God's kindness is meant to lead you to repentance?* ⁵*With your hardness and in your impenitent heart you are heaping up wrath for yourself on the day of wrath, namely, the revelation of the righteous judgment of God.* ⁶*He will render to every man according to his works:* ⁷*to those who, steadfastly concerned for good works, seek glory and honor and immortality, eternal life;* ⁸*but to those who from egotism resist the truth but obey unrighteousness, wrath and fury;* ⁹*affliction and distress on every human being who does evil, the Jew first and also the Greek,* ¹⁰*but glory, honor, and peace on every one who does good, the Jew first and also the Greek.* ¹¹*For there is no respect of persons with God.*

Bibliography: H. Schlier, "Von den Juden. Römerbrief 2,1-29," *Die Zeit der Kirche,* 38-47; E. Flückiger, "Die Werke des Gesetzes bei den Heiden," *TZ* 8 (1952) 17-42; Joest, *Gesetz und Freiheit;* C. Haufe, *Die sittliche Rechtfertigungslehre des Paulus* (1957). 1: A. Fridrichsen, "Quatre conjectures sur le texte du Nouveau Testament," *RHPR* 3 (1923) 439-442. 4: H. Pohlmann, *Die Metanoia als Zentralbegriff der urchristlichen Frömmigkeit* (1938); E. Molland, "Serta Rudbergiana," *Symbolae Osloenses* Fasc. Suppl., IV (1931) 44-52; K. Stendahl, "Rechtfertigung und Endgericht," *Lutherische Rundschau* 11 (1961) 3-10. 6: E. Jüngel, "Das Gesetz zwischen Adam und Christus," *ZTK* 60 (1963) 42-74; K. Grobel, "A Chiastic Retribution-Formula in Romans 2," *Zeit und Geschichte. Dankesgabe an Rudolph Bultmann zum 80. Geburtstag* (ed. E. Dinkler; 1964) 255-261; J. Jeremias, "Paul and James," *ExpT* 66 (1954/55) 368-371; S. Lyonnet, "Gratuité de la justification et gratuité du salut," *Stud.Paul.Congr.,* I, 95-110. 11: D. Rahnenführer, "Das Testament des Hiob und das Neue Testament," *ZNW* 62 (1971) 68-93; K. Berger, "Zu den sogenannten Sätzen Heiligen Rechtes," *NTS* 17 (1970) 10-40. See also the bibliography for 1:18–3:20.

What follows can be understood only as a polemic against the Jewish tradition which comes out most clearly and with much the same vocabulary in Wis 15:1ff.

(Daxer, "Lehrauffassung," 68ff.; Lietzmann; Nygren): "But thou, our God, art kind and true, patient and ruling all things in mercy. For even if we sin we are thine, knowing thy power; but we will not sin, because we know that we are accounted thine. For to know thee is complete righteousness, and to know thy power is the root of immortality. For neither has the evil intent of human art   [⁵ misled us." Here Gentile idolatry is judged. The pious person, freed from this basic sin, can appeal to his knowledge of God as his righteousness and thus deal lightly with his own guilt.

The contrast to the depiction in ch. 1 is unmistakable. It extends even to the style, which at least in vv. 1-6 reflects the lively dialogue of the diatribe with address, question, and argumentation. Typically Pauline are the absurd motives ascribed to the adversary (Bultmann, *Stil*, 67). Finally, the abundance of legal terms should not be overlooked. A distinction from 1:18-31 is that these are now combined with the apocalyptic outlook which is dominant here too.

The Jew comes from a history which is not primarily shaped by the secret or sinister nexus of guilt and destiny. God's word has been spoken to him in law, promise, and curse. He knows about the goal of the last judgment and he can be addressed in terms of this. Painful experience lets him bear with comparative patience the historical fluctuation of good and evil. As he hopes for justification from the end, so the most serious threat can come to him only from the end of history in divine judgment (Bornkamm, "Revelation," 59f.). Paul's argumentation sees Jewish reality as exemplary for humanity as a whole. But this does not mean that the Jewish situation depicted here is any the less grave (Murray). Only the contrast between the world of Gentile vices and that of the pious who judge them can show in all its seriousness the depth and breadth of the divine wrath on all existence. Nothing suggests that these are Jewish-Christians (*contra* Minear, *Obedience*, 47ff.).

Verse 1 might be an early marginal gloss which originally drew the conclusion from v. 3 and was then put at the beginning (Bultmann, "Glossen," 200). διό at any rate does not have an inferential sense, requiring frequently the insertion of ideas left out or (Fridrichsen, "Conjectures," 439ff.) explained as a mistake for an original δίς. It is always used consecutively in Paul (Jervell, *Imago*, 319), but according to other parallels (cf. Lietzmann; Molland, "Serta," 44ff.) it can be a colorless transitional particle (also Michel). It takes on significance, however, if it introduces the expected answer to the rhetorical question of v. 3. Then it also is easier to understand the generalizing and repetitive πᾶς ὁ κρίνων, which certainly cannot be referring to the rabbi (*contra* Michel). It disturbs the antithesis of "judge" and "do the same" because it places the accent entirely on the first word. It is perhaps a reminiscence of the prohibition against judging in Matt 7:1 and Luke 6:37. But Paul's concern is not with judging others, and by suggesting this the gloss is misleading to expositors (cf. Zahn; Schlatter). Furthermore, the partial overlapping of v. 1 and v. 3 is avoided if we accept v. 1 as an interpolation. Verse 2 with its antithetical summary οἴδαμεν δέ moves on smoothly from 1:32. To be sure, ἀναπολόγητος εἶ cannot then be ascribed to Paul, even though it points back to 1:20 and is appropriate to the situation.

Verse 2 aptly brings out the agreement between Paul and the partner in the conversation. τὸ κρίμα τοῦ θεοῦ means the pronouncing of judgment on the last day. According to 'Abot 3:20 Rabbi Akiba says of this: "The judgment is a judgment of truth." This is later interpreted as follows (Billerbeck): "He judges all according to truth and right." If Paul follows this tradition, κατὰ ἀλήθειαν indicates the norm of judgment. There is no important change of sense if the expression is taken in Greek fashion to refer to the objective facts (BAGD, 36a; Bultmann, TDNT, I, 243; Nygren; Murray). τὰ τοιαῦτα overlaps a ταῦτα and is repeated in v. 3, meaning "all such." The attack begins in v. 3 with λογίζῃ δέ, which is normally used of a conclusion to be drawn, and which in this context means "imagine" (Heidland, Anrechnung, 62f.). We find a traditional form of this in Wis 15:8: "Those who do evil do not escape the judgment of the Lord." This applies even when we make ourselves co-critic with God (Barth).

Verse 4 does not bring an alternative to v. 3, but makes it concrete. Judgment is not escaped but confirmed when God's kindness is despised. Dependence on Jewish tradition, possibly (Michel) on the language of prayer, is again unmistakable. The catchwords χρηστότης, τὸ χρηστόν, μακροθυμία occur already in Wis 15:1. 2 Apoc. Bar. 21:20 speaks of those who take God's forbearance for weakness. On the other side Paul draws upon a conception already at hand. Wis 11:23 declares that God overlooks sins with a view to repentance, and 2 Apoc. Bar. 59:6 connects the postponement of wrath with the great measure of God's forbearance. The last passage shows that ἀνοχή means here the delay of wrath (Schlier, TDNT, I, 359f.; Stählin, TDNT, V, 431; but cf. Kühl). The three divine predicates are in Hellenistic genitive constructions and in typical Pauline fashion (Michel contra Zahn; Kühl) are dependent on πλούτου.

The individualizing of the charge softens the tenor of 1:18ff. but does not abolish it (cf. Strobel, Untersuchungen, 198ff.). In this respect it is plain how strongly the apostle identifies himself with the opponent and his premises in order to lay hold of him from that perspective. In ἀνοχή one sees how broad is μακροθυμία, which Judaism relates particularly to omnipotence (Billerbeck). χρηστότης, however, is generous "kindness" as in 11:22 (Weiss, TDNT, IX, 490f.). The rhetorical plerophory gives emphasis to the demand of v. 4b. ἄγειν εἰς is in the conative present (BAGD, 512b). μετάνοια is alien to the Greek world (cf. Norden, Agnostos Theos, 134ff.) and means "turn around" (Hebrew שׁוּב) rather than "change of mind." If, surprisingly, Paul uses this word elsewhere only in 2 Cor 7:9 and the verb in 2 Cor 12:21, it is because πίστις replaces it in missionary preaching. The constant demand is thus accentuated. The danger of the pious person is that of isolating God's gifts from the claim which is given with them, and of forgetting to relate forbearance and patience to the Judge of the last day. Humans always crave security. They seek to obtain it through moralism, worshiping the gods, or trusting the divine goodness. The Lord who is known as Judge, however, does not ensure security; he destroys it. In fact Gentile and Jewish piety constantly plays off God against God, the Giver against the Judge. In this context repentance as an integral element of faith can only say that there must be a turning from the religiously perverted desire of mankind, that one must submit himself to the Judge. μετάνοια is thus conceivable only as a change in the existence of man as he is. Hence v. 5 does not introduce a new theme (contra Flückiger, "Werke," 20). It is not a refutation of the Jewish view of justification in judgment. Instead, it is its radical confirmation.

55

The person represented typically by the Jew is determined by σκληρότης and, in explication, by the καρδία ἀμετανόητος. These two terms are based on typical OT/Jewish preaching of judgment, as in Deut 9:27 and also in Qumran (Michel; Behm, *TDNT*, IV, 1009). In these earlier passages also they denote obstinacy and the resultant hardness which is not open to the claim of the Lord and   [thus means that the person is constitutively closed in upon himself. The gifts given us are then regarded as our booty with which we may protect ourselves against the Giver himself, as though he were our enemy. When this happens we have the same paradoxical process as that depicted in 1:22ff. God actually becomes what we see in him and make of him, namely, the wrathful adversary.

The difference from 1:22ff. lies in the apocalyptic vocabulary and motivation. The ἡμέρα τῆς ὀργῆς καὶ ἀποκαλύψεως δικαιοκρισίας τοῦ θεοῦ here becomes the center of proclamation. Conversely it is now clear that all historical destiny presses not merely toward its consummation (Dodd) but also toward the disclosure of its meaning, or, better, of the will at work in it. The revelation of wrath from heaven in the temporal dimension is, in spite of its boundless breadth and unsearchable depth, something that must be endured but whose true character is not yet understood. God's right even over rebels remains remarkably concealed, not yet speaking to us directly. Judgment is executed without the Judge himself coming on the scene. Only with the manifestation of δικαιοκρισία does eschatological clarity penetrate the twilight of destiny. The Judge makes himself known.

Paul adopts here a rare Hellenistic word (BAGD, 195b) which according to *T. Levi* 3:2; 15:2 (cf. the equivalent "righteous judgment" in 1QS 5:12 and on this Braun, *Qumran*, I, 172) links the two motifs of judgment on the guilty and the established right of God. In this light the relation between God's righteousness and wrath, which has hitherto remained a problem, can be more closely defined. In both cases it concerns making known God's right in relation to the world, so that the one cannot be detached from the other. In will and work, of course, the declaration is basically different. The solution of the dialectic is that with the revelation of righteousness in the gospel the destiny of wrath, which rules and may be detected already, is manifested in its eschatological orientation, namely, as the hidden epiphany of the final Judge and the anticipatory execution of his sentence on a rebellious world. Only now is God's unrestricted lordship proclaimed universally and unconditionally as salvation (Heil). In this light perdition (Unheil) is explained.

On the other hand, the righteousness of God as salvation remains a gift which can be received only in faith. Unbelief as disobedience to the offer does not cancel the gift and certainly does not set aside the Lord who expresses himself therein. Yet the disdained Lord, since he does not give up his claim to creation or relativize the salvation consisting in his lordship, can reveal himself only as Judge and that to our destruction. The doctrines of justification and judgment are inseparably linked in Paul (cf. Mattern, *Gericht*, 71ff.), because the concern in both is the Creator's right as Lord of creation as this works itself out in the creature. To those who open themselves to him this Lord appears as salvation, but to those who resist him as perdition, since in this resistance they misplace the source, goal, and way of their own lives. A doctrine of justification which avoids the concept of judgment loses its character as proclamation of the lordship of God

and loses therewith the only basis of the humanization of mankind. A concept of judgment which does not receive its meaning from the doctrine of justification leaves no more room for assurance of salvation. For the apostle doom lies not only over the world but also over the individual whose existence heaps God's
3] wrath upon itself. θησαυρίζειν is not used ironically (*contra* Michel). It derives from the good Jewish view that a person accumulates capital in heaven with his works when he is alive (Billerbeck, I, 429ff.; Stählin, *TDNT*, V, 438; for other figurative uses cf. BAGD, 361b). Paul, however, changes the Jewish expectation into its opposite. The use of ἐν for εἰς in the sense of "for" is characteristic of the *koine*.

The argument reaches its sharpest climax when in v. 6 (cf. 1 Cor 3:13ff.; 9:17; 2 Cor 5:10; 9:6; Gal 6:7ff.) Paul, with the citation from Ps 61:13 LXX; Prov 24:12, adopts the fundamental Jewish idea (Billerbeck) of eschatological retribution according to our works. Protestantism has always found serious difficulty with this theologoumenon (cf. the historical survey in Braun, *Gerichtsgedanke*, 14-31; Oltmanns, "Verhältnis," 110ff.; Roetzel, *Judgement*, 2f.) and Roman Catholics have seized on it, not without malicious joy, as support for their dogmatics (cf., e.g., Gutjahr). Some solutions may be dismissed at once as artificial, even if they are championed interconfessionally. This applies especially to the thesis that the statement is hypothetical, that Paul is adopting a pre-evangelical standpoint in order to expose the guilt and judgment of the Jew even if there were no gospel and the law could be fulfilled (Lietzmann; Sickenberger; J. Knox; contrast Eichholz, *Paulus*, 89). The many Pauline parallels refute this theory, which in any case finds no support in the text. The only particle of truth in it is that, as in ch. 7, the non-Christian world is seen from the Christian point of view. But the stylistic forms of the diatribe should not allow us to forget that the apostle is addressing the congregation, not giving missionary instruction to the world around.

Also unacceptable is any explanation that simply establishes Paul's attachment to Jewish tradition, thus being content with the history of religions and psychology but ignoring the theological interpretation. Naturally one cannot rule out in principle a Judaizing relapse, even by Paul. Yet he has thoroughly thought through the tradition, and here in particular he radicalizes it (Braun, *Gerichtsgedanke*, 48ff.). If our interpretation thus far is not completely wide of the mark, the element of God's eschatological right plays, especially for him, a role that forbids us from limiting it to certain parts of his theology or phases of his biography.

In view of the doctrine of justification we are also to reject, thirdly, any theory which pleads in different ways a "not only–but also," which has been attempted in many variations. Paul may not always argue with strict logic. His individual statements and even his intentions may sometimes contradict one another. In no circumstances, however, may one blunt the central point of his message. For him faith certainly is not one work among others, not even the most important, and he just as certainly does not teach that faith and works are complementary (Sanday and Headlam; Filson, *Recompense*, 127ff.), which would necessarily bring with it either a sequence of justification and sanctification, or the assumption of a double justification in baptism and in the eschatological judgment (J. Jeremias, "Paul and James," 370f.; Lyonnet, "Gratuité," 106; Black), and hence a possible compromise with Jas 2:14ff.

Again, one cannot simply establish the contradiction and demand that it be upheld (Joest, *Gesetz und Freiheit*, 165-176, cf. Jungel, "Gesetz," 73; for criticism, Stuhlmacher, *Gerechtigkeit*, 229ff.). Otherwise Paul becomes schizophrenic. Christ as the fulfilment of the law is not yet treated in this passage (*contra* Flückiger, "Werke," 23), so that the problem also cannot be blunted in this way.

The decisive thing is that the doctrine of judgment according to works not be ranked above justification but conversely be understood in the light of it (Mattern, *Gericht*, 214f.), although this perspective is not yet apparent here. Again, the difficulties in exposition are largely connected with a failure to pay due regard to the power-character even of the righteousness of God received as a gift, since this involves a radical separation of gift and Giver, and of Giver and Judge. If the gift is finally the sign and content of Christ's lordship on earth, we can no longer live by our own will and right but constantly stand in responsibility and accountability (Furnish, *Ethics*, 120f.). To this degree the last day does not differ from each earthly day.

It should also be recalled that here, as in 1:22ff., the Judge always comes upon the scene in conflict with human illusion. Illusion is any state which attacks the lordship of the Creator by forgetting one's creatureliness. It is a state of not living out of the Creator's lordship, whether in Gentile or Jewish form, or of living, as Jas 2:14ff. rightly points out, in a faith which understands itself in terms of experiences and dogmatic or ecclesiastical ties instead of standing or falling by the Lord, as in Rom 14:4ff. This is why Paul could take over the OT/Jewish maxim.

The contexts of the passages quoted show that he did this in a Christianizing way (rightly H. W. Schmidt). According to the OT view, man lives as one who acts and is on the path of pilgrimage, therefore as one who hopes, and (Phil 3:12f.) always has to press on anew to meet his Lord. According to Gal 5:5 faith itself waits for its definitive justification from the eschatological future. The earthly path does not end in the contestable character of faith, which now determines it, but in the full freedom of being with the Lord and therefore (2 Cor 5:10) before Christ's judgment seat. Here it will be seen (1 Cor 3:12f.) on what foundation a person has built, and this is described by the alternative of obedience or illusion. If retribution according to works is no longer a recognition of human achievement, as in the Judaism which Paul combats, but the definitive revelation of the lordship of Christ in judgment on all human illusions, the believer stands with Gentile and Jew under the same measure of the same Lord (Roetzel, *Judgement*, 178ff.), and the law of the last day is none other than the "law of faith" which is already experienced now, namely, acceptance and confirmation of the lordship of Christ. Here "by works alone" in fact coincides with "by faith alone" (Althaus). The misunderstanding of "partly by faith and partly by works" is ruled out. It is not that faith has to be succeeded by moral conduct which alone will be judged at the last (e.g., Kühl).

Faith itself is at issue when God judges illusions. He does this already and all the time. As surely as God's righteousness is salvation, just as surely the faith which receives this righteousness is set before the Judge, and only as it is set thus is it faith. In anticipation of the chapters which follow one may say already that true faith represents the only human reality of not living by illusion. For faith alone sees its salvation in the lordship of Christ. Faith receives it from the hand of its Judge as it constantly stands before him, faith being the ability to stand outside oneself and before God in Christ. Where the concern is the necessity of the revelation of God's righteousness, this reality is not yet discussed; it is shown that God's righteousness and illusion are mutually exclusive. This is the point in the present verse and its context.

By no means accidentally are vv. 7-10 hymnic and highly stylized rhetorically (Grobel, "Retribution," 255ff.). Verses 9f. repeat vv. 7f. chiastically. Verse 11 is a conclusion which formally parallels v. 6, but which also gives the reason for its content. The verbs are completely absent in vv. 7-10. To speak of an anacoluthon in v. 8 (Lagrange; contrast BDF, §469) is to miss its character as acclamation. Verse 6 is not developed but is solemnly confirmed by Paul as a representative of the Christian community. Blessing and curse are prophetically proclaimed here on those who conform or rebel in face of the law of the last day (v. 6). In the style of holy law, which rules out any hypothetical interpretation of what precedes, the criterion of the last judgment is unveiled in its universal scope and in its present validity, as in the acclamations of Revelation.

In face of this criterion there is an eschatological division of mankind which relativizes the distinctions between Jew and Gentile in the same way that this happens in the proclamation of justification. This is a fresh indication that the message of judgment in Paul must be understood in the light of his doctrine of justification and is posited along with it. Where the gospel is preached there is spread abroad (2 Cor 2:16) both the fragrance of life to life and also that of death to death, and those who are called to salvation are separated from those who go to perdition (1 Cor 1:18; 2 Cor 2:15). The parallelism in these passages cannot possibly be overlooked, and the present verses belong to the same context.

We have here a strict parallel to the transition from 1:16f. to 1:18. When salvation is revealed, perdition is also disclosed, and the uniqueness of our passage lies not in the thought of judgment as such but in the apocalyptic, universal dimension of its proclamation. Obviously Jewish tradition is followed in its richness. Nothing, however, justifies assuming an original Semitic text (*contra* Grobel, "Retribution," 259 and his analysis). With the contradictory juxtaposition of ζωὴ αἰώνιος and the ὀργὴ καὶ θυμός, which Paul takes from the OT and LXX only here, eternal salvation and perdition are denoted. To the same sphere of Hellenistically influenced Judaism belong, according to 1 Pet 1:7; Rev 4:9, δόξα and τιμή as praise and heavenly recognition. ἀφθαρσία, which is used, e.g., in Wis 2:23, is interchangeable with εἰρήνη, and is the opposite of purely earthly affliction and trouble in 4 Ezra 7:95f. Semitic features are the characterization of essence by origin with the formula οἱ ἐκ and the meaning of ἀλήθεια as God's demand (cf. 2:20) in the antithesis to ἀδικία (Bultmann, *TDNT*, VI, 4). The meaning of ἐριθεία is uncertain. It probably does not derive from ἐρεθίζειν, "be refractory," as in Deut 21:20 LXX (Lagrange), but from ἐριθεύειν, "work for wages and act accordingly." The conjecture that Paul connects it in a false etymology with ἔρις (Lietzmann; Pallis; Murray) does not fit the context and lacks cogency on other grounds. The meaning "selfishness" or "selfish ambition" is more prevalent today (Sanday and Headlam), although "baseness" (Büchsel, *TDNT*, II, 661) and "striving for recognition" (Schlier, "Juden," 40) also call for consideration.

καθ' ὑπομονὴν ἔργου ἀγαθοῦ is to be taken with the participle. In distinction from the genitive construction in 2 Cor 1:6 the idea is not so much that of enduring as of perseverance—the consistent pursuit of a goal (Murray). This goal lies transcendently outside the sphere of earthly possibilities but is the reward for constant concentration on it as indicated by ζητεῖν and the related prepositional phrase. The antithesis in v. 8 makes it clear that what is being described is the obedience that allows no deviation. With obedience the goal is reached, with disobedience it is missed. Obedience is accordingly the one good work, the "good" in v. 10 as such, the criterion of retribution in the judgment, and the standing in eschatologically anticipated blessing. In contrast, disobedience derives from a self-centered will and is a simple equivalent of evil. It is a mark of that human illusion which is disclosed in the judgment and which even now stands under wrath.

A common view is that the repetition of vv. 7f. in vv. 9f. is more plainly directed against Jewish claims and that this is the reason for the recurrence of the formula of 1:16, "to the Jew first and also the Greek." But in the acclamation and the modification of the terminology the point is that coming judgment in blessing and curse already reaches into the present. In a prophetic function Paul with effective power pronounces both on those concerned (Zeller, *Juden*, 151). One can explain this only as an occurrence of holy law, no matter how one explains the religio-historical background (*contra* Berger, "Sätze," who does not take seriously my starting point in the Pauline phenomenon).

What follows should not be interpreted psychologically. θλῖψις, the eschatological tribulation, is strengthened, as in 2 Cor 4:8, by στενοχωρία, which stresses the idea of hemming in with no way out. The two terms had previously been used together in extrabiblical Greek and in the LXX (Lagrange; Schlier, *TDNT*, III, 139f.; Bertram, *TDNT*, VII, 606f.). What is meant objectively is the reality of a life hemmed in on all sides, which is abandoned to the Judge's wrath with no chance of flight. The converse of this is peace as standing in the truce of God and of the anticipated kingdom of freedom in which a person receives room to breathe and space for action. The compound κατεργάζεσθαι replaces the simple form, as often in the *koine*. The situation for both Jew and Gentile is that they are already on the way to divine judgment and have fallen into its reach. The precedence of the Jew in salvation history is not affected (*contra* Kühl), but it is not a privilege on which he may rely. As in 4:11ff., it must be authenticated by obedience. Precisely the Jew stands all the more strongly in the alternative of curse and blessing.

The closing sentence (v. 11) does not establish uniformity. God is not a leveller like death. He gives to each his own, as Paul tirelessly insists (Schlatter). The πρῶτον of v. 10 applies also to judgment, whose premise is not uniformity but the measure of the imparted gift. The transition to the dimension of salvation history is especially instructive here. It shows us that the apostle is especially critical of Judaism but also warns us against exaggerating the individualizing tendency of the passage. Anthropology must not relativize or eliminate the problem of salvation history. Otherwise, what follows is redundant. As the consequence of the first verses and the presupposition of the next section, v. 11 shatters Jewish claims in particular. The statement goes back to 2 Chr 19:7, which in Judaism is also reflected in *Jub.* 5:16ff.; 33:18; *2 Apoc. Bar.* 44:4. Paul radicalizes it by applying it to both Jews and Gentiles (Billerbeck; Limbeck, *Ordnung*, 109, 112). The LXX knows only πρόσωπον λαμβάνειν or θαυμάζειν. The noun occurs for the first time in the NT in Paul. Nevertheless, its use in the household rules in Col 3:25; Eph 6:9 and also in Jas 2:1 suggests a pre-Pauline tradition (Lohse, *TDNT*, VI, 779). This seems to be confirmed by *Testament of Job* 43:13 and the adverbial use in 4:8 (Rahnenführer, "Testament des Hiob," 75f.).

2. The Possession of the Torah is No Privilege (2:12-16)

[12]*For those who have sinned without the law will perish without the law, and those who have sinned under the law will be judged by the law.* [13]*For not hearers of the law (are) righteous before God, but doers of the law will be pronounced righteous.* [14]*When, therefore, the Gentiles, who do not have the law, fulfil of themselves the (demands) of the law, they are law to themselves, even though they do not have the law.* [15]*For they show that the work of the law is written in their hearts, witness also being borne by their conscience, and the thoughts which accuse or excuse them,* [16]*on the day when God will judge the secrets of people according to my gospel through Christ Jesus.*

Bibliography: W. Mundle, "Zur Auslegung von Röm 2, 13ff.," *ThBl* 13 (1934) 249-256; W. Brandt, "Das Gesetz Israels und das Gesetz der Heiden," *Kirche und Erziehung* 8 (1934); R. Leichtenhahn, *Evangelium wider Gesetz im Neuen Testament* (1940); F. K. Schumann, "Bemerkungen zur Lehre vom Gesetz," *ZST* 16 (1939) 600-628; G. Bornkamm, "Gesetz und Natur, R. 2, 14-16," *Studien*, 93-118; R. Bultmann, "Anknüpfung und Widerspruch," *TZ* 2 (1946) 401-418; O. Kuss, "Die Heiden und die Werke des Gesetzes (nach Röm 2, 14-16)," *Auslegung*, I, 213-245; J. B. Souček, "Zur Exegese von Röm 2, 14ff.," *Antwort. Karl Barth zum siebzigsten Geburtstag am 10. Mai 1956* (1956) 99-113; B. Reicke, "Natürliche Theologie nach Paulus," *Svensk Exegetisk Årsbok* 22/23 (1957/58) 154-167; R. Walker, "Die Heiden und das Gericht. Zur Auslegung von Röm 2, 12-16," *EvT* 20 (1960) 302-314; F. Kuhr, "Römer 2₁₄f. und die Verheissung bei Jeremia 31₃₁ff.," *ZNW* 55 (1964) 243-261; J. Riedl, "Die Auslegung von R 2, 14-16 in Vergangenheit und Gegenwart," *Stud.Paul.Congr.*, I, 271-281; R. Hirzel, νόμος ἄγραφος (Abhandlungen der Philologisch-historischen Klasse der Königlich Sachischen Gesellschaft der Wissenschaften 20, 1; 1900); I. Heinemann, "Die Lehre vom ungeschriebenen Gesetz im jüdischen Schrifttum," *Hebrew Union College Annual* 4 (1927) 149-171; W. Kranz, "Das Gesetz des Herzens," *Rheinisches Museum für Philologie* N.F. 94 (1951) 222-241; M. Pohlenz, *Die Stoa. Geschichte einer geistigen Bewegung* (2 vols.; 1948, 1949); F. Heinimann, *Nomos und Physis* (1945); H. Osborne, "Syneidesis," *JTS* 32 (1931) 167-179; J. Dupont, "Syneidesis," *Studia Hellenistica* 5 (1948) 119-153; C. A. Pierce, *Conscience in the New Testament* (SBT 15; 1955); B. Reicke, "Syneidesis in Röm. 2, 15," *TZ* 12 (1956) 157-161; J. Stelzenberger, *Syneidesis im NT* (1961); H. Sahlin, "Einige Textemendationen zum Römerbrief," *TZ* 9 (1953) 92-100; J. Riedl, *Das Heil der Heiden, nach R. 2, 14-16. 26. 27* (1965); H. Saake, "Echtheitskritische Überlegungen zur Interpolationshypothese von Römer ii. 16," *NTS* 19 (1972/73) 486-89.

For H. E. Weber, *Beziehungen*, and Pohlenz, "Paulus," see the bibliography for 1:18–3:20; for M. Barth, "Speaking," and Bonhöffer, *Epiktet*, see the bibliography for 1:18-32; for Flückiger, "Werke," and Schlier, "Juden," see the bibliography for 2:1-11.

γάρ elucidates what is implied in v. 11. The gifts granted to the Jew in salvation history do not protect him against universal judgment. This is directed first against any reliance on the reception and possession of the Torah as the true mark of the difference between Jew and Gentile. The anti-Judaistic thrust of what follows may be seen in the fact that now for the first time Paul expounds the concept of the law thematically. In a way characteristic of the whole theology of the apostle, the Mosaic Torah is so identified with the divine law that there is no overall species νόμος, and that as a result the lack of the article is without significance (Lietzmann; Bläser, *Gesetz,* 1ff.). Certainly the more general use of the term in the sense of "norm" is familiar to the apostle from the Greek world. But he does not limit the Torah by making it one law among others. On the contrary, the Torah reaches out in a distinctive way beyond the sphere of Israel to the world, as will be shown in a moment. Its distinguishing mark is the fact that it is fixed in writing. This is how it has the clarity and the binding force which, according to Paul's view and that of Judaism, the so-called unwritten laws do not have to the same degree (Heinemann, "Lehre," 150ff.).

The uniqueness of the Torah means that the non-Jew can be called ἄνομος. On these premises the unconditional validity of the principle in v. 11 is established in v. 12 by two parallel sentences. Sin brings judgment no matter where it is committed. Outside the sphere of the Torah this happens in the fateful retribution of ch. 1, which leads to death. Against the sinful Jew, however, the imparted gift of the law, which represents the Giver, acts as the accuser and also as the means of personal judgment, declaring therein its character as power.

In giving a basis v. 13 shows that the emphasis is on the second sentence. The antithesis of ἀκροαταί–ποιηταὶ νόμου derives materially from the Jewish tradition, may be found also in Jas 1:22, and at least earlier has the same accent as here (Billerbeck). The future tense of the verbs, whose passive denotes divine action, is plainly eschatological. δικαιοῦσθαι, corresponding to κρίνεσθαι, means "be declared righteous" (Stuhlmacher, *Gerechtigkeit,* 217ff.). The typically Semitic formula δίκαιοι παρὰ θεῷ (Michel) clearly shows δίκαιος to be a relational concept.

In v. 14 Paul, again using the γάρ of argument, makes the transition, not to an excursus, but to a concrete application. The initially surprising reference to the Gentiles is logical to the extent that those without the law (v. 12a) are not without an accuser or without any law at all, and are thus subject to possible punishment. The ἀνόμως of v. 12a is in a sense corrected now (Bornkamm, "Gesetz," 100). But the attack on the Jews is sharpened hereby: the law is not their inviolable private possession.

The direction of the argument is now reversed. Earlier the movement was from law to act; now it is from act to the law effecting it. This has nothing to do with a suddenly more optimistic evaluation of the Gentiles (Dodd; M. Barth, "Speaking," 290) or with the Pelagian question of a morally established righteousness (Bornkamm, "Gesetz," 99 is right here *contra* Flückiger, "Werke," 26). The exclusive point is that there is no escaping universal judgment.

Finally, the careful formulation as well as the radical intention is to be noted. In analogy to 1:20f. (Bornkamm, "Gesetz," 99) Paul relates what he is saying to experience. ὅταν means "whenever" (BAGD, 587b). Omission of the article before ἔθνη can hardly be unintentional. The reference is not to all Gentiles (correctly van Dülmen, *Theologie,* 76f. *contra* Walker, "Heiden," 304) but not to exceptions either (Lagrange). Similarly, with some ambivalence τὰ τοῦ νόμου is used instead of νόμος. This does not mean concern for fulfilment of the law (Lackmann, *Geheimnis,* 222ff.), nor the full work (Flückiger, "Werke," 28; Gaugler), nor the whole law (Gutjahr). Instead the reference, in accordance with the ὅταν, is to the demands of the law encountered in the concrete situation (Eichholz, *Paulus,* 92), which do not in any sense have to be recognized as such (Bläser, *Gesetz,* 69; differently Walker, "Heiden," 305). It happens repeatedly that those who are without the law do in fact fulfil the intention of the law (Maurer, *Gesetzeslehre,* 68). They do so φύσει.

Concerning the interpretation of φύσει, which again poses the problem of natural theology in Paul, theologians and philologists are engaged in hot debate with little prospect of agreement. Does the apostle mean that there is a generally known law of nature (many Roman Catholic scholars; Fuchs, *Natural Law,* 19f.; Dodd; Black; Lietzmann; Bornkamm, "Gesetz," 101; Norden, *Agnostos Theos,* 122; Pohlenz, "Paulus," 69ff.; Kranz, "Gesetz," 222ff.) from which the principles of natural justice may even perhaps be drawn? Is he offering a variation and modification of the Greek idea of the νόμος ἄγραφος which is the basis and norm of legal codes or which in its primal and universal character stands opposed to the arbitrary θέσεις of political rulers (cf. Huby; Kuhr, "Verheissung," 255ff.)? The fact that a person may be or become law to himself reminds us of statements like Aristotle *Nicomachean Ethics* iv.8.10 (1128a.31): ὁ δὴ χαρίεις καὶ ἐλευθέριος οὕτως ἕξει, οἷον νόμος ὢν ἑαυτῷ, "thus will the tasteful gentleman conduct himself, and be, as it were, a law to himself" (additional parallels in Lietzmann; Bornkamm, "Gesetz"; Kleinknecht, *TDNT,* IV, 1032; Pohlenz, *Stoa,* I, 133, 201f.; II, 101). The expression γραπτὸν ἐν ταῖς καρδίαις αὐτῶν can undoubtedly mean unwritten law. Finally, the reference to συνείδησις is possible only on Greek soil.

That Paul might have known and adopted the idea of the νόμος ἄγραφος is hardly in debate. It is not only attested in Philo (Gutbrod, *TDNT,* IV, 1052-54) and 4 Macc 5:25 but even found a home in Palestinian Judaism (Heinemann, "Lehre," 163ff.; Hengel, *Judaism,* I, 173f.). There, of course, it served the purpose of being able to ascribe the knowledge of the Torah to the age of the patriarchs, as in *2 Apoc. Bar.* 57:2, or as in 1QS 10:6, 8, 11 of setting forth an exposition of the law, engraved on heavenly tablets, of the divine cosmic order and especially of the course of the aeons (cf. also Koester, *TDNT,* IX, 273f.; against him Walker, "Heiden," 305f.).

Nevertheless, great caution is needed in regard to the present passage (Kuss; Ridderbos). No convincing proof has been adduced that it should be understood in terms of the Greek view, nor has it even been made probable. Apart from the special case of 1 Cor 11:14, φύσις is used in a very colorless way in Paul. That the dative, which is not in any case typical for the philosophical use (Bonhöffer, *Epiktet,* 148), provides instrumentally the basis for doing the law may be deduced neither from its adverbial position nor from the next clause (*contra* Bornkamm, "Gesetz," 103). On the contrary, ἑαυτοῖς forms a material parallel. The only appropriate sense of φύσει is "of themselves," "by nature," "as such," since the apostle in Gal 2:15; 4:8 and also Eph 2:3 neither can nor will trace back to nature the being of the Jews, the children of wrath, or idols.

Various paraphrases have been suggested: "natural disposition" (Kühl; Lietzmann; Althaus; Brunner; Kuhr, "Verheissung," 256ff.; BAGD, 869b), "moral consciousness" (Huby), "sense of order," "order of creation" (Kuss), "trueness to type" (Souček, "Exegese," 109), or "creatureliness" (Michel). But these give the word an emphasis which may fit the whole predication but in part goes beyond it. In v. 14 the apostle is not characterizing the constitution of man but specific action not based on the Torah. The point of the second clause is blunted if reflection on the possibility of such an action is imported into this first clause. Nor is Paul concerned about man's integration into an ordered nexus, as is assumed when natural law is inferred from a Greek view. His true concern, as may be seen from v. 15, is with the crisis of existence.

There is an intensification from τὰ τοῦ νόμου to the second clause. Paul is unquestionably not saying that the Gentiles are a law to themselves nor that they have in a different way the same divine law as the Jews (*contra* Bornkamm, "Gesetz," 101). For the apostle does not restrict the Torah to the moral law (*contra* Moule; Gutjahr; Bardenhewer; Riedl, *Heil*, 200f.) and thereby dilute it. For him everything depends on the fact that the Gentiles also experience the transcendent claim of the divine will and thus become, not *the* law or *a* law, but [⸱ law to themselves. Thus, although they do not stand in identity, they stand in some analogy (Michel) with the Jews. They sense that a person is set in question and that a demand is laid on him from outside, and paradoxically they do so in their inner beings.

Verse 15 is confirmatory and is thus introduced (cf. 1:25,32) by explanatory οἵτινες. ἐνδείκνυσθαι is used as in 9:22; 2 Cor 8:24 but it has here a forensic sense (Schlatter): "demonstrate by acts." Judaism, as 4 Ezra 3:33-36 shows, already took account of pagan ethics, or asserted pagan guilt, by speaking of Adamic or Noachic commandments, which, as it acknowledged, individual Gentiles had fulfilled (Billerbeck). Paul, however, says more than this when he speaks about the work of the law being written in their hearts.

Since no eschatological facts are made known, the promise of Jer 38:33 LXX is not at issue (*contra* Zahn; Lietzmann; Nygren; Souček, "Exegese," 101f.; Riedl, *Heil*, 202f.). Even a reminiscence is doubtful (*contra* Bornkamm, "Gesetz," 107; Kuss; cf. Kuhr, "Verheissung," 259). The point of the expression γραπτὸν ἐν ταῖς καρδίαις αὐτῶν is that the Gentiles do not share the Jewish advantage of having a written as distinct from a non-fixed law. They do not have that which is written on the tables of God. Nevertheless, something is written within. They have an analogue to the γραφή and are accountable to this as the Jews are to the Torah received by them. They can as little escape it as they can themselves.

The expression thus has the same goal as the idea of the νόμος ἄγραφος, namely, that of setting mankind under an unconditional obligation. Yet it does this on Jewish premises. Hence we have, not unwritten law, but law written in a special way, *T. Jud.* 20:3f. being very instructive for our text. The "work" of the law is obviously a reference back to τὰ τοῦ νόμου. The singular is most unusual (Nygren; Michel; though cf. Bornkamm, "Gesetz," 106) and so is the genitive, especially in a non-disparaging sense (Mattern, *Gericht*, 144f.). The rendering "core" (Lietzmann; Kuss), or "epitome" (Schlier, "Juden") is off the mark. What is meant is the concrete act demanded by the law (Lagrange; Schlatter; Asmussen) in a general sense (Kühl). Otherwise we arrive at a *nomos* such as the

Jews maintain in the case of the patriarchs and which only Christians fulfil according to Paul. Here, however, it is a matter of Gentiles experiencing God's will, not from the Torah as such, but in outline, as it were, from what is written in their hearts.

If the text is not left imprecise but worked out metaphysically, fear of Pelagianism might lead us to make Augustine's mistake of referring ἔθνη to Gentile-Christians (Mundle, "Auslegung," 249ff.; Flückiger, "Werke," 34ff.; Souček, "Exegese"; cf. Leenhardt; Schrage, Einzelgebote, 191ff.). This is possible only lexically (cf. Kuhr, "Verheissung," 243ff.; history of interpretation in Riedl, Heil, 7-172). For the spontaneity of acting in the Spirit is not expressed by φύσει instead of Spirit and the Christian is not law to himself, nor is he ἄνομος, for he is subject to the law of Christ. It is absurd to refer v. 15 to the Christian if one will not refer 7:7ff. to him also. The final point of the whole argument (Schrage, Einzelgebote, 192f.) is that possession of the Torah cannot be defended as an unlimited privilege vis-à-vis the Gentiles. This is self-evident for the Christian (cf. Bornkamm, "Gesetz," 109f.). The discussion shows, however, that great caution is needed in interpretation at this point.

In v. 15b conscience is called a witness, not for the law nor for the subject of the verb, but for the process described. It cannot be proved that reference is made here to the rule of Deut 19:15. Prior biblical use of συνείδησις is found only in Wis 17:10, then T. Reub. 4:3. Paul introduces it into the NT. It is a common mistake to ascribe the concept to Stoicism. It belongs in fact to popular philosophy (cf. Maurer, TDNT, VII, 898ff.) and in the first instance designates (cf. Dihle, RAC, VI, 686) perception of a claim made on mankind. It is distinguished from νοῦς by the fact that this claim is absolutely obligatory and enforces critical testing of one's own reaction (Bultmann, Theology, I, 216ff.; Enslin, Ethics, 101). If one reflects on orientation to God's command (Michel) or the inner law (Dodd; against him Furnish, Ethics, 229), one is propelled toward an understanding in the sense of a consciousness of norms, as in the later view. At issue for Paul is a consciousness of oneself which can turn a critical eye on one's own conduct of life.

An attractive suggestion (Bornkamm, "Gesetz," 111ff.) is that the passage follows the Pythagorean rule of self-examination by conscience. According to Seneca De ira iii.36.1 the Roman philosopher Sextius offers an example of daily self-scrutiny along these lines ("What bad habit have you cured today? What fault have you resisted? In what respect are you better?" [LCL]), and Seneca himself commends it in Epistula 28.10 ("Therefore, as far as possible, prove yourself guilty, hunt up charges against yourself; play the part, first of accuser, then of judge, last of intercessor" [LCL]). This seems to provide an excellent illustration of v. 15c.

Nevertheless, this theory cannot be upheld. While Paul binds the accusing and excusing thoughts very closely to the conscience and its function as described elsewhere, here and in 9:1 (as also for the most part in secular usage) συνείδησις clearly has only the task of a witness. Nor does v. 15c refer to an organ of meditation (Bornkamm, "Gesetz," 115 contra Flückiger, "Werke," 35f.). In particular, one must not lose the nuances in the sharply differentiated materials of vv. 14b-15 by laying all the stress from the outset, in modern style, on the role of conscience (contra Barrett; Kuss) and then construing the introductory καί of

v. 15c explicatively (Lagrange). Even more erroneous is the relating of λογισμῶν as an objective genitive to συνείδησις (Reicke, "Natürliche Theologie," 158ff.): "consciousness or feeling for thoughts." Another serious mistake in the context is to take αὐτῶν in v. 15b and μεταξὺ ἀλλήλων in v. 15c antithetically and to understand by λογισμῶν, as in the case of the reading διαλογισμῶν in G, the judgments which people pass on one another (Kühl; Gutjahr; Schlatter; Althaus; Heidland, TDNT, IV, 288; Gutbrod, TDNT, IV, 1057f.; correctly Maurer, TDNT, VII, 916f.).

In Paul the issue is the forensic situation (cf. Maurer, TDNT, VII, 911-13 on Philo; Lackmann, Geheimnis, 221ff.) in the inner person (Sanday and Headlam; Ridderbos), as the juridical vocabulary already shows. This finds expression in the clash of accusation and—ἢ καί as in 2 Cor 1:13—excuse, as in the very un-Greek function of conscience as an eschatological witness. This does not mean that the apostle has no interest in man's self-judgment in self-criticism (contra Bornkamm, "Gesetz," 115). The point is that such self-criticism anticipates the last judgment, as in Wis 1:5-10 (Behm, TDNT, V, 810).

In the action of his decisions for the transcendent claim, which he experiences in his own existence instead of from the Torah, as in the reaction of self-criticism and the unceasing dialectic of his judgments on himself, it is clear, according to the apostle, that there are criteria for a person which he himself has not set. Since in general they tend to accuse him, he may deny them or set up defenses against them. But he cannot silence them. Instead, his controversy with them shows that he is in severe contradiction with himself, as expressed in 7:7ff.

In distinction from the Greek view of the νόμος ἄγραφος, Paul does not speak of the law which sets us in a metaphysical nexus of order and in harmony with the universe around us, in a moral world order (Dodd; J. Knox), or even in a moral law of nature (Sickenberger; Best; Baulès), and he certainly does not have in mind an innate sense of right or a guiding moral ideal. Instead he speaks of the great disturbance which affects those who encounter in themselves what is written by another hand and who find themselves engaging in self-criticism and self-defense before an alien forum. Precisely in his innermost being a person is not his own master. He does not himself establish the criteria which are directed against him, and if he could he would end the split in his ego and the dialectic of his existence. Someone else observes us as we have to criticize ourselves and he contradicts us in the contradiction of our life. The shadow of the Judge does not just surround us on the outside as in 1:22ff. It falls on our inner being (cf. Schlatter) and makes it the tribunal. That is the advance made on 1:18ff. To the wrath which rules the Gentile world in the form of destiny there corresponds (Pierce, Conscience, 85) the secret judgment day within. Life may be depraved. Conscience and judgment may be subject to various influences and constant vacillations. But we do not at all judge ourselves throughout life in accusation and defense apart from the compulsion of a Judge who is still hidden to us. Only faith, of course, can proclaim this (Schlier, "Juden," 43). All the same, ancient tragedy and the Hellenistic discussion of the problem of conscience show that this proclamation could connect up with Gentile experience.

It is in this light that we are to interpret v. 16. Difficulties abound here, too. Materially the variants in the introduction are of no significance (cf. Lietzmann).

Their rise is best explained from the singular reading of B, ἐν ᾗ ἡμέρᾳ. Inadvertent omission of the ᾗ led to the Egyptian text and the Byzantine text favored by most witnesses. Almost all commentators find it hard to see how the event described in v. 15 will also be future. All conceivable solutions have been attempted. Verse 16a has been related to the earthly day of encounter with the Word of God (H. E. Weber, *Beziehungen*, 142ff.) or to that of conversion (Reicke, "Natürliche Theologie," 161). Some have argued that originally v. 16 came after v. 13 (Sanday and Headlam; Dodd; Kirk). Many suggest that vv. 14f. are in parentheses. Since this is implausible on the ground of length, others restrict the parenthesis to v. 15b (Mundle, "Auslegung," 255). To proposals to strike ἡμέρᾳ and to connect the relative ἐν ᾗ with συνείδησις (Sahlin, "Textemendationen," 93), one may add the radical proposal to explain vv. 14f. and vv. 26f. as glosses because of their content (J. Weiss, "Beiträge," 218).

Such obviously desperate measures are unnecessary. If there is doubt about the original text, it is best to take v. 16 as a gloss. In this case the difficult κατὰ τὸ εὐαγγέλιον, which occurs elsewhere only in the deutero-Pauline 16:25 and 2 Tim 2:8, can be taken as a reminiscence of 1 Cor 4:5 (Bultmann, "Glossen," 200f.; Bornkamm, "Gesetz," 118; but cf. Walker, "Heiden," 311; Saake, "Überlegungen," 487). There is general agreement that the sentence is too long and that it is brought to a forced end with a loosely attached subsidiary clause. A link might be supplied; e.g.: "All this will be made plain" (Michel; Leenhardt; Huby). This is unnecessary, however, if ἐνδείκνυνται, like κρίνει (unless κρίνει is indeed the true reading), is given a future sense (H. W. Schmidt; Ridderbos). As v. 5 spoke of heaping up ἐν ἡμέρᾳ ὀργῆς, so here the demonstration will come on the day of judgment.

An argument against taking v. 16 as a gloss is that this reference to the judgment is indispensable (Eichholz, *Paulus*, 92f.; Saake, "Überlegungen," 488f.; Riedl, *Heil*, 204). The context remains a torso without it unless what precedes is related to the righteousness of faith of Gentile-Christians. The legal process depicted in v. 15 demands a final clarification and decision in which the previously hidden Judge is manifested. Verses 14f. are not so closely related that proof of the coming judgment is offered by them (Bultmann, "Glossen," 200f.). Verse 14 moves to a climax in v. 15: Those who cannot simply from a Jewish standpoint be said to be without law, since their good deeds point to some sort of law over them, are at the same time in a forensic situation. With their existence in contradiction they point to a day of judgment, to which v. 16 refers openly. The idea that this reference is sufficient on its own, and does not need to be completed in v. 16, is unsatisfactory (Bornkamm, "Gesetz," 118). For taken alone, vv. 14f. show nothing more than that the Gentile is not wholly without law and thus falls into self-contradiction.

All explanations that diminish the importance of v. 16 have the unfortunate result of putting the stress on v. 14a and finding the heart of the statements in a variation of the motif of the νόμος ἄγραφος. What follows is then a consequence and not the goal and true concern of the argument. That Paul with great boldness projects apocalyptic into anthropology in v. 15 and then in v. 16 protects himself against a psychological misunderstanding of this anthropology, is not perceived even though he does the same in ch. 5 and ch. 7 when these are seen to be complementary. Phenomena which can be provisionally established are by no means incontestable or apparent to all men (*contra* Bultmann, "Glossen," 201). They are so in their psychological givenness, but not in their eschatological meaning (H. W. Schmidt; Walker, "Heiden," 313), and for this reason Paul intentionally reckons them among the κρυπτὰ τῶν ἀνθρώπων. They have still to be deciphered. A person is responsible on that basis, but not determinable. Only God can make the determination.

The goal of the section is thus reached: the Gentile, like the Jew, can understand the proclamation of the last judgment and the criteria which will apply in it. A solemn formula is used at the end in emphasis. Gospel here simply means the apostolic preaching. Seen from the other side, Paul's gospel is that, when apparently inviolable privileges end, illusions are unmasked, and the coming judgment is thus intimated. The problems seen by liberal exegesis are not present, since what the chapter shows is that, and how far, the proclamation of judgment inseparably belongs to the gospel. This gospel is, of course, constitutive for primitive missionary preaching (Molland, *Euangelion*, 96). The unique feature in Paul is simply the radicalness with which this message is intensified from the doctrine of justification. The recurrence in deutero-Pauline writings of the formula used here is best explained as a reference to the apostle. διὰ Χριστοῦ Ἰησοῦ, in virtue of its position, should not be related to κρίνει (Schlatter). It offers a liturgical conclusion to the section.

3. Jewish Transgression of the Law (2:17-24)

[17]*But if you call yourself a Jew and rely on the law and boast of God* [18]*and know his will and can tell what really matters, having been instructed in the law,* [19]*and are sure you are a guide to the blind, a light to those in darkness,* [20]*an instructor of the foolish, a teacher of children, having the very shape of knowledge and truth in the law*—[21]*you then who teach others, do you not teach yourself? You who preach: Do not steal, do you steal?* [22]*You who say: Do not commit adultery, do you commit adultery? You who abominate idols, do you rob temples?* [23]*You boast of your law*—*by transgression of the law you dishonor God.* [24]*For it is written: The name of God is blasphemed among the Gentiles because of you.*

Bibliography: G. Bornkamm, "Paulinische Anakoluthe," *Ende des Gesetzes*, 76-92; G. Klein, "Studien über Paulus," *Beiträge zur Religionswissenschaft* 3 (1918); A. Fridrichsen, "Der wahre Jude und sein Lob. Röm 2, 28f.," *Symbolae Arctoae* 1 (1927) 39-49; R. Hermann, "Über den Sinn des μορφοῦσθαι Χριστὸν ἐν ὑμῖν in Gal 4, 19," *TLZ* 80 (1955) 713-726; M. Philonenko, "Le maître de justice et la Sagesse de Salomon," *TZ* 14 (1958) 81-88; L. Goppelt, "Der Missionar des Gesetzes," *Basileia* (Festschrift W. Freytag, 1959) 199-207 (reprinted in Goppelt, *Christologie und Ethik* [1968] 137-146); J. Murphy-O'Connor, *Paul and Qumran* (1968) 179-250.

The new section passes over to a concrete attack on the Jews (*contra* Ulonska, *Paulus*, 163, who refers it to Jewish-Christians in Rome). The phrase in v. 3, ὁ κρίνων . . . καὶ ποιῶν αὐτά, is now established. The claim of the pious Pharisee and his rabbinic leaders is not acknowledged from the Christian standpoint, although it is not treated ironically (Schlatter; Nygren *contra* Kühl; Lagrange *et al.*). Jewish practice is advanced against it, with an even stronger orientation of the attack to extreme perversion than in 1:22ff.

Judaism itself bitterly bewailed its moral collapse in the disturbances prior to the Jewish War (Billerbeck). In general the life of Pharisees was strict and not infrequently even attracted Gentiles. This does not justify us, however, in not taking vv. 21ff. literally (*contra* Barrett; Goppelt, "Missionar," 204ff.). Nor can it be said (*contra* Goppelt, 203) that types are presented, as in Essene writings. Instead, an apocalyptic approach is again presenting what may be empirically an exception as representative of the community.

In vv. 17-20 we have an anacoluthon, which, as is characteristic for Pauline diction, not only brings out the temperament of the apostle and his rhetoric but also aims at a materially appropriate effect. The advantages of the Jew are impressively accumulated, and then when they reach their crest they break to pieces like a wave. Similarly the harsh and sharp accusation in the brief questions in vv. 21-22 are like a barrage which completely traps the one who is addressed. Stylistically the discrepancy between claim and performance could hardly be more impressively emphasized (Bornkamm, "Anakoluthe," 78). The influence of the diatribe is unmistakable (Bultmann, *Stil*, 70). This is shown by the excellent parallels in Epictetus *Discourses* ii.19.19ff.; iii.7.17, which inquire about the essence of the true Stoic (Fridrichsen, "Der wahre Jude," 45).

The Byzantine reading ἴδε in v. 17, which eliminates the anacoluthon (BDF, §467), is a classic example of itacism. The five verbs in vv. 17f. characterize the attitude brought on by possession of the Torah. The participial expression in v. 18c forms a first resting-point which prepares for the further attack in vv. 19f. Four nouns now replace the preceding verbs. The participial clause in v. 20c, providing the basis for the Jewish self-predications, creates a rhetorical pause before the four incisive questions in vv. 21f. bring out the contrast between the teaching and the life of Paul's opponent. The change from the participle-style in v. 23 is an indication that we have a summary of the whole, backed by the words and authority of Scripture in v. 24. The analysis shows that we have here a masterpiece of rhetoric.

The title "Jew" (v. 17), used first by the surrounding world, became (cf. Kuhn, Gutbrod, *TDNT*, III, 359ff.) in the Diaspora a self-predication of the adherents of OT monotheism (Billerbeck). Inscriptions use it as a cognomen. But ἐπονομάζειν here hardly means more than "(to) name." Nor must ἐπαναπαύεσθαι, "boast," "rely on," have the secondary censorious sense of Mic 3:11. This is even more true of καυχᾶσθαι ἐν θεῷ. The Jew was summoned to all this by the OT. The attack has yet to come. Even the list of titles in vv. 19f. simply enumerates the claims that result from the position of the Jews (Conzelmann, *TDNT*, IX, 345, with parallels). These claims lose their credibility only when they no longer coincide with reality. To be sure, the heaping up of predications prepares the way for what Paul wants to assert.

The καυχᾶσθαι of vv. 17, 23, which stems from Jer 9:23, is a key word in Paul's theology and serves to differentiate true and false religion. It is parallel to πεποιθέναι. Both times the element of trust expressed in word and conduct is constitutive (Bultmann, *TDNT*, III, 649; *Theology*, I, 243). Whether it is right or wrong depends solely on its object, which is defined by the alternative of God or the flesh. The problem is that even religiously God and flesh can be confused.

As in 1 Cor 16:12 θέλημα (v. 18) in the absolute denotes in good rabbinic fashion the divine will which in the OT and Judaism is the proper content of γινώσκειν. This knowledge does not exist without critical testing which establishes τὰ διαφέροντα in distinction from ἀδιάφορα (BAGD, 190; K. Weiss, *TDNT*, IX, 63; Lietzmann; Ridderbos), i.e., things that count, what is decisive. Phil 1:10 shows that understanding the situation plays an important part in this, and not just moral evaluation. To refer it to a correct distinction between Judaism and paganism (Michel) is exaggerated (K. Weiss, *TDNT*, IX, 63).

When the apostle speaks of κατηχούμενος, we are to think of the fixed catechetical traditions of Judaism. Primitive Christianity adopted both the practice and also to a large degree the contents of Jewish instruction, and it is impossible to believe that Paul was the first to use the verb technically (*contra* Beyer, *TDNT*, III, 639).

Surprisingly the Jewish cultus is not mentioned. The more strongly then, as in 2 *Apoc. Bar.* 48:22-24, the Torah emerges as the one possibility of access to God and as the center of Jewish piety, as corresponds especially to the situation in the Diaspora. There is a sense of being heir and fulfiller of the eschatological promises to God's servant (Isa 42:6f.; 49:6), as the first two titles ὁδηγός and   [6 παιδευτής (vv. 19f.) show. If there are no rabbinic parallels, Matt 15:14; 23:16, 24 reflect the claim of the first predication and 1QH 4:27, fr. 28b from Qumran Cave 1, *126*, col. ii, 27f. the claim of the second. According to 1QS 3:13; 9:12 there is an office of instructor, and according to 1QpHab 7:4; 1QH 2:13 the teacher of righteousness is the possessor and proclaimer of the divine mysteries. *T. Levi* 14:3f. and the statement about the priestly Messiah in 18:3, 9 bear witness to the same tradition. Materially the predicates are much the same since they always involve the transmission of the Torah. The first two, however, stress enlightenment and the next two instruction, or, as 1QH 2:9 puts it, "wisdom for the simple."

Reminiscence of Jesus' conflict with the Rabbinate and Pharisaism (Dodd; Schlatter; Althaus, etc.) is unnecessary and out of place. There might well be an allusion to missionary work in the Diaspora. This was restricted in Palestine and even viewed with horror (Billerbeck; G. Klein, "Studien," 7ff. simply proves that there were proselytes and that not all the rabbis were hostile). The situation was different in Hellenized Judaism. One hears its voice in Wis 18:4: δι' ὧν ἤμελλεν τὸ ἄφθαρτον φῶς τῷ αἰῶνι δίδοσθαι; cf. also *Sib. Or.* iii.195: "who point out the way of life to all mortals." Josephus says in *Ap.* ii.293: "I might boldly affirm that we Jews are originators in respect of most things and the best for all others." According to Philo *De Abrahamo* 98 Israel has the office of priest and prophet for all mankind; cf. also *De vita Mosis* i.149; *Sib. Or.* iii.582f.

The fact that Paul is using existing formulations taken from the Diaspora synagogue (Lietzmann; Behm, *TDNT* IV, 754) becomes particularly clear (cf. Norden, *Agnostos Theos*, 296ff., though cf. Kuss) in v. 20b. In context μόρφωσις cannot mean, as in classical Greek, "formation" (Schlatter), "summary," "outline" (Hermann, "Gal. 4:19," 721), or "structure" (Pallis). The usage is that of

70

the *koine*. In distinction from 2 Tim 3:5 the original *nomen actionis* is almost synonymous with χαρακτήρ, and designates the result of an "impression" (Michel; H. W. Schmidt; Black). As in the OT and Judaism γνῶσις refers to the divine will with its requirements (Bultmann, *TDNT,* I, 706). ἀλήθεια is probably related particularly to monotheism, with the formula of *2 Apoc. Bar.* 44:14—"truth of the law"—as a possible basis. The reference, then, is not to behavior that is not deceptive (*contra* Schlatter).

Judaism sees an advantage in possessing the will of God in fixed form and not just *actualiter* (cf. Murphy-O'Connor, *Paul,* 187ff.). νόμος could even mean the book of the law (cf. BAGD, 543a), which in the Diaspora was read from the standpoint of divine *paideia* (Schoeps, *Paul,* 30f.).

The questions, too, belong to the style of the diatribe. Between διδάσκων, κηρύσσειν, and λέγων in vv. 21f. there is only a rhetorical distinction (*contra* Michel; Leenhardt; H. W. Schmidt). For διδάσκειν does not concern doctrine but teaching itself. κηρύσσειν and λέγειν relate to the instructions of the Decalogue. Philo *De confusione linguarum* 163 has the same combination of stealing, adultery, and robbing temples, while *Corpus Hermeticum* XII:5 has the last two (BAGD, 373b). CD 4:15ff. speaks of the "three nets of Belial," which bear some connection to our text. Rabbinic discussion shows that these offenses were in fact committed (Billerbeck; Michel). There is no reason to remove v. 22b from the parallelism of the previous sentences (*contra* Goppelt, "Missionar," 204f.) and to understand ἱεροσυλεῖν in the broader sense of sacrilege or in a figurative (Nygren) sense (Schrenk, *TDNT,* III, 256). Naturally, as the first clause shows, Jewish temples are not in view. βδελύσσεσθαι, of which the only other NT instance is at Rev 21:8, refers to abhorrence of idolatry, and the Jewish-Greek term εἴδωλα means the gods (Büchsel, *TDNT,* II, 377f.). For the Jew these were nonexistent, so that in spite of Deut 7:25f. he did not have to treat their property as sacrosanct, especially when they were offered to him as stolen property (Billerbeck; Black). Acts 19:37 bears witness to this possibility. Verse 23 sums up the section in striking contrast to *Sib. Or.* iii.234ff. The Jew is in truth a transgressor of the law to which he appeals, and dishonors the divine name thereby. Paul sees his judgment confirmed by Isa 52:5, which he quotes in v. 24. This interpretation does, of course, change the meaning of the original text, which the LXX had already expanded by adding δι' ὑμᾶς and ἐν τοῖς ἔθνεσιν, into its exact opposite. What causes the Gentiles to blaspheme is no longer the suffering of Israel but the behavior which denies its mission. Possibly the missionary polemics of primitive Christianity had already used this biblical proof prior to Paul. At any rate, a more effective conclusion could hardly be found.

4. Circumcision Does Not Justify (2:25-29)

²⁵*Circumcision is indeed useful if you keep the law. But if you are a transgressor of the law, your circumcision becomes uncircumcision (before God).* ²⁶*Again, if the uncircumcision observes the statutes of the law, will not his uncircumcision avail as circumcision (before God)?* ²⁷*Hence what is in itself uncircumcision but keeps the law will judge you, the transgressor of the law,*

in spite of the letter and circumcision. [28]*For he is not a (true) Jew who (is) one visibly, nor is true circumcision that which is visible in the flesh.* [29]*The Jew (is so) inwardly and circumcision is of the heart, in the spirit and not according to the letter. His praise (comes) not from men, but from God.*

Bibliography: S. Lyonnet, "La circoncision du coeur, celle qui relève de l'Esprit et non de la lettre," *L'Évangile hier et aujourd'hui. Mélanges offerts a Franz-J. Leenhardt* (1968) 87-97; G. Schrenk, "Der Segenswunsch nach der Kampfepistel," *Judaica* 6 (1950) 170-190; B. Schneider, "The Meaning of St. Paul's Antithesis 'The Letter and the Spirit,' " *CBQ* 15 (1953) 163-207; E. Käsemann, "The Spirit and the Letter," *Perspectives,* 138-166. For Flückiger, "Werke," and Schlier, "Juden," see the bibliography for 2:1-11; for Sahlin, "Textemendationen," and Bornkamm, "Gesetz," see the bibliography for 2:12-16; for Fridrichsen, "Der wahre Jude," see the bibliography for 2:17-24.

In the Jewish view only circumcision grants a share in God's covenant with Israel (cf. the excursus in Kuss). The question of its usefulness, to which 3:1 refers, is not an open problem for the Jew. Paul already diverges from orthodoxy by raising the question. He does so even more when he sets circumcision in antithesis to fulfillment of the law, since for the religious this takes place already with circumcision and at least in Palestine cannot be thought of apart from circumcision (Barrett). Things are different in the Diaspora insofar as "god-fearers" cluster around the synagogue and Hellenized liberalism can open itself to the problem, as in Josephus *Antiquities* xx.41f.; Philo *De specialibus legibus* i.1-11 (cf. K. G. Kuhn, *TDNT,* VI, 731f.). Apologetics and propaganda here ask about the meaning of the rite, give it a moral sense, and accept the possibility of worship of God without it. On the other hand, the common view that there could be "semi-proselytes" is mistaken. There were no uncircumcised Jews. In asserting the contrary in vv. 28f. Paul diverges from the liberalism that might have been the first to accept his question and argument.

Paul does not speak solely or primarily about a relation to God (*contra* Michel). Rather, he attacks Judaism at its basis and in relation to an inalienable feature. The argument of vv. 12-16 is now repeated in relation to a new theme and directed against the almost obvious assumption that circumcision as such has saving force (cf. Billerbeck; Stummer, *RAC,* II, 159ff.). It should be noted, however, that Paul is not simply engaging in an anti-Jewish polemic. He uses the same argument in 1 Cor 10:1-11 to combat the enthusiasts' misunderstanding of baptism, whereby sacramental realities in Israel's history are fully recognized. Already, then, the text raises the sacramental problem, with a focus on circumcision and an anti-Jewish thrust. Circumcision is an initiation rite, whose sacramental character for the Jews is not denied. In contrast to the religious world of his time Paul does not recognize any sacraments that work *ex opere operato* and that provide escape from judgment. If they do not open the path of obedience, their ὠφέλεια is illusory.

This is brought out by the sharp antithesis in v. 25, which opens up the new round of debate with an argumentative γάρ, and which disposes at once of a Jewish objection that has not in fact been made. The concept of the useful tells us on what front the apostle is fighting, since it is always raised in answer to enthusiasts. περιτομή and the purely biblical and ecclesiastical (K. L. Schmidt, *TDNT*, I, 225) ἀκροβυστία denote the action, the resultant state, and the fellowship established therewith. νόμον πράσσειν and τελεῖν (used only in v. 27) reach further than the statement in v. 14. The expression τὰ δικαιώματα τοῦ νόμου φυλάσσειν in v. 26 characterizes unequivocally the attitude of strict adherence to the law which demonstrates membership in the saved community (cf. the examples in Rössler, *Gesetz*, 85ff., 101f.). The reference of δικαιώματα, as in Deut 30:16, is to the whole Torah (Flückiger, "Werke," 29), defined by legal statements. γέγονεν of v. 25 is not construed with the dative and the particle of comparison ὡς, and it cannot then be equivalent to כ נעשה in the sense of "is reckoned as" (*contra* Billerbeck; Michel), although λογισθήσεται in v. 26 corresponds to it. Paul argues that without obedience circumcision is annulled (in the perfect) but on the basis of his obedience the uncircumcised will be placed on the same footing as the religious Jew in the judgment. His opponents cannot agree with either of these statements. They make sense only on the premise that only circumcision of the heart avails before God. That takes up a theme of OT prophecy (cf. Deut 10:16; 30:6; Jer 4:4; 6:10; 9:25; Ezek 44:7) which the Palestinian Rabbinate handles only hesitantly but Philo deals with much more frequently (Billerbeck). Paul, then, is probably following the spiritualizing of cultic matters in the Diaspora synagogue, although he for his part has no spiritualizing interest (*contra* Moule; H. W. Schmidt). Neither OT prophecy nor the apologetics and propaganda of the Diaspora synagogue dismissed circumcision as irrelevant because of circumcision of the heart, whereas this is precisely what Paul does. Verse 26 robs the spiritualizing interpretation entirely of its basis.

Circumcision here is simply a directive to obedience for the Jew, and it is superfluous for all others. As in Gal 6:13 it simply serves to mark transgression of the law. This is the Christian judgment in a discussion which is, of course, purely fictional, since no serious debate is possible on this basis. That is shown by the diatribe style of the question in v. 26b. The possibility considered here is also fictional, at least in the immediate context. If the apostle cannot allow that the Jew keeps the law in its unity and totality, he can hardly agree that the Gentile does. The formula does not characterize the obedience of the Christian, so that one should not drag in Gentile-Christians at this point (Zahn; Bultmann, *Theology*, I, 261). Instead the statement unquestionably refers back with increased intensity to the unhypothetical assertion of vv. 14f. It is highly improbable that Paul's polemical zeal and dialectical leanings would drive him to the point, contrary to his own convictions, of fashioning in radical consistency a constantly more favorable picture of the Gentile and then measuring against him, in spiritualizing fashion, the ideal Jew who has been freed to become a true human being (*contra* Fridrichsen, "Der wahre Jude," 43f.). The apostle does not proceed in this wrongheaded fashion.

To be sure, the atmosphere of the argument here is instructively lit up by referring to the Stoic reinterpretation of the concept of political freedom, the related differentiation between being and appearance, between what is within and what is without, and the resultant question of authentic existence. Nevertheless this does not adequately explain the text, as the eschatological aspect in v. 27 makes clear. For the future of the verb, as in v. 26b, is not logical (*contra* Kühl).

73

If the passive there described God's judicial action, Paul now adopts the rabbinic view, familiar from Matt 12:41 and indirectly 1 Cor 6:2f., that a person will be measured by others in the last judgment (Billerbeck).

This does not mean that Paul was influenced by the gospel text (contra Lagrange; Dodd; Nygren). What is there prophetic proclamation in extreme polemic, is here very naturally inferred, with an introductory consecutive καί (Lagrange), from what precedes. The paradox is thrown into accentuated relief by antitheses both within and between the two clauses. What is "physically" uncircumcision fulfils the law. What can point to Scripture and circumcision is shown to be a transgressor of the law. Hence Gentiles will judge the Jews. To Jewish ears this is a blasphemous utterance, which is part of the primitive Christian message of the eschatological transvaluation of all earthly values. The same applies to the antithesis of γράμμα and πνεῦμα in v. 29, found also in 7:6; 2 Cor 3:6, which always expresses the contrast between the old and new aeons. It is obviously the culmination of the section. It is triggered by the phrase διὰ γράμματος καὶ περιτομῆς, in which διά is not instrumental (Schlatter; Schrenk, TDNT, I, 765) but indicates the accompanying circumstance (BDF, §223[3]; Lietzmann). διὰ γράμματος seems to be contrasted with ἐκ φύσεως: It is natural to the uncircumcision, but comes in virtue of the written commandment to the circumcision. The Jew who transgresses the law denies both his circumcision and the commandment of Scripture which directs it.

This adequately explains the expression, but it remains to be asked what leads Paul to overload the sentence with the new antithesis. The basic decision has already been made in v. 25. What is the point of the apparent surplus which, with its heaping up of antitheses, presses beyond the theme into an eschatological horizon? Only as we answer this question can we say why the apostle obviously reaches back to vv. 14f. but in an inexplicable crescendo. For there can no more be a Gentile who as such fulfils the Torah than there can be anyone else who of himself does what the law specifically requires. Is Paul losing himself in hypotheses?

We receive an answer from vv. 28f., which do not repeat vv. 25-27 in other [7● terms (Kuss), but show their result. The statement is constructed in such a way that 'Ιουδαῖος and περιτομή, which are plainly used here as honorary religious predicates, are predicates in v. 28 but subjects in v. 29. Hence the subject of the first sentence is missing, and there are no predicates in the second, lest the same nouns should follow one another directly. An effective chiasmus is thus achieved. Verse 29c, referring to 'Ιουδαῖος in v. 29a, artistically offers an additional member of the conclusion, common in Pauline rhetoric, in which the waves of the accumulated antitheses roll to a stop. This indicates that antithetical development of the section now reaches its climax and simultaneously the theme which led to the appendix in v. 26 is brought to light. The apostle is not content to have pushed aside the problem of circumcision almost by sleight of hand. He now sets the theme of the true Jew over against it as the secret core and decisive criterion of the problem he has taken up. In so doing he moves into an eschatological dimension, since the true Jew is an eschatological phenomenon.

In this regard Paul can use the Hellenistic tradition in which Epictetus, for example, asks concerning the true Stoic. Here the appearance, which depends on the evaluation of spectators, is set over against the inward and essential existence. According to the Stoics the latter rests in itself (cf. Fridrichsen, "Der wahre Jude," 44f.) and pays attention to harmony with God and the all. Paul, of course, modifies this motif and in so doing is helped by the Diaspora synagogue. For the antithesis of ἐν τῷ φανερῷ–ἐν τῷ κρυπτῷ does not wholly coincide with that of outer and inner (*contra* Althaus). What Paul calls "hidden" (cf. 1 Pet 3:4) is not just what is within but total existence in the mystery of its personality, which will be revealed only eschatologically. In contrast piety is part of what is visible. For this reason further definition is indispensable.

ἐν σαρκί refers to the bodily sphere as the generally accessible and present concretion of the visible. The proposal to excise what seems to be a repetitive ἐν τῷ φανερῷ in v. 28b (Sahlin, "Textemendationen," 95) disturbs the balance with the even fuller v. 29. The accent falls on v. 29b. The Jewish tradition present here presupposes the eschatological-dualistic variation of the motif of the circumcision of the heart which in Qumran replaces the ethical-allegorical interpretation of Philo. In distinction from the conduct of the sacrilegious priest depicted in 1QpHab 11:13, 1QS 5:5 issues the command: "They shall circumcise in the community the foreskin of impulse and stiffneckedness to lay a foundation of truth for Israel, for the community of an eternal covenant." From this there is a bridge to *Jub.* 1:23: "I will circumcise the foreskin of their heart and make a holy spirit for them," and also to *Odes Sol.* 11:1-3: "My heart was circumcised and its blossom appeared; grace grew in it and brought forth fruits to the Lord. For the Most High circumcised me by his Holy Spirit . . . hence circumcision was for me redemption." The final link in this chain is Col 2:11ff. with its understanding of baptism as the circumcision of Christ effected by the Spirit.

This background explains the combination of circumcision of heart with the Spirit. In this regard it makes little difference whether ἐν is taken instrumentally (Zahn; Kuss) or, better, locally: in the sphere of power. The reference is not a spiritualizing one to a denationalized Jew liberated for pure humanity but an eschatological one to the working of the Holy Spirit. All the preceding eschatological statements are directed toward it. Only the motif of the true Jew, for which there is no parallel in the rabbis (Billerbeck), is Hellenistic. If this religio-historical reconstruction of our passage is appropriate, Paul is not dealing with hypotheses but with a reality. What seem to be highly theoretical arguments do not relate to a sham position (Bornkamm, "Gesetz," 110). It is not for nothing that vv. 14f. are intensified in such a way that the reality seems to be lost to view and everything is pressed into an eschatological horizon. What is weighed as a possibility until v. 28 ceases to be understood as a mere fiction in v. 29. There is a true Jew who fulfils the law even as a Gentile while Jews do not do so. He exists in the form of the Gentile-Christian (Schrenk, "Segenswunsch," 176; Maurer, *Gesetzeslehre*, 40, though cf. Dahl, *Volk Gottes*, 238, following Fridrichsen). The Gentile-Christian has received through the Spirit the circumcision of the heart which alone avails. The Spirit allows him to fulfil the law according to 8:4 and integrates him into the new divine covenant according to 2 Cor 3:6.

It cannot be objected that this interpretation is out of context and that it spoils the conclusion that the Christian is not regarded as circumcised before God (e.g., Nygren following Schlatter). The very opposite is true. Only thus does the context make sense and achieve a theological climax. The rhetorically skilful construction of the chapter culminates in the last sentence which alone brings out the point and unveils the intention of the whole (Lyonnet, "Circoncision," 96f.). If this view be rejected, v. 29 is full of difficulties. One may then rightly ask where is the Gentile of whom vv. 26f. are true (Zahn). It may also be asked where Paul allows that the Jews lived in full operation (Schlatter; Schlier, "Juden," 46), in the order of the Spirit (Lagrange), in a spiritual way (Barrett), or in the inner movement of joyous self-giving (Althaus). Exposition which cannot accommodate the antithesis in context, and has at least to reduce it (Kuss), demands critical scrutiny. Although they will not accept it, the interpretations listed show that in principle Paul here steps beyond the boundaries of Ἰουδαισμός (so R. Meyer, TDNT, VI, 82f.; von Stromberg, Studien, 105f.). This is completely clear from the antithesis of γράμμα and πνεῦμα, which has become so significant but hard to interpret.

A noteworthy fact is that the apostle always uses both terms in the singular, although the former may have arisen in dependence on the customary expression ἱερὰ γράμματα (Schrenk, TDNT, I, 751, 763f.). Whether Paul coined the typical singular is impossible to say. It is certainly characteristic of his theology but it is also used without any introduction, as though familiar to the reader. It has the advantage of being able to designate a power, as clearly happens in 2 Cor 3:6 from a world-historical angle. The reference is no doubt to the Torah as instruction (Schrenk, TDNT, I, 746) but always in a pejorative sense in distinction from the use of nomos. To this degree the translation "letter" carries the proper nuance. On the other hand this translation also gives rise to serious misunderstandings (cf. Ebeling, RGG, II, 1290ff.).

Idealistic exposition has spiritualized the relation between the two words. γράμμα is the non-living thing which the human person as a spiritual being cannot assimilate and which he cannot integrate into his essential being. It is, then, that which remains outside and is contingent. Conversely spirit is the faculty of achieving profound inwardness and of grasping the world that meets us from this standpoint. It is thus reduced to inwardness and a right disposition. This understanding [72 is still at work even when the usual distinction between legality and morality is rejected (Bläser, Gesetz, 98), but all the same defines γράμμα as the outwardly fixed precept which does not penetrate the inner core of a person and leaves him to himself (ibid., 133). The Greek source of this understanding, and perhaps even the setting of Paul's antithesis, may be found in the statement of Archytas in Stobaeus iv.1.135: νόμος ὁ μὲν ἔμψυχος βασιλεύς, ὁ δέ ἄψυχος γράμμα, "The living law is the king, the lifeless law is the letter." Nevertheless, even if Hellenism offered the apostle the term γράμμα for the fixed law, it nearly always presents the relation between spirit and law in a positive light (Kleinknecht, TDNT, IV, 1024, 1032ff.). It does not help us to understand what is for Paul the decisive eschatological-dualistic component of the antithesis; and the doctrine of the unwritten law, if it may be brought into the discussion at all (against this Schrenk, TDNT, I, 768f.), helps prepare the ground for this antithesis. This means that interpretation can rest on no clear religio-historical derivation. It is referred solely to the context. It must also abandon in advance the misunderstanding of a spiritualizing idealism which has been so persistent in the church's history.

Two things relate to γράμμα according to Paul. First, it signifies codified law as a collection of individual statutes (Schrenk, *TDNT*, I, 746f., 765; Michel, *Bibel*, 174ff.; Rössler, *Gesetz*, 87ff.). Secondly, by representing the universal obligation of the letter of the Torah with its demand for works, it is for the Christian part of the old aeon and for this reason can find no "fulfilment." When one considers the connection with the γραφή in the Jewish exegetical tradition on the one side and the antithesis to spirit on the other, it may be said that γράμμα is the written OT, which is separated from the Spirit and from the exposition which the Spirit makes possible, in which the Torah universally demands a hearing and obedience. The γράμμα in this sense does not produce the eschatological circumcision of the heart and hence it does not produce the "true Jew." Neither of these is to be found in empirical Judaism as this is committed to the Scripture as Torah, but only in the sphere of the Spirit as the power of the new covenant.

If this is a correct interpretation, the doctrine of the righteousness of faith not only stands opposed to legal piety. It is simultaneously the criterion for a true interpretation of Scripture, as is explicitly stated in 10:5ff. Scripture is promise only insofar as it is not allowed to be γράμμα. If this distinction and separation is not made, the OT γραφή will always become γράμμα again, for it is expounded aright only by the Spirit who is given through Christ and who proclaims the righteousness of faith.

Paul's conclusion is almost doxological. Yet this is concealed behind a Hellenistic view. With ascetic energy the Stoic fought the desire for the ἔπαινος of onlookers, which is inseparably connected with the Greek ideal of ἀγών (cf. Fridrichsen, "Der wahre Jude," 46ff.). His concern was for the truth of existence freed from appearance, for the inwardness of a person looking dispassionately on the outside world and living in harmony with reason. This is why Marcus Aurelius asks in iv.19.2 πρὸς τὸν ζῶντα τί ὁ ἔπαινος, "to the living, what is praise?" and in xii.11 proudly answers ἐξουσίαν ἔχει ἄνθωπος μὴ ποιεῖν ἄλλο ἢ ὅπερ μέλλει ὁ θεὸς ἐπανεῖν, "mankind has authority to do nothing other than what God will praise." Even if Paul did not know this view, he offered a Christian modification with a characteristic eschatological orientation as in 1 Cor 4:5. The praise of the true Jew does not come from humans but from the God who alone knows and judges τὰ κρυπτὰ τῶν ἀνθρώπων. A long and initially English tradition explained the surprising introduction of the motif of ἔπαινος by a play on words identifying Judah with praise as in Gen 29:35; 49:8 (J. Knox; Ridderbos). If Paul really had this in mind, it would hardly have been intelligible to the Roman community.

5. Objections (3:1-8)

¹*What (remains), then, the advantage of the Jew, what is the value of circumcision?* ²*Much in every respect. First, God's words are entrusted to the Jews.* ³*What does it matter if some became unfaithful? Does their unfaithfulness nullify God's faithfulness?* ⁴*In no way! Let God show himself to be true and every man a liar! It is written, That thou mayest be justified with thy words and win when men go to law with thee.* ⁵*If, however, our wrong shows God to be right, what does this mean? Is God unjust when he inflicts wrath? I speak in human fashion.* ⁶*Not at all! For how, then, could God judge the world?* ⁷*But*

if through my untrustworthiness the truth of God achieves superabundant glory, why should I still be condemned as a sinner? [8]*Is it perhaps true, as is blasphemously reported of us, and as some people have us say, Let us do evil that good may come? Judgment rightly falls on such.*

Bibliography: J. Jeremias, "Zur Gedankenführung in den paulinischen Briefen," *Studia Paulina,* 146-154; *idem,* "Chiasmus in den Paulusbriefen," *ZNW* 49 (1958) 145-156; A. Fridrichsen, "Exegetisches zu den Paulusbriefen," *ThStKr* 102 (1930) 291-301; K. H. Fahlgren, *ṣᵉdāḳā, nahestehende und entgegengesetzte Begriffe im AT* (1932); J. W. Doeve, "Some Notes with Reference to τὰ λόγια τοῦ θεοῦ in Romans III, 2," *Studia Paulina,* 111-123; T. W. Manson, "Some Reflections on Apocalyptic," *Aux sources de la tradition chrétienne. Mélanges offerts à M. Maurice Goguel* (1950) 139-145; H. Ljungvik, "Zum Römerbrief 3, 7-8," *ZNW* 32 (1933) 207-210; G. Bornkamm, "Theologie als Teufelskunst," *Geschichte und Glaube,* II, 140-48; C. J. Bjerkelund, " 'Nach menschlicher Weise rede ich.' Funktion und Sinn des paulinischen Ausdrucks," *ST* 26 (1972) 63-100. For Hanson, *Wrath,* see the bibliography for 1:18-32.

As if taking a breath before stating his conclusion, Paul finds a place for two objections. The first asks whether the precedence of the Jews in salvation history has been completely cancelled according to 2:12-29. The answer in vv. 2-4 shows that the apostle cannot escape the problem, not because he is a Jew (Lietzmann; Dodd), but on theological grounds. The second objection is directed against Paul's doctrine of justification, because it seems, according to vv. 5f., to make God an unjust Judge, and, according to vv. 7f., to push us into libertinism. (Bornkamm, "Teufelskunst," 143f. thinks v. 3 opens the second round and v. 5 the third.) From v. 8c it would seem that Paul is reproducing an actual criticism directed against him. He possibly has Jews or more probably Jewish-Christians in view. Yet he is reminded of their attack only by the paradox stressed by him in v. 4. Hence he did not intend in advance to enter into this debate and he cuts it short in v. 8c.

In contrast the questions in v. 1 and v. 3 are put to him in the style of the diatribe (Bultmann, *Theology,* I, 108f.). No specific controversy is in mind. There is no reason to think of a sermon to the Jews which is interrupted by objections and protests (*contra* Jeremias, "Gedankenführung," 147). Even apostles do more [7 than preach. There is no need of dramatic incidents to explain Paul's dialectic. Whether the argumentation is weak and obscure, and the defense of so doubtful a cause might have been better omitted (Dodd), exegesis must decide.

The adjectival noun τὸ περισσόν denotes surplus, then privilege. The reference is to the Jew. πολὺ κατὰ πάντα τρόπον is just as plerophorous as the introductory question. In view of the radical demolition of Jewish privileges in what precedes, the exuberance is astounding unless one sees that the problem of chs. 9-11 is already in view. The πρῶτον of v. 2 is supposed to introduce a list as in 9:4f. and should not be translated "above all" (Gutjahr). The reading πρῶτοι γάρ in Origen removes the offense of the continuation that is lacking as in 1:8; 1 Cor 11:18. The decisive "plus" of Judaism is that it has the λόγια τοῦ θεοῦ. In the first instance this expression means "oracular sayings" (Murray), but very quickly the element of sacred tradition comes to the fore. In Hellenistic Judaism it means God's revelation in Scripture (Doeve *contra* the sense of salvation event in Kittel,

TDNT, IV, 137ff.). As in 1:2; 3:21b, the reference is to the promise of the gospel. Then it is natural to take πιστεύεσθαι to mean "be entrusted" in the technical sense found in ancient law governing deposits (J. Ranft, *Der Ursprung des katholischen Traditionsprinzips* [1931] 195ff.; cf. *RAC,* III, 780; Ljungman, *Pistis,* 14f.). It is hard to see (*contra* Stuhlmacher, *Gerechtigkeit,* 85) that he refers back to the demands of the law from 2:26 as an expression of God's covenant law (cf. Manson, "Reflections," 142ff.).

The new question in v. 3 shows plainly that Paul is bringing the objections himself. For τί γάρ cf. Phil 1:18; it means "What does it matter?" (BAGD, 819b). The common μὴ γένοιτο is to be derived from the typical style of the diatribe (Bultmann, *Stil,* 33). The OT and rabbinic חלילה, sometimes rendered μὴ γένοιτο in the LXX, has a religious sense and does not stand alone (Billerbeck), so that it is unlikely to be Paul's source. The uniqueness of the passage lies in the mixture of OT and Jewish terminology and argumentation with the rhetoric of the diatribe.

Verses 2b-3 are unmistakably oriented to the theme of πίστις. This means covenant faithfulness and corresponds to ἀπιστία as defection from the covenant. Apart from the formula πιστὸς ὁ θεός in 1 Cor 1:9; 10:13; 1 Thess 5:24 (which Ljungman, *Pistis,* 17ff. puts in the setting of synagogue benedictions), the motif of God's faithfulness is explicitly expressed only here in this way. Nevertheless, it is given extraordinary emphasis by its relationship to the antitheses that follow: "truth" and "falsehood," "righteousness" and "unrighteousness." Relations within the covenant are indicated thereby. In good OT fashion God's truth is his reliability, which upholds covenant and promise, while human falsehood characterizes human inconstancy even within the covenant. It is only here, then, that Paul identifies πίστις and δικαιοσύνη τοῦ θεοῦ by making them parallel, as is possible from the OT understanding of God's righteousness as his prevailing covenant faithfulness. Along the same lines ἀδικία is not primarily moral defection but rejection of God's law as this is established with the covenant.

Oddly the bearing of these statements both on the interpretation of our text and also on Paul's doctrine of justification has seldom been recognized or adequately investigated. It is no help to exegesis to say that we have here a departure from Paul's usual thought or mode of expression. Interpretations (cf. Ridderbos) which speak of a divine attribute are wide of the mark. The issue is not a quality of God's nature but a declaration of the power of God working itself out forensically in the sphere of the covenant. Even when this is seen, however (Schrenk, *TDNT,* I, 155f.; Braun, *Gerichtsgedanke,* 78; Bornkamm, "Teufelskunst," 143ff.), there is still need to explain why this complex emerges clearly only at this point, and what it means for the apostle's theology.

The first question is easy to answer. When Paul pursues his own intentions he does not think in terms of the schema of the one covenant, but in terms of the contrast between the two covenants. His theology has a universal thrust and is thus oriented to the antithesis of Adam and Christ, of the first and last creation. When tradition offers him the concept of the covenant he uses it universalistically and therefore in a transferred sense. Hence he almost never speaks of the renewed covenant with the holy remnant. In analogy to the καινὴ κτίσις he speaks of the καινὴ διαθήκη. This modification of the OT and Jewish view affects his eucha-

79

ristic teaching and, in close connection therewith, his christology and ecclesiology. But it also determines, as our text shows, his doctrine of justification. God's righteousness comes to expression, not in a renewing of the old covenant, but in the founding of the new. If the Sinai covenant is still polemically in view in 2 Cor 3:6ff.; Gal 4:24ff., the parallelism between the new creation and the new covenant indicates that when the apostle thinks of the covenant he no longer thinks of Moses and Sinai, but in a transferred sense of the creation of the world. He can find support for this in that Jewish-apocalyptic literature in which the law is understood from the standpoint of the order of creation and is a manifestation of the cosmic order which determines all of reality, directs history, and reflects heavenly relationships (Limbeck, *Ordnung,* 49ff., 75ff., 150ff.). Only thus can redemption be for Paul the second and last creation, a covenant valid for all men. God's righteousness is the power which has its legal title in this first and most comprehensive covenant of creation and which therefore eschatologically re-establishes and enforces its law in this covenant as its sphere of lordship (Stuhlmacher, *Gerechtigkeit,* 83ff.).

The present text is to be understood against this background. It is now evident that Paul can speak of God's covenant faithfulness and of his constantly abiding truth verified therein. The objection of v. 3 that the Jews have become unfaithful (disloyal) makes no difference here. This objection results necessarily from the whole history of Israel, which reaches its logical culmination in the rejection of the gospel (Kuss). But it does not affect God's covenant faithfulness, since otherwise God's deity itself would be ambivalent and his truth would no longer be reliable, as it is constitutively according to 11:29. Paul likes to use the indefinite τινές for his opponents when they are numerically superior. This is particularly striking here, since almost all Judaism is in view. It would be easier to understand if he were already thinking of the message of 11:25ff. (Althaus), but this is very unlikely. A better solution is that τινές is to be explained in antithesis to the new world defined by the obedience of faith. καταργεῖν is a common and specifically Pauline term which usually means "destroy" in an eschatological sense but which is emphatic here. The future is a logical one. This is the first conclusion from v. 2. When calling accompanies God's promise, human unfaithfulness cannot nullify God's faithfulness.

The apostle is not content, however, with the counterquestion of v. 3. His true answer comes in v. 4 with the two quotations from Ps 115:2 LXX and 50:6b LXX. The antithetical introduction of the first word from Scripture changes the   [*
sentence into a petition (Michel), although this neither expresses a demand of the religious consciousness (Lietzmann; Lagrange) nor does it reflect personal experience (H. W. Schmidt). γινέσθω is odd and is usually poorly understood. One might indeed render it: "May it become apparent." But it is wrong to add: always and in all circumstances (Kühl), or to maintain that the concrete experience of the psalmist is now radically extended (Kuss). The underlying idea that God cannot "become" but can only "be confirmed" is a specifically modern one and does not correspond at all to the apocalyptic view. For this God's deity still awaits its definitive revelation, and prayer is to be made for it. From the perspective of the end of history (Schlatter) γινέσθω ἀληθής really means: May it become true and attest itself so. In this light every person appears as fallen into falsehood.

At this point one sees plainly that Paul regards history as God's trial with the world which will come to an end only in the last judgment and will result solely in the victory or defeat of one or the other party (Gaugler; C. Müller, *Gottes Volk*, 65ff.; Stuhlmacher, *Gerechtigkeit*, 85f.). In this struggle for vindication the issue is who is truthful and constant and who is the liar, or the victim of illusion and falsehood. Since this is the only alternative, only God or man can triumph as the representative of the world (typical of complete misunderstanding is the moral interpretation of Ulonska, *Paulus*, 166f.). Paul already knows the outcome and wishes it almost in the form of an incantation. For him God's truth is not metaphysically a religious *a priori*, the primary axiom of all Christian philosophy (Calvin). It manifests itself eschatologically and the struggle for it is the content, center, and meaning of world history.

Logical consistency leads from this to the second quotation. The psalmist's confession of guilt, which acknowledges God's judgment, is again interpreted eschatologically, as the wording of the LXX alone permits. Hence the LXX subjunctive, original notwithstanding ‭א‬ A D, is replaced by the future νικήσεις and the middle sense of ἐν τῷ κρίνεσθαι by the passive, as follows from the situation of a trial and the parallel in v. 7 (Lagrange; Kuss *contra* Schlatter; Ridderbos). Similarly the δικαιοῦν of God no longer relates to cultic exhomologesis in which God's right is acknowledged as in *Pss. Sol.* 2:15; 3:3, 5; 4:8; 8:7, 26; *2 Apoc. Bar.* 78:5. Also νικᾶν no longer has the originally cultic sense of the equivalent זכה, "be clean," the piel of which, in the sense of "declare righteous," designates the result of a legal procedure. The meaning "win in a trial," which occurs in the Aramaic period, is correctly rendered by νικᾶν in the LXX (BAGD, 539a). The forensic aspect of the verbs allowed a transposition of cultic into eschatological terminology, as often in Jewish apocalyptic. God is no longer declared to be righteous in his temporal judgment. He triumphs over his earthly opponents in the last judgment and shows himself to be justified in the words of his revelation. What Paul gathers from the Psalm quotation is that world history ends with God's victory over his foes and with the manifestation of his justice over his creatures. This makes the Scripture the promise for whose fulfilment prayer is made in v. 4a, and it corresponds precisely to the apocalyptic expectation of 1 Cor 15:24-28 and Rev 15:3f. If this interpretation is correct, this text (*contra* Bornkamm, "Teufelskunst," 148; Zeller, *Juden*, 181) is to be regarded as a key passage for the whole of Paul's doctrine of justification, since it lays bare the connection of this doctrine with apocalyptic and explains its cosmic dimension.

77]   It is extremely important to make the distinctiveness of the argument clear. The starting point is the question whether destruction of the Jewish claim to privilege and exposure of Israel's unfaithfulness means that the once elect people has lost its significance in salvation history. Paul vigorously contests this by pointing to the ongoing promises, and in further proof he adopts the terms and motifs of the covenant. This can only mean that the covenant violated by the people is still maintained from God's side. Now the argument does not continue, however, as might have been completely possible according to 15:8, in such a way that Christ has become a servant of the circumcision to confirm the promises made to the fathers and thereby to confirm God's covenant faithfulness to Israel. In a most remarkable way the problem is extended to every human being and to God's trial with the whole world. This makes sense only if the faithfulness of God to Israel is a special instance of his faithfulness to all creation. The idea of the covenant then, as already often established, is oriented not merely to Moses and Sinai but to the creation of the world. The promises given to Israel are fulfilled in no other way than elsewhere and everywhere.

As the third stage of the argument, then, we have the statement that salvation means always and everywhere the victory of God over the world contending with him. Israel is not mentioned again. Yet it is included in the proposition. For only thus does its unfaithfulness not have to lead to the loss of the divine promises and the abrogation of the covenant. God's victory is always over the unfaithful or over rebels, as is summarized in 11:32. It is always—to anticipate 4:5—the justification of the ungodly. The point lies in the fact that it is said here from the other side: The justification of the ungodly means God's victory over the world that strives against him. It is to be seen from the perspective of the forensic situation which plays so great a role in our text. Always and everywhere it implies that mankind is presented as deceived by illusion regarding itself and God, that God's truth is manifested in his word, and that God's right prevails over rebels who have to give him the right. By using the special case of Israel to exemplify God's dealings with the whole world, Paul can establish both Israel's guilt and God's faithfulness to his creation, which also means hope for those who bear the promise. Verse 4 is not a rhetorical digression (*contra* J. Weiss, "Beiträge," 221). It is the key to a solution of the problem and beyond that of Paul's message of justification, which applies equally to Jews and Gentiles and which gives the epistle its unity.

This being so, it is completely consistent that Paul's doctrine of justification is the object of the second objection in vv. 5ff. There can be no question of abstract reflection (*contra* Bornkamm, "Teufelskunst," 147). Paul is personally attacked. Since this happens in view of what he has just said about God's righteousness, this cannot be his distributive justice (*contra* Bornkamm, ibid., 145). Such a misunderstanding simply shows that the whole text is incomprehensible if God's righteousness is regarded merely as a gift and the apocalyptic horizon of Paul's teaching is eliminated in favor of the anthropological aspect. The theme of the covenant in fact no longer needs to be treated (ibid., 147). In contrast the Pauline doctrine of justification, in terms of which this theme was expounded, is now the object of debate in two respects. First, it seems to be blasphemous because it makes our unrighteousness the presupposition of God's righteousness. [7 Secondly, it leads in practice to the slogan in v. 8. Paul has to defend himself against both objections, for everything is now at stake.

The new objection in v. 5 links up not merely with the ὅπως of the last quotation, as is often maintained, but with the whole argument of v. 4. Verse 5a resumes what is said in v. 4 and sharpens it. Opponents have quite rightly understood that the quotation asserts the justification of the ungodly. But they draw from this a false conclusion. The striking antithesis of ἀδικία–δικαιοσύνη τοῦ θεοῦ does not indicate Paul's use of the expressions of others (*contra* Jeremias, "Chiasmus," 155). It points back to OT usage, and although the question may have arisen in discussions with Jews and Jewish-Christians, this objection, unlike that in v. 8, is one that Paul can bring himself. The verb συνιστάνειν, which Paul uses only in the sense of "demonstrate" (BAGD, 790b), points us again to the presupposed legal situation (Michel). ὁ ἐπιφέρων τὴν ὀργήν falls in line with the participial divine predications, which may be traced back to Jewish and primitive Christian liturgy. There is not the slightest ground for relating ὀργή to anything but eschatological judgment (Bultmann, *Theology*, I, 288f. *contra* Lietzmann; Hanson, *Wrath*, 88). The sense of the objection is given added precision in v. 7. Can the presupposition of God's glorification simultaneously be the ground of his judgment upon us without God himself being unrighteous? To speak of sin in the service of God at this point (Jeremias, "Chiasmus," 155; Leenhardt; H. W. Schmidt) is to get the point exactly.

Paul energetically rejects such a question and interpretation of his teaching. He calls it blasphemous. Only humans can argue thus (Lietzmann). κατὰ ἄνθρωπον λέγω, which recurs in 6:19; 1 Cor 9:8; Gal 3:15, finds no matching phrase in the rabbinic literature (Billerbeck). In our text, however, the apostle might have been following a fixed rabbinic tradition which uses כביכול "in some sense, *sit venia verbo,*" to show that statements which sound blasphemous are not being advanced seriously (Daube, *Rabbinic Judaism,* 394ff.). The learned derivation of this expression (understandable in itself) from the argumentation of rabbinic disputations, which like parables lay the foundation for theological discussion (Bjerkelund, "Nach menschlicher Weise," 67ff., 88ff.), seems very farfetched, especially since Paul does not use parables. God cannot be unrighteous simply because he is Judge of the world. ἐπεί in v. 6, as in 11:6, means "otherwise" (BDF, §456[3]). τὸν κόσμον κρίνειν stands as a formula also in 1 Cor 6:2; John 3:17; 12:47; *Sib. Or.* iv.184 (Billerbeck).

That this is not an argument but an appeal to knowledge about a moral order of the world (Dodd) is no longer a modern insight. Against that it is very important that here, without saying it explicitly, God's righteousness is linked to world judgment. This is consistent materially, for it is always the action of the Judge who establishes his justice by being gracious because he always puts an end to human illusions. God's truth is his lordship over the creature. It shatters as such our self-assertion and when accepted sets us in the power of grace. Grace is granted only from the Judge's hand.

The objection of v. 5 takes a more concrete form in v. 7. What has previously been discussed in general terms is now given a personal thrust. The prepositional expression in v. 7a is to be taken instrumentally. Exposure of mankind's fallenness into illusion brings overwhelming glory to the truth of God, namely, to God's lordship over his creation. This should be enough for God. Why does he insist on judging the person who is unmasked as a sinner, a rebel? κἀγώ does not mean "I as well as the Gentile." The Jew would have to ask this in the light of v. 1, and Jewish-Christians are most probably mangling Paul's message in v. 8. Nevertheless, it is clear from v. 4 on that Paul is no longer debating with the Jews but is simply taking the Jews as examples of mankind and extending the idea of the covenant to creation. The loose position of the καί, which is to be taken with the verb (though cf. BAGD, 393a), finds parallels in 5:3; 1 Thess 2:13; 3:5 (Lietzmann's other examples are questionable). A protest is being made against the preaching of judgment in connection with Paul's doctrine of justification. Mankind has been humbled enough through the latter. God has been glorified enough. May

83

not both, then, dispense with judgment? Would it not even be cruel for people now that they have been so profoundly exposed as sinners?

It should be noted that God's righteousness and glory are interchanged almost incidentally. The OT and Jewish apocalyptic provide a basis for this. This circumstance will become important in v. 23 and 8:30. Here it proves that v. 5 does not speak of distributive justice but of the power which establishes its right to the creature.

The pious take offense at the justification of the impious. If it is true, in the view of Paul's opponents, both God and man are put in a false position and future judgment is absurd since it has already been anticipated on earth. If this interpretation is correct, v. 8 cannot move in the same direction as vv. 5-7, and it certainly cannot (with Fridrichsen, "Exegetisches," 24f.; Ljungvik, "Römerbrief," 207; Jeremias, "Chiasmus," 155) be combined with v. 7 in a single sentence dependent on τί in v. 7b (K. Beyer, Semitische Syntax im Neuen Testament, I [1962] 95). The protest is no longer merely against Paul's doctrine of justification in the name of the pious because it makes sin the presupposition of grace and anticipates the judgment. It must also have libertine consequences and thus involves a reductio ad absurdum.

There can be little doubt that we have here objections actually raised against Paul, whereas previously it was at least possible that he was raising objections himself after the style of the diatribe. He himself complains now that ideas which he regarded as blasphemous were being urged as necessary deductions from his message. The enthusiasts at Corinth show that these were not merely imaginary (Schlatter; Althaus; Barrett). Libertinism really could develop out of Paul's view of justification, and his adversaries claim that it is an unavoidable result.

We thus have a crescendo of objections from v. 5 on. The question in v. 5 is still more or less theoretical. It becomes more concrete in the characteristic I-style of v. 7. As this style is limited to v. 7, v. 8 brings, with a new theme, the culmination of the section by drawing an inference which radically discredits the apostle's teaching. Thus v. 8 cannot be made parallel to v. 7. We do not have the monstrous structure of a double question in a single sentence. καὶ μή in v. 8 corresponds to μή in v. 5b. Its function is not one of coordination. It is to be translated as intensifying by "even" (BDF, §442[8]). The ὅτι after λέγειν, from which a λέγομεν may be deduced for the main clause, is recitative: "Are we even supposed to say?" or: "Is that even true what some . . . have us say?" The apostle describes what follows not merely as slander but also as blasphemy, since it is an attack on his gospel. Hence he no longer answers as he had done in v. 6 when he referred to God as the Judge of the world to whom no unrighteousness can be ascribed. Basically the conclusion of v. 8 is a curse (Kuss), just as v. 4a is not a religious postulate but a prayer of entreaty.

The whole argument makes sense only as it is seen to hinge on v. 4. The advantage of the Jew in salvation history will never be lost so long as God does not abandon his own cause. Jewish apostasy has not led him to do this. God always glorifies himself over the ungodly, to whom the Jews now belong as well. Only thus can he triumph over them. Only thus will the end of the litigation between God and the world demonstrate the faithfulness of the Creator to his promises. The common assertion, then, that Paul has lost sight of the goal of his discussion from 1:18 on is wrong. The problem of Israel has not been put in the proper perspective where in fact merely its guilt has been established and its special claims have been struck down. The result of this whole part of the epistle can be seen only when Israel also is drawn into fellowship with the ungodly. The Pauline doctrine of the justification of the ungodly demands this. Necessarily, then, it becomes the target of the objections raised: that it violates God's deity, v. 5; that it passes human comprehension, v. 7; that it leads to libertinism, v. 8. Instead of being a digression, vv. 1-8 are a logical preparation for vv. 9-20. Only from the perspective of the Jew as the representative of the religious person can universal godlessness be proclaimed.

6. Conclusion (3:9-20)

9What then? Have we any advantage? Not at all! We have already charged that all men, both Jews and Greeks, stand under the power of sin. 10Hence it is written: None is righteous, no, not one. 11There is none that understands, none that seeks after God. 12All have turned aside, all have become unusable. None does good, no, not one. 13An open grave is their throat, with their tongues they deceive, the poison of asps is under their lips. 14Their mouth is full of cursing and bitterness. 15Swift are their feet to shed blood. 16Ruin and misery are in their ways, 17and the way of peace they have not known. 18There is no fear of God before their eyes. 19Now we know that what the law says it says to those who are in the sphere of the law, that every mouth may be stopped and the whole world may be guilty before God. 20Hence by the works of the law no flesh will be justified before God. For by the law (comes only) the knowledge of sin.

Bibliography: E. Lohmeyer, "Probleme Paulinischer Theologie, II, 'Gesetzwerke,' " *ZNW* 28 (1929) 177-207; R. Gyllenberg, "Die paulinische Rechtfertigungslehre und das AT," *Studia Theologica* (Riga) 1 (1935) 35-52; J. A. Fitzmyer, "The Use of Explicit OT Quotations in Qumran Literature and in the NT," *NTS* 7 (1960/61) 297-333; R. A. Kraft, "Barnabas' Isaiah Text and the 'Testimony Book' Hypothesis," *JBL* 79 (1960) 336-350; O. Kuss, "Nomos bei Paulus," *MTZ* 17 (1966) 173-277; P. Vielhauer, "Paulus und das AT," *Studien zur Geschichte und Theologie der Reformation. Festschrift E. Bizer* (1969) 33-62; U. Wilckens, "Was heisst bei Paulus: 'Aus Werken des Gesetzes wird kein Mensch gerecht'?" EKK, *Vorarbeiten 1* (1969) 51-77; J. Blank, "Warum sagt Paulus: 'Aus Werken des Gesetzes wird niemand gerecht'?" EKK, *Vorarbeiten 1* (1969) 79-107. For Bornkamm, "Teufelskunst," see the bibliography for 3:1-8.

1] Verse 9 returns to v. 1 not because the intervening argument has been inconclusive (Dodd), but because all the world can really be pronounced guilty if even the religious person is. For Jews, not just Jewish-Christians (Zahn) and Paul, are the subject of the question in v. 9 and the object of the statement in vv. 19f., which in view of vv. 9b and 19f. can now be generalized. The associated quotations in vv. 10b-18 also apply primarily to the Jews. These are not a liturgy of lament in three strophes (vv. 10-12, 13-14, 15-18) nor are they a primitive Christian psalm developed out of the OT (*contra* Michel; Leenhardt). They are a message of judgment (Schlatter). Scripture anticipates Christian experience and accusation since it is eschatologically oriented.

In v. 9a the problems of the more difficult reading (Lietzmann) have produced variants. In the style of the diatribe an answer follows two brief questions. In the middle the verb in classical Greek (cf. Sanday and Headlam; Ridderbos) means "throw up as a defense," but in the *koine* without object it has to mean the same as the active "have an advantage" (Maurer, *TDNT*, VI, 693). Since in context Paul is not offering a self-defense, the meaning "look for excuses" (BAGD, 705-706) is off the mark. οὐ πάντως offers an energetic rejection as in 1 Cor 5:10: Not at all (Sanday and Headlam; Gutjahr; Murray; Ridderbos). In view of vv. 1f., however, a restriction should be considered: Not in any respect (Lietzmann; Lagrange; Huby). No claims are supported by precedence in salvation history.

ἁμαρτία in the singular, which is characteristically Pauline, always means, in almost hypostatizing fashion, the power of sin. The reality of the world is determined by being subject to this power and hence delivered up to God's wrath. Each individual represents it in his own way. Even the pious person is not exempt, as primitive Christian prophecy has already proclaimed in its accusations. The convicting function of this prophecy, which characteristically makes use of the OT, is now elevated to the plane of reflection and is literarily transformed.

The complex of quotations, which is introduced by the usual formula, is so comprehensive, colorful, and varied in detail that it is hard to think of it (with Michel, *Bibel*, 39f., 80) as a product of the apostle's memory. That is all the more so since there is a briefer parallel in Justin *Dialogus cum Tryphone* xxvii.9-12 which can hardly be derived from this passage (E. Hatch, *Essays in Biblical Greek* [1889] 203ff.). Perhaps the series has its source in oral tradition (Smits, *Citaten*, 483f.), but the idea of a florilegium is more convincing here (Vollmer, *Zitate*, 40). The findings at Qumran show that these already existed in the primitive Christian era (cf. H. Chadwick, *RAC*, VII, 1131-1160; Braun, *Qumran*, II, 304f.; Luz, *Geschichtsverständnis*, 95ff.). Missionary apologetics and polemics necessarily feed from a relatively fixed body of usable OT material. Taking a sentence out of context, weaving together passages with different thrusts, and inserting an interpretation into the particular citation reflect rabbinic exegesis of the Bible (Black; though cf. Bonsirven, *Exégèse*, 334ff.), which Jewish Christianity followed. Naturally this robs such proofs of their cogency for historical criticism.

Definite structuring is hardly possible (*contra* Sickenberger; Baulès), even though the beginning and end summarize and sins of word are especially stressed in vv. 13-14. Verses 10b-12 abbreviate and alter Ps 13:1-3 by inserting the decisive catchword δίκαιος. There is literal quotation of Ps 5:9 in v. 13a-b and of Ps 139:4 in v. 13c. Ps 10:7 is altered in v. 14 and Isa 59:7-8 is abbreviated in v. 15. Ps 36:2 is quoted almost word for word in v. 18. The LXX is always the basis.

In Judaism sinlessness was popularly ascribed not merely to the righteous of [past days but also to some in the present (Billerbeck). In contrast especially apocalyptic taught universal sinfulness; cf. 1QH 4:29f.; 7:17, and in almost literal agreement with Paul, 9:14f.: "None is righteous according to thy sentence nor guiltless in thy judgment." Confession is also made in 12:31f.: "Thou art righteous and none stands before thee." From this it is concluded, as in Paul, that mankind is silenced. In the light of Phil 3:6 it is most unlikely that the apostle is drawing on his own pre-Christian knowledge here. From v. 13 on, Jewish hatred of the gospel seems to come into consideration (Schlatter). Too much should not be made of the details. The rhetorical force of the passage is unmistakable, especially in the emphatic negations. The conclusion gives added emphasis to the beginning with a picture also used by the rabbis of the most extreme wrongdoer who, having no fear of God, throws off every divine claim (Billerbeck; Hengel, *Judaism*, I, 150f.).

Three weighty assertions are made in v. 19 which sum up the passage and state the goal of this part of the epistle. The first statement confirms our view that the Jew as a representative of the pious person is the real opponent in the discussion. The common phrase οἴδαμεν ὅτι here does not so much call to mind the doctrinal tradition in the community but emphatically stresses the conclusion of the argument. Only the premise will command Jewish assent.

At this point the problem of Paul's concept of the law arises (cf. the survey in Gutbrod, *TDNT*, IV, 1069ff.; Kuss, "Nomos," 177ff.). It does so primarily in Jewish dialectic. Since the Torah proper has not been adduced in the quotations, νόμος in v. 19a, as in 1 Cor 14:21 and frequently in the Rabbinate (Billerbeck), means Scripture as a whole (*contra* Zahn). Nevertheless, the OT has its material center in the Torah as the declaration of God's will in the strict sense. ἐν νόμῳ denotes the sphere of the law's validity as a factor in salvation history. This merits attention, since it warns against interpreting ἐν as obviously "mystical" in the parallel phrases "in Christ" and "in the Spirit." A salvation-historical meaning must always be considered (Neugebauer, *In Christus, contra* Deissmann and his school). A final point is that νόμος for Paul is not a generally valid norm, an abstract "legality" as such. It is the concrete Torah of Moses which retains its character only in relation to the history of Israel.

In context the ἵνα clause offers not merely the conclusion (Lietzmann; Ridderbos) but also the divine purpose (Kühl; Nygren; C. Müller, *Gottes Volk*, 76), which is, of course, proclaimed and known only through the apostle's preaching. The general statement at least, which v. 20b elucidates, is one that the Jew cannot accept (Zahn; Foerster, *TDNT*, III, 1021f., *contra* Schlatter). Characteristically Billerbeck can offer no parallel for it. *2 Apoc. Bar.* 48:40 simply says that the Gentiles could have known their sins from the law which they arrogantly despise. When, however, the *Hodayoth* have the religious person recognize his as well as human lostness, this insight does not come from the law. In its thrust against Judaism (Bruce; Baulès), the assertion is typical of Paul's understanding of the law.

In the parallelism between πᾶν στόμα and the OT πᾶς ὁ κόσμος one may see afresh how Paul's anthropological understanding of the world and the cosmic horizon of his anthropology mutually interact. "World" here is not just defined by the totality of mankind, but concretely by the contrast between Jew and Gentile. The "every" and "all" have the Jew specifically in mind. Hence the relation of the individual to the world is complex. It presupposes a religious fellowship from which one must not abstract away. On the other hand, if the antithesis of Jew and Gentile dissolves into the comprehensive unity of "world," Paul achieves a nuance which is dominant in the Fourth Gospel: The cosmos is represented in exemplary fashion by the Jew, since religiosity most profoundly characterizes the nature of the world. Paul's concept of the law constitutively presupposes dialectic between the Jew as recipient of revelation and the Jew as typical representative of human piety directed to performance. The law which God has given is not simply identical with that which the Jew seeks to fulfil. When the apostle speaks of the law polemically, he has in view the *nomos* interpreted and practiced by the Jew. There is thus a fluid interplay between different aspects first of the documentation of God's will in Scripture, secondly of the function of the law given to the Jew as revelation, and thirdly of the law's inability to effect salvation.

Verses 19c and 20b speak of the factual working of the law. The popular Hellenistic (ἐμ-)φράσσειν στόμα is also used in Ps 107:42; Job 5:16; 1 Macc 9:55. The only function of the law in the Jewish tradition is to silence all pious claims and to show that man is ὑπόδικος, i.e., under accusation with no possibility of defense (Maurer, *TDNT*, VIII, 558). Hence the statement in v. 20a is necessary. The decisive words ἐξ ἔργων νόμου are interpolated into the quotation from Ps 142:2 by way of interpretation. πᾶσα σάρξ is substituted for πᾶς ζῶν as in *1 Enoch* 81:5. The parallel in Gal 2:16 shows that the passage is of constitutive importance for the apostle.

Flesh here simply means human life. The background and meaning of the formula "works of the law" may be taken as explained (cf. Billerbeck, III, 160ff.; IV, 559ff.; Bertram, *TDNT*, II, 645; Lohmeyer's article, which is stimulating although it should be read critically). These are works that, explicitly demanded by the Torah, at the same time fulfil it. They take precedence over "good" works, for example, the activity of love, and stand in contrast to self-selected works at one's own discretion. The technical equivalent in rabbinic works is מצות, "fulfilment of the law," or sometimes מעשים. When *2 Apoc. Bar.* 57:2 speaks of *opera praeceptorum* (statutory works), apocalyptic prepares the way for Paul's formula and in some cases it even attests to pre-Pauline use. The stress is on the genitive, which indicates the sphere of the power that demands these works and makes them possible. The consistently used plural ἔργα and the abbreviation which simply has the technical "works" in 4:2, 6; 9:11; 11:6 make clear that specific deeds are in view. On the other hand, examples of the various possibilities are not given. In 10:5; Gal 2:21; 3:11; 5:4; Phil 3:6, 9 Paul can even refer instead to the law itself.

In these works the issue is keeping and fulfilling the whole Torah as a never-ending service (Lohmeyer, "Gesetzeswerke," 183ff.; Rössler, *Gesetz*, 79ff.). In this regard Paul's understanding necessarily diverges from Jewish tradition. The apostle does not renounce work and works, and according to 2:6ff. he views them in the same way Judaism does, as obedience to the divine will. He has to show, however, in what relation the service of the law stands to that of Christ. In sharp opposition to the Jewish view we have the result of this distinction in v. 20a.

In *2 Apoc. Bar.* 51:3 the Jewish view speaks of the glorious appearing of those who have acted justly on the basis of the law, while 67:6 refers to the "incense of the righteousness which has its source in the law." Paul, however, says: οὐ δικαιωθήσεται. If this refers primarily to the eschatological declaration in God's judgment this can also be prophetic anticipation. Proclamation and actualization coincide, so that the future is gnomic (Bultmann, *Theology*, I, 274). This makes sense when the service of the law and that of Christ are mutually exclusive, and this can be so only if Paul does not see authentic obedience realized in the works of the law.

Passionate protest has been raised against this view in order to head off a liberal retreat into mere disposition (Schlatter, *Glaube*, 325ff.; *Theologie*, 281). But the distinction between works of the law as the good and Christ's work as the best (loc. cit.) is thoroughly non-Pauline. It simply proves that the radicalness of Paul's theology lies decisively in its doctrine of the law and that only sharp antithesis does justice at this point to the message of Christ. The actual law as it has been handed down does not bring about genuine obedience for the apostle since the religious seize it and make it the ground not only of their attainment but also of their boasting. However, that is simply sacrilege. Because Paul sees this sacrilege incessantly in progress in the works of the law, he can only sharply reject it.

The point of the whole is completely missed if, in accordance with Qumran statements, only the general transgression is supposed to be established in our text, but no basic disputing of works of the law is in view (so U. Wilckens, "Was heisst . . . ," 54ff., 72ff., and in ironical criticism the Roman Catholic Blank, "Warum sagt . . . ," 89ff.). This misunderstanding fails to explain why Paul speaks of works of the law rather than the deeds and efforts of the pious, and especially the polemic against the law as a whole and against Moses.

What, under such circumstances, is the task of the law? The answer in v. 20b is oracular in its brevity. Its sententious character, however, should not mislead us into thinking that it is presenting a general truth which can be known even before Christ, namely, through the law which convicts of sin (*contra* Wilckens, "Was heisst," 75f.; Baulès; in clear-cut opposition Schlatter: "No one read this in the law"). Paul is not speaking, then, of a pedagogic task of the law (with Kühl against Nygren). We have here a Christian insight which God's presence alone makes possible and which Paul finds to be a judgment on his earlier religiosity. Hence the statement is not saying the same thing as the almost verbally identical statement of Epicurus in Seneca *Epistulae morales* 28: "Knowledge of sin is the beginning of salvation." It is not merely that a person learns from his mistakes. Certainly ἐπίγνωσις is the knowledge of experience which leads to acknowledgment of a situation (Bultmann, *TDNT*, I, 707), and this experience is imparted through dealings with the law. Yet it happens, not progressively, but at the end of a path at which an insurmountable abyss opens up.

When Judaism points to actual transgression of the law, as, for example, in 4 Ezra 3:20; 7:46, 72; 9:36, it combines it with a call to repentance which spurs to closer observance of the law. Not being able to do it is not seen here as a sign that one should not take this way (Bultmann, *Theology*, I, 267; Bornkamm, "Teufelskunst," 147, though cf. Gutbrod, *TDNT*, IV, 1050). It simply pushes one deeper into the vicious circle of demand and effort from which Paul breaks free. Paul's reference is not to a provisional situation but to the definitive situation. This part of the letter ends, then, with a statement of general hopelessness.

The service of the law, according to 2 Cor 3:6ff., is a service of condemnation. According to Rom 7:7ff. it provokes sin. For the sake of the scope, the point is made differently here. Not just theoretically, but through experience, a person learns what sin really is at its deepest level. It is the human attempt to rob God of his power. Naturally this insight is not acknowledged by servants of the law. It is accompanied, then, by the insight into God's wrath which only the gospel makes possible, although it is foreshadowed earlier and does determine the world in fact. False religion is what makes plain that sin is not just weakness or specific wrongdoing but actual blasphemy. That with the law nothing else is provided is the decisive point. For thus it is shown that even the way of the pious is hopeless prior to and apart from Christ. When only sin can find a place under the law and in piety, Christ alone can make a new beginning.

III. The Righteousness of God as the Righteousness of Faith (3:21-4:25)

In sharp antithesis to the depicted hopelessness of mankind, 3:21-31 speaks of the manifestation of the righteousness of faith and its basis. The thesis proper is stated in 3:21-26, and it is elucidated in its anti-Jewish thrust in 3:27-31. 4:1-25 offers scriptural proof that the thesis corresponds to God's direction of salvation history and to his will as it is documented in the OT. Sometimes ch. 5 is included in this part of the epistle, but this is to be explained and rejected as due to a false juxtaposition of justification and sanctification.

A. The Thesis (3:21-26)

[21]But now the righteousness of God has been manifested without the law, being attested by the law and the prophets, [22]namely, the righteousness of God through faith in Jesus Christ for all believers. For there is no difference: [23]All have sinned and (therefore) lack the glory of God. [24](So) all are justified freely in his grace by the redemption in Christ Jesus. [25]Him God has publicly set forth as an expiation, (which is appropriated) through faith in virtue of his blood. (This took place) to show his righteousness in such a way that in divine forbearance former sins were remitted; [26]to show his righteousness in the present hour of destiny, that he might be righteous and might justify him who lives by faith in Jesus.

Bibliography: W. Michaelis, "Zur Frage der Aeonenwende," *ThBl* 18 (1939) 113-18; E. Lohse, "Imago Dei bei Paulus," *Libertas Christiana. Friedrich Delekat zum 65. Geburtstag, 1957* (ed. W. Mattias; BEvT 26; 1957) 122-135; E. Käsemann, "Zum Verständnis von Römer 3, 24-26," *Exegetische Versuche und Besinnungen,* I (6th ed., 1970) 96-100; J. Jeremias, "Das Lösegeld für Viele," *Abba,* 216-229; E. Schweizer, "Mystik"; F. Grandchamp, "La doctrine du sang du Christ dans les épîtres de saint Paul," *Revue de Theologie et de Philosophie* ser. 3, 11 (1961) 262-271; S. Lyonnet, "De Iustitia Dei in Epistola ad Romanos 3:25-26," *VD* 25 (1947) 129-144; S. Schulz, "Zur Rechtfertigung aus Gnaden in Qumran und bei Paulus," *ZTK* 56 (1959) 155-185; P. Valloton, *Le Christ et la foi* (1960); G. Fitzer, "Der Ort der Versöhnung nach Paulus," *TZ* 22 (1966) 161-183; C. H. Talbert, "A Non-Pauline Fragment at Romans 3:24-26?" *JBL* 85 (1966) 287-296; W. Schrage, "Römer 3, 21-26 und die Bedeutung des Todes Jesu Christi bei Paulus," *Das Kreuz Jesu* (ed. P. Rieger; *Forum* 12; 1969) 65-88; W. G. Kümmel, "πάρεσις und ἔνδειξις," *Heilsgeschehen und Geschichte. Gesammelte Aufsätze 1933-1964* (1965) 260-270; W. H. Cadman, "Δικαιοσύνη in Romans 3:21-26," *SE,* II, 532-34; D. Zeller, "Sühne und Langmut. Zur Traditionsgeschichte von Röm 3, 24-26," *Theologie und Philosophie* 43 (1968) 51-75; K. Wennemer, "'Ἀπολύτρωσις Römer 3, 24-25a," *Stud.Paul.Congr.*, I, 283-88; H. Rosman, "Justificare est verbum causativum," *VD* 21 (1941) 144-47; A. Deissmann, "ἱλαστήριος und ἱλαστήριον," *ZNW* 4 (1903) 193-212; C. Bruston, "Les conséquences du vrai sens de ἱλαστήριον," *ZNW* 7 (1906) 77-81; T. W. Manson, "'Ἱλαστήριον," *JTS* 46 (1945) 1-10; W. Manson, "Notes on the Argument of Romans (Chapters 1-8)," *NT Essays, Manson*, 150-164; L. Moraldi, "Sensus vocis ἱλαστήριον in R 3, 25," *VD* 26 (1948) 257-276; L. Morris, "The Meaning of ἱλαστήριον in Rom III, 25," *NTS* 2 (1955/56) 33-34; J. Heuschen, "Rom 3, 25 in het Licht van de OT Zoenvoorstelling," *Revue Ecclésiastique de Liège* 44 (1957) 65-79; H. J. Schoeps, "The Sacrifice of Jesus in Paul's Theology," *JBL* 65 (1946) 385-392; H. G. Meecham, "Romans 3:25f.; 4:25—the Meaning of διά c. acc.," *ExpT* 50 (1938/39) 564; C. Blackman, "Romans 3:26b: A Question of Translation," *JBL* 87 (1968) 203-204; A. Pluta, *Gottes Bundestreue; ein Schlüsselbegriff in Röm. 3, 25a* (1969).

This section has rightly been called one of the most obscure and difficult in the whole epistle (J. Weiss, "Beiträge," 222). But the reason for this is not clear. It is not that the apostle wanted to deal exhaustively with his theme or was wrestling with new thoughts or was trying to avoid misunderstanding. If the doctrine of justification forms the center of his theology and of the present epistle, brevity is to be expected rather than obscurity, and in fact he could hardly have stated the matter in shorter compass. Misinterpretations come into view only in v. 31. The jumbled nature of the passage can be explained only if it be noted that we have here a heaping up of non-Pauline terms and liturgical motifs. In other words, fixed tradition is drawn on by way of both introduction and conclusion to support the doctrine of justification both here and in 4:25, as it is also in the case for the message of Christ in 1:3f. The sentence structure becomes obscure because Paul as elsewhere does not identify as such the tradition which he uses and, moreover, he interprets it through additions (Bultmann, *Theology*, I, 46f., 293; J. Jeremias, *TDNT*, V, 706; also in broad agreement Zeller, "Sühne," 52, but cf. Barrett; Kuss; Fitzer, "Versöhnung").

νυνὶ δέ characterizes both the logical antithesis and especially the eschatological turn (Stählin, *TDNT*, IV, 1117). In its very objectivity the statement corresponds to the counter-statement in 1:18. But the antithesis is not captured with the categories of the old and the new aeons (Nygren), and even the Jewish view of the two aeons, although presupposed by Paul, is adopted only dialectically and never explicitly (Michaelis, "Aeonenwende," 116, is too radical). For Paul the new aeon has already broken into the old aeon in Christ and it is spread abroad with his death. On the other hand, only in the sphere of Christ's lordship is there worldwide salvation for a cosmos under the wrath of God into which Christians can fall back and whose reality will be ended only with the parousia. The fact that salvation is present has for cosmology and anthropology, as its projection, the structure of a "No longer" and "Not yet." This is why 8:22 will speak of the woes in which creation now finds itself. The thrust of historical movement is decided by the coming of Christ. The presence of Christ's lordship gives definitiveness to the "now" and yet the temptation (*Anfechtung*) of that which still is imposes on faith the provisional character of a not yet concluded way on which it will be necessary to stand the test. Pauline eschatology, then, does not remove historicity or history, but bases both on God's saving action toward a world which barricades itself against him.

As denoted by the perfect of the verb, which indicates duration, the eschaton is paradoxically present but the present is not the eschaton. Contrary to many modern commentators, for the apostle God's righteousness is not exhausted by the assurance of salvation for faith which is under assault. Like the Spirit, faith is rather the firstfruits of future fulfilment. Hence the question is justified (Lütgert, *Römerbrief,* 42ff.) why he does not simply speak of grace and forgiveness.

Roman Catholic interpretation especially moves repeatedly in this direction when, appealing to the OT, it defines God's righteousness as saving action and more or less unequivocally subsumes it under love. But this is to shorten Paul's perspective, according to which only the Judge can posit salvation and, as the forensic expression indicates, establish his right to his creation with the power of grace. Mankind's justification is the actuality of God's right to his creation as this reveals itself as saving power, and this remains the basis, force, and truth of justification—a truth which transcends the individual and is directed toward a new world.

Without such a distinction the doctrine of justification dissolves into an anthropology of faith and the *extra nos* of salvation, which is given with the Christ event, cannot be strongly preserved. As surely as justification loses its reality unless it happens to the individual, just so surely it cannot remain an eschatological event unless it is the Creator's grasping of his world and not of the individual alone. In the primacy of christology over anthropology and cosmology these two are included and Paul's eschatology is distinguished from ideology.

For this reason the verb φανεροῦν, which, like ἀποκαλύπτειν, belongs to the vocabulary of revelation, and means more than merely becoming visible (*contra* Cerfaux, *Christian,* 420; J. Knox), does not imply (Zahn) that the righteousness of God has always been present already in hidden form. Rather, God's ultimate victory manifests itself now. It is neither correct that grace for Paul, for the sake of his positive attitude to the law, is simultaneously justification (Lütgert, *Römerbrief,* 47f.) nor that as the ongoing norm of the relations between God and mankind grace transcends the law (W. Manson, "Notes," 156). Since God's eschatological salvation is for creation, it excludes the law understood as a call for the righteousness of works and yet there is no total breach with salvation history (v. 21b), as Marcion believed.

The revelation of righteousness has been made public, and is proclaimed with legally binding force. This is the sense of the forensic expression μαρτυρεῖν (Asting, *Verkündigung,* 458ff.). The rabbinic "law and prophets" (Zahn), which Paul uses only here, means the whole OT (Billerbeck). The law is concretely the Pentateuch as the Torah in the strict sense (Barrett; Gutbrod, *TDNT,* IV, 1070f.). Hence we are not to think primarily of the messianic prophecies as the mention of the prophets probably intends. Nothing indicates that the apostle here distinguishes between a legalistic and a prophetic strand in the OT (*contra* Dodd), and the explanation that Paul is basing his argument on the Torah (Nygren) is too weak. It fails to take into account Paul's dialectical concept of the law and its basis. Just because the *nomos* is originally intended to be a witness to salvation, its interpretation as a summons to achievement is a Jewish misunderstanding. On the other hand the law actually reaches people only in this religious perversion, so that only Christian faith can give it back its character as promise by putting an

93

end to pious achievement. Even in the Pentateuch, then, it is a witness to salvation, since it demands the obedient heart which Christ creates (cf. Schlatter). The obedience of faith abrogates the law as a mediator of salvation, sees through the perversion of understanding it as a principle of achievement, and in eschatological retrospect restores to the divine gift the character of the original will of God. Verse 22 answers the question whether new support is not given to the piety of works with this dialectic.

The righteousness of God manifests itself as the righteousness of faith. The whole statement is a single expression. The elucidatory δέ catches up and attributively defines the subject of v. 21. Whatever else God's eschatological righteousness may be, at any rate it is a gift that comes to man διὰ πίστεως. Faith is basically human receptivity, as actively as it may express itself in obedience. If the original 'Ιησοῦ has dropped out in part of the tradition this eliminates the mistaken idea that the reference is to Jesus' own faith (J. Haussleiter, *Der Glaube Jesu Christi und der christliche Glaube* [1892]; Valloton, *Le Christ*, 47) or, in modified form, that the genitive is both subjective and objective (Deissmann, *Paul*, 161ff.; O. Schmitz, *Christusgemeinschaft;* Asmussen; Leenhardt). Correct in this is only that for Paul the Giver always comes on the scene with the gift, so that in Gal 3:23 πίστις can even be hypostatized. Here v. 26 supports an objective genitive. It is generally present to the extent that the non-Greek paraphrase of the subject by relative clauses or ὅτι statements, and by the linking of the verb with εἰς or, more rarely, ἐπί is characteristic (Bultmann, *Theology*, I, 89f.).

The strange pleonasm εἰς πάντας καὶ ἐπὶ πάντας is obviously a compilation of variants present in the *koine* and Western text (Lietzmann, though cf. Zahn, Kühl, Nygren, etc.). In contrast to the universal fall in 1:18–3:20 the universality of the gift is emphasized by πάντες in vv. 22b-23, cf. 1:16f. Although it is received only by believers, it is the worldwide power of grace. The antithesis of 5:12ff. is announced (introduced) when, in the contrast, the correspondence between the two aeons is stressed in respect to the universality of their sphere of operation, which relativizes every empirical distinction. Paul does not use the vocabulary of Jewish apocalyptic here, because the future world has already begun as he sees it; nevertheless he takes up the same motifs. It is noteworthy that both the absence of apocalyptic vocabulary and his adoption of its motifs derive from his doctrine of justification.

When God's righteousness comes upon the scene, the kingdom is present simultaneously in a sense that is to be defined more closely. Nevertheless, it is present in such a way that the world of Adam and of Christ confront one another and at the same time correspond to one another as the only eschatological realities. Salvation history is not the superstructure of the doctrine of justification, but the latter is its criterion. In its antithesis to the lordship of Christ given with God's righteousness, v. 23, like 1:18ff.; 7:7ff.; 8:19ff., from an apocalyptic view designates the solidarity of a world in guilt and need as the place of the salvation event. The καί between the verbs has a consecutive sense (Cambier, *L'Évangile*, 73). Luther's rendering of δόξα τοῦ θεοῦ misses the point, for the phrase does not mean, as in the objective genitive of John 12:43, the good opinion (Lagrange) or honor of God (BAGD, 204a), but the radiance which according to the apocalyptic view awaits the justified in heaven. Unlike 1 Cor 15:43, however, this verse

94

does not look toward the future glory (*contra* Kühl; Schlatter; Althaus; Nygren) but toward the lost glory to which 1:23 alludes already and of which *Apoc. Mos.* 20, in a most characteristic parallelism with former righteousness, says: "I am estranged from my glory with which I was clothed." Similarly *Gen. Rab.* 12:6 states that Adam lost his glory through sin.

In contrast to current rabbinic tradition (cf. Kittel, *TDNT*, II, 393; Foerster, *TDNT*, III, 1020f.; Larsson, *Vorbild*, 128-169) the divine likeness is here regarded as lost since the fall (Jervell, *Imago*, 44f., 92, 100ff., 113ff.; J. B. Schaller, "Gen. 1–2 in antiken Judentum" [Diss., Göttingen, 1961] 76, 148ff., though cf. Larsson, *Vorbild*, 186f.). In spiritualized form, i.e., with reference to immortality, this motif occurs already in Wis 2:23f., and the christological use of the εἰκών predicate can be understood only in the light of this branch of Jewish tradition (cf. Lohse, "Imago," 123ff.), which Paul consistently follows. As in 1:23 he is not interested in the mythological connections. Yet in this way he can radically characterize the human plight and, in contrast to it, sharply profile the eschatological promise. The correspondence of δόξα and δικαιοσύνη τοῦ θεοῦ derives from the antithesis in the context (Bardenhewer; Best). From it one may also infer that with righteousness the lost image will be restored to a person in his participation in Christ's lordship and the fallen world will be eschatologically changed into the new creation of 2 Cor 5:17. To put it more precisely, the δόξα τοῦ θεοῦ is δικαιοσύνη within the horizon of the restoration of paradisaical perfection, while conversely δικαιοσύνη is the divine δόξα within the horizon of controversy with the world, thus of temptation (*Anfechtung*). The apostle does not understand the divine image as a *habitus* but as a right relation of the creature to the Creator (Jervell, *Imago*, 180ff., 325ff.). Thus the new obedience appears as the fruit and the reverse side of justification. Justification and creation are unmistakably intertwined here and both are connected in a salvation-historical perspective; therefore they cannot be played off against the Pauline eschatology. It is worth noting that the text merely hints at all this, although it profoundly determines all further interpretation. The way in which Paul takes it for granted shows that he can count on the agreement of his readers at this point.

He can do so because he is building on a settled tradition. This may be seen especially in the abrupt change in sentence structure in v. 24. There is, of course, an antithetical correspondence to v. 23 in vv. 24ff., but not in such a way that the sentence is continued with the characteristic πάντες and the contrast is sharply developed as in 5:18 (*contra* Wengst, *Formeln*, 87). Since expositors feel the break, they have to treat vv. 22c-23 as a parenthesis, although the participle in v. 24 goes neither with v. 22b (*contra* Murray) nor even with the noun δικαιοσύνη (Michel). Not even the suggestion that there is an echo of oral tradition here (Cambier, *L'Évangile*, 75ff.) solves the syntactical difficulty. The only solution seems to be that Paul is quoting the fragment of a hymn.

It is theologically important that the same Paul who in 1:16f. interpreted the christological statement of 1:3f. soteriologically now conversely gives the righteousness of faith a christological basis and connection (Schrage, "Bedeutung," 71). While it is true that for Paul christology must be interpreted and established in terms of the doctrine of justification, it is equally true that the doctrine of justification makes sense and is necessary only when viewed christologically. It can in no way be anthropologically rendered independent via a religious doctrine.

It is and remains applied christology. Only thus is it gospel. On the other hand, it enables us to decide between true and false christology. Whenever a person leaves this circle, Paul's theology as a whole is misunderstood and thrown in doubt.

In the context δικαιοῦσθαι in non-Greek fashion, yet derivable from the causative hiphil of צדק, can only mean "to be made righteous" (Barrett; Cambier, L'Évangile, 83, 153, cf. the excursus in Lagrange). As may be seen from baptism, the restored divine image means eschatologically transformed existence. This observation does not, as commonly assumed, eliminate the problem of the forensic meaning of the verb, as ch. 4 will show. The argument that legal terminology is unsuitable for the ethical relation between God and man, and that it can be used only paradoxically (Dodd), is a relic of what is now an illegitimate liberalism. The question must on the contrary be pressed all the more sharply by turning it around: To what extent can the incontestably forensic "declaring righteous," which is not to be taken out of the context of eschatological judgment, come to present expression in the creative act of "making righteous"?

The present participle in v. 24, which replaces the past forms of v. 23, offers a first answer to this question by pointing to gracious liberation through Christ. Here again χάρις is not a divine disposition nor (Bultmann, Theology, I, 289f.) the act of grace but eschatological power. The use of δωρεάν, which is materially superfluous and non-Pauline as in Rev 21:6; 22:17 (Michel), strengthens it.

ἀπολύτρωσις is still constantly interpreted in terms of the sacral manumission of slaves (Deissmann, Light, 327ff.; Paul, 172ff.; Lietzmann; Althaus; etc.). But there is no basis for this understanding (Eichholz, Paulus, 195f.). Not even legal language is probable (contra Stuhlmacher, Gerechtigkeit, 88). What we probably have is liturgical use as in 1 Cor 1:30; Col 1:14; Eph 1:7, which emphasizes the eschatological event (Büchsel, TDNT, IV, 355). For this reason no object is mentioned but the solemn formula ἐν Χριστῷ 'Ιησοῦ is appended, the preposition being instrumental. That this formula designates "a divine event in respect of its eternal validity" and thus differs from the parallel phrases ἐν Χριστῷ and ἐν κυρίῳ (Schmauch, In Christus, 47 and passim) is refuted precisely here by the fact that while ἀπολύτρωσις refers to an event, the formula points exclusively to the mediator of salvation. The whole expression relates to the concrete act of salvation and not to ongoing redemption (Schlatter; Murray; Wennemer, "'Απολύτρωσις"). Christ's death has effected once and for all what grace continually applies to us.

There can be no doubt that materially the statement fits in well with Paul's theology. This is no reason, however, to ascribe it to him and to begin the piece he uses only at v. 25 (contra Talbert, "Fragment"; Schrage, "Bedeutung," 78; Wengst, Formeln, 87; Fitzer, "Versöhnung," 165). Apart from the break in style occasioned by the introductory participle, against that view one also must consider that ἀπολύτρωσις does not denote the ransom mentioned in 1 Cor 6:20; 7:23; Gal 3:14; 4:5 (contra Fitzer) and that it has a present reference in 1 Cor 1:30 only within the framework of a formula that is at least liturgical and probably depends on tradition, whereas Paul himself according to 8:23 reserves it for the eschatological future. The relative addition, which is typical of hymnic material, fits in smoothly if the quotation begins already in v. 24 (cf. Zeller, "Sühne," 52f.; the survey in Cambier, L'Évangile, 81; Pluta, Bundestreue, 42ff.).

In any case vv. 25f., as the history of exposition shows, cannot be understood unless a fixed tradition be assumed. προέθετο does not refer to God's predestination (Bruston, "Conséquences," 77; Cambier, *L'Évangile,* 90f.; Pluta, *Bundestreue,* 59ff.) nor to apostolic proclamation (Schrenk, *TDNT,* III, 321), since then a further verb would be almost indispensable. A reminiscence of Gen 22:8 in the OT (Schoeps, "Sacrifice," 385; critically Barrett, *First Adam,* 26ff.), or of Exod 25:17 (Smits, *Citaten,* 469), also has little credibility. The material parallel in 4QpPsª 3:16 is closer. Here the Teacher of Righteousness is "appointed" by God. The idea is that of public manifestation (cf. Zeller, "Sühne," 57f.). As often in the *koine,* the preposition strengthens the simple form (though cf. Zeller, "Sühne"; Fitzer, "Versöhnung," 166).

Debate focuses most sharply on whether ἱλαστήριον refers, as in Heb 9:5, the LXX, and Philo (cf. Billerbeck's excursus; Pluta, *Bundestreue,* 62ff.), to the cover of the ark or its top. In the expiatory ritual of the great Day of Atonement this, or, after the destruction of the temple, its former site, was sprinkled with sacrificial blood by the high priest and for this reason it was called the place of the divine presence, or, in the targums, the place of expiation. In Jewish-Christian tradition this reference cannot easily be ruled out here, as Heb 9:5 shows (cf. Kühl; Althaus; Gaugler; Nygren; Murray; Bruce; Schrenk, *TDNT,* III, 320f.; H. W. Schmidt; Manson, Moraldi, and Heuschen in their essays; Schoeps, *Paul,* 130ff.; with reservations Barrett; Kuss; rejected by Ridderbos; sharp criticism in Morris, "Meaning"; Wengst, *Formeln,* 88; Schrage, "Bedeutung," 81).

The main argument against the conjecture is that the predominantly Gentile-Christian community in Rome would scarcely have understood so ambiguous an allusion (Kümmel, "πάρεσις," 265), and Jewish-Christian tradition would probably have clarified it (Taylor, *Forgiveness,* 39; Seidensticker, *Opfer,* 153f.). Furthermore, Jesus could not easily be simultaneously the site of the offering and the offering itself. Likewise one cannot prove any concrete reminiscence of the motif of the sin-offering in Isa 53:10 (*contra* Jeremias, *TDNT,* V, 706) or the use of the masculine adjective ἱλαστήριος as a noun (Zahn already, *contra* Sanday and Headlam). One can certainly manage with the meanings of the Greek word which denote something related to expiation, concretely the gift or sign of expiation, in general the means of expiation. The word occurs in the last sense in 4 Macc 17:22 with reference to the death of martyrs. Cultic language can hardly be contested (e.g., Seidensticker, 194 *contra* Schrage, "Bedeutung," 81). It is supported by the stereotyped use of blood in the NT for the death of Jesus (but cf. Grandchamp, "Doctrine," 262ff.; Fitzer, "Versöhnung," 167ff., 183). What follows shows in any case that here, as in 2 Cor 5:18ff., we have the premise, not (*contra* Leenhardt) the main thrust of the text. The satisfaction theory cannot be based on it (*contra* Lietzmann with Kümmel, "πάρεσις," 270). As blood brings the covenant into effect, so it also belongs to its eschatological renewal, which will be dealt with shortly. God himself makes this expiation and hence makes possible again the fellowship which had been disrupted. The translation "means of forgiveness" (Schlatter; Dodd) is thus too weak.

The sentence is difficult syntactically. It seems that ἐν τῷ αὐτοῦ αἵματι should go with ἱλαστήριον, corresponding to 5:9 (Lietzmann; Ridderbos). But the position and the sense prevent διὰ πίστεως from being linked to the verb. The appositions jostle one another. Ign. *Smyrn*. 6:1 is not to be used as a parallel. The expression "to believe in the blood of Christ" would be singular in the NT (Zahn; Kühl), and Paul does not use πίστις with ἐν (Schlatter; Dodd). When commentators think they must speak of the means of expiation which is grasped in faith and which becomes effective through blood, this is obviously a stop-gap, since it reverses the order of the words. The phrase διὰ πίστεως, which is not accidentally dropped from A, and which does not (*contra* Pluta, *Bundestreue*, 105ff.) designate God's covenant faithfulness, should be treated as a parenthesis (Seidensticker, *Opfer*, 161, though cf. Cambier, *L'Évangile*, 120f.), in which Paul's reworking of the tradition can be seen, as in Phil 2:8 or Col 1:18, 20. The apostle has made this rough interpolation in order to be able to relate salvation and faith to one another.

Only now, however, do we come to the worst difficulty. The verses are plainly conjoined by the two purpose clauses in v. 25b and v. 26a, and these in turn are summed up in the infinitive purpose clause in v. 26b. Are we to interpret the parallelism in the sense of an intensification or a restatement (cf. the surveys in Kümmel, "πάρεσις," 263ff.; H. W. Schmidt; Cambier, *L'Évangile*, 124ff.)? In general the intensification is preferred. As the change of prepositions and the presumably anaphoric use of the article in the second member (Zahn) differentiate the expressions, δικαιοσύνη is supposed to designate initially the divine attribute or distributive justice (Ridderbos, *Paul*, 186ff.; Cerfaux, *Christian*, 406) and later the eschatological act of salvation. From this standpoint v. 25b speaks of the guilty past and v. 26a of the present age of salvation, whereby πάρεσις means freedom from punishment through personal clemency, upon which actual justification follows in v. 26 (Kühl; Gutjahr; Bardenhewer; Huby; Murray). A variation of this understanding sees in διὰ τὴν πάρεσιν . . . θεοῦ a parenthesis (Lagrange; Althaus; J. Weiss, "Beiträge," 222 with reference even to v. 26a).

Intensification in the verses necessarily rests on the other presupposition that vv. 25f. are a non-Pauline fragment (Talbert, "Fragment"). The decision as to the correctness or incorrectness of this view depends on the interpretation of πάρεσις. The earlier almost obvious translation by "overlooking" or "letting pass" is certainly possible, but has become dubious since the technical legal sense of "remission of penalty" has been demonstrated to be predominant (Lietzmann; esp. Kümmel, "πάρεσις," 262f.). In fact a distinction from ἄφεσις in the latter case is scarcely present (Bultmann, *TDNT*, I, 508), and one might ask why this word, which was so common in primitive Christianity, is not used (Michel; Barrett). The only possible answer is that in a divergent tradition the legal nuance is given a stronger emphasis than by the already polished ἄφεσις. ἔνδειξις has precisely this nuance; it can mean "proof" (cf. Michel; Kümmel, "πάρεσις," 263), but here it must have the sense of "demonstration" as in 2 Cor 8:24 (Kümmel, ibid., 265f.).

God, however, does not submit to human judgment, especially as righteousness would then be his attribute, whereas in the context it is his action. In the death of Jesus he has cancelled guilt stored up in pre-Christian times (Schrenk, *TDNT*, II, 204f.). In so doing he has manifested his saving action as earlier indicated by προέθετο. Again the mode of expression speaks against Pauline authorship. Paul's concern is with the disarming of sin, of which he therefore always speaks in the singular, and he uses the term forgiveness so astonishingly seldom because for him it is not just a question of the remission of pre-Christian offenses. Nevertheless, not only the vocabulary and thinking are non-Pauline, but also the overloaded style, which is reminiscent of the deutero-Pauline letters, with its wealth of genitive constructions and prepositional phrases. This is particularly true of the final member, which speaks of the divine ἀνοχή and which cannot go with what follows on account of the parallelism of the verse. One might point to the motif of God's clemency toward human guilt in Acts 17:30 (Murray; Leenhardt; H. W. Schmidt) or to the μαϰροθυμία of 2:4 (E. Schweizer, "Mystik," 256). But this is little help here. 1:18–3:20 sets the past under the theme of the revelation of wrath, not of the clemency which practices patience (Jülicher; Fitzer, "Versöhnung," 153f. can thus see in v. 25b only the gloss of a none too intelligent reader), and in 2:4 forbearance and patience are not clemency but the postponing of full wrath and therefore the legal basis of the final judgment, as in 9:22; 2 Apoc. Bar. 59:6. The motivation present here simply contradicts Paul's theology. Hence vv. 25f. also can hardly be regarded as originally a single unit (contra Talbert, "Fragment"), and absolutely nothing speaks for a later interpolation of the two verses. On the contrary, both are in fact indispensable here since they present justification as an eschatological gift of salvation and as the theme of the present part of the epistle.

Some results of the foregoing analysis may now be considered. Everything speaks against considering v. 26a as either an intensification or a resumption of Paul's thought after a previous parenthesis. Hence we cannot accept the translation (Lietzmann): "To show his righteousness to the extent that he forgives sins committed earlier in the time of his patience so as to prove his righteousness in the present." As God has nothing to prove (Kümmel, "πάρεσις," 267), this brings v. 26a into conflict with v. 26b and pointlessly repeats the beginning of v. 25b. If, however, the two verses are parallel, then we have in v. 25b a Jewish-Christian view upon which Paul comments in v. 26. This tradition was important to Paul because, like him, it saw salvation in the justification of the sinner. To put it more accurately and precisely, because it did not speak of the individual (Kümmel, 267 contra A. Schweitzer, Mysticism, 219; Mundle, Glaubensbegriff, 88): already in the original, forgiveness and justification characterized the change of aeons (cf. Kertelge, Rechtfertigung, 48ff.; Schrage, "Bedeutung," 83f.). For διά with the accusative has here as in 8:20; Rev 13:14 and often in the koine the sense of "through" (BAGD, 181b; Meecham, "Romans," 564).

The same conception occurs liturgically in Col 1:14. It has a long history, as emerges if one studies the connection between God's righteousness and patience, and the resultant forgiveness (cf. Zeller, "Sühne," 64ff.), and is thus led to the interpretation of Exod 34:6f. in the OT and Judaism. Here, in the confession to the breach of the covenant, appeal is made to God's patience and, identical with that, to his righteousness as covenant favor, which will make atonement. Two passages from Qumran stand at the end of the complicated history (cf. Zeller, "Sühne," 70). CD 2:4f. reads: "Patience is with him and rich forgiveness, to make expiation for those who have turned aside from sin." This has a parallel in 1QS 11:12ff.: "When I slip through the wickedness of the flesh, my justification stands in the righteousness of God in eternity. . . . Through his mercy he has brought me near and through his demonstrations of grace comes my justification. . . . With the riches of his goodness he expiates all my sins and through his righteousness he purifies me from all the uncleanness of mankind and from the sin of human children." This is sharpened to the point of heresy in 4 Ezra 8:31-36: "For we and our fathers have passed our lives in the ways that bring death; but thou, because of us sinners, art called merciful. For if thou hast desired to have pity on us, who have no works of righteousness, then thou wilt be called merciful. . . . For in this, O Lord, thy righteousness and goodness will be declared, when [9 thou art merciful to those who have no store of good works."

If the present text grows out of this tradition, it is not concerned with distributive righteousness (contra Jülicher; Lietzmann; Gutjahr; Althaus; Brunner; Kuss; Cadman, "Romans," 532ff.; Schrenk, TDNT, II, 204, but not Lyonnet, "Iustitia," 142). The concern is with the patience of God which demonstrates his covenant faithfulness and which effects forgiveness. The concluding phrase ἐν τῇ ἀνοχῇ τοῦ θεοῦ is not to be taken with προγεγονότων, and in spite of the tempting antithetical parallelism to ἐν τῷ νῦν καιρῷ it should not be understood as a period of patience (contra Pallis; Gutjahr; Kümmel, "πάρεσις," 268; Schrage, "Bedeutung," 83). Asyndetically appended, the phrase looks to that patience with the covenant partner which makes its faithfulness concrete through God's intervention in the act of the death of Jesus (Zeller, "Sühne," 71). Greeks too (cf. BAGD, 703b adducing scholia on Apollonius of Rhodes iv.411ff. and Diodorus Siculus xix.1.3) might have spoken of προγεγενημένα ἁμαρτήματα or ἀδικήματα. But the concern in our text is with the sins of the people of God in its past history. These have been set aside with the change in aeons effected in the death of Jesus, so that already in v. 25b there is contrast between past and present. The themes and individual motifs can be understood quite well in terms of the eucharistic liturgy (Bultmann, Theology, I, 295f.; Stuhlmacher, Gerechtigkeit, 88ff.; Michel; Zeller, "Sühne," 75; Pluta, Bundestreue, 91ff.). Here at any rate the eschatological restitution of the covenant is celebrated and characterized as a demonstration of the divine righteousness. Paul saw that this statement fitted in with his own preaching and he could thus adopt it in a legitimating way. With its catchword it offered him his own theme, as the repetition of v. 25b in v. 26a shows, and it set this theme, as he himself did, into the eschatological horizon of the salvation mediated through Christ's death.

Paul underscores this motif in his restatement (Kühl). For ὁ νῦν καιρός naturally does not mean (contra Sasse, TDNT, I, 205; cf. Kümmel, "πάρεσις," 266) the earthly aeon but the νυνί of v. 21. Hence with this expression, although at first glance it seems to be formulated in antithesis to the end of v. 25b, Paul is not diverging from his original any more than from a supposed penal righteousness. All the same he is not in total agreement with the original. This is shown by the repetition in v. 26a, which would otherwise be superfluous, and very plainly by the solemn infinitive clause, which fits with the hymnic fragment. The participial divine predication is both biblical and liturgical. A final sense is preferable to the consecutive sense, since the εἰς τὸ εἶναι refers back to the motif of ἔνδειξις. The combination of adjective and participle is singular but not incomprehensible, if one regards as at hand the doxological combination of predicates in, e.g., "living and life-giving" or "holy and making holy." At any rate, the two are not to be torn asunder, since otherwise the first member would be speaking of the attribute of God and not his faithfulness. Paul is here combining the tradition and his own interpretation.

καί has almost an explicative sense (Blackman, "Question," 203f.; Schrage, "Bedeutung," 87). 1 John 1:9 is to this extent a parallel (Zeller, "Sühne," 73). The Giver himself makes himself known in the gift. He makes himself known as the Almighty who intervenes in righteousness. Paul's correction of the original is perhaps the reason for the heavy accent on *kairos* in v. 26b. The issue is not merely the once-for-all renewal of the covenant in the death of Jesus, nor merely the forgiveness of past guilt, but the shining forth of righteousness in the kingdom of Christ.

Above all, the addition of διὰ πίστεως in v. 25a gains meaning. This is now taken up and clarified. For the apostle the demonstration of divine righteousness is no longer the renewal of the covenant with God's ancient people. It is universally oriented to faith. πίστις 'Ιησοῦ naturally does not (*contra* H. W. Schmidt) mean Jesus' own faith. As in v. 22 'Ιησοῦ is excised in some variants, probably under Marcionite influence, or else it is assimilated to v. 22 by the addition of Χριστοῦ. In contrast to the standpoint in v. 25b the category of the individual is intentionally introduced (Zahn). This is the reverse side of πάντες in v. 22. God's righteousness reaches beyond the covenant people and is valid for everyone who believes in Jesus the Crucified. Indirectly this says that God's covenant faithfulness becomes his faithfulness to his whole creation and his right which is established in this relationship. The catchword righteousness of God was most welcome to Paul as indication of the change in aeons; nevertheless, he interpreted it in terms of his own theology. Precision is given to *sola gratia* by *sola fide*. The salvation history of the old covenant moves out into the broader dimension of world history. The ὁ ἐκ πίστεως, which characterizes faith as the source of the new life, relativizes all other conditions of existence. The justification of the ungodly, expressed already in the original, is radicalized. It reaches beyond Jewish Christianity as the holy remnant and thus breaks through a final barrier (for other argumentation see Zeller, *Juden,* 183ff.). This will be the theme of the verses that follow.

B. Polemical Development (3:27-31)

[27]*Where is then the possibility of boasting? It is excluded. By what law? (Perhaps) of works? No, but by that of faith.* [28]*For we judge that a person is justified without the works of the law (only) by faith.* [29]*Or is God the God of Jews only? Is he not the God of Gentiles, too? Yes, of Gentiles too.* [30]*For (the truth is) God is one, who will justify the circumcision on account of faith and the uncircumcision through faith.* [31]*Do we then abolish the law because of faith? By no means! Instead we establish the will of God.*

Bibliography: G. Friedrich, "Das Gesetz des Glaubens. Röm 3, 27," *TZ* 10 (1954) 401-417; G. Delling, "Paulusverständnis"; U. Wilckens, "Die Rechtfertigung Abrahams nach Römer 4," *Studien zur Theologie der alttestamentlichen Überlieferungen* (ed. R. Rendtorff and K.

Koch; 1961) 111-127; *idem*, "Zur Römer 3,21–4,25," *EvT* 24 (1964) 586-610; G. Klein, "Römer 4 und die Idee der Heilsgeschichte," *Rekonstruktion*, 145-169; *idem*, "Exegetische Probleme in Römer 3,21–4,25," *Rekonstruktion*, 170-79; E. Peterson, Εἷς Θεός (FRLANT 41; 1926); L. Baeck, "The Faith of Paul," *Journal of Jewish Studies* 3 (1952) 93-110. For Cremer, *Rechtfertigungslehre* see the bibliography for 1:16-17; for Joest, *Gesetz und Freiheit* see the bibliography for 2:1-11; for Wilckens, "Was heisst" see the bibliography for 3:9-20.

This section does not draw inferences (Michel; Lyonnet, *Quaestiones*, I, 129) like chs. 5–8, nor is it a summing-up (Cambier, *L'Évangile*, 146). It does not deal exhaustively with the validity of the law for believers, although a short statement is required. Otherwise Paul's thesis would not be clear. Hence there is reference back to v. 9 and v. 20 and now in such a way that the question of the prerogative of the Jew becomes more concrete in the specifically Jewish question as to possible καύχησις. When God's will is perverted into a principle of achievement this culmination (*contra* Delling, "Paulusverständnis," 110) is unavoidable. Standing on faith alone without the law is also the end of boasting.

The arguments of vv. 27f. and vv. 29f. give a final polemical edge to the theses of vv. 21-26 from the reverse side. The style of the diatribe is again used, with a rapid series of brief questions and answers. Paul's doctrine of justification is in fact a militant one. We are not to weaken this element in the least by letting (cf. Cambier, *L'Évangile*, 410ff., 417ff., 421ff.) the "polemical coloring" serve only to underline the *sola gratia*, as it was understood as early as the Pastorals. Nor should we relativize the material significance of the polemic historically (as Cerfaux, *Christian*, 383f.) by relating it to the phase of the most intense discussion with Jewish Christianity. It is the inalienable spearhead of justification because it attacks the religious person and only in so doing preserves the sense of the justification of the ungodly. Otherwise the Christian message of grace will become a form of religion and Paul's doctrine of justification will be reduced, as happens throughout modern exposition, to a proclamation of salvation which speaks profoundly of the love of God and therefore does not seriously set the pious person before his Judge, no matter how much it may talk about future judgment. Grace is simultaneously judgment because it fundamentally sets even a religious person in the place of the godless. This is the criterion of Paul's theology and the consequence of his christology. So long as the δικαιοσύνη τοῦ θεοῦ is understood only as God's saving action the militant doctrine of the apostle will be levelled down either psychologically or historically.

In the *koine* καύχησις can be used for καύχημα (Bultmann, *TDNT*, III, 649). Here, however, the act is denoted rather than its basis or object. Faith and self-boasting are incompatible, for the believer no longer lives out of or for himself. The eschatological end of the world proclaims itself anthropologically as the end of one's own ways of salvation, whereas the law in fact throws a person back upon himself and therefore into the existing world of anxiety about oneself, self-confidence, and unceasing self-assurance. To the extent that this finds expression in self-glorying it is the mark and power of the world which does not believe even in its religiousness. Faith puts an end to boasting, also among Gentiles according to 1 Cor 1:29. In so doing it overthrows the dominion of the law. It does it so unrestrictedly and forcefully that Paul again plays on the word *nomos*, as in 2:14.

What is meant, of course, is not the principle of faith as a demand (Bläser, *Gesetz*, 24; Bruce; Murray) but the rule, order, or norm of faith (Gutbrod, *TDNT*, IV, 1071; Bultmann, *Theology*, I, 259f.). This makes possible the transition to the antithesis "the law of works." Faith ends the operation of the Torah, not in the opinion of the believer, but in virtue of the new order which establishes him and appears in him, and which is paradoxically called νόμος πίστεως. The thrust of the context stresses the antithesis (Kuss). Hence the genitive of quality designates neither transcending of the Torah (Kühl), nor the law of Israel which points to faith as in v. 21 (Friedrich, "Gesetz," 409ff.; Furnish, *Ethics*, 160), and especially not (Zahn; Lietzmann; Sickenberger) the law which demands faith and must make it a religious work (Friedrich, "Gesetz," 407ff.). ἐξεκλείσθη in v. 27 rules out all such ideas.

Verse 28 sums up the first line of argument and formulates what has just been called "law." In this context λογίζεσθαι does not mean "think," "assume" (Bauer; H. W. Schmidt) but "pass judgment in a dispute" (Heidland, *TDNT*, IV, 288; Lyonnet, *Quaestiones*, I, 136). In non-Greek fashion it is, of course, the insight of faith, not reason, that decides (Heidland, *Anrechnung*, 62). Hence v. 28 takes the form of a doctrinal statement and ἄνθρωπος without the article does not refer categorically to mankind, eliminating the distinction between Jew and Gentile (*contra* Klein, "Römer 4," 149), but has the force of "one" (Wilckens, "Zu Römer," 588; Michel). Thus v. 20a is varied in such a way that πίστει inserts the catchword of the thesis of v. 22a and draws the weight of the sentence to itself. "By faith alone" is the only adequate rendering of the situation.

What is new, then, in these verses? The answer is this: If v. 20a has summarily said that a person cannot be justified by the works of the law, v. 28 with its catchword points out that he is not supposed to be justified in this way (*contra* Wilckens, "Was heisst," 54ff., 72ff.). God's intervention in Christ has made this plain. Simultaneously the nature of justifying faith is further elucidated to the extent that antithesis to the works of the law includes antithesis to the boasting of the pious person necessarily intended with such works (Furnish, *Ethics*, 150f., 193f.). As the motivating element of works of the law is the attempt to achieve security before God (Bultmann, *TDNT*, VI, 223f.), so faith grows out of the premise of v. 19b and is thus devotion to him who alone establishes salvation and therefore always justifies the ungodly. The law is of no value to the ungodly. Since it does not presuppose the power of God alone to save, it simply provokes the possibility of boasting even when this is hidden in its opposite, namely, despair. Inasmuch as the works of the law respond to this provocation, they are for Paul a higher form of godlessness than transgression of the law and are thus incompatible with faith. In vv. 27f., on the basis of the nature of faith, the end of the law is proclaimed in terms of its anthropological outworking (Eichholz, *Paulus*, 225; though cf. Cambier, *L'Évangile*, 153).

The same result is achieved in vv. 29f. from the standpoint of salvation history. There is no reference now to any Jewish objection (*contra* Michel; Wilckens, "Zu Römer," 588). With incomparable audacity this thesis is directed instead against the dominant idea of God in rabbinic teaching (Billerbeck), cf. *Exod. Rab.* 29 (88d): "I am God over all that come into the world but I have joined by name only with you; I am not called the God of the idolaters, but the God of Israel."

Here, in terms of the concept of the covenant, and as in fact later in Marcion, the saving action of God is separated from his work as Creator and Judge. The person called to performance also binds God to it (Gutbrod, *TDNT,* IV, 1057) and separates him in his essential nature from the impious, as the Jewish sharpening of the Torah shows (Bläser, *Gesetz,* 108f.). Since the Gentiles are not left to themselves, this leaves room for false gods and demons alongside God. With the universality of grace the singularity of God simultaneously becomes questionable. A religious sphere, not the world as such, becomes his domain. In contrast to all this Paul links justification, as eschatological salvation, to the faithfulness of the Creator (Klein, "Römer 4," 148f., fails to see this). For this reason he recalls the Jewish Shema and instructively varies the acclamation εἷς θεός (cf. Peterson's [⁹ book). Paul turns Israel's own presuppositions against itself.

The one God can only be the one who has a claim to all and who encounters all, not just as Creator, but also as he who establishes salvation. *Solus deus* cannot be separated from *sola gratia,* as is perceived already in 1QH 10:12–13:16f. (Schulz, "Rechtfertigung," 167). Indeed, Paul is even more radical. *Sola gratia* has its only basis in *solus deus,* namely, in the omnipotence and freedom of the Creator and Judge of the world. Hence it cannot be restricted to the covenant on Sinai. The monotheistic confession shatters a conception of the law which makes salvation a privilege of the religious. As Creator and Judge God is also the God of the Gentiles and therefore the salvation of the ungodly. As merely the God of the Jews he would cease to be the only God. The full force of this revolutionary statement is seldom perceived. Hence the argument is necessarily made irrelevant that takes the Torah as an example of the moral law and only hears from these verses the universal validity of the gospel (Kirk, 65, 70f.).

εἴπερ means "if else" (BDF, §454[2]), here "then certainly" (BAGD, 220a). δικαιώσει is (*contra* Lagrange; Schlatter) a logical future, since justification already follows. By accepting *solus deus* faith lays hold of God's sole efficacy as its only basis and hence it can no longer rely on the works of the law. The religious differences between περιτομή and ἀκροβυστία, which profoundly determine life and the world in the pre-Christian era, are thus overcome. Jews and Gentiles are both called to faith alone. The use of the two different prepositions ἐκ and διά is rhetorical as in 4:11f.; 5:10; 1 Cor 12:8; 2 Cor 3:11. Yet it is not without material significance (*contra* Cambier, *L'Évangile,* 156f.). Religious differences are overcome. But there are still Jewish- and Gentile-Christians. The former are not to despise the history from which they derive; this would be too much to ask of them. They are simply to grasp their origin afresh in Christ beyond this history. As for Gentile-Christians, it is evident from them that salvation history does not follow an immanent continuity which can be calculated. Faith for them is not a door to this history which they have themselves pushed open; it has been miraculously opened for them. The differences are relativized in the solidarity of faith. They mark the path and place where salvation is experienced and are not factors in salvation or perdition as the religious person thinks.

In face of the polemic of vv. 27-30 the question and answer in v. 31 seem to be paradoxical. The expression νόμον καταργεῖν and ἱστάνειν correspond to rabbinic usage presupposed also in 4 Macc 5:25 (Schlatter). As the conclusion of the passage (e.g., Kühl) the verse is incomprehensible. Paul gives not the slightest indication that νόμος here is "an expression of moral truth" (Cremer, *Rechtfertigungslehre,* 390), the sum of the law in the NT sense (Schlatter; Althaus; Gaugler; Murray), not even in its transcending by the gospel (W. Manson, "Notes," 156f.; cf. Bultmann's criticism in *Theology,* I, 260), or the divine order (Kühl) or legal system (Lyonnet, *Quaestiones,* I, 140ff.). The statement makes sense only as a transition to ch. 4 (Lagrange; H. W. Schmidt; Friedrich, "Gesetz," 416; cf. the survey in Cambier, *L'Évangile,* 157ff.). It refers back to v. 21b in which the law is also witness to the righteousness of faith and νόμος is the will of God stated in the OT (Lietzmann; Bardenhewer; Huby; Dodd; Schrenk, *TDNT,* I, 760f.; Bläser, *Gesetz,* 37; Wilckens, "Rechtfertigung," 120f.; "Zu Römer," 589ff.; *contra* Klein, "Römer 4," 150f.). Paul, then, does not have merely the judicial function of the law in mind (Nygren; Grundmann, *TDNT,* VII, 649), nor is he attacking its present validity while acknowledging its significance for the past (Baeck, "Faith," 106f.). Finally he is not defending the law dialectically in the sense that the act of faith is possible only in antithesis to it (Joest, *Gesetz und Freiheit,* 178; Baulès, a Roman Catholic variation). Instead, the OT will of God can be manifested only when the *nomos* comes to an end as a principle of achievement (G. Bornkamm, *RGG,* V, 183). Hence the law does not contradict the righteousness of faith; it summons us to it.

C. Scriptural Proof from the Story of Abraham (4:1-25)

In three arguments Paul's thesis is now shown to be vindicated by the OT (cf. Schlatter). The example of Abraham shows that there already faith was justified, that this took place before circumcision, and therefore that the promise is fulfilled only for believers. Use of Abraham as a model corresponds to the Jewish tradition which closely connects the covenants with Abraham and Moses and in the light of Isa 51:2 emphatically calls the patriarch "our father." Paul attacks his opponent anew at the very point where the latter feels that he is strongest and least vulnerable. In a way highly typical of his polemical style, Paul wrests from him the right of appeal both to the fathers and to Scripture. In no sense is the example chosen at random (*contra* Conzelmann, *Outline,* 169f., 190; Ulonska, *Paulus,* 170). Jewish tradition, of course, has to be decisively reinterpreted, with the help of rabbinic methods, to serve the apostle's purpose.

1. Abraham Justified by Faith (4:1-8)

¹*What shall we say, then, that Abraham our forefather according to the flesh has found? ²For if Abraham was justified by works, he is entitled to boast. But (this will not stand up) before God. ³For what does scripture say? "Abraham believed God, and it was reckoned to him for righteousness." ⁴Now to him who works wages are not reckoned as a gift but as a due. ⁵But to him who does not work but believes in him who justifies the ungodly, his faith is counted as righteousness. ⁶So David also calls the man blessed to whom God imputes righteousness without works: ⁷"Blessed are those whose iniquities are forgiven*

105

and whose sins are covered; [8]*blessed is the man to whom the Lord does not impute his sin."*

Bibliography: Cf. the bibliography for 3:27-31. O. Schmitz, "Abraham im Spätjudentum und im Urchristentum," Aus *Schrift und Geschichte. Theol. Abhandlungen A. Schlatter dargebracht* (1922) 99-123; A. Meyer, *Das Rätsel des Jakobusbriefes* (BZNW 10; 1930); J. Jeremias, "Zur Gedankenführung in den Paulinischen Briefen," *Studia Paulina,* 149-151; G. von Rad, "Faith Reckoned as Righteousness," *The Problem of the Hexateuch and Other Essays* (Eng. tr. 1966), 125-130; C. Dietzfelbinger, *Paulus und das Alte Testament* (1961); E. Jacob, "Abraham et sa signification pour la foi chrétienne," *RHPR* 42 (1962) 148-156; C. Butler, [1] "The Object of Faith according to St. Paul's Epistles," *Stud.Paul.Congr.*, I, 15-30; H. M. Gale, *The Use of Analogy in the Letters of Paul* (1964); E. Jüngel, "Theologische Wissenschaft und Glaube im Blick auf die Armut Jesu," *EvT* 24 (1964) 419-443; K. Berger, "Abraham in den paulinischen Hauptbriefen," *MTZ* 17 (1966) 47-89; H. Binder, *Der Glaube bei Paulus* (1968); E. Käsemann, "The Faith of Abraham in Romans 4," *Perspectives*, 79-101; D. Lührmann, "Pistis im Judentum," *ZNW* 64 (1973) 19-38. For Cremer, *Rechtfertigungslehre* see the bibliography for 1:16-17.

In the style of the diatribe the proof is now introduced with a question. The corruption of the text in v. 1 (cf. Zahn; Lietzmann; Lagrange) can hardly be described as beyond remedy (Bultmann, *TDNT,* III, 649). εὑρηκέναι has perhaps been put before κατὰ σάρκα and related to it because the statement about Abraham as our forefather according to the flesh did not fit a later situation. Since, conversely, the righteousness of faith also could not be regarded as a fleshly discovery, the verb was left out in B Or 1739 (Zahn; Sanday and Headlam; Kühl; Schlatter; Barth). In context, however, there is little point in asking how far Abraham is our forefather according to the flesh. Dissection of the question is no help (Zahn; Kühl; Luz, *Geschichtsverständnis,* 174) since a negative answer would then be expected. The dominant reading is the only possible one, since it asks about Abraham's "gain," perhaps in reminiscence of Gen 18:3 (Michel, *Bibel,* 57; Jeremias, "Gedankenführung," 47, 2; Wilckens, "Rechtfertigung," 116). κατὰ σάρκα is not said in disparagement of the earthly reality.

Clarification is offered in v. 2 with a reference back to 3:27ff., i.e., to the relation between the works of the law and boasting. Here καύχημα means the reason and basis for boasting. An imaginary understanding of the statement (Bultmann, *TDNT,* III, 649; Kuss) is possible in view of what follows but it is not necessary and a different construction would in that case be more suitable (H. W. Schmidt). Paul can agree hypothetically with his opponent's view in order to reject his premise in v. 2b. In this case v. 2b does not have to have the restrictive sense for which nothing in the argumentation thus far has prepared us: before men but not before God.

The quotation comes from Gen. 15:6. γραφή, as in 9:17; 10:11, means Scripture as a whole and not the individual saying (Schrenk, *TDNT,* I, 753). Paul's appeal to Abraham as a physical ancestor finds its closest parallel in Josephus *B.J.* v.380 (BAGD, 709a). As in Gal 3:6ff. the apostle as a Jewish-Christian conducts the discussion with the material and methods of the synagogue (Schmitz, "Abraham"; Billerbeck; A. Meyer, *Jakobusbrief,* 100). For the rabbis the patriarch is completely righteous, and especially in Hellenistic Judaism he is a model of faith. Discussion of Gen 15:6 is old and widespread (Billerbeck; Heidland, *TDNT,* IV, 289). In direct or indirect polemic against sacrificial acts the saying originally meant that God in free appraisal regards trust in the promise as a fulfilment of the covenant relation (von Rad, "Faith"; Heidland, *Anrechnung,* 79f.). Later juridical exposition of the idea of the covenant takes the saying legally. Thus חשב is translated by the commercial phrase λογίζεσθαι εἰς, "to reckon as." From the perspective of its effect, then, faith is a meritorious work, as in 2 Macc 2:52. As trust and existential obedience it may be distinguished from fulfilments of the commandments as their basis. Concretely, e.g., as a monotheistic confession, it becomes one work among others (Billerbeck; Heidland, *Anrechnung,* 93ff.). This combination of faith and works, which also determines the interpretation of Gen 15:6 in Jas 2:23, stands in antithesis to Paul's position (Conzelmann, *TDNT,* IX, 388). Hence the apostle's argument is in no way conclusive for Judaism.

Indeed, this argument is probably attacking (A. Meyer, *Jakobusbrief,* 99f.) the expository tradition of Judaism. At least a new understanding of faith controls it. Philo's description of the hero of faith should not be adduced at this point (*contra* Billerbeck; Schoeps, *Paul,* 200ff.; Sickenberger; cf. the excursus in Sanday and Headlam). For πίστις (*contra* Lagrange) is not a διάθεσις of the soul leading to solid character (cf. Schlatter, *Glaube,* 60-80). Philo too, of course, can say in *Quis rerum divinarum heres* 95: δικαιοσύνης δ' αὐτὸ μόνον ἔργον, thus espousing the dominant view of Palestinian Judaism that faith is an act—a view which influences Paul as well when he speaks of obedience. Nevertheless this passage shows that Paul's concept of faith is complex (cf. the excursus in Kuss). More strongly than elsewhere, but as in 9:33; 10:11, exegesis of Gen 15:6 causes the accent to fall on the element of trust in the divine promise. πιστεύειν with ἐπί or with a simple dative is not typical of Paul and he does not develop it into the formula πιστεύειν εἰς (Bultmann, *TDNT,* VI, 203). For this reason the language about a personal relation of faithfulness (Brunner) is highly questionable, to say nothing of language about union with Christ (many Roman Catholic commentators, e.g., Cambier, *L'Évangile,* 345ff., 370). Even if it is correct that Paul never offers a definition (Bornkamm, *Paul,* 141), we cannot be content to point to the co-existence of different nuances. The very multiplicity of possible aspects raises the question of their material center and unity and demands sharp demarcations.

In fact the Jewish (*contra* Lührmann, "Pistis," 20ff.) and Christian mission gave the concept its predominant meaning (Bultmann, *TDNT,* VI, 181f., 208f.) In its specifically Christian use we must always start with, and continually refer back to, the relation of πίστις to the word of proclamation. Even as "believing" persons, who as such stand "in the Lord" and "in grace," believers are and remain (10:16) hearers of the preaching and stand "in the gospel" (1 Cor 15:1). In no sense, whether as *fides qua* or *fides quae creditur* (the faith with which or the faith which we believe), can faith stand on its own apart from the word. By nature it is the relation of reception and preservation of the message of salvation. This emerges in the formula πιστεύειν εἰς, which not by chance in Paul is continually resolved by participial, relative, or ὅτι clauses. Faith is neither a virtue, a religious attitude, nor an experience. It is faith by hearing. It enters into the promise of salvation and becomes obedient to it.

This means that one may not arbitrarily extend its "object," which in reality is its "basis," whether to supraterrestrial life (Amiot, *Key Concepts*, 74), or to the religious order in Christ (Cambier, *L'Évangile*, 347, 376), or to being overwhelmed by salvation history whose facts are imparted and interpreted in the message (Cullmann, *Salvation*, 323). Since faith differs from sight, it is always bound to the word of the gospel, and exclusively so, as the prepositions ἐϰ and διά make plain. That says conversely that faith also is not dogmatic acceptance of certain events of salvation even though this be inner conviction (Weinel, *Paulus*, 88) and even though it is true that the gospel does speak of the events of salvation, as in 3:24ff. or 1 Cor 15:3ff., and these can and should be reflected upon in dogmatics. The essential danger of theological thinking arises out of the false alternatives to which the Pauline dialectic has constantly misled people. For the apostle Christian faith is not the development and deepening of a general trust in God (cf. on this Ridderbos, *Paul*, 246), and it cannot therefore be seen in analogy to a relationship of love (*contra* Baulès, 147f., 159f.). Nor is it orientation to a number of salvation events which continually extends its hold in the church and the world (*contra* Butler, "Object of Faith," 28ff.).

Strictly speaking it is just as inappropriate to speak of experience or a disposition as it is to speak of the object of faith or of the acceptance of a system of truths or facts of salvation. Either way christology is shortchanged. The Lord whom we experience has on this view nothing to offer us that we could not say to ourselves or experience in some other way. If we make him an object as the mediator of the facts or truths of salvation, he then becomes an entity that we can control or at least count on in the church—an entity which can be represented by a system or fused with ecclesiology and anthropology. Faith is constituted by the fact that with the preaching of the gospel the Lord who is the basis of the gospel comes upon the scene and seizes dominion over us. The saving events recounted in the gospel qualify him so that he cannot be confused with others or remain unrecognized. Hence the cross and resurrection are the center. Because as Lord he does not allow himself to be taken in, we are constantly dependent on his word. Faith is living out of the word which bears witness to his lordship, nothing more and nothing less.

This enables us to decide two hotly debated questions. The first arises out of the expressions ἐϰ and διά πίστεως and discusses whether and in what way faith is a condition of salvation. For the apostle this is obviously no problem at all, at least not in the manner or from the standpoint of the discussion. If one insists on putting the question in this form, faith is not just *a* condition but *the* condition of salvation as such. This has to be so, since salvation comes to us in the gospel and has to be, and can only be, appropriated in the gospel. Materially we thus have a "condition" but only in its exclusiveness, and therefore only in antithesis to other possibilities of salvation which might be offered or demanded.

According to Paul's anthropology man lives by the fact that he must let the decisive thing be said to him and this decisive thing is always the addressed claim and promise of him who is or wants to be our lord. Thus a person can live only in faith or superstition, since always and everywhere it is a matter of which lord's voice we must, can, and will listen to. Faith and superstition are lived out hearing and to that extent, and only to that extent, both are in their own way obedience.

The prepositional formulae make it plain that only the hearing lived out on the basis of the gospel relates to the Lord who in distinction from all others is salvation. They mirror the *solus Christus* and maintain the *sola fide* on the premise that each person belongs to the one whom he hears. Faith is thus the "condition" of salvation, not as a human achievement, but as receiving and keeping the word which separates us from all lords and all salvation outside Christ, and which causes us to live herein.

The second problem is at the moment more dangerous. It arises out of the use of "faith" and "believe" in the absolute, which is incontestably typical of Paul. A radical form of this is Gal 3:23, 25, which speaks of the epiphany of faith as release from the Jewish Torah. Accordingly faith is not supposed to be a human work, but something that is done to a person (Jüngel, "Wissenschaft," 430). It is not an individual attitude but a power which invades the world (E. Schweizer, "Mystik," 200), a supraindividual total phenomenon (Stuhlmacher, *Gerechtigkeit,* 81f.; cf. Wilckens, "Zu Römer," 588), a divine occurrence and a transsubjective entity (Binder, *Glaube,* in exaggerated form; cf. 12, 53, 56ff., 64ff., 73). Such statements are inspired by the assessment that faith is primarily God's decision (Neugebauer, *In Christus,* 165ff.). This is possible, however, only if the singular OT use of πίστις for the faithfulness of God in 3:3 were the dominant one in Paul and characterized God's eschatological act of salvation (rejected also by Neugebauer, 163). The truth in all these aspects is that the gospel intends to embody itself in the apostolate and also in the disciples and hence to set up signs, admittedly always ambiguous, in the world. It is equally correct that no one believes in isolation but only in the community and that the new aeon has dawned in this community. Paul, then, speaks of "faith" and "believing" in the absolute in the same way that he makes faith and the Spirit parallel, namely, to denote the mark of the members of Christ's body who are summoned into the new aeon.

It should not be overlooked, however, that this faith is one which is always tempted, exposed to the danger of backsliding. Hence there can be no faith by proxy and no implicit faith. So also the confession is not a person's "answer to the faith" (Neugebauer, *In Christus,* 169) but a statement of faith which is frequently problematic and which has always to be tested, interpreted, and proved. There is a confession which is understood and manipulated as a way of dispensing with faith. To emphasize the *fides quae creditur* at the expense of the *fides qua creditur,* and isolation from it, is to misunderstand the apostle just as badly as in the reverse case (Ridderbos, *Paul,* 246). If faith is hypostatized in Gal 3:23, 25, this takes place in no other sense than with the righteousness of faith in 10:6ff., namely, in antithesis to the Torah and as the equivalent of the gospel as the true *fides quae creditur.* We must insist strongly that faith in Paul, even when it is oriented to the *fides quae creditur,* thus to "homology," is the act and decision of the individual person (Bouttier, *En Christ,* 77f.; Conzelmann, *Outline,* 173) and is thus an anthropological and not primarily an ecclesiological concept (*contra* Neugebauer, *In Christus,* 167; Jüngel, "Wissenschaft," 429; Cerfaux, *Christian,* 143ff.). Otherwise we will have a renewal of the liberal antithesis of justification and Christ piety (e.g., Deissmann, *Paul,* 168-170), which is an offshoot of the distinction between Paul's juridical theology and his mystical theology (Lüdemann, *Anthropologie;* Schweitzer, *Mysticism*).

Now obviously it is not enough simply to exhibit the existential structure of a movement between the "No longer" and the "Not yet," which may also be found in superstition (*contra* Bultmann, *Theology*, I, 322). Faith certainly exists only in negation of superstition and therefore in temptation and victory, in exodus and hope. For the apostle, however, the present and future are no less threatening dimensions than the past and it is an illusion to separate them from the dominion of the powers and of death. The crying of the children of God for freedom always characterizes faith, and in this respect too it is always reception of the word which even as gospel does not cease to be promise. In "homology" faith also tells us that the promise of the word has already become reality and its reception creates new life. Hence faith can be defined even if new interpretation of the definition is always required. It is hearing of the word of the gospel which cannot be regarded as done once and for all but which also cannot be broken up into individual points as though it had never happened and as though there were no community [▶ of believers. Faith is not a venture in the sense that every life must be a venture and sacrifice; it is a venture upon and with Christ (Eichholz, *Paulus*, 233). The word does not simply call to it so that it is then an achievement, whether by assent or by following an example (cf. Bultmann, *Theology*, I, 283f. in criticism of Mundle, *Glaubensbegriff*, 99f.; Schlatter, *Glaube*, 335ff.). The word also creates faith, since we continually come out of an existence and world of superstition and are thus incapable of true hearing on our own. Only in the address of grace does faith achieve its knowledge, trust, certainty, hope, and task. Apart from this word, which sets faith at once both in contradiction with the world and also under the assault of its fleshliness, there is no guarantee of salvation for it.

Only along these lines can one understand the thrust of the passage and Paul's understanding of the πίστις of Abraham and of the quotation from Gen 15:6. He does not have in mind here either a quality or a meritorious work of the patriarch but the latter's devotion to the issued word of promise, according to which God wills and acknowledges nothing but faith. This proves the absurdity of a desire for fame or a reliance on works. Devotion to the word implies looking away from self and expectation of salvation from God alone.

Verses 4-5, in authentically Pauline fashion, ground v. 3 in such a way that the most important thing, namely, the mutually exclusive antithesis of faith and works, "to believe" and "to work," is presupposed. In v. 4 the argument consists of a reference to a generally accepted rule which catches up what is said in v. 2. Here, then, the mode of expression is non-theological. ἐργάζεσθαι means simply "work" and λογίζεσθαι εἰς means "credit," as in commercial language. The emphasis is on the secular antithesis, found formally (cf. Hauck, *TDNT*, V, 565) in Thucydides ii.40.4, between χάρις and ὀφείλημα. We find a theological application of the same rule in the rabbis (Billerbeck).

Verse 5a is obviously an antithetical development of the analogy of v. 4. But the apostle no longer has enough patience to round off his metaphors and comparisons well. The application is mingled with the comparison and overlaps it. This means that the terminology, now used theologically, receives a different sense (Heidland, *Anrechnung*, 119f.; Gale, *Analogy*, 173ff.). The "one who does not work" is identified with Abraham, and ἐργάζεσθαι no longer means "to work" but "to be concerned about works." Since the reckoning now refers to

God's gracious action toward those who have no accomplishments, he can talk of "to credit" only in a transferred sense. Materially it concerns a spoken judgment fixed in the OT, thus an award (Schlatter, *Glaube,* 359f.). Paul thus comes closer again to the original sense of Gen 15:6 (Dietzfelbinger, *Alte Testament,* 16, 26).

If it is asked why the technical formula from commercial language is retained, the answer is that the apostle's concern is first with the dimension of the word-event and secondly with the paradoxical character of grace. Faith is not in itself righteousness. In responding to the promise it finds fulfilment in the gospel, journeying between them. Its justification cannot be separated from the act of the divine address. We do not have it (*contra* Baulès) alongside and apart from this address. To this extent (*contra* the protest of Lagrange, 123ff.) it is "forensic" and "imputative." Faith is not a substitute for righteousness (Cremer, *Rechtfertigungslehre,* 341), and one may not infer from the "reckon" that God treats faith as though it were righteousness (*contra* Weinel, *Paulus,* 89; for a correct view cf. Schlatter, *Glaube,* 348ff.). It is a condition as poverty is, or waiting for blessing. It is the place where the Creator alone can and will act as such.

This may be seen most clearly in Paul's further characterization, which is nowhere so fully developed although it is the basic theme of his soteriology. It stands in sharp contrast to the Jewish view which, to cite an example from Qumran (CD 1:19), maintains that justification of the sinner can be only a sign of ungodliness and thus stands opposed to the heretical statement of *4 Esdr.* 8:33ff. (Schrenk, *TDNT,* II, 215f.; Stuhlmacher, *Gerechtigkeit,* 226f.). Even if the sinfulness of the pious is radically asserted, the Torah is also intensified. It is obvious, then, that grace can be imparted only to the pious, who then doxologically confess their sin.

Expositors, then, constantly find trouble with Paul's radical and obviously polemical formulation and weaken it by contesting the antithetical element (Cambier, *L'Évangile,* 166), speaking of gross exaggeration (Kirk), and disputing the relation to Abraham (H. W. Schmidt; Berger, "Abraham," 65f.). The statement is misplaced psychologically in the empirical realm (Dodd) and expounded in terms of strict ethical self-judgment for which the distinctions between the pious and the ungodly are relative and ultimately irrelevant (Zahn; Kühl). It should be noted that the formula is fashioned on liturgical predications of God. Hence it is a basic characterization of the divine action. For this reason one is not to deduce from it a process of development: a person is indeed ungodly prior to justification but does not remain so, being set on the path of sanctification (Taylor, *Forgiveness,* 57f.; Bruce). Even if Paul in fact asserted a change of existence for Christians, a reason must be given why the apostle in this context defines the nature of faith at the deepest level by the justification of the ungodly.

The decisive question of the doctrine of justification, the epistle, and Paul's theology as a whole, is whether this sharp and rhetorically exaggerated sentence is an extreme case or the truth of Christian faith as such (so Schlatter; Leenhardt), whether reception of grace always presupposes and brings a person's reduction to nothing (Bultmann, *Theology,* I, 284). Indubitably Paul means it in the latter sense. Then neither psychology nor the moralizing, which speaks without understanding of the justification of the wicked (Lietzmann), provides further help.

Here as in 1:18ff. it is presupposed that the nature of sin and the corresponding understanding of self are known only in the light of the gospel. According to this gospel the achievements of works and faith are mutually exclusive, while in Jewish and pagan thought there is no εὐσέβεια, and therefore no true relation to God, without human achievement. If Abraham did not have this, he could no longer be, as in Judaism, "an example of an outstanding religious personality" (Dodd; Bruce). Measured by the world around, he would be irreligious and ungodly (Bornkamm, *Paul*, 142; Jacob, "Abraham," 154). If Gen 15:6 tells us that the nature of faith is non-achievement, then faith as a consequence has to do with him who makes the ungodly righteous. With Abraham as the example, what is said about him serves as a model of faith in general, and it is thus formulated in the present tense and in a general maxim (Wilckens, "Rechtfertigung," 113). The antinomian polemic, which can speak with the same definiteness of the God of the Gentiles too in 3:29 and without which the doctrine of justification would not be Pauline, does not allow us to understand *sola gratia* positivistically and edifyingly (*contra*, e.g., Huby). For Paul faith is not the same as piety. For the apostle the strictest piety and morality can be the garment of ungodliness. Unlike Philo, he does not view faith as a human capability and therefore it also cannot be defined in terms of mankind. To define faith, he has to say who God is. He does this in his doctrine of justification by speaking of the *creator ex nihilo*. Faith is the Yes to the message of this God. It is thus confession that this God always and only makes the ungodly righteous. Ungodly means more than "impious" (*contra* Michel). It is a predicate of the person who has to do radically with his Creator and who learns that he must be created anew in grace. He has nothing to which to appeal and will produce nothing that might prejudice God's creative act. He is the man who has no ground of boasting before God.

In this light we may now interpret the relation between πίστις and δικαιοῦσθαι (cf. the excursus in Kuss). The use of the verb is controlled, not by secular Greek, but by OT and Jewish thought, especially in the LXX (Stuhlmacher, *Gerechtigkeit*, 217ff.). What is meant is pronouncing righteous. This is an eschatological act of the Judge at the last day which takes place proleptically in the present. As already in the analysis of the noun, it is to be established again that a saving action is designated thereby. Although the forensic sense is plain, condemnation is not meant as with κρίνειν. The OT and Jewish tradition of the covenant idea continues in the meaning "pardon."

This finding, which clearly indicates a declaratory event, has run into problems now that history-of-religions research, especially in view of the sacramental statements of the apostle, has shown irrefutably that δικαιοῦσθαι has also the sense of effectively making righteous as in 3:24 and as Roman Catholicism has constantly maintained. The difficulty can no longer be forcefully resolved by alternatives (*contra* H. W. Schmidt). We are again confronted by the Pauline dialectic which protects a central concern against misunderstanding on two fronts. This very passage makes this plain. The declaratory element is retained through the whole chapter and it is emphasized by the link with the reckoning-formula. On the other hand, interpretation along the lines of an "as if" has already been warded off and the relation to the idea of creation has been brought to light. God makes the ungodly person a new creature; he really makes

112

him righteous. The two strands can be united only when the creative power of the divine word is presupposed and the link between justification and this word is not snapped. The new creature comes into being through the word and will be preserved only under the word. There is Christian existence only in the right and ongoing hearing of the word which thus forms the constitutive mark of the new obedience and of sanctification. Such a hearing includes perception of him who as Creator is also the final Judge and who as Judge sets us where creation began, namely, before his face where grace alone avails, since without grace there can be no life (Furnish, *Ethics*, 152f.). As eschatological address, then, justification is that act by the Judge which sets us free for new creation (Schrenk, *TDNT*, II, 215f.) and alone makes us capable of it. Faith is recognized to be righteous because, in a way that is past human comprehension, it allows God to act on it instead of wanting to be and do something in itself and thereby seeking a ground of boasting. It lets itself be placed by the word in the possibility of standing outside self before God through Christ.

According to a basic Jewish principle there have to be two witnesses to the truth, and according to rabbinic practice the Prophets or Writings are quoted alongside the Torah (Michel). In vv. 6ff. what has been said is thus confirmed by Ps 31:1f. LXX, the psalm being ascribed to David. Since the psalm contains the catchword "not impute," which will be emphasized in vv. 9f., Paul is in fact proceeding according to the *gĕzērâ šāwâ*, the second of Hillel's seven criteria of exposition (J. Jeremias, "Gedankenführung," 149ff.; Barrett; Cambier, *L'Évangile*, 168). In virtue of the analogy between them two similar phrases in Scripture mutually interpret one another.

The quotation interrupts the argument from the example of Abraham but does not end it. For the type of the messiah king stands as a witness (Lagrange), not as a second example (Schlatter; Nygren), alongside Abraham. The highest authority in Judaism apart from Abraham and Moses agrees with the statement concerning the righteousness of faith. As often, καθάπερ provides a basis, not just a comparison. μακαρισμός is already used technically (Hauck, *TDNT*, IV, 367) and in the context it appears as a prophetic promise of salvation, although this does violence to the original sense of the saying (Kuss). As always in the NT beatitudes μακάριος means eschatological salvation and not merely heavenly bliss. The conclusion from v. 6 is the anticipated Pauline interpretation of the quotation. Not to reckon sin is to reckon righteousness. In content this is given greater precision as forgiveness. Since forgiveness finally happens only to the sinner, the quotation proves that God creates salvation, not on the basis of works, but for the godless. This rounds out the proof. What remains surprising is that Paul never speaks of forgiveness except when he adopts πάρεσις in 3:25, and only here in the quotation does he refer to forgiving (though cf. Hauck, *TDNT*, IV, 369; not noted by Nygren), although this catchword, which is common in Qumran and the deutero-Pauline corpus, characterizes the earliest baptismal message and in Matt enters into the eucharistic tradition too. For the apostle salvation, as avoidance of the plural "sins" also indicates, is not primarily the setting aside of the past guilt (*contra* Kühl) but freedom from the power of sin (Bultmann, *Theology*, I, 287; Schlatter, *Glaube*, 334; Schrenk, *TDNT*, II, 205). A different theological horizon results in a different set of terms.

2. Abraham Justified Before Circumcision (4:9-12)

⁹(Is) this blessing (only) for the circumcision or also for the uncircumcision? For we quoted: "Faith was reckoned to Abraham for righteousness." ¹⁰How then was it reckoned? In the state of circumcision or of uncircumcision? Not in circumcision but in uncircumcision! ¹¹He received the sign of circumcision as a seal of the righteousness of faith in uncircumcision. In this way he was to become the father of all uncircumcised believers, so that righteousness might be reckoned to them. ¹²(At the same time he was to be) also the father of the circumcision, namely, of those who not merely belong to the circumcision but also follow in the steps of the faith of our father Abraham (demonstrated) in uncircumcision.

Bibliography: F. J. Dölger, Sphragis (Studien zur Geschichte und Kultur des Altertums 5/ [ ]
3-4; 1911); W. Heitmüller, "Σφραγίς," Neutestamentliche Studien. Georg Heinrici zu seinem
70. Geburtstag (1914) 40-59; E. Maass, "Segnen, Weihen, Taufen," Archiv für Religionswissenschaft 21 (1922) 241-286; E. Dinkler, "Jesu Wort vom Kreuztragen," Neutestamentliche Studien für Rudolf Bultmann zu seinem 70. Geburtstag (ed. W. Eltester; BZNW 21; 2nd
ed. 1957) 110-129; G. W. H. Lampe, The Seal of the Spirit (1951). For Jeremias, "Gedankenführung" and Dietzfelbinger, Alte Testament see the bibliography for 4:1-8; for Wilckens,
"Rechtfertigung," "Zu Römer," and Klein, "Römer 4" see the bibliography for 3:27-31.

Paul now considers the objection that the beatitude quoted relates to Israel and is thus valid only in the sphere of the circumcision, as in fact was asserted by the rabbis since Sir 44:20 (Billerbeck). Is not the righteousness of faith, then, restricted to the same sphere? Judaistic opponents actually thought so. Hence the question is important in practice as well as principle.

Abraham again serves as an example. This time Gen 15:6 confirms the quotation from the Psalm, the converse of the order in vv. 7f. The assumption of an argument from analogy (Jeremias, "Gedankenführung"; H. Müller, "Auslegung," 143) is probable but not compelling (Kuss). In rabbinic argumentation as in the diatribe counterquestions are typical. Proof with the help of scriptural chronology clearly corresponds to Jewish exposition. Official synagogue reckoning puts Gen 17:10f. some 29 years later than Gen 15:6 (Billerbeck). Paul again smites his foes with their own weapons. Even Jewish interpretation has to concede that the Judaistic objection is untenable. Circumcision is not an indispensable presupposition of justification.

Yet the apostle is not satisfied with this answer. Not only for the reader of the Bible and the Jew, but for the theologian, the question now arises what significance circumcision had for Abraham anyway. The fact that the problem occurs only here, but is not relativized (Dietzfelbinger, Alte Testament, 13), is not unimportant. Looking at the matter in terms of salvation history leads deeper than the actual debate, which in the first instance brought to light the structure of justifying faith (Wilckens, "Rechtfertigung," 121).

The reference in Gen 17:11 is to a sign of the covenant. Paul intentionally replaces that with "sign of circumcision." Epexegetically circumcision counts as a sign (Zahn; Michel; Barrett, but cf. Lagrange). Textual emendation (Rengstorf,

114

TDNT, VII, 258) is neither necessary nor justified. Yet the change is materially important and has considerable consequences. In context the apostle cannot use the thought of the covenant. This has been reduced to the point of complete removal (Klein, "Römer 4," 154 refers with some exaggeration to a usurpation of the text for which there is no analogy; Wilckens, "Zu Römer 3:21ff.," 597 does not agree that the idea of the covenant has been left out intentionally). While it uses synagogue methods, Paul's argument from Scripture is worthless for us, since it ignores the historical meaning of the text (Dodd; Lagrange refers to difficulties of exegesis in the fathers).

Because σημεῖον can mean "impress of a seal," "stamp" (BAGD, 747-48), it can be taken up again in σφραγίς, "sealing" (Murray). From the chronological sequence it then follows that circumcision confirmed the righteousness of faith received previously. This has broad implications. It is unclear and hotly debated whether the use of σφραγίς is to be explained in terms of the train of thought, as in 1 Cor 9:2, or whether it presupposes fixed traditions to be noted here. The rabbis have a phrase "seal of circumcision," although attestation of this is late (Billerbeck, IV, 32f.; Fitzer, *TDNT,* VII, 947f.). Hence the text might be alluding to a technical usage (Sanday and Headlam). The problem becomes important when it is linked with the description of baptism as a seal, for which there is plain attestation from Hermas, and when this is derived from what is postulated to be the earlier language of Judaism relating to circumcision. Then baptismal language would have at least an indirect influence on our passage (von Stromberg, *Studien,* 92f.; Michel; Althaus; probable, Maass, "Segnen," 53, 77ff., 107; possible, Bultmann, *Theology,* I, 137f.; Klein, "Römer 4," 154; negative, Fitzer, *TDNT,* VII, 949f.; Lampe, *Seal, passim*).

The question is more complex than it is usually made out to be. In *Barn.* 9:6 it is presupposed that the adversary knows the term. But the sense "confirmation" will fit in there as it does here (BAGD, 796-97; Heitmüller, "Σφραγίς," 40ff.; Lietzmann; Barrett; Kuss). σφραγίζειν should not be derived as a baptismal term solely on the basis of the vocabulary of circumcision. According to Rev 7:3ff. sealing was meant originally for the last judgment, so that the meaning of σφραγίς as a mark of protection and possession was used. This sense has a long prior history with an eschatological orientation already in the OT and Judaism (Dinkler, "Jesu Wort," 117f.). The understanding of circumcision, and by derivation of baptism, as a "seal" has at most latched onto this older tradition.

Nevertheless, since Col 2:11ff. presupposes a traditional typology of circumcision and baptism in primitive Christianity, the possibility has to be seriously considered that "to seal" in 2 Cor 1:22; Eph 1:13; 4:30 belongs to the fixed vocabulary of baptism. When relating the noun to circumcision here and in *Barn.* 9:6, the tradition of Col 2:1ff. can hardly be left out of the picture. That Paul could interpret OT events sacramentally may be seen from 1 Cor 10:1ff. If certainty cannot be achieved, it is probable that the Jewish vocabulary of circumcision is adopted through the mediation of baptismal language.

Yet the juridical nuance must not be overlooked either (Rengstorf, *TDNT,* VII, 258). For Paul Abraham's circumcision is the documentation and validation of the righteousness of faith. εἰς τὸ εἶναι points not just consecutively (Lagrange; H. W. Schmidt) but finally (Kühl; Bultmann, *TDNT,* VI, 206) to the will of God confirmed in circumcision. The second infinitive can hardly be a parallel but is to be subordinated as consecutive (*contra* Kühl; Lagrange). The Jewish theologoumenon of Abraham as the father of all proselytes (Billerbeck) acts as a foil. It is not just extended but in its concrete context reversed (Klein, "Römer 4," 155f.). As Abraham already received righteousness before his circumcision, so one does not have to become a proselyte to attain to righteousness. Abraham is thus the father of all believers. His example shows that everything depends only on faith. Becoming a proselyte is not a prior condition of this. In fact, then, Judaism is robbed of both Abraham and circumcision (Nygren; C. Müller, *Gottes Volk*, 52; Dietzfelbinger, *Alte Testament*, 18; Wilckens, "Zu Römer," 598f.).

This roughness is softened in v. 12. As often, Paul hastens to qualify an exaggerated statement. An ongoing relation of the patriarch to Judaism is now acknowledged. In fact the apostle is concerned to be able to call Abraham also the father of the circumcision, since any other course would take the promise away from Israel and contest its salvation history (Wilckens, "Zu Römer 3:21ff.," 599ff.). Yet one should not find merely the coordination of a "just as–so also." Everything depends on the accent. If it is already intolerable for Jews to be mentioned only second, a further reduction follows at once in the participial clause, in which the stress is on the conclusion.

From an early date καὶ τοῖς has given constant trouble to expositors. This is inevitable if the point of the antithesis is not accurately clarified. Like 2:15ff. it says what alone can count as true circumcision and can lay claim to Abraham. What is the factual situation and the claims based on it mean nothing. What is not circumcision of the heart in virtue of obedience does not merit the name. Here again, only the Christian is the true Jew, and Abraham is called the father of the circumcision only as the father of Jewish-Christians. To that extent the antithesis contrasts Jews and Jewish-Christians (*contra* Kuss). This explains the readoption of the article (Luz, *Geschichtsverständnis*, 175; Cambier, *L'Évangile*, 171; Michel; though cf. Lietzmann; Kuss).

In reality the slogan περιτομή no longer belongs to the Jews. Like the sonship of Abraham, it appertains only to believers, to Christians from among Gentiles as well as Jews. Trust should not be placed in a sign. Everything depends on the reality of a change in obedience. The metaphor is found already in the rabbis (Billerbeck) and occurs also in 2 Cor 12:18; 1 Pet 2:21. It means staying in rank. Strong emphasis is again laid on the fact that the faith of Abraham was that of someone not yet circumcised and that it led thus far to the justification of the ungodly. The solemn concluding title no longer applies to the forefather according to the flesh as in v. 1, but to the father of Christianity (Schrenk, *TDNT*, V, 1005).

The theological significance of the passage is not just that in it Paul with the help of Jewish methods of exegesis energetically proves and defends the righteousness of faith from Scripture. His understanding of salvation history is given sharper contours than in vv. 1-8. For if one cannot say that salvation history is the core of Pauline theology (*contra* Cullmann, *Salvation in History*), one also cannot deny (*contra* G. Klein) that salvation history is inseparably connected with the apostles' doctrine of justification, and that this is evident here. The "theological indifference" of Jews and Gentiles (Klein, "Römer 4," 153) is not the point either in 3:29f. or in this passage. It is a modern inference from *sola fide*. If it is maintained that the history of Israel is "radically desecularized and paganized" (ibid., 158, etc.), not only is the proof from Scripture in its historically demonstrable argumentation rendered questionable, but the whole appeal to the OT is rendered meaningless. If the experience of the righteousness of God is limited to the post-crucifixion period (ibid., 148) and prior to that related to Abraham exclusively (ibid., 155), both the exclusiveness and the choice of Abraham as an example are absurd and constitute a hopeless difficulty for exegesis. Marcion's example should then be followed and this chapter, along with much else in the NT, eliminated.

On the other hand, the text in fact makes it clear that "the category of a salvation history which runs in chronological continuity is ill adapted to serve as a hermeneutical principle in elucidating Paul's view of Abraham" (ibid., 169). If a particular understanding of salvation history becomes clear here, another, namely, the Jewish one, is undoubtedly shattered (ibid., 164). Paul does not establish unbroken continuity between Abraham and Christ or promise and fulfilment (ibid., 157f. contra Wilckens, "Rechtfertigung," 121-27). Except in 9:27ff.; 11:13ff. Paul does not use the motif of the holy remnant. It is true that he does not detach faith from history. It is a complete misunderstanding, however, to argue that for him faith is in principle trust in history and to find in history its primary basis (Wilckens, "Rechtfertigung," 123, 127). It is also ridiculous to claim that Abraham had to believe in prospect of the eschatological ratification of the promise (ibid., 125). Salvation history as Paul presents it is marked by paradoxes. In its earthly course, then, it is discontinuous and cannot be calculated (cf. the fine if exaggerated statement of Barth that its heroes are a question to which it gives no answer). The next section will show that its continuity is the power of God (Bornkamm, *Paul*, 148f.) which awakens the dead, and that will of God which cannot be read off from history but is heard in the word of promise. For Paul salvation history is the history of the divine promise which runs contrary to earthly possibilities and expectations. Thus the OT and NT coincide in it while Jewish history and Christian history diverge. Salvation history is the history of the divine word which finds faith and gives rise to superstition, but which cannot be an address to remarkable, isolated individuals nor the basis of a speculative interpretation of history.

3. On the Model of Abraham the Promise is Only to Faith (4:13-25)

[13]*For the promise to Abraham or his seed that he should be heir of the world (did not come) on the strength of the law but on the strength of the righteousness of faith.* [14]*If those who keep the law are heirs, then faith is meaningless and the promise is void.* [15]*For the law brings wrath. But where there is no law, there is also no transgression.* [16]*This is why (it is true): By faith and consequently by grace, so that the promise may be valid for all his descendants, not just for those who are of the law, but also for those who are of the faith of Abraham. He is the father of us all,* [17]*as it is written: "I have made thee the father of many nations." He believed in the presence of the God who gives life to the dead and calls that which is not into being.* [18]*Against (earthly) hope*

he believed in hope that he should become the father of many nations accord-
ing to the saying: "So (great) shall thy seed be." [19]*Without weakening in faith*
he considered his own body which was as good as dead—he was almost one
hundred years old—and also the barren womb of Sarah. [20]*He did not doubt*
God's promise in unbelief but, strong in faith, gave God the glory [21]*and was*
fully assured that what God had promised he could also do. [22]*For this reason*
it was reckoned to him for righteousness. [23]*But the words "it was reckoned to*
him" were not put in Scripture for his sake alone [24]*but for ours too, to whom*
it will be reckoned (as well). We believe then in him that raised from the dead
our Lord Jesus, [25]*who was put to death for our offenses and raised again for*
our justification.

Bibliography: P. L. Hammer, "A Comparison of KLĒRONOMIA in Paul and Ephesians,"
JBL 79 (1960) 267-272; E. Sjöberg, "Neuschöpfung in den Toten-Meer-Rollen," *ST* 9 (1955)
131-36; A. Ehrhardt, "Creatio ex Nihilo," *The Framework of the NT Stories* (1964) 200-233;
O. Hofius, "Eine altjüdische Parallele zu Röm IV.17b," *NTS* 18 (1971/72) 93f.; H.-M.
Schenke, "Aporien im Römerbrief," *TLZ* 92 (1967) 881-88; R. Bultmann, "Ursprung und
Sinn der Typologie als hermeneutischer Methode," *TLZ* 75 (1950) 205-212; L. Goppelt,
"Apokalyptik und Typologie bei Pls.," *TLZ* 89 (1964) 321-344; J. R. Mantey, "The Causal
Use of *Eis* in the NT," *JBL* 70 (1951) 46f.; D. M. Stanley, "Ad historiam exegeseos Rom.
4:25," *VD* 29 (1951) 257-274; K. Romaniuk, "L'origine des formules pauliniennes 'Le Christ
s'est livré pour nous . . . ,' " *NovT* 5 (1962) 55-76; G. Delling, "Partizipiale Gottesprädikationen in den Briefen des Neuen Testamentes," *ST* 17 (1963) 1-59. For K. Berger, "Abraham" and Dietzfelbinger, *Alte Testament* see the bibliography for 4:1-8; for Klein, "Römer
4" and Wilckens, "Rechtfertigung" see the bibliography for 3:27-31.

The word "promise" is the connecting link in vv. 13-25. The argument is grouped [
around three statements. In vv. 13-17a the idea that the promise is attached to
the law is contested. In vv. 17b-22 the promise is characterized by the fact that
only faith in the resurrection of the dead corresponds to it. The conclusion is
drawn in vv. 23-25 that Abraham's faith is an anticipation of Christian faith. Hence
Scripture really testifies to Paul's thesis by the example of Abraham. Verses 13-16
do not form an independent section (*contra* Kühl; Lagrange; Schlatter; Nygren;
Wilckens, "Rechtfertigung," 124) any more than do vv. 13-17 (*contra* Barth;
Michel; Kuss), since it is hard to find any clear break. Finally, the antithesis of
the righteousness of faith and the law was the determinative point already in
vv. 1-8. This is taken up again here with a focus on the promise as the background
of what follows. The characterizing of the promise in v. 13b is decisive for all
else.

The theme of the ἐπαγγελία has central theological significance for Paul and
the NT writings influenced by him. It designates the incalculable continuity in
salvation history of the divine word in its eschatological orientation. As the act
and object of the προευαγγελίζεσθαι of Gal 3:8 it is a complement of the gospel
(Schniewind, *TDNT*, II, 579), namely, the gospel as a reality already in salvation
history and as hidden in history (cf. 1:1f.). Conversely the gospel is the promise
realizing itself eschatologically. Paul's concept is truncated, however, if we do not
take this complementarity with full seriousness by making the promise merely the
announcement and the gospel the fulfilment as the result of a process of devel-

opment (Zeller, *Juden*, 83, *contra* H. W. Schmidt who for this reason can speak of the assurance of salvation in a highly non-Reformation manner). The two are materially identical but each marks a different aspect (Moltmann, *Hope*, 147f.). The mutual relationship shows that eschatological occurrence breaks into real history with the word and thus qualifies history already as the sphere of divine creation and direction (Asmussen). The distinction makes it clear that history and eschatology are not the same but are related only by the word as God's self-address. The word, then, enters into history in such a way that it makes a place for itself and also conceals itself in it, as misunderstanding, offense, and obduracy show. The gospel does not sever the promise as it does the law, and only as promise does it retain its eschatological character and horizon. One may speak of realized eschatology only very dialectically and even then not exclusively in the anthropological category of "futurity" (*contra* Bultmann's basic thesis in *History and Eschatology*).

The Hellenistic concept of ἐπαγγελία acquired its terminological sense only when it merged with the Jewish tradition, developed especially in apocalyptic (Berger, "Abraham," 53), of the promises and assurances of God (Billerbeck; Schniewind, *TDNT*, II, 579f.; Moltmann, *Hope*, 144f.). In particular this explains the fixed eschatological usage which makes the future world the theme of hope in *2 Apoc. Bar.* 14:13; 51:3; 4 Ezra 7:119. In this regard the promised occupation of the land by Israel is obviously transferred to the end-time as in Hebrews. The problem of the relation between promise and law, which is an important one for Paul, is also discussed in Judaism. According to 2 Macc 2:17 the law is itself the bearer of the promise, and thanks to this function it was already known to Abraham and his generation in unwritten form (*2 Apoc. Bar.* 57:2; 59:2). Since fulfilment of the law is also a condition of performance of the promise according to *2 Apoc. Bar.* 46:6, despair can be voiced in 4 Ezra 7:119: "For what profit is it to us if the eternal age is promised to us but we have done works which bring death?" Paul is thus arguing against the background of Jewish tradition and problems, and he is using the methods these provide with the same conciseness as the rabbis do.

Nevertheless, he does this polemically and with a very different intention. The promise has nothing in common with the law positively. Rather it is antithetical to it. The antithesis has salvation-historical depth to the extent that, as in Gal 3:6ff., it implies the contrast between Abraham and Moses as the two prototypes of the conflict, and thus acquires a global dimension. The lack of understanding of an existentialist interpretation of Paul for the theological significance of these connections is grotesquely brought to light when it is seriously maintained that Paul lived wholly for the moment (Ulonska, *Paulus*, 216) and that his quotations are nothing more, then, than golden words for a past generation (ibid., 207ff.).

Naturally he is not thinking here of a general law (*contra* Zahn; Kühl; Murray). Jewish tradition allows us to take διὰ νόμου instrumentally (Michel). But διὰ δικαιοσύνης πίστεως refers more to the sphere of power in which promise becomes possible (Barrett). Its content is provided by the infinitive with its allusion to Gen 22:17: "Thy seed will inherit the cities of their enemies." In good rabbinic fashion (Behm, *TDNT*, III, 779f.; Zeller, *Juden*, 91) Paul extends the promise, presumably inspired by the blessing of all nations in the following verse. To be sure, "inheriting the earth," which is undoubtedly a technical formula, has not yet been adequately explained thereby. It occurs with reference to Jacob and Israel in *Jub.* 19:21; 22:14; 32:19, cf. Philo *De vita Mosis* i.155. In *Jub.* 17:3 and the saying of R. Nehemiah (*c.* 150) preserved in *Mekilta Exodus* 14:31, it is connected with Abraham (Berger, "Abraham," 69; Billerbeck): "Thus wilt thou find of Abraham that he has taken possession of this and the future world as a reward of faith, as it is written, He believed in Yahweh and he reckoned it to him for righteousness." Clearly, then, we can follow a process of development at the beginning of which stands the worldwide extension of the blessing of Abraham in Sir 44:21: "They shall take possession from sea to sea and from the river (Euphrates) to the end of the earth." The motif of the conquest is first given a cosmic reference. This could be all the more readily accepted in Hellenistic Judaism because Abraham embodied the type of the wise man to whom, according to the Stoics, world dominion belongs (cf. Cerfaux, *Christian,* 224ff. on spiritualizing in Philo). All the same, this hypothesis is not necessary. The earthly promise is applied apocalyptically to the future world. This leads to what has become the traditional messianic predicate in Heb 1:2 of "heir of the world." It also leads to the adoption of the Jewish tradition for Christianity in Matt 5:5; 1 Cor 6:2. The present text presupposes this final stage, as will be shown, and it does so with express appeal to Abrahamic sonship.

σπέρμα is not given a messianic interpretation as in Gal 3:16, as v. 13c shows (Michel). In negatively formulated sentences ἤ can be coordinative (BDF, §446). Paul spoke of "seed" mostly, as he obviously does here (Lagrange; Dietzfelbinger, *Alte Testament,* 19ff.), with a view to believers. This is in sharp contrast to the Jewish view. The argument is not so parallel to that in Galatians 3 that the promise as a gift has to be set in antithesis to a contract (*contra* Kühl; Nygren; Barrett; Bultmann, *Theology,* I, 282). Then in the light of the impossibility of fulfilling the law, stress would be laid on the necessity of the promise which waives works of the law (Lietzmann; Dodd; Althaus). Either way a contrary view, which sees the text as a general discussion (Kühl) in which the specific content of the promise is not at issue (Nygren), appears ridiculous (Jülicher; Kuss). This is refuted by the adoption of κληρονόμοι in v. 14a, the conclusion in v. 16b, and the continuation of the thought in v. 17. Precisely the content of the promise is at issue, namely, its universalism, which could not be attained through the law (Moltmann, *Hope,* 147). The details are to be seen accordingly.

The reality of the law does not correspond to that of the promise. In origin the Semitic οἱ ἐκ again refers to commitment to a sphere of lordship which is confirmed by human action. One is tempted to translate: "Those who stand under the principle of the law." But this (Bultmann, *TDNT,* VI, 213; H. W. Schmidt) would force us to speak erroneously of the principle of faith as well. The formula οἱ ἐκ νόμου makes sense only if there are not several origins and commitments for existence. The alternative is clearly stated in v. 14b. καταργεῖσθαι, which is often used eschatologically, denotes here the radicalness, although not the violence, of the event (Michel). The promise and faith would be pointless if the law could produce the heirs of Genesis 22. But according to 7:8 the law provokes transgression and therefore brings one necessarily (Michel *contra* Stählin, *TDNT,*

V, 433, who speaks of *opus proprium* on p. 443, however) under the wrath of the Judge. This is not a second argument (*contra* Kuss; Barrett; Bläser, *Gesetz*, 168). It is the basis of v. 14b.

Verse 15a omits the intermediate thought that wrath is reached by way of transgression, but it is added in v. 15b. The negative formulation, however, makes it a transition to v. 16a, where grace can take the place of wrath. The transitional δέ is not merely better attested than γάρ (Lietzmann) but it is materially preferable. The statement, for which there are rabbinic parallels (Billerbeck), has the form of a legal gnome (Michel) and expresses a general truth (Zahn), so that νόμος has a transferred sense (*contra* H. W. Schmidt; Luz, *Geschichtsverständnis*, 176), and it is thus not an exact parallel to 5:13. The point of the statement, however, is that in the days when the promise was given to Abraham there was no Jewish law, which for Paul is inseparably related to Moses.

The conclusion is drawn in typical rabbinic style in v. 16a. The omitted subject is not God's plan in general (Lagrange; Barrett; possible, Kuss), but the promised inheritance which is achieved by faith and therefore by grace. The infinitive does not have a final sense (*contra* Zahn; Michel; Oepke, *TDNT*, II, 430). It is consecutive, offering the conclusion. βέβαιος does not here mean "believable" (Zahn) nor "legally valid" (Schlier, *TDNT*, I, 600ff.) but "firm, certain," as in 2 Cor 1:7. The stress is on παντὶ τῷ σπέρματι.

The theme in vv. 16c-17a is the universalism of the promise of salvation. It thus follows that one may not from the general context refer τῷ ἐκ τοῦ νόμου to Jews as distinct from Christians (*contra* Kühl; Jülicher; Lietzmann; Dodd; Michel; Klein, "Römer 4," 160f.). The formulation is parallel to that in v. 12b and is to be understood in the light of it (H. W. Schmidt). The predication of Abraham as our father is aimed polemically at the Jewish claim. It radicalizes the idea of Abraham as the father of proselytes along the lines of Matt 3:9, which says that God can raise up children to Abraham even from the stones. That purpose is also served by the quotation from Gen 17:5, in which ἔθνη incontestably (*contra* Zahn) means the Gentiles, so that Christians alone can be in view in v. 16c as in v. 12. Strictly the formulation fits only Jewish-Christians, who alone can show the characteristics of deriving both from the law and from the faith of Abraham. But since Gentile-Christians are included in what follows, the antithesis characterizes in loose fashion Christians from both Jews and Gentiles (Zahn; Jülicher; Barrett; Kuss; Althaus; Wilckens, "Rechtfertigung," 125).

The transition to definition of Abraham's faith as faith in the resurrection in v. 17b is a hard one. This is because a liturgical predication of God is quoted and is then linked to the biblical citation, which is not to be understood as a parenthesis (Lagrange *contra* Lietzmann). Dependence of the new statement on the end of v. 16, and the resultant conclusion that Abraham alone is the father of believers before God (Schlatter; Althaus), have to be forced on the text. κατέναντι οὗ is loosely connected with the subject in τέθεικα: "to be set before this one."

As in 2 Cor 1:9 Paul (Billerbeck) makes use of the second benediction in the Prayer of Eighteen Benedictions: "Yahweh who makes the dead alive." This is why the unusual ζωοποιεῖν is used instead of the usual ἐγείρειν. Characteristic of the apostle is the christological variation on the Jewish predication: "Who raised the Lord Jesus from the dead."

The second attribute is also traditional. Like ζωοποιεῖν, καλεῖν is used in the present, not just of a generally valid statement (Delling, "Gottesprädikationen," 31), but of an ongoing event. As in Isa 48:13; Wis 11:25 it denotes God's sovereign creating in the Word (K. L. Schmidt, *TDNT,* III, 489f.). The hymnic style, the immediate context, and parallels in *2 Apoc. Bar.* (Lietzmann) all suggest liturgical tradition. *2 Apoc. Bar.* 21:4 reads: "Thou who from the beginning of the world hast called forth what was not previously there." 48:8 reads: "By a word thou dost call into life what is not there." The later church continues the same tradition: *2 Clem.* 1:8, "He has called us who are not and resolved that we should be out of non-being"; *Herm. Man.* 1:1, "who called all things out of non-being into being"; *Apostolic Constitutions* viii.12.7, "Who brought all things out of non-being into being." It is anticipated almost word for word in Philo *De opificio mundi* 81, and in *De specialibus legibus* iv.187 in the same formula the verb "call" replaces "bring forth," as in our text. Further variations may be found in *De migratione Abrahami* 183; *Legum allegoriae* iii.10; *De mutatione nominum* 46; *Quis rerum divinarum heres* 36. In Qumran (according to Sjöberg, "Neuschöpfung," 131ff.) 1QH 3:19-24; 11:10-14 regard entry into the fellowship as a new creation and thus set in parallel remission of sins and resurrection. Closest to the Pauline statement is the saying in Joseph and Asenath 8:9: "Thou supreme and mighty God, who givest life (ζωοποιήσας!) to all things and callest out of darkness into light and out of error to truth and out of death to life."

The debate about the theme of creation out of nothing, which is sometimes introduced into this text, has importance only for the history of religions. It should not be overlooked that the motif plays a part in some philosophical discussions in the Greek world (Ehrhardt, *Creatio,* 210ff.; BAGD, 341b). Rabbinic Judaism also discussed the problem (Ehrhardt, 218f.; Weiss, *Untersuchungen,* 100ff.; Foerster, *TDNT,* III, 1016f.). Nevertheless, speculations about it were regarded as unprofitable and it was found hard to think of creation apart from the ἄμορφος ὕλη specifically mentioned in Wis 11:17. The statement ὅτι οὐκ ἐξ ὄντων (Codex A, variants ὅτι ἐξ οὐκ ὄντων) ἐποίησεν αὐτὰ ὁ θεός in 2 Macc 7:28 attacks this Greek cosmology, and Philo too speaks of non-being as non-ordered matter (Weiss, *Untersuchungen,* 59ff., 72f.) in the same way as rabbinic Judaism (ibid., 140ff.). On the other hand, because of the certainly appropriate observation that Judaism was more interested in the question of the "whence" than the "out of what," we cannot ignore the fact that the expression "non-being" can have been taken only from the Greek world, as is plain in Philo. Mere rejection of the influence of Greek cosmogony is inadequate for the apocalyptic hope in a new cosmic creation. This began already in Qumran and necessarily had some impact on the doctrine of creation. If in Judaism the worldview is in general not very important at this point, and the main stress is on God's omnipotence instead (Weiss, *Untersuchungen,* 88ff., 140ff.), nevertheless the nihil is important, since it represents the reverse side of this omnipotence (*contra* Weiss), and the corresponding Christian statements cannot be explained in terms of anti-Gnostic polemic (ibid., 167). Along these lines the apocalyptic tradition is not taken seriously. In the debate with a philosophical doctrine a theory which is untenable for primitive Christianity is advanced and theological interpretation is reduced to a minimum (ibid., 178f.).

The present passage is by no means unclear, and its significance for Paul's

122

theology as a whole (cf. 1 Cor 1:28) cannot be overvalued (*contra* Ehrhardt, *Creatio*, 214ff.). The context makes this clear. If the two traditional formulae are related here, this happens according to the principle stated in *Barn.* 6:13: ποιῶ τὰ ἔσχατα ὡς τὰ πρῶτα, which shaped most profoundly both Jewish and Christian eschatology (cf. H. Gunkel, *Schöpfung und Chaos in Urzeit und Endzeit* [1895]). The very wording of the text makes it inconceivable that there should be polemic against the use of the concept of creation (Berger, "Abraham," 72). It also makes it obvious in what sense Paul can and must speak of a creation out of nothing. He is concerned with the justification of the ungodly. But this is not a rhetorical exaggeration of the *sola gratia*. It is an anticipation of the resurrection of the dead, which as no other event deserves to be called a creation out of nothing and presents the eschatological repetition of the first creation. As hardly anywhere else the full radicalness of Paul's doctrine of justification is brought out here. When the message of this justification is accepted, there is unavoidably linked with it a reduction to nothing which deeply shakes the righteous by associating them with the ungodly. No one has anything of his own to offer so that a new creature is both necessary and possible.

Paul's bitter attack on works of the law finds its root here, and at this point no mediating compromise is possible, but only the alternative of rejection of Pauline theology at its core. This polemic is of course a doctrine for battle, but as such it should not be relativized as "time-bound" for this reason, since it is the criterion for understanding or misunderstanding the doctrine of justification and what Paul calls faith: With the gospel one has to accept oneself as completely new and as changed by Christ.

This is, however, only one side of the matter at hand, although one cannot stress it too strongly in opposition to an interpretation which understands faith as experience of the love of God and infilling with spiritual power (Baulès represents this important trend in exposition). The other side comes to light in the fact that here creation, resurrection, and justification declare in fact one and the same divine action. This means that justification, as the restitution of creation and as resurrection anticipated in the stage of trial (*Anfechtung*), is the decisive motif of Paul's soteriology and theology and that these have always to be interpreted in terms of it. It also means that justification cannot be located and isolated in soteriology, and especially not in anthropology, but is rooted in the apostle's christology and his doctrine of God.

When God's omnipotence comes on the scene, as it has done in creation and will do in the resurrection, and as it does here in justification, the world and history are always involved in justification. In the anthropological reality the Creator's grasping of his whole creation is announced. Only when this cosmological dimension is overlooked can one deny that the standpoint of the chapter is that of salvation history. This plunges the universalism of the verse and the relation between promise and gospel into obscurity. Finally, there is again manifested here the validity of the distinction between justification which is granted to the individual as a gift and the power of divine righteousness, expressed therein, as the claim of lordship over creation. The two aspects are related by the fact that the sovereignty of God in grace and his omnipotence which effects resurrection finally coincide for Paul and are eschatologically actualized at every moment through his creative word.

ὡς ὄντα, which Philo uses in the same way in *De Iosepho* 126, does not mean then (contra Zahn; Kühl; Billerbeck; undecided, Michel) that what is not is treated as though it were. It is consecutive (Lietzmann; Barrett; H. W. Schmidt; Hofius, "Parallele," 93): "so that it is." The paradoxical formulation of v. 18a rests on the fact that always God creates only where from the earthly standpoint nothing exists. That then defines the peculiarity of faith, which, as trust in the miracle addressed in the promise (Bultmann, TDNT, VI, 206f.), is hope transcending all mere earthly hope, which always counts on what can be controlled (Bultmann, TDNT, II, 206). What is meant is not the venture of the amor fati, which in forward flight abandons itself to the current of futurity, nor of believing the absurd, which waits for illusory miracles. It is instead an exodus from the sphere of the calculable into horizons opened up by the word, namely, the horizons of a future under the saving will of God. Primarily Paul is here setting the Greek concept of hope in juxtaposition with another concept which can be understood only in terms of the biblical tradition. The paradox of the expression defines exactly the paradox of the conduct demanded.

The infinitive in v. 18b does not relate to God's purpose (Kühl) nor to the content of faith (Bultmann, TDNT, VI, 206; Kuss), since the ἔθνη of the quotation are Gentile-Christians. It is consecutive (Lagrange). Abraham is a model of the faith of those who as Gentiles must rely on the God who calls non-being into being. They are the seed whose origin and number the patriarch could not foresee.

What is basically stated in vv. 17b-18 is elucidated in vv. 19-21. The argument holds only if one overlooks the story of the sons of Keturah in Genesis 25 (Lietzmann). For (contra Kuss; Gutjahr) it does not seem to be assumed that Abraham retained his miraculously restored generative power. τῇ πίστει is not instrumental (Sanday and Headlam). It is a dative of closer definition. τῇ ἀπιστίᾳ in v. 20 has a causal sense (Kühl). κατενόησεν is emphatically made the predicate instead of the preceding participle. The strongly attested introduction of οὐ in D G K L P et al. ruins the point (Bardenhewer; Bruce; Ridderbos, Paul, 250; K. A. Bauer, Leiblichkeit, 146). The patriarch was not weak in faith because, even though aware of the human reality, he trusted in what is from a human point of view impossible (Leenhardt; Franzmann). Faith does not first show itself as such in reckoning with the impossible. Nevertheless, by trusting in God, what is from the earthly standpoint impossible, even though it be recognized as such, is not the boundary of hope. If the paradox of v. 18a illustrates this, it now emerges that hope in the promise of the God who raises the dead is the true mark of faith and that this has to stand the test already in the present. Faith arises over the graves of natural possibilities. νενεκρωμένον σῶμα occurs in the funerary inscription cited in Inscriptiones Graecae III/2 (repr. 1974), No. 1355. νέκρωσις is common in the koine (Deissmann, Light, 97f.).

In what follows we have an antithesis to v. 19 and not a psychological sequence (Michel contra Lagrange). ἀπιστία as lack of trust (Bultmann, TDNT, VI, 207) catches up the phrase "not weak in faith." Naturally εἰς is not causal (contra Mantey, "Use") but expresses the relation of doubt which measures the word by earthly realities and for this reason is not radically bound by the promise. ἐνεδυναμώθη is not to be supplemented with "in his body" (contra Zahn). The verb goes with τῇ πίστει. Faith is not an organ by which power is received (Grundmann, Kraft, 117). As in the whole context it is reception of the word. If we let ourselves be bound to this alone, the power of God grasps us and makes possible the doxology which the Gentiles did not raise according to 1:21. God is given the glory only when we let him be God, namely, omnipotent and sovereign. Constantly and not just cultically the believer stands in such a doxology when he looks away from himself and in doing so responds to the promise.

πληροφορεῖν is a rare word expressing the *koine* love of emphasis. It first means "to fill," "to be filled" and "full," and then full certainty and firm conviction (Delling, *TDNT*, VI, 310). Like the passive elsewhere ὃ ἐπήγγελται describes God's work. δυνατὸς καὶ ποιῆσαι is proverbial (Billerbeck) and in the Diaspora at least it is a predicate of God (cf. Philo *De Abrahamo* 112, 175; *De Iosepho* 244; *De specialibus legibus* i.282; *De Somnis* ii.136).

Faith here is characterized in exemplary fashion as unconditional and joyful devotion to the promise of the divine omnipotence. If such statements are connected with Philo's fine depiction in *Quis rerum divinarum heres* 92f., Paul could not, of course, speak of the "work of a great and olympian reason." For him gnosis is obedience to the word only as a firm clinging to God's faithfulness even in trial. Verse 22 returns to the beginning and offers the result. Very clearly here ἐλογίσθη means address. Equally clearly faith is not yet salvation. If it may be dangerous to call it a condition (cf. Schlatter, *Glaube,* 174), the apostle does use the prepositions ἐκ and διά to indicate the place and limits of the reality of salvation. Faith is not a preparatory condition of grace (as especially in Roman Catholic exegesis). Nor is it the subjective form of the spiritual experience of salvation (Baulès, 73). It is the answer to the promise, which does, of course, have to be proved. Human beings do not precede God; God does not bypass mankind. The relation between justification and faith dialectically combines these two statements.

The biblical proof of the thesis of 3:21-26 concludes with v. 22. Further proof is not offered in vv. 23-25 (*contra* Klein, "Römer 4," 163). They are an appeal to the reader: All this concerns him. Indirectly this has already happened when in vv. 16f. Abraham is named the father of all, including Gentiles, and the quotation from Scripture is actualized when the liturgical formulae in v. 18 remind us of God's constant work and the argument in v. 19 is pointed toward faith in the resurrection. Nevertheless, what is said in vv. 23ff. develops the relationship of Scripture to the present thematically. The distinctiveness of the passage is illuminated by a comparison with Sir 44:10-15, which discusses the significance of the pious in covenant history for the living. There the permanence of their inheritance and remembrance in the community is extolled. In this passage, however, the distinction of Abraham is seen in the fact that his story was preserved in Scripture (Klein hopelessly misunderstands this in "Römer 4," 163f.).

Verse 23 does not merely underscore the antithesis in v. 24 (*contra* Kuss). When promise and gospel complement one another, and when these terms indicate the continuity between the OT and the NT, Scripture as such necessarily moves into an eschatological horizon and therefore also has eschatological significance. The dimension of historical tradition and illustration (Ulonska, *Paulus,* 174; Klein, "Römer 4," 163) is thus transcended. If events and acting personages are not taken out of history they are also not limited to it. They mark basic situations in salvation history and hence there is no going beyond them. They constantly proclaim the future and serve as criteria for understanding the present. The generation of the end-time that has come with the gospel finds in them an anticipation and prophecy of its own destiny with all its possibilities, dangers, and realities. Conversely they too, if they are not removed from historicity as illustrations of timeless truth, stand in a peculiar concealment which ends only when the light of the end-time falls on them and removes them from the sphere of purely moral example such as we find, e.g., in 1 Clement.

Here then for the first time we come up against the problem of Pauline typology. If, seen in terms of the history of religions, this develops out of thinking which counts on a cyclical course of the world (Bultmann's thesis!), the NT use presupposes the schema of the two aeons as its framework. If thereby the old and new aeons initially succeed one another, a variation sets them in spatial confrontation as the heavenly and the earthly aeons. Each of these understandings has its distinctive function. The schema of succession deals with the prefiguring of the eschatological events in the old aeon, while the schema of spatial levels deals with the shadows of the heavenly in the earthly. The two aspects can merge into one another as in Hebrews, or as in the case of Paul in Gal 4:25f. When this happens the earthly shadow is simultaneously an incomplete or even antithetical prefiguring of the future.

In view of this complex situation typology cannot be explained in terms of mere comparison (Galley, *Heilsgeschehen,* 161ff.), analogy (H. Müller, "Auslegung," 93ff., 175ff.), or repetition (Bultmann, "Typologie," 205). Nor (*contra* Goppelt, *Typos;* E. Fuchs, *Hermeneutik* [4th ed. 1970] 192; H. Müller, "Auslegung," 175ff.—93 is right here but inconsistent) can one get by with the idea of "prefiguration" alone, since type and antitype can be seen in an opposite movement, as in Rom 5:12ff. For the same reason NT typology cannot be adequately characterized in terms of the element of intensification between type and antitype or, as 1 Cor 10:1-13 shows, be subsumed under the schema of promise and fulfilment. Christ and Adam stand in contrast as do blessing and curse, and they correspond precisely in this universally valid contrast. Over against this the elements of repetition and intensification have only secondary significance (H. Müller, "Auslegung," 95). This means, however, that typology in Paul can be related neither to cyclic thinking nor to thinking that is in the strict sense salvation historical, true though it is that salvation history is proclaimed in it (Cullmann, *Salvation,* 162f.). Not just any historical events are used in typology but only those which positively or negatively correspond to the relation between the primal and final times (*contra* Galley, *Heilsgeschehen,* 190). Typology is constitutively for Paul an apocalyptic mode of expression (*contra* Goppelt, "Apokalyptik," 328; perceived in germ in Schoeps, *Paul,* 233; Kertelge, *Rechtfertigung,* 140; Luz, *Geschichtsverständnis,* 56, 60). Hence it cannot be systematized, and it presents only one form of biblical interpretation (*contra* Goppelt, *Typos,* 154) along with occasional allegory and the common proof from Scripture.

What marks it off from these other forms? In Paul typology relates exclusively to Scripture and interprets events rather than biblical sayings (Goppelt, "Apokalyptik," 329f.). Prophecy and allegory begin with concrete texts, assert fulfilment rather than mere correspondence, and are possible from the whole of Scripture. If in prophecy Scripture points directly to the future, in typology and allegory the future reference may be established only later by a comparison, since it is present in a concealed way in the historical. If in allegory the historical element is a concealing garment and the hidden future reference is the decisive thing, in typology the historical side has its own full reality and significance. The future reference belongs to a hidden dimension of depth which is first brought to light by an eschatological understanding. It then receives salvation-historical importance as well. When primal time and end-time correspond or contrast, the law of all history may be discerned, although its continuity cannot be controlled immanently and permanently as in a process of development. What is stressed is not the element of example but that which is pregnant with destiny, which transcends individual existence and determines the world as a whole.

This provisional analysis shows (Goppelt, "Apokalyptik," 333f.; otherwise Bultmann, "Typologie," 210) that the story of Abraham is treated typologically in this passage. Like 1 Cor 10:11, v. 23 establishes the correspondence between primal time and end-time. In the patriarch as the prototype of faith (Wilckens, "Rechtfertigung," 114f., 122; Asmussen; Franzmann), not as merely one example among others (Weinel, *Paulus*, 35 [*St. Paul*, 59]), nor as a model in salvation history (Goppelt, *Typos*, 166), nor as the cipher of a contingent historical figure (Klein, "Römer 4," 158, 164), God's plan of salvation is announced in accordance with the law of the end-time. Insofar as he belongs to primal time, as the recipient and witness of the promise he is simultaneously the beginning of the gospel of the righteousness of faith. One sees from this that the element of repetition and intensification should not be made the starting point and measure of Paul's typology, but probably the periodizing of world history, represented by Adam, Abraham, Moses, and Christ, is connected with it. Thereby Abraham and Christ are parallel, Moses and Christ antithetic, and Adam and Christ dialectically related to one another. Creation is not abandoned, although it in fact lies under the curse and needs new creation. The promise courses through history in hidden form before coming to the light of day, and the law comes to an end with the end-time. Abraham and Christ are separated from one another by Moses so that the common features and correspondences in their histories are discovered only eschatologically and cannot be pursued chronologically by means of a postulate of election. The individual is determined by his position amidst this debris. He cannot deny the forefather of his history. Revelation reminds him that promise and miracle make possible even before him the exodus from the history of fallenness into freedom. Faith as devotion to the promise has already always actualized not merely membership in the heavenly world but also in the fellowship of the people of God on its pilgrimage through earthly history. Christian existence can never be isolated from the world or history.

If v. 23a tells us that God's reckoning was recorded in Scripture not just for Abraham's sake, this not only prepares the way negatively for what follows (*contra* Kuss). The story of Abraham has its own validity and importance, and putting it in Scripture adds significance to the historical side too. If according to 15:4; 1 Cor 9:9f.; 10:11 the primary interpretation must be eschatological, one may see that the historical and eschatological approaches are not always or necessarily alternatives. The latter, however, marks the horizon in which the former retains its place. God's action points toward the end, which, nevertheless, has a prior earthly history from which it must not be abstracted if eschatology is not to evaporate in spiritualizing.

μέλλει λογίζεσθαι possibly is directed to the present, which logically appears as future from the standpoint of the past time of the scriptural statement (Zahn; Kühl; Lagrange; Kuss; Luz, *Geschichtsverständnis*, 113). In this case, however, one would expect a past form of the verb. Hence a genuine future, related to the parousia, is to be preferred (Schlatter; Michel; Barrett). Verse 24b mentions the correspondence on which the typology rests. As has been clear from v. 11 on, the generation of the end-time is qualified by faith. The preceding argument makes sense only if this faith is not different from that of Abraham (Gaugler; Leenhardt; Cerfaux, *Christian*, 272; Kertelge, *Rechtfertigung*, 193; Berger, "Abraham," 72ff., though cf. H. W. Schmidt; Kirk; Murray; Luz, *Geschichtsverständnis*, 114; Huby; Bonsirven, *Exégèse*, 269f.). If Paul in adopting the divine predication modifies it christologically, this does not permit us to play off faith in the facts of salvation against faith in the promise (*contra* Kühl; Schlatter), to see in the latter only a prefiguring of the former, or to distinguish the two from the standpoint of structure and content. The patriarch believed in the same God who raises the dead and was confirmed therein, while Christian faith experiences realization only outside the self in Christ and not yet in one's own resurrection. The content of the promise which Abraham anticipated in hidden and isolated form has been made public with Christ so that it is now confessed in the community. Here then is an element of intensification. But it relates to the circumstances under which one believes and not to the content, which not unintentionally was formulated earlier in v. 17b.

The christological variation of the divine predication makes it possible for this part of the letter to end, as it began, with a liturgical formula. Scepticism in relation to this (Kuss) or to pre-Pauline tradition (Kramer, *Christ*, 30f.) has no basis (Bultmann, *Theology*, I, 82; Michel; Althaus; Barrett; H. W. Schmidt; Bruce; Best). The solemn introduction in v. 24c already prepares the way for it. It is [possible that πιστεύειν ἐπί does not follow the model of ἐλπίζειν ἐπί (Bultmann, *TDNT*, VI, 212) but denotes the confession of faith (Michel). The interchanging of participle and relative clause is common liturgically. The careful construction may be seen in the parallelism of the equal lines and also in details. The verbs, in Semitic style, come first, as in 1 Tim 3:16. The two διά's correspond and the conclusions form a deliberate antithesis. The first line is not based on the context, which puts all the stress on ἠγέρθη (Kühl), while the relating of Christ's resurrection to our justification is singular. The phrase "was put to death for our offenses" is a fixed formula of the passion tradition (cf. 8:32; 1 Cor 11:23) (K. H. Schelkle, *Die Passion Jesu in der Verkündigung des Neuen Testaments* [1949] 70f., 249, though cf. H. E. Tödt, *The Son of Man in the Synoptic Tradition* [Eng. tr. 1965] 160f.). In its reflexive form it is perhaps baptismal too (Gal 2:20; Eph 5:2, 25; Tit 2:14) (Romaniuk, "L'origine," 61). The first line is obviously based on Isa 53:5, 12 LXX. This explains the absolute use of παρεδόθη, whose passive denotes God's action, and also διά with the accusative, which provides the basis, instead of Paul's familiar ὑπέρ (Jeremias, *TDNT*, V, 706; H. W. Wolff, *Jesaja 53*, 95). This by no means makes it obvious that the idea of the Suffering Servant is applied to Jesus (*contra* Schweizer, *Erniedrigung*, 73 [*Lordship*, 50f.]), since the NT does more "atomizing" quotation than we often want to allow (*contra* Wolff, *Jesaja*

53, 150f.). Decisive, in any case, is the soteriological function according to which God, as in 3:24, has acted graciously toward us through Jesus' sacrificial death, with no cooperation on our part.

The justification of the godless, proclaimed here too, holds the two lines together. The cross and resurrection are a single event, so that their juxtaposition is in the first instance a result of the rhetoric of antithetical parallelism (Weiss, "Beiträge," 172; Dodd). Yet in Isa 53:11 (H. W. Wolff, *Jesaja 53*, 95), and in the NT in John 16:10; 1 Tim 3:16, justification and glorification are related as a sign of the triumph of the risen Lord. In spite of the parallelism the διά in the second line cannot be viewed as causal like that of the first (Schlatter). Rhetorically repeated (Schrenk, *TDNT*, II, 223f.; Oepke, *TDNT*, II, 70), it undoubtedly denotes purpose. Perhaps one might sum up the thought as follows: The sacrifice of Jesus for the sake of our transgressions took place once and for all on the cross. The relating of the event of justification to the resurrection makes it clear that this event constantly wins new ground in encounter with the risen Lord. While it is true that here, as in 1:16f., the christological tradition is interpreted in terms of the doctrine of justification (Stuhlmacher, *Gerechtigkeit*, 207ff.), nevertheless one must be on guard against exaggeration. For it is also true that christology alone forms the basis of the doctrine of justification and protects it against misunderstandings. Both faith as assent to historical event and mysticism are ruled out. Grace is tied to the Christ event, although this does not mean that it is limited to a specific period of time in the past. It is a reality eschatologically present with the reign of Christ. Christian faith relates to a non-interchangeable event. Yet it gains access to the cross only in virtue of the resurrection of Jesus, while on the other side faith in the resurrection of Jesus does not mean hope of eternity but the victory and rule of the Crucified. With this formula, which he no doubt took from Hellenistic Jewish Christianity (cf. Hahn, *Titles of Jesus*, 59f.; Wengst, *Formeln*, 56ff., 101f.), the apostle brings the preceding portion of the epistle to a fine conclusion and also formulates the theme of the part which is to follow.

IV. The Righteousness of Faith as a Reality of Eschatological Freedom (5:1–8:39)

Paul's thesis has now been presented and proved. But will it do justice to the reality of the believer's life? The Jew especially must object that attained righteousness frees from death and sin and coincides with life by the Spirit of God. Paul agrees to that with the distinctive extension that it also frees from the law. The reality of the righteousness of faith is Christian freedom and herein it is life by the Spirit. A structuring which brings chs. 1–5 under the title "justification" and chs. 6–8 under that of "sanctification" (cf. Huby; Prat, *Theology,* II, 14, who argues that the abstract thesis of justification is forgotten after the controversy) distorts Paul's basic position, apart from all else, for justification is not for him (*contra* Dodd; Cerfaux, *Christian,* 421ff.; Prat, *Theology,* I, 210; J. Knox; Black) the first stage in the moral life of the redeemed. Our understanding of ch. 4 as a proof from Scripture does not allow us to attach 5:1-11 to the preceding section (*contra* Leenhardt; correctly: Dupont, "Structure," 376; Kümmel, *Introduction,* 306; survey in Paulsen, *Überlieferung,* 15ff.).

A. Freedom from the Power of Death (5:1-21)

The chapter falls into two parts, vv. 1-11 and vv. 12-21. These describe Christian freedom as standing in the peace of God and as participation in the reign of Christ the Life-giver.

1. Paradoxical Standing in the Peace of God (5:1-11)

¹Justified, then, by faith, we have peace with God through our Lord Jesus Christ, ²through whom in faith we have attained access to our standing in grace, and we boast of the glory of God in which we hope. ³Nor only that, but we boast also of affliction. For we know that affliction produces endurance, ⁴endurance confirmation, and confirmation hope. ⁵Hope, however, does not let us be confounded. For the love of God has been poured into our hearts through the Holy Spirit who has been given us. ⁶For when we were still weak, even then Christ died for the ungodly. ⁷Hardly anyone will die even for a righteous man. For a good man perhaps someone will dare even to die. ⁸But God shows his love to us in (the fact) that Christ died for us even when we were still sinners. ⁹Justified now by his blood, we shall the more certainly be

131

saved by him from the wrath of judgment. [10]*For if as enemies we were reconciled to God by the death of his Son, the more certainly as those who are reconciled we shall be saved by the power of his life.* [11]*Even more than that, we boast in God through our Lord Jesus Christ, through whom we have now (already) received reconciliation.*

Bibliography: N. A. Dahl, "Two Notes on Romans 5," *ST* 5 (1951) 37-48; W. S. van Leeuwen, *Eirene in het NT* (1940); R. Bultmann, "Adam and Christ in Romans 5," *The Old and New Man* (Eng. tr. 1967) 49-78; M. Dibelius, *James* (Hermeneia; Eng. tr. 1976); W. Nauck, "Freude im Leiden," *ZNW* 46 (1955) 68-80; A. M. Festugière, "'Υπομονή dans la tradition grecque," *RSR* 21 (1931) 477-486; S. Spicq, "'Υπομονή, patientia," *Revue des sciences philosophiques et théologiques* 19 (1930) 95-106. **6ff.:** G. Bornkamm, "Paulinische Anakoluthe," *Ende des Gesetzes*, 78-80; H. Sahlin, "Einige Textemendationen zum Römerbrief," *TZ* 9 (1953) 92-100; G. Delling, "Der Tod Jesu im der Verkündigung des Paulus," *Apophoreta: Festschrift für Ernst Haenchen* (BZNW 30; 1964) 85-96; C. Maurer, "Der Schluss a minori ad majus als Element paulinischer Theologie," *TLZ* 85 (1960) 149-152. **10f.:** J. Dupont, *La réconciliation dans la théologie de Saint Paul* (1953); D. E. H. Whiteley, "St. Paul's Thought on the Atonement," *JTS* N.S. 8 (1957) 240-255; E. Käsemann, "Some Thoughts on the Theme 'The Doctrine of Reconciliation in the NT,'" *The Future of Our Religious Past: Essays in Honour of Rudolf Bultmann* (Eng. tr. 1971) 49-64; L. Goppelt, "Versöhnung durch Christus," *Christologie und Ethik* (1968) 147-164; U. Luz, "Aufbau." For A. Schlatter, "Durch Christus," K. Müller, "Rechtfertigungslehre," Hanson, *Wrath*, and G. Fitzer, "Ort der Versöhnung" see the bibliographies for 1:8-15; 1:16-17; 1:18-32; and 3:21-26, respectively.

One can discuss whether this section forms an introduction to the new division corresponding to the conclusion in ch. 8 (Dahl, "Notes"; Feuillet, "Citation," 57; contrast Dupont, "Structure," 389f.). The close relation between ch. 7 and ch. 8 is an argument against this, as we shall see later. We are thus to see in these verses a prelude to the pericope which follows (Kuss). Yet the two views are not fully exclusive, since many of the motifs do in fact recur in ch. 8. A description of standing in the peace of God (*contra* Michel) is given in vv. 1-5. After a chiastic sequence in v. 5a-b, this is established as standing in the love of God in vv. 6-8 and in hope in vv. 9-10. The motifs of vv. 1-2 are then taken up again chiastically in the final verse.

Whereas rabbinic Judaism is very strongly marked by uncertainty of salvation (Billerbeck), peace is a characteristic of the Christian life. It is not just equanimity of mind (Kühl; Jülicher; Schettler, "Durch Christus," 19; K. Müller, "Rechtfertigungslehre," 100; Baulès) but relation to God, as the prepositional phrase shows. As in 2:10 it exists only for the justified as standing in God's triumph over his enemies (van Leeuwen, 203, cf. the discussion of apocalyptic, 144-179). To speak of good order (Lennhardt) is thus to say too little. Under the dominion of Christ strife with God ends and so does subjection to the power of wrath. The fulness of salvation is realized on earth—what the Semite describes as peace. The verse sums up the preceding part of the epistle and thus clearly introduces the next one.

Evaluation of the well-attested and ancient (Lietzmann) reading ἔχωμεν is difficult but it is strongly defended (Sanday and Headlam; Lagrange; Kuss; J. Knox, *Life*; Neugebauer, *In Christus*, 61; Dinkler, *RAC*, VIII, 463f.; worth considering: Bardenhewer; Murray). But the content with its indicatives and the general thrust of the section are against it. In dictation the indicative and subjunctive could not be distinguished (Foerster, *TDNT*, II, 415) and later hortatory interests would support the latter, which is by no means without sense (Kuss *contra* Lietzmann).

Verse 2a uses a cultic motif in interpretation of v. 1 (Michel). προσαγωγή, which is not used transitively for "conducting" (Schlatter; H. W. Schmidt), means unhindered access to the sanctuary as the place of God's presence (Ridderbos). The next clause shows that χάρις here is standing in the power of grace (Lietzmann; Bultmann, *Theology*, I, 290f.). καί gives emphasis, but should not be pressed (Lietzmann). The omission of τῇ πίστει in B sa D G Or is arbitrary (Lietzmann *contra* Kühl; Dodd; Weiss, "Beiträge," 226). The catchword of the last two chapters is emphatically repeated.

Verse 2b extends v. 1 almost provocatively and at any rate in paradoxical antithesis to 3:27. καυχᾶσθαι is a second mark of the state of salvation and is the response of faith to the dawning δόξα, and its point is lost if we translate it by "praise." In spite of the lofty speech and the liturgical expressions, the section does not call for doxology (*contra* Michel). It offers an argument which sets boasting against the background of Christian resistance to the world and its powers. In good Semitic fashion it is presupposed that "boasting" is an existential factor in human existence (Schlatter; Kuss), namely, an expression of human dignity and freedom. For this very reason it is easily perverted, whether in terms of its object or the way it is demonstrated. If as Paul sees it existence is defined by its lord, the basic understanding of existence comes to expression in boasting. In this, a person tells to whom he belongs. In his fallen state he boasts of himself and the powers. The apostle attacks this, since it is a denial of creatureliness. It is plain here that Paul as man, author, and theologian has no interest whatever in *ataraxia*. From Jer 9:23ff. he derives not just the permission but the justification of a καύχησις proper to the creature. The present text is one of many different reflections on the OT saying. According to 3:23ff. the Lord of whom we can and should boast is the one who with the gift of righteousness restores mankind's lost image. The apostle's reserve with respect to the latter motif should, of course, not be overlooked. Like resurrection, the divine image is for him in the first instance primarily a christological predicate, which, apart from the divergent tradition in 1 Cor 11:7, is transferred to the Christian only apocalyptically. Here again the trial of faith resists an unprotected realized eschatology. On the other hand apocalyptic makes it possible to develop the motif anthropologically as in 1 Cor 15:49. The travail of the present time under the aegis of the Messiah transforms believers back into the image lost by Adam (8:19-29; 2 Cor 4:7-18). Reference may thus be made to the dawn of the glory of the children of God as this comes upon mankind.

The text is to be understood in this context. The thrust of the tradition used, however, should not be allowed to conceal Paul's interpretation, so that moral growth of the life initiated by justification becomes the theme of these verses (*contra* Jülicher; Dodd; Kirk; Lagrange; Enslin, *Ethics*, 309; Richardson, *Theology*, 236). From the eschatological perspective from which Pauline ethics must also be viewed, what is involved, nevertheless, is not merely the hope of future salvation (contra Mattern, Gericht, 88). The δόξα τοῦ θεοῦ is the fulfilment of the righteousness already given and is anticipated in the righteousness in such a way that hope still waits for the remaining fulfilment and yet is certain of it beyond the gift already received. ἐλπίς is no longer in Greek fashion the prospect of what might happen but the prospect of what is already guaranteed. The dialectic of the Christian life is characterized thereby.

On the one side there is faith only face to face with the threat of the powers still dominant on earth, i.e., under temporal assault. On the other side, when God has worked to save, faith stands in the sign of victory, confidently seeing that the threat is transitory, and thus in spite of all appearances encountering the world with the power and confidence of the victor. This explains the strange circumstance that while Paul everywhere presupposes and adapts the apocalyptic doctrine of the two aeons, he never deals with it thematically (Furnish, Ethics, 115f.). Christian dialectic bursts open the schemata of this doctrine. The old aeon has not simply vanished with the inauguration of the new. It still radiates temptation and mortal peril. But precisely this is the sphere which the new aeon invades. In the time ushered in with Christ the two aeons are no longer separated chronologically and spatially as in Jewish apocalyptic. The earth has become their battleground. Assailed faith and the vanquishing of the powers mark the place where Christian boasting paradoxically proclaims that peace and freedom are already secured even in the midst of the ongoing conflict.

Formally vv. 3-5 continue the motif of v. 2b, but materially they are a development. εἰδότες does not introduce a parenthesis (contra J. Knox; Bultmann, "Adam and Christ," 52), nor does it express a general truth, as the underlying parenetic tradition might have understood it. Christian experience speaks here. God's triumphant glory can be extolled in hope only when sufferings can also be extolled as the sphere in which according to 2 Cor 12:9 the reality of χάρις also seeks to manifest itself. This does not mean that καυχᾶσθαι ἐν θλίψεσιν is to be taken locatively (contra Zahn; Dodd; Harder, Gebet, 34; considered by Michel). The verb, constructed with ἐν as in the LXX, designates the object of boasting. Only thus is the paradox of what follows brought out clearly.

The elliptical οὐ μόνον δέ, which is used by Paul elsewhere and which also occurs in Greek authors, serves a rhetorical rather than a material intensifying. This is equally true of the rabbinic chain (examples in Dibelius, James, 74ff., 94-99; Billerbeck), which corresponds to the Greek crescendo (cf. BAGD, 846a), and which causally derives the fruits of trial (Anfechtung) the one from the other. Obviously there is no dependence on James (contra Zahn). Both passages and also 1 Pet 1:6f. are linked by a common hortatory tradition (Grundmann, TDNT, II, 258), which develops the theme of T. Jos. 10:1: πόσα κατεργάζεται ἡ ὑπομονή. It may have its origin in the days of the Maccabean persecution (Nauck, "Freude," 72ff.). Suffering is not integrated here (contra H. W. Schmidt) into a system of world-affirmation. Nor is it understood purely as a means of divine instruction (cf. Billerbeck; Bultmann, TDNT, III, 650). It reflects the shadow of the cross in which God's eschatological power alone intends to work. θλίψις is the end-time affliction which comes on the Christian as a follower of the messiah Jesus. ὑπομονή, regarded from Plato on as the ἀνδρεία which resists evil (cf. Festugière's article), also means steadfastness here, with an OT and primitive Christian (Spicq,

134

PARADOXICAL STANDING IN THE PEACE OF GOD   5:1-11

"'Υπομονή," 102) orientation to the hoped for salvation. δοκιμή is a specifically Pauline term for being proved in a test. The power expressed therein is divinely given and to that extent gives to life an openness to the future (Bultmann, "Adam and Christ," 53). The same situation is depicted in 1QH 9:11-14.

In the saying in v. 5a, which is based on Ps 21:6; 24:20 LXX, καταισχύνεσθαι does not mean "to be ashamed" (Zahn; Kühl; J. Knox) but "to be put to shame" in the eschatological situation (Bultmann, *TDNT*, I, 189). If the Jewish tradition may have described how solid character arises in life (so Lietzmann; Baulès; Franzmann), Paul has something else in view. His concern is for the eschatological miracle of the humanization of man which is prefigured by the crucified Christ and in which the coming of the new world takes place. Apocalyptic is anthropologically deepened and made concrete, so that the text corresponds antithetically to 1:24ff. If the creature falls step by step under the wrath of God, he does not climb up again to heaven after justification, as enthusiasts think. But in the earthly state and its difficulties he proves his calling to give honor to God. This interpretation is shown to be right by v. 5b, where the earlier tradition is obviously abandoned.

Verses 6-8 make it clear that ἀγάπη τοῦ θεοῦ is not an objective genitive as Augustine thought, i.e., love for God. Nor does it denote infused charity as a loving disposition (Gutjahr; Kirk). Nor can it be construed as God's act of love (Bultmann, *Theology*, I, 291f.; Ridderbos; Blank, *Paulus*, 282), since the verb speaks against this. As in similar constructions with the genitive the reference is to the encompassing power of God, with a special orientation to being for us, as 8:31ff. clearly indicates. As the apostle's anthropological terms characterize existence in its different relations, something of the same is true of these genitive constructions. They, too, speak of a relation of divine power, or, more accurately, of the powerful God, the relation being to the creature. In wrath this power reveals itself as destruction to rebels, in God's righteousness it creates salvation for rebels, in faithfulness it means that the Creator holds firmly to his will and work in salvation history. In love this power shows itself to be the solidarity which overcomes the opposition between Creator and creature, which upholds the miracle of the new existence, and which at the same time continually brings awareness of it.

The verb expresses the final element. It derives (Michel) from OT language and encompasses supreme fulness. When God pours his power of love into our hearts, this takes control of us in the center of our personality and makes us its own, in fulfilment of Jer 31:31ff. The tense suggests an ongoing state established by a once-for-all act. What is in mind is probably the baptismal event in which the Spirit is imparted, according to the common view of primitive Christianity. In a striking formulation, God's love is said to be imparted to us by the Spirit. This is not said merely in edification. The not understandable label "mystical-ethical" (Dodd) is of as little help here as psychological considerations (Zahn; Kühl). Paul is saying three things.

First, when God's love has seized us so totally and centrally, we no longer belong to ourselves; a change in existence has taken place. Secondly, since the Spirit is a down payment (8:23; 2 Cor 1:22), we have an "objective" pledge that our hope will not be confounded. Finally, when the Spirit who is given us makes

135

us constantly sure of this love, we can praise God in the midst of earthly affliction as in 8:37ff., standing in everyday as well as eschatological service of God. No longer left to ourselves and the world, already in time we are set in the kingdom of freedom, which is no other than the openness of access to God and of the peace granted therewith.

The apostle is not saying, then, that the Spirit and love are identical (Kirk; J. Knox), or that love justifies (Lagrange; Dodd; Dibelius, "Vier Worte," 4) or is justification (Kirk), or that love as a moral principle and the sphere of moral experience unleashes justification (Dodd). Behind all these interpretations there lurks the ancient idea, which constantly takes new forms, of faith formed by love. The significance of this idea for confessional division should not go unperceived, and in spite of all interpretations to the contrary there is not the slightest support for it in this epistle. Also lurking in the background is an outmoded approach which thinks that the ethicizing of the ecstatic or the juridical is characteristic of [Paul's concept of the Spirit (Gunkel, *Wirkungen,* and Lüdemann, *Anthropologie*). Whichever form it takes, this understanding is unable to break free from the shackles of idealistic interpretation. It confuses the symptoms with the reality and tries to find forces wherewith to play down the historically decisive phenomenon of Pauline eschatology.

In an age in which the significance of the Dead Sea Scrolls for the NT has been stressed sometimes almost to the point of the grotesque, it is hard to understand how with the help of these texts the material relevance of eschatological thinking for Paul and his contemporaries can be watered down ethically or ecclesiologically. As the Spirit determines Christian life as a whole, not just its extraordinary manifestations, so conversely it sets the whole of this life in the sphere of miracle. "Being in the Spirit" becomes the proclamation of "being in Christ" both as the crucified and as the resurrected one. The event of justification is saved from the threat of historicization and the love of God from that of a mystical theory of the removal of the remaining distance between God and mankind, or Christ and the church, with the help of the motif of union between the two. The new creature stands, not on our morality, but on "God for us and with us." New insights from religious history no longer permit us to uphold the liberal schemata, and traditional dogmatic positions need to be rethought at least in the light of them, and submitted to possible or necessary correction. If not, the result will be schizophrenia between history and theology.

But how can one be sure of God's love through the Spirit? A point rarely considered here is that there is also a lying spirit and that according to the witness of the NT this lying spirit is in the church. Verses 6-8 provide an answer to the question with their reference to the death of Jesus. Paul, to be sure, did not formulate his thought precisely. Verse 6 is disjointed. Verse 7a introduces an unhappy analogy which is not very skilfully corrected in v. 7b. Only in v. 8, which takes up v. 6 and also forges a link with v. 5b, is the point properly made. What is the reason for this unusual jumble?

Obviously the apostle wants to show how inconceivable is the divine action in the death of Jesus and to demonstrate therewith the greatness of his self-revealing love. He measures this action by those on whose behalf it is performed, but does it under the guiding theme of his doctrine of justification: for the ungodly

(Eichholz, *Paulus*, 167f.). This makes it clear that God's saving act is incommensurable and that although God's love proclaims itself even the sharpest contrasts offer no basis of comparison.

Commentators old and new have rightly found difficulty with the argument, but their alterations have not improved matters. Neither vv. 6-7 (Fuchs, *Freiheit*, 16), nor v. 7b (Jülicher), nor the whole of v. 7 (Sahlin, "Emendationen," 97) can be convincingly explained as glosses. The theory of a copying mistake which was badly corrected later (Sahlin, 96f.) also lacks plausibility. The clumsy duplication of ἔτι in v. 6 has led to variants to the original ἔτι γάρ at the beginning or the omission of the second ἔτι (Zahn; Lietzmann; Bornkamm, "Anakoluthe," 79; Eichholz, *Paulus*, 165; though cf. Sanday and Headlam). The duplication, however, corresponds to that of the genitive absolute and to the catching up of ἀσθενεῖς in ἀσεβεῖς. Elsewhere Paul attributes ἀσθένεια to Christians.

If the pre-Christian period is envisaged here (though cf. Schlatter), the stronger and more unequivocal term in the second member is a correction. The construction thus becomes confused, and even more so by the fact that in this part of the verse there is heavy stress on the time of the death of Christ. κατὰ καιρόν does not mean the right moment (Michel; Leenhardt; cf. also Ridderbos) but (BAGD, 394f., 406; H. W. Schmidt) "then," and, as is common, is to be taken with the predicate. The point is that Christ did his saving work at an unexpected and, morally considered, even inappropriate moment. Unworthy, genuinely ungodly people benefitted from it (Furnish, *Ethics*, 166f.). In this argument the historical aspects of the passion are already overlaid completely by the soteriological and dogmatic aspects. The statement is given two stresses by the fact that the ἔτι γάρ is linked with the genitive absolute and the ἔτι κατὰ καιρόν with the verb. Both should present the same paradox: We were the very opposite of strong when Christ died, and he died when we were still ungodly. As in 4:5 this is no mere rhetoric or moralizing. One should not translate the adjective by "wicked" (Lietzmann) and "almost ungodly" (Jülicher); this is to change the doctrine of justification along the lines of edification.

The analogy in v. 7 has a conclusion *a minori ad majus*—the rabbinic *qal waḥ ōmer*—but after the correction of v. 7a in v. 7b this is dropped as inadequate in v. 8. In antithesis to v. 6 death even for the righteous is described as rare. μόλις means "scarcely" (BAGD, 526). But then the apostle remembers that sacrificial deaths are common enough. He thus concedes quite tortuously this possibility as regards the good, by which he means not individuals but a type (Barrett) and, to be sure, not (Billerbeck; Michel) the kindly person but the particularly worthy person. A neutral interpretation as the good does not fit in view of the parallelism and intensifying in relation to δίκαιος, which has the sense of "upright" (Gutjahr; Ridderbos; though cf. Sanday and Headlam). The analogy pushes Christ's death into the sphere of the heroic and is of no help for this reason.

The point is finally made in v. 8. As against variants which omit it, ὁ θεός is the subject, for only thus is support given to the statement in v. 5b. ὅτι is explicative, while συνίστησιν has the sense "to demonstrate" as in 3:5 (Kasch, *TDNT*, VII, 897f.). As may be seen from 1 Cor 8:11; 1 Thess 5:10; Rom 14:15, the statement borrows from liturgical and possibly eucharistic language (Riesenfeld, *TDNT*, VIII, 508ff.). One may contest the usefulness of arranging it under the heading of a "faith formula" (Kramer, *Christ,* 26f.) or a death formula (Wengst, *Formeln,* 78ff., 82). In any case it involves substitution according to Gal 2:21; 2 Cor 5:14, and the characteristic ὑπὲρ ἡμῶν means both "on behalf of" and "in place of," substantively at any rate "without us." God's love is more than an action which makes good our deficiencies. It is the almighty power which effects salvation, brings forth the creation out of nothing (*creatio ex nihilo*), and puts an end to wrath. This almighty power produces and maintains eschatological justification. Four times, in clarification of the theme of the section, sentences close with ἀποθνῄσκειν. Because for Paul Christ's death has concretely manifested the love of God, the basis of Christian assurance lies in it. This is why the presence of the Spirit is described in v. 5b as the presence of God's love, about which one can and may speak according to Paul only from the perspective of Jesus' passion. If this is constitutively defined from the very outset by the categories of the doctrine of justification, the theology of the cross is according to our text the key to the Pauline doctrine of God, soteriology, anthropology, and eschatology. Who God is, who mankind and the world are, and what salvation and perdition are, find their criterion in it.

Verses 9-10 offer a further basis of Christian hope. The conclusion *a minori ad majus,* for which the way is prepared in vv. 6f., controls the statement with its [1. twofold πολλῷ μᾶλλον, for which there are rabbinic equivalents (Billerbeck). While the phrases are liturgical the statement is not (*contra* Maurer, "Der Schluss," 150f.) either doxological or prophetic. Like the section as a whole, it is argumentative. The beginning is parallel to that in v. 1, for here too justification opens the door to the eschatological present. As in 3:25 the liturgical metaphor of the blood of Jesus is used to show that justification is effected by the death of Jesus. But now the present and the future of final judgment are separated. This ultimate future is doubtless marked by ἡ ὀργή, and again there is not the slightest reason, for fear of anthropomorphism, to make of this an objective principle (Dodd) or impersonal process (Hanson, *Wrath,* 89) or even to relate wrath to the sufferings of vv. 3f. What is meant is the consuming power of the World-Judge which according to 1:18ff. has already announced itself in hidden form in earthly history. In contrast σῴζειν clearly has the sense of eschatological deliverance (Foerster, *TDNT,* VII, 992f.).

Verse 10 repeats the statement in somewhat altered terminology and with a climax at the end which again clarifies v. 5 and the explanatory γάρ at the beginning. As πολλῷ μᾶλλον and σωθησόμεθα both recur, διὰ τοῦ θανάτου τοῦ υἱοῦ αὐτοῦ interprets the phrase about the blood of Jesus. There is a rhetorical change of prepositions; both, however, are instrumental. From all this it follows that "to justify" and "to reconcile" are also the same in content (Schlatter; Nygren; Barrett; Kuss; Bultmann, "Adam and Christ," 51; Furnish, *Ethics,* 149; though cf. Sanday and Headlam; Büchsel, *TDNT,* I, 255; Dupont, "Réconciliation," 20ff.). As a technical term "to reconcile" occurs only in the Pauline corpus but may have been taken from the liturgical tradition (Käsemann, "Theme," 51; though cf. Goppelt, "Versöhnung," 150ff.). The concept does not refer (so Kühl; Leenhardt; Baulès) to an inner event but to the objective ending of enmity (Bultmann, *Theology,* I, 285ff.; Dupont, "Réconciliation," 19f.; Kümmel, *Theology,* 203ff.; Ridderbos), without belonging to the legal sphere or having sacrificial significance (*contra* Dupont, "Réconciliation," 28ff., 40ff.; rightly Fitzer, "Ort der Versöhnung," 180ff.). The idea of substitution is not intrinsic to it but may be combined with it, as here by way of the prepositional phrases (Whiteley, "Atonement," 240; Käsemann, "Theme," 56ff.). Paul uses it to characterize the event of salvation as the justification of enemies (Ridderbos, *Paul*, 182) and the peace of Christ as its goal, as the participial clause shows. ἐχθροί, like ἔχθρα in 8:7 though not as in 11:28, has an active sense and means rebels (Foerster, *TDNT*, II, 814; Zahn; Kühl; H. W. Schmidt; for a passive sense cf. Lietzmann; Gutjahr; Murray; Ridderbos; Dupont, "Réconciliation," 27; ambivalent Michel; Bultmann, *Theology*, I, 286; Büchsel, *TDNT*, I, 256f.; Taylor, *Forgiveness*, 74f.; Kuss). For those who are reconciled in that way the future has no more terrors.

A surprising shift of thought lifts the negatively formulated conclusion of v. 9b into a positive one in v. 10b. The change in prepositions is rhetorical as in vv. 9-10a. But this is hardly true of the statement itself (with Schlatter against Barrett; Kuss). The reference is to ζωὴ αὐτοῦ as in 2 Cor 4:10ff. The power of the life of the risen Lord embraces and preserves the community. To be sure, the death and resurrection of Jesus belong together. Nevertheless they can be differentiated, as in 4:25, to clarify the two aspects of the event of salvation, namely, the eschatologically once-for-all and the permanent. The Christ who died for us also lives for us, and destroys the threats of the future as he destroyed the evil power of the past. He is in person the irreversible "for us" of God; hence the change in destiny of vv. 12-21.

The repeated crescendo in the οὐ μόνον δέ, ἀλλὰ καί of v. 11 is not merely connected with v. 10 (*contra* Lietzmann) but steers us back rhetorically to the theme of καύχησις with which the section began. It has now become clear, however, to what extent Christians can be "boastful." Paul's concern is that they remain so continually in the light of the salvation which has befallen them and in spite of all afflictions. In context the participle is indicative, not cohortative (*contra* Kuss). Real consideration may now be given to what takes place in Christian worship. For the liturgical style of v. 11a is unmistakable (Weiss, "Beiträge," 226; Bousset, *Kyrios*, 159f.), and the stereotyped formula διὰ τοῦ κυρίου ἡμῶν Ἰησοῦ Χριστοῦ (cf. the excursus in Kuss) clearly points to the exalted Lord as the author and mediator of inspired doxology. Almost plerophorically the relative clause again states the basis and theme of Christian boasting, and almost all the motifs of the section are collected under the catchword of the reconciliation that exists in the eschatological present. As in 3:21; 5:9 the νῦν has in this regard a force corresponding to the theme of this new portion of the epistle (Fuchs, *Freiheit*, 17).

2. The Dominion of the Last Adam (5:12-21)

¹²*Thus (it is true): As by one man sin came into the world and death through sin, and death came thus on all men, since all sinned—. ¹³For up to the law sin was (already) in the world. But when the law was not present sin was not (specifically) imputed. ¹⁴Yet between Adam and Moses death reigned even over those who had not sinned according to the transgression of Adam. He is the type of the future (humanity). ¹⁵The work of grace, of course, is not like the*

fall. For if through the fall of one many died, the grace of God, namely, the gift granted with the gracious power of the one man Jesus Christ, abounded the more richly to many. [16]*What is given is not like that which the one sinner (did). For judgment led from the one to condemnation, but the work of grace led from many transgressions to justification.* [17]*For if with the transgression of one death gained dominion through that one, the more surely will those who receive the fulness of grace with the gift of justification reign in the sphere of life through the one Jesus Christ.* [18]*Hence (it is true that) as through one man's transgression condemnation came on all men, so through one man's act of justification life in justification comes on all men.* [19]*For as by the disobedience of one man many were made sinners, so by the obedience of one man many will be presented as righteous.* [20]*The law interposed itself in order to increase the transgression, and where sin expanded grace became all the more overwhelming.* [21]*It did so to this end: As sin won dominion in virtue of death, so the power of grace, in virtue of justification, must reign to eternal life through Jesus Christ our Lord.*

Bibliography: J. Freundorfer, *Erbsünde und Erbtod beim Apostel Paulus* (1927); A. E. J. Rawlinson, *The NT Doctrine of the Christ* (1926); C. H. Kraeling, *Anthropos and Son of Man* (1927); B. Murmelstein, "Adam ein Beitrag zur Messiaslehre," *Weiner Zeitschrift für* [13. *die Kunde des Morgenlandes* 35 (1928) 242-275; 36 (1929) 51-86; A. Vitti, "Christus-Adam," *Bib* 7 (1926) 121-145, 270-285, 348-401; E. Hirsch, "Zur paulinischen Christologie," *ZST* 7 (1930) 605-630; H. W. Robinson, "The Hebrew Conception of Corporate Personality," *Werden und Wesen des AT* (ed. P. Volz *et al.*; Beihefte zur Zeitschrift für die Alttestamentliche Wissenschaft 66; 1936) 49-62; A. Vögtle, "Die Adam-Christus-Typologie und 'der Menschensohn'," *Trierer Theologische Zeitschrift* 60 (1951) 309-328; *idem*, " 'Der Menschensohn' und die paulinische Christologie," *Stud.Paul.Congr.*, I, 199-218; M. Black, "The Pauline Doctrine of the Second Adam," *SJT* 7 (1954) 170-79; F. G. Lafont, "Sur l'interprétation de Romains V, 15-21," *RSR* 45 (1957) 481-513; W. Barclay, "Romans V, 12-21," *ExpT* 70 (1958/59) 132-35, 172-75; W. Grundmann, "Die Übermacht der Gnade," *NovT* 2 (1958) 50-72; E. Schweizer, "The Son of Man," *JBL* 79 (1960) 119-129; A. R. Johnson, *The One and the Many in the Israelite Conception of God* (2nd ed. 1961); S. Lyonnet, "Le péché original en Rom 5, 12," *Bib* 41 (1960) 325-355; *idem*, "L'Universalité du péché et son explication par le péché d'Adam," *Étapes*, 55-106; K. Smyth, "Heavenly Man and Son of Man in St. Paul," *Stud.Paul.Congr.*, I, 219-230; K. Barth, *Christus und Adam* (2nd ed. 1964); R. Scroggs, *The Last Adam. A Study in Pauline Anthropology* (1966); A. Feuillet, "Le règne de la mort et le règne de la vie (Rom. V, 12-21)," *RB* 77 (1970) 481-521; J. de Fraine, *Adam and the Family of Man* (1965); H. Conzelmann, *1 Corinthians* (Hermeneia; Eng. tr. 1975); H.-M. Schenke, "Die neutestamentliche Christologie und der gnostische Erlöser," *Gnosis und NT* (ed. K.-W. Tröger; 1973) 205-229. **12:** C. E. B. Cranfield, "On Some of the Problems in the Interpretation of Romans V, 12," *SJT* 22 (1969) 324-341; A. J. M. Wedderburn, "The Theological Structure of Romans V, 12," *NTS* 19 (1972/73) 339-354; **13:** G. Friedrich, "Ἁμαρτία οὐκ ἐλλογεῖται Röm 5, 13," *TLZ* 77 (1952) 523-28; E. Jüngel, "Das Gesetz zwischen Adam und Christus," *ZTK* 60 (1963) 42-73. **14:** J. Gewiess, "Das Abbild des Todes Christi (Röm 6, 5)," *Historische Jahrbücher* 77 (1958) 339-346. **15ff.:** H. Müller, "Der rabbinische Qal-Wachomer-Schluss in paulinischer Typologie," *ZNW* 58 (1967) 73-92; L. Schottroff, *Der Glaubende und die feindliche Welt* (WMANT 37; 1970). For Bornkamm, "Anakoluthe," Bultmann, "Adam," and Dahl, "Two Notes" see the bibliography for 5:1-11.

According to the last section freedom from death can be asserted only paradoxically as standing in the peace of God and in certain hope in spite of ongoing afflictions and the required trial. To this extent it participates in the paradoxical circumstance of the justification of the ungodly, which seeks to take effect as a life-giving power in the existence of the Christian (*contra* the basic thesis of Feuillet, "Citation," 56f.; "Règne," 515f., which detaches the theme of death and life from that of sin and justification; rightly Dupont, "Structure," 381). Naturally, this initial statement does not suffice. Since death is a force which shapes the cosmos, freedom from it, like the justification which underlies this freedom, has to have universal validity if it is to be seriously maintained. This is the theme of the new section.

This means that the section is a consistent development of what precedes (*contra* Feuillet, "Règne," 481, 509, etc.; cf. the bibliographical survey in Luz, "Aufbau," 178). If one does not from the beginning deny to the apostle the systematizing power which is evident throughout the epistle, there is no reason to characterize the passage as an erratic block (Luz, *Geschichtsverständnis*, 193; Kirk) or to ascribe it essentially to an earlier source (Fuchs, *Freiheit*, 18ff.). If, of course, Paul's doctrine of justification is seen predominantly from the standpoint of individualistic anthropology, and the cosmic dimension of 1:18–3:20 is viewed only as a dark foil and not as an antithetical correlate, the logical connection with the context will have to be disputed. This can even be done when the uniqueness of the passage is stressed, when it is seen as the climax of the epistle, and when its interpretation is said to be the primary task inasmuch as it offers an expository key (Nygren). The section is not formally an excursus (*contra* Bornkamm, "Anakoluthe," 80f.). It does not offer a framework of salvation history for the preceding proclamation (*contra* Michel; Kuss). In content it is neither a philosophy (Kühl) nor a theology of history (Jülicher; H. W. Schmidt; Luz, *Geschichtsverständnis*, 204, 210). The latter designation is correct only to the degree that the apostle does not know any existence outside the reality of the history of salvation or judgment between the first Adam and the last (Barrett, *First Adam;* Asmussen). All the same Paul does not lose himself in historical speculation (cf. Kuss, 275ff.).

If, in relation to existence, the depth of the salvation event is in view, so is the universality of grace with the historical perspective. In each individual God is concretely reaching for the world. This would be arbitrary if the whole breadth of creation were not at issue. The two approaches alternate and complement one another in this epistle (Cambier, *L'Évangile*, 203). Neither the person in isolation nor history abstracted from the individual, but the person in his world is as the reality of creation simultaneously the object and the field of salvation. Hence the next chapters might well be entitled a verification of the theological thesis by reality (Luz, "Aufbau," 173).

If freedom from death is at issue, the aspect of a world qualified by the power of the risen Lord has to come into view. This can take place only kerygmatically and not by demonstration. It is, however, not merely an elucidation and substantiation of vv. 1-11 (*contra* Bultmann, *Theology*, I, 252; Brandenburger, *Adam*, 257; Barth; Ridderbos; H. W. Schmidt; Gibbs, *Creation*, 49; Lyonnet, *Quaestiones*, I, 225). What we have is a second argument continuing the first.

In this argument there is an obvious reference back to the apocalyptic idea

141

of the two aeons. This formulates most sharply the antithesis between subjection to death and eschatological life in a cosmic view. Nevertheless (*contra* Nygren) we should not make this idea a key to interpretation of the text. As already indicated, there is good reason to think that Paul did not adopt the historical schema of the succession of the two aeons, even though in Gal 1:4 he speaks of the present evil aeon, awaits the heavenly consummation, and contrasts primal time and end-time (H. Müller, "Qal-Wachomer," 76f.; Furnish, *Ethics,* 134). Since the end-time has already begun for Paul, his theme is not the relation of the aeons but the presence of life (Brandenburger, *Adam,* 262ff. *contra* Nygren). To talk of two ages or forms of existence (Nygren, also Müller, "Qal-Wachomer," 88) obliterates the constitutively apocalyptic aspect of the text (the basic error in Barth, *Christus und Adam*). Thus the presentation of eschatological salvation, in distinction from the dominant Jewish view, is at bottom messianically determined. The reign of Christ confronts the reign of sin and death initiated by Adam.

This leads to a series of correspondences which have decisive significance for the whole. Formally it hardly suffices to speak of analogies (Barrett; Murray). For at the same time the incomparable charcter of the effects on both sides is established. Primal time and end-time confront one another in mounting antithesis (Kuss). Typology strictly adhered to is clearly indicated by the use of the word "type" in v. 14 (Eichholz, *Paulus,* 172f.; though cf. Scroggs, *Adam,* xxii). The apocalyptic rootage of typology in Paul emerges clearly here. Scripture is not quoted directly as in 4:17ff. The apostle undoubtedly has Genesis 3 in mind, although under haggadic control (Bultmann, "Adam and Christ," 61; Brandenburger, *Adam,* 45ff.; Kuss; Leenhardt *contra* Freundorfer, 1ff.). Hence Adam is for him a historic personage and not just the mythological personification of every human being (Luz, *Geschichtsverständnis,* 201). Typology fundamentally presupposes history. The world and history of the first Adam stand over against those of the last, and are overcome by the latter.

Such an observation leads us, however, into a difficulty whose size is reflected   [1.
in the literature. In spite of strenuous efforts no adequate explanation in the history of religions has been found for the rise of Adam-Christ typology (Schottroff, *Glaubende,* 117, though cf. Murmelstein, "Adam," 246ff.; Schenke, "Christologie," 220f.). Its setting can be localized. But we are hardly carried further by the greatly overworked Semitic idea of "corporate personality," although in many circles this is regarded as a pat solution (begun by Robinson's article; exemplified by de Fraine, *Adam*; also in Dodd; Leenhardt; Hanson, *Unity,* 68f.; Barclay, "Romans V, 12-21," 173f.; J. Knox, *Life,* 41ff.; Larsson, *Vorbild,* 176ff.). In the Judaism of the age it was probably much less vital than among contemporary expositors, who have discovered in it what seems to be a way out of a much too crude mythology. To resort to the idea of the ancestor who potentially decides the fate of his descendants (e.g., E. Schweizer, "Son," 128; Scroggs, *Adam,* 22f., 41ff.; Kuss, 280) misses the point of the text. Christ is not a patriarch nor can Adam be brought under this category.

At issue is the uniqueness of both. They do not characterize stages in history but its beginning and its end (Eichholz, *Paulus,* 185f.). The issue, then, is the apocalyptic antithesis of primal time and end-time. Undoubtedly it is an important aspect of the text that the fate of the descendants is settled in the forefather. To this extent, recollection of the idea of corporate personality is useful. It was indeed applied to the patriarchs, but remained related to Israel. Decisive in the interpretation of our text, however, is not the comparison of two heads of a generation, but of the two figures, in sharp dualism, who alone inaugurated a world of perdition and salvation, so that they cannot be listed in a series of ancestors (Schottroff, *Glaubende*, 117ff., 131; Cambier, *L'Évangile*, 214ff. for this reason would limit the schema to Adam). At best, then, the idea is only an aid to understanding.

Almost grotesque is the attempt, on the basis of the term *anthropos*, to emphasize the humanity of the person of Jesus, to develop something like an anthropology of Jesus, and finally to speculate on its material priority over that of Adam and his successors (K. Barth, *Christus*, 10ff., 73ff.; with limitations, Gibbs, *Creation*, 50ff.). Paul did not reflect on the human nature of Christ or derive from this the idea of the true man who bears witness to hidden continuity in the lordship of the Creator (correctly Bultmann, "Adam and Christ," 75ff.). Christ is not original man and fallen Adam derived man. Anthropology as such is not at issue. Cosmic disaster and grace which universally intervenes and prevails over it are traced back to bearers of destiny as their temporal and material authors.

It has become customary in theology to steer clear of the idea of destiny and to limit as much as possible the undeniable mythological element in the passage. Detailed exegesis is forced into debate here. Provisionally one can say only that for Paul the *anthropos* Christ undoubtedly does not abstractly represent humanity, nor is he concretely one individual among and alongside others. He is the pre-existent one, the risen one, and the designated cosmocrator. As such, as in 1 Cor 15:44ff., he confronts the protoplast, who thus receives a unique dignity and cannot be compared even with the patriarchs or Moses. Quite apart from the question whether or not we can and must speak of collective persons within properly defined limits, the whole stress should not at least be placed on this in relation to Christ. If it is, he is necessarily robbed of his character as ruler, which is constitutive for Pauline christology, and the difference between him and his kingdom is effaced. This is precisely the weak point which can be seen every-where when the idea of corporate personality is used. The lordship of Christ is weakened in favor of the thought of union with him. Consciously or uncon-sciously, ecclesiology covers over christology (as typically in J. Knox). Interest in anthropology is the Protestant version of this shift. The shift in the interpre-tation of Paul happens differently according to whether christology is determined by the idea of corporate personality and the related idea of union or whether the necessary and responsible adoption of the motif of corporate personality with its ecclesiological and anthropological implications is determined by christology with the sharpest stress on the dignity of the *kyrios*. At least that unavoidable measure of reflection must be demanded of interpretation which considers this theological question and reaches a clear answer that will inevitably involve conflict. The idea of a "bearer of destiny" is not, of course, a theological one in the true sense. But it, too, is an aid, since it indicates the lines along which the theologoumenon of Christ's lordship should be made more precise. It should also be noted, how-ever, that the motif of destiny is related by the apostle to the gospel in 1 Cor

9:16f., to the word of the cross in 1 Cor 1:18ff., and to apostolic work in 2 Cor 2:16f., and we shall often come across it.

Our first task is to fix as clearly as possible the main religio-historical problem. It is not just a matter of showing the context which determines how far Adam and Christ can be correlated with one another as archetypes of their respective worlds (Schottroff, *Glaubende*, 124). The real question is whether the antithesis between the protoplast and the Messiah under the common denominator of *anthropos* can be derived from pre-Pauline tradition. That this may be assumed rests above all on the variations in 1 Cor 15:21f., 45ff. Added in Paul is the combination of the messianically interpreted texts Ps 110:1 and 8:6 in 1 Cor 15:25, 27, the point being to characterize the Messiah as the eschatological Adam. Finally the idea is taken up in the context of the baptismal exhortation in Col 3:9f.; Eph 4:24 and, in antithetical allusion, probably also in the liturgical fragment in Eph 2:15: What was divided in the old aeon will be united in the heavenly man of the end-time. Eph 5:25ff. has a variation on this final motif with explicit appeal to the paradise story. The horizon is the motif of the *eikon* in Gen 1:27, which also plays an important role in the apostle. It is very unlikely that Paul and his followers would have created such different versions of the same idea, with quotations from such different scriptures, unless there was an underlying tradition.

This is all the more true since in 1 Cor 15:46f. we find an emphatic attack on a point of view which knows of a pre-temporal primal man in heaven (Schottroff, *Glaubende*, 127ff.; Conzelmann, *1 Corinthians*, 284ff. with helpful material and bibliography). This idea is in competition with that of Christ's pre-existence, and [1 this competition is not removed by identifying the heavenly primal man with the pre-existent Christ. Hence it is hard to think that Christians held it in Paul's day. Paul's polemic can only be directed against the views of Hellenistic Judaism, which follow a primal-man mythology already altered by Philo. An immense literature has been devoted to the reconstruction of this mythology. The whole problem is unavoidably bound up with the hotly contested question of pre-Christian Gnosticism, and the basis for the debate is almost completely contradictory post-Christian materials (cf. Conzelmann, *loc. cit.*; Schottroff, *Glaubende*, 120ff.; Schlier, *RAC*, III, 445ff.).

In terms of the history of religions the debate is characterized at the moment by two negative results. First, the myth of the "redeemed redeemer" is not the center of a pre- and extra-Christian Gnosticism, as was assumed for decades, especially in Germany, on the basis of the work of R. Reitzenstein. Secondly, and irrespective of the as yet unclarified matter at issue, the Pauline Adam-Christ typology in its central problematic is not even grasped, let alone solved by it. For in Paul Adam and Christ are antipodes unrelated by any original consubstantiality. Not Adam who is only earthly protoplast, not a fallen heavenly being, but the world implicated in Adam's fall, is redeemed. Christ is no Adam redivivus; he is the eschatologically manifested Son of God. Adam and Christ are commensurable, not in terms of nature, but solely in terms of function; the world is changed by both. The only thing that might be clarified by the myth of the primal man is that both bear the title *anthropos* and even this is possible only by way of a very complicated reconstruction.

To be rejected is any combining of the *anthropos*-predicate with the idea of the Son of Man in primitive Jewish Christianity (Colpe, *TDNT,* VIII, 410ff., 470ff.). Neither in Paul (so Hirsch, "Christologie," 616ff.; Cullmann, *Christology,* 166ff.), nor in the pre-Pauline Hellenistic field, where Aramaic titles were no longer understood, is this idea transformed into an *anthropos*-teaching (*contra* J. Jeremias, *TDNT,* I, 143; Barrett; Michel; in opposition Kuss; Vögtle, "Adam-Christus-Typologie," 310ff.; "Menschensohn," 204ff.; Black, "Second Adam," 174; Vitti, "Christus-Adam," 139; Smyth, "Heavenly Man"). It is conceivable, though not incontestable, that both ideas come from a common root. Yet the eschatological World-Judge has nothing antithetically to do with Adam (correctly Kümmel, *Theology,* 156f.) nor with the resurrection of the dead. This difficulty is not avoided by dubiously finding an allusion to the Servant of the Lord in v. 19 (Jeremias, *TDNT,* VI, 442ff.; Cullmann, *Christology,* 171ff.; Feuillet, "Règne," 492, etc.), or, as is often done today, by coupling the ideas of the Servant of the Lord and the Son of Man in order thus to speak of the Incarnated (*contra* Brandenburger, *Adam,* 235). Apart from the doubtful nature of the combination, there is no reference to an antithesis between the Servant and Adam, the text does not speak expressly of Christ's atoning work, nor is representation dealt with in the strict sense. The questions are not made any easier by such suggestions. The exegetes' notices of embarrassment simply fog the interpretation. In all circumstances this has to keep in view the central motif of Christ's dominion, and it must not end up with archetypes. On the other hand, it must be stated that all sorts of mythological speculations came to be bound up with Adam in orthodox Judaism, but no myth of primal man ever developed in the strict sense. The motifs of such a myth were adopted and changed. Unlike Abraham and Moses Adam was not a mediator of salvation and hardly any traces of his eschatological redemption can be found in his function as protoplast. To be sure, the expression "all the glory of Adam" is used as an end-time promise in 1QS 4:23; CD 3:20; 1QH 17:15. What is meant, however (Scroggs, *Adam,* 26f., 54f.), is the eschatological restitution, not of the primal man, but of his progeny, although naturally with restriction to Israel with its legal piety.

The beginnings of another view, which came into Judaism from the surrounding world, may be found in pre-Christian days only in connection with speculations on heavenly wisdom as the mediator of creation (cf. Wilckens, *TDNT,* VII, 507ff.; Hegermann, *Schöpfungsmittler*). As this wisdom is generally identified with the Torah, in Hellenistic Judaism it is identified with the *logos,* and also, as in Philo *De confusione linguarum* 146, with the *anthropos,* namely, as the heavenly primal man. This probably took place in order that a tradition current in heretical circles might be related strictly to the existing motif of a mediation of creation and deprived of its dangerous independence (Hegermann, 75f., 85f.). There is a clear parallel when in *I Enoch* 48:1ff.; 49:3f. wisdom and the Son of Man are interrelated, so that the pre-existence of the Son of Man is affirmed as well as the eschatological return of wisdom (Hegermann, 80f., 83).

Two things may thus be stated. In the Hellenistic period Judaism came under the influence of the motifs of the myth of the primal man. It adapted these motifs by incorporating them into the *sophia* myth and with no interest in them except for the idea of the mediator of creation. Nevertheless, the possibility opened up that in new circumstances the motifs might become independent in the sense of their originally basic conception. The new conditions arrive with primitive Christianity and especially with Gnosticism. Gnosticism cannot be discussed here because of its far-reaching problems. It is sufficient to establish the transfer of *sophia* speculation to christology in the NT. This happened both in relation to the earthly Jesus, in whom wisdom speaks again, and in relation to the pre-existent Christ, who thereby receives the function of the mediator of creation. In Paul the process may be seen in 1 Cor 10:4, the doxology in 1 Cor 8:6, and in the deutero-Pauline letters especially in Col 1:15ff., thus in an already existing hymn. One is thus led to the hypothesis that Hellenistic Judaism passed on to primitive Christianity both the idea of the mediator of creation and also the title of this mediator as Logos and Anthropos. Christians accepted this complex because in this way it could characterize the pre-existent Christ as the inaugurator of a new humanity. Acceptance was made all the easier by the fact that the voice of wisdom had been heard already in the earthly Jesus.

Along these lines the path is presented along which the pre-existent Christ could come to be called the eschatological primal man—an idea which was then developed further in Christian Gnosticism. On the other hand this does not yet explain the Adam-Christ typology as such. Transfer of the title Anthropos to the protoplast must at any rate be regarded as secondary compared with its transfer to the pre-existent Christ. Paul's polemic in 1 Cor 15:45f. attests this, as does also the motif of the old man in baptismal exhortation. The new step becomes possible only when the apocalyptic idea of the two aeons also enters the picture. Then the first and second Adam can be contrasted with one another, and the two can be set in the antithetical correspondence of primal time and end-time. There then arises also the possibility of understanding the mediator of creation as the beginning and author of the general resurrection and finally of finding an anticipation of the eschatological work of the last Adam in the event of baptism. In dualistic contrast Christ and Adam are now the bearers of destiny for the world determined by them. It should be noted once again that in all this we have attempted a reconstruction whose hypotheses demand discussion. Nevertheless, as already shown, it is unlikely that Paul initially created the typology himself. How helpful it was for him in the present passage is obvious. We must now attempt a detailed exegesis.

The complex sentence of this section up to v. 17 forms a giant anacoluthon. As elsewhere, this is not due to any clumsiness on the apostle's part. It is due to the wealth of ideas and associations which crowd in upon him, and here especially to the balancing of given motifs with his own purpose. Already by reason of the prepositional introduction v. 12 cannot be merely a superscription (*contra* Barth, *Christus*, 73). If διὰ τοῦτο is viewed weakly as a transitional particle (Zahn; Lietzmann; Lagrange; Barrett; Bultmann, "Adam and Christ," 62), this overlooks the break in thought and leads to a new argument. It marks the beginning of this and also substantiates vv. 10f. (H. W. Schmidt; Brandenburger, *Adam*, 258) or vv. 1-11 as a whole (Michel; Cranfield, "Problems," 325; Luz, "Aufbau," 179f.). Eschatological life is already present in the reign of Christ.

In relation to the origin of sin there is no speculation by reference to Satan as in Wis 2:24 (*contra* Feuillet, "Règne," 428f.) nor on the basis of the evil impulse asserted by the rabbis (Zahn; Schlatter; Bultmann, *TDNT*, III, 15; Brandenburger,

146

Adam, 159). All the same, the Kierkegaardian formula that sin came through sinning is exaggerated (Bultmann, *Theology*, I, 251; Bornkamm, *RGG*, V, 181; Brandenburger, *Adam*, 159). It obscures the importance of Adam in the typology (E. Brunner; Eichholz, *Paulus*, 182; Murray *contra* Dodd). Conversely the western theory of original sin and death (defended by Freundorfer, "Erbsunde"; Gutjahr; Sickenberger) is much too rationalistic, especially when both are taken to be sexual transmission (survey in Lyonnet, *Quaestiones*, I, 182ff.). As in 1:18–3:20 Paul's concern is with the reality of earthly life as faith perceives it. From the time of Adam's fall people always find themselves in this reality. As there, this reality evades rational or speculative basis. No process of development is depicted. Of course, the nexus of sin and death is asserted in the categories of cause and effect, but there is no further explanation or discussion (Wedderburn, "Structure"). Characteristically there is no differentiation with regard to the individual. The fulness of possibilities respecting his conduct, and the resultant differences in concrete life and death, play no part.

9]   The spheres of Adam and Christ, of death and life, are separated as alternative, exclusive, and ultimate, and this happens in global breadth. An old world and a new world are at issue. In relation to them no one can be neutral. There is no third option. The style is thoroughly mythological. Hence Paul is definitely not speaking of personal guilt or naturally necessary death but of the forces of sin and death which have invaded the world (Kuss; Cambier, *L'Évangile*, 223ff.; Brandenburger, *Adam*, 160, 164; though cf., e.g., Schlatter). The cosmos here is the human world, as the parallel "all men" in v. 12c shows. But it is neither the sum of individuals nor the field of personal relations and decisions (*contra* Bultmann, *Theology*, I, 255f.; cf. Kuss; H. W. Schmidt). The person is not seen primarily as the subject of his history; he is its object and projection. He is in the grip of forces which seize his existence and determine his will and responsibility at least to the extent that he cannot choose freely but can only grasp what is already there. Verse 12a-c speaks with the objectivity characteristic of mythology. For this reason διῆλθεν in v. 12c does not merely bear witness to the love of the *koine* for compounds. Visibly (cf. Michel; Sasse, *TDNT*, III, 889) it allows death to spread across the generations like an infectious disease. It is a curse in the texture of earthly life which ineluctably affects every individual.

The real problem in interpretation lies in v. 12d, where the motif of destiny which dominates v. 12a-c is abruptly set aside by that of the personal guilt of all mankind. Related to this change of thought is the fact that the verse ends as an anacoluthon and excursuses follow. From an early period various attempts have been made to eliminate the difficulty, but without attaining persuasive results. Rejection of an anacoluthon (Scroggs, *Adam*, 79; cf. against this Cranfield, "Problems," 326ff.) presupposes that Paul, following a rhetorical pattern ABBA, begins and ends with a human act and speaks of the related destiny in the intervening statements. This thesis is refuted by the fact that it has to understand καὶ οὕτως as though it were οὕτως καί: "correspondingly" or "consequently" (Brandenburger, *Adam*, 163f.; Lyonnet, *Quaestiones*, I, 227).

Especially debated is the meaning of ἐφ᾽ ᾧ (cf. the survey in Kuss; Cranfield, "Problems," 330ff.). The older Latin translation which has dominated the west from the time of Augustine is *in quo*. This gives the theory of original sin and death an anchor in the text. In terms of this theological trend at least it is to be rejected from the outset, for the apostle does not know of inheritance of sin and death in the strict sense. Nevertheless, at least implicitly, this idea is even today everywhere present in fact when the typology of the passage is understood along the lines of the idea of corporate personality with no discussion of the grammatical and lexical question of the prepositional expression. Oddly, people in general seem to be unaware of that. If Paul used this idea, or if it formed the background of his statements, he must at least have corrected it unless he wanted in fact anthropologically to teach original sin and ecclesiologically to teach the church as collaborator in salvation. The theological implications of history-of-religions explanations must be considered if schizophrenia is not to result.

Champions of the idea can at any rate oppose the translation *in quo* only on grammatical and not on material grounds. If, however, the translation is grammatically and lexically incorrect, the theory of corporate personality can no longer [be used exclusively in interpretation of the text. More consistent are those who find the motif of destiny in v. 12d. In this case ἐφ' ᾧ relates to death or to the whole verse and has the sense "on the basis of which," "through which" (Zahn; Nygren; Cerfaux, *Christ*, 232f.) or "in which circumstances" (Cambier, *L'Évangile*, 238, 241; Lyonnet, "Universalité," 96ff.). The same result is attained by a final understanding "to which end" (Stauffer, *TDNT*, II, 437; *New Testament Theology* [Eng. tr. 1955] 270 n. 176; Eichholz, *Paulus*, 182f.; Feuillet, "Règne," 490ff.) or a pluperfect reading of the verb: "for they all had original guilt" (Lagrange; Bardenhewer; Ligier, *Péché*, 269ff., though cf. Brandenburger, *Adam*, 171ff.; Cambier, *L'Évangile*, 236f.; Lyonnet, "Universalité," 99). The variations show that these interpretations are attempts to solve the problem that do not want to admit the break in thought in v. 12d. The problem itself supports the view that the expression is to be rendered by "because." It is used causally in this way in 2 Cor 5:4; Phil 3:12; 4:10 as well (Bardenhewer; Huby; and most commentators). In this case the verb means concrete sinning, so that there is in this verse an ambivalence between destiny and individual guilt (Bultmann, *Theology*, I, 251; Kümmel, *Man*, 63ff.; Michel).

Only too understandably modern exegesis has tried to tackle the problems of the passage from the opposite side too. In this case v. 12d is the key to an understanding at least of Paul's concern, if not of the text as a whole. Existentialist interpretation is most radical in this regard, ascribing the motif of destiny to pre-Pauline tradition and finding this ostensibly transcended by the apostle's interest in man's concrete decision and responsibility (begun by Bultmann, *TDNT*, III, 15; *Theology*, I, 251ff.; taken up by Bornkamm, *RGG*, V, 181; "Anakoluthe," 84; Fuchs, *Freiheit*, 18ff.; especially Brandenburger, *Adam*, e.g., 229ff.; opposed by Jüngel, "Gesetz," 43ff., 57ff.). Even if Paul has no model (*contra* Fuchs, *Freiheit*) he unquestionably stands in a solid Jewish tradition which finds expression in Sir 25:24; 4 Ezra 3:7, 21f., 26; Wis 1:13; 2:23; *2 Apoc. Bar.* 23:4 and which shows the same ambivalence between destiny and guilt most plainly in *2 Apoc. Bar.* 54:15, 19; "For if Adam sinned first and brought untimely death on all, each of those who descended from him, each individual has brought future pain upon himself. Adam is thus the cause for himself alone; each of us has become his own Adam, each for himself." Clearly the emphasis here is on personal responsibility, and for this reason *Šabbat* 55a (cf. Billerbeck) has the basic formulation: "No death without sin and no punishment without guilt." Later the idea gains strength of a mortal destiny (Scroggs, *Adam*, 36), which does not very clearly imply a sinful destiny. It seems to have been espoused first by Jewish heretics. It is still sharply contested in 4 Ezra and *2 Apocalypse of Baruch* (cf. the basic analysis in Harnisch, *Verhängnis*) and is only gradually accepted by the rabbis (Brandenburger, *Adam*, 49ff., 64f.; uncritically Murmelstein, "Adam," 253ff.). Paul radicalized this latter view by positing the actualization of the power of sin in concrete sinning (Brandenburger, *Adam*, 183ff.).

On the other hand it should be noted that in 2:12 he lays explicit emphasis on sinning outside the law and that in 4:15 he makes an emphatic distinction between sin and transgression (Brandenburger, *Adam*, 202f.). The same thing occurs here and leads on to the first excursus in vv. 13f. Verse 12d does not restrict or correct v. 12a-c. Otherwise vv. 13-14, with a basic and transitional γάρ at the beginning, could not let the power of sin invade the sphere of transgression of the law (Murray; Cambier, *L'Évangile*, 250ff.; Lyonnet, "Universalité," 104ff.), which is what causes the existentialist interpretation the greatest difficulty. Verse 12 portrays the same impenetrable nexus of destiny and guilt as 1:18ff. (though cf. Bultmann, *Theology*, I, 250f.). The issue in v. 12d is not primarily or even exclusively the transition from a cosmic outlook to an individual outlook, from the sphere of mythical curse to that of responsible decision. If it were, the next verses would make no sense and the thrust of the passage would be missed. The undeniable individualizing in v. 12d gives depth to what is said about the scope of the disaster, as later reflection on the individual believer gives existential depth to the universal event of salvation. Paul's concern unites what seems to us to be a logical contradiction and what does in fact become antithetical in Judaism: No one commences his own history and no one can be exonerated. Each in his own conduct confirms the fact that he finds himself in a world marked by sin and death and that he is subject to the burdening curse (Lafont, "Interprétation," 500). The alternative between free will and natural behavior is alien to the apostle. He is not oriented to principles but, as in 1:20ff., to experience. He does not view a person as a being who can be isolated but as a manifestation of the world represented by him. For him sin is an offense against the deity of God and therefore against the first commandment. For this reason it and the death which is its consequence have the character of universal forces which no one escapes and to which each in his way is subject both passively and actively.

If, taking up 2:12f., v. 13a maintains that the power of sin ruled in the world prior to the law, v. 13b modifies the statement in 4:15 that transgression is made possible only by the law. Sin prior to the law has not been imputed. Whether a Jewish legal statement is being quoted here (Zahn; Friedrich, "Röm 5, 13," 526f.), or reference is at least being made to an established legal tradition (Brandenburger, *Adam*, 195 disputes this), is problematic, although one might suppose that Paul is using the Jewish idea of the recording of merits and demerits in heavenly books (Friedrich, "Röm 5, 13"; Michel; Brandenburger, *Adam*, 197ff.). If so, the verb is to be vividly translated by "chalking up," as in Phlm 18.

But what is the point of the argument? The context allows only one answer. Under the law judgment is to be expected on the last day. Even before its enact-

149

ment, however, punishment falls on committed sin according to the nexus of act and consequence described in 1:24ff.; the world is "handed over" by the wrath of God to general corruption. This clarifies the transition to v. 14. Even the world which is not yet determined by law stands already under the sign of involvement in the general rebellion against God and thus suffers the corresponding retribution of consignment to the destiny of death. Thus v. 12a-c is not corrected but readopted, and v. 12d is interpreted to mean that the sinful act of the individual is a manifestation of the general fall into guilt and is to that extent the presupposition of the cosmic destiny of death.

Hence Paul comes back to v. 12a-c with ἀλλά, "nevertheless." Death, whose power is characterized particularly clearly by the verb, reigned unrestrictedly [¹ between Adam and Moses. It exercised judgment on the sin which, unlike that of Adam, could not be classified as transgression of the law. When the old Latin versions and Origen omit the μή before the participle, they miss the point (Zahn; Lietzmann). They could think of sin only as a repetition of Adam's act, namely, as transgression of the command. This anticipated the modern lack of understanding of the passage (cf. Bultmann, *Theology,* I, 253; Kümmel, *Theology,* 183). It brings clearly to light the weakness of an interpretation which reduces sin to the personal guilt of responsible existence, finds a barrier which is not really there between v. 12a-c and v. 12d, distinguishes between the tradition and Paul's view, and causes the cosmology of the apostle to evaporate into individual anthropology with its personal relations. The text points in exactly the opposite direction. Paul is not speaking primarily of act and punishment but of ruling powers which implicate all people individually and everywhere determine reality as destiny (Cambier, *L'Évangile,* 272; Ridderbos).

Anthropology is here the projection of cosmology. Individual existence is not thematically reflected upon. Even Adam as the primal man is not an interchangeable example. As a transgressor of the law—this is decisively important in 7:7ff.—he represents the Jewish community. Insofar as one must speak of existence at all, its relation to the world which determines it is its constitutive mark. It is the concrete form of a sphere of lordship in personal life. Because the world is not finally a neutral place but the field of contending powers, mankind both individually and socially becomes an object in the struggle and an exponent of the power that rules it. His basic definition derives from the category of belonging. He is no more neutral than the place where he stands. If creation has already set a lord over him, he is in no sense autonomous in the fall. Even though the Creator maintains his claim to him, he falls under another lordship. Concretely he falls under sin and death. This approach must not be rationalized either moralistically by forcing it into the framework of individual responsibility, guilt, and expiation or causally by associating guilt with lineal descent and making death a natural phenomenon. The excursus in vv. 13f. is against such an interpretation. After Adam's fall mankind always finds itself in the power of sin and death, even before and outside that law which proclaims eschatological judgment on our works and summons us with our transgressions before the final Judge.

As will be considered especially at 6:4, the meaning of ὁμοίωμα is disputed wherever it occurs in Paul and possibly no unequivocal explanation can be given. It is now generally assumed that the term should not be taken abstractly in the sense of "similarity," "resemblance" (BAGD, 567; Lietzmann; Michel; Brandenburger, *Adam*, 191) but concretely, as in the LXX, in the sense of "image" or "form" (Schneider, *TDNT*, V, 191ff., 195). Sometimes this is made more precise by speaking of a model, prototype, or, obviously under etymological influence, likeness (Zahn; H. W. Schmidt; Gewiess, "Abbild," 342). This is made possible by the fact that ὁμοίωμα and εἰκών can be synonymous since Plato (Schneider, *TDNT*, V, 191f.; Schwanz, *Imago Dei*, 33f.), although the latter term leaves room for various nuances. At this point we need not spend time on the differences of interpretation, since the meaning of the statement is clear. Materially it is undoubtedly a matter of conformity and agreement, so that the translation "likeness" is appropriate, although to be cautious one might prefer the more neutral "image." In B ἐν replaces ἐπί before the noun, probably to avoid too close repetition of the preposition (Lietzmann). In unusual and perhaps Semitic fashion it means the norm (Zahn) rather than the basis (Gewiess, "Abbild," 342f.). The whole phrase characterizes those who do not become sinners by transgression of the concrete commandment as Adam did.

In a further development the last part of the verse (14c) brings out the point of what has been said thus far, which immediately motivates a second digression in vv. 15-17. The apostle has been speaking of Adam and the damage he did in order to be able to present the effect of the act of salvation against this background. No matter how different Adam and Christ might be, even if they can both be called Anthropos, for all the antithesis there is also correspondence between them. This is expressed by the word τύπος.

Originally τύπος did not mean the impression but the hollow form (H. Müller, "Auslegung," 87ff.). In distinction from 1 Cor 10:6, the meaning here cannot be prototype or model, because what we have in the context is contrast. To speak of a specifically Pauline usage raises problems. But to speak in terms of the foreshadowing of a future and superior figure (Goppelt, *TDNT*, VIII, 252f.; H. Müller, "Qal-Wachomer," 89ff.) is to interpret the train of thought rather than the word and to put the emphasis on the development in the verses that follow. The meaning "antitype" (Nygren) does not fit badly and possibly could be supported by the τυπικῶς of 1 Cor 10:11, but there is no other example of it. An important point is that in 1 Cor 10:6 the relation between primal and end-time is governed by the term. "Prototype" brings this out best.

Unlike ὁ ἐρχόμενος in Matt 11:3, the participle ὁ μέλλων is hardly a mysterious messianic predication (*contra* Nygren; Michel; H. W. Schmidt), nor does it concern the future glory of Christ (LaFont, "Interpretation," 502), and certainly not Moses (Robinson, *Body*, 35; Scroggs, *Adam*, 81). Along apocalyptic lines the author and representative of the new aeon confronts that of the old in a way that is characteristic of Paul's typology. This does not mean that continuity is maintained, as the parallel in 1 Cor 15:47f. makes perfectly plain. Otherwise one could in fact reverse the relation and see in Christ the true Adam (Barth, *Christus;* in opposition Bultmann, "Adam and Christ," 75f.; Brandenburger, *Adam*, 267ff.). Thus one can achieve an emphasis on anthropology as the true theme of the passage (Barth, *Christus*, 73, 86f.; Robinson, *Body*, 92, 100ff.; Scroggs, *Adam*, xxii). It is true, of course, that the new humanity is the goal of Paul's argument. Nevertheless, the antithesis between the two primal men should not be relativized in terms of the intended result. Only from christology does the way lead to anthropology and ecclesiology, which for their part denote standing in the dominion of Christ.

Verse 14c is also the superscription of the digression that follows in vv. 15-17 (Bultmann, "Adam and Christ," 64; though cf. Scroggs, *Adam*, 81). In a specific manner which is made more precise in these verses it is also the theme of the whole section. If the two primal men correspond as inaugurators of their different worlds, the difference between them has now to be described. To do this a sec-   [ondary motif of eschatological superiority is now introduced in the diacritical and apparently "illogical" (Jülicher) πολλῷ μᾶλλον. As elsewhere Paul is adopting the rabbinic *qal-wāḥōmer* argument (Billerbeck, 223ff.). It is not so easy to follow here, however, as it is in 5:9f. The very diversified interpretations prove this.

One may rule out at once the psychological understanding which makes the loving will of God stronger than the wrath, which must almost be forced out of him (Kühl; cf. Zahn; Dodd; Schlatter). The context refutes any idea that goodness is broader than judgment (H. W. Schmidt). Can one say in general that good is more real and vital than evil (Dodd; cf. Bultmann, "Adam and Christ," 65; Althaus)? In support of this, appeal is made to *Sifre Levi* 5:17: "Only one commandment was laid on Adam in the form of a prohibition, and he transgressed it. Lo, how many cases of death have come as a punishment on him and his generations and the generations of his generations up to the end of his generations. And how? Which measure is greater? Is the measure of the divine goodness greater or the measure of the punishments? Say: The measure of goodness. . . ." Paul's concern, however, is not with the outcome of approaching judgment and a moralizing generalization of the quotation is illegitimate.

No more convincing is a reference back to vv. 13f. and the deduced thesis that the law has broken the analogy between Adam and Christ, so that πολλῷ μᾶλλον denotes a logical and not a qualitative intensification (Dahl, "Two Notes," 43ff.; cf. Schrenk, "Missionsdokument," 96). For Paul Moses is on Adam's side and vv. 13f. distinguish between transgressors of the law and the rest of humanity. Hence they do not break the analogy nor do they form the basis of the "how much more," which for its part expresses a most profound qualitative superiority.

One may say, of course, that the phrase is uttered in the judgment and logic of faith (Althaus), although one should not incautiously call this faith "securely grounded" (Brandenburger, *Adam*, 223f.; H. Müller, "Auslegung," 80f.). The statement as such is thereby again placed in the psychological realm. Finally, we do not get at the real point if we say speculatively that God's act sets us in passivity and overcomes the sin-oriented activity of mankind (Jüngel, "Gesetz," 62). The antithesis is between Christ and Adam, not God and man. Our destiny is in view, not our deeds.

All these attempts at interpretation are examples of the way in which modern exposition tries to avoid apocalyptic. For in the apocalyptic horizon the end-time is infinitely superior to fall-determined primal time, as may be seen from 11:12, 15f. and 4 Ezra 4:31f.: "Consider now for yourself how much fruit of ungodliness a grain of evil seed has produced. When heads of grain without number are sown, how great a threshing floor they will fill." One should not emphasize the conclusion in vv. 15ff. in such a way that the thought of correspondence in the typology seems to be inappropriate (*contra* Brandenburger, *Adam*, 276ff.; H. Müller, "Auslegung," 84f.). Conversely one should not let the motif of intensification and superiority be decisive for the typology. Predominant here is the antithetical correspondence according to which Adam and Christ are both bearers of destiny for the world although they do not have the same significance in their functions. The bearer of eschatological salvation is the only alternative to the first Adam. These two—and basically these two alone—have determined the world as a whole. But he who ends disaster is infinitely superior to him who brings disaster, for he shatters destiny in order to build up his reign on earth.

In v. 15a παράπτωμα and χάρισμα are set in rhetorical antithesis (Barrett). They can hardly designate concrete acts, although v. 15b already has in view an action to which vv. 16b, 17a, 18a, and the δι' ἑνὸς ἁμαρτήσαντος of v. 16a also refer. χάρις τοῦ θεοῦ denotes the power whose result is indicated by ἡ δωρεά ἐν χάριτι in v. 15c, δώρημα in v. 16a, and δωρεά in v. 17b. The connection between action and result is emphasized. Hence the nouns παράβασις and παρακοή are avoided at least initially, and juridical terms are used in v. 16. The objective manner of speech characterizes afresh the fatefulness of the event (Michaelis, *TDNT*, VI, 171f.). Verse 15b takes up v. 12a-c and very unclearly derives universal death from Adam's fall. Decision about the world does not depend on the responsibility and offenses of individuals, of whom Adam is the representative. Rather, he is continually set over against the many. In his singularity as Anthropos he can be compared only with Christ and is to be differentiated from his descendants in the same way as Christ is from believers. This singularity is at issue when the two are constantly given emphasis by the use of εἷς, which is not to be understood here in terms of the Semitic εἷς–εἷς, "the one–the other" (correctly Cullmann, *Christology*, 171 *contra* J. Héring, *Le Royaume de Dieu et sa venue* [1937] 155ff.). This theme is so important to Paul here that, in distinction from 1 Cor 15:21, 45ff., he blurs the contrast between the primal men by using δι' ἑνὸς ἀνθρώπου of both; only adoption of a mythological tradition makes this possible. Added stress is given by counterposing the "many" to Adam as well as to Christ. This expression, which points to Dan 12:3 Theodotion and is explicitly used in Isa 53, denotes inclusively first of all the crowd and then the people as a totality (Billerbeck; Jeremias, *TDNT*, VI, 536ff.). It is extended universally here, as the parallel πάντες in v. 18 shows. The view that there is allusion to the Servant of the Lord, and that this explains that the one is spoken of with and without the article (Jeremias, *TDNT*, VI, 542ff.; in opposition Brandenburger, *Adam*, 235), has already been rejected. The antithesis of Adam as well as Christ to the many strictly rules out such an assumption. Although the Western reading ἁμαρτήματος in v. 16a obviously takes δι' ἑνός as a neuter, the context and especially the conclusion in v. 17 support the view that the stereotypically repeated δι' ἑνος is always masculine (Schlatter; Michel; Cambier, *L'Évangile*, 257 *contra* Kuss; Barrett; Ridderbos; also for v. 18 H. W. Schmidt).

Unmistakable rhetoric brings out the superior power of grace when the χάρισμα of v. 15 is taken up in the hendiadys χάρις καὶ ἡ δωρεά ἐν χάριτι and the ἐπερίσσευσεν is illustrated thereby. In Semitic fashion the prepositional combination replaces the genitive. Sharp stress is laid on the character of unmerited gift, which δώρημα in v. 16a also emphasizes. There is no reason to take δωρεά in the legal sense of "honorary gift," "legacy" (Büchsel, *TDNT*, II, 167). Grace again denotes, not the disposition (*contra* Kuss; Murray; Baulès), but the power which takes concrete shape in the gift as its result. This suggests already that χάρισμα in v. 15a should be rendered by "work of grace." The repetition of the introduction of v. 15a in v. 16a shows that v. 16 does not continue but intensifies the preceding verse. The ἐϰ denotes the sphere (Brandenburger, *Adam*, 224f.) and not the ground.

The legal terms which now appear do not make it clear that v. 16 looks back to v. 13b and v. 17 to v. 14 and that the verses are thus occasioned by recollection of the law (*contra* Jüngel, "Gesetz," 64). What they show is that the apostle does not view man tragically but as a wrongdoer, even though he speaks of the ongoing curse of guilt. The message of 1:24ff. is repeated. Judgment on the sin of the protoplast leads in anticipation of eschatological wrath to condemnation of the world dependent on him. The intensifying of ϰρίμα to ϰατάϰριμα corresponds, then, to the διὸ παρέδωϰεν. It is not unconsciously nor under the pressure of circumstances that moral breaches of unshakable laws produce hopeless entanglements as in Greek tragedy. Rebellion against the first commandment cannot be limited to the individual. It has productive force and spreads like a contagion. On the other hand a person cannot advance the excuse that he has no option. Even a heroic pose is denied him. In our lives we confirm the fact that a world in revolt surrounds us. The cycle of sin and destiny cannot be rationalized in terms of individual existence. All is fruit and all is seed.

Paul is not offering aetiology. Hence he begins at once with the judgment on Adam. His concern is with the reality of the present world in which personal accountability can be neither eliminated nor isolated. We are not bearers of history like the characters in a tragedy. Precisely in our acts we are exponents of a power which transforms the cosmos into chaos. Always before us is the unknown Judge who turns the intentions and weapons of rebels against them and lets us execute his sentence upon ourselves. Any moralistic or idealistic idea of a basically healthy world is dispelled here by an apocalyptic nightmare. The image has been lost (cf. 3:23) universally and not just privately.

Only against this background is it clear what the supremacy of grace really means. Verse 16c relates specifically to the sphere of the worldwide fall in transgression of the divine law which determines the present. This sphere has been invaded by the power of grace to effect a new creation. The noun χάρισμα does not have here the usual sense of individuations of grace, but as in 6:23 it can denote only the basic work of grace already accomplished. It finds its outcome in διϰαίωμα. Undoubtedly we have here rhetorical assimilation to other nouns with the same ending. For this reason the common translation is "justification" (BAGD, 198; Schrenk, *TDNT*, II, 226; Lietzmann; Schlatter; Barrett; Ridderbos). The reference is to the work of charisma (Bultmann, "Adam and Christ," 67) and certainly not, as in 1:32; 2:26; 8:4, to the demand of the law (*contra* Kühl), nor to God's righteous order. Conversely it is going too far to speak of the "dimension" of the Christ act (Nygren). What is meant is the objective reality of the justification that results. The statement has great significance for Pauline theology. What Paul elsewhere calls charismata are emanations and manifestations of the power of grace which has come on the scene with Christ. In context, however, they are also testimonies to accomplished justification and they lose their character if instead they are understood as privileges granted by the Spirit. Thirdly, they build a bridge from justification to what is usually called sanctification, and they do so in such a way that the latter is integrated into the event of justification.

Only in the third approach in v. 17 does Paul reach the goal of his argument. In the protasis he takes up terms from vv. 12, 14, and 15; in the apodosis πολλῷ μᾶλλον is again the central motif and it is characterized in its eschatological inconceivability (Barth, *Christus,* 83). The γάρ then does not just establish v. 16b (*contra* Jüngel, "Gesetz," 64); it also resumes it. This makes possible transition from the two digressions to the resumption of the anacoluthon of v. 12 in v. 18. Here again the genitive constructions develop rhetorically the περισσεία of grace. With the prepositional phrase they lead to a sharp climax. The διὰ τοῦ ἑνός in v. 17a seems to be redundant after the introductory τῷ τοῦ ἑνὸς παραπτώματι. In its parallelism to διὰ τοῦ ἑνὸς Ἰησοῦ Χριστοῦ at the end, however, it underscores again the antithetical correspondence of the two bearers of destiny and hence stresses that the Adam-Christ typology is the main concern of the section. Only thus can Paul's decisive theological summation be drawn. Later copyists emended the text to avoid the repetition in v. 17a (Lietzmann).

Here again grace is not to be understood as kindness for the sake of a distinction from δωρεά (*contra* Kuss). It is again the power which takes concrete form in the gift. With an epexegetical genitive the gift is defined as righteousness which is Christ's work pure and simple, and hence a mark of the new world. Thus v. 16c is elucidated and at the same time the connection with vv. 1-11 and the theme of the epistle is brought to light. The context proves that the justification of the ungodly is at issue. We do not have a mere change of course or expunging of prior guilt but transition from one aeon to another and to that extent existential change. This is sharpened in v. 17c so that the concrete goal of the previous argument is named. The plus of grace consists in transfer from the sphere of death to that of life as resurrection power (Schrenk, *TDNT,* II, 223f.).

Even this, however, does not satisfy the apostle. In deliberate correspondence to the dominion of death in vv. 14a, 17a, participation in the *basileia* is promised as in 1 Cor 15:25, and, to be sure, as it is anticipated in justification. It will be shown in ch. 6 that the tension between the present participle and the future verb is significant (Kuss). Only Christ has already been raised. His reign, however, represents God's lordship before its final victory and it finds expression precisely in the justification of the ungodly as the sphere of the commenced new creation. Even now, then, we participate in the life of the future world.

The λαμβάνοντες are undoubtedly believers. These now take the place of the earlier "many." This implies no restriction since "all" are mentioned in v. 18 and the "many" reappear in v. 19. The point is that even under grace and as a believer a person remains dependent on the one who, with the expression διὰ τοῦ ἑνὸς Ἰησοῦ Χριστοῦ, is with solemn emphasis opposed again to Adam as a bearer of destiny. For this reason it is doubtful whether one should (with Bultmann, "Adam and Christ," 68f.; *Theology,* I, 302f.) understand the participle in terms of decision and choice and see in Christ the possibility opened thereto (Jüngel, "Gesetz," 65 is right). For Paul the reign of Christ replaces that of Adam. The ontological structure of his anthropology remains determined by lordship as in the old aeon.

Analogy can arise between Adam and Christ only because both establish dominion over existence and the world.

Of course, it is valid to see that when this is said the analogy remains structural (Jüngel, "Gesetz," 60). The difference in the antithetical correspondence which establishes the infinite superiority of Christ and his kingdom arises out of the reality. This enables us to see the limit of the concept "bearer of destiny," at least so far as Christ is concerned. Its justification lies in the analogical structure. We never stand at the beginning in such a way that the alternative of Adam and Christ is not already present. In fact, the whole world is determined by this alternative and our existence becomes the place of the concrete battle between them. Insofar as we are integrated into Christ's reign, and remain in him, we owe this not to ourselves, but to the grace which possesses and sustains us as the ability to stand outside ourselves before God through Christ. As from Adam on the curse that has invaded all time and space is already present to us, no less is the blessing which is established universally throughout time and space by Christ and which spreads abroad in his kingdom. We do not constitute either the one or the other but we are instruments of either the one or the other and to that extent we receive "destiny" therefrom for ourselves and our world. Christ, however, shatters subjection to the Adamic world of sin and death by setting the world before its Creator again and by setting us in the state of creatureliness. Since the Adamic world is present and seems to prevail, this has to be continually reaccepted in faith. Received blessing brands us but it also sets us in conflict (*Anfechtung*) and contradiction. It places us before the need to persevere and in the possibility of relapse. It is not an irrevocable destiny which puts an end to the history of existence and the world. It gives free play to real history by making it the place, not of fallenness and doom, but of the assaulted freedom of faith and of the grace which is to be seized unceasingly in renunciation of the old aeon.

Verse 18, which is characteristically introduced by ἄρα οὖν (Kühl) and given its basis in v. 19, sums up the matter. In context δι᾽ ἑνός is again not a neuter (*contra* H. W. Schmidt; Murray). For the last time the premise, as in vv. 12, 14, 15b, and 17a, characterizes with the πάντες of v. 12c the universal doom hanging over Adam's world. In the final clause there is a rhetorical correspondence (BDF, §488[3]) to the same type of objective expression as governs the whole section, which demonstrates the change of aeons which has been effected with no cooperation on our part. As in v. 16c δικαίωμα in antithesis to παράπτωμα cannot be the legal requirement or the fulfilment thereof in a legal order (Zahn; Kühl), nor can it mean the verdict of justification (Lietzmann; Kuss; H. W. Schmidt) nor the righteous conduct of Christ throughout his life (Schrenk, *TDNT*, II, 221f.; Leenhardt; Murray). The deed alone corresponds to the fall (Brandenburger, *Adam*, 233; Ridderbos). Thus v. 19 refers to ὑπακοή, probably with the crucifixion in view as in Phil 2:8. The deed does, of course, involve an outworking. If this was described by δικαίωμα in v. 16c, it is now developed as δικαίωσις ζωῆς, taking up v. 17b. The genitive is qualitative and not one of direction (*contra* Bornkamm, "Anakoluthe," 88; Brandenburger, *Adam*, 233; Lafont, "Interprétation," 492; Cambier, *L'Évangile*, 265; Murray; Ridderbos).

Two things become apparent thereby. The goal of the argument is the doctrine of justification (Bultmann, "Adam and Christ," 69; Jüngel, "Gesetz," 66f.; Murray). But it is so in such a way that in the light of it the eschatological περισσεία of grace is set forth which causes the universal validity of the resurrection power of Christ already to break out of the future into the present. This is the advance on vv. 1-11. To be sure, precisely this point raises a problem. Does not the hope of general restoration (*apokatastasis*) come to expression here (cf. Grundmann, "Übermacht," 53f.; Oepke, *TDNT*, I, 392) if we take seriously the πάντες of v. 18b and the inclusive οἱ πολλοί of v. 19b in antithetical correspondence to the first clauses? Certainly believers are meant, yet they alone are not mentioned (*contra* Zahn; Murray) and nothing justifies the assumption (Jülicher) that at the end only they remain for Paul. If conversely one asserts rhetorical overstatement (Lietzmann), one has still to clarify what it means. The parallels in 1 Cor 15:22 and particularly 11:32 should not be overlooked. Common to all these passages is that all-powerful grace is unthinkable without eschatological universalism (Schlatter; Barrett) and that cosmology overshadows anthropology as its projection. As in vv. 18f. the antithetical correspondence of primal time and end-time undeniably determines the typology present (*contra* Brandenburger, *Adam*, 238f., 241ff.), Christ appears, in the problematic mode of expression which we can scarcely accept uncritically (without *Sachkritik*), presented as the predestined cosmocrator. The intention of the apostle is to present the universality of the reign of Christ in antithesis to the world of Adam. New creation is proclaimed and this points to the end when, as 1 Cor 15:28 puts it, God will be all in all.

Verse 19 repeats, supports, and elucidates what is said in v. 18. Undoubtedly Genesis 3 is in view when disobedience is spoken of instead of transgression and the obedience of the second Anthropos is contrasted with the disobedience of the first. If in relation to the former Paul has the cross especially in mind, as in the existing tradition in Phil 2:8f. and corresponding to Heb 5:8f., the statement is not limited to that and there is certainly no reference to the atonement (Brandenburger, *Adam*, 235; Cullmann, *Christology*, 171). Hence there is not the least reason to introduce the motif of the Suffering Servant into the text. The important thing is only the antithesis to Adam's disobedience and therefore again the antithetical correspondence of primal time and end-time.

Disobedience is of the essence of sin, and the revelation of the new obedience in Christ is eschatological salvation. Christ has thus been exalted to be the hidden Ruler of the world (Phil 2:9ff.; 1 Cor 15:24). His people, being obedient, participate for the time being in the freedom from the powers which he has won and will one day share openly in the kingdom (*basileia*, v. 17b). Even more plainly than before, the dawn of the new creation is now proclaimed.

καθιστάναι τινά τι means "make someone something," passively "become something" (BAGD, 390b; Oepke, *TDNT*, III, 445). After the past form in the first clause the verb in the second clause, as in v. 17b, is not in the logical (Sanday and Headlam; Zahn; Kühl; Lagrange; Althaus; Bultmann, *Theology*, I, 274) but the eschatological future (Lietzmann; Kuss; Ridderbos; Schrenk, *TDNT*, II, 191, 218). We thus have a parallel to Gal 5:5, where righteousness is awaited as a gift of the consummation. Naturally this does not mean that suddenly there is doubt as to the reality of accomplished justification, or that this is restricted. It has already been shown that righteousness and God's glory are different aspects of the same thing. If we now have an eschatological future, the divine righteousness granted to faith is characterized as a mark of the end-time and of the rule of God which has dawned for the "many" as the new world. The obedience of Christ, which cancelled the disobedience of the primal man, and reinitiated history, stands at the beginning of the kingdom of fulfilment.

Unexpectedly v. 20 returns to the question put in v. 13. There is a reason for this digression (contra Kuss). But (contra Michel) it does not consist in the fact that the context contains a legal argument and that salvation is understood in terms of law, as in Judaism. To the extent that Paul is in fact opposing a Jewish approach, he is not in any sense affirming the inner connection between a first and a last period (contra Bultmann, "Adam and Christ," 71), nor is he christologically transcending both (Barth, Christus, 105f.), nor is he (contra Jüngel, "Gesetz," 67ff.) declaring the law to be the structure of the world. Such speculations are refuted by παρεισῆλθεν, although one should not relate this to the secret and hostile "slipping in" of Gal 2:4 (correctly Zahn; Cambier, L'Évangile, 267). Rather, what emerges is that the law offers no possibility of contact for the world of Christ. It is not even considered (contra Jüngel, "Gesetz," 68) that the spheres of sin and death are the place of the new history. In relativizing fashion the verb marks an interlude (Althaus; van Dülmen, Theologie, 170; contra Gutjahr; Murray). The final clause shows that the law has no significance for the antithesis of Adam and Christ but only for the world of Adam. It radicalizes sin, by allowing it to increase through transgression. We are not told how this happens, and it is idle to ask for information about that here (contra Luz, Geschichtsverständnis, 202), especially as 7:7ff. will give the answer. The only point for the moment is that between Adam and Christ, and the worlds inaugurated by them, there is no third alternative, namely, legal piety (Barth, Christus, 100). In a way that is blasphemous to Jews, Paul finds in the law no legitimate answer to the question of eternal life (Michel). It does not mark the way of salvation but belongs in both fact and effect to the side of sin and death. The pious who set themselves under it also stand under the reign of Adam, which is indeed more sharply articulated in them than elsewhere. To this there corresponds afresh the eschatological extravagance of grace in the hyperbolical ὑπερπερισσεύειν, for which one finds a parallel in the "superabound" of 4 Ezra 4:50 (Hauck, TDNT, VI, 60). Now that the last chance of bridging the antithesis has gone v. 21 presents again the πολλῷ μᾶλλον of vv. 15ff. along with the break between the two aeons. If ἵνα has a final sense in v. 20, the consecutive is more likely here, since 21a and 21b are parallel. ἐν τῷ θανάτῳ can hardly be meant instrumentally (contra Lietzmann; Kuss; Barrett; Michel; Bornkamm, "Anakoluthe," 87; Brandenburger, Adam, 254). It designates the sphere. In v. 21b the verb is in the logical future. Grace, righteousness, and eternal life can no longer be separated chronologically or causally. In them we encounter under different aspects the same thing, namely, the basileia of Christ. As often in Paul, the liturgical heaping up of prepositional phrases and the concluding christological formula mark the end of the argument (Bornkamm, "Anakoluthe," 89).

B. Freedom from the Power of Sin (6:1-23)

The logic of the context will not let us separate the themes of freedom from death, from sin, and from the law. There is no question here of a systematically forced and "linear" construction (*contra* Luz, "Aufbau," 164). All these things belong together in the reality of justification. For this reason one should not put ch. 5 in the previous division of the epistle and find the beginning of the new one only with ch. 6 (especially Kühl; Sanday and Headlam; Lagrange; Huby; Ridderbos; Black; Dupont, "Structure," 383, 387f.). Nor are chs. 6–7 an excursus (J. Knox, *Life*, 49).

Nevertheless the uncertainty of exegetes shows that we have here a problem that should not go unnoticed. The proposed structure gives rise to a number of difficulties of which at least the most important ought to be listed. What is the nature of the relation between ch. 8 and chs. 5–7? Why is the theme of freedom from the law dealt with briefly in 7:1-6 and then almost paralyzed by the long section that follows? What motivates Paul to incorporate exhortation into ch. 6 and ch. 8 even though this latter in its fundamental character contrasts with the admonitions of chs. 12ff.? What significance does the Adam-Christ typology have for what follows if it is not regarded as an excursus?

The questions are not adequately answered or connected with one another by saying that in the next chapters (Kuss) Paul is dealing with the paradoxical relation of indicative and imperative. At the same time this does provide at least an indirect insight which can set us on the way to solving the problems and indicate the relevance of 5:12ff. for what follows in such a way that a thematic superstructure for this section results.

Freedom from death is presented so universally and therefore with such mythological objectivity that individual existence threatens to be lost to view. If in a certain respect Christ is a bearer of destiny for the world as Adam was, the destiny which he brings is not a fate like that of Adam. In what sense, then, can it still be called destiny? The apostle stands before the task of making intelligible in terms of the reality of everyday life, of the community, and of the individual, the universal realization of eschatological life which he has set forth in ch. 5. He does this by characterizing it as freedom from the powers of sin and the law and therewith summons Christians with inner necessity to confirm in their personal life the change of aeons that has been effected. He still maintains both the cosmological horizon and the fact that the Christ event precedes faith. With the new themes, however, both are more clearly projected into the sphere of anthropology (Blank, *Paulus*, 279) and also are verified by the presence of the community. The other questions will be clarified from that perspective.

1. Dead to Sin by Baptism (6:1-11)

[1]*What shall we say then? Must we remain under the power of sin that grace may increase?* [2]*Impossible! How can we who are dead to sin still want to live in it?* [3]*Or do you not know that we who were baptized into Christ Jesus have been baptized into his death?* [4]*We were even buried with him by the baptism of death. The aim was that as Christ was raised from the dead by the glory of the Father, we too should walk in newness of life.* [5]*For if we have been united and fashioned into the likeness of his death, we shall be no less so into that of his resurrection.* [6]*We must realize that our old man was crucified with him so that the body of sin might be destroyed. For this reason we can no longer serve the power of sin.* [7]*For he who is dead is set free from sin.* [8]*If we then*

have died with Christ, we believe that we shall also live with him. [9]*For we know that Christ, being raised from the dead, dies no more. Death has no more power over him.* [10]*In that he died, he died to sin once and for all, and in that he lives, he lives to God.* [11]*Draw the conclusion then that you too are dead to sin but alive for God in Christ Jesus.*

Bibliography: G. Wagner, *Pauline Baptism and the Pagan Mysteries* (Eng. tr. 1967); E. Lohmeyer, "Σὺν Χριστῷ," *Festgabe für Adolf Deissmann zum 60. Geburtstag 7. November 1926* (1927) 218-257; J. Dupont, Σὺν Χριστῷ, *L'Union avec le Christ suivant saint Paul. I: "Avec le Christ" dans la vie future* (1952); G. Otto, *Die mit σύν verbundenen Formulierungen im paulinischen Schrifttum,* Diss. Berlin (1952); P. Bonnard, "Mourir et vivre avec Jésus Christ selon saint Paul," *RHPR* 36 (1956) 101-112; H. Braun, "Das 'Stirb und werde' in der Antike und im NT," *Gesammelte Studien,* 136-158; W. T. Hahn, *Das Mitsterben und Mitauferstehen mit Christus bei Paulus* (1937); O. Kuss, excursus "Mit Christus" in his commentary, 319-381; E. Schweizer, "Mystik"; O. Casel, *The Mystery of Christian Worship* (Eng. tr. 1962); S. Stricker, "Der Mysteriengedanke des hl. Paulus nach Röm 6, 2-11," *Liturgisches Leben* 1 (1934) 285-296; H. G. Marsh, *The Origin and Significance of the NT Baptism* (1941); O. Cullmann, *Baptism in the NT* (Eng. tr. 1950); H. Schwarzmann, *Zur Tauftheologie des hl. Paulus in Röm 6* (1950); M. Barth, *Die Taufe—ein Sakrament?* (1951); K. H. Schelkle, "Taufe und Tod. Zur Auslegung von Röm 6, 1-11," *Vom christlichen Mysterium. Gesammelte Arbeiten zum Gedächtnis von Odo Casel* (ed. A. Mayer, *et al.*; 1951) 9-21; G. Bornkamm, "Baptism and New Life in Paul (Romans 6)," *Early Christian Experience,* 71-86; W. F. Flemington, *The NT Doctrine of Baptism* (1953); R. Schnackenburg, "Todes- und Lebensgemeinschaft mit Christus. Neue Studien zu Röm 6, 1-11," *MTZ* 6 (1955) 32-53; H. Schlier, "Die Taufe nach dem 6. Kapitel des Römerbriefs," *Die Zeit der Kirche,* 47-56; idem, "Zur kirchlichen Lehre von der Taufe," ibid., 107-129; G. Delling, *Die Zueignung des Heils in der Taufe* (1961); idem, *Die Taufe im NT* (1963); G. R. Beasley-Murray, *Baptism in the NT* (1962); V. Warnach, "Taufe und Christusgeschehen nach Römer 6," *Archiv für Liturgiewissenschaft* III/2 (1954) 284-366; idem, "Die Tauflehre des Römerbriefs in der neueren theologischen Diskussion," ibid., V (1958) 274-322; O. Kuss, "Zur paulinischen und nachpaulinischen Tauflehre im NT," *Auslegung,* I, 121-150; idem, "Zu Röm 6, 5a," *Auslegung,* I, 151-161; H. Frankemölle, *Das Taufverständnis des Paulus* (1970); E. Dinkler, "Die Taufaussagen des NT," *Zu Karl Barths Lehre von der Taufe* (ed. F. C. Viering (1971) 60-153; W. Bieder, *Die Verheissung der Taufe im NT* (1966). 3-6: L. Fazekaš, "Taufe als Tod in Röm 6, 3ff.," *TZ* 22 (1966) 305-318; E. Stommel, "'Begraben mit Christus' (Römer 6, 4) und der Taufritus," *Römische Quartalschrift für christliche Altertumskunde und Kirchengeschichte* 49 (1954) 1-20; idem, "Das Abbild seines Todes (Römer 6, 5) und der Taufritus," ibid., 50 (1955) 1-21; F. Mussner, "Zur paulinischen Tauflehre in Röm 6, 1-6," *Praesentia Salutis* (1967) 189-196; J. Gewiess, "Das Abbild des Todes Christi (Röm 6, 5)," *Historische Jahrbücher* 77 (1958) 339-346; K. G. Kuhn, "Rm 6, 7," *ZNW* 30 (1931) 305-310; W. Diezinger, "Unter Toten freigeworden," *NovT* 5 (1962) 268-298; R. Scroggs, "Romans vi.7," *NTS* 10 (1963) 104-108; C. Kearns, "The Interpretation of Rom. 6:7," *Stud.Paul.Congr.,* I, 301-307.

From the very beginning historical study has been kindled by Paul's sacramental teaching as well as his eschatology. The question of the influence of Hellenistic mystery-religions on his doctrine of baptism is still debated, and an affirmative or negative answer has far-reaching theological consequences even in the Roman Catholic camp. It is in order, therefore, to anticipate this problem of exegesis. Here again we find two extremes. Initial over-evaluation yielded first to a more sober estimate and today in many circles to absolute scepticism. The basic and most impressive study by G. Wagner concludes that the mystery cults adduced either do not merit their name or in their principal views do not coincide with the Pauline tradition of dying and rising again with the Redeemer so that they are of no importance in understanding this passage. To be sure, he remains obligated to his own explanation, and rules out with methodological care any questions that might lead to a different conclusion. If, as we shall try to show, the apostle was correcting the tradition of the community here, he must have used an understanding which was current in the Hellenistic community, since the idea of dying and rising again with the Redeemer can even less be explained in terms of Judaism. It is obvious at least that Wagner does not give due weight to the Isis initiation depicted in Apuleius *Metamorphoses* xi.11ff., 23f. (Gäumann, *Ethik*, 41ff.; Wengst, *Formeln*, 39f. against Wagner, *Problem*, 98ff.; cf. already Lietzmann). If a general Hellenistic mystery piety is rejected as a vague postulate, not even Philo and Hermetica I and XIII are taken into account, and it remains inconceivable in what way the early church saw in the mysteries a devilish perversion of its own cult (cf. the judicious discussions in Kuss, 322, 344ff., 369ff.; Friedrich, *RGG*, V, 1141). Again it is neither fish nor fowl for historians and exegetes when similarities in structure and motifs are accepted but direct connection is denied (Larsson, *Vorbild*, 22f.). The present passage cannot be treated in isolation. In the background stand the groups from Corinth and elsewhere which regard the future resurrection as superfluous since they imagine that baptism has already set them in an angelic state. Liturgically stamped tradition in Col 2:11ff.; Eph 2:14ff.; 5:14 undoubtedly permits us to state that in these circles at least baptism was celebrated as a Christian cultic mystery. So long as the problems of such data are not seen and solved, one misses the starting point for any possible detailed investigation.

Decisive for this passage is the origin and meaning of the formula "with Christ," which Paul varies in many ways. In 1 Thess 4:14; 2 Cor 4:14 the reference is only to the resurrection, in Gal 2:19 and here to crucifixion with Christ from the perspective of baptism. The expression receives its point (characteristic for the apostle) in the antitheses which in 2 Cor 4:10 relate present participation in Christ's death to future participation in his life and in Rom 8:17 relate suffering with Christ to glorification with him.

Especially interesting is 2 Cor 13:4b, since here the same antithetically formulated motif in the first member replaces the σὺν αὐτῷ of the second member with ἐν αὐτῷ. In this way Paul obviously wants to characterize the state of earthly temptation as overcome by the exalted Lord. But this is presupposed in all the passages mentioned. The change of prepositions shows that Paul was not dependent on the formula σὺν Χριστῷ when he wanted to depict Christian suffering and death in the service and discipleship of Jesus. "In Christ," which is far more common in Paul, was completely sufficient for this purpose. The same is true when it is a matter of living fellowship with the exalted Lord and the future glorification of Christians. 5:10; 14:8f.; 2 Cor 5:15 refer simply to abiding membership which according to other passages is guaranteed by the Spirit as resurrection power.

This finding makes it highly improbable that Paul himself coined the expression "with Christ" (*contra* Lohmeyer, "Σὺν Χριστῷ," 257; Grundmann, *TDNT*, VII, 767, 781; Prat, *Theology*, II, 18ff.; Kuss, 328, 378; Schnackenburg, *Baptism*, 174f.; Siber, *Mit Christus*, 196ff., 213). That is all the more so since the formula obviously is connected with the idea of being conformed with Christ as God's image, an idea which probably derives from liturgical tradition according to 8:29; Phil 3:21 and is also taken up in Phil 3:10. In Phil 3:10 and 1 Thess 4:14ff. it is related to the traditional idea of apocalyptic "meeting" (ἀπάντησις). One sees here the various complexes of tradition which were present already, which the apostle used and adapted, but whose prior history still needs illumination. If 1 Thess 4:14-17 is taken as a starting point, the supposition lies at hand that the original apocalyptic idea that Christians will be caught up with their Lord into eternal fulfilment with him formed the initial stage and that this was extended in the face of the speculations of enthusiasts to the earthly being with Christ (A. Schweitzer, *Mysticism*, 186ff.; augmented by Lohmeyer, "Σὺν Χριστῷ," 219ff.; E. Schweizer, "Mystik," 184ff.; Thyen, *Studien*, 209f.; Kuss; Grundmann, *TDNT*, VII, 781; criticism of Lohmeyer in Schnackenburg, *Baptism*, 172f.; Bieder, *Verheissung*, 199f.; Siber, *Mit Christus*, 10f.).

It is true enough that for Paul the earthly "with Christ" reaches its climax with the eternal being of consummation, as especially in Phil 1:23. Yet this does not decide the origin of the formula. Phil 1:23 is not apocalyptic. Characteristically, no noun takes up the verbal sayings, which at the crucial points do not speak of a being but of an event which allows two stages to follow one another antithetically. While this antithetical sequence cannot be explained in terms of anticipation of the future heavenly state, we know it from the hymns to Christ. It is proper, then, not to insist on a single root for the total complex.

Two independent ideas come together at this point. The one describes fulfilment at the parousia, or after death, as being "with the Lord." The other transfers the stages of Christ's way to believers as the disciples of their Lord (Otto, *Formulierungen*, 86; Schnackenburg, *Baptism*, 175; Bonnard, "Mourir," 101ff.). The latter undoubtedly has its locus in ideas about baptism, which as a rite of initiation gives a share in Christ's destiny (Schnackenburg, *Baptism*, 172ff.; Dupont, "L'Union," 112, 181-191; Prat, *Theology*, II, 19f.). The liturgical texts Col 2:11ff.; Eph 2:4ff.; 5:14 show that originally baptism itself was understood as translation into the world of the resurrection out of the sleep of sin, or as participation in the death and resurrection of Christ, or, according to 8:29, his glory. The Corinthian enthusiasts held a similar view. A Christianity directed against such enthusiasm, to which Paul belonged, viewed baptism as participation in the death of Christ and a pledge of future glorification. The apostle seems to have heightened the tension by bringing the motif of "being crucified with" into the baptismal statement and making suffering in discipleship the mark of the earthly state of the Christian (E. Schweizer, "Mystik," 194).

This reconstruction yields the following conclusions. In the pre-Pauline community outside Palestine baptism was really understood as a mystery event which incorporated one into the fate of the cultic God, Christ. Christ was thereby the heavenly *eikon* who trod the way of redemption first and to whom believers had to be conformed. This must not be reduced in modern style (*contra* Larsson, *Vorbild*, 25 and *passim*) to the idea of a pattern or model. Otherwise the connection with the motif of the eschatological primal man in 5:12ff. and the connection between the two chapters, or the understanding of baptism as incorporation into the body of Christ, are not taken into account. Even more mistaken is exposition under the catchword "contemporaneity" of Christians and Christ (Hahn, *Mitsterben*, 90ff.). In both cases it is not perceived that the tradition of the "with Christ," which does not belong constitutively to Paul's theology and which therefore overlaps the formula "in Christ," is used by the apostle to give precision to his concept of Christ as a bearer of destiny. In baptism the new world initiated by Christ seizes the life of the individual Christian too, in such a way that the earthly path of the exalted Lord is to be traversed again in this life and Christ thus becomes the destiny of our life. Baptism is projection of the change of aeons into our personal existence, which for its part becomes a constant return to baptism to the extent that here dying with Christ establishes life with him and the dialectic of the two constitutes the signature of being in Christ (not perceived in Siber, *Mit Christus*, 186ff.).

For most exegetes the structure of the chapter is determined by the parallel questions in diatribe style in v. 1 and v. 15. Verse 11, however, solemnly sums up a first train of thought (K. Barth; Lagrange; Kuss; Bornkamm, "Baptism," 78f.; Schnackenburg, *Baptism*, 32) according to which Christians are set free from sin with a definitiveness which death alone can achieve. This is a thoroughly dogmatic statement to which the label "ethical and hortatory" (Kühl; Schnackenburg, *Baptism*, 32) fails to do justice. For here, too, sin is viewed as a power and not just as an offense. In the sphere of Christ the conclusion of 5:20b is irreversible, as the indignant denial of the question in v. 1 shows. The problem of possible relapses into the pre-Christian state certainly comes into view in the rhetorical clothing of introduction and conclusion, but it is not discussed in a fundamental way as it would have to be in a systematic exposition of the relation of the Christian to sin. Paul instead proclaims the freedom from the power of sin which is given with the change of aeons and baptism as its projection in the individual life.

Verses 12-14 form the theme of the second section, which is more broadly developed in vv. 15-23. It is not unintentionally dominated by imperatives. It deals with the result of such a message in its practical verification. What emerges most clearly is that the righteousness of God, which is predominantly described as a gift in the preceding chapters, is the eschatological manifestation of its Giver, so that, like sin, it has the character of a power that determines existence. As such it enables us to maintain the break with the world of Adam accomplished in baptism and to show in the new obedience that the dominion of the obedient man of 5:19 is an earthly reality. It is quite out of the question, then, that Paul is leaving the main theme of the epistle in chs. 6–8. He stays close to this theme (*contra* Luz, "Aufbau," 181), although approaching it from a different angle.

The first section does not offer an explicit statement of Paul's doctrine of baptism (Thyen, *Studien*, 194ff. *contra* many scholars, e.g., Warnach, "Tauflehre," 279), although it is a locus classicus for this and the apostle nowhere deals more extensively with this complex. Important theologoumena in the primitive Christian and Pauline view of baptism are missing, such as the conferring of the Spirit as a constitutive element and sacramental incorporation into the body of Christ (Hegermann, *Schöpfungsmittler*, 143f.). The widespread idea that this passage too is determined by the idea of corporate personality (Dodd; Nygren; Beasley-Murray, *Baptism*, 128ff.; Grundmann, *TDNT*, VII, 789; Thyen, *Studien*, 200) can appeal to v. 3 but overlooks the surprising reserve with regard to this motif in general. We learn nothing about what probably was already then the necessary preparation of those who sought baptism and next to nothing about the rite as such (contra Dodd; Nygren; Sickenberger; Flemington, Doctrine, 59; Schwarzmann, Tauftheologie, 40; Warnach, "Taufe," 299; "Tauflehre," 295ff., 326f.; cf. for a correct view Ridderbos; Mussner, "Tauflehre," 194; Gäumann, Ethik, 74, 108; E. Schweizer, "Mystik," 192; Marsh, Origin, 141; Stommel, "Abbild," 3f.; Braun, "Stirb," 25). We are not told whether it is related to the gathering of the community, administered by office-bearers, accompanied by invocation of the name of Jesus, vows, hymns, and laying on of hands, or given by immersion or aspersion, nor whether many people or families are baptized together, let alone whether infants are also baptized. βαπτίζειν already has a technical sense (Larsson, Vorbild, 56; Fazekaš, "Taufe," 307f.; Frankemölle, Taufverständnis, 48f., 51f.). It is at least questionable whether it still carries the sense "to dip," "to immerse." An understanding of the process as an efficacious symbol (e.g., Sickenberger; Huby; Cerfaux, Christian, 331), which leads Casel and his school to speak of a Christian cult mystery, may once have been present but it cannot be convincingly read from the text (Murray; Ridderbos, Paul, 402; Schnackenburg, Baptism, 33ff., 127ff.; Dinkler, "Taufaussagen," 72; Siber, Mit Christus, 193). The phrase about being crucified with Christ is incompatible with it, and only pious imagination can link the other phrase about burial with Christ to going under the water. Since we lack fuller information about the rite, there is no justification for making the admittedly connected element of confession the central point (contra M. Barth, Taufe, 228ff.; Bieder, Verheissung, 191ff.) or for playing off the "cognitive" against the causative effect (contra Thyen, Studien, 200ff.). In distinction from Judaism, in any case, it does not involve self-baptism, and the activity of believers recedes completely behind what is done to them.

Finally, it must be stressed that the text tells us nothing about the prior history of baptism. We learn nothing about its relation to Jewish practices of washing, especially the much cited baptism of proselytes, whose practice at this period is highly problematic, nor about the institution of baptism by Jesus and the probable connection with John's baptism, nor about the Jewish-Christian understanding of the eschatological sealing and transferal of the baptized to the risen Lord. The style of the passage is not at all hymnic (contra Michel) nor confessional, and only wishful thinking can discover here an early Christian "creed" (Gäumann, Ethik, 64). Of course, v. 3 is not merely polite pedagogics (Lietzmann; Wagner, Problem, 277ff.), but it also carries no reminiscence of the primitive Christian view (contra Larsson, Vorbild, 24, 75ff.) and it is probably reminiscent of fixed tradition already present at least in the Hellenistic community (Bultmann, Theology, I, 141ff.). This had come to expression in formulae which could harden into confessional statements, unless they derive from these. Such formulae and statements are found already here. If we say more we are no longer on solid ground. From the various epistles of Paul all kinds of material can be collected on the theology and practice of baptism, and it is obvious that he valued it no less than the eucharist (contra Siber, Mit Christus, 192, who claims a lack of any interest in it). Nevertheless, Paul never gave a comprehensive account of it. This implies that the rite and its meaning were not disputed in his circles. Hence it was necessary to emphasize only the basic motifs, in this case the fellowship of our destiny with that of Christ.

The introductory question is rhetorical (with Kuss; Frankemölle, *Taufverständnis*, 40) in such a way that one could assume an objection posed by Paul himself as a means to move to a new theme. Yet according to 3:5ff. Paul in fact was accused of inviting to libertinism, so that one has to take it into account that he is defending himself against misunderstanding of the doctrine of justification (Kühl). The apostle answers the charge in v. 2 with a single assertion which is broadly developed in what follows. Verses 2-4, 5-7, and formally at least, with a material displacement, vv. 8-10 are parallel to one another (Bornkamm, "Baptism," 74f.; Michel; Frankemölle, *Taufverständnis*, 23). In baptism Christians are freed from the power of sin by death.

οἵτινες (= *quippe qui*) gives the reason and the future in v. 2b is logical, while variants make it cohortative (Kuss). ἐν αὐτῇ refers to the sphere of sin (Kuss; Schnackenburg, *Baptism*, 33), over against which dialectical vacillation is ruled out from the outset (Bornkamm, "Baptism," 73f.). The ἢ ἀγνοεῖτε means the same as the more common οἴδατε and points to familiar tradition. As in 1 Cor 12:13 the parallel between "in Christ" and "into his death" suggests that the force of εἰς is local. It is true that according to 1 Cor 1:15 Paul knew the conception which expressed transferal to Christ through the formula "baptized in his name." But he does not pick this up here (with Kuss; Leenhardt; Ridderbos, *Paul*, 403 *contra* M. Barth, *Taufe*, 225; Larsson, *Vorbild*, 55; Delling, *Zueignung*, 73ff.; Siber, *Mit Christus*, 206), nor does he even presuppose it as the basis of his phrase (with Tannehill, *Dying*, 84; Gäumann, *Ethik*, 74; Frankemölle, *Taufverständnis*, 43ff.; *contra* Barrett; Schnackenburg, *Baptism*, 107; Warnach, "Taufe," 294; Stommel, "Abbild," 5).

As in 2 Cor 1:21; Gal 3:27 the baptized are integrated into the new Adam. This should not be abstractly brought under the denominator of the "reality of salvation" (*contra* Delling, *Zueignung*, 77ff.), though one is right to reject the idea of a mystical union. As will be shown, and as has been intimated already in 5:12ff., it is ultimately a matter of participation in the reign of Christ. To achieve this, however, the old man must die. This is done causatively and effectively by baptism (Schlier, "Taufe," 48; Larsson, *Vorbild*, 58; Mussner, "Tauflehre," 190). Verse 3a is Paul's formulation of the premise for the traditional statement in v. 3b. In context the past tenses point to an event which lies in the past and happened once-for-all. Hence dying with Christ is not to be psychologized as repentance (Leenhardt) or as a sacramental experience of the death of Jesus (Huby; Schnackenburg, *Baptism*, 37). Otherwise the apostle could not proclaim freedom from the power of sin as a reality. Conversely the speculative assertion can compel theologically very dangerous consequences, as though the general baptism took place on Golgotha and we have died already on the cross with Christ (cf. Kümmel, *Theology*, 215f. *contra* Cullmann, *Baptism*, 23, 32f.; M. Barth, *Taufe*, 229, 271ff.; Delling, *Taufe*, 127ff.; Otto, *Formulierungen*, 32ff.; Thyen, *Studien*, 198f.). Whereas in 1 Cor 15:22 all died in Adam, in 2 Cor 5:14 Christ died for all and, as the context shows, he has caught up Christians into his death; this took place in baptism. The concept of vicariousness controls and interprets here that of the fellowship in his fate. Otherwise the cross of Jesus loses its fundamental significance and becomes the mythical cipher of a cosmic drama, as in the case of Adam's fall. Christ alone died on the cross. Only inasmuch as he died for us are we too brought into his death and does baptism arise as reception of his act and participation in his fate (Eichholz, *Paulus*, 211f.).

The verb in v. 4a sharpens v. 3b. Hence εἰς τὸν θάνατον goes with βαπτίσματος (*contra* BDF, §272; Zahn; Lagrange; Kuss; Bornkamm, "Baptism," 74; Ridderbos; with Kühl; H. W. Schmidt; Larsson, *Vorbild*, 56; Schnackenburg, *Baptism*, 34). It is hard to see why the article should be repeated before εἰς or an αὐτοῦ added to θάνατον. The idea of a burial into death seems a forced one. In baptism a death takes place to such an extent that in analogy to the christological tradition of 1 Cor 15:4 this effects burial (Michel; Thyen, *Studien*, 196f.; Stommel, "Begraben," 6). The once-for-all event has a definitive character (Fazekaš, "Taufe," 308f.).

As in v. 3a, however, a premise is named, and this in formal terms. Hence the verb should not be made the center of the context (Dinkler, "Taufaussagen," 72 *contra* M. Barth, *Taufe;* Otto, *Formulierungen*, 40; Stommel, "Begraben," 9f.; Thyen, *Studien*, 202f.). The sharpening of v. 3b arises from the fact that the second element in the view adopted by Paul, namely, resurrection with Christ, can now be brought into the argument. As in 5:12, 15ff. the motif of correspondence in ὥσπερ–οὕτως has materially supportive significance (Warnach, "Taufe," 300). The solemn "by the glory of the Father" may be pre-Pauline, since it speaks of the Father with no further definition and δόξα is identified with δύναμις or πνεῦμα (Fuchs, *Freiheit*, 29; Michel). Where graves cannot hold the dead, the deity of God is at work (Murray). This is true for Christ, who is simply called the Son as in 1:4, and by participation in his destiny it is true also for the baptized. In the non-Palestinian, pre-Pauline community faith focuses on this last aspect, as the Corinthian enthusiasts, Col 2:12, and Eph 2:5f. all show. Here, too, Paul is dealing with fixed tradition.

The tradition is important for Paul, since he can base the new life in Christ upon it. Note should be taken, however, of the care with which he expresses himself (Barrett; Siber, *Mit Christus*, 205). It need not be more than a different nuance that he speaks of καινότης ζωῆς instead of resurrection, and in the verb avoids the present indicative. καινότης undoubtedly denotes that which is eschatologically new. As in 7:6 the stress is on the noun, which in Semitic fashion can represent an adjective. The permanence of the resurrection power, which cannot be undone, is emphasized. The aorist subjunctive possibly replaces a logical future (Zahn; Kühl; Larsson, *Vorbild*, 71; Schnackenburg, *Baptism*, 37). Yet the eschatological futures in vv. 5b and 8b are against this (Lietzmann; Leenhardt; Gäumann, *Ethik*, 48; Thüsing, *Per Christum*, 70f., 139ff.). Hence one is forced to say (with Bultmann, *Theology*, I, 140f.; Braun, "Stirb," 26; Merk, *Handeln*, 24) that Paul modifies his tradition, differentiating between the already risen Lord and believers. As in 2 Cor 13:4 the power of the resurrection which is in fact at work in them asserts itself initially by setting them contrariwise (*sub contrario*) under the shadow of the cross and makes this in a special way the mark of the new life.

It is astonishing how obviously most expositors, following the dominant exegesis of the early church (cf. Schelkle, 16ff.), fail to observe the caution required by the apostle's eschatology (e.g., Kühl; Lagrange; Sickenberger; Kuss; Baulès;

Cullmann, *Baptism*, 23, 30, 35f.; Stricker, "Mysteriengedanke," 286; Warnach, "Taufe," 301, 313ff.; Stommel, "Abbild," 10f.; Schwarzmann, *Tauftheologie*, 26f.; Schlier, "Taufe," 48ff.; Delling, *Taufe*, 130f.; with some differentiation Huby; Cerfaux, *Christian*, 187f.; in opposition Gäumann, *Ethik*, 75f.; Dinkler, "Taufaussagen," 72). An important influence in this regard is doubtless the idea of mystical union with Christ, which (even in Sanday and Headlam; Murray; J. Knox) is maintained as a central theme and is thought to involve an ontological change of the human *physis* (Warnach, "Taufe," 301; Stommel, "Abbild," 19ff.; Seidensticker, *Opfer*, 236f.; Schnackenburg, *Baptism*, 182, 190f.; Otto, *Formulierungen*, 47ff.). Over against this the verb περιπατεῖν should call attention to the fact that the apostle expects our resurrection only in the future and, as vv. 12-23 show, sees in the new obedience an anticipation of it and the sign of the already present reality of its power (Furnish, *Ethics*, 174f.; Siber, *Mit Christus*, 240ff.).

Verses 5-11 (*contra* Larsson, *Vorbild*, 51) do not explicate vv. 2-4. Nor is v. 5 a parenthesis (*contra* Kühl). Verses 2-4 are repeated for clarification in vv. 5-7 (Gäumann, *Ethik*, 83; Frankemölle, *Taufverständnis*, 60ff.). Exegetical difficulties are concentrated in v. 5 (cf. Schelkle, 11ff. on patristic exegesis; Kuss and Schnackenburg, *Baptism*, 44ff., 129ff. on modern problems). The reading ἅμα for ἀλλά in v. 5b is a correction caused by the dominant interpretation (Lietzmann). Today there is widespread agreement on only two questions.

σύμφυτος, originally an organic term, gradually weakened in sense to "connected" and finally came to indicate only the hyphen between two things (Kuss; Gäumann, *Ethik*, 78) which does not even presuppose a personal relation (*contra* Kühl). An interpretation which appeals to the process of growth in 11:17ff. (Schwarzmann, *Tauftheologie*, 28f.; cf. Frankemölle, *Taufverständnis*, 63) is off the track and is conceivable only in terms of a specific cultic interest. In general the trend nowadays is to follow the concrete understanding of ὁμοίωμα in the LXX and either to translate very weakly as "picture," "copy" (Schlatter; Althaus; Kuss; Bieder, *Verheissung*, 198) or "form" (Tannehill, *Dying*) or more sharply as "image" (Michel) or "likeness" (Bornkamm, "Baptism," 77). "Imitation" (Lietzmann) is possible only if one thinks (rather dubiously) of baptism as such. The problem of this kind of understanding has already arisen in relation to 5:14. An abstract sense of "likeness," "similarity" has been defended here too (BAGD, 567b; M. Barth, *Taufe*, 240; Fuchs, *Freiheit*, 30; Delling, *Taufe*, 130; Gewiess, "Abbild," 340; originally Schnackenburg in *Baptism*, 47ff., modified in "Todesgemeinschaft," 37, 44). The nuances and objections show that the trend has not brought any clarity in the matter. This is quite understandable when one remembers the breadth of variation of such nouns with the -μα ending in the *koine* and also considers intentional ambiguity possible for Paul (BAGD, 567b). 8:3 and Phil 2:7 make it clear that the same form does not have to include ontic likeness (Bornkamm, *loc. cit.*; Gewiess, "Abbild," 344; Delling, *Taufe*, 130; Murray; Ridderbos). It is in the best interests, therefore, not to cling too closely to the LXX or to postulate a standardized usage but to let the particular context be decisive (Mussner, "Tauflehre," 196). In the present case, certainly, this is difficult.

For interpretation depends on whether one understands τῷ ὁμοιώματι instrumentally (Mussner, "Tauflehre," 191; Schwarzmann, *Tauftheologie*, 48) or associatively (Bornkamm, "Baptism," 78; Kuss, "Zu Röm 6, 5a," 152f.; Gewiess,

"Abbild," 339; Beasley-Murray, *Baptism*, 135) and whether one links it with τοῦ θανάτου (Schlier, "Lehre von der Taufe," 111; Schnackenburg, "Todesgemeinschaft," 37) or not (Warnach, "Taufe," 298). Related to the latter assumption and an instrumental understanding is the hypothesis that accordingly an αὐτῷ should be supplied, since a genitive cannot follow σύμφυτοι (BAGD, 567b; Schnackenburg, *Baptism*, 34, 45f.; in opposition Lietzmann; Kuss; Schneider, *TDNT*, V, 191ff.; Tannehill, *Dying*, 54ff.). Again, interpretation as a whole is determinitive. Yet one should not change the sentence and have the dative with the ensuing genitive, as dependent on σύμφυτοι, be rendered associative.

This leads us to the heart of the problem: What precisely is meant by ὁμοίωμα τοῦ θανάτου? The interpretations differ widely (cf. Gewiess, "Abbild," 340ff.; Siber, *Mit Christus*, 219ff.). Extreme solutions, however, are questionable (Ridderbos). This is true when in aversion to sacramentalism refuge is sought in a salvation-historical historicism which makes the outworking of the "general baptism" on Golgotha effectively present for believers and bases this in a supposed "space-time continuum" (Wagner, *Problem*, 292ff.). The mystery concept is decisively preferable to such modern mythology. This also applies, however, to a view which equates ὁμοίωμα with baptism itself (Stricker, "Mysteriengedanke," 290f.; cf. in opposition Bornkamm, "Baptism," 78) and which thus claims that the Christian is in the state of death (Stommel, "Abbild," 9, 20).

The fact remains, of course, that, parallel to the eucharist, the act of baptism must make present what happened on the cross (Bultmann, *Theology*, I, 39ff.; Schlier, "Lehre von der Taufe," 111; Bornkamm, "Baptism," 75ff.; Kuss; Dinkler, "Taufaussagen," 75f.). The death which takes place in baptism, then, is no mere copy of the crucifixion (*contra* Gewiess, "Abbild," 345f.) nor is it simply analogous thereto (correctly Bornkamm, "Baptism," 76f., though cf. Mussner, "Tauflehre," 191ff.). Conversely, it is not a "carrying out together with" as the premise of the union with Christ, as a cultic mystery would be (*contra* Warnach, "Tauflehre," 281, 287, 315, 322). Kierkegaard's concept of "contemporaneity" (Hahn, *Mitsterben*, 97ff.) could be used meaningfully only in connection with the work of the Spirit (Hahn, 119ff., 180; Schnackenburg, "Todesgemeinschaft," 44f.; *Baptism*, 158ff.), but there is no reference to this in the present context. Finally, the thesis that ὁμοίωμα relates directly to Christ's person cannot be sustained, since all constructions with σύν would do that (Bornkamm, "Baptism," 77f.; in opposition Kuss, "Tauflehre," 125; Michel). Paul is speaking of the death of Jesus (Kuss), which is both a historical and an eschatological event, and which cannot be fixed to a single time alone but concerns the whole world. In baptism it lays hold of him who submits to this act and it does so in a documentary, visible, existence-changing fashion. ὁμοίωμα thus distinguishes from the event of Golgotha as much as it connects with that event (cf. Ridderbos, *Paul*, 406ff.).

The historical and theological priority of the cross is not contested. Baptism, however, is not made its repetition. The cross is actualized in the act of baptism. The abstract sense of "likeness" does the most justice to this. In trying to describe exactly the mode of making present, exegetes are doing something which can be meaningfully done elsewhere with the help of such words as Spirit, Word, or Christ's lordship, but which in this case demands too much of the text. This insight has an important implication. In our context the primary concern is the fact that we have died in baptism with Christ and have thus escaped from the power of sin. To the extent that this is generally recognized it needs no further explanation. But to the degree that in the Hellenistic congregation it is simply a presupposition of resurrection with Christ, it has to be stressed. This is not restricted by the next clause which opens with the intensifying ἀλλά (BAGD, 38b). Usually a τῷ ὁμοιώματι is supplied in v. 5b in conformity with the first clause and thus the apparent connection of σύμφυτοι with the genitive is avoided. In this case, however, one would expect to see a reference to Christ's resurrection and not just to ἀνάστασις in general. The presence of a partitive genitive at least cannot be ruled out (Stricker, "Mysteriengedanke," 292; Fuchs, Freiheit, 30). The future is plainly eschatological (contra Thyen, Studien, 206ff.; Frankemölle, Taufverständnis, 61). We have yet to participate in the resurrection even though its power already rules us and sets us in the new walk.

τοῦτο γινώσκοντες in v. 6 resumes and governs the statement, replacing an indicative (Kuss, contra Kühl). Paul is interpreting in his own mode of expression the tradition used by him (Bultmann, TDNT, I, 708; though cf. Michel; Frankemölle, Taufverständnis, 73f.). The motif of crucifixion with Christ, which determines his theology, is thus put in the center (Bornkamm, "Baptism," 76f.; Gaugler; E. Schweizer, "Mystik," 194; Eichholz, Paulus, 208f.). As in vv. 3a and 9a an understanding of what happened to him is ascribed to faith, which here, as in Phil 3:10, characterizes participation in the cross of Jesus as the gift and place of resurrection power. Although the apostle understands the sacrament as incorporation into Christ and his body, mystical union is not so crucial for him as it is for his interpreters. His concern is that we take the place occupied by the earthly Jesus and thus declare the lordship of the exalted One. To the extent that this is not done exclusively by the word, it is indisputable that Paul held the sacraments as constitutive and irreplaceable for every Christian. There is no faith which does not let itself be put publicly and visibly in its allotted place and which does not continually grasp its task afresh in the light of such a process. Without this historical singularity of the process the declaration of once-for-allness is without orientation. Only thus has the statement that we are freed from the power of sin a basis in reality. The man who comes from the cross, and remains beneath it, has a Lord who necessarily separates him from the powers and forces which rule in the world (Furnish, Ethics, 174) and thus stands in fact in the change of aeons.

It is no accident, then, that the obviously pre-Pauline term παλαιὸς ἄνθρωπος, which comes from Adam-Christ typology, comes into use. According to Eph 2:15; 4:24 Christ is the "new man" and the exhortation in Col 3:9f. carries the antithesis of the old and new man into anthropology. Here the "old man" is Adam individualized and represented in us (Barrett; Murray; K. A. Bauer, Leiblichkeit, 149f.). σῶμα τῆς ἁμαρτίας means the same thing from the standpoint of fallenness. The expressions are not collective (correctly E. Schweizer, TDNT, VII, 1065; K. A. Bauer, Leiblichkeit, 152 contra Fuchs, Freiheit, 31f.; Thyen, Studien, 203f.). They characterize (H. W. Schmidt) existence in sin's power. Materially the ἵνα clause is parallel to what precedes and elucidates it. The conclusion comes only with the infinitive. As usual καταργεῖν has an eschatological sense (BAGD, 417). It is not true, then, that the old and the new existence stand alongside one another and have only to be separated (contra Zahn). Nor is the stress merely on moral and religious change (*contra* Delling, *TDNT,* I, 452ff.; Mussner, "Tauflehre," 192). The ending of bondage is movement into the freedom of the new aeon and is possible only in the dominion of the Crucified (Oepke, *TDNT,* II, 336). Verse 7 supports the conclusion of v. 6 with a statement (Sanday and Headlam; Kühl; Lagrange; Huby; Ridderbos; Dinkler, "Taufaussagen," 74) which argues in legal fashion (Althaus; Michel; sceptical Nygren; Scroggs, "Romans 6:7," 106-108). It resembles (Billerbeck; Dodd; Gäumann, *Ethik,* 66, 82) the rabbinic saying in *Šabbat* 151b *Baraita*, which is attributed to Rabbi Shimeon ben Gamaliel (*c*. 140): "When a man is dead he is freed from fulfilling the law." This explains the strange expression δικαιοῦσθαι ἀπό, "to be free from" (BAGD, 197b), for which there are parallels in Sir 26:29; *T. Sim.* 6:1; Acts 13:38; *Herm. Vis.* 3:9:1, but hardly the Syrian burial inscription εὐνὴ δικαίων ἀφ' ἁμαρτιῶν (quoted by Lietzmann). It is most unlikely that there is a reference here to the expiatory force of death (Kuhn, "Rm 6, 7," 305ff.; Schrenk, *TDNT,* II, 218f.), whether or not such force is really ascribed to ordinary death in Judaism. Paul's concern is not with guilt but with the power of sin (Schnackenburg, *Baptism,* 40f.). It is completely fantastic to interpret ἀποθανών christologically (Kearns, "Interpretation," with a fine history of exposition; Thyen, *Studien,* 204f.; Murray; Frankemölle, *Taufverständnis,* 77ff.) and hence to conjecture that we have an exposition of Ps 87:5 LXX (Diezinger, "Unter Toten," 275ff.). It seems inconceivable to many theologians that an apostle should ever utter trivial truth. In this way, however, Paul underscores what is important to him.

The principal point is reached in the third argument in vv. 8-10. The new life is envisioned as the theme of the next section (Frankemölle, *Taufverständnis,* 81). Verse 8 takes up the schema of v. 5 while v. 9 supports the apodosis and (*contra* Gutjahr; Murray) its eschatological future. πιστεύειν can hardly relate homologically (Michel) to reception of the kerygma (Gäumann, *Ethik,* 84) but means the hoping confidence which rests on the "with Christ" (Kuss). For the sake of this "with Christ," faith, which for Paul always involves understanding (Bultmann, *Theology,* I, 318), is assurance of salvation, as εἰδότες shows. It is this neither as rational knowledge nor as ecstatic illumination concerning the eschatological future. It is so to the extent that a pledge of hope is given to it in the Christ event. We do not quite catch the sense if we talk of dogmatic knowledge. For vv. 9f. do not emphasize the fact of Christ's resurrection as such but the life of the Ruler who is no longer threatened by death. By leaving this power behind through death, he has definitively escaped it. Faith responds to this in obedience.

The second accent in the verse arises out of the fact that v. 10a with its exclusively christological statement is only formally parallel to the sentence in v. 7. The relative pronoun ὅ is to be construed as an accusative of object; the two datives designate the relation. The stress is on the ἐφάπαξ of v. 10a in the sense of "once and for all," unrepeatable (Stählin, *TDNT,* I, 383). Christ's life, which can no longer be taken away, is described in the conclusion as being for God and therewith as the only true and abiding life. Verses 9-10 thus support v. 8b in such a way that out of the σὺν Χριστῷ the destiny of the prototype is indicated to which we are destined to be conformed. Verse 11 is not to be taken with v. 10 (*contra* Thüsing, *Per Christum,* 74). The verse draws the now necessary conclusion (Bornkamm, "Baptism," 78f.; Gäumann, *Ethik,* 86; Merk, *Handeln,* 25; Dupont, "Structure," 385). λογίζεσθαι has the same sense as κρίνειν in 2 Cor 5:14; it does not mean "to take stock of oneself" (Kühl) or "to regard oneself" (Larsson, *Vorbild*, 72) or "to think as if one were" (J. Knox, *Life*, 53ff.) but "to judge" (Schlatter; Asmussen). The salvation event which has been established "with Christ" is to be grasped by the Christian as binding on himself, and while it is not to be repeated (*contra* Huby) it is to be verified in discipleship. He who has died to the power of sin can exist on earth only for God unless he denies his Lord. The solemn concluding formula does not lack material content: Such an existence is possible only in Christ Jesus and this should not be taken only ecclesiologically (*contra* Merk, *Handeln*, 27).

2. *Freed for Obedience (6:12-23)*

[12]*Sin, therefore, should not have power in your mortal bodies so that you obey its desires.* [13]*Do not yield your members to sin for use as weapons of unrighteousness but present yourselves to God as those who have been raised to life from the dead, and your members as weapons of righteousness for God.* [14]*For sin should not rule over you (any longer), since you are not under the law but under grace.* [15]*What then? May we sin because we are not under law but under grace? Not at all!* [16]*Do you not know that if you present yourselves as slaves to someone to obey, you are slaves of the one whom you obey, whether it be of sin to death or of obedience to righteousness?* [17]*But thanks be to God that you were the slaves of sin but have now become obedient from the heart to the form of doctrine to which you were committed.* [18]*Having been set free from sin, you have become the slaves of righteousness.* [19]*I am speaking in human terms because of the weakness of your flesh. For as you once yielded your members slavishly to impurity and lawlessness upon lawlessness, so now yield your members to righteousness for sanctification.* [20]*So long as you were slaves of sin, you were free from righteousness.* [21]*But what fruit did you have then? You must now be ashamed of it. For death was its result.* [22]*But now, freed from sin and set in the service of God, you have sanctification as the fruit and the goal eternal life.* [23]*For the wages of sin is death, but the gracious gift of God is eternal life in Christ Jesus, our Lord.*

Bibliography: R. Bultmann, "Das Problem der Ethik bei Paulus," *ZNW* 23 (1924) 123-140; H. Windisch, "Das Problem des paulinischen Imperativs," *ZNW* 23 (1924) 265-281; W. Mundle, "Religion und Sittlichkeit bei Paulus in ihrem inneren Zusammenhang," *ZST* 4 (1927) 456-482; G. Staffelbach, *Die Vereinigung mit Christus als Prinzip der Moral bei Paulus* (Freiburger Theologische Studien 34; 1932); E. Lohse, "Taufe und Rechtfertigung bei Paulus," *KuD* 11 (1965) 308-324 (= *Einheit*, 228-244); M. Müller, "Freiheit. Über Autonomie und Gnade von Paulus bis Clemens von Alexandrien," *ZNW* 25 (1926) 177-236; H. Jonas, *Augustin und das paulinische Freiheitsproblem* (FRLANT 44; 1930; rev. ed. 1965); J. Ellul, "Le sens de la liberté chez St. Paul," *Paulus-Hellas-Oikumene* (ed. P. I. Bratsiotis; 1951) 64-73; J. Cambier, "La Liberté chrétienne selon saint Paul," *SE*, II, 315-353; H. Schürmann, "Die Freiheitsbotschaft des Paulus—Mitte des Evangeliums?" *Catholica* 25 (1971) 22-62; A. Dietzel, "Beten im Geist," *TZ* 9 (1953) 13-32; E. Käsemann, "On the Pauline Anthropology, *Perspectives*, 1-31. **12f.:** E. Schweizer, "Die Sünde in den Gliedern," *Abraham unser Vater.* Festschrift für Otto Michel zum 60. Geburtstag (ed. O. Betz et al.; 1963) 437-39. **16f.:** J. Moffatt, "The Interpretation of Romans 6:17-18," *JBL* 48 (1929) 223-38; A. Fridrichsen, "Exegetisches zum NT," *ConNT* 7 (1942) 4-8; H. Greeven, "Propheten, Lehrer, Vorsteher bei Paulus," *ZNW* 44 (1952/53) 1-43; H. Sahlin, "Einige Textemendationen zum Römerbrief," *TZ* 9 (1953) 92-100; J. Kürzinger, "τύπος διδαχῆς und der Sinn von Röm 6, 17f.," *Bib* 39 (1958) 156-176; F. W. Beare, "On the Interpretation of Romans 6:17," *NTS* [▮ 5 (1958/59) 206-210; K. Aland, "Interpretation, Redaktion und Komposition in der Sicht der neutestamentlichen Textkritik," *Apophoreta: Festschrift für Ernst Haenchen* (BZNW 30; 1964) 7-31. For Bornkamm, "Baptism" and Schlier, "Taufe" see the bibliography for 6:1-11.

Exegetical and systematic problems overlap in this chapter more than they do elsewhere. This has to be thoroughly weighed as we move into the new section. For centuries Protestantism also has regarded justification as the beginning of Christian life, which sanctification necessarily must follow and verify. This view has not been outdated although it has been much modified and has lost its former clarity. Obviously the present text could provide it exemplary support (cf. Moule; Kirk; Murray; Huby; Amiot, *Key Concepts*, 133; Stalder, *Werk*, 192ff., 210). Nevertheless it is untenable (Furnish, *Ethics*, 153ff.), since Paul does not limit the event of justification in time and he understands the new walk also as the work of grace in which resurrection power projects itself on earth. The distinction between justification and sanctification and the sequence derived from it were possible only when the gift was separated from the Giver, justification was no longer viewed at its center as transferal to the dominion of Christ, and instead anthropology was made its horizon. Almost inevitably, then, room was created for the idea of an inner development in the Christian life, the more so as Paul speaks of sanctifying and perfecting. The spiritual growth of the believer replaced the question how one remains under the rule of Christ through the changes of times and situations and in face of the provocation of the world and its powers.

Liberal theology at the same time systematized and diluted the traditional schema by expanding it, through a return to ancient categories, to the problem of religion and morality in their mutual relation and distinction. The "ethics" of the apostle now became the independent subject of numerous investigations (survey in Furnish, *Ethics*, 242ff.). The religio-historical research, which rediscovered Jewish apocalyptic and the Hellenistic mysteries, sharpened the question in discussion of the relation between this ethics and the eschatology or sacramental statements of Paul. That this was a justifiable line of investigation cannot be contested insofar as in Pauline theology justification, sacrament, and eschatology are in fact connected and the coherence of such relationships must be determined. The fragile ground upon which the investigation moved, however, became apparent when one was compelled to make a distinction between the juridical-ethical and the sacramental approach of the apostle (Lüdemann, *Anthropologie*), or when his ethics had to be derived from religious enthusiasm, or when, in a variation of the same premise, the doctrine of justification had to be made into a subsidiary crater of eschatological mysticism as the basis of Pauline ethics, and the relation between the two had to be radically contested (A. Schweitzer, *Mysticism*, e.g.; 225).

The circle of possibilities was thus staked out on all sides insofar as one maintained the distinction between justification and sanctification. What price had to be paid for this may be seen most clearly from the equally serious and pene-

172

trating discussion of the question whether and in what sense the baptized, being set in a new life, are without sin for the apostle (cf. esp. P. Wernle, *Der Christ und die Sünde bei Paulus* [1897]; Windisch ["Problem," 280] espouses an ethics of sinlessness; cf. Wetter, *Vergeltungsgedanke*, 101). The levelling down of Pauline exhortation to a general ethics and the underlying concentration on anthropology separate the two foci of Pauline theology, play off the subjective and objective perspectives against one another, change the thesis of freedom from the power of sin into morality, and thus make individual acts of sin the real subject of debate. The resultant contradictions are then blamed without inhibition on the apostle. Historically his true concerns could be separated from relics of his past or the modes of expression available to him from his environment. If one does not simply capitulate as a systematician and assert irreconcilable contradictions (following Lüdemann, *Anthropologie*, e.g., Kirk, 83ff.), one could affirm the same result from an idealistic standpoint as an antithesis between "theory" and "practice" (e.g., Dodd; J. Knox; also Cerfaux, *Christian*, 449 on which cf. Schrage, *Einzelgebote*, 26ff.). Theoretically, on this view, present sinlessness is postulated. The ethical demand designates this in contrast as a future goal worth striving for. We thus have a combination of ineradicable antinomianism and a morality exercised in voluntary matter-of-factness (Lietzmann). Whereas speculation at its height does not find in 5:12ff. the redemptive word of far-reaching moral renewal, in complete dissociation and absolute antithesis there is an appeal to moral energy (Jülicher, 263f.). The antinomy is resolved at two levels. In terms of the history of religions it is seen as the result of a syncretistic combination of Jewish and Hellenistic tradition. Theologically one had to overcome it with the help of the idea of development which goes beyond Paul and corrects him. The basic metaphysical concept of *posse non peccare* (ability not to sin) leads by way of the battle for verification to the result of Christian perfection (Lietzmann). Redemption requires moral cooperation. Hence the solution is not: "Become what you already are in fact by baptism," but: "Become what you now can become" (Kühl, 212ff.).

The discussion which follows stands under the sign of the various interpretations of the almost magical formula, intimated already in the last sentence: "become what you are." There has been little concern that as such this slogan comes from our idealistic legacy and just as little that it leads necessarily to an intolerable formalizing of the problem. When being and becoming are dialectically related and opposed in this way, it seems to be enough to speak of the tension between the indicative and the imperative in Paul. Pushed wholly into the background is the question why the apostle not only formulates basic statements and demands in relation to the new life but also why he spends so much time on concrete exhortation (Schrage, *Einzelgebote*). Finally, there is at least no direct or unavoidable wrestling with the ancient and very impressive doctrine of faith formed by love, although there is always a temptation to slip into it. Even when faith is not understood psychologically and morally as the ethical act of obedience and trust (Staffelbach, *Vereinigung*, 51), as a new order (ibid., 65), or as the ethical norm of changed ideals (Mundle, "Religion," 460ff.), there is widespread acceptance of the pointed statement that love is the vitality of the life of faith (Spicq, *Agape*, II, 324), its true definition (ibid., 310), the sole principle of morality by which all that the Christian does may be comprehensively described (ibid., 340f.; cf. Dodd, *Gospel*, 25ff.; Mundle, "Religion," 473 and critically Schrage, *Einzelgebote*, 9ff., 59ff., 82f.). It is true, of course, that only Roman [Catholic authors speak of the constant participation in accomplishing Christ's saving work (Seidensticker, *Opfer*, 237), or of saving love which coincides with saving faith (Spicq, *Agape*, II, 312), as a description of the Christian life complementary to "in Christ" and "in the Spirit" (ibid., 320). Nevertheless, these writers are simply working out the consequences of the widespread idea of mystical union with Christ and showing in their own way how "become what you are" can be understood (cf. Niederwimmer, *Freiheit*, 191ff.; Enslin, *Ethics*, 133 and *passim*). The basic consensus behind such an approach is finely brought out in the statement that Pauline ethics relates to what transcends other ethics but that the religious principle can be expounded only ethically (Dodd, *Gospel*, 44f.). Only with Bultmann's essay on the problem of ethics do we have at least a new turn in the discussion, as is emphasized by the resultant protest of Windisch ("Problem") in which the liberal view is again championed.

Bultmann's new interpretation lifts the problem out of the spheres of mere ethics and a combination with mysticism ("Problem," 126, 130ff.) and sets it into the dimension of Pauline eschatology (cf. Furnish, *Ethics*, 262ff.). The apostle's concern is not with sinlessness as freedom from guilt, but with freedom from the power of sin. Secondly, he is not concerned with development to perfection but with a constantly new grasping of the once-for-all, eschatological, saving act of justification, since man is always and totally thrown back on grace. Third, the imperative of moral demand does not merely presuppose the indicative which speaks of God's gift; it paradoxically coincides with the indicative to the extent that it calls for obedience as verification of the gift, which for its part also can only be received as a gift. The demand is simultaneously a promise, since in the last resort it demands no more than reception of the gift and its attestation. Hence neither indicative nor imperative loses its seriousness or significance, and "become what you are" (taken up first in Bultmann, *Theology*, I, 332f.) receives its meaning from the message of the epistle. The act of salvation neither becomes actual nor is developed through what we do. It makes one responsible, without basing salvation on this responsibility, and has ethical consequences which, even though recognized and possible elsewhere, are shown to be Christian as the verification of grace. Sanctification here is justification maintained in the field of action and suffering.

This interpretation has been able to prevail beyond Bultmann's own school (cf. Kuss, 397, 409; Kertelge, *Rechtfertigung*, 251ff.; Merk, *Handeln*, 37f.; Wendland, *Ethik*, 49; Stalder, *Werk*, 192ff.). Yet it is bound to tradition in the sense that it does not break free from the restriction of anthropology, that it can thus take up the idealistic formula, and that it thus leaves the possibility open of interpreting the Pauline imperative as a summons to Christian "self-realization" (Kertelge, *Rechtfertigung*, 283). The reference to genuine paradox and antinomy is then also dubious and is comprehensible only within the framework of the basic anthropological conception. The argumentation from the union with Christ at least is justified in the fact that in our text the demand arises out of the sacramentally grounded σὺν Χριστῷ, or, in 8:12ff., out of the interchangeable ἐν Χριστῷ and ἐν πνεύματι, and the coherence of both chapters describes participation in the reign of Christ as the gift of the eschatological act of salvation. This means, however, that in reality the gift is the Giver himself, just as the pneuma means nothing other than the earthly manifestation of the exalted Lord in his community. If salvation is made autonomous over against him who brings it, one comes into dangerous proximity to the enthusiasts of Corinth, who understand christology merely as the premise of anthropology and of a basically realized eschatology, or into dangerous proximity to a Christian nomism in which salvation has to be assured by human action and perfection.

Not for nothing the demand is derived from baptism. But this does not mean in the traditional sense setting up the cult as the final goal of personal and ethical life (*contra* K. H. Schelkle, *Theology of the New Testament*, III: Morality [Eng. tr. 1971] 219f.). Here the Kyrios takes possession of us. The much debated question of the relation between faith and baptism cannot be answered by speaking of complementarity, in such a way that what would otherwise be lacking were dialectically related in occasional supplementation (*contra* Schnackenburg, *Baptism*, 121ff.). The statements about baptism characterize faith as reception of the lordship of Christ, and the description of the Christian state as faith protects baptism against an *ex opere operato* understanding (*contra* Prat, *Theology*, I, 223). It also prevents us from thinking that Christ's lordship is not contested or from not connecting it with the ever necessary summons to its grace and its service.

If this is so, it is highly debatable to speak of a Pauline "ethics" (cf. Wendland, *Ethik*, 2f.). Naturally the lordship of Christ has consequences in the field of ethical behavior. Under it, as the individual exhortations show, in a concrete situation a particular practice is excluded under all circumstances and another demanded with equal absoluteness (Schrage, *Einzelgebote;* Merk, *Handeln*, 232ff.). At the same time, Paul does not develop a system or casuistry of morality and he draws his instruction largely from Jewish and Hellenistic tradition, although these can be established in a different way. He certainly cannot be described as the first Christian ethicist (Furnish, *Ethics*, 209ff. *contra* Wendland, *Ethik*, 49). As his exhortation is rooted in primitive Christian tradition, it is not determined by a principle of synthesis or selection. If, as in the present passage, he sets it fundamentally under some such catchword as obedience or freedom, in so doing he is not naming leading ideas but stressing the totality and indivisibility of the obligation of the Christian and the community to the Kyrios (Schrage, *Einzelgebote*, 52ff.), as many concrete admonitions show in exemplary fashion. In this chapter the issue is freedom from the power of sin. The premises are given in vv. 1-11, and vv. 12-23 make it clear that this freedom, grounded in the act of salvation and with baptism as the coming of the change of aeons, can be maintained only in the practice of service. What is usually called ethics (*contra* Enslin, *Ethics*) goes beyond the moral sphere, as certainly as it asserts itself in that sphere, because sin has moral implications for Paul even though it is not a moral phenomenon. Resistance to its power and victory over it depend on Christ remaining Kyrios over us as the One who imparted himself to us in baptism. The so-called imperative is integrated into the indicative and does not stand paradoxically alongside it, since the Kyrios remains Kyrios only for the one who serves him. Gift and task coincide in the fact that both designate standing under Christ's lordship, which only inadequately, namely, from the truncated anthropological

view, can be brought under the idealistic formula: "Become what you are" (Fur-   [
nish, *Ethics,* 225ff.). The point is that the lordship of the exalted one be declared
in the following of the crucified one. Justification and sanctification belong together to the extent that being conformed to Christ is valid in both. They are
distinct because this is not effected once and for all but, having begun in baptism,
has to be experienced and suffered always afresh in changing situations. Paul's
ethics cannot be independent of either dogmatics or the cultus. It is part of his
eschatology (Furnish, *Ethics,* 114, 213ff.; Eichholz, *Paulus,* 265ff., 276). More
exactly, it is the anthropological reverse side of his christology.

Verses 12-14 are not just transitional (*contra* Lagrange; Tachau, *Einst,* 116).
Thematically (cf. 1 Thess 5:6-8) they take up v. 11 with a baptismal exhortation
(Fuchs, *Freiheit,* 39; Kertelge, *Rechtfertigung,* 266). What v. 11 calls "to live for
God" is now described as the obedience of the free (Murray; Ridderbos). Verses 12
and 13 are parallel, with heightened concreteness in v. 13 (Horst, *TDNT,* IV, 561;
K. A. Bauer, *Leiblichkeit,* 154). The basis of the imperatives is given in v. 14.
Christian obedience derives from the power of grace and resurrection (K. Barth).
The power of sin from which the Christian has been removed in baptism still rules
in the world and from that standpoint threatens us in our bodily existence. For
Paul's view of the body the most important passages are 6:12; 8:13; 1 Cor 6:12ff.
People still maintain the ultimately Greek interpretation in terms of the idea of
the organism (Dodd, *Meaning,* 60; Ridderbos, *Paul,* 114), obviously in view of
the fact that the apostle speaks almost synonymously of our members. But like
the view that the body is for Paul the principle of individuality (Dodd, *Meaning,*
60) or, as for most, the person, this interpretation is no longer possible now that
Bultmann has shown that all Paul's anthropological terms mean existence in a
specific orientation. Only in the light of 8:13 can it be considered whether the
body characterizes that human self-relation in which a person can set himself at
a distance from himself as the subject of action and object of suffering and can
experience himself as under the dominion of alien powers (Bultmann, *Theology,*
I, 197ff., 200ff.; Conzelmann, *Outline,* 176f., 198; cf. my criticism in *Perspectives,*
16ff.). The present text justifies only the latter motif in this definition. Corporeality
is standing in a world for which different forces contend and in whose conflict
each individual is caught up, belonging to one lord or the other and representing
this lord both actively and passively. If in such a context Paul speaks of our
members, or even our bodies themselves are called members, it is clear that we
are never autonomous, but always participate in a definite world and stand under
lordship (Robinson, *Body,* 29f.; E. Schweizer, *TDNT,* VII, 1065f.; Asmussen; cf.
K. A. Bauer, *Leiblichkeit*). There thus arises a dialectical understanding of Christian existence. It belongs to the sphere of power of the risen Lord, but it does so
on earth and therefore it is still exposed to the attack of the powers which rule
this aeon, is always under assault (*Anfechtung*) (Merk, *Handeln,* 29ff.), and is
constantly summoned to preserve and verify eschatological freedom in the service
of its true and only Lord.

Paul can distinguish, then, between the body of sin and death, the mortal
body and the glorified body, and thus contrast existence in the fallenness of this
world, in the temptation (*Anfechtung*) which accompanies earthly temporality,
and existence in the resurrection reality which is no longer exposed to threat.

θνητὸν σῶμα certainly does not mean the "body of sin" from which the "essential I" should distance itself (contra Bultmann, Theology, I, 192ff., 200). We died to this in baptism, and exhortation relating to it would be pointless. It concerns the corporeality or secularity of the Christian which is threatened not only from without by the world but also by its own mortality; it concerns our "worldliness." It is precisely to this that God lays claim as the Creator who is bringing back his world in his justice (K. A. Bauer, Leiblichkeit, 154f.). Its mortality, however, causes its ἐπιθυμίαι, which are not to be understood psychologically as purely sensual or immoral impulses (contra Zahn; Jülicher; Lagrange; Huby). In keeping with the deepened anthropology of the apostle, what is in view is that which binds us in our actuality to the rest of creation and which leads to self-will and self-assertion (Bornkamm, "Baptism," 80f.). If one yields to this, sin can reign afresh over us and set our members in its service.

It is customary to speak of sin in the members (E. Schweizer, "Sünde in den Gliedern"). μέλη does not refer primarily to parts of the body (contra Zahn; Dodd; Murray). As in 1 Cor 12:12ff. it refers functionally to our capabilities (Barrett; Black). παριστάνειν can hardly be taken from sacrificial language. It has the general meaning "place at the disposal" (Horst, TDNT, IV, 562; Reicke, TDNT, V, 840, etc.). Polybius Historia iii.109.9 shows that a military use is possible. This is the most likely sense here, since ὅπλα probably does not mean "tools" (BAGD, 575b) but "weapons." As in 13:12; 2 Cor 6:7; 10:4 the motif of the militia Christi is present (Kuss, 405ff.; Leenhardt; Thüsing, Per Christum, 93; Eichholz, Paulus, 271).

One should not for this reason stress the dominant ethical factor in the OT-Jewish antithesis of weapons of righteousness and unrighteousness (contra Jülicher; Schrenk, TDNT, II, 209f.; K. G. Kuhn, "πειρασμός," 212f.). Paul goes beyond the contrast between good conduct and bad. For him, as the context shows, unrighteousness is ungodliness, while righteousness is the power of God which has come on the scene in Christ and with justification, which effects new life in anticipation of bodily resurrection, and which sets us in its service.

With the basic ὡσεὶ ἐκ νεκρῶν (Kühl; Michel; Kuss; Ridderbos; Kertelge, Rechtfertigung, 268) there is a reference back to vv. 4f., although with no denial of the restrictive sense of ὡσεί (Zahn; Barrett; H. W. Schmidt). The eschatological reservation earlier expressed by the futures is still in force here. Christians participate provisionally in the resurrection of their Lord only in the form of new obedience. Conversely, their service makes known the fact that resurrection power has already taken possession of them and set them in new life and the new aeon (Furnish, Ethics, 195f.; Siber, Mit Christus, 240ff.).

We thus have confirmation that Paul's "ethics" is a constituent part of his eschatology and, to the extent that as baptismal exhortation it characterizes discipleship, his christology. Resurrection power does not establish merely a new and better morality or a different cultus. It does not seize our bodies and members in such a way that these are drawn into the essentially inward service of God (Zahn; Cerfaux, Christian, 297). Bodily obedience is necessary as an anticipation of the reality of bodily resurrection. Otherwise it would not be clear that we are engaged in the eschatological struggle for power (Merk, Handeln, 37ff.), which was familiar in Judaism both at Qumran and elsewhere (Kuhn, "πειρασμός,"

203ff.; Brandenburger, *Adam,* 22ff.). In this struggle the deep question is: To whom does the earth belong? This question can be answered only if the part of the world which we are in our bodies is taken out of its supposed neutrality and placed before the alternative of service for righteousness or unrighteousness, and identical with that for God or against him. That the decision goes in God's favor even in the sphere of mortality, and that it is taken permanently, as shown by the transition from the present to the aorist, points beyond the present which is marked by the power of sin, and, as in 1 Cor 10:1-13, is not only the demand and promise of baptism, but is also a standing in conflict. It is thus set up on earth where we no longer live under the power of sin but under that of grace.

A surprising feature in v. 14b is the antithesis to νόμος, which is not initially obvious from the context. Does it mean that the apostle is thinking in schemata and drawing necessarily rhetorical antitheses from these? The taking up of the question of v. 1 in v. 15 ought to warn us against this superficial explanation, although, as in v. 1, the diatribe style and not only the repetition of the question as such, but the antithesis of v. 14b give evidence of rhetoric. There is, however, no material changing or intensifying of v. 1 in the sense that Paul is now speaking of life-fulfilment instead of the order of being (Schlier, "Taufe," 52; cf. Lagrange; Tachau, *Einst,* 117; in opposition Gäumann, *Ethik,* 92; Merk, *Handeln,* 137). It is also impermissible (*contra* Stalder, *Werk,* 279f.) to speak only of the curse of the law and not of its power, which is plainly parallel to that of sin. The sudden shift in thought, the rhetoric of a new start, and the repetition of the antithesis of v. 14b in v. 15 make sense on the assumption that Paul now sharpens the baptismal exhortation of vv. 12-14a in terms of the dialectic of Christian freedom and Christian obedience. This is introduced in the phrase "not under the law." Christian obedience is not to be equated with obedience under the Torah, for as standing in grace it is also freedom.

In a way which is hard to fathom it has been maintained that freedom is not a basic theme in Pauline theology (Nestle, *RAC,* VIII, 280ff.; but cf. Ellul, "Liberté," 64ff.; Cambier, "Liberté," 317ff.; Niederwimmer, *Freiheit,* 69; Schürmann, "Freiheitsbotschaft," 25ff.). This part of the epistle proves the opposite. Freedom is the anthropological result of the doctrine of justification, and it has to be so if justification means the Creator's reconciliation with the rebellious creature and the inauguration of the new creation. At the same time we have to say precisely what is meant by this. The problem is misunderstood from the outset if seen in terms of autonomy and emancipation (M. Müller, "Freiheit," 187ff.). For all the connections (cf. Jonas, *Augustin,* 13ff.) the independence which Stoicism and popular philosophy promise as human self-realization must not be read into Paul's statements.

If it has become customary in many circles to differentiate between "freedom from" and "freedom for" (cf. M. Müller, "Freiheit," 183ff.)—a rich formula which can be interpreted in many different ways—the emphasis on the positive side should never be weakened. Nevertheless, one has to begin with the negative side (with Schlier, *TDNT,* II, 496ff. against Bultmann, *Theology,* I, 330ff.; Jonas, *Augustin,* 13ff.; Schürmann, "Freiheitsbotschaft," 39f.) if one is not to restrict or distort what Paul has in mind either existentialistically by "openness to the authentic future" and "authenticity of existence," moralistically as fulfilment of

178

what natural law requires (J. Fuchs, *Natural Law*, 28f.), mystically as the exaltation of human freedom into the supernatural, as a quality in the sphere of ecclesiological freedom (Schürmann, "Freiheitsbotschaft," 27ff.) which is rooted in Christian being and which moves in the direction of church unity (Cambier, "Liberté," 315ff., 326ff., 340ff.). The mythological form according to which freedom means escape from the elements of the world that are superstitiously associated with the stars is to be set in the foreground, as is even plainer in the deutero-Pauline letters than in the apostle. This is true even when one remains aware of its close connection with παρρησία and thus sees established with it a new Christian self-understanding. For this self-understanding cannot be characterized, as it often is, merely as inner or religious freedom. It involves a different relation to the world, sees through its demonic aspects, and recognizes that Christ has overcome them.

At this point we have to break free from our idealistic heritage. What is ultimately at issue is the opposite of the idealistic view. In contrast to this Paul does not regard obedience as a possibility, expression, or variation of freedom. He regards freedom as the determinative relation of Christian obedience vis-à-vis the world. It is presupposed here as elsewhere that a person belongs constitutively to a world and lies under lordship. With baptism a change of lordship has been effected (Furnish, *Ethics*, 176ff., 194f.; Siber, *Mit Christus*, 227ff.). The new Kyrios sets those who are bound to him into freedom from powers and necessities. 1 Cor 8:6 expresses this clearly and in a christologically pointed way takes up the first commandment as both demand and promise. If the relation between obedience and freedom is turned around, the distinction between Christ and his disciples is obliterated. He is the free one who became obedient, whereas we receive our freedom in allegiance to him and as a result of the right of lordship which God has graciously established over us. Freedom is the world-oriented reality of justification. This is why it can be dealt with only after 3:21ff. He who belongs to the true cosmocrator strides erect through his sphere of power, breaks all the barriers and taboos arbitrarily set up there, and thus walks no less confidently through the sphere of the Torah, bearing witness thereby, in spite of appearances to the contrary, to God's peace on the earthly battlefield and to openness for brethren as the truth of the reign of Christ and as an announcement of the world of the resurrection. The future in v. 14a permanently equates the command and the promise.

The judgment that nowhere in the epistle would so much be said on the same subject without perceptible development of thought (Jülicher) fails to take into account the fact that the apostle's concern here is with the center of Christian conduct, so that the dialectic presented is constantly set before us as a question in new and concrete forms, and with eschatological radicalness a strict either/or is demanded of us (K. Barth; Fuchs, *Freiheit*, 41; Merk, *Handeln*, 31f.). Precisely standing in grace has a hardness which must not be weakened. It is therefore characterized, with an exclusive claim intolerable to the Greeks (Rengstorf, *TDNT*, II, 267), as a servile existence. There is nothing here (*contra* Lietzmann; Kürzinger, "Sinn," 162ff.) to suggest the ancient custom of redeeming slaves. The statements in v. 16 are tautological (Kuss). Thus the first δοῦλος does not denote (*contra* Barrett; Leenhardt) the servant who adopts service voluntarily and the second δοῦλος the slave.

There is, however, a shift of accent from the verb in the first statement to the noun in the second. Paul's concern is to rule out the possibility of neutrality. οὐκ οἴδατε appeals to general experience. A statement about human life is first made, and then this is given a Christian application in the alternative at the end. We may give ourselves to a bondage which determines us totally, as is underscored by the materially superfluous εἰς ὑπακοήν and the relative clause ᾧ ὑπακούετε. From a Christian standpoint it becomes apparent that the example is not merely one possibility among others but the basic constitution of mankind as such (Furnish, *Ethics*, 195; Siber, *Mit Christus*, 230; missed by J. Knox). For the baptized this means that he can fall back from Christ's reign only into that of Adam described in 5:12ff.

Logically one would expect that the antithesis would lead at the end to the phrase ἢ δικαιοσύνης εἰς ζωήν (J. Weiss, "Beiträge," 181). But Paul loves nuances. It has been shown already in 5:18ff. that eternal life is anticipated and is present in righteousness. Here ὑπακοή no longer has, as in the first clause, the general sense of dependence. As shown in v. 17 it has now a concrete Christian sense. As in 1:5 obedience is faith (Schlatter) which grasps the promise of the gospel and evidences it in action. Ever-present temptation (*Anfechtung*) is overcome only by him who hears the word and obeys it. This can take place continually as and because it has taken place in baptism.

The thanksgiving renews in the sharp antithesis of vv. 17a and 18 the reality thus established. The dominion of sin is ended. Liberation from it, however, does not leave us unrestrained. It places us in the service of righteousness. The combination, the context, and the parallels in v. 13 prevent us from seeing in the moral norm of uprightness a new ideal (*contra* Cerfaux, *Christian*, 409). The power of sin is confronted by eschatologically manifested righteousness as a power (Ridderbos; Quell, *TDNT*, II, 209f.; Zeller, *Juden*, 167f.; Ziesler, *Meaning*, 201). It is particularly plain here that for Paul righteousness cannot be detached from God's self-revelation (Furnish, *Ethics*, 156). Serving it is parallel to serving God in v. 13 and v. 22. It designates the reality of the God who seeks us in grace, which is actualized in our justification. What God gives eschatologically is not just one of his gifts, not even the supreme and final gift. He gives us himself by drawing us into his right as our Creator. Along any other lines the connection with the reign of Christ, which is the theme of the chapter, is not at all comprehensible. The gift is the Lord himself so long as one does not separate the doctrine of justification and christology. Justification means that God is there for us. The apostle speaks of it instead of love because the subject is God's right even and precisely over the ungodly and because we as such are set in his lordship. Standing before and under God alone is freedom. It releases us both from our own control and also from the powers of the world, and opens up the place from which Adam fell.

A problem is raised by the parenthetic expression in v. 17b, which undoubtedly disrupts the fine antithesis of vv. 17a and 18 (J. Weiss, "Beiträge," 229) and which for this reason is often viewed as a gloss (Bultmann, "Glossen," 202; Fuchs, *Freiheit*, 44; Gaümann, *Ethik*, 94ff.; Tachau, *Einst*, 117; Bornkamm, "Baptism," 86; Leenhardt; Furnish, *Ethics*, 197f.; rejected by Kuss; Goppelt, *TDNT*, VIII, 250; Aland, "Interpretation," 29; Greeven, "Propheten," 20ff.; extended to the whole context Sahlin, "Textemendationen," 98). The theory is not strengthened by the argument that ἐκ καρδίας and τύπος διδαχῆς are non-Pauline, that the latter phrase refers to Paul's teaching from the standpoint of a glossator (opposed by Lietzmann; Gutjahr; Murray), and that, in context, obedience to this τύπος is trivial. For what would cause a glossator to presuppose that Rome already had the teaching which the epistle is giving? Formal expressions from the tradition are not surprising in baptismal exhortation. Without the intervening expression the solemn statement would simply repeat v. 16b and rhetorically overlap the thanksgiving. Little can be built on the innocuous ἐκ καρδίας. The conclusion of v. 16 has already demanded that Christian obedience be defined in terms of hearing the message. This is now confirmed and only thus do we have development in v. 17.

The question to which everything points, then, is what is actually meant by τύπος διδαχῆς. If we refer it to Christianity in general and without support in the text as an antithesis to the Torah (Lietzmann), then the formula sounds intolerably stilted. This is true even if what is meant is Christian teaching as a whole, the gospel as orally transmitted (contra Sickenberger; Baulès; Schrage, Einzelgebote, 130; Delling, Worship, 96). On the other hand, one can hardly suppose that Paul's message is being differentiated here from other forms of teaching (correctly Sanday and Headlam; Schlatter against Jülicher; Kühl), since it could not apply to the Romans. Restriction to moral instruction is impossible (Lagrange; Huby; Bruce; Murray; Beare, "Interpretation," 209f.). Even the "sound doctrine" of the Pastorals refers to the tradition of faith, and τύπος does not mean the norm (contra Althaus) but the specific form or model. The baptismal hymns of the NT, the catechetical tradition of 1 Cor 15:3ff., and the later development of the Roman Creed (already presupposed here by Gutjahr and Kürzinger, "Sinn," 173ff.) support the view that a summary of the gospel was given at baptism (Sanday and Headlam). Paul himself, using technical terms, appeals to the basic tradition in 1 Cor 11:23; 15:2 (Ridderbos). If unfortunately a clear example cannot be given, it is not impossible that the apostle is reminding this community not personally known to him of something like a baptismal creed (Norden, Agnostos Theos, 270f.; P. Feine, Die Gestalt des apostolischen Glaubensbekenntnisses [1925], 76; Schlier, TDNT, II, 499; "Taufe," 53; Bornkamm, "Baptism," 83; Kürzinger, "Sinn," 169ff.; Kertelge, Rechtfertigung, 270; critically Kuss).

In this light it makes good sense that the reference is not to the giving of the tradition to the baptized but the commitment of the baptized to the tradition. The attraction expressed by τῷ τύπῳ . . . εἰς suggests a Jewish form of expression for the commitment of a student to the teaching of a rabbi (Fridrichsen, "Exegetisches," 6f.; Oepke, TDNT, II, 426). If this is not to the point, it should be considered that faith means more than personal engagement. Eph 4:5 with its threefold acclamation, which probably derives from the act of baptism, shows that steps had to be taken quite early against heretical doctrines of salvation. Romans as a whole gives evidence of the process of linking proclamation with a clear interpretation of the gospel and presupposes not uniformly established but christologically centered confessions which serve the same purpose. τύπος διδαχῆς corresponds in antithetical parallelism to the Jewish μόρφωσις τῆς γνώσεως καὶ ἀληθείας of 2:20, which likewise means commitment to a specific teaching.

181

As the baptized is committed to the Lord, he is also claimed for a creed (Furnish, *Ethics*, 98ff., 106ff.) which sets out in binding form the significance of this Lord. The context receives therewith a perspective which has not yet been sharply contoured. Christian obedience involves more than moral behavior (this is often overlooked, e.g., J. Knox). It is always oriented to faith by hearing, to which one is committed in baptism and which one simultaneously accepts from the heart   [and therefore radically and willingly. Freed from the compulsion of the powers, one submits voluntarily to new service. Appeal can and must always be made to this. But if this is so, the sacramental statement can no longer be separated from the proclamation of justification. Only gross misunderstanding of the saying can restrict its application to the moral and legal side of the sacramental act (Schlier, "Taufe," 53). In indissoluble complementarity baptism and proclamation set us in the sphere of divine righteousness (Merk, *Handeln*, 19ff.; Lohse, "Taufe," 321ff.). As the sacrament displays the externality of the act of revelation and protects it against spiritualizing, the word stresses the fact that relations are established and protects against an impersonalizing of revelation. In both cases the central concern is not the individual but the lordship of Christ, which is objectively erected over the individual and is to be subjectively grasped and maintained. This is why δουλεία is the key word in the passage.

Exposition finds the importance of δουλεία a problem because in 8:15 the apostle expressly contests the idea that there is slavery for the Christian (Zahn; Dodd; Althaus; Michel; *et al.*). Paul anticipates this objection. Nevertheless v. 19a does not weaken and excuse his statement (as many suppose); it offers the reason for it (Sand, *Fleisch*, 139f.). When he used the concept of slavery to show the parallel between the structures under sin and in righteousness, he was speaking in human fashion, namely, as people must see it, corresponding to the κατὰ ἄνθρωπον in 3:5. The explanatory prepositional phrase envisions neither ethical (Kühl; Bardenhewer; Gutjahr; Stählin, *TDNT*, I, 491) nor intellectual weakness (BAGD, 115a; Lietzmann; Michel; Kuss; E. Schweizer, *TDNT*, VII, 125) nor immaturity (Sand, *Fleisch*, 139f.). In Paul ἀσθένεια never means some kind of feebleness but the temptation (*Anfechtung*) of Christians through the impulses of the flesh. It is conceded that to describe the Christian state as slavery is inadequate and applies only to the earthly aspect (Ridderbos). But this is at once balanced dialectically by the otherwise superfluous expression at the end: It was necessary to speak thus (Wetter, *Vergeltungsgedanke*, 99) because the flesh desires autonomy and thus rejects the idea of slavery as too much to demand. While it is good to stress the sonship and freedom of Christians, one should not enthusiastically presume on them and thereby deny dependence on the Lord. On this interpretation ἀσθένεια is not the impotence of the weak who cannot be helped by the demand for radical obedience but the defiance of the strong who would like to be free of all bonds and who thus protest against the apostle's exposition. These are told that what preceded certainly described only the earthly aspect but that it cannot be retracted or restricted lest encouragement be given to the flesh.

Paul calls himself a slave of Christ. The truth of sonship in faith establishes from an earthly standpoint the reality of slavery. In this regard Paul is distinguishing himself both from the Jewish view which regards slavery as a necessary but oppressive earthly reality and from the enthusiasm which believes that it is already ended on earth. Grace establishes corporal obedience so radically that comparison with slavery is justifiable—did not Christ take the form of a slave according to Phil 2:7? At issue is the total and exclusive obligation of the first commandment, which has to be developed according to both of its sides. Being total, it means bondage. Being exclusive, it creates freedom. Again the relation between sacrament and ethics comes to light. So little does Paul think "sacramentally" in the usual sense that for him only obedience counts as the fruit of baptism. Conversely, he thinks so "sacramentally" that this obedience is made possible only by the address of divine love and orientation to the lordship of grace. The one who is loved empties himself and becomes lowly. Only he can do this.

This leads to the third subsection, under the catchword ἁγιασμός. The history of exposition has already shown how dangerous this theme is. The danger is all the greater here because it seems to be the goal of the Christian life (Grundmann, *TDNT*, I, 313; Kertelge, *Rechtfertigung*, 272; Thüsing, *Per Christum*, 94). A current view is that forensic justification is the basis of ethical authentication. This comes to expression in progressive perfecting (Dodd, *Meaning*, 125f.; Taylor; Cerfaux, *Christ*, 304ff.; Schürmann, "Freiheitsbotschaft," 46), and it finally makes possible the state of holiness or at least brings it into view (Sanday and Headlam; Kühl; Sickenberger; Lagrange; Schlier, "Taufe," 54; but cf. Stalder, *Werk*, 227; Kertelge, *Rechtfertigung*, 272).

What is first needed, however, is to realize that the term is part of the baptismal vocabulary (Tachau, *Einst*, 105; Furnish, *Ethics*, 154f.). According to 1 Thess 4:7 the baptized are called to holiness, and as those who belong to the eschatological world they are called ἅγιοι. The baptismal formula in 1 Cor 6:11 draws a parallel between the state of justification and that of sanctification. This shows that, as elsewhere, an originally cultic term has already been taken up by Judaism into both the ethical and the eschatological spheres of language (cf. the parallels to Qumran in Dietzel, "Beten," 23). In primitive Christianity the second aspect is the more prominent. If there seems to be development in the present text, it is because sanctification is described as the daily task of the living out of justification (Gaugler; Merk, *Handeln*, 33; Furnish, *Ethics*, 157, 239f.).

It is not accidental that that is related to the members. At issue is the bodily obedience which in 12:1 will be characterized as service of God in the everyday world (Thüsing, *Per Christum*, 94f.). Here then, in contrast to v. 13, παριστάνειν seems in fact to point to sacrificial language. The scope and background of the text are missed if attention is not paid to the antithetical pairs which control it: law and grace in v. 15, sin and obedience in v. 18, sin and righteousness in v. 20, and death and life in vv. 22f. To these should be added ἀνομία and ἁγιασμός. Presupposed is the conflict of spirit and flesh described in Gal 5:17ff., in which the two aeons clash. This constantly goes on in anthropology and is constantly decided afresh. The Christian must not let himself be misled into ἀνομία as lack of commitment. Sanctification means a being for God manifesting itself bodily in the secular world and in face of temptation, because in Christ God graciously sets us in his lordship and is there for us. Justification claims the whole person in all his possibilities and relations and therefore in his worldly reality, since God wills and creates a new world. In sanctification it is a matter of this intention and dimension of justification which has to be represented individually and by way of example.

No matter what may be the religio-historical origin and form-critical setting in life of the formula of contrast "once–now" (cf. on this Tachau, *Einst*), here and in other important passages it undoubtedly occurs in the context of baptismal [exhortation (Tachau, *Einst*, 80, 119). In contrasting the present of believers with their pre-Christian life, it describes a definite history characterized by a break. The change of aeons is thus reflected in the baptism and the existence of the baptized (*contra* Tachau, 109f.). The contrast of times is constitutive, then, for that of the antithetical statements and here these statements unambiguously serve, not as an assurance of salvation, but as a summons to battle and resistance (*contra* Tachau, 109f., 112f., 115f., though cf. 120ff.). From a specifically Jewish standpoint the past of the readers is described with loathing as typically heathen. What was formally called sin is here ἀκαθαρσία and ἀνομία. As in 1:24ff., the wild sexuality and licentiousness, in which a person makes his lusts the measure of his action and behaves autonomously, leads to anarchy (Schlier, *TDNT*, II, 496f.). Only the Christian is aware that this life is one of bondage. δοῦλα is also used biblically in Wis 15:7.

εἰς τὴν ἀνομίαν clashes with the preceding dative. Hence a series of MSS omit it and it is sometimes viewed as a gloss (Sahlin, "Textemendationen," 99). The point is that capricious and deceitful freedom is infectious and carves out an earthly sphere for itself. Against this background the same can be said antithetically for the service of righteousness. It, too, sets up a field of relations in which the lordship of the holy God is demonstrated. Belonging to God should find earthly manifestation. It can do this only if we bear witness to it with our members, thus in the whole of our physical existence. Only then does there arise the fruit which in Jewish terminology (cf. Delling, *TDNT*, VIII, 55; Kuss, 404f.) represents the harvest of life. Here Paul seems to be replacing the motifs of the *militia Christi* and sanctification with a picture drawn from the process of organic growth. But the idea of development has already been ruled out. Life is not to be led in vain or to remain empty. Act and effect are its signs. This mode of expression is dangerous, since it might favor the idea of achievement. For the apostle, however, action, result, and fruit, and even a non-self-justifying καύχησις, cannot be abandoned, since a person is not a nomad and leaves traces in society if he does not live to himself alone. Bearing fruit, of course, also stands under the apocalyptic alternative. It can also be borne to sin and death. With both statements Paul removes the catchword sanctification far from the horizon of individual perfection, setting it in the relations of being in the world. The holy person is the one upon whom God looks and who stands in the presence of Christ. But his sanctification means that the world around perceives the service of God in earthly secularity reflected in his bodily (social) expressions of life, as in a mirror, and it thus catches a glimpse of the God who looks on his creature. The world is confronted by its true Lord through his servants and the questionability of cosmic powers is thereby exposed.

Verse 20 makes the same thing clear from the opposite side by speaking very formally of freedom from righteousness and thus maintaining the basic antithesis of the section. In this way, as already happened at Qumran (cf. Becker, *Heil*

Gottes, 87ff.), righteousness is envisioned as the sphere of a lordship which God's creature is supposed to represent on earth but which is abandoned in pagan fashion in favor of the lordship of sin. ἐφ' οἷς (*contra* Zahn) should not be taken with v. 21. It is the answer to the question posed there. ἐπαισχύνομαι does not come from the vocabulary of confession (*contra* Gäumann, *Ethik*, 101). Its reference is to objectively present shame. The reason is given in v. 21c. This shows that καρπός is the result of the service of sin, not the end denoted by τέλος. We thus have a circle. If uncleanness and licentiousness lead to cosmic anarchy, they conversely are the consequence and manifestation of the power of sin already present. We thus have the same dialectical relation of guilt and destiny as in 1:24ff.; 5:12ff. In a universal nexus everything is both fruit and seed at the same time. Death is not just the end. It is the secret goal of the life which is not controlled by Christ and which thus falls victim to sin.

Verse 22, speaking formally of freedom in exact correspondence to v. 20b, formulates for the last time the antithesis of the past and the salvific present. As in 3:21, the eschatological νυνὶ δέ again denotes the change. The apostle can speak of freedom so formally because in content the concept primarily denotes deliverance from the compulsion of the powers. If he now refers to God again in the place of righteousness (Murray; Tachau, *Einst*, 105), the conclusion is unavoidable that in Paul righteousness cannot be restricted to the judgment of justification or even to the gift of the righteousness of faith. God's reign in the sign of grace is its material center and justification is the participation in it, in which one is set in the reign of Christ as the obedient Adam and in the new obedience. Also here service does not remain without fruit. ἀνομία is replaced by ἁγιασμός, namely, a life in open access to the presence of God (5:2) and hence in earthly openness, which as a token to the world bears witness to the Lord Christ.

This life has, of course, an end and goal which is anticipated in service. If it is called eternal life, this shows yet again that in reality Christian ethics is lived-out eschatology. The apostle does not share the modern interest in continuity of being and (*contra* Enslin, *Ethics*, e.g., 309) in the ethical development of character. The break between past and present, and the related dividing alternatives of our section, are signs of this. We are certainly on the way to a goal. Yet this has already been given in Christ's work and is present in our service. Conversely, we have continually to receive afresh the freedom granted with baptism, which will be ours unassailably only in the resurrection.

Verse 23 provides a basis by summarizing not only v. 22 but the whole preceding exhortation. It is solemnly stylized in such a way that v. 23a relates to v. 21 and v. 23b to v. 22. ὀψώνιον does not mean compensation (*contra* BAGD, 602b) but the soldier's pay (Heidland, *TDNT*, V, 592; Black). The genitive that follows is a genitive of agent: Sin is already making the payment, death. The same image cannot be used for the God who gives, so that to construe χάρισμα as a gift of honor (Zahn, etc.) is highly doubtful. As in 5:15, what is said to be already given is not an extraordinary gift (*contra* Kühl; Gutjahr; Michel; Kuss; Gaugler; H. W. Schmidt) but the comprehensive gift of salvation (Barrett; Thüsing, *Per Christum*, 96). The specific charismata all derive from this as concrete forms. It is received by those who in baptism receive Christ as Lord. The additional clause after symmetrical parallelism is used elsewhere by Paul to conclude a train of thought (J. Weiss, "Beiträge," 189, 1).

C. The End of the Law in the Power of the Spirit (7:1–8:39)

Only detailed exegesis can establish a convincing link between the two chapters. The same applies to the structure of ch. 7. It is a provisionally open question whether there is an inner logic behind sections 1-6, 7-13, and 14-25.

1. Free from the Law (7:1-6)

¹Do you not know, brethren—I speak to those familiar with the law—that the law rules over a man only so long as he lives? ²For a married woman is bound by the law to her husband while he is alive. If he dies, however, she is released from the law in respect of her husband. ³While her husband lives she will be called an adulteress if she gives herself to another man. But if her husband dies she is free from the law, and therefore she is not an adulteress if she marries another man. ⁴Similarly, my brethren, you are dead to the law through the body of Christ, so that you may belong to another, (namely) him who has been raised from the dead, and therefore we have to bear fruit for God. ⁵For when we were still in the flesh, our sinful passions, stirred up by the law, were at work on our members to bear fruit for death. ⁶But now we are fully freed from the law, dead to that in which we lay captive. We can thus serve in the new being of the Spirit and not the old one of the letter.

Bibliography: W. G. Kümmel, *Römer 7 und die Bekehrung des Paulus* (1929); E. Lohmeyer, "Probleme paulinischer Theologie, III: Sünde, Fleisch und Tod," *ZNW* 29 (1930) 1-59; E. von Dobschütz, "Wir und Ich bei Paulus," *ZST* 10 (1933) 251-277; G. Bornkamm, "Sin, Law and Death (Romans 7)," *Early Christian Experience*, 87-104; E. Ellwein, "Das Rätsel von Römer VII," *KuD* 1 (1955) 247-268; E. Giese, "Römer 7 neu gesehen im Zusammenhang des gesamtes Briefes" (Dissertation, Marburg, 1959); H. Hommel, "Das 7. Kapitel des Römerbriefes im Licht antiker Überlieferung," *Theologia Viatorum* 8 (1961/62) 90-116; K. Prümm, "Röm 1-11 und 2. Kor 3," *Bib* 31 (1950) 164-203; S. Schulz, "Die Decke des Moses," *ZNW* 49 (1958) 1-30; S. Zedda, "L'uso di gar in alcuni testi di San Paolo," *Stud.Paul.Congr.*, II, 445-451; H. Hübner, "Anthropologischer Dualismus in den Hodayoth?" *NTS* 18 (1971/72) 268-284; J. D. M. Derrett, "Romans vii.1-4," *Law in the NT* (1970) 461-471.

The spearhead of the Pauline doctrine of justification is that along with sin and death it ascribes the law to the old aeon. If this is not perceived the apostle's view is domesticated in the interests of edification. 2 Corinthians 3 in particular shows that Paul understands the law as a universally effective power, which therefore continues to threaten the Christian from outside even though it no longer has any claim on him. It must also be remembered that through the law as in nothing else Paul was confronted by his own past. As a former Pharisee he could not distinguish between the cultic and ethical Torah, as later Christianity did, for to him the law was indivisible. Hardly any theme, then, moves him more strongly and is reflected upon by him more passionately. The law is the true counterpart of the gospel, and radical criticism of the Torah is the inalienable mark of Paul's theology (Eichholz, *Paulus, passim*). It is no surprise, then, that the exposition of Christian freedom leads to the thesis of freedom from the law. What is surprising is the caution, fussiness, and consideration with which he opens the section. Possibly the apostle was aware that he was treading on dangerous ground as far as the Roman community was concerned, or important groups within it. At any rate the present verses do not refer back to ch. 6 (Feuillet, "Citation," 58f.) and they are not to be regarded as transitional (*contra* Best; Tachau, *Einst,* 126f.; Black). They represent a fresh start.

As in 6:3 Paul begins with a question and with the ἢ ἀγνοεῖτε of the diatribe, which points here, not to the tradition, but to general experience, and thus is followed by an example. The readers are addressed as people who know the law. Insofar as the Roman community consisted mainly of Gentile-Christians, even the existence of an active Jewish-Christian minority and liturgical contact with the OT could hardly justify our referring this predication to the Torah (*contra* Zahn; Schlatter; Murray; van Dülmen, *Theologie,* 101; Minear, *Obedience,* 64). The context also does not treat the marriage law of the Torah (*contra* Schlatter; Gaugler; Bläser, *Gesetz,* 221; Maurer, *Gesetzeslehre,* 42f.; Schoeps, *Paul,* 171f., 192). The legal and not especially religious argument of the example (BAGD, 91b, 526a) would certainly be familiar to the Jew from his own tradition, but it does not have to remind us of the Torah (*contra* Lietzmann; Huby; Althaus; Leenhardt; H. W. Schmidt; Bläser, *Gesetz,* 88ff.; correctly Ridderbos). νόμος here is simply the legal order (Sanday and Headlam; Bultmann, *Theology,* I, 259f.) to which citizens of the capital were subject and which would not be beyond their legal knowledge. They were not barbarians. The γάρ is not basic but introductory (Zedda, "L'uso," 445f.).

The comparison that follows has a pedagogic function like the statement in 6:7. In the social sphere death severs ties, as the special instance of marriage shows (Kümmel, *Römer 7,* 37). The same is true of Christians in relation to the law of Moses. For the sake of the analogy the term νόμος is ambiguous. Hence there is not the slightest basis for the common practice (Sanday and Headlam; Pallis; Althaus; Bornkamm, "Sin," 88; Hommel, "7. Kapitel," 93f.; correctly Zahn; Nygren; Kümmel, *Römer 7,* 38f.) of allegorically importing the subject matter of vv. 4-6 already here. Nor is this justified by the fact that the illustration, as so often in Paul, does not work out very well (Lietzmann; Dodd; Gale, *Analogy,* 192ff.). Belonging to Christ does not presuppose the end of obligation to the law; it establishes it. Unlike the woman depicted, the Christian does not become his own master but receives a new lord who replaces the old. Hence the husband in the illustration is not the Torah (*contra* Derrett, *Law,* 466ff.). The only point of comparison is that death dissolves obligations valid throughout life. The principle is enunciated in v. 1b. κυριεύειν may imply legal force rather than lordship. The statement is applied concretely to marriage in vv. 2-3. The Hellenistic expression ὕπανδρος corresponds (Billerbeck) to the rabbinic equivalent. καταργεῖν does not have the eschatological sense of radical dissolution, while χρηματίζειν, originally (BAGD, 885b; Lagrange; Michel) "to do business," acquires, to the extent

187

that that happens in a particular change, the sense "to be called." The closing infinitive is consecutive (Lagrange). Verse 4 draws the conclusion. The aorist and the total context unmistakably look again to baptism. What is said in 6:4ff. in relation to the power of sin is self-evidently transferred to the relation to the law. As in 6:11 the dominion of the risen Lord is the basis of the new existence. This comes to expression, as in 6:22, in bearing fruit for God, which, as there, does not mean achievement but passing on the blessing, and which is shown to be God's will by ἵνα. The change from the third person to the first person marks a lasting determination.

The motifs of the previous chapter are also repeated in v. 5. What is called ἐπιθυμίαι in 6:12 is now described as παθήματα τῶν ἁμαρτιῶν. What is said about the old man in 6:6 is now described by ἐν σαρκί. The members, as before, perform the actions in which the power which controls us manifests itself and enters the world of the body. Yet the nuances are to be noted. The old man within us who is to be crucified is now replaced by the universal dimension of the flesh which was introduced by the first Adam, and which is represented by, although not confined to, our existence in subjection to the earthly. Here for the first time we come up against the technical formula ἐν σαρκί which is so characteristic of Pauline anthropology (for the history of interpretation, Sand, Fleisch, 3-121; excursus in Kuss; Brandenburger, Fleisch, 42ff.). No adequate equivalent is available. It cannot be understood in terms of classical Greek. There flesh is material one has bodily without being "in it." It is used in the OT and Judaism to denote the difference between the creating God and the creature, not only in the sense of weakness, but also in that of resistance to the Creator. It thus goes beyond the individual sphere. Creaturely fellowship in family, people, and even the world is presupposed. One may thus speak in principle of being "in the flesh."

Yet obviously a certain dualistic influence is needed before "flesh" and "spirit" can oppose one another in metaphysical contrast as the realities of the old aeon and the new, being defined as powers by distinctive prepositional constructions with κατά and as spheres of lordship by the parallel constructions with ἐν. Undoubtedly a number of Qumran passages tend in this direction, so that one may read out of them a concept of "demonized flesh" (Kuhn, "πειρασμός," 209ff.). Yet they do not have in this connection a technical use in the absolute but use a qualifying genitive such as flesh of wickedness (Kuss, excursus). We certainly do not have a technical and absolute antithesis of flesh and spirit, and no explicit doctrine of the spirit is formulated (Davies, "Paul," 176ff.; Brandenburger, Fleisch, 96f.; Hübner, "Dualismus," 268ff.). If intensification of the Torah meant anything, this was impossible, and being in the flesh could not be regarded as the abolished past as in the present passage. The unmistakable heightening of the antithesis as compared with OT statements does not attain the radicalness of Paul even when it seems to press beyond the ethical to the border of a metaphysical contrast. Transition to cosmic dualism comes only with Philo (Brandenburger, Fleisch, 86ff., 140ff.), to be sure, not with the fixed statements of Paul's antitheses, but in a wealth of analogies (ibid., 115ff., 197ff.) which distinguish between the two spheres of power. So far, then, the religio-historical derivation of Paul's formulae in the absolute has not been fully traced, although it seems unlikely that they are to be attributed to the apostle himself. One may conjecture that he came across them and put them to use in his conflict with enthusiasm.

Not to be overlooked is the breadth of possible variations (cf. Bultmann, *Theology*, I, 232ff.) ranging from corporeality, designation of the personal and its social ties to creatureliness in weakness and vulnerability (*Anfechtung*), all the way to the antithetical spheres of power of the old aeon and the new. One can understand such a scale to the extent that subjection to the world and its powers goes hand in hand with the earthly state outside the rule of Christ. Even the technical formulations are not rigid. In 2 Cor 10:2f. subjection to the power of the world κατὰ σάρκα is differentiated from vulnerable creaturely existence ἐν σαρκί, but here ἐν σαρκί plainly means the nature of the old aeon and is thus identical with what is usually called κατὰ σάρκα. The qualitative genitive construction τὰ παθήματα τῶν ἁμαρτιῶν names the energies of the flesh, which in many ways, as the plural shows, is subject to the world and in revolt against God. It is a moot point whether παθήματα instead of ἐπιθυμίαι is calling attention to the fact that these impulses cannot be directed by us but use us as a field of force, so that basically they are suffered by us (Schlatter; Horst, *TDNT*, IV, 562; for this reason Kühl thinks the verb is middle: "become effective"). The wording does not support this nuance and the context makes it even more improbable. Sinful passions are activated by the law as was already indicated in 5:20a, is expressly supported in 1 Cor 15:56, and the development, already envisioned here, in 7:7ff. will reveal. Paul is thus laying the foundation of the section.

There can be no question of the law having regained its original function of being an aid to righteousness (*contra* Beare, *BHH*, III, 1612). καταργηθῆναι, which radicalizes the ἐθανατώθητε of v. 4, does not speak of a new understanding and use of the Torah. Without restriction it means the end of the Torah for Christians after baptism (Thüsing, *Per Christum*, 96ff.). Incorporation into the rule of Christ and total separation from the law coincide. This is what characterizes the salvific present, here again denoted by νυνὶ δέ.

Why this is so is obviously shown by the very enigmatic and as yet undiscussed expression διὰ τοῦ σώματος τοῦ Χριστοῦ in v. 4. The reference is not to our participation in the dead body of Jesus (Nygren; Robinson, *Body*, 47). It is also arbitrary in the context to relate σῶμα Χριστοῦ, as in 12:4; 1 Cor 12:12ff., to the body of the risen Lord in the church (A. Schweitzer, *Mysticism*, 188 n. 1; Prat, *Theology*, II, 223; Dodd; J. Knox; Kümmel, *Theology*, 212f.; considered by Barrett; rejected by Kuss). This would have had to be expressed more clearly and would demand that the verb be in the present. It is best (E. Schweizer, *TDNT*, VII, 1067) to take the expression as a formula. 1 Cor 10:16 shows that in probably pre-Pauline eucharistic language it denoted the crucified body (Bultmann, *Theology*, I, 147). By this, through baptism, we are released not only from sin but also from the law. We have died to it. Hence 6:7 applies to us. This is underlined in v. 6. What is done away is not just the curse of the law (*contra* Stalder, *Werk*, 288f.) or the tyranny of an idea of legality and moral order of retribution (Dodd, *Meaning*, 71ff.). It is the Torah itself. According to the parallels in v. 4a the relative clause can refer only to the law (Schlatter; Kuss; Gaugler; Ridderbos; Bläser, *Gesetz*, 224; Giese, *Römer 7*, 61; probable, Michel). Hence ἐν ᾧ is not to be taken as neuter (*contra* Zahn; Kühl; Lagrange; undecided: Lietzmann; Leenhardt) nor related to the flesh (contra Jülicher). The meaning of Gal 3:23f. is clearly shown herewith. The pedagogue is here the jailer (Ridderbos; Brandenburger, Fleisch, 56). We do not have in fact the smooth transition from law to gospel and vice versa on which other exegetical traditions have placed so much emphasis.

Paul is thus advancing the thesis which is logically connected with the two preceding chapters. The freedom of Christians from the power of the Torah is proclaimed. Remarkably it usually escapes notice how seldom the apostle does this. According to the apostle's theology his argument in this section of the letter reaches a climax here and thus is connected with a detailed presentation as in Galatians. The captatio benevolentiae at the beginning and the illustration which follows make sense only if Paul is fully aware how important and how difficult the new theme is. The more surprising, then, is the brevity with which he treats it and even more so the apparent distaste for the matter. The illustration is not merely lame. In content it does not lead beyond a simple assertion, which is stated adequately enough in v. 4 and v. 6ab that the illustration is really superfluous. Nor do vv. 4-6 add anything new to the thesis. Both formally and materially the argument about freedom from sin is repeated and is transferred to the relation to the law. Baptismal exhortation remains decisive (Nygren; Michel; Kuss; Leenhardt; Luz, "Aufbau," 170, 176f.), and what is to be demonstrated is presupposed rather than proved. Hence it is not surprising that many commentators find in this section an appendix to what precedes, especially as the conclusion of the chapter does not seem to advance the train of thought. Has not the apostle said all that needs to be said on this theme in 2:1-3:20, so that the thesis is enough and what has already been discussed is merely summarized? In this case no climax is reached here. If a new question is raised with ch. 7 and another change in course comes in ch. 8, this portion of the epistle is also without logical structure and there can certainly be no talk of a theological system in the strict sense.

These matters have to be raised if the significance of the conclusion in v. 6 is to be grasped. At a first glance the exhortation of vv. 4f. simply seems to be reinforced with an emphasis on the service of the liberated along the lines of 6:12ff., the whole being crowned rhetorically by a restatement of the formal antithesis of 2:29. The antithesis has already been interpreted. It clearly characterizes the standing of the Christian after the change of aeons, which is still at issue in 2:29. The nouns καινότης and παλαιότης here show plainly what was implicitly intended there. Semitically they can replace adjectives, but they probably mark the two contrasting epochs characterized by the old covenant and the new (Conzelmann, Outline, 170). In this case "spirit" and "letter" do not have the character of timeless concepts (contra Conzelmann). The decisive question is why Paul repeats the formula in the present context.

Rightly it has often been pointed out that it presents something like a summary of the main theme of chs. 7-8 (Prümm, "Röm 1-11," 187f.; Luz, "Aufbau," 166; Schunack, Problem, 125; Conzelmann, Outline, 229; Paulsen, Überlieferung, 29; only as far as 8:11 Bornkamm, "Sin," 88; Michel; Kuss). To be sure, no consequences have been drawn from this. They lie at hand once the oddness of the section is perceived. In its brevity, with its application of baptismal exhortation to the new theme, and with its gentle approach and preparatory illustration, it has

190

the task of an introduction in which for the moment only the thesis as such is set forth. With the formula at the end of v. 6, which perhaps grew out of the conflict with the adversaries of 2 Corinthians (Duchrow, *Weltverantwortung,* 104; D. Georgi, *Die Gegner des Paulus im 2. Korintherbrief* [WMANT 11; 1964], 168ff., 257, 272), the theme of the argument which follows is stated in thesis form. If Paul in his reliance on baptismal exhortation used a tradition familiar to his readers, he at this stage develops his thesis out of his own theology. Previously it was only stated that in virtue of the death of their Lord Christians are loosed from the law and are dead to it. Now the central statement is made that only under the dominion of the Spirit, who according to the common view is imparted at baptism, is the dominion of the law broken and vanquished.

Therefore, chs. 7 and 8 form a unity. This part of the epistle reaches its climax in them. The disproportionate length of the discussion corresponds to the importance of this question in Pauline theology. Freedom from the powers of sin and death takes concrete shape in freedom from the law. Made possible by the Spirit, this can be maintained only "in the Spirit." Christianity is not just a Jewish sect which believes in Jesus as the Messiah. It is the breaking in of the new world of God characterized by the lordship of the Spirit. The intensification of the Torah which shaped Judaism in the days of the apostle is impossible for Paul even in the form of an internalizing of the law. He does not set up a new law as his interpreters do when they oppose living religion to book religion (Weinel, *Paulus,* 79 [*St. Paul,* 115f.]), or the statutory commands to the living will of God (Schrenk, *TDNT,* I, 766; Seesemann, *TDNT,* V, 720; Stalder, *Werk,* 283f.), a purified law (J. Knox, *Life,* 63f.), ethical activity (Dodd, *Gospel,* 65ff., 72), or inner moral power (cf. Huby; Sickenberger). All this would presuppose that God has to do primarily with the pious and not with the ungodly as Paul's doctrine of justification maintains, so that the order of the world and existence would be proclaimed as salvation under the banner of the law (cf. Limbeck, *Ordnung*). For Paul the antithesis of letter and Spirit is the same as that of flesh and Spirit. As he sees it, the presence of the risen Lord in the power of the Spirit takes the place of the Torah of Moses and makes holy the world which otherwise, even in its piety and ethics, is unholy. The break with the law has to be proclaimed wherever the justification of the ungodly is the premise. This is the point in the two chapters. On this is built both the discussion of the problem of unbelieving Israel in chs. 9–11 and the exhortation of chs. 12–15. The immediate question, of course, is that of the place of vv. 7-25 in this context.

2. The Work of the Law (7:7-13)

⁷What are we to say then? Is the law itself sin? Not at all! I should not have come to know sin except through the law. I should not have known what covetousness is if the law had not said: "Thou shalt not covet." ⁸Sin received a push from the law and worked all kinds of covetousness in me. For apart from the law sin was dead. ⁹I was once alive—apart from the law. But when the commandment came, sin revived. ¹⁰In contrast I died. Thus the law which was (given) for life proved to be (what leads) to death for me. ¹¹For sin, being put on the offensive by the law, deceived me and by it killed me. ¹²The law,

191

then, is holy, and the commandment is holy, just, and good. ¹³*Did that which is good, then, become death for me? Not at all! Sin, in order that it might be seen to be sin, worked death in me through that which is good. (It did it) in order that sin might be exceedingly sinful through the commandment.*

Bibliography: G. de los Rios, "Peccatum et Lex," *VD* 11 (1931) 23-28; R. Bultmann, "Romans 7 and the Anthropology of Paul," *Existence and Faith* (Eng. tr. 1960) 147-157; H. Braun, "Römer 7, 7-25 und das Selbstverständnis des Qumran-Frommen," *Gesammelte Studien*, 100-119; P. Benoit, "La loi et la croix d'après St. Paul," *Exégèse et Théologie*, II (1961) 9-40; S. Lyonnet, "L'histoire du salut selon le ch. 7 de l'épître aux Romains," *Bib* 43 (1962) 117-151; idem, "Quaestiones ad Rom 7, 7-13," *VD* 40 (1962) 163-183; idem, " 'Tu ne convoiteras pas' (Rom. VII, 7)," *Neotestamentica et Patristica* (Cullmann Freundesgabe; NovT Sup 6; 1962), 157-165; E. Fuchs, "Existentiale Interpretation von Römer 7, 7-12 und 21-23," *ZTK* 59 (1962) 285-314; O. Modalsli, "Gal. 2, 19-21; 5, 16-18 und Röm 7, 7-25," *TZ* 21 (1965) 22-37; K. Kertelge, "Exegetische Überlegungen zum Verständnis der paulinischen Anthropologie nach Römer 7," *ZNW* 62 (1971) 105-114. See also the bibliography for 7:1-6.

7:7-25 is nearly always regarded as an excursus. This is understandable, since it seems possible and meaningful to move on directly from 7:6 to ch. 8. But on this premise one has to inquire into the reason for Paul's digression. A common German view is that we have here an "apology for the law" (Kümmel, *Römer 7*, 9ff.; Bultmann, "Romans 7," 58f.; Bornkamm, "Sin," 88f.; Braun, "Selbstverständnis," 101; Hommel, "7. Kapitel," 101; Brandenburger, *Adam*, 206; Friedrich, *RGG*, V, 1141; Lagrange; Kuss; H. W. Schmidt). The apologetic motif is in fact evident at vv. 7a, 12, 13a, 14, so that the section might be given this heading (Fuchs, *Freiheit*, 55; Kertelge, "Überlegungen," 109; Luz, *Geschichtsverständnis*, 155). Nevertheless it is hard to contest the point that even here the effectiveness of sin is more strongly emphasized (Luz, "Aufbau," 166f.; critically Kirk; Stalder, *Werk*, 290; Giese, *Römer 7*, 52), and that the transition to vv. 14-25 can more easily be made from this perspective. For there, except in v. 14a, the Torah recedes completely into the background and everything focuses on anthropology, which in turn is no less important than the question of the law in vv. 7-13. One may thus doubt whether the title mentioned does justice to the apostle's intention. Detailed exegesis alone can offer an alternative.

In contrast light seems to have been shed on the other question that has bothered exegetes, namely, that of the subject of the "I" in these verses (cf. Schelkle, 232ff.; surveys in Kümmel, *Römer 7*; Kuss; Ellwein, "Rätsel"; Giese, *Römer 7*, 64ff.). A specific aspect of Christian existence is hardly being described (*contra* Althaus; Nygren; Giese, *Römer 7*) when vv. 7ff. speak of a distinctive past event and not of present experience, when in v. 14c the I is said to be carnal and sold under sin, and when the antithesis to ch. 8 is taken into account. Paul is depicting pre-Christian being from a Christian standpoint (as is generally agreed since Kümmel's monograph). Nevertheless further delimitation of this insight is required. We do not have an autobiographical reminiscence (*contra* Zahn; Kühl; Dodd, commentary and *Meaning*, 76ff.; Bruce; W. L. Knox, *Church*, 99; Gutjahr; Sickenberger; Bardenhewer; Hommel, "7. Kapitel," 99f.). This is refuted by Phil 3:6. Nor is there a reference to the experience of the pious Jew. No pious

Jew regarded the law as impossible to fulfil in principle or as a spur to sin (*contra* Bläser, *Gesetz*, 115f.; J. Knox; correctly Enslin, *Ethics*, 3). For this reason there is no point in recalling the Jewish duty of binding a boy at 12 years of age to observance of the Torah (*contra* Billerbeck; Deissmann, *Paul*, 92; Davies, *Rabbinic Judaism*, 24f.; Franzmann; Best; considered by Kuss; Michel; Bruce; rejected by Schlatter; Bornkamm, "Sin," 92f.; Leenhardt; Benoit, "Loi," 12; Lyonnet, *Étapes*, 115; Conzelmann, *Outline*, 233). In spite of this obligation all Jews knew already of the existence of the law. The idea of childish innocence (Dodd; Baulès; Prat, *Theology*, I, 231) is completely unbiblical and part of our modern mythology. One result of all this is at least that a psychological interpretation is out of place no matter whether it refers to the person of the apostle (characteristically Weinel, *Paulus*, 53ff. [*St. Paul*, 68ff.]) or to the rise of sin (*contra* Lietzmann; Althaus; Baulès; J. Knox, *Life*, 65ff.; Kirk; even Kuss; Cerfaux, *Christ*, 227f.; Murray) and constitutes a drama which is both psychological and salvation historical (Sanday and Headlam; Black). This approach is not complementary but invincibly antithetical to 5:12ff. Both passages are equally objective. If one is prepared to accept the expression, then, both are salvation historical.

As regards the I-statements this implies the use, stylistically, of a rhetorical figure with general significance (BDF, §281). This is encountered not only in the Greek world but also in the OT psalms of thanksgiving when divine deliverance from guilt and peril of death is confessed (Kümmel, *Römer 7*, 118f.; Stauffer, *TDNT*, II, 358ff.; Bornkamm, "Sin," 85, 89f.; Leenhardt; H. W. Schmidt; etc.). Impressive examples of this are to be found in the Qumran *hodayoth* (H. Braun, "Selbstverständnis," 103ff., 112; Schulz, "Rechtfertigung," 160ff.; Michel). To say this, of course, is not enough. Why does Paul use this stylized figure here (Dodd; Kuss; Ridderbos; Schunack, *Problem*, 110; Kertelge, "Überlegungen," 107f.) even though a Christian survey of the vanquished past could have been presented differently as in 1:18–3:20 and 5:12ff.? Certainly the element of confession in the passage is not to be pressed to the point (Michel) of referring to rhythm in the text or even strophes. Here again the problem has not yet been fully discussed. Exegesis begins with open questions.

If an attempt is made to bring vv. 7-13 under a common theme, the original intention and the actual function of the law have to be set in contrast (J. Knox). The question posed again in diatribe style and its indignant rejection in v. 7a reflect Jewish-Christian objections as in 3:5; 6:1, 15. If the Mosaic *nomos* belongs to the old aeon like sin and death, it might be regarded as a manifestation of sin, as by Marcion later. The answer, to the extent that it connects with 3:20; 5:20, is dialectical. The law is not as such and originally sinful, but in fact it leads to experience of sin. It puts an end to the naïvete not merely of wickedness but also of a religiosity which misunderstands the will of God and brings about palpable transgression. ἀλλά in v. 7b is probably adversative, not restrictive. Notwithstanding the subjunctive use of the verb, οὐκ ἔγνων and οὐκ ᾔδειν point to knowledge really attained (Maurer, *Gesetzeslehre*, 46). Verse 7b and v. 7c are only formally parallel. The quotation, a surplus member of the sentence, shows that v. 7c forms the basis of what precedes (Brandenburger, *Adam*, 206; Schunack, *Problem*, 126). Sin, here defined as the power and reality of covetousness, is both stimulated and unmasked by the law as the divine commandment. Paul obviously has the Decalogue in view. Characteristically he leaves out the positive commandments, but unlike the rabbis (Billerbeck) he does not separate the last commandment from the others, in such a way that covetousness becomes one among many sins or represents the intention of transgression.

In understanding the commandment against covetousness as the core and sum of the law the apostle follows a Jewish tradition. 4 Macc 2:6 reads: ὅτε μὴ ἐπιθυμεῖν εἴρηκεν ἡμᾶς ὁ νόμος (Büchsel, TDNT, III, 171; Bornkamm, "Sin," 102 n. 7). In Apoc. Mos. 19:3 and also in Philo De Decalogo 142, 150, 173 covetousness is described as the beginning of all sin, and Jas 1:15 develops this psychologically (Michel; H. W. Schmidt; Mauser, Gottesbild, 156f.). The Talmud takes the same view (Lyonnet, "Rom. VII, 7," 159ff.). This does not mean merely that all other sins stem from covetousness, and sexuality is certainly not meant (contra Lohmeyer, "Sünde," 33ff.; considered by Kuss). The point is that it is absolutely the basic sin (Lagrange) against which the whole law is directed and which the law in fact provokes. Similarly it appears as the key concept in 1 Cor 10:5ff. (Mauser, Gottesbild, 156; Lyonnet, "Röm. VII, 7," 160). For Paul ἐπιθυμεῖν is not primarily psychological. What it denotes is not the intention of blasphemous transgression but the passion to assert oneself against God and neighbor (Grundmann, TDNT, I, 311; Schlier, TDNT, II, 496ff.; Bultmann, Theology, I, 264f.; etc.). As such it can come to expression religiously in the striving for achievement (Bornkamm, "Sin," 90). The sentence thus stands in the comprehensive context of Pauline theology.

Verse 8 elucidates. ἀφορμὴν λαμβάνειν is a common phrase (BAGD, 127b). ἐντολή is not to be identified simply with the law (contra Kümmel, Römer 7, passim; Schrenk, TDNT, II, 550f.; van Dülmen, Theologie, 130f.). Referring to the quotation, the word means in this context, as elsewhere, the specific commandment. πᾶσαν ἐπιθυμίαν does not merely emphasize multiplicity but in Pauline fashion includes already the form of religious perversion of which vv. 10b-11 speak. The meaning of v. 8c is debated. Certainly 5:13, which speaks of actual sin which is not reckoned, does not say the same thing (Kümmel, Römer 7, 48f.). On the other hand, already through the participial phrase the power of sin is characterized also here as already lying in ambush and present (Lohmeyer, "Sünde," 11, though cf. Kümmel, 51). Since it is called "dead" in anticipation of v. 9, the idea is that sin is "latent" (Kuss) or "powerless" (Kühl; Huby; Ridderbos). It does not yet have the form of transgression. The expression, which further develops 4:15, is too oracular (Brandenburger, Adam, 209ff.) not to need the more concrete statements in vv. 9-11 (Kuss). In v. 9 ἔζων corresponds to sin being dead. As ἀπέθανον in v. 10 shows, however, what is meant is not just relative liveliness (Zahn; Huby; Ridderbos; Benoit, "Loi," 16), or a life in self-complacency (Murray). Apart from confrontation with the nomos a person really lived. The ποτέ indicates the loss of this status, which what follows narrates expressly and almost dramatically (Sanday and Headlam) in the form of a report. This element should not be overlooked. The relation between sin and law is not reflected on in a basic way (contra Brandenburger, Adam, 207ff.). Nor is ἀφορμή in v. 8 opposed as a secondary function (contra Benoit, "Loi," 13ff.) to the primary one of information, so that the whole emphasis falls on the inability of the law to overcome sin and its condemnatory role is underscored (ibid., 33ff.). An event is called to mind by the commandment.

This insight is lost if the general I-style of confessional speech is allowed to remain so formal that a vague reference to everyman is seen. This approach covers up the difficulty, which nevertheless emerges in debate and imprecise exposition. For example there is the claim that we have here a mixture of experience and exaggeration (Dodd, *Meaning,* 88ff.) or the summary explanation that the reference is to neither Adam nor Paul, nor the Jewish people, nor humanity (Schunack, *Problem,* 136). What is left then? Two considerations can bring us further.

First, it is to be maintained under all circumstances that the apostle is speaking of mankind under the law, or specifically of the pious Jew. Here lies the difference from vv. 14ff., where the perspective is at least broadened. To be sure, the problem of this assertion must also be seen. No Jew experienced the depicted situation of a time without the law and a moment when it came to him (correctly Gaugler against Bardenhewer; cf. Braun, "Selbstverständnis," 105ff.). At least from the time of Moses, according to 5:12ff., the law was always there along with sin and death. He could only confirm such givenness through his own transgression. Furthermore the Jew would regard it as blasphemy to describe the law as a spur to sin and a means of deception leading to death. Even if Paul saw the past in a different light as a Christian, he could hardly make assertions depicting a fictional Jew. The adequacy and reality of what he said had to be perceptible even if it was not accepted.

Secondly, strict attention should be paid to the way in which the verbs in the past tense are related to a definite moment when sin passes from "being dead" to its awakening and from a person's life to his death, in short to a fall into sin. It is no accident that in v. 9 the coming of the commandment is spoken of in exact analogy to the coming of faith in Gal 3:25. To change this "chronologically" fixable date into a constant present is to depart from the text and to involve oneself in insuperable difficulties. This is particularly clear when an attempt is made to take the temporal moment into account and, as is widely done, a reminiscence of the fall of Adam is sensed through the mode of speech (Bultmann, *Theology,* I, 250f.; Goppelt, *Typos,* 157; Brandenburger, *Adam,* 214ff.; Kühl; Kuss; Michel; H. W. Schmidt; cf. Bornkamm, "Sin," 93). For this brings the two tendencies of the text into conflict. The reference to Adam explains the temporal element but does not seem to fit the reality of a pious person under the law, while conversely this reality for its part does not permit a dating to a concrete event. Various ways out of this impasse have been tried. At root certainly the interpretation always runs in the direction of understanding the fall of Adam paradigmatically (Kuss). Adam remarkably lives on in "my reality" which cannot be adequately described either in terms of salvation history or mythologically (Bornkamm, "Sin," 94). The "primal history of the I" has to be narrated (Brandenburger, *Adam,* 206, 214), or the encounter of Adamic humanity with the law as its essential origin (Goppelt, *Christentum,* 104f.). People (cf. Kuss for a good survey of the literature) think of the reproduction of a psychological process which repeats itself in one way or another in the Adamic world (Black), or holds to be possible an ambiguous mingling of everyman with Paul and Adam (Luz,

Geschichtsverständnis, 166f.), if they do not even assert a universal experience in confrontation with the moral demand (Jülicher; Benoit, "Loi," 18ff.). In face of the multiplicity of interpretations and the predominantly unclear mode of expression, might it not be better simply to express resignation (Luz, *Geschichtsverständnis,* 163)? But this would mean dropping any understanding of a text which is obviously of supreme importance for Paul himself.

Methodologically the starting point should be that a story is told in vv. 9-11   [and that the event depicted can refer strictly only to Adam. That this takes place in the style of confessional speech, and this is a supra-individual I as in Gal 2:20 (Kertelge, "Überlegungen," 108), does not mean (*contra* Conzelmann, *Outline,* 170, 233f.) that the story of Adam is projected into the present as the story of the I and that it forms the horizon of this present. On the contrary, it means that we are implicated in the story of Adam. In the full sense only Adam lived before the commandment was given. Only for him was the coming of the divine will in the commandment an occasion for sin as he yielded covetously to sin and therefore "died." Even the motif of deception is part of the paradise story. If there and in 2 Cor 11:3 it is Eve who is deceived, the variation in our text is easily explained through the adoption of different forms of tradition. There is nothing in the passage which does not fit Adam, and everything fits Adam alone (Lyonnet, "L'histoire," 130ff.; "Quaestiones," 179ff.; *Étapes,* 118ff. *contra* Kümmel, *Römer 7,* 54f., 86f.; Brandenburger, *Adam,* 216f.; Ridderbos, *Paul,* 144).

If in Genesis nothing is said about the prohibition of covetousness, Jewish tradition, which Philo allows to speak of the source of evil and original wickedness in *De specialibus legibus* iv.84f., interprets the Genesis story in the light of it (Lyonnet, "Rom. VII, 7," 163ff.). According to this tradition (Lyonnet, *Étapes,* 129ff.) Adam received the whole law with the commandment which he was given. This disposes of the chief objection, namely, that since the text refers to the Mosaic Torah and quotes the Decalogue it cannot be related to the paradise story (Kümmel, *Römer 7,* 86f.; Bornkamm, "Sin," 93f., 97; Brandenburger, *Adam,* 214; Benoit, "Loi," 11; Gaugler). A branch of Jewish exegesis, which Paul follows, made Adam the prototypical recipient of the law and thus linked his story materially with that of Moses. Here precisely is the central concern of the apostle. He is concerned to distinguish the original intention of the law as the declaration of God's will from its actual effect, and, on the other side, to derive the awakening of sin with all its consequences from the factual Torah. This intention cannot be realized either autobiographically or in view of the Jew in general and out of his experience, since the true nature of sin as the desire to assert oneself against God and human beings cannot be learned from experience even by the pious but is brought to light by the gospel. The work of the law as a spur to sin can be demonstrated only by Adam, and Jewish tradition offers the means for doing this.

If one defends oneself against harmonizing 5:12ff. and the present text (Kümmel, *Römer 7,* 86f.; Brandenburger, *Adam,* 209, 212ff.), this leads to begging the question (*petitio principii*). It is more likely that the two passages are parallel than antithetical (Furnish, *Ethics,* 141). Protest against this presupposes a prior understanding of vv. 14ff., namely, it considers the central theme to be man's personal responsibility before and under the law (Benoit, "Loi," 13ff., 17) and the experience of moral inability (Brandenburger, *Adam,* 217). If one cannot agree with this, it may be asked whether the supposed harmonization is not in fact the solution to the riddle. Salvation history and universality are integral to both arguments. The only question is why Paul uses "I" instead of naming Adam. It is not enough to refer to the character of the confession so long as this merely supports the possibility of the stylistic form used and not its inner necessity. That can be done theologically in the light of the history of religions as well as the sense of the confession.

Here is the point where one should refer to the concept of corporate personality, although for some strange reason this is not done. On this basis one can establish logical continuity between 5:12ff. and 7:7ff. There is not the slightest reason to contest or destroy this. Every person after Adam is entangled in the fate of the protoplast. The fate of every person is anticipated in that of Adam. With Adam every person has lost both the divine glory of 3:23 and also life and righteousness. Before Christ Adam is continually repeated. The difference from 5:12ff. is that vv. 7-13 look primarily to people under the Torah (Eichholz, *Paulus*, 253) and Adam is portrayed as their prototype. This is necessary because Paul wants to depict the work of the law factually in terms of the recipient of the law and of Jewish piety, and he can exemplify this only through the first recipient of the law.

He can do this, of course, only as a Christian. The Jew with his understanding of the law necessarily defends freedom of decision. He thus rejects Paul's interpretation. As we have seen, only heretical circles dared to think of sin radically as destiny. Paul made this point already in 5:12ff. For him there is the conquest of the law in daily life only through the Spirit, as the antithesis of v. 6 showed. Hence only the "pneumatic" grants that standing under the law repeats the situation of Adam, namely, that through the law a person is driven to desire self-assertion, self-glory, and pious ungodliness. The experiences of the Jew, who is able to see his faults and to understand his life as a battle against sin, are unable to bring to light such a repetition and the resultant destiny. Only the gospel enables us to recognize both. Looking back on his own past under the law, the pneumatic learns the truth about his "once" and the religious threat, still given by his existence in the world, posed to his "now" in continuity with Adam. In the stylistic form of confessional speech he can thus identify himself with Adam (Mauser, *Gottesbild*, 154; Eichholz, *Paulus*, 259), having learned through Christ the "coming in" of 5:20a and the ending of the Torah in the apocalyptic change.

To a large degree our interpretation of the details of vv. 9-11 has been given already. ἀνέζησεν in v. 9b naturally means "awake," not "come to life again" (BAGD, 53b). The compound is a strengthening of the simple form (Lyonnet, "Rom. VII, 7," 157). The fall of the sinner is a dying which intimates both physical and eternal death. Since the apostle sees the source of life in the relation to God, he sees death in the same light. Life and death are the alternatives of human existence given therewith, which according to 14:7f. are transcended and relativized by the "in Christ." εὑρέθη μοι means: "it proved to be for me." The phrase therefore is not to be psychologized (*contra* Huby) nor related to enlightenment by the law. The paradoxical statement in v. 10b sets forth the consequences of the fall. The intention of the law was the promise of 3:21: It aimed to keep us in life. This should not be weakened (*contra* Bläser, *Gesetz*, 196f.) as though it could do this only by grace. The point is that grace revealed itself originally in the law. This was perverted when the law was misunderstood as a demand for achievement. In this perversion, however, the law brings death, as every gift, when perverted, avenges itself on mankind. Verse 11 explains the contradiction between intention and actual function with a reference back to v. 8 (Bornkamm, "Sin," 91). διὰ τῆς ἐντολῆς is to be taken with the verb (*contra* [1 Kühl; H. W. Schmidt). The superfluous repetition of δι' αὐτῆς is for emphasis and does not support a link with ἀφορμήν. Here again sin is a power which, as in 5:13, is posited already by the fate of Adam even before the giving of the Mosaic Torah. It has a demonic character (Grundmann, *TDNT*, I, 311; Michel). As in 2 Cor 11:14 Satan changes himself into an angel of light, so here sin disguises itself and is thus able to deceive us (though cf. Benoit, "Loi," 17, who speaks of an unmasking of man). It is not just a matter of subjective error but of objective deception as in the paradise story. The promise is usurped and it is thus perverted. Sin creates an illusion (Bornkamm, "Sin," 91). People die in and of the illusion about themselves and God, while life as God's gift creates and is freedom from the illusion of human self-assertion.

Verses 12-13 sum up. Verse 10b is solemnly repeated. In good Jewish fashion the law thus has the predicates of divine wisdom and heavenly power. Although law and commandment seem to be identical here, their juxtaposition allows some differences to be grasped. In the commandment as the concretion and sum of the law (Leenhardt) stress is laid on God's will as the intention of the law. It is not a matter of the objective ethical ideal (*contra* Dodd) or the ethical demands (*contra* Bultmann, *Theology*, I, 341). The adjectives holy, just, and good in their rhetorical pleonasm (Althaus) characterize not so much the origin and nature of the law (Leenhardt; critically Kuss) as its work on human beings, which has the power of the divine will unimpeded by illusion. Verse 13 takes up the question of v. 7 again and broadens it. Paul is no antinomian (*contra* Lietzmann). The law in its truth does not belong with sin and death. It has been misused by the power of sin, which always perverts the good, and now effects the opposite of what was intended. The two ἵνα clauses in v. 13a and v. 13b are not consecutive but final (Kümmel, *Römer 7*, 57). The second discloses in rhetorical crescendo the point of the first. Precisely in and by the law light is shed on what sin is. In concrete encounter with the law, sin reveals its force, which exceeds every conceivable measure and which by blinding us uses the good to do its work of death. Herein lies its ὑπερβολή. According to Paul it is not to be viewed morally. Misleading even the righteous, it creates the demand for autarchy which is the mark of pure ungodliness (Bultmann, *TDNT*, III, 16; cf. Bornkamm, "Sin," 95). As may be seen from what follows, God's wrath is provoked thereby, which delivers up to death the person who has perverted the law.

3. The Complaint of the Enslaved (7:14-25)

[14]*We know of course that the law is spiritual. But I am fleshly, sold under the power of sin.* [15]*For I do not know what I do. I do not do what I want but I do what I hate.* [16]*If, however, I do what I do not want, I agree (thereby) that the law is good.* [17]*Then it is no longer I that do it but sin dwelling in me.* [18]*For I*

198

know that the good does not dwell in me, that is, in my flesh. If I can will what is good, I cannot do it. [19]*For I do not do the good that I want but I do the evil that I do not want.* [20]*If, however, I do what I do not want, it is no longer I that do it but sin dwelling in me.* [21]*Wanting to do the good, I thus find it to be a law that evil clings to me.* [22]*For according to the inward man I delight in the law of God.* [23]*I see another law, however, in my members. This is at war with the law of my reason and takes me captive to the law of sin which is in my members.* [24]*O wretched man that I am! Who will deliver me from this body of death?* [25]*Thanks be to God through Jesus Christ our Lord! So then I serve the law of God with my reason but with my flesh I serve the law of sin.*

Bibliography: J. Blank, "Der gespaltene Mensch," *Bibel und Leben* 9 (1968) 10-20; J. I. Packer, "The 'Wretched Man' in Romans 7," *SE*, II, 621-27; F. Müller, "Zwei Marginalien im Brief des Paulus an die Römer," *ZNW* 40 (1941) 249-254; O. J. F. Seitz, "Two Spirits in Man: An Essay in Biblical Exegesis," *NTS* 6 (1959/60) 82-95; W. Keuck, "Dienst des Geistes und des Fleisches," *TQ* 141 (1961) 257-280; J. Kürzinger, "Der Schlüssel zum Verständnis von Röm. 7," *BZ*, N.F. 7 (1963) 270-74; E. W. Smith, "The Form and Religious Background of Romans VII 24-25a," *NovT* 13 (1971) 127-135; H. Jonas, *Augustin und das paulinische Freiheitsproblem* (1930). See also the bibliographies for 7:1-6 and 7:7-13.

The new section is distinguished from the previous one by the present tenses of the verbs. From this it may not be concluded that now it deals with the Christian present (*contra* Nygren; Packer, "Wretched Man," 626; Franzmann; J. Knox; Asmussen; Modalsli, "Rom. 7, 7-25," 34ff.; cf. also Bruce; Murray; correctly Kertelge, "Überlegungen," 108). Nor do we have a new excursus (*contra* Hommel, "7. Kapitel," 102; van Dülmen, *Theologie,* 112), or a proof (Jülicher; Lietzmann; Dodd), or a commentary (Fuchs, "Interpretation," 293), or support for the previous section (Kühl). Instead, the results of vv. 7b-11 are presented in their cosmic breadth (Bornkamm, "Sin," 95; Kertelge, "Überlegungen," 108). The statements are parallel to those about the pre-Christian world in 1:18–3:20 and 5:12ff. Corresponding to this, the theme of the Torah is taken up only in the backward glances of vv. 14a and 16b and in the variant formula ὁ νόμος τοῦ θεοῦ in v. 22 (*contra* Kümmel, *Römer 7,* 57f., 61). The play on a transferred meaning in vv. 20ff. certainly reminds us of it, but it has already another scope, namely, that of the burdensome plight hanging over all mankind even in its piety. This is described through the contradiction of will and act in vv. 14-20, and as complete self-estrangement of the creature in vv. 21-24.

The reading οἶδα μέν in v. 14 is not original (*contra* Zahn); it is an assimilation to the context. It sets the accent on knowledge, whereas Paul takes up v. 12 in summary fashion in v. 14a so as to be able to set forth the contrast in v. 14b. The same purpose is served if πνευματικός, which is identical with ἐπουράνιος, goes beyond the predicates of v. 12. The will of God, originally recorded in the law, gives testimony to its heavenly origin and nature. Verse 14c shows that σάρκινος does not simply characterize the person of flesh and blood (Zahn; Dodd; Nygren) in his weakness as in 1 Cor 3:1 (Murray), nor the physical basis of our ethical constitution (Kühl). Synonymous with the σαρκικός of 2 Cor 10:4, it qualifies a person in his cosmic fallenness to the world (Schweizer, *TDNT,* VII, 144).

It is more than doubtful to try to derive the figurative expression in v. 14c from 1 Kgs 21:25 (Schlatter) or other OT passages (Michel). We certainly should not ask who has sold us to sin. ἐγώ means mankind under the shadow of Adam; hence it does not embrace Christian existence in its ongoing temptation (*contra* Zahn; Nygren; Murray; Ellwein, "Rätsel," 266f.; Maurer, *Gesetzeslehre*, 46; Stalder, *Werk*, 306; cf. on this Kümmel, *Man*, 49ff.; Ridderbos). What is being said here is already over for the Christian according to ch. 6 and ch. 8. The apostle is not even describing the content of his own experience of conversion.

If v. 14c presents the theme of the sub-section, it has already left the plane of what can be experienced morally and psychologically (*contra* Kümmel, *Römer 7*, 132ff.; Althaus; Kirk; Gutjahr; Ridderbos, *Paul*, 124ff.; correctly Kertelge, *Rechtfertigung*, 110ff.; Schrage, *Einzelgebote*, 195ff.). It has been shown in 1:24ff. that sin has moral consequences and one may agree that it will necessarily express itself in the moral field, but this is not to say that here is its primary sphere of activity (*contra* Schrage, *loc. cit.*). What sin really is, and the nature of its dominion, escape the category of what may be experienced even in standing under the law (*contra* Gaugler). They are brought to light only by the gospel. The pneumatic alone can perceive them. Paul's theology as a whole stands or falls with this statement, since the justification of the ungodly is its center. For it the moral man is the very one who is most deeply engulfed in the power of sin without being able to recognize it according to 9:31 or 10:3 (H. W. Schmidt). If this were not so, the debate with Judaism's faithfulness to the law would be pointless and debate with pagan idealism would be necessary.

If v. 14c is to be recognized as a title for the argument that follows, the ethical cleavage between will and act or wish and reality does not have to be overlooked. It is no more than an indication of what Paul has in mind. A purely or primarily moral interpretation of the text cannot be harmonized either with v. 14c or with what would otherwise be a superfluous reference back to the fall of Adam in vv. 9-11. Yet it constantly dominates exposition because unquestionably there arises from vv. 15-20 the reminder of the universally experienced ethical conflict, especially when emphatic exaggeration is ascribed to the apostle. On the other hand, paganism as well as the OT and Judaism so willingly admits the moral frailty of mankind that only the radical nature of Paul's presentation would then be worthy of note. Indeed, even this is not new. Correctly Ovid *Metamorphoses* vii.19f. has constantly been adduced as a representative statement in this regard: "Desire persuades me one way, reason another. I see the better and approve it, but I follow the worse" (LCL). This statement stands (cf. Hommel, "7. Kapitel," 113f.) in a solid line of tradition which goes back to Euripides' criticism of the Socratic doctrine of *paideia* in virtue, which finds expression in many different variations in antiquity (cf. Hommel, "7. Kapitel," 106ff.; Lietzmann; Dodd), and which can be traced through the history of the west (Huby). The influence of this tradition on the apostle is all the more easily accepted since the Jewish diaspora was affected by it and Paul, as will be shown, incontestably uses certain expressions and motifs from its line of argument in the present passage (Duchrow, *Weltverantwortung*, 92ff., 96ff.). No less close to him, of course, were the basic ideas of Qumran in which the rabbinic concept of the evil impulse was radicalized. More is at issue there than the war between duty, or the wish for perfection, and the passion of the individual. It concerns the cry of the pious, who are brought to salvation but are also exposed to creatureliness and the entangling power of sin (cf. K. G. Kuhn, "πειρασμός," 210ff.; Braun, "Selbstverständnis," 102ff.; Schulz, "Rechtfertigung," 162ff.). In the typical passage 1QS 11:7ff. one finds with the characteristic I-style the statement of 11:9: I belong to wicked humanity, to the fellowship of the sinful flesh.

The differences between the traditions are obvious. Whereas the first emphasizes the contrast between intention and act in the life of the individual, the second goes beyond the sphere of the individual in a dualistic cosmology in which two spheres of power clash and the creaturely being as well as the factual action of the pious is subjected to the dominion of sin (Braun, "Selbstverständnis," 105ff.).

The differences between the two traditions and Paul's anthropology are even more to be noted. One makes the exegesis too easy if one finds in the passage a development of the psychology of sin in principle (Kümmel, *Römer 7*, 125ff.; Hommel, "7. Kapitel," 96, 105; Schrenk, *TDNT*, II, 551f.; III, 50; Nygren; Althaus; correctly H. Braun, *TDNT*, VI, 480f.). Apart from the gloomy formulation, there cannot be ascribed to the apostle, according to 2:12ff., 26f., a pessimism which leaves no room in the human sphere for good acts or the demand for them, which conceals the differentiated reality with global statements, and which has in view only the wretchedness of our existence. Paul was attacking the strong, not the weak. If he were simply bewailing our lack of will-power, he would have to be resisted in the name of mankind, even though the lamentable aspect cannot be overlooked. The hopelessness of a theology for which all cats are grey in the dark is concealed with the meaningless formula "psychology of sin." Here not even the level of Qumran is reached. Yet Qumran also stands in a different horizon from Paul. When the most extreme tightening of the Torah is practiced, and grace opens the way to this, the complaint of the pious about belonging to the world of wickedness expresses the fact that he remains dependent on grace to fulfil the law. This does not conflict with required and possible obedience to the Torah. It is the summons to a battle with sin which never ends on earth and which has to be fought with all vigor. These two things go together (Braun, "Selbstverständnis," 114ff.) in an anthropological dualism which makes the cosmic struggle for power concrete. It is the task of the pious to endure this conflict and constantly to conquer anew with his action. For Paul, however, the existing Torah is neither grace nor help. Its fulfilment is not the goal. It is the religious mode of human self-assertion. Our text, therefore, does not speak of the state of salvation; it speaks of fallen and lost humanity.

If this is clear, vv. 15-20 differ so sharply both from the Greek tradition and from Qumran that in them there can be no question at all merely of the ethical conflict, which most commentators find here. The key to a correct understanding of the verses has to be the fact that they illustrate the superscription in v. 14c. The ethical conflict as such, however, does not demonstrate the "sold under sin," as precisely Qumran is able to show. It might lead to resignation, or a more intensive effort of will, or stricter observance of the demand. It does not show us what sin is as resistance to the right of the Creator. This is reflected on a lower level only to the extent that a person is never finished with himself. If the apostle were to rest content with this truism of experience he would be working with inadequate means and would be presenting a weak theology, or, more accurately, no theology at all, but a psychology oriented to the ethical problem. Naturally, one cannot rule out this possibility. But this should be suspected only if no other solution remains.

In fact a different possibility is already set before us by vv. 9-11. The only change is in vocabulary, not in content. What is there described as confrontation with the commandment is now sketched as orientation to the good (Black) in which we accept and correspond to the divine will. What is there the deception of sin and illusory action is now disclosed to be the reality of every illusion that does not reach the intended goal. The change of vocabulary, and the alteration of perspective manifested thereby, derives from the difference between our own situation and that of Adam. We already have the fall before us as a destiny imposed by the power of sin and we confirm it by our conduct, which shows that we are standing in illusion. We, too, want life in all our acts, but even with this aim we always bring about the death which Adam first died when confronted with the law.

This understanding of the text (established by Bultmann, "Romans 7") must be tested out in an exegesis of the basic statement in v. 15a and the variation on this in v. 15b, which are underscored heavily by the repetitions in vv. 16a, 18c, 19, and 20a and elucidated by the other statements. The variations of the verbs κατεργάζομαι, ποιῶ, and πράσσω are undoubtedly rhetorical (Ridderbos), so that an intensive meaning "bring about" can hardly be claimed for the first in view of the parallels (contra Bultmann, Theology, I, 248; cf. already Augustine and Luther). In contrast to v. 13, the effect is not being set forth as such, although act and effect cannot be separated (Schlatter; H. W. Schmidt). Every act produces a result, which does not have to be the one intended. That the result is death, however, cannot be taken directly from the text (contra Bultmann, Theology, I, 248f.). The αὐτό in vv. 17, 20b corresponds to the τοῦτο in vv. 15b, 16a, and 20a and contrasts in a completely formal way will and act. The stress is on οὐ γινώσκω, which also comes to expression in the indefinite way of speaking. If it is related to θέλειν in vv. 15b, 16a, 18c, and 19f. and the contrasting μισεῖν in v. 15b, such knowledge, as usually in Paul, is not theoretical knowledge (contra Hommel, "7. Kapitel," 96f.) but practical experience which renders account of the motives and results of its acts. Existence, in the antithesis of willing and hating, seeks one thing and rejects another. Verse 15a maintains that the person in view is not without direction but fails to understand the course which his intentions take as he tries to put them into effect. The opposite of his wishes, plans, and expectations results, to be sure without exception, when he tries to realize them in action. This shows that the reference is not to human practice in general, whose many possibilities cannot be limited to one alternative and which does not always end up in failure. That cannot even be said of the ethical domain, in whose field there are continual compromises and incontestable victories accompany the many defeats, and thus there is the unity of what is intended and what is effected and the good is realized (for this reason J. Knox relativizes the statement).

Verse 16b shows what sphere is in view. It is when there has to be fulfilment of the will of God disclosed in the law that verification and offense, "good" and "evil," stand in sharp antithesis (Goppelt, *Christentum*, 105). The experience which Paul envisions consists in the fact that the pious, who alone come into the picture here, do not succeed in realizing the will of God as the true good so long as the Spirit of Christ is not given to them. Instead, in their very acts they give a place and reality to evil, although that is not their intention. Their helplessness in face of this perversion of their intentions shows that they are in fact oriented to the good, that they feel themselves to be under obligation to the will of God, and that they accept it as the norm of their existence. Obviously this is in the first instance a depiction of the situation of the Jew who is faithful to the law. The situation is present among the Gentiles only in the shadow of 2:14ff. It is presented in the confessional style of vv. 7ff.; thus precisely as in that passage, the Christian is looking back at his own past. Similar confessions at Qumran do not end in hopelessness. Realization that one belongs to the world of sinful flesh triggers the impulse genuinely to observe the intensified Torah and establishes the hope that radical obedience is possible and will ultimately prevail. The Christian, however, can no longer connect this hope with standing under the law. For him the situation of the pious before and outside Christ is hopeless. It is therefore an impenetrable riddle, since it stands under a burdensome destiny, as vv. 17c and 20 show. In the case of an ethical conflict we know what we are doing, why things happen, and what results follow if passion proves stronger than duty. The pious of Qumran know that because they belong to the world of the flesh there will continually be transgressions. This does not lead them to despair, however, but causes them to arm themselves more firmly for further warfare under the banner of the Torah. Paul, in contrast, depicts the situation of the pious as objectively a desperate one. Before and apart from Christ he cannot escape disaster. Rather, he constantly creates it anew in all his acts without being able to understand this compulsion as the Christian can, who knows about the doom of the power of sin, the perversion of the law which follows, and the fulfilment of the will of God only in Christ and in the power of the Spirit. Soteriological rather than ethical experience leads to the statements in this passage and is the reason for the confessional style.

What a person wants is salvation. What he creates is disaster. This is also true, and especially so, of the pious who are faithful to the law (Furnish, *Ethics*, 142). This is what is meant by "good" and "evil" in these verses. A person thinks he knows what he is doing and what he can expect. But he lives under an illusion, since the will of God becomes the basis of one's own pious self-assertion and thus leads to one's own destruction. The exegetical key to the text is to be found in 9:31f. and 10:3. The description of the conflict as "transsubjective" (Bultmann, "Romans 7," 151, 155) has met with furious criticism, for it ostensibly does not do adequate justice to the subjective element (Kuss; Ellwein, "Rätsel," 259f.; Bläser, *Gesetz*, 122ff.) or to the specific application in the ethical sphere (Schrenk, *TDNT*, III, 51; Giese, *Römer 7*, 33; Schrage, *Einzelgebote*, 195ff.). It is undoubtedly misleading and yet it leads the way beyond a purely psychological and ethical interpretation and is not at all as abstract as it sounds. It starts with the concrete will and act of a person and therefore with the "subjective" field. If it does not enter into the ethical problems more strongly or find reflected in these the basic conflict envisioned here (cf. Grundmann, *TDNT*, III, 481f.; Braun, *TDNT*, VI,

481; Blank, "Mensch," 13f.), in this respect it follows the steps of the apostle, who also does not provide examples. Its concern is that the statements of the text transcend the sphere of concrete events no less than that of general experience. It might have done better to speak of mankind as under destiny and illusion. When we take our fate in our own hands, even in the name of a particular ethics or religion, God is no longer recognized as Creator; we have to put greater trust in ourselves than is possible and become less than we are meant to be. Even in the ethical field we constantly show ourselves to be the captives of our own arrogance, passions, caprice, and stupidity.

In adopting the language and motifs of his age, Paul has infinitely deepened them. He affirms, not just the contradictoriness of existence even in the pious, but the entanglement of a fallen creation in all its expressions in the power of sin. Hence he does not need to differentiate, as he would have to do from an ethical or psychological point of view. He does not leave open even the possibility of a battle which is not yet decided, so that it would be adequate to speak of torn or divided man as many do (e.g., Blank). Only when the arguments of 1:18–3:20, 5:12ff., and 6:3ff. are forgotten can one postulate a middle state between the fallen person and the saved person. The passage stands under the heading of "sold under sin." It is characterizing lost mankind. It views the death of Adam of vv. 7b-11 as continued in the present. This is made perfectly plain in vv. 17f.

νυνὶ δέ has a logical, not a temporal, sense (contra Zahn; Nygren). Verse 17b provides the basis for what is described in vv. 15f. and summed up in the antithesis of v. 17a. Thereby an expression is used which elsewhere motivates ecstatic inspiration or characterizes possession (Grundmann, TDNT, I, 311; Lagrange; Kuss; Schoeps, Paul, 183ff.). According to T. Naph. 8:6 Satan dwells in the sinner as in his own vessel. A demonological state of affairs is asserted which corresponds to the end of v. 14. Here at least it is clear, then, that the field of ethical conflict is vastly transcended. To give way to weakness is not demonic but human, and the person who is conquered by his passions can never evade responsibility for his acts or claim that fundamentally he was not guilty. He would have to be sick, cowardly, or childish to try to get off that way. Even in the greatest confusion he is at least the one who wills what is done, and it can be shown later that he desired and did what was wrong.

Paul, however, really means that the I who speaks here is demonically enslaved (Gaugler; Blank, "Mensch," 17f.) and therefore did not will or grasp the effect of his action. Verses 18f. carry this a stage further. Again the compulsory exchange of the desired good with the unwanted evil, and even more the total incapacity for good, is derived from possession. οἶδα γάρ has the same sense as οἴδαμεν in v. 14 and formulates a Christian insight which had already, perhaps, been recognized dogmatically. How far this can be conceded to the natural person is a problem that can be solved only in the light of vv. 22f. The good is in any case what is willed by God, and as such includes salvation. To restrict it to the moral sphere (on this cf. Schrage, Einzelgebote, 196f.) seems to be doubtful in context, since the demonic power of sin reaches beyond this sphere.

A new point is that the dwelling of sin in me is established by the statement that I am σάρξ. The parenthesis obviously does not have a limiting sense (contra Zahn; Sanday and Headlam; Kühl; Jülicher; Pallis; Huby; Lietzmann; Schlatter;

Althaus; H. W. Schmidt; Kümmel, *Römer 7,* 61; possibly Bultmann, *Theology,* I, 245). The ἐν ἐμοί is not corrected (van Dülmen, *Theologie,* 153) but identified (K. Barth; Bornkamm, "Sin," 98; Leenhardt; Michel; Gaugler; Ridderbos; Braun, "Selbstverständnis," 101; Ellwein, "Rätsel," 249; Kertelge, "Überlegungen," 109; Sand, *Fleisch,* 190). Flesh is, terminologically, the workshop of sin, the whole person in his fallenness to the world and alienation from God, and to this extent existence in the mode of possession. παράκειταί μοι, already used in a profane sense in the LXX (Giese, *Römer 7,* 35) means "to be ready, available" (Büchsel, *TDNT,* III, 656).

A résumé is given in vv. 19-20. The argument is not advanced here. Paul is concerned to underscore the fact of possession and hence the conclusion of v. 14. Attention should again be directed to the general mode of speech, which is not orienting "good" and "evil" to an individual case or a concrete duty. A human being is not seen as one who can fight against his destiny and can change his fate, as the moral will tries to do. If this is not possible, however, the formula of a rift in existence is misleading if it has in view anything other or more than an impotent spectator of the tragedy played out in one's own life (Schweizer, *TDNT,* VII, 133f.).

Verses 21-25 sharpen vv. 15-20 by making the impotent spectator of self the central object of what is said, so that the problem of the ἐγώ is again posed with a special urgency. The new terminology in v. 22 and the play on the concept of law in vv. 22f. show that the result of the preceding argument is now being presented with a final radical intensification. Verse 21, as a summary of the preceding verses (Kümmel, *Römer 7,* 61f.), marks the new turn, εὑρίσκω introduces the next sentence (J. Weiss, "Beiträge," 231; van Dülmen, *Theologie,* 115) and with it the conclusion of the argument. There is no longer any express reflection on the Torah as such. νόμος in v. 21 means in an extended sense the rule or necessity and the genitive construction νόμος τοῦ θεοῦ in v. 22 does not mean the fixed law but God's will in a general sense which allows the antithesis to the law in my members. In v. 23 the phrase therefore is taken up by νόμος τοῦ νοός and is set in contrast to the cosmic νόμος τῆς ἁμαρτίας. The statement has, then, a universal breadth and applies to every existence in the wake of Adam.

The fourfold use of the term law expresses in different ways a basic antithesis (Kuss; though cf. Kühl; van Dülmen, *Theologie,* 116). As in 6:11ff., God and the power of sin are opponents. Both lay claim to a person. Both have something like a foothold in his existence, namely, the ἔσω ἄνθρωπος or νοῦς on the one side and the members on the other. A difference from 6:11f., however, is that the received will of God does not have the upper hand. The members make themselves independent of it, so that sin can operate with them and triumph. The reference is plainly to unredeemed man. Paul thereby no longer speaks primarily of the pious Jew, as in the previous sections. Insofar as he still has not vanished from the field of view he represents pious humanity and the problem of the Torah is replaced by that of human existence.

Each of us, as in 1:20, is addressed by the will of God. Each of us, as in 3:20; 5:12ff., is characterized as unable to fulfil this will. In a modification of the exposition in 1:18–3:20—and this is highly significant for our understanding of the chapter and its place in the composition as a whole—the theme of our verse is humanity under the curse of Adam's fall, seen now from the standpoint of the individual. A logical step forward leads consistently from the history of Adam in vv. 9-11 to that of the pious person represented by the Jew in vv. 14-20 and then [to everyman in the present verses.

The central problem of the conclusion is the remarkable anthropology which finds expression in terms different from those used by the apostle elsewhere. νοῦς is the diacritical faculty of mankind which offers its services in a concrete situation and judges the various means and ends (Bultmann, Theology, I, 211f.). Even rhetorically and in a transferred sense one cannot correctly equate it, as some do, with a νόμος in the sense of order (BAGD, 542a). Its opposite, then, is lack of judgment, not another nomos as in the present text. Like conscience, reason, on the basis of the Spirit, can achieve greater clarity on what is necessary and purposeful, so that 12:2 can speak of a renewed reason. But that does not make it an organ of revelation (Ridderbos, Paul, 119), not even of the ethical consciousness (Sanday and Headlam; Behm, TDNT, IV, 958), and certainly not self-consciousness (Kühl) as a person's higher spiritual nature (Dodd; H. W. Schmidt; Cerfaux, Christian, 303ff.; Prat, Theology, I, 235; II, 50ff.; Cambier, L'Évangile, I, 292). Hence one cannot appeal to 1 Cor 2:16. For there the νοῦς Χριστοῦ is synonymous with the πνεῦμα Χριστοῦ. It can thus distinguish the spirits as in 1 Cor 12:10 and is a Christian charisma, whereas the present verse is concerned with the reason of the unredeemed. Obviously Paul follows Hellenistic tradition here.

This is very clearly shown by the identification with the ἔσω ἄνθρωπος. Elsewhere only 2 Cor 4:16 uses this expression in antithesis to the outward man as our corruptible nature. Yet this should not seduce us (cf. J. Jeremias, TDNT, I, 365) to think again of spiritual existence, especially as this, for Paul, is no less exposed to decay than the body. What is meant is the pneumatic who must go through suffering and death and grow therein. The inward man of 2 Cor 4:16 is thus the opposite of the "old man" of 6:6; Col 3:9f.; Eph 4:22ff., and in a dualistic context it is identical with the "new man" of which Christ himself is the prototype in Eph 2:15. Undoubtedly this view derives from the tradition of the man within man as our true existence which participates in the divine reason and which in its rationality is constitutively open to the divine will. Philo took it over from the heritage of Plato and sharpened further the dualistic aspect (cf. Brandenburger, Fleisch, 155f., 172; Duchrow, Weltverantwortung, 92ff.), dealing with it under the theme of the divine image (cf. Jervell, Imago, 58ff.; Eltester, Eikon, 43ff.). In Paul and his school, as 3:23 already shows, it is varied through the eschatological antithesis of the old aeon and the new. The fact that in the Greek world νοῦς and πνεῦμα could be synonymous was particularly helpful at this point. The pneumatic, determined by a heavenly nature and belonging to the new world, is true human being, and he is this in participation in Christ as his prototype, in whom the divine image has manifested itself again at the end of the times. He has in the pneuma the νοῦς Χριστοῦ.

In this eschatological context it is inadequate to speak of the ἔσω ἄνθρωπος. The religio-historical roots of the view are brought to light herewith. Nevertheless in a different setting it draws attention to the fact that in this world and in our corporeality the heavenly nature has only begun in hidden form and has yet to come to consummation. We need only sketch the way in which this tradition was taken over and adapted here, since the real problem can be tackled only when this has been done. For the dilemma now arises that the terminology and motivations of the verse, which are unusual in Paul's anthropology (Packer, "Wretched Man," 625), can be understood only in the light of such a tradition and yet their projection into the life of the unredeemed poses a riddle if it otherwise occurs only with regard to the pneumatic (and then seldom). The riddle is all the greater when note is taken of the verbs which characterize reason and the inner man here.

In v. 16 σύμφημι τῷ νόμῳ derives from a logical conclusion by way of negation. If, however, v. 22 says that I delight in God's will according to the inner man, this shows that σύμφημι also denotes a positive agreement which is not simply forced on a person. Here, then, reason and the inner man have the ability, which is accorded to them in the Greek tradition, namely, that of accepting and recognizing the divine will. Paul does not say this so unrestrictedly even of the conscience as the human power of self-criticism in face of a last judicial court. For he realizes that conscience can go astray or be overpowered, so that its norm shifts. Joyful agreement with the will of God is everywhere reserved, in fact, for the pneumatic.

It is astounding that the problem has not been sharply pinned down. How can the predicates and capacities of the redeemed person be ascribed to the unredeemed? For it is incontestable that for Paul reason, too, is subject to the power of the flesh (Kümmel, *Man*, 57f.), so that the "inner man" here is simply an aspect of the "outward man" of 2 Cor 4:16. Interpretation has commonly been in terms of the Greek tradition. Sometimes, in gross misunderstanding of Pauline anthropology, a person has been divided into two parts (Lietzmann). People have even gone so far as to talk of an "imperishable element of nobility," or an "unconscious Christianity," at least from the standpoint of redemption (Jülicher). Thus the shadow of a dualistic anthropology is nowhere avoided. In a particularly sublimated form one still meets it in the assertion that in this verse, as distinct from other passages, νοῦς has the "full sense" of the "authentic I" in distinction from the "objectified I" of corporeality (Bultmann, *Theology*, I, 212). For at root this is simply a variation on the contrast between nature and spirit (cf. also Lietzmann; Lagrange; Althaus; Leenhardt; Kuss; Hommel, "7. Kapitel," 105f.; Behm, *TDNT*, II, 698f.). This necessarily leads to the theme of the "divided I" (Bultmann, *Theology*, I, 201ff., 245f.; Braun, "Selbstverständnis," 102, 114; Blank, "Mensch," 19f.; Eichholz, *Paulus*, 257).

Does not this view become unavoidable, however, through the antithesis of v. 23? One can agree to this only if one does not pay sufficient attention to the parallelism with 6:12ff. and to the underlying concepts there. In both cases, not accidentally, military metaphors are used which characterize human existence as the place and instrument of the conflict of the powers and which thus support the "transsubjective" interpretation of vv. 14-20, which reaches beyond ethical conflicts. What was depicted in the previous section reflects cosmic strife projected into existence. In both cases, then, there is reference to the "members," with three things in view. Human reality exists only in the sphere of corporeality, of earthly communication. The battle for world dominion necessarily takes concrete shape as the battle over existence in its relation to the world and not just over individuals and their "authenticity." To the extent that the members are [2 spoken of rather than the body, the fact is expressed that actively and passively we do not take part in the conflict independently but only as those who belong to a lord and his rule. Those who take a different view there must consistently do so here also, and therefore already in vv. 14-20, and especially here, they are caught in the problems of ancient and modern idealism with its antithesis of will and act, spirit and nature, I in orientation to God or I in rebellion against him.

Now Paul undoubtedly uses the idealistic terms and motifs of the Greek tradition. This does not mean, however, that he takes over their original scope. If it is seen (Kümmel, *Man,* 59f.) that in some sense the Christian situation of Gal 5:16ff. is here transferred to pre-Christian existence, the reasons for this must be sought. An answer can be given only if one includes in consideration the antithetical relation of this passage to 6:11ff. and the common concern in both texts is investigated. In contrast to current exegesis, which reads an anthropological dualism precisely out of the passage, Paul in both instances has the totality of existence in mind. This cannot be sundered in its bodily reality (cf. Bornkamm, "Sin," 98ff.), since corporeality means service, and service excludes a person from belonging to two masters simultaneously. It should be stressed again that v. 14c set all that follows under the heading: Sold under the power of sin. One should not paralyze this fallenness by finding a counterpart to it in the good will. Everything depends on the fact that the will does not reach its goal and thus shows itself to be powerless.

The theme is given final force in v. 23. The existence depicted here, in its bodily relation to the world with all its capacities, is the basis of the operation of the power of sin which uses our members as its instruments. Indeed, we are the booty of sin, and as such we are in slavery to it. The intrinsically superfluous phrase τῷ ὄντι ἐν τοῦς μέλεσίν μου at the end of the verse is not just a rhetorical repetition of the opening. It makes it plain that the compulsion of sin does not remain outside us and leave us at least a little personal room for play. It takes concrete form as compulsion in our members and embraces us totally. If we cannot overcome it according to vv. 15ff., in our verse we cannot even fight and resist it using delaying tactics. Yet even under this alien rule we are still the creatures of God. Neither our power nor the power of sin can obliterate this. When otherwise we sink into fallenness to the world, it still displays itself in the fact that we cannot cease to lament, as happens in v. 24.

No one is going to argue that this lament and the accompanying cry for redemption are simply taken schematically from pre-Pauline tradition. Conversely, there is such a tradition in whose chain the apostle fits, perhaps, without knowing it. The closest parallels, which go beyond the usual laments and cries for help in prayer (cf. Michel), are to be found in the Hermetic tractate *Kore Kosmou* §§34-37 and the Hellenistic-Jewish story of *Joseph and Asenath* 6:2ff. (Smith, "Background," 128-133). Despair at imprisonment in earthly corporeality and at the related blindness causes the question of redemption to be brought to utterance here. The destiny of the soul reflects a cosmic drama which can be formulated most succinctly in the equation σῶμα–σῆμα. Paul uses related vocabulary as well as the style of speech present in this tradition.

1]   In a rhetorically effective way the adjective is separated from the noun and put first. ταλαίπωρος means more than harassed (Schlatter). It has the sense of wretched and smitten by misfortune in every respect (BAGD, 803a). τοῦ σώματος τοῦ θανάτου τούτου may be a single phrase "this body of death," the demonstrative thus not merely referring to θανάτου (Kühl; Lietzmann; Lagrange; Kuss contra Schlatter; Bardenhewer; Gaugler; Murray; Kümmel, Römer 7, 64; H. W. Schmidt). Where sin reigns, the power of death qualifies our bodily existence in its total relationship to the world, as in 5:12ff. Salvation can be seen here only in deliverance from this corporeality and, as in the parallels, through liberation from it. It is perfectly clear, then, that the antithesis of will and act in vv. 14-20 does not primarily concern contradictions in the moral plane. The will which continually fails is ultimately concerned to attain life and salvation even in its concrete acts, so that the pious person and not the sinner represents its destiny. Since the intention is most evident in him, his fate is also particularly puzzling.

Here is the heart of Paul's teaching. It is not just that the creature repeatedly comes up against its limits after the fall, but precisely the religious person crashes and the pathway under man fails. The path which leads by the Mosaic Torah blinds him like Adam and delivers him up to sin. He agrees with the will of God, which is oriented to the salvation of the creature. He delights in it, so long as he desires salvation and strives to attain it by obeying the commandments. In the process, however, he becomes entangled in his own desire for life which tries to snatch what can only be given and thus falls subject to the powers of the world. This pious person typifies as no one else can the nature of self-willed, rebellious, perverted, and lost creation.

This perspective enables us to understand the adoption of the νοῦς and ἔσω ἄνθρωπος in vv. 22f. The apostle reaches beyond the sphere of the Torah in vv. 21-24. The person curved in upon himself who undergoes the fate of Adam, exists everywhere. There is an analogy to the law in which according to 2:13ff. a person is law to himself. What was previously called conscience is now presented as "reason" and "inner man," since the issue here is the sense of the divine will of 1:19ff., not confrontation with the judge. The play on νόμος also becomes intelligible. Paul is forging a link with the preceding sections as well as going beyond them. As there is a sphere of the Torah, so there is that sphere of the analogy to it of which 1:19ff. and 2:13ff. spoke, that order of creatureliness which even the fallen creature cannot totally destroy. No one is completely abandoned by the will of God. Our inner being bears witness to it, even if very hazily and simply in the desire for life and salvation. The fact that confrontation with God's will is not enough, however, has been shown by the example of Adam and manifests itself constantly not only in the life of the pious Jew but also in every human existence. After Adam this confrontation simply brings to light our weakness and the fate of "delivering up" which governs us (1:24ff.), as well as our possession by and bondage to the powers of the world. What remains is finally only the lament and the cry for redemption. Thereupon our creatureliness is, so to speak, shriveled up. What is brought to light is the depth of our fall, not our relatedness to God. We are no longer masters of ourselves and only the cry for the deliverer and his help can do justice to this situation.

In paradoxical fashion this also marks the possibility of reversal which, in an

abrupt change even of style, provides the reply of v. 25a to the complaint of v. 24. [2
In the same way 8:19ff. will connect the hope and promise of the glorious liberty
of the children of God with the sighing of creation in its unwearying cry for
redemption. When man comes to an end of himself, creation out of nothing can
follow, the pneuma can clothe the shadow with new corporeality, and the possessed of the world can become the eschatological freedmen of God. The anxiety
of the creature in which its need of help comes to expression permits a Christian
interpretation of pre-Christian existence. The fact that it still cries in piety and
transgression is, for all the demonic entanglement and possession, a sign of the
humanity of that "inner man" whose question about a deliverer God has answered.

From this perspective the sense of our chapter is illuminated. Verses 1-6a are
shown to be an introduction to the theme in v. 6b. What follows in vv. 7ff. is not
an excursus but an exposition of this theme which distinguishes the old aeon and
the new in the antithesis of law and Spirit (Lyonnet, *Quaestiones*, II, 15), so that
freedom from the law can be proclaimed. If this is so, the argument in vv. 7-24
cannot be meant as an apology for the law. To be sure, the law in the intention
of the Giver of the law must be distinguished from its reception by those to whom
it comes. It is a declaration of the divine will, but it is perverted by mankind and
made an incitement to sin. How this is possible is shown by the example of Adam
as the first recipient of the law. Verses 15-20 are not to be given the heading of
"man in contradiction" or "divided man." The issue is possession and destiny,
not the undecided conflict of flesh and Spirit. It concerns that person who lives
in the illusion that he can and should help himself and thereby repeats the story
of Adam even when he is acting piously and ethically. Finally, vv. 21-25 show that
necessarily and objectively this person is despairing. This is the true mark of
every creature after Adam's fall.

Paul does not grant himself the luxury of digressions. His argument is consistent. He develops it in three broadening circles. The whole makes it plain what
mankind is under the sign of law. He thus sets up a foil for what ch. 8 will describe
as existence in the sign and sphere of the Spirit (Kertelge, "Überlegungen,"
112f.). The apostle thus follows a schema which his message of 3:21ff. already
presents against the background of 1:18–3:20 (Dupont, "Structure," 390) and
which his promise for Israel in ch. 11 will again display in antithesis to the exposition in chs. 9–10. It always concerns the eschatological break and the miracle
by which what is not is called into being. This schema is particularly apt here.
Freedom from death and sin could be handled with relative brevity. But when the
issue is freedom from the law, Paul's doctrine of justification is under debate at
its most offensive point. The Christian message of baptism already enables him
to proclaim the end of the law in vv. 4-6a. For the apostle, however, this is
simply a prologue to his own argument which in virtue of the importance of the
subject matter is again set in the schema of the contrast between then and now.
The Spirit has replaced the law in the Christian. Christian freedom stands opposed
to bondage under the *nomos*. The liberated person looks back on his past, which
from the perspective of the world still threatens him, so that he can be kept from
it only "in the Spirit." The figure of the confession in the I-style is the suitable
way of expressing this. The reference back to the story of Adam does not merely
make clear the fateful role which the law plays for mankind and the world in   [20

210

general but also paves the way (cf. 5:12ff.) for the history of Christ whose present(ness) is governed by the Spirit. The lament and the cry for deliverance in v. 24 confirm the "sold under sin" of v. 14. The Christian understands it as an expression of the sighing of every creature, as the truth of real human being to which the true God responds by accomplishing the freedom of the bound, deliverance from the compulsion by cosmic forces, and the justification of the godless. Only the Christian can see it thus, since he is rescued from the power of the illusion which rules the world under Adam and Moses.

There are no very cogent arguments for a liturgical background to vv. 24-25a (Smith, "Background," 133ff.). The eulogy in v. 25a is very Pauline (Paulsen, *Überlieferung,* 34, 38ff.). It was later adapted verbally to current speech and made into a clearer introduction to ch. 8, but this destroys its paradoxical character (Zahn; Kühl; Lietzmann; Lagrange; survey in Sanday and Headlam). Verse 25b poses many difficulties for expositors (cf. Keuck, "Dienst," 257ff.). It can be given a key position in the chapters (Kürzinger, "Schlüssel," 271) and regarded as a summary of ch. 7 (Lagrange; Gutjahr; Bardenhewer; Schlatter; Kümmel, *Römer 7,* 65ff.; Giese, *Römer 7,* 40; Barrett; Murray) only if vv. 14ff. are interpreted in terms of an ethical conflict and a process of struggle for perfection is thought to be described here (Huby). To say that the apostle's logic leaves something to be desired elsewhere as well (Kühl; Lietzmann; Schlatter; in opposition Packer, "Wretched Man," 626f.) is off the mark. It would indeed be illogical if after v. 25a there were a flashback to the time before the change of aeons. This would shatter not merely the logic but also the anthropology and the whole theology of the apostle. The sentence would in fact show that the Torah was not done away with for Paul (Cranfield, "Law," 158) and that a substantive dialectic united the person under the law with the person under grace (Jonas, *Augustin,* 48f.; cf. on the assumption of authenticity Bornkamm, "Sin," 99ff.). An anthropological dualism would, precisely as in Qumran (Kuhn, "πειρασμός," 215ff.; Braun, "Selbstverständnis," 113), ascribe a doubly oriented δουλεύειν to the same existence.

How precarious it is to assert there is a gloss here against the whole textual tradition merely on material grounds cannot be minimized in the slightest. There is no historical evidence for this. On the other hand, the price which has to be paid for assuming authenticity should not be underestimated. For in this case it is not just our interpretation of the context that falls. All that Paul says about baptism, law, and the justification of the ungodly, namely, all that he says about the break between the aeons, will have to be interpreted differently. The νοῦς which sees the flesh, here understood as corporeality, to be subject to sin but still for its part subservient to the will of God is not yet at the end of its possibilities. Its lament portrays, not the possession and destiny of the creature, but its insufficiency. He is convinced that he can serve God, and he remains so in spite of every defeat in the conflict. Undoubtedly the reference is not just to the Jew (H. W. Schmidt) or to the I which makes itself independent over against grace (Zahn; J. Weiss, "Beiträge," 232; Keuck, "Dienst"; in opposition Packer, "Wretched Man," 625). αὐτὸς ἐγώ means the true I which can be separated from the flesh in non-Pauline fashion. The material problem is not solved by putting the sentence after v. 23 (Jülicher; Dodd; F. Müller, "Marginalien," 251; Michel;

Black; Eichholz, *Paulus*, 257). Here if anywhere we have the gloss of a later reader (Bultmann, "Glossen," 199; Fuchs, *Freiheit*, 82f.; Luz, *Geschichtsverständnis*, 160; K. A. Bauer, *Leiblichkeit*, 159; Paulsen, *Überlieferung*, 23ff.; probable Schweizer, *TDNT*, VII, 133n; Bornkamm, "Sin," 99), which presents the first Christian interpretation of vv. 7-24.

4. Man in the Freedom of the Spirit (8:1-39)

Chapter 8 is clearly structured. Verses 1-11 deal with the Christian life as being in the Spirit. Verses 12-17 expound this as the state of sonship. Verses 18-30 portray it as the hope of eschatological freedom. Verses 31-39 depict it as triumph. The reality of the dominion of the law is far transcended in all this.

Paul's view of the divine Spirit reflects many traditions and is thus very complicated (cf. my article on Spirit and spiritual gifts in *RGG*, II, 1272-79). Apart from the Johannine view, it is the most sharply delineated in the NT. The still effective idealistic interpretation, resting on the singular passage 1 Cor 2:11, regards God's Spirit as his self-consciousness and hence views the impartation of the Spirit as participation in the self-understanding of a heavenly being. This orientation to classical Greek has been shattered religio-historically by the discovery of the Hellenistic world in which *pneuma* is the power of miracle and ecstasy. If the OT and Jewish apocalyptic already related the gift of the Spirit to the end-time, primitive Christianity connected it with the resurrection of Jesus and the work of the exalted Lord in his community, in which it saw the dawn of the new aeon. Baptism imparts the Spirit to every believer and thus assures him of his share in the world of the resurrection (incomprehensibly contested by Stalder, *Werk*, 429).

Primitive Christian enthusiasm, which results from this experience, regards the community as the sphere in which the forces of the supernatural world unceasingly manifest themselves. When an attempt is made to demonstrate this, the Spirit becomes a kind of metaphysical vitality which finds embodiment especially in miracle-workers and ecstatics. This view has persisted to our own time and must even be described as the dominant one. It is the basis whenever people speak of the "life-principle" (cf. Amiot, *Key Concepts*, 157; Knox, *Life, passim*; Pfister, *Leben*, 32). Already in the post-Pauline period, however, steps were taken to guard against the dangers of religious individualism by domesticating the gift ecclesiastically and regulating it by the counterweight of fixed offices.

Over against this position the apostle develops his doctrine of the Spirit, not systematically, but with astonishing clarity and with a practical orientation (e.g., Schrage, *Einzelgebote*, 63, etc.). Traditional ideas are adapted. The Spirit, of whom he characteristically speaks in the absolute, is the power which works in all the baptized and which also empowers for ecstasy and miracle. Sometimes indeed, since antiquity knows no energy without substratum, the Spirit appears substantially as radiance, as the concept of the resurrection body irrefutably shows (though cf. Kleinknecht, *TDNT*, VI, 357f.; E. Schweizer, *TDNT*, VI, 415, 432; Stalder, *Werk*, 28ff.; Delling, "Paulusverständnis," 102f.). The connection between gift and power, which is so important in the theology of the apostle, comes out most plainly at this point. The Spirit unites the community to the body of Christ and thus creates for itself spatially a field of earthly activity, a sphere of power which corresponds antithetically to the sphere of the rule of flesh or of the "letter." The cosmic dualism toward which Hellenistic Judaism was already tending (cf. Brandenburger, *Fleisch*) is apocalyptically changed. The power of the resurrection world breaks into the old aeon and brings about a worldwide conflict into which (cf. Gal 5:16ff.) every believer is drawn both as the battleground and as the instrument of his Lord (Schweizer, *TDNT*, VI, 420ff.).

History-of-religions research (from the time of Gunkel's *Wirkungen des Geistes*, 1888) has regarded ethicizing as a distinctive feature in Paul. But it is already characteristic of Judaism (Sjöberg, *TDNT*, VI, 383ff.), and insofar as it applies to Paul one has to take into account the dialectical fact that for Paul the "ethical," at least in the Christian life, is an eschatological possibility; thus it derives from the work of the Spirit, and can be paralleled with ecstatic and cybernetic capabilities. The supposed antithesis is a modern one and usually follows a pastoral concern to present love as the supreme Christian virtue (Dodd; Kühl; Kirk; J. Knox, *Life*, 72ff.), which is a misunderstanding.

The Pauline doctrine of the Spirit is constitutively shaped by the fact that the apostle, so far as we can see, is the first to relate it indissolubly to christology. In the Spirit the risen Lord manifests his presence and lordship on earth. Conversely the absolute criterion of the divine Spirit is that he sets the community and its members in the discipleship of the Crucified, in the mutual service established thereby, and in the assault of grace on the world and the sphere of corporeality. The difference from enthusiasm is that the Spirit is to be tested in terms of christology, and christology is not set under the shadow of ecclesiology. In this way the history of primitive Christianity enters a new phase.

Theological reflection begins a critical rethinking of traditional ideas without this process being already terminated in principle. The connection to christology can be viewed as a first step to the later doctrine of the Trinity if this is not already seen embryonically in the Pauline corpus itself (Schweizer, *TDNT*, VI, 433f. *contra* Lagrange; Amiot, *Key Concepts*, 162ff.; J. Bonsirven, *Theology of the New Testament* [1963] 239, etc.; cf. the excursus in Kuss, 580ff.). Rhetorical and possibly liturgical texts in which God, Christ, and the Spirit are linked together are not decisive in this regard. That powers can be personified in a certain manner in antiquity is also shown in the use of the terms flesh and law, sin and death. Paul does not even go as far as John, who equates Pneuma and Paraclete. Probably Spirit and gospel are already closely related in him (7:6; 10:6ff.; esp. 2 Corinthians 3–4). Spirit and faith correspond to one another (Schweizer, *TDNT*, VI, 425ff.), as Christ or righteousness is related to faith. But the relations are not explained logically. Since the apostle's concern was the assault of grace on the world of the body, he could not ignore the ecstatic and thaumaturgic gifts of the Spirit, he had to stress charismatic ministries, and he could not confine the work of the Spirit to the sphere of the word. The controversy with nomism and enthusiasm hampered the development of a self-enclosed systematics at this point, but conversely set one in a great openness to reality and raised crucial points which are unavoidable.

213

a. Christian Life as Being in the Spirit (8:1-11)

¹There is thus no more condemnation for those who are in Christ Jesus. ²For the law of life given with the Spirit in Jesus Christ has freed you from the law of sin and death. ³(There has been done) that which was impossible for the law, in which it showed itself to be weak because of the flesh: God sent his own Son in the likeness of sinful flesh and as an expiatory sacrifice, condemning sin in the flesh. ⁴The claim of the law should thus be fulfilled by us who do not walk according to the flesh but according to the Spirit. ⁵For those who are determined by the flesh orient themselves to the things of the flesh, but those who are determined by the Spirit to the things of the Spirit. ⁶For the tendency of the flesh is death, but the concern of the Spirit is life and peace. ⁷Hostility to God is the intent of the flesh. For it does not submit to God's law; indeed, it cannot do so. ⁸Those who are bound to the sphere of the flesh cannot please God. ⁹But you are not (any more) in the power of the flesh but in that of the Spirit if the Spirit of God dwells in you. If anyone does not have the Spirit of Christ, he does not belong to him. ¹⁰If, however, Christ (is) in you, the body is dead in view of sin, but the Spirit is life in view of righteousness. ¹¹If the Spirit of him who raised up Jesus from the dead dwells in you, he who raised up Christ Jesus from the dead will give life to your mortal bodies through his Spirit dwelling in you.

Bibliography: W. Schmauch, *In Christus. Eine untersuchung zur Sprache und Theologie des Paulus* (1935); F. Büchsel, " 'In Christus' bei Paulus," *ZNW* 42 (1949) 141-158; C. H. Dodd, "Ἔννομος τοῦ Χριστοῦ," *Studia Paulina*, 96-110; F. Gerritzen, "Le sens et l'origine de l' ἐν Χριστῷ paulinien," *Stud.Paul.Congr.*, II, 323-331; J. Beck, "Altes und neues Gesetz," *MTZ* 15 (1964) 127-142; P. Benoit, "La loi et la croix d'après St. Paul," *Exégèse*, II, 9-40; S. Lyonnet, "Gratuité de la justification et gratuité du salut," *Stud.Paul.Congr.*, I, 95-110; idem, "Le Nouveau Testament à la lumière de l'Ancien," *NRT* 87 (1965) 561-587; E. Schweizer, *Jesus* (Eng. tr. 1971); idem, "Zum traditionsgeschichtlichen Hintergrund der 'Sendungsformel' Gal 4, 4f. Rm 8, 3f. Joh 3, 16f. 1. Joh 4, 9," *ZNW* 57 (1966) 199-210; K. Berger, "Zum traditionsgeschichtlichen Hintergrund christologischer Hoheitstitel," *NTS* 17 (1970/71) 391-425; E. Lohse, "ὁ νόμος τοῦ πνεύματος τῆς ζωῆς. Exegetische Anmerkungen zu Röm 8, 2," *Neues Testament und christliche Existenz. Festschrift für Herbert Braun zum 70. Geburtstag* (ed. H. D. Betz and L. Schottroff; 1973) 279-287. For Bornkamm, "Sin" and Müller, "Marginalien" see the bibliographies for 7:1-6 and 7:14-15, respectively.

Like 7:25b, 8:1 is a dogmatic sentence, which is certainly not a question (*contra* Zahn) but according to the ἄρα νῦν that follows, which is parallel to the ἄρα οὖν in 7:25b, is to be understood as a foundation. As such, however, it does not fit in either (*contra* Kühl; H. W. Schmidt) with the depiction of existential tornness in 7:25b, the lament in 7:24, or the thanksgiving in 7:25a, which needs an explanation rather than a basis and is given this in 8:2. Again 8:1, unlike 7:25a and 8:2, does not maintain deliverance from the body of death but from eschatological judgment. A relation can be seen to 7:7ff. as a whole (Lagrange) only if one argues for a new and antithetical beginning embracing all that follows (Bornkamm, "Sin," 103 n. 33; Hoppe, *Heilsgeschichte*, 117f.; Mattern, *Gericht*, 91f.; Kuss; Paulsen, *Überlieferung*, 26ff.). However, the inferential introduction of the sentence speaks against this. Both textual tradition and the close relation between vv. 2 and 3 are against reversing vv. 1 and 2 (Müller, "Marginalien," 251; Michel). Again therefore we are forced to consider the possibility of a gloss (Bultmann, "Glossen," 199f.; Fuchs, *Freiheit,* 83) which a later period expanded. In sharp contrast to 7:7-24 but in elucidation of 7:25a, vv. 2-4 characterize the new life of the Christian as grounded in the act of salvation and standing in the sphere of the Spirit, in which the will of God is actually fulfilled as it could not be under the rule of the law. This does not mean (*contra* Cranfield, "Law," 166f.; Fuchs, *Freiheit,* 85; H. W. Schmidt; Lohse, "Anmerkungen," 284ff.) that the law as such is restored by the Spirit or—an even greater error—that it is replaced by a Christian variation on natural law (*contra* J. Fuchs, *Natural Law,* 24f., 31). It concerns the circumstances described in 2:26ff. Exposition deriving from Western and Gentile-Christian tradition does not usually make it clear that for the apostle the moral and ceremonial law in the Torah of Moses forms an indissoluble unity (Enslin, *Ethics,* 85). Only when one reduces this to a moral law can one postulate its ongoing validity in the church and adduce as proof of this the sayings of Jesus (Dodd, "Ἔννομος," 99ff., 110; Davies, *Rabbinic Judaism,* 144f.; opposed by Furnish, *Ethics,* 60ff.), Gal 6:2 (Jüngel, *Paulus und Jesus,* 54ff., 65), and exhortation in general. To do this, however, is to understand not only the law but the Spirit, too, otherwise than Paul does. Verses 5-8 are not a digression. A predominantly negative basis is offered for v. 4. What is done by bearers of the Spirit after the change of aeons was not yet possible for the flesh. Here one sees yet again that Paul does not oppose law and Spirit abstractly. Since powers are at issue, what both of them involve can be appropriately defined through their relation to the one ruled by them. The anthropology of the apostle has a verifying function, as was clear already in ch. 7. Verses 9-11 correspond to vv. 5-8. The Spirit effects eschatological life in righteousness and simultaneously gives assurance of bodily resurrection, which is anticipated in the new obedience made possible by him. He is the power of the new creation of the end-time and as such links the present of faith to the future consummation. He does this by claiming bodily existence for God.

According to the context in ch. 7, it is not accidental that v. 2 sets all that follows under the heading of liberation. The address in the second person, taken up in v. 9, is quite provocative, and excellent readings apparently thought it had to be altered in view of the preceding I-style (Lietzmann; Ridderbos *contra* Sanday and Headlam; H. W. Schmidt). Confession becomes evangelical encouragement (Paulsen, *Überlieferung,* 30f.). This justifies the solemnity of the piled up opening, which is to be regarded as a single genitive construction. The genitives have qualifying significance, as does the appended prepositional phrase. This shows that the "law" is spoken of in a transferred sense as in 3:27—a commonly accepted view. Undoubtedly a person should thereby be reminded of the Torah (Schweizer, *TDNT,* VI, 429). Yet the contrast is heightened in this way; no bridge is built. The third use of the law is still inconceivable to the apostle, who thinks in terms of the apocalyptic idea of the change in aeons. (*contra* Lohse, "Anmerkungen"). This verse is found in the alternative of 2 Cor 3:6ff. The law of the Spirit is nothing other than the Spirit himself in his ruling function in the sphere of

Christ. He creates life and separates not only from sin and death but also from their instrument, the irreparably perverted law of Moses.

In this regard Paul agrees with the enthusiasts. God's will is learned only through the Spirit. An essential part of Christian freedom is that it does not stand under a new law and that its obedience is oriented in the last resort, not to the Torah, but solely to the Kyrios. Allusions to Jeremiah and Ezekiel (*contra* Lyonnet, "Testament," 563ff.) are not to be seen in the verse even if it may subsequently be understood as an echo of them.

Verse 3 elucidates. Historical and material reasons support an anacolouthon. Verse 3a-b must end: God has accomplished this in us by the power of the Spirit. The premise sums up 7:7ff. In spite of its combination with the genitive, διά does not mean "through" but, as in 7:10; 2 Cor 9:13, "on account of," "in virtue of" (BAGD, 181a; Lietzmann; Kuss). ἀδύνατον can mean both "incapable" and "impossible" (BAGD, 19a); the latter is to be preferred here for the sake of the antithesis (Zahn; Lagrange; Leenhardt, though cf. H. W. Schmidt). The verb in the relative clause,· however, shows that actual inability underlies the verdict of impossible. ἐν ᾧ can hardly be causal (Zahn; Lagrange; Ridderbos). It is modal "wherein" (Sanday and Headlam; Kuss). Paul is sharply rejecting the Jewish view which finds in the law the strength of the pious (Grundmann, *TDNT,* II, 297, 308). The anacolouthon sharpens the "by grace alone" and presents the paradox of 5:15ff.; 1 Cor 1:21, according to which God begins where the earthly reaches its end. The ὁ θεός of v. 3c, which is put first for emphasis, shows that there can be no bridge from the one to the other. With the Christ event eschatological action brings another reality in which the Spirit does not simply make possible a better or an original understanding of the law but replaces it. Seen from the perspective of the history of traditions the break in the verse and the anacoluthon arise because Paul refers to fixed proclamatory material as in 3:24 (Schweizer, "Sendungsformel," 107ff.; Mauser, *Gottesbild,* 168; Kramer, *Christ,* 115; Eichholz, *Paulus,* 156).

Comparison with Gal 4:4; John 3:16f.; 1 John 4:9 suggests a liturgical statement which describes the incarnation of the pre-existent Son of God as the salvation of the world. The christologically applied motif of the sending of the pre-existent Son is typically Johannine. It also occurs in Phil 2:6ff., but it is not common in Paul. It is tempting to ascribe the prepositional phrases to the tradition. They can hardly have been composed *ad hoc.* If the second merely means "on account of sin" it would be plerophoric and in part would anticipate v. 4 (Lietzmann; Fuchs, *Freiheit,* 90; Jülicher even considers a gloss). Nevertheless the phrase makes good sense, and develops the argument, if περὶ ἁμαρτίας, used technically as in Lev 16; Heb 10:6, 8; 13:11, means "sin-offering" (Moule; Schweizer, *TDNT,* VIII, 383f.; "Sendungsformel," 210; Riesenfeld, *TDNT,* VI, 55; Bruce; Pfister, *Leben,* 39; contested by most others). In this way a bridge would be built to v. 3d, which does not speak of the overcoming of sin (Michel; Lyonnet, *Étapes,* 168ff.) but of its condemnation (Stalder, *Werk,* 398ff.). The first prepositional phrase, coming between two traditional formulae, has a solid place in pre-Pauline tradition, whether it originally belongs to the context or not. Phil 2:7b as the closest parallel supports this supposition. However, there can be no final certainty about this. A certain likelihood should be recognized.

This makes it at least worth considering whether the vigorously debated ὁμοίωμα in its christological relation is not taken and used by Paul from the tradition present in Phil 2:7, so that its employment in the difficult texts does not have to be explained solely in terms of the LXX. One cannot avoid here the dogmatic dispute whether the incarnation means unrestricted entry into human nature even to the point of kenosis (cf. Pallis). Stress is laid explicitly on the sending of the Son into the flesh of sin, which corresponds to the formula "flesh of iniquity" in 1QS 11:9; 1QM 4:3; 12:12 (Brandenburger, *Fleisch*, 101). To the extent that commentators take the harsh expression seriously, they speak of susceptibility to the power of sin and emphasize victorious obedience, which the verse hardly permits. This is precluded by the common view, which is pre-Pauline, that the earthly Jesus was already God's Son and that as such he could not be subject to temptation to sin (Wrede, *Paul*, 98). Interest in the true human being conflicts with interest in the true God, although this relates to a phase in dogmatic history which had not yet been reached in Paul's day even if the problem was beginning to take shape. If a tradition also present in Phil 2:7 underlies the present verse, it is methodologically necessary to interpret the verse in terms of this passage. Two emphases may be seen there. Christ gave up his pre-existent deity when he took human μορφή, which is Hellenistic for "nature." At the same time the conclusion of Phil 2:7 distinctively limits the statement by using ὡς ἄνθρωπος. That can only mean that Jesus could and must die in earthly fashion but did not become subject to sin. In this context the term ὁμοίωμα has the function of protecting such a dialectic. It has the same function here, especially as the verse even sharpens the statement of Phil 2:7. God sent his Son so deeply into the sphere of sinful flesh that from the very first he ordained him a sin-offering. Nevertheless the term ὁμοίωμα denotes a limit (J. Schneider, *TDNT*, V, 195f.). Jesus came in the likeness of sinful flesh. He was passively exposed to sin, but in distinction from us he did not actively open himself to it. What is decisive for such a perspective is not the susceptibility to sin, but the reality of the sin-offering which was made for us and which represents us. ὁμοίωμα is thus used because of its ambivalence, and one should not try to render it either by "identity" or on the other side by "similarity." The use of "in the likeness" shows that it can go in both directions (BAGD, 567b with a reference to *1 Enoch* 31:2; but cf. Mauser, *Gottesbild*, 168ff.).

Paul changed the tradition of the sending formula, which stresses the incarnation of the pre-existent Son, in order to draw attention to the act of salvation on which the accent falls in v. 3d (Schweizer, *TDNT*, VIII, 383f.; "Sendungsformel," 209; Mauser, *Gottesbild*, 174). He was no longer concerned with the incarnation as such (*contra* Zahn; Kühl; Lagrange) but with the crucifixion (cf. Benoit, "Loi," 21ff. and most scholars). This could have been the case already in his tradition if a coherent tradition underlies the whole statement up to v. 4a and he does not take up merely individual motifs. The remarkable mythical idea of a condemnation of sin in the flesh of the Crucified has its closest parallel in the sentence in 2 Cor 5:21 and is not far from the statement in Col 2:14f. The beginning of the final statement in v. 4 describes the Christian fulfilment of the law as a fruit of the saving act, which goes beyond 12:8-10 and reminds us of the Jewish-Christian view in Matt 5:17ff. δικαίωμα τοῦ νόμου means the legal claim as in

1:32, and correspondingly πληροῦν means the keeping of a norm (Delling, TDNT, VI, 293). It would be more than strange if after 7:1-6 Paul had spoken of such a claim of the law on Christians. But if he is taking over an existing formulation, he can apply it to the doing of the will of God of which he speaks also in 12:8ff. Exposition shows, however, how dangerous and misleading the statement is. If one finds here a proclamation of the divine ideal of morality (Gutjahr; Barden-hewer), or an explicit linking of the new morality with justification (Dibelius, "Vier Worte," 8f.), or an equation of the practice of love with the guidance of the Spirit (e.g., Kühl), the gospel is in fact made into a means to fulfil the law. The reference to the legal claim is natural enough, just as it is natural at Matt 5:17ff. to see in love a radicalizing of all the commandments and a new law (Paulsen, Überlieferung, 65, though cf. Blank, Paulus, 293f.). This is what leads to the idea of faith formed by love. From the actual wording a clear decision is scarcely possible. Yet it should be noted that there is no reference to love. Instead there is a strong stress on the passive of the verb and the concluding participial phrase. This corresponds to the thrust of v. 3. What counts is not first of all what we do but what God has done and made possible when he let Christ die. This is why we have an anacolouthon which obviously disturbs the logic of the train of thought, and why pre-Pauline tradition is fragmentarily cited which moves christology into the foreground.

In contrast to his interpreters Paul unmistakably sets forth the alien work (opus alienum) and in so doing pays the price for the fact that his argument is affected by motifs from another source. His intention is clear. Only the Spirit gives freedom from the powers of sin and death. Since the Torah has been per-verted by the flesh it cannot enable us to fulfil God's will, without which that freedom does not exist. As he releases us from the dominion of the powers, the Spirit evokes the new obedience and thus establishes the rights of the divine will which had been originally manifested in the law. The christological interpolation, however, stands in the way of the natural assumption that the Spirit is simply the law correctly understood by illumination and restored to its original meaning, and thus the principle of Christian life and morality. The Spirit is the supernatural power of grace which is based on the act of salvation and constantly directs us to it. God alone fulfils what he demands. He does it paradoxically on the cross with the sending of his Son as a sin-offering, and therefore apart from and even in opposition to our cooperation (Asmussen; Lyonnet, "Gratuité," 108f. typically resist this view). κατέκρινεν τὴν ἁμαρτίαν, which is a surprising expression in Paul, must be understood from this perspective (Lyonnet, "Testament," 573ff.). It does not simply refer to Christ's penal suffering (contra Brunner). If God representatively on the cross judged and condemned sin in the fleshly sphere, the Spirit is for the apostle the power which sets us under the cross and under the judgment executed there. In so doing he rescues us from our autonomy and illusions and manifests the Crucified as the end of our own possibilities and the beginning of the wonderful divine possibilities by which we shall henceforth live the life of grace. He does not do this by continuing the religiosity and morality which are demanded by the letter and which are possible even in the old aeon. He does it by fashioning a new creature under the sign of the fulfilment of the divine will. For this is the point of the emphatic ἐν ἡμῖν, which does not just introduce the participial phrase but varies Gal 2:20 and confirms Rom 2:28f. What is meant is not an instrumental "through" or modal "with or to us" (Kühl; Bardenhewer) but, as in Gal 2:20, a local "in us," with an anthropological reference to individual Christians and an ecclesiological reference to the whole community (Stalder, *Werk,* 406). The reality of the new life is characterized by the fact that Christ takes possession of it in the power of the Spirit. The community and its members are the sphere of his life and work, his sphere of lordship (Brandenburger, *Fleisch,* 26ff., 54ff., 186ff., 203ff.), which is wrested from the powers of the world and set in antithesis to them, as the characteristic κατά shows. That this means lasting conflict may be seen from περιπατεῖν, which in good Semitic fashion describes living as being under way (Pfister, *Leben,* 53f.).

If this interpretation is correct, the motif of the justification of the ungodly, as in 4:17ff., is taken up in and maintained by that of the fashioning of a new creature. There can be no talk of mystical relations, which is usually associated with the common but obscure and dangerous idea that union with Christ is the true work of the Spirit. The Spirit points us back to the cross of Christ as the place of salvation. He thus continually actualizes justification, sets us unceasingly in the sphere of power of the Crucified, and is (Eichholz, *Paulus,* 274f.) the earthly presence of the exalted Lord. If the motif of union is to be used at all, it must be precisely understood as incorporation into the lordship of the Crucified.

The many negative statements from vv. 5-8 expound this. The slogan φρονεῖν denotes the direction not merely of thought but of total existence, which on the Semitic view is always oriented consciously or unconsciously to a goal. The dualistic alternative already mentioned at the end of v. 4 corresponds to Pauline eschatology. The alternative distinguishes the kingdom of this world from the kingdom which has dawned with Christ. Here, too, the axiom of Pauline anthropology is presupposed. A person cannot live on his own. He is what he is because of his Lord and the power of his Lord, and he shows this in his acts. When all other differences and limitations are eschatologically relativized, commitment to flesh or Spirit and their possibilities and necessities marks a final and abiding distinction. Verse 6 gives precision to the eschatological alternative along the lines already indicated from ch. 5 onward and confirms our exposition of 7:14ff. The issue is always the antithesis between true, eternal life and death. A person naturally wants life. As flesh, however, he can effect only death. Life and peace are not inner harmony (Sanday and Headlam; Dodd), but as in 14:17 they are the *basileia* (Foerster, *TDNT,* II, 412f.) to which the beatitude in 2:7ff. points, namely, full salvation. This is not given gradually or step by step (Zahn). It is given in the new birth announced by baptism, and therefore by the Spirit. Verses 7-8 are explicatively introduced by διότι (Lagrange). They establish why the flesh must be directed toward death. Having fallen victim to the world it can do nothing other than live in active hostility to God (Kühl). For, as the example of the Jews will show in 10:3, it neither can nor will subject itself to God's will, here denoted by νόμος. ὑποτάσσεσθαι characterizes the state proper to the creature, from which the rebel, manifesting his enmity to God, has fallen, whereas the Spirit brings him back to that and thus into the good pleasure of God. The twofold οὐ δύνανται marks the depth of the breach which runs across all mankind and is defined as the antithesis of flesh and Spirit (vv. 4b-8). "In the flesh" and "in the

Spirit" now replace the κατά formulations. In terms of the history of religions that can be explained only against the background of a non-Jewish (R. Meyer, *TDNT*, VII, 114) metaphysical dualism, as strongly as this view is resisted (cf. Schweizer, *TDNT*, VII, 131ff.). The explanation is inadequate, however, since the whole of Paul's theology has to be taken into account in interpretation. At least one should see that the apostle is forced into this approach by his eschatology and is thus following the tracks of the Jewish doctrine of the two aeons (Furnish,   [
Ethics, 130ff.). In the end-time it will be revealed that the powers which rule the world fight for each individual person to make him their representative on earth. They do this with an exclusiveness which demands total commitment, as the alternative κατά shows. The result is denoted by the preposition ἐν. Commitment to one or the other power makes one a member of a worldwide domain which can be defined by the alternatives of righteousness and unrighteousness, Christ and Adam, Spirit and flesh, or Spirit and law.

Verses 3b-4a made it clear that this matter must be approached from a christological perspective. Thus it is now necessary to go into the much-debated formula "in Christ" and its variations. We find it solemnly in v. 2 and it is reciprocally taken up in v. 10 by Χριστὸς ἐν ὑμῖν. It is closely connected, then, with the antithesis of Spirit and flesh in the present section. Modern debate about the formula began with Deissmann's *In Christo Jesu* in 1892, in which the ἐν was resolutely given a local sense and interpreted mystically in terms of the idea of union with the exalted Christ. This had the advantage of making the reciprocal nature of the formula immediately understandable. The hypothesis was able to establish itself with the victorious march of history-of-religions research and its assumption of the dogmatically important motif of mystical union, and it still occupies an unshakable place in view of the attractive result. More recently, however, it has been no less resolutely contested (Büchsel, "In Christus"; Schmauch, *In Christus*; Delling, *Worship*; Neugebauer, *In Christus*). A driving force behind the attack obviously is dislike for the idea of a Pauline mysticism and its Hellenistic derivation. Behind the religio-historical debate there undoubtedly stands a typically Protestant concern, namely, the emphasis on faith and on the primacy of christology, which opposes the ecclesiological motif of union, especially as it is represented in Roman Catholic and Anglo-Saxon circles. Characteristically, one thereby falls into a historicizing liberalism. The ἐν is taken instrumentally as equivalent to the Hebrew ב and union is replaced by the believer's integration into what is quite vaguely described as the ongoing Christ event. In fact this means the relation between the once-for-all event and its historical radiation, in which Spirit and tradition tend to merge.

The two interpretations are not at root so far apart as might initially appear. Both stress the incorporation of the Christian and the community into a higher field of force and are distinguished chiefly by the fact that the former speaks of a metaphysical relation of mutual union between Christ and his people whereas the latter speaks of a working historical relation grasped in faith. Both obviously suffer from the same defect that their slogans remain remarkably formal and obscure. Mysticism is so many-layered that one ought to speak of it precisely. The inclination to call Paul a mystic (cf. Bousset, *Kyrios Christos*) disappears to the same degree that one becomes aware of his eschatology. The attempt to build a bridge from one to the other by speaking of "eschatological mysticism" (A. Schweitzer, *Mysticism*) remains unfruitful, and must be so as a contradiction in terms. On the other hand, faith for Paul is not just the acceptance of the events of salvation history, and the continuation of these events has to be distinguished basically and with theological adequacy from other intellectual processes. The most important result of the controversy is negative. It reflects a confrontation between metaphysics and historicism and shows that on neither side have the premises been sufficiently thought through theologically.

In spite of this, special studies have certainly made it clear that the Pauline material is more complicated and richer in nuances than a first glance would suggest (Kümmel, *Theology*, 218; Schrage, *Einzelgebote*, 80ff.). Undoubtedly "in Christ" is often used in a weak sense and in such cases means no more than "Christian." Secondly, the formula is parallel to the other "in the Lord," not an "in Jesus," which relates to fellowship with the earthly person. To be in Christ is to be determined by the crucified and risen Lord. ἐν κυρίῳ, which is not related reciprocally, was probably coined by Paul on the model of ἐν Χριστῷ. It occurs especially in exhortations, although not exclusively so (correctly Bouttier, *En Christ*, 59ff., 68f.; Kramer, *Christ*, 138ff., 169ff. *contra* Neugebauer, *In Christus*). It clearly differentiates the Lord from his disciples, as is natural in admonition, and thus speaks against an undifferentiated view of union with Christ.

Obviously there is today a tendency to avoid extreme and one-sided solutions. The local sense of the preposition can be neither upheld outright nor rejected outright. In each instance one must ask whether the usage is local, instrumental, or modal (Oepke, *TDNT*, II, 537ff.; Schweizer, *Jesus*, 106f.; Bouttier, *En Christ*, 65ff.; Gerritzen, "Sens," 330f.; Merk, *Handeln*, 17ff.). A further point of agreement is that the labeling of the passages with the local sense through the catchword "mystical" is inappropriate, since no less than others they have an eschatological orientation and thus denote the reality of the new aeon which has come.

The question of the history-of-religions classification of the locally intended formula remains, however, and widely varying answers are given. One might try to avoid the question with the thesis that the formula is constitutively instrumental and refers to the ongoing Christ event. But then the problem is reduced to that of the meaning of the preposition as such, and with the help of OT analogies (Berger, "Hoheitstitel," 403ff.; Gerritzen, "Sens," 330f.) and a reference to the phrase "in the law" (Schmauch, *In Christus*, 167f.) the formula can be explained as a contrasting construction to the latter phrase. Naïveté and a desire to prove that everything derives from Judaism are remarkable here in the same way. The argument that one cannot start with the parallels "in the Spirit" and "in the flesh" because the former usually designates inspiration (Gerritzen, "Sens," 328ff.) is an absurd one. It disregards the contrast between the two phrases, the character of the worldwide forces described by them, and the background of the Jewish doctrine of the aeons. It also skates nonchalantly over the context in which the phrases are very closely related to "in Christ," and "in the Spirit" is interchangeable with "in Christ." Exegesis often betrays more of what scholars do not want to see than what they do see.

If it is true that the linking of pneumatology and christology is a decisive feature and perhaps even an original insight of Pauline theology, this is also the starting point for interpreting the formulae at issue. Probably it is too bold to suggest that initially the apostle changed and sharpened the conception "in the Spirit," which he had found in enthusiasm, through the "in Christ." Nevertheless the reciprocity in the use of the formulae makes sense only if they are derived from pneumatology and understood in the light of it. By the Spirit Christ seizes power in us, just as conversely by the Spirit we are incorporated into Christ. Familiar to both the Jewish and the pagan environment of primitive Christianity was the idea that the Spirit comes into a person ecstatically, removes him beyond the purely human sphere, and associates him with the heavenly world. If this concept is applied in a new way to Christ, the dualistic perspective goes along with it and an eschatological modification is possible. Christ and the Spirit divide the old world and the new.

If one asks what "in Christ" means for Paul himself, a common answer is that it is to be seen as an abbreviation of the theologoumenon of the body of Christ (Bultmann, *Theology*, I, 311, 327f.; Dodd, *Gospel*, 36f.; J. Knox; A. Schweitzer, *Mysticism*, 122f.; Cerfaux, *Church*, 207ff.; *Christ*, 328; Richardson, *Theology*, 249; Schrage, *Einzelgebote*, 80). The church is for the apostle the irruption of a new world and the field where the power of the Spirit is manifested and the rule of Christ unites believers and separates them from the sphere of Adam. Nevertheless, one may scarcely limit the formula to this meaning. Only in terms of enthusiasm can one abstract away from misunderstandings and aberrations in the community, which was not for Paul a mere mystery group. The parallel ἐν κυρίῳ sees to it that even where one would like to establish something like union with Christ, the primacy of christology even over the church is retained. The community is not an extension of Christ nor is Christ merely the vitality which animates it. Both in terms of history-of-religions development and in terms of the theological center it is completely misleading to interpret being in Christ in the light of being in the Spirit. The very opposite is both true and necessary if Christ is not to be merely one interchangeable power among others and the church is not to be a mere band of enthusiasts who glory in the integration into the supernatural world.

The formula σὺν Χριστῷ indicates the community of the disciples with the destiny of the leader. Champions of an instrumental understanding in fact reduce the ἐν Χριστῷ to no more than this. The latter phrase, however, goes further than the former in the sense of the specific Kyrios christology of the apostle. Naturally a sign of Christ's lordship is that we continue his earthly way. Baptism has set us in this nexus of tradition. But the process is not to be approximated to analogies in the history of thought, as is rightly pointed out by representatives of the doctrine of union. The Kyrios was not just there in the past, as though we had today no more than the results of his revelation. He is present in the medium of his Spirit, both in the lives of individual believers and in the community, and through both in the world at large.

Paul knows no invisible Christ whom one can localize only in heaven. He sees Christ at work on earth and describes a sphere of power in which he can be found. He is not afraid of making this extremely concrete. Baptism has given the Spirit and thereby set up his rule. In baptism, according to Gal 3:27ff., believers

222

have put on Christ like a garment which cannot be simply slipped off. A change in existence has taken place so that earthly distinctions and contrasts are relativized. Undoubtedly the church is also for Paul a mixed body with false witnesses, unworthy members, and many sins. Yet it is not an invisible church, for the gospel is more than an idea, the sacraments are more than religious rites, worship is the gathering of the saints, and each Christian is an earthly representative of his exalted Lord. According to 1 Cor 14:24f. unbelievers declare that "God is really among you." No disciple can leave it an open question whether there really applies to him what the apostle, with apparent audacity, and abandoning the anonymity we so much love today, confesses in Gal 2:20: "I live, yet not I, Christ lives in me." This is the point of the reciprocal formula. It is not just a matter of Christ's sphere of dominion in the world. Paul uses the vocabulary of enthusiasm (Conzelmann, *Outline*, 208ff.) in order to be able to say as concretely as possible (Schrage, *Einzelgebote*, 84ff.) that Christ has taken total possession of our lives. ἐν Χριστῷ means in fact standing in a field of force (Grundmann, *TDNT*, IX, 550; Ridderbos; Kuss, *Paulus*, 371; Becker, *Heil Gottes*, 248ff.). Everything is spoiled, however, if the primary focus (Cerfaux, *Christ*, 328ff.) is on participation in a supernatural life instead of on the reign of Christ.

Verses 9-11 are to be understood in the light of this. As the kingdom of Christ the community stands in conflict with the flesh as the sphere of subjection to the world. As in 14:17f. it enjoys God's good pleasure and can respond to the imparted pneuma as its distinguishing mark. εἴπερ does not have a conditional (Sanday and Headlam; Fuchs, *Freiheit*, 96) and limiting sense but an affirmative sense (cf. the survey in Kuss). If the indwelling of the Spirit is spoken of here as that of sin is in 7:17ff., in both cases radical possession is indicated which also affects our will according to 5:5. It is not just that we are given an ideal to admire (Lagrange). Verse 9c, like 1 Cor 2:16, defines Christian existence in its total orientation. There is no restriction to ethics (*contra* Hanse, *TDNT*, II, 819f.). Christians are recognized as such when they have the Spirit. This can be said in this unequivocal way only if the Spirit means standing under the present Lord. The claim of enthusiasts to a special position is herewith refuted. Ecstatics and thaumaturgists are simply representatives of a community in which each has everything only through his Lord, so that he must always serve with his particular charisma. For with the relationship to himself this Lord gives a special gift as the possibility of a specific service, since he wants to penetrate every corner of the world in all its breadth and depth. The onslaught of grace cannot succeed with ecstatics alone. It presupposes the activity of every member of the community in his own place. Each must participate with his abilities and weaknesses in the victorious march of the exalted Lord (2 Cor 2:14ff.).

Whether v. 9c is a pre-Pauline separation formula like 1 Cor 16:22 or *Did.* 10:6 (Michel) is doubtful, although the saying has the structure of pronouncements of sacral law (Paulsen, *Überlieferung*, 37) which were proclaimed with apostolic authority. In any case it is one of the most important sayings in Paul's theology and is the basis of his exhortation. At the same time one sees in it the characteristic Pauline dialectic in which a postulate of the enthusiasts is adopted and simultaneously torn away from an exalted enthusiasm. If "in Christ" interprets "in the Spirit," the supernatural heavenly power becomes the power of grace, and isolated pneumatica as demonstrations of the new aeon are replaced by charisms as concretions and modifications of the universal priesthood. No one in the community should deny or disregard the special mandate given him by his Lord. One cannot belong to the Lord without manifesting his lordship with one's own existence. The buried talent is a sin against the Spirit and treason against the Lord. The ministry of grace is entrusted to everyone and is thus rendered concretely in everyday life. This leads on to the consideration of the body in vv. 10-11.

Service which does not include the body is imaginary. As the reality of our communication with the earth the body can be the instrument of the subjection of the flesh to the world. Standing in the Spirit sets us under the lordship of Christ not merely in our individuality but also in our relationship to the earth, since otherwise this would be illusory. The apostle's intention is clear even if his mode of expression is difficult to understand. The antithetical parallelism of the two parts of the sentence is obviously rhetorical, although to say this is not enough, as many think. In Paul rhetoric always has a material function, and here it points once again to the change in aeons and the transformation of existence which has taken place. Not for nothing the accent now rests on "Christ in us." It would be a gross misunderstanding for pneumatics to regard themselves as happy owners. They do not possess the heavenly; Christ possesses them. Verse 10bc shows what this means.

In the context the reference is always to the divinely given Spirit (Pfister, *Leben*, 44f., though cf. Ziesler, *Meaning*, 204). In contrast to that the σῶμα, called νεκρόν, can only be the body of sin (6:6) or death (7:24), i.e., σάρξ (Bultmann, *Theology*, I, 201; Jervell, *Imago*, 193f.; K. A. Bauer, *Leiblichkeit*, 162f.; Ridderbos). Since the reference is not to the inner life of a person (*contra* Sanday and Headlam; Kühl; Bardenhewer; Gutjahr; Zahn; Lagrange; Schlatter; Gaugler), νεκρόν cannot possibly mean "mortal" (Zahn; Lagrange), "subject to death" (Grundmann, *TDNT*, I, 313; Sickenberger; Jülicher; Pfister, *Leben*, 46), "dead in the eyes of God" (Michel). If one does not psychologize, the only possible reference is to the death of the body of sin effected in baptism (Bultmann, *TDNT*, IV, 894; Barrett; Leenhardt; Kuss; Paulsen, *Überlieferung*, 69ff.). The repeated διά constitutes the main difficulty. If we think of the deadly work of sin, it must be seen as causal the first time and then final (Weiss, "Beitrage," 181), brought to a formula: "On account of sin committed, on account of righteousness being exercised" (Lietzmann; Lagrange, but cf. Stalder, *Werk*, 449). If one cannot accept this premise, then διά with the accusative means "with reference to" (Dibelius, "Vier Worte," 8f.): the body is dead since baptism so far as sin is in question, but the Spirit who is given us makes alive so far as concerns righteousness (opposed by Siber, *Mit Christus*, 83). The Spirit effects the life in righteousness described in 6:14ff. For in the context of the antithesis δικαιοσύνη cannot refer to the sentence of justification (*contra* Schrenk, *TDNT*, II, 209). It is rather walking by the Spirit in bodily service in a way which is pleasing to God.

As in 6:11, this is an anticipation of the resurrection and here, too, it is set under the characteristic eschatological reservation. Christ is already risen and we are on the way thereto, whereby our new obedience reflects on earth the future glory. That Paul is following fixed tradition here (Wengst, *Formeln*, 31ff.) is not unlikely if τὸν 'Ιησοῦν is to be regarded as the original object of predication. The predication of God is similar to that in 4:17. But here the Spirit is obviously regarded as the true resurrecting force, as is evident in Eph 1:19f. For us he is the pledge that we shall be made like the resurrected Christ (Asmussen)—and this in new corporeality as the sign of a creation which is no longer subject to assault. The promise, then, is not for the present life (contra Lietzmann; Leenhardt; Siber, Mit Christus, 83ff.; for a correct view cf. Schweizer, TDNT, VI, 422; K. A. Bauer, Leiblichkeit, 165f.). The loosely attached conclusion has an accusative with διά in B and other important readings (accepted by Zahn; Kühl; Gutjahr; Pallis; Schweizer, loc. cit.). This is not necessarily the more difficult reading because the Spirit appears elsewhere as creative power only in 1 Cor 15:45. It can be explained by the later preference for the use of the accusative after prepositions (Sanday and Headlam; Lietzmann; Leenhardt; suvey in Kuss). Materially it makes no difference.

b. Being in the Spirit as Standing in Sonship (8:12-17)

¹²So then, brethren, we are not under obligation to the flesh to live according to the flesh. ¹³For if you live according to the flesh you will die. But if by the power of the Spirit you put to death the works of the body you will live. ¹⁴For those who are led by the Spirit of God are the sons of God. ¹⁵You have not received a spirit of slavery (which sets) you in fear again. You have received the Spirit of sonship in which we cry "Abba, Father." ¹⁶The Spirit himself bears witness to our spirit that we are the children of God. ¹⁷If we are children, however, we are also heirs, namely, heirs of God and co-heirs with Christ, so long as we suffer with him so that we may also be glorified with him.

Bibliography: C. Fabricius, "Urbekenntnisse der Christenheit," Reinhold Seeberg Festschrift (1929) 21-41; W. Twisselmann, Die Gotteskindschaft der Christen nach dem NT (1939); W. Bieder, "Gebetswirklichkeit und Gebetsmöglichkeit bei Paulus," TZ 4 (1948) 22-40; S. V. McCasland, "Abba, Father," JBL 72 (1953) 79-91; T. M. Taylor, " 'Abba, Father' and Baptism," SJT 11 (1958) 62-71; W. Marchel, "Abba Pater: Oratio Christi et christianorum," Bib 42 (1961) 240-47; K. Romaniuk, "Spiritus clamans," Bib 43 (1962) 190-98; E. Haenchen, Der Weg Jesu (1966); J. Becker, "Quid locutio πάλιν εἰς φόβον in Rom 8, 15 proprie valeat," VD 45 (1967) 162-67.

The christological relation of the Spirit finds expression in the new section in the fact that Christ as the prototype, as in Heb 2:10ff., creates new sons for God, i.e., the bearers of the Spirit. The antithetical parallelisms of vv. 12-13 take up those of vv. 5-8 at the hortatory level and form a transition to the new theme. ἄρα οὖν draws the conclusion from what precedes. The Christian necessarily stands in conflict with the power of the flesh if he is not to fall under the doom of death which this brings. ὀφειλέται ἐσμέν means "to be under obligation." What is at issue is not the relation of idea and reality (Michel is right here over against Lietzmann) but the maintaining of the new life against temptation. The infinitive of v. 12 is final, while μέλλετε in v. 13a has the sense "you must" (BAGD, 501a). πράξεις does not refer abstractly to a mode of conduct (contra Maurer, TDNT, VI, 643f.) and even less to the wicked impulse against which the rabbis summon us to fight (Billerbeck). The reference is to the autonomous actions of earthly existence. These cannot just be fixed in the moral sphere (contra Zahn; Dodd; Michel), especially since they are spoken of very objectively and adjectives are avoided.

The real difficulty, indicated already by variant readings, lies in the interpretation of σῶμα, which is unquestionably authentic. It certainly does not mean the organic individuality which persists through every change (Dodd) and whose moral renewal is demanded (Jülicher). As at 6:12 one must reject an understanding which sets the "true" I at a distance from its works, which the body is presented here as doing (Bultmann, Theology, 197f., 201). The eschatological difference between the pneumatic and the earthly person must not be outmaneuvered by an anthropological ontology whose interest rests in the continuity of existence. If the body is the reality of human communication, this in isolation from the Creator can act autonomously out of the πρόνοια mentioned in 13:14. It is not yet identical with the σάρξ as subjection to the world (Pfister, Leben, 73 contra Zahn; Lietzmann; Kuss), but is threatened by it, since the power of the flesh has a point of attack in our body, which is still dominated by the earthly (Schweizer, TDNT, VII, 131f.; K. A. Bauer, Leiblichkeit, 168f.). If it is no mere matter of a sham fight, our task in the conflict with the flesh according to 1 Cor 9:27 is also to put to death the striving of the body to secure autonomy. The genitive probably replaces an adjective. The accent is on the instrumental dative and the verb. The pneumatic life provisionally authenticates itself in the overcoming of temptation, not as an inalienable possession. As in 6:11ff. only dogged service triumphs over our constant vulnerability.

The phrase "driven by the Spirit" in v. 14 is taken from the vocabulary of the enthusiasts according to 1 Cor 12:2. It therefore should not be weakened to "be led by" (Dodd; Brunner; Gaugler; Ridderbos; Pfister, Leben, 56f., 76f.) in order to preserve the free ethical decision (Sanday and Headlam; Kühl; Gutjahr; Lagrange; Dodd; Kuss; Stalder, Werk, 470f., also Bultmann, Theology, I, 336f.; Schrage, Einzelgebote, 73f.), of which there is no talk here (correctly perceived by Wetter, Vergeltungsgedanke, 100). Paul was not so timid as his expositors. He could appropriate the terms of the enthusiasts because he took "Christ in us" seriously, as in Gal 2:20, and regarded the Spirit as a power distinct from us. Even in relation to our acts he maintained the "outside us" (extra nos) of grace, since only thus could our authentication and our ability to overcome be safeguarded. He recognized only the objective earthly I. For him the body was never a subject in the true sense but a battleground over which we ultimately are not the ones who decide. We bear responsibility only in the sense that we must not misuse or leave unused the gifts and possibilities that we are given. This means, however, that we must let our Lord work through us instead of thinking about our "true I" as modern ideology demands. Whether or not the justification of the ungodly is grasped and maintained radically may be seen from the test question of christology, which cannot be evaded anthropologically. A doctrine of the Spirit which is not afraid of the catchword "being carried off" is the reverse side of the justification of the ungodly since it connects this with abiding in the reign of Christ in which as constant recipients we are under constant demands. If the righteousness of God is seen solely or primarily in terms of justification as a gift, justice cannot be done to Paul's "ethics." The struggle between Spirit and flesh no longer has as its deepest issue, as in 1 Cor 15:25, the question whether Christ reigns but whether I find myself. Correctly understood this is not an alternative, but it necessarily leads to a different interpretation if the irreversible thrust is not observed. The divine sonship is and remains an eschatological reality. Of course, it allows creation again to come into view, but its continuity arises only in relation to God's word, as vv. 15-16 show.

The original sense of "adoption" is scarcely present in υἱοθεσία (correctly Zahn but cf. Schlatter; Leenhardt). Sonship is not always present (*contra* J. Knox, *Life,* 14) as though the Spirit were simply confirming it (Kühl; Lagrange). Imparted by baptism, it is expectation of and present participation in the *basileia* (Schlatter; Furnish, *Ethics,* 128). The title "son of God," at first reserved in the OT for the people of God and its kingly representative, was later and infrequently transferred to the pious individual. In the Hellenistic sphere, however, it is applied to the θεῖος ἀνήρ, in the mysteries to the initiate, and in Gnosticism to the believer as a member of the heavenly world. The eschatological orientation differentiates primitive Christianity from this environment, and enthusiasm uses it of pneumatics. ὅσοι has both an exclusive and an extensive sense: All (BAGD, 586a; Lagrange).

Verses 15-16 are not (*contra* Lagrange; Siber, *Mit Christus,* 135) a parenthesis addressed to doubters (Lietzmann) but a proof of v. 14. In a common Pauline figure found also in Gal 4:6f. sonship is contrasted with slavery. The apostle is not afraid of formally contradicting 6:12ff. His statements always relate to the situation and the readers. Radical obedience is pointedly defined as slavery. But insofar as this is offered to the gracious Lord as a joyful sacrifice (1 Cor 9:17), it also denotes genuine freedom and sonship. Paul's dialectic is always fighting on two fronts and cannot, therefore, dispense with paradoxes. Thus Phil 2:12 can call for fear and trembling, while here φόβος as a result of bondage and a mark of unredeemed creation seems to be irreconcilable with sonship (Becker, "Locutio," 163 thinks the antithesis is purely rhetorical). The ambivalence of the concept also originates in the substantive dialectic. The servant lives in the fear of God which recognizes his transcendence. Yet our God is not a despot. His saving will is revealed. His service frees from every other rule. Just because the Christian fears God, then, he is delivered from the anxiety into which all other creatures are driven by the incalculability of an uncertain destiny (Bultmann, *TDNT,* VI, 221; Balz, *TDNT,* IX, 214). Assurance of salvation differentiates the two types of fear, just as the rabbis oppose the joy of Israel to the trembling of the Gentiles (Billerbeck).

Verses 15f. obviously are related to a liturgical event (Zahn; Kuss; Delling, *Worship,* 71; Nielen, *Gebet,* 113; Blank, *Paulus,* 277). The plural points to the congregation. The aorists in v. 15a-b refer to the reception of the Spirit in baptism (Schweizer, *TDNT,* VIII, 391f.). κράζειν is in the first instance loud crying as in incantations (Grundmann, *TDNT,* III, 898ff.), then the inspired proclamation of the biblical witnesses (Romaniuk, "Spiritus," 197), or ecstatic outcry (Bultmann, *Theology,* I, 161; Michel). In a world that is hostile to God the Spirit grants the community the possibility of crying Abba, in which open access to the peace of God of 5:1 is manifested.

227

The influence of the Jesus tradition has continually been seen here, since we have the same Ἀββὰ ὁ πατήρ in Mark 14:36. In fact the proclamation of Jesus is shaped by the promise of eschatological sonship and the motif of the heavenly Father. It is hard to believe, however, that with Abba Jesus was adopting the familiar term used in the family and especially by children (Kittel, TDNT, I, 5f.; J. Jeremias, The Central Message of the New Testament [1965] 22ff.; for criticism cf. Haenchen, Weg, 492ff.) and that with the term he was specifically expressing loving devotion (Thüsing, Per Christum, 120; Twisselmann, Gotteskindschaft, 65). It is not even certain that the Jesus tradition is present at all here or in Gal 4:6 (Delling, Worship, 70f.), and one may rule out altogether the common assumption that the opening phrase of the Lord's Prayer is being quoted (correctly Schrenk, TDNT, V, 1006 contra Kittel, TDNT, I, 6; Grundmann, TDNT, III, 902f.; Zahn; Dodd; Lietzmann; Cullmann, Christology, 208f.). Naturally Jesus did not address God in two languages; Mark 14:36 is carried over from later practice in the community. The Lord's Prayer also did not begin in two languages. Behind the mistake is the idea that κράζειν in analogy to the invocations of the Psalter refers self-evidently and primarily to prayer (Grundmann, TDNT, III, 899f.; Marchel, "Abba," 245; Ridderbos; for a correct view Greeven, Gebet, 144ff.), when it should in fact have been recognized as a technical term of acclamation. For there is an acclamation in Ἀββὰ ὁ πατήρ as there is in the cries κύριος Ἰησοῦς and μαραναθά. In it the congregation is uttering an ecstatic cry in response to the message of salvation. Hence it is neither a primitive Christian confession (Fabricius, "Urbekenntnisse," 22f.) nor a baptismal formula (Taylor, "Abba," 2; Paulsen, Überlieferung, 88f.), let alone glossolalia, as surely as acclamations have a confessional character and could have followed baptism. Whereas Maranatha and Amen were handed down unchanged, the cry Abba had a Greek translation added to it in the Gentile-Christian sphere. That its interpretation as acclamation is correct is shown by v. 16.

Against the almost universal view, πνεῦμα ἡμῶν, which is distinct from αὐτὸ τὸ πνεῦμα, is by no means our inner life which is identical with reason (contra BAGD, 675b; Strathmann, TDNT, IV, 509; Greeven, Gebet, 154; Bultmann, Theology, I, 205ff.; Lietzmann; Althaus; Kuss; for a correct view cf. Schweizer, TDNT, VI, 435f.). What would cause Paul to stress the union of the Spirit of God with our insight, which as such cannot at all perceive divine sonship? Paul has in view the situation of worship, not a process in the soul (contra Ridderbos; Pfister, Leben, 81ff.). Finally, the juridical nature of the verb should also be noted. Acclamation is inspired. It is thus an act of sacral law. When it takes place, the Spirit ruling in the congregation manifests objectively to the individual Christian what the Spirit given to him personally says. Like the pagan in 1 Cor 14:25, the congregation learns from the acclamation of ecstatics that God is present in their midst and that both to the whole and to the individual he gives assurance of sonship as participation in the basileia (Paulsen, Überlieferung, 100f.). The host of the assaulted always needs new revelation and consolation.

As often in the koine the compound verb replaces the simple form of the verb (Strathmann, TDNT, IV, 509; Leenhardt; H. W. Schmidt; survey in Kuss). But it also makes good sense to stress the preposition and to understand it as emphatic (Schlatter; Barrett). The Spirit who speaks in worship bears witness to what the

228

Spirit who dwells within us must acknowledge. Verse 16 is thus an interpretation of v. 15c (Kuss).

υἱοί and τέκνα θεοῦ are obviously interchangeable. The statement proceeds link by link as in Gal 4:7 and is expanded in view of a legal relationship. For if κληρονομία refers in a transferred sense to the eschatological occupation of the land, namely, participation in the *basileia,* the nouns can be related only against a legal background. The consequences of sonship are mentioned in order to show its irreversibility. The heir of God is he who participates in his rule, as in 5:17. One can do this only as a co-heir with Christ, the future cosmocrator, who as the exalted one already rules in a hidden way. The use of "heir" means that Paul has to speak in the eschatological future, which also manifests itself in the final clause in v. 17. On the other hand the promise implies qualification of the present already in keeping with the general tenor of the section. For all our vulnerability the coming glory is also already anticipated.

The double aspect comes out in the surprising finish to v. 17 (Furnish, *Ethics,* 128), which obviously leads on to the subsection which follows and gives it emphasis by way of contrast. In all Paul's theology participation in coming glory does not mean that the cross can be dodged. This substantive dialectic is reflected in a typically Pauline argument. With unmistakable pathos the verses begin with the ideas of enthusiasts and hence refer by no means incidentally to what takes place ecstatically in worship. For Paul too the Spirit is the miraculous power of the heavenly world which breaks into the earthly sphere to fashion a new creature. If the enthusiasts are supported thus far, Paul breaks with them when they draw from the premises shared with him the conclusion that they are made safe from worldly threats. Then he confronts them with the theology of the cross and reminds them that the Spirit who makes Christ present on earth is the very one who imposes on them a pilgrim theology. In the final verse, then, we do not simply have, as in Jewish piety (Billerbeck), an insistence that expectation of the *basileia* presupposes earthly suffering, though this is not contested. The preposition σύν in both verbs imposes discipleship of Christ and proclaims its promise. Only he who participates on earth in the passion of the Kyrios will participate in his glory. As in 2 Cor 13:4, suffering with him is the paradoxical guarantee of sharing the *basileia.* εἴπερ might well refer to the reality of the standing and experiences of the Christian (Leenhardt; Michel; Siber, *Mit Christus,* 139f.). But the final sentence which follows and the sharp break in thought more naturally suggest a hortatory and conditional understanding (Michaelis, *TDNT,* V, 925), which directs us back to vv. 12f. (Kuss). Only those who resist the flesh with suffering can overcome. Where Christ is present in the Spirit, one can in no way escape following the Crucified. The enthusiastic premises of the section lead to a markedly anti-enthusiastic conclusion.

c. Being in the Spirit as Standing in Hope (8:18-30)

[18]*For I judge that the sufferings of the present time do not have the same weight as the future glory which is to be revealed in us.* [19]*The eager longing of creation watches for the revealing of the sons of God.* [20]*For creation was subjected to futility, not willingly, but (left) in hope, looking to him who sub-*

jected it. [21]*Hence even creation will as such be freed from bondage to corruption for the glorious freedom of the children of God.* [22]*For we know that all creation groans together and is in pain until now.* [23]*And not only that. We ourselves who have received the Spirit as a firstfruits groan together, waiting for (full) sonship, the redemption of our bodies.* [24]*For in this hope we are saved. Seen hope, however, is not hope. For what does a man still need to wait for patiently when he already sees?* [25]*But if we hope for what we do not see, we look forward to it with patience.* [26]*In the same way the Spirit also comes to the aid of our weakness. For we do not know what we should pray for as we ought. The Spirit himself, however, intercedes for us with inexpressible sighs.* [27]*He who searches the hearts knows what is the Spirit's concern, because the Spirit intercedes for the saints according to God's will.* [28]*We know that everything works together for good to those who love God, namely, to those who are called according to the election.* [29]*For those whom he elected he also foreordained to be conformed to the image of his Son, so that he should be the firstborn among many brethren.* [30]*But those whom he foreordained he also called, and those whom he called he also justified, and finally those whom he justified he also glorified.*

Bibliography: E. Käsemann, "The Cry for Liberty in the Worship of the Church," *Perspectives*, 122-137; U. Gerber, "Röm VIII, 18ff. als exegetisches Problem der Dogmatik," *NovT* 8 (1966) 58-81; G. W. H. Lampe, "The NT Doctrine of Ktisis," *SJT* 17 (1964) 449-461; H. Hommel, "Das Harren der Kreatur," *Schöpfer*, 7-23; W. D. Stacey, "God's Purpose in Creation—Romans viii. 22-23," *ExpT* 69 (1957/58) 178-181; B. R. Brinkmann, *Creation and Creature* (1958) 27-35; S. Lyonnet, "Redemptio cosmica secundum Rom 8:19-23," *VD* 44 (1966) 225-242; A. Debrunner, "Über einige Lesarten der Chester Beatty Papyri des NT," *ConNT* 11 (1947) 33-49; E. Hill, "The Construction of Three Passages from St. Paul," *CBQ* 23 (1961) 296-301; H. Schlier, "Das, worauf alles wartet. Eine Auslegung von Römer 8, 13-30," *Interpretation der Welt. Festschrift für Romano Guardini zum achtzigsten Geburtstag* (ed. H. Kuhn *et al.*; 1965) 599-616; G. Bertram, "ἀποκαραδοκία," *ZNW* 49 (1958) 264-270; P. Benoit, "Nous gémissons, attendant la délivrance de notre corps (*Rom.*, VIII, 23)," *Exégèse*, II, 41-52; J. Swetnam, "On Romans 8:23 and the Expectation of Sonship," *Bib* 48 (1967) 102-107; J. Cambier, "L'espérance et le salut dans Rom 8:24," *Message et Mission. Recueil Commémoratif du Xe Anniversaire de la Faculté de Théologie* [Kinshasa] (1968) 77-107; W. Grundmann, "Die Übermacht der Gnade," *NovT* 2 (1958) 50-72. 26ff.: J. Schniewind, "Das Seufzen des Geistes," *Nachgelassene Reden und Aufsätze* (1952) 81-103; R. Zorn, *Die Fürbitte im Spätjudentum und im NT* (diss. Göttingen; 1957); A. Dietzel, "Beten im Geist," *TZ* 13 (1957) 12-32; E. Gaugler, "Der Geist und das Gebet der schwachen Gemeinde," *Internationale Kirchliche Zeitschrift* 51 (1961) 67-94; K. Niederwimmer, "Das Gebet des Geistes, Röm. 8, 26f.," *TZ* 20 (1964) 252-265. 28ff.: B. Allo, "Encore Rom. VIII, 28-30," *RSPT* 13 (1924) 503-505; W. Michaelis, "Die biblische Vorstellung von Christus als dem Erstgeborenen," *ZST* 23 (1954) 137-167; J. B. Bauer, "τοῖς ἀγαπῶσιν τὸν θεόν, Rm 8, 28; I. Cor 2, 9; I. Cor 8, 3," *ZNW* 50 (1959) 106-112; M. Black, "The Interpretation of Romans VIII, 28," *Neotestamentica et Patristica* (Cullmann Freundesgabe; NovTSup 6; 1962) 166-172; K. Grayston, "The Doctrine of Election in Romans 8,28-30," *SE*, II, 574-583; (Bishop) Cassien, "Le fils et les fils, le frère et les frères," *Paulus-Hellas-Oikumene* (ed. P. I. Bratsiotis; 1951) 35-43; J. Kürzinger, Συμμόρφους τῆς εἰκόνος τοῦ υἱοῦ αὐτοῦ (Röm 8, 29)," *BZ* N.F. 2 (1958) 294-99; A. R. C. Leaney, "Conformed to the Image of his Son (Rom viii. 29)," *NTS* 10 (1963/64) 470-79; C. E. B. Cranfield, "Romans 8:28," *SJT* 19 (1966) 204-215.

A basic insight if we are to understand this section is that possession of the Spirit is here described as standing in hope and that the established anti-enthusiastic trend of v. 17c is very clearly set forth herewith. For Paul it is beyond dispute that salvation is present. This is maintained, however, within a theology of the cross, and thus it is not by chance that in 1 Cor 15:24ff. he distinguishes the lordship of Christ from the consummated lordship of God. For the moment the latter is present only in the mode of the former. Hence the Spirit is simply an earnest and pledge of what is to come. Present eschatology means the time of the gospel in the twofold sense of *promissio* as assurance and promise. This is put in a way which is highly provocative for enthusiastic Christianity in the Hellenistic sphere when life in the Spirit is defined as standing in hope, as post-Easter Jewish Christianity had already defined it (Gerber, "Problem," 59).

One must keep that in view if one wants to understand the position of the passage in the context, its inner thrust, and even its structure. Assurance of salvation determines both vv. 14-17b and vv. 28-30. The thesis of v. 18, which confirms 2 Cor 4:17 (Vögtle, *Zukunft*, 191), fits in with this. Not entirely without reason, then, a psychologizing interpretation perceives a "mood of victory" here and thinks that Paul is speaking poetically in what follows (Kühl; Dodd), although the sharp contrast of vv. 19-27 ought to have been noted. Dominant here are the ideas of troubled expectation and groaning.

The theme of hope is obviously approached from the standpoint of struggle. Hence vv. 19-27 cannot be the basis of v. 18 as though "guarantees" and "supports" were being offered for the assurance of salvation (*contra* Jülicher; Gaugler; Murray; Vögtle, *Zukunft*, 191f.; Balz, *Heilsvertrauen*, 101; in effect, Kuss also). Nor do we have in these verses a justification of suffering judged from the perspective of v. 18 (H. W. Schmidt). That well-founded hope is expressed is incontestable. But the tension with the context, the unmistakable break between vv. 18 and 19, and the meaning of the triumph song in vv. 28-30, which does not immediately follow v. 18, are relativized if insufficient justice is done to vv. 19-27 as a counterthrust to vv. 18 and 28ff.

In that case one would also easily disregard the total structure, which is governed by the concentric constructions in vv. 19-22, 23-25, and 26-27, and which demonstrates clear introductions and a material climax (Zahn; J. Schneider, *TDNT,* VII, 601f.; Balz, *Heilsvertrauen*, 33f.). οἴδαμεν in v. 28 indicates a new start and vv. 28-30 are distinguished from v. 31 by their hymnic style. Verses 20f. and 24f. cannot then be regarded as parentheses, and v. 23 is not the conclusion of a first part to which vv. 25f. are added (*contra* Vögtle, *Zukunft*, 196f., 199, 202). Nor is v. 24 a résumé followed by development (Cambier, "L'espérance," 77), and creation and Christians are not divided into two sections (Luz, *Geschichtsverständnis*, 377ff.; cf. Balz, *Heilsvertrauen*, 34). This oversimplifies the train of thought and fails to appreciate the rhetorical skill of the whole. At least the transition from v. 22 to v. 23 does not allow us to find throughout the schema of statement, proof, and summary (*contra* Balz, *Heilsvertrauen*, 33f.).

In a typically Pauline paradox (cf. 2 Cor 4:10-13) the sequence of suffering and glorification with Christ (v. 17c) is set in the mode of contemporaneity (*contra* Cambier, "L'espérance," 8f.). In adoption and reversal of the first beatitude those who are already set in the state of sonship, and who anticipate heavenly glory therein, are also those who wait and suffer, sharing the groaning of every creature.

Otherwise their stigma through the fate of Christ is not visible, as must happen according to vv. 17c and 28-30. Grace relates us more deeply to the earthly because it thrusts the community as a whole and each of its members beneath the cross where extreme assault and victory coincide. In opposition to the enthusiasts Paul had to go back to Jewish apocalyptic to present it thus. The widespread dislike for this tradition is a chief obstacle in interpreting the text, since avoiding Scylla inevitably means being caught on Charybdis. The Gentile-Christian enthusiasm of a radically realized eschatology has finally gained the upper hand in church orthodoxy too, and in so doing has obscured the theology of the cross.

Verse 18 is not just introductory and transitional (*contra* Lagrange; Gaugler), but the theme. It opens heavily with λογίζομαι, which expresses a firm judgment (Gaugler; Murray; Cambier, "L'espérance," 84) and not just a conviction (Gutjahr; Bardenhewer). ἄξια . . . πρός links up with rabbinic school language (Billerbeck; Rössler, *Gesetz*, 88ff.; Balz, *Heilsvertrauen*, 95ff.); it occurs especially in discussions of the problem of the sufferings of the pious. ἄξιος means "of equal weight" (Foerster, *TDNT*, I, 379), then "of value," and in acclamations "worthy." πρός means "with regard to." ὁ νῦν καιρός is not just the earthly present but also not the evil αἰὼν οὗτος nor to be equated with the age of salvation of 3:21. The phrase remains peculiarly ambivalent, which is explained by the prepositional link that follows. It involves the moment of destiny which precedes the revelation of future glory, with the brevity of παραυτίκα τῆς θλίψεως in 2 Cor 4:17. The construction makes the aorist infinitive dependent on μέλλουσα. This is not unusual according to Gal 3:23; 1 Pet 5:1 (BDF, §474 [5]), but it seems here to indicate the immediate proximity of the awaited event (BAGD, 501a). What is in view is the parousia. This characterizes the moment according to the verb συνωδίνειν in v. 22 as the time of the messianic woes (Bruce; Kirk; Michel; Vögtle, *Zukunft*, 191f., 198, 206; Gerber, "Problem," 61; Balz, *Heilsvertrauen*, 52; Schlier, "Worauf," 600, 606; *TDNT*, III, 145). This concept of Jewish apocalyptic is broadly developed in Mark 13:5ff. but also has a pagan parallel in the Fourth Eclogue of Virgil (Hommel, "Harren," 19f.). Paul offers a variation to the extent that in him it does not precede the coming of the Messiah but characterizes the period between the first coming and the second. Therefore it unites cosmic and Christian suffering, with the Spirit helping the embattled witnesses. In Gal 4:19 it relates to the apostolic ministry which effects the formation of the new creature. When all this is added up, v. 18 is not just speaking of assurance of salvation in face of the enduring afflictions, which are unavoidable in discipleship to Christ, and these afflictions are in no way minimized (*contra* Vögtle, *Zukunft*, 208). The reverse is the case, as with Abraham in 4:19. Nevertheless, although sufferings are taken seriously, they hardly count (cf. 2 Cor 4:17), since their end is near. Imminent expectation comes to expression here. This provides a transition to vv. 19-22.

In general, exposition of these verses has concentrated on the question what is meant by κτίσις (cf. Gerber, "Problem," 64ff.). Obviously the intensification in v. 23 contrasts it with Christians. A passionate plea has been made for the world of mankind (Schlatter; Pallis; Grundmann, "Übermacht," 60f.) and support has been sought in the personifying verbs in the context. In fact cosmos is usually understood in this sense by Paul, and it seems absurd to oppose to this view rich speculations about plants, animals, or even spiritual powers (cf. the survey in K. A. Bauer, *Leiblichkeit,* 171f.). There can be no doubt that non-Christians are included (Vögtle, *Zukunft,* 184ff.). Hence it is a mistake to speak of "irrational creation" (e.g., Bardenhewer), and even the word "nature" can hardly be used so self-evidently as modern man might think. Nature plays a very small role for the apostle. He lays the whole stress on creation as a historical phenomenon, so that the universe is regarded as the setting of human history (Dahl, *Volk Gottes,* 250f.; Schlier, "Worauf," 601). All the same, the main emphasis today is rightly put on non-human creation (cf. the survey in Kuss), and the phrase πᾶσα ἡ κτίσις in v. 22 supports this. The contrast with vv. 23ff. achieves added sharpness in this manner.

In this regard Paul is grounded in a solid tradition which may be traced already in the OT (Billerbeck; Lietzmann; Balz, *Heilsvertrauen,* 42ff.). A few examples will show how strongly this tradition set the fall and redemption of man against a cosmic background. In 4 Ezra 7:11ff. we read: "And when Adam transgressed my statutes, what had been made was judged. And so the entrances of this world were made narrow and sorrowful and toilsome." 2 *Apoc. Bar.* 15:7f. reads: "In so far as thou hast said of the righteous that this world came into being for their sake, so again will the future world come for their sake." To this corresponds the saying which is attributed to R. Shemuel (260), according to *Gen. Rab.* 12:6: "Although things were created in their fulness, when the first man sinned they were corrupted, and they will not come back to their order before Ben Perez (the Messiah) comes." Hence one cannot speak of the obscure words of our text (*contra* Jülicher; Bultmann, *Theology,* I, 230; cf. Gerber, "Problem," 62f.). Mankind for the apostle represents the world, but is also the world's exponent. Life always has a cosmic dimension, since it is always integrated in creation. In the light of v. 22 κτίσις is all creation including mankind, with no sharp line of differentiation. As in Jewish apocalyptic, historical destiny counts for more than nature as such. A difference is that there is no express reference to the participation of creation in the fall nor directly to a general redemption. The uniqueness of the passage is not sufficiently brought out if one too hastily introduces the opposite (correctly Vögtle, *Zukunft,* 187ff., 194). Creation in vv. 19f. is not the object of a revelation of promise. It becomes so only in v. 21, although even there Paul speaks very reservedly only of participation in eschatological freedom, not of a new heaven and a new earth. According to v. 20 creation has to suffer the consequences of man's fall. Hence it is wrong to deny any reference to primal history in our verses or to find only a prophecy of the eschatological Christ event (*contra* H. W. Schmidt). On the other hand the verses do not proclaim an eschatologically restored rule of the world by Christians (*contra* Leenhardt). Only on the basis of these delimitations can one see the decisive point of the argument.

Paul certainly does not presuppose Gnostic mythology (*contra* Bultmann, *Theology,* I, 174, 177f.) but the tradition of Jewish apocalyptic with its idea of the loss of the divine image in the fall into sin. Hence 3:23; 5:2, 12ff. come into the picture again. Paul, too, expects a restoration in eschatological glory, to which 4:25 and 6:4ff. point, along with the combination of justification, new creation, and resurrection in 4:17ff. He sets both against the background of the indissoluble interrelation of mankind and world (Gibbs, *Creation,* 40f.). Nevertheless the picture usually given in Jewish apocalyptic is missing. Everything focuses sharply

233

on the center, which is designated by the word "freedom" (Balz, *Heilsvertrauen*, 49f.). The whole context serves this interest, and it is no accident that the emphatic genitive construction at the end of v. 21 crowns the argument.

It makes no difference whether τῆς δόξης in Semitic fashion represents an adjective or is a narrower independent description. Materially ἐλευθερία and δόξα coincide, so that the latter should not be referred to God's absolute transcendence (*contra* Schlier, "Worauf," 600, though cf. 604ff.; Gerber, "Problem," 72f.). Eschatological glory is perfected freedom and this in turn is the content of the [eschatological glorification of the children of God. This is pressed to the point where it represents the true revelation of the parousia.

Comparison with 1 Cor 15:24ff. shows how unusual such a reduction is within the general framework of Paul's eschatology. Christians certainly look forward to their salvation at the parousia, since this is the consummation of their being "with Christ." Yet nowhere else is the parousia seen from an exclusively anthropological angle, namely, as the manifestation of the children of God (Vögtle, *Zukunft*, 187ff.; Schweizer, *TDNT*, VIII, 399). At most one can recall only the OT view of the new Zion to which the nations make pilgrimage, or the depiction of the procession of believers into the eternal *basileia* in 2 Pet 1:11. Both cases, however, lack the decisive catchword of freedom as the true epiphany of the last day, although the concept is present in the background.

A provisional summary is now in place. The sufferings of the messianic age, whose difficulties are recognized, count for little in Paul's eyes, since he stands in the imminent expectation of eschatological freedom and anticipates the glory of this freedom in divine sonship. The sequence of v. 17c is retained, as is also the eschatological restraint of the futures of 6:4ff. Only Christ is exalted. Disciples are still stigmatized by his cross and must occupy the place on earth which he has left. Suffering, however, is so permeated by the assurance of imminent salvation that the sequence of v. 17c dialectically becomes simultaneity, corresponding to 2 Cor 3:18; 4:16. By allowing Christians to suffer with Christ, the Spirit brings about the transforming of the old creation into an expectancy of glorification and an initial participation in this. Hope, then, reaches beyond believers to creation as a whole. For since Adam's fall the world lacks nothing more than eschatological freedom, which alone means salvation for it too. Since Paul understands eschatological freedom as salvation in a cosmic dimension, he here singularly describes the event of the parousia from the standpoint of anthropology. He could not say that the world was on the way to Christ even though he regarded Christ as the designated cosmocrator and oriented world history to him. He was concerned to show, however, that within the world, in remarkable connection with ecstatic events during Christian worship, and by contrast in the community which suffers with Christ, eschatological freedom as salvation for all creation appears in outline. Hence Christianity, which witnesses to sonship and in the fellowship of suffering points to Christ as the coming Lord of the world, seemed to him to be the great promise for all creation even beyond the human sphere. This is not to be regarded as mere exhortation after the manner of Calvin. For all the mythical form of expression it brings, it concerns here the core of the Pauline message. This is what necessarily made him a world missionary. In these verses the justification of the ungodly appears in a new cosmological variation as salvation for the fallen and groaning world (Siber, *Mit Christus,* 150ff. with an anthropological emphasis).

The mythical features in the message should not be overlooked. Nor should one fail to see how close it comes to the modern view of the profound alienation of the world. Demythologizing should be on guard at least against using the yardstick of the nineteenth century, and present experience should be taken no less seriously than that of the Enlightenment. Paul has more to say to us than the theological guild is largely prepared to accept even when he makes use of ancient mythology. The very wording of the following verses differs from what we normally find. The catchword ἀποκαραδοκία, found elsewhere only in Phil 1:20, is taken up in ἀπεκδέχεσθαι (Delling, *TDNT,* I, 393; Grundmann, *TDNT,* II, 56) and according to the prior interpretation has less the sense of uncertain expectation than that of wistful and impetuous desire in a state of anxiety (Schlier, "Worauf," 601f.). The verb denotes impatient straining for a glimmer of hope. Paul was neither a Stoic nor a Gnostic. Hence he came to terms with existing relationships in the world neither with resignation nor contempt. He passionately wanted a new world. Yet he did not lose himself in illusions about the future. He kept earthly reality firmly in view, faithful to the hoping against hope which he had portrayed in 4:17ff. (using Abraham as an example) as persistence in the promise. ἀποκαραδοκία does not accept the earthly status quo and whether it knows and wills it or not is in quest of eschatological freedom. This cannot be otherwise if God holds fast his creation. The status quo of fallen creation is ματαιότης, which 1:21 spoke of already as the result of human guilt, and which the verb characterizes here as an enduring fate. It is not precise and is usually construed as spiritual emptiness (Bauernfeind, *TDNT,* IV, 523; Delling, *TDNT,* VIII, 41; Vögtle, *Zukunft,* 194, cf. Lyonnet, *Étapes,* 199f.; Cambier, "L'espérance," 87f.). It misses existence and opts for illusions (Schlier, "Worauf," 603; Gerber, "Problem," 68). The verb, which has the specific sense of "to be subject," according to apocalyptic tradition refers to the consequences of the fall. Hence it is not at all unclear who the ὑποτάξας is (*contra* Bultmann, *Theology,* I, 230). The οὐχ ἑκοῦσα, which was later softened to οὐ θέλουσα, indicates that creation did not incur guilt for itself as mankind did, and the verb, as in 1 Cor 15:27ff., relates to the divine omnipotence. διά with the accusative does not exclusively refer to cause (*contra* Balz, *Heilsvertrauen,* 41) but to author (BAGD, 181b). Neither Satan (Pallis) nor Adam (Foerster, *TDNT,* III, 1031; Delling, *TDNT,* VIII, 41; Fuchs, *Freiheit,* 109; Lampe, "Doctrine," 458; Lyonnet, "Redemptio," 228) implicated the destiny of creation in the fall of mankind (Michel; Gaugler; cf. the survey in Vögtle, *Zukunft,* 194f.). Apart from its own action God subjected it to futility along with mankind (the usual view). Bondage to decay, the rule of death, is not merely its result (Ridderbos; Cambier, "L'espérance," 88) but its reality (Harder, *TDNT,* IX, 104). We have here a backward glance at the παρέδωκεν of 1:24 and also at the depiction in 5:12ff. The aorist of the verb refers to the actual curse, not to a judicial decision (*contra* Michel; Gaugler). It concerns the handing over to the power of the curse immanently at work.

The difference from 1:24; 5:12ff. comes out (Hill, "Construction," 297 views the first prepositional expression as a parenthesis!) in the loosely attached ἐφ' ἐλπίδι (cf. on the rough breathing BDF, §14), which obviously interprets the ἀποκαραδοκία of v. 19 in Christian terms. What 7:21ff. says of the νοῦς and the ἔσω ἄνθρωπος and what is expressed in 7:24 as the cry of the enslaved person, now applies to creation as a whole. By looking for liberation from the forces which rule it, for a Christian understanding it manifests the hope in the midst of hopelessness which makes sense only to faith. This is not a mythological extension of 7:14ff. but its cosmic basis. Unredeemed mankind is spokesman for his world. Hence the text is not in any way extravagant. It stands in a context which elucidates it. The only new point in the passage is that, corresponding to the doctrine of the justification of the ungodly, it links the promise of salvation with a description of the most extreme ruin and boldly finds the basis of hope in the groaning of enslaved creation. But this is anchored in the will of the Creator (Schlier, "Worauf," 604).

Anticipated here in a different way is the summation drawn in 11:32, namely, that all are held under disobedience in order that mercy may be shown to all. Where things behave that way the liberation of the children of God is the answer to the cry of the unredeemed, namely, the dawn and actualization of the new world. This is the glory of the Christian state which is at present still hidden in suffering with Christ. The world makes sense as creation only if it is oriented constitutively to Christian liberty, which is not to be equated with autonomy (*contra* Rengstorf, *TDNT*, II, 278). This is to be seen as the pledge also of its participation in eschatological liberation. If Marcion was forced by the inner logic of his theology to cut out vv. 18-22, he is followed today by an existentialism which individualizes salvation and thereby truncates Paul's message by describing freedom formally as openness to the future. In fact it is a term for the earthly reality of Christ's lordship (Schlier, "Worauf," 604). The truth in the existential interpretation is that it recognizes in pride and despair the powers which most deeply enslave mankind. Its theological reduction derives from a world view which no longer knows what to do with Pauline apocalyptic, allows anthropological historicity to conceal the world's history, obscures the antithesis of the aeons of 1:20ff. by natural theology and here through the assertion of mythology, and for this reason can no longer speak adequately of the dominion of Christ in its worldwide dimension.

Verse 22 resumes with an introductory οἴδαμεν, which is spoken of faith (Schlier, "Worauf," 606). Verse 20 established that στενάζειν, the catchword also of the next subsection, replaces the earlier term of expectation. The compounds of the verbs do not relate to the attitude of Christians (*contra* H. W. Schmidt), previously unmentioned. Theodore of Mopsuestia saw already that they replace a συμφώνως. The chorus from the depths fills the whole world. συνωδίνει, obviously corrected to ὀδυνεῖ ("lament"), in obvious assimilation to συστενάζει, occurs also with the first verb in 4 Ezra 10:7ff. (Luz, *Geschichtsverständnis,* 378), although in a different sense. συνωδίνειν makes the sighing concrete in the light of the messianic woes so impressively described in 1QH 3:7ff. (Black; Bertram, *TDNT,* IX, 668ff.). ἄχρι τοῦ νῦν, on which the accent falls (Vögtle, *Zukunft,* 198), is, then, more than chronological dating (*contra* Lagrange). It takes up the ὁ νῦν καιρός of v. 18. What is meant is the eschatological moment (Stählin, *TDNT,* IV, 1110; Balz, *Heilsvertrauen,* 52) which precedes the parousia, i.e., the end seen in Rev 21:4 when sorrow, crying, and pain will cease with the first creation.

In a new section vv. 23-25 see in this also the consummation for believers of v. 21. The heightening of the argument may be seen in the introductory οὐ μόνον δέ, ἀλλά. The sentence construction would be easier if one could excise the doublet καὶ αὐτοί with P⁴⁶ (Debrunner, "Lesarten"). It is so well attested in so many variations, however, and is so strongly supported by the material paradox in the statement, that the elimination is to be regarded as a correction for the sake of clarity (Lietzmann). The repetition is originally stressed both in ℵ A C and, in a stylistic smoothing, in K L P by ἡμεῖς. The participial phrase at the beginning has a concessive, not a causal sense, and states thematically the paradoxical nature of the Christian state set forth in v. 18.

In detail the verse offers further difficulties. ἀπαρχή, synonymous with ἀρραβών in 2 Cor 1:22; 5:5, can hardly come from the sacrificial vocabulary of the OT (contra Michel). The rare meaning "birth-certificate" (cf. Balz, Heilsvertrauen, 56) is most improbable. The reference is to a deposit on a purchase. The genitive is not (contra Sanday and Headlam; Lietzmann; Murray; Delling, TDNT, I, 486; Larsson, Vorbild, 293) partitive but epexegetical (the common view). Christians do not sigh because they do not yet have the Spirit totally but in spite of the fact that they have him, and the repetition "even we ourselves" brings this out. We are thus to avoid an interpretation which relates ἐν ἑαυτοῖς to the inner life and thus brings back the element of imperfection (contra Bardenhewer; Althaus; Leenhardt; H. W. Schmidt). In context the groaning even affects worship and thus involves the whole of existence. ἐν ἑαυτοῖς could mean "in view of us" (Vögtle, Zukunft, 202), but "with" or "among us" is more likely. If later readings omit υἱοθεσίαν, this is not to be taken as original (contra Grundmann, "Übermacht," 61; Benoit, "Nous gémissons," 41ff., cf. Swetnam, "Expectation," 103ff.). Tendency criticism avoids apparent contradiction to vv. 14ff. and smooths the lectio difficilior (more difficult reading). Thus there is no real contradiction, since Paul never regards the gift of salvation as an undisputed possession. He always characterizes it dialectically as now present and now future in order to balance its reality with its vulnerability on earth. Sonship will be unassailable and complete only in the ἀπολύτρωσις τοῦ σώματος.

This is undoubtedly a variant on the motif of the future revelation of glorious freedom, and it also takes up the idea of the waiting of creation for liberation from decay. In the earthly body we are constantly exposed to the grasp of bondage. Hence even in its wording the phrase is open to misunderstanding. The debate whether we have an objective genitive or a genitive of separation (e.g., Jervell, Imago, 279) is unnecessary. Redemption naturally takes place ultimately when the earthly body is put off, but it also involves the conferring of new corporeality. The idea of immortality (Baulès) or the resurrection of the flesh (Sickenberger) is non-Pauline. The apostle passionately longs for the liberation of existence from temptation and decay in favor of a mode of being in a world that belongs to God alone. This is the object of the groanings of Christians as they wait for the parousia (Schlier, "Worauf," 608). In the light of this the recollection, which is not to be thrust aside, that ἀπολύτρωσις means concretely the redeeming of slaves is absurd here.

Paul does not let assaulted faith be the final word of Christian proclamation. In face of enthusiasm his theology of the cross pays due tribute to earthly reality and places us in the discipleship of the suffering Christ. Simultaneously, however, just because he knows the stress and severity of the struggle, he has an ardent longing for God's complete victory over the forces of the cosmos. For him the resurrection of the dead was no mere symbol of openness to the future but the end of earthly pain. Hence the gospel for him was more than ideology; it was promise. Under it he knew that he was in solidarity with unredeemed creation as it cried out for perfect freedom. Verse 24 supports and confirms this by now depicting faith with the strongest emphasis as hope.

The first sentence seems to run contrary to any realized eschatology. In particular, exposition of τῇ ἐλπίδι has always been a problem (Schelkle, *Paulus*, 305; Cambier, "L'espérance," 78f.). An instrumental sense (Schlatter) is ruled out, since the aorist of the verb can point only to the Christ event mediated in baptism. A dative of advantage (Kühl) would be possible only if one were to find here a correspondence to the ἐφ' ἐλπίδι of v. 20 (Lietzmann; Gaugler, but cf. Schlier, "Worauf," 609). It is completely non-Pauline that deliverance should simply lead to hope, as a dative of advantage would say if taken seriously. To be sure, the context does not completely exclude the idea that deliverance brings assured hope. But this would make it merely a preliminary stage of total salvation, which again is hardly reconcilable with the apostle's theology. Hence the most common assumption that we have a modal dative is the simplest and most probable. Hope is the situation in which we live as those who are saved (cf. also 12:12).

Putting the dative first and linking it to the aorist verb provides a pointed attack on enthusiasm. Certainly the longing of creation is given its interpretation by Christian hope. Conversely, Christians with their assurance of salvation are not at all in the sphere of sight according to 2 Cor 4:18; 5:7 (Bultmann, *TDNT*, II, 530f.; VI, 221), and they are not even set in a process of development (*contra* Cambier, "L'espérance," 96f.). Paradoxically they share the ἀποκαραδοκία of creation even to the point of groaning at corruptibility. As bearers of the Spirit they do not transcend the earthly. In the time of the messianic woes their participation in heavenly glory takes the form of ταπεινοφροσύνη. Saved because Christ brought salvation, they are so only in the hope that through the Spirit salvation will constantly be imparted to them afresh from Christ. They are saved as they can stand outside themselves before God through Christ. This does not involve self-actualization, but remaining under the word. In a sentence which appeals to the rationality of the readers, and which both presupposes and transcends the Greek meaning of ἐλπίς as uncertain expectation, the nature of Christian hope is defined in v. 24b-c (Michel; Vögtle, *Zukunft*, 204). It is not clear whether the mood of βλεπομένη is passive or middle, i.e., whether the reference is to what is hoped for (as most expositors see it) or to the act of hope, as the preceding and following clauses suggest. In content it makes little difference, since in both cases the point is that we do not yet see. Assurance of salvation is not salvation secured. Faith always remains hope, even when earth seems to offer no hope.

Like v. 23, the succeeding clause raises textual problems. Important readings surprisingly have ὑπομένει as the verb. This might be assimilation to δι' ὑπομονῆς in v. 25b, although this phrase is some distance away. The verbs merge into one another in the LXX (Spanneut, *RAC,* IX, 255). On the other hand, emendation

238

of an original and unexpected ὑπομένει to ἐλπίζει is so natural in the context that the principle of the more difficult reading is against an original ἐλπίζει (Lietzmann; Gaugler; Debrunner, "Lesarten," 35f.; Cambier, "L'espérance," 101ff.; in opposition most others, cf. Balz, *Heilsvertrauen*, 61). If one decides for ὑπομένει the variant τις, τί καί in A *et al.* is the clearest. For the sake of the surprising verb τί καί is used in an intensifying way, and for the sake of contrast a subject is explicitly named in the first clause. In the contrast of βλέπειν and ἐλπίζειν these clarifications are not needed, so that P⁴⁶ simply presents the schema and the other readings indicate the uncertainty of the tradition or the concern of copyists for clarity. ὑπομένει is to be preferred because it advances the thought and prepares the way for v. 25b. Hope which does not see implies steadfast waiting. The groaning of Christians for final redemption and their solidarity with unredeemed creation (Cambier, "L'espérance," 105ff.) are more understandable in this way.

Verse 25 again draws the conclusion. δι' ὑπομονῆς names the accompanying circumstance (Murray; Balz, *Heilsvertrauen*, 68). ἀπεκδέχεσθαι takes up the keyword of vv. 19 and 23. Hope is separated from sight of the heavenly by patience, which is still directed away from the earthly to its goal. Paul argues in this way because for him the goal is the overcoming of temptation in bodily resurrection. He does it polemically in the face of the self-elevation of the pneumatics, who no longer see that their place is beneath the cross. He thus creates room for love and service not just in the community but also to tormented creation. If disciples are no longer on the road they have no more to say and give either to themselves or the world. They can thus be regarded only as the champions of one ideology among others. Those who groan with creation, and this not merely in fervent prayer (Pallis; Herrmann, *TDNT*, II, 786), are truly potential and called instruments of the Spirit.

The third subsection in vv. 26-27 brings the paradox to its climax. It has no parallels in the NT and is an alien body even in Paul (Niederwimmer, "Gebet," 252). Hence misinterpretation abounds. An initial error is to take as a starting point the experience of difficulty in prayer, widespread both in antiquity and today, and to draw Paul into this (Harder, *Gebet*, 130ff., 138ff., 161f.; Ridderbos). There are hardly any traces of this problem in the NT. Thus the point of the text also is not correct prayer, for which an introduction has to be provided. The most important statement is completely unfamiliar for primitive Christianity, namely, that we do not know what we should pray for. Earnest prayer was in fact offered everywhere, and the Lord's Prayer must have been generally known and embedded in worship as handed down in liturgical formulae. Many forms of petition, intercession, thanksgiving, praise, hymnic adoration, and prayers in glossolalia contradict the idea that a problem of the early church is discussed in this passage.

Understandably the statement has often been weakened for this reason (cf. the survey in Niederwimmer, "Gebet," 257ff.). If the parallelism with κατὰ θεόν in v. 27 is not heeded, καθὸ δεῖ is taken with οἴδαμεν (Zahn; Kühl) and translated: We do not know in the required measure what we should pray for. Others shift the emphasis from τί to an interpolated πῶς (Kühl; Lagrange; Sanday and Headlam; factually Michel; Schlier, "Worauf," 610), as though it were a matter of the correct technique of prayer, not the subject-matter. A common solution is that

Paul has in view exceptional circumstances in the situations also experienced by him (Jülicher; Gutjahr; Althaus; Asmussen; Brunner; Murray; H. W. Schmidt). An earlier aid to interpretation was to raise the question of the hearing of prayer (Luther; Calvin). Today the whole concept is radicalized with the assertion that a person has no understanding at all of true prayer (Gaugler; J. Knox, Life, 107; Niederwimmer, "Gebet," 255ff.) or with the general claim that prayer is the proper work of the Spirit (Schweizer, TDNT, VI, 430f.), which as such is unfathomable. A presupposition of all these theories is that ἀσθένεια in v. 26a denotes inner inability (Sanday and Headlam; Schlatter; H. W. Schmidt), imperfection (Dodd), or weakness in prayer (Nygren). In fact, however, Paul is not referring   [here to a psychological or moral circumstance, but to the external temptations (Anfechtung) of Christian existence. The interest of exegetes usually shifts from v. 26a to the continuation of the verse and the passage is cut off from its context or treated as an appendix to vv. 23-25 (Vögtle, Zukunft, 192, 202). But the argument advances the farthest here, as is shown by ὡσαύτως, which is not comparative (Asmussen) but conclusive (cf. Mark 14:31; 1 Tim 5:25) (Balz, Heilsvertrauen, 69). Primarily it is not a matter of what we can or cannot do but of the work of the Spirit, and he does not take over a share of the work (Zahn) but comes with divine power to the aid of those who are assaulted on earth.

This is made precise by the rare second verb ὑπερεντυγχάνειν, which as in 8:34; Heb 7:25 denotes intercession (Schniewind, "Seufzen," 83, 92; Barrett; Kirk; Murray; Franzmann; Sickenberger; Balz, Heilsvertrauen, 75f.). The motif of the intercessor is widespread, and in Judaism many figures discharge the function (cf. Balz, 83ff.; Behm, TDNT, V, 810f.: already the Spirit!). In the NT the office is reserved for Christ except in this text, since the Paraclete of John's Gospel has a different task (Niederwimmer, "Gebet," 261). With the intercession of the Spirit, then, there has to be some special circumstance, particularly as it takes place, in distinction from that of the exalted Christ, in στεναγμοῖς ἀλαλήτοις. Modern interpretation relates this in edifying fashion to wordless sighs (Sanday and Headlam; Schlatter; Dodd; Nygren; Asmussen; Greeven, Gebet, 153; Schlier, "Worauf," 611; Taylor, but cf. Ridderbos; Balz, Heilsvertrauen, 81). In primitive Christianity, however, there can be no question of this (Schniewind, "Seufzen," 86; Gaugler, 71f., 74). Instead it can only be a matter of ecstatic cries (Gaugler; Murray; Kirk). In 1 Cor 14:15 the apostle expressly mentions praying in the Spirit during worship and this phenomenon, not attested in the rabbis but presupposed in the Qumran Hodayoth (cf. Billerbeck and Dietzel, "Beten," 24ff.), is confirmed by Eph 6:18; Jude 20; Rev 22:17. Naturally there is also private ecstasy. But the sighs mentioned here are regarded as visible manifestations of the Spirit and they are associated with the legal act of the Spirit's intercession which takes place in them. This is meaningful only in liturgical processes (Zahn; Althaus; Fuchs, Freiheit, 112; Balz, Heilsvertrauen, 91, though cf. in opposition Gutjahr; Bardenhewer; Leenhardt; Michel; Murray; Delling, Worship, 23). Broad deductions have already been drawn from this type of ecstatic crying in the Spirit in v. 15, and here as in v. 16 the formula αὐτὸ τὸ πνεῦμα is used, which designates the Spirit acting objectively in the congregation as distinct from the Spirit in the individual.

The meaning of v. 26b is now clear. The apostle is not dealing with the problem and technique of prayer nor is he speaking primarily of infused mystical prayer (*contra* Lietzmann; Dodd). He is speaking with reference to certain practices in congregational life which are open to misunderstanding and have in fact been misunderstood (Gaugler, "Geist," 67, 70ff., 76), namely, inexpressible sighings. These can hardly be acclamations as in v. 15, for they are thoroughly understandable. It makes good sense, however, if what is at issue is the praying in tongues of 1 Cor 14:15 (Zahn; Althaus; N. Q. Hamilton, *The Holy Spirit and Eschatology in Paul* [1957] 36; Cullmann, *Salvation,* 256; Balz, *Heilsvertrauen,* 79f.; possible Delling, *TDNT,* I, 376; Harder, *Gebet,* 169f.; unlikely Barrett; rejected by Sickenberger; Huby; Schlatter; Gaugler; Michel; Greeven, *Gebet,* 155).

The objection that tongues is an individual and not a congregational affair (Schlatter; Gaugler; Leenhardt) is not convincing. For in 1 Cor 14 praying in tongues represents worship as a whole. As there, Paul accepts it as heavenly speech and an expression of the eschatological event. At most one has to ask why he speaks of στεναγμοὶ ἀλάλητοι instead of praying in the Spirit. We learn the answer from 2 Cor 12:4. In his rapture Paul heard ἄρρητα ῥήματα, which in context cannot mean "wordless" but only "inexpressible in earthly language." Paul was counted worthy to hear angelic speech and he could not reproduce it. The reason why the Corinthians prized tongues above all other gifts was that they viewed it as the language of angels (1 Cor 13:1), and it thus demonstrated the participation of pneumatics in heavenly being. The apostle has to take issue with this notion, and he does this by finding a different meaning in glossolalia at worship from that espoused by the Corinthians. Since he glories in his own gift of tongues in 1 Cor 14:18 he does not deny that the Spirit expresses himself in heavenly speech, and he sees in this a sign of the end-time in which the prophecies of Isa 28:11f. and Deut 28:49 come to fulfillment.

To characterize glossolalia in this way he speaks of "inexpressible sighs" in the present passage. Heavenly speech can be heard in worship as a work of the Spirit. But what enthusiasts regard as proof of their glorification he sees as sign of a lack. Praying in tongues reveals, not the power and wealth of the Christian community, but its ἀσθένεια. The Spirit himself has to intervene if our prayers are to have a content which is pleasing to God. He does so in such a way that even in worship he brings us to that groaning of which the unredeemed creation is full and which speaks out of the longing of the assaulted for the redemption of the body. In tongues at worship there sounds forth in a singular way, and in such a manner that we do not ourselves comprehend the concern of the Spirit who drives us to prayer, the cry for eschatological freedom in which Christians represent the whole of afflicted creation. In this the Spirit manifests himself as the intercessor of the community before God and he takes it up into his intercession. By its ecstatic cries prayer is made for the whole of enslaved and oppressed creation. The intercession of the exalted Christ takes place at the right hand of God. The Spirit, however, is the earthly presence of the exalted Lord and does his work, intercession included, in the sphere and through the ministry of the community. If this intercession is regarded as possible only in the heavenly world (Michel; J. Schneider, *TDNT,* VII, 602; Zorn, *Fürbitte,* 117), the point is missed that the reference here is to the intercession of the Spirit and that this coincides with the cries of those who speak in tongues. This makes sense, however, if it is

241

the earthly reflection of what the heavenly High Priest does before the throne of God.

Verse 27 draws the conclusion. In the tradition of the OT and Judaism God is here regarded as the one who knows the heart (Balz, *Heilsvertrauen*, 81). He sees through human beings and even grasps what they are not able to recognize on their own. He thus understands the φϱόνημα of the Spirit manifested in the unintelligible cries of ecstatics. The ὅτι clause (*contra* Sanday and Headlam; Gaugler, "Geist," 90; Balz, *Heilsvertrauen*, 80f.) is not explicative but causal (the accepted view). Otherwise the content of φϱόνημα, namely, the cry for freedom, would have to be indicated. Instead the first clause is given a basis in the fact [. that the Spirit really comes before God in intercession and prays according to his will (Gaugler, "Geist," 75 can hardly be right: after the manner of God). He does this for that community which is here given the primitive Christian self-designation "the saints," a designation merited by the fact that it is ruled by the Spirit.

The climax of the argument is thus reached. Three times in the course of it the glory of the children of God has been paradoxically linked to their vulnerability. This glory is so great that all creation waits for its approaching and definitive revelation. In Christian life it is hidden under its opposite, namely, in assaulted faith as hope which is steadfast and certain of salvation. It finally expresses itself in ecstatic practices at worship, in such a way that not even the community itself knows its true meaning and is represented by the Spirit.

Since eschatological freedom is always at issue, the parts are constructed concentrically. As bearer and heir of the promise the Christian community is the inbreaking of the new creation and the representative of all creatures. It is this, however, in the sense of the first beatitude, in solidarity with the host of those who wait, suffer, and groan, who are not yet redeemed, in short, who hope. This has to be so because in the present time this community still stands in the shadow of the cross, showing itself thereby to be the community of him who is distinguished from all other lords by the cross.

The Spirit as the power of the exalted Lord manifested on earth sets it in this place. Only there is it truly "with Christ" and "in Christ," since there the destiny of Jesus is accepted by it and he is visibly confessed as Lord. It also stands, then, in solidarity with creation, which God has not abandoned but from which enthusiasts, for the sake of their own salvation, break away in denial of the Crucified. Enthusiasts are thus called back from the imaginary heaven of a radical realized eschatology to the messianic woes which still govern even Christian worship. When it is a matter of the justification of the ungodly, God does not just want a new religiosity but a renewed creation under the cosmocrator Christ. True theology, then, cannot be a theology of glory. It has to remain a pilgrim theology under the message of the gospel as a promise for the whole world—a theology of hope. If eschatological freedom is its content, only the resurrection of the dead can fully work this out. The new obedience and liturgical events symbolically indicate this future. Faith is no longer faith if it ceases to be patience, to make possible love, to be the basis of hope, to draw us into deeper solidarity with all creation instead of elevating us above it. The constitutively cosmic rather than purely individual dimension of the justification of the ungodly has to achieve liturgical visibility in worship (Schniewind, "Seufzen," 91ff.; Eichholz, *Paulus*, 278).

With v. 27 the countermovement begun in v. 19 comes to an end. οἴδαμεν in v. 28, which reproduces the experience of faith (Grayston, "Election," 575f.), clearly marks a break and returns to the starting point in v. 18. The sufferings of the present time cannot be denied. If in v. 18 it was said that they could not be compared with the future glory, such a statement is now surpassed. Everything, included the sufferings named, must work out for good to believers. The climax thus continues, reaching a new high point in vv. 29f. Verse 28 takes the form of a doctrinal statement (Michel; J. B. Bauer, "Rm 8, 28," 106) and falls back on a common axiom of antiquity (BAGD, 787b; Billerbeck; Lietzmann; Cranfield, "Romans 8.28," 212f.; J. B. Bauer, 106ff.). R. Akiba (*Ber.* 60b) taught: "One should accustom oneself to say that everything the mercy (of God) does, it does for good."

A decisive point is whether and how far the apostle is giving precision to this tradition or whether and how far he is departing from it. The strongly attested and widely accepted reading with ὁ θεός as subject (Kühl; Pallis; Dodd; Huby; Kirk; Barth; Bertram, *TDNT*, VII, 875; probable Gaugler; Schlier, "Worauf," 612) is probably an edifying emendation (Lietzmann; Michel; Ridderbos; for a full discussion Cranfield, "Romans 8.28," 206ff.). The reason for thinking that πάντα is a scribal error for an original πνεῦμα (Black, "Interpretation," 166ff., cf. Cranfield, 207; Balz, *Heilsvertrauen*, 103f.) probably lies only in fear of an ostensible synergism. συνεργεῖν, to which subject the πάντα relates, means "to work together" and perhaps has the specific Hellenistic sense "to be serviceable" (cf. *T. Iss.* 3:8; *T. Gad* 4:7; *T. Benj.* 4:5) (Cranfield, 211; J. B. Bauer, 107; Balz, 106). Also derived from the OT and Jewish tradition (cf. *Pss. Sol.* 4:25; 6:6; 10:3; 14:1) is the description of the pious as those who love God (cf. also 1 Cor 2:9; 8:3) (Cranfield, "Romans 8.28," 205; Larsson, *Vorbild*, 294; Balz, 104f.). In adopting the formula Paul parts company in some respects with the Jewish ideal of righteousness (J. B. Bauer, "Rm 8, 28," 108ff.). Characteristically he usually inverts it, speaking of God's love for us, not in an emotional sense, but in the sense of his "being for us." Here, then, the phrase is interpreted by the elucidating and causal (Ridderbos) apposition at the end along the lines of 1 Cor 8:3. A person can love God only if he is "known" by him in election.

This comes to expression in κατὰ πρόθεσιν κλητοί, which is not to be related only to the community (*contra* Huby). In Hellenism πρόθεσις is a public statement, an official decree. Here, as often in the Qumran literature, it means God's decree of salvation (Michel; Maurer, *TDNT*, VIII, 164ff.). Since difficulty is often found with the doctrine of predestination the apparent problem is raised (Luz, *Geschichtsverständnis*, 251f.) whether or not the reference is to a pre-temporal decree as in Eph 3:11; 2 Tim 1:9. According to vv. 29f. as explanatory of v. 28b (Balz, *Heilsvertrauen*, 102) an affirmative answer must be given as befits the Creator. But 1 Cor 1:18ff.; 2 Cor 2:15f. show that the saving decree encounters us in the word which summons us, and which appears here in the κλητοί.

Our remaining task is to examine what εἰς ἀγαθόν means. In the underlying tradition of antiquity it means the happy outcome of strange earthly events, and the use in Judaism is much the same (Billerbeck). In our context, as in 10:15, it can only designate eschatological salvation, although this certainly does not exclude present experience.

Verse 28 is thus made up of fragments of Jewish tradition which conform to the thinking of Paul only as they are assembled. Verse 18 is thereby varied, preparing the ground for vv. 29f. Earthly troubles are set in the shadow of God's saving decree, which in spite of them and through them achieves its goal in us (Dupont, *Gnosis,* 100f.), without for that reason speaking of a process of development (Sanday and Headlam). They form stages of our earthly path, on which light falls from the divine past and the divine future.

The careful rhetorical construction of the members, which are linked in a mounting chain, and a vocabulary not typical of the apostle indicate that we have here a traditional liturgical piece (Jervell, *Imago,* 272ff.; Cassien, "Fils," 38ff.). In content it seems to be a kind of confession (H. W. Schmidt). If, however, this term is reserved for Christ hymns, which do not have the chain-like form, and if [the emphasis here is on enumeration of the saving experiences of the community, it is best to see an affinity to texts like Eph 2:5. Verses 29b and 30b-f suggest a setting in life (*Sitz im Leben*) in the event of baptism. The conjunctions and the final clause in v. 29c might well be Pauline.

Differentiating between the first two verbs is difficult. They have been related earlier to foreknowledge and predestination (Bardenhewer; Gutjahr; Huby; Lagrange; Murray; not clear Gaugler). Paul, or the source he cites, offers a key to interpretation by relating the second verb to a statement of the goal (Michel; Schlier, "Worauf," 613), as happens also in Eph 1:5. προγινώσκειν refers to eternal election, which was already named in κατὰ πρόθεσιν in v. 28c. προορίζειν makes this more precise. Eternal election is also foreordination to fellowship with Christ in which God's saving decree becomes concrete. Passages like 1 Cor 15:49; 2 Cor 3:18; Col 1:18; Phil 3:10f. have seduced some to think in terms of the risen Christ and participation in his resurrection body as in Phil 3:21 (Sanday and Headlam; J. Knox; Lietzmann; Gutjahr; Huby; Gaugler; Larsson, *Vorbild,* 303f.; Schlier, "Worauf," 613). In this case, however, one would have to weaken συμμόρφους to relationship (Kürzinger, "Röm 8, 29," 296ff.; Thüsing, *Per Christum,* 121ff.). Against that it is to be objected that in the text Paul consistently establishes the present salvation by use of the aorist and he does not speak merely of the exalted Christ (Balz, *Heilsvertrauen,* 110ff.). In reality Christ as the manifestation of eschatological divine likeness is the divine image in the absolute, as in 2 Cor 4:4; Heb 1:3 (Jervell, *Imago,* 205, 287; Eltester, *Eikon,* 133ff.). He is thus the mediator of creation as in Col 1:15 and the prototype of every creature, which Philo calls ἀρχηγέτης νέας σπορᾶς (cf. Eltester, 34-42). We are made like him in the birth of which Gal 4:19 speaks in baptismal language and which leads to participation in his death according to Phil 3:10. The final clause states unmistakably that this takes place already in our earthly existence.

As in the hymn in Col 1:15ff. the predicate εἰκών is replaced with πρωτότοκος, which was used originally of Israel (Michaelis, "Vorstellung," 137ff.), then the Torah (parallel to *sophia*), Adam, and Jacob, and was rendered in Philo as the *logos* (Billerbeck; Eltester, *Eikon,* 34ff.), so that it could become a predicate of the Messiah. The reference is not simply to the self-evident relation to God (Michaelis, *TDNT,* VI, 877) but also to primacy in the fellowship of God's people, which explains the mention of the many brethren here. Elucidation may be found in Heb 2:11ff., where the Son creates sons and recognizes them as brothers. We obviously have here the established tradition of the eschatological Adam as the prototype of the sons of God, a tradition which fits in best with baptismal teaching (G. Schille, *Frühchristliche Hymnen* [1965] 89f.; Jervell, *Imago*, 275ff.; Luz, *Geschichtsverständnis*, 251ff.; Paulsen, *Überlieferung*, 159). This is supported by the surprising use of δικαιοῦν, which, as in the baptismal statement at 1 Cor 6:11, has in view the righteousness which characterizes the band of the consecrated in the Hellenistic community (cf. R. Reitzenstein, *Die Hellenistischen Mysterienreligionen* [3rd ed., 1927] 257ff.; Schlier, "Worauf," 614). Appropriate in this context is the aorist ἐδόξασεν, which has constantly confused exegetes in view of the fact that elsewhere Paul expects heavenly δόξα only at the parousia. In distinction from the preceding verbs, then, it has been regarded as anticipatory (Lietzmann; Kühl; Gutjahr; Lagrange; Bardenhewer; Leenhardt; Gaugler; Michel; Larsson, *Vorbild*, 306f.; Bultmann, *Theology*, I, 348f.; Thüsing, *Per Christum*, 123ff., 130). This is unnecessary, however, in an enthusiastic baptismal tradition such as we have in Eph 2:5f. This spoke of change into a heavenly nature (Kittel, *TDNT*, II, 396; Behm, *TDNT*, IV, 758f.; Eltester, *Eikon*, 24f., 165; Schwanz, *Imago Dei*, 18; Cassien, "Fils," 42; Balz, *Heilsvertrauen*, 113). In baptism the divine image which was lost according to 3:23 is restored by conformation to the Son. Although this statement seems to be in contradiction with his eschatological caution, Paul adopts it here, as in 2 Cor 3:18; 4:6, in order that in the context of vv. 19-27 he may paradoxically set forth the link between suffering with Christ and the glory of divine sonship. At the same time he makes the transition to the theme of victory which follows.

d. Being in the Spirit as the Reality of Victory (8:31-39)

[31]*What, then, are we to say to this? If God (is) for us, who (can be) against us?* [32]*He did not spare his own Son but gave him up for all. How, then, shall he not give us all things with him?* [33]*Who can raise any charge against God's elect? God justified.* [34]*Who will condemn? Christ Jesus, who died, indeed, who was raised again, is at the right hand of God, our intercessor.* [35]*Who shall separate us from the love of Christ? Affliction, distress, persecution, hunger, nakedness, peril, or sword?* [36]*It is written: "For thy sake we are killed all the day long, we are viewed as sheep for slaughter."* [37]*Nevertheless, in all these things we triumph in the power of him who loved us.* [38]*For I am fully certain that neither death nor life, neither angels nor principalities, neither present, nor future, nor powers,* [39]*neither height nor depth nor any other creature can separate us from the love of God in Christ Jesus our Lord.*

Bibliography: H. Schlier, "Mächte und Gewalten im NT," *ThBl* 9 (1930) 289-297; *Mächte und Gewalten im NT* (Quaestiones Disputatae 3; 1958); K. L. Schmidt, "Die Natur- und Geisteskräfte im paulinischen Erkennen und Glauben," *Eranos-Jahrbuch* 14 (1946) 87-143; J. Schoeps, "The Sacrifice of Isaac in Paul's Theology," *JBL* 65 (1946) 385-392; K. Romaniuk, "L'origine des formules pauliniennes 'Le Christ s'est livré pour nous,' 'Le Christ nous a aimés et s'est livré pour nous,' " *NovT* 5 (1962) 55-76; G. Münderlein, "Interpretation einer Tradition. Bemerkungen zu Römer 8, 35f.," *KuD* 11 (1965) 136-142; G. Schille, "Die

Liebe Gottes in Christus. Beobachtungen zu Rm 8, 31-39," *ZNW* 59 (1968) 230-244; N. A. Dahl, "The Atonement—An Adequate Reward for the Akedah? (Ro 8:32)," *Neotestamentica et Semitica: Studies in Honour of Matthew Black* (ed. E. E. Ellis and M. Wilcox; 1969) 15-29.

It has always been felt that Paul's fervor finds strongest expression in these verses. The tradition in vv. 29f. has prepared the way for it. But we do not have here a mere development of what precedes nor, in connection with v. 28, a contrast to vv. 19-27 (Schille, "Liebe," 231; Paulsen, *Überlieferung,* 133). Undoubtedly the argument of the chapter is brought to a final climax even though the theme "in the Spirit" is no longer explicit. If in Paul this theme is a variation on "in Christ," it makes good sense that it is now brought to this, its ultimate reality.

Notwithstanding widespread views to the contrary, the apostle constructed the epistle very carefully and structured it systematically. This section transcends the context and forms the conclusion to the whole division (chs. 5–8). Freedom from death, sin, and law is the freedom of the vulnerable insofar as Christians look to themselves. It is the freedom of the victorious, however, insofar as the Lord reveals his power in and through them. This helps us to understand the emotional and rhetorical force of the passage. The modern judgment of its "poetic beauty" (Kühl; Jülicher; Dodd; H. W. Schmidt) is understandable but completely inappropriate, especially when it is accompanied by a warning against overcritical analysis (Jülicher). It will not do to characterize it as a doxology (Balz, *Heilsvertrauen,* 116) or as a hymn (Huby; J. Weiss, "Beiträge," 195f. also inclines in this direction), though certainly hymnic style and dependence on confessional formulations are present. The interplay of question and answer, objection and response, shows that we again have a Christian diatribe with an approximation to the rhythmic prose of antiquity. The effect on modern readers should not be allowed to obscure the place and character of the passage in the history of traditions.

Its structure is to be discussed accordingly. The climax of the construction is not to be undervalued. To speak of strophes, however, corresponds to a hymn rather than to the argument of a diatribe (J. Weiss, "Beiträge," 195f.; Lagrange; Leenhardt; Paulsen, *Überlieferung,* 135-151). If four smaller units usually are seen, or two from the perspective of the keyword "separate" (Balz, *Heilsvertrauen,* 117ff.), we do most justice to the development of thought if we see in v. 31a the typical introductory question and then a first exchange in vv. 31-32, a second in vv. 33-34, and a third in vv. 35-39 (Leenhardt; Schille, "Liebe," 232). Verses 38-39 are not, of course, a mere answer to v. 35 but form a conclusion to the whole (Michel). In content the circles overlap as in vv. 19-27. The climax is not psychological (*contra* Leenhardt), for behind the diatribe form stands the content of the struggle with the world powers and indirectly at least the idea of God's legal contest with them for dominion over Christians (C. Müller, *Gottes Volk,* 72).

The initial rhetorical question does not merely prepare the way for what immediately follows. It sets the whole message of chs. 5–8 under debate. It already emerged at 5:5 that God's love is not to be seen merely as an emotion (*contra* Kühl, *et al.*). Here one may see plainly that it designates his "being for us" and that it thus embraces the predestinating event of vv. 28-30. Paul knows neither the autonomous existence of a person and the world nor of God existing for himself. He therefore provides no footing for metaphysics in the traditional sense. The uncontestable mythology serves the eschatological perspective. For in spite of the established motifs of predestination the relation of Creator and world cannot be dealt with protologically. This very section proves that the saving event of the death and resurrection of Christ forms the center from which the beginning and end of history may then be seen. Not a concept of God but the saving act centered in the death of Jesus characterizes the God for us (Luz, *Geschichtsverständnis*, 371; Balz, *Heilsvertrauen*, 118) of whom 1 Cor 8:5f. also speaks. In the light of the cross alone this God is truly known (1 Cor 1:21), the face of the world is perceived, and the world and the community are seen both in unity and contrast. On the ground of the cross Christianity attains its standing in victory. For the cross is the place where divine power is manifested as aiming from the very first at resurrection and therefore as omnipotence, and where the gospel has its origin as the power of God. If the justification of the ungodly sets forth the θεὸς ὑπὲρ ἡμῶν as the Creator out of non-being, it also sets forth his love as the God who protects the new creation with the power of resurrection and enables it to withstand heavenly and earthly powers. Thus here in fact God's Spirit and love converge with one another. The Spirit makes it clear that God's love is not just a general attribute but the ongoing action of the one who effects salvation on earth. The old aeon, rebellious, threatening, and perverted, is still present, so that Christians are under attack. On the other hand no creature can do anything against his Lord and those who hold to him and are upheld by him. In the Spirit God does not merely maintain his right. He also graciously brings them home and preserves them. In this way he manifests his love as Creator. This is the triumph of the assaulted. As is almost universally recognized today, it comes to expression, at least in vv. 32-34, in confessional fragments.

This insight (*contra* Schille, "Liebe," 33) should not be overstated, as though we had here a common kerygma in a Pauline form. The style of the whole is thoroughly prosaic. We must view as Pauline the verbs φείδεσθαι and the eschatologically meant χαρίζειν in the sense "to give graciously." Pauline, too, are the antithesis in v. 32ab, the question in v. 32c, the τὰ πάντα, which (*contra* Zahn) does not mean "the all" but emphatically "everything," and the weak σὺν αὐτῷ ("along with" — Gutjahr), not technically "in fellowship with" (Michel). ὅς γε = *qui quidem* (BDF, §439[3]) is confirmatory, not the hymnic introductory relative. The phrase "gave him up for all" undoubtedly has a liturgical character, but this does not mean that it comes from the baptismal confession or eucharistic language (*contra* Schille, "Liebe," 232f.; Romaniuk, "L'origine," 61). It may be taken from the catechetical tradition. A reminiscence of formulated material is probably also present in the expression about his own Son, which is sharpened to the expression "beloved Son" in the baptismal exhortation at Col 1:13. It is at least possible that v. 32a has in view the typological prototype of Abraham in Gen 22:16 LXX (Zahn; Schoeps, "Sacrifice," 390; *Paul*, 146; Michel; H. W. Schmidt; Ridderbos), although this can hardly be considered certain (cf. Dahl, "Atonement," 16ff.; Blank, *Paulus*, 295ff.; Paulsen, *Überlieferung*, 165ff.). In

247

spite of some fixed formulae, then, one cannot say that vv. 31b-32 is a pre-Pauline confession or one which the apostle has adopted.

The quintessence of the rhetorically effective argument is an elucidation of the "God for us" and an appeal to the reason of the readers to recognize that the God who has given up his only Son will not refuse us anything that is needed for our salvation. The situation changes in vv. 33-34. The diatribe style continues when to a brief and purely hypothetical question answers follow in vv. 33a and 34a which show the question to be meaningless. It is impossible to understand whole statements as questions and to introduce them with "perhaps" (*contra* Lietzmann; correctly Ridderbos). Verse 34b is so expanded by the apposition which follows that we have a statement, and the same then applies also to v. 33b. It need not be asked who the accuser of v. 33a is, and one need not think of Satan (possible Barrett; Leenhardt). To do so is to fail to pay sufficient attention to the apostle's rhetoric, which can ask impossible questions and make that clear in the answers. The future is not eschatological (Gaugler; Black; Schille, "Liebe," 233) but logical. For this reason past tenses are used in the secondary clauses. The trial to which the juridical language points has been closed by the salvation event (Balz, *Heilsvertrauen,* 119) and there can be no question of moral concerns (Jülicher;   [Dodd). It may be correct that the divine predicate ὁ δικαιῶν is probably taken from Isa 50:8 and the questions in the text stand in some analogy to the situation in Isa 50:7-9. It is going too far, however, to speak seriously of a paraphrase of the Servant Song (Michel; Romaniuk, "L'origine," 72, 75; cf. also J. Jeremias, *TDNT,* V, 710). The individual motif adopted no longer expresses expectation but with the divine predicate points toward the fulfilled promise. There is no reference to God's servant and it is highly unlikely that the question of v. 34a develops the κρίνειν of Isa. 50:8f.

Things are different with v. 34b, which, not without reason, is expanded by the following statements, each of which goes beyond the preceding line. Again it is quite dubious whether one can speak of a self-contained hymnic fragment. The intensifying μᾶλλον δέ of v. 34c is probably Pauline. It prepares for the two relative clauses, of which the first, based on Psalm 110, is the basis of the decisive second clause. Once the logical structure is clearly perceived, nothing more results than that Paul is combining here basic affirmations employed christologically and liturgically. His first concern is with the death of Jesus which sets aside all condemnation. This event certainly belongs to the past but not to a past that has been overcome (cf. 4:25; 5:10). For he who died for us is now the risen Lord who according to the interpretation of messianic prophecy current in primitive Christianity sits as the exalted One at the right hand of God. He can thus be our constant Intercessor like the High Priest of Heb 7:25 or the Paraclete of 1 John 2:1 (Behm, *TDNT,* V, 809ff.), warding off even future accusations against us. The use of participial and relative clauses is typically hymnic (Norden, *Agnostos Theos,* 201ff.) and the motifs of the relative clauses are not specifically Pauline. The use of Ἰησοῦς strengthens the solemnity of the statement and may be original (Kühl; Michel; Ridderbos). The eschatological freedom of the children of God is, in good Pauline fashion, won by Christ alone.

The conclusion of v. 34 offers the apostle the possibility of a new climax in a third movement. The stress is on the verb χωρίσει, which no longer has a juridical character and does not contain any material development of what precedes (contra Balz, Heilsvertrauen, 121). On the other hand the motif of Christ alone slips over into the technically used motif of σὺν αὐτῷ, certainly described by the slogan the love of Christ. In very ancient readings assimilation to the context (Lietzmann) results instead in speaking of the love of God. The point is, however, that "God for us" is now expounded as the being of Christ for us, namely, as the indissoluble union of the community with its Lord. Unlike the questions of vv. 31b, 33a, 34a, that of v. 35a is no longer a purely rhetorical one, as the seven-membered list in v. 35b shows. It presents the manifold and frightful attack to which we are inescapably subject, according to the quotation from Scripture. The list, which unlike those of popular philosophy does not include happier circumstances too, has been given a Christian form, namely, it has been related to the sufferings of Christ. It does not concern the person who is exposed to the incalculable whims of chance, but the follower of Jesus who is stigmatized by the cross. The apostle's own experiences are typical of those of all Christians, and they make clear the difference between secular life and apocalyptic life. We should not trivialize this by treating it as a hyperbolical statement (contra Jülicher) of the fact that we are never safe in any moment of our life, nor is any pride in suffering discernible.

θλῖψις is again eschatological tribulation. Since all the other nouns depict external experiences, στενοχωρία does not portray objectively constriction of space (contra Asmussen; Schille, "Liebe," 239) but blocked exits. μάχαιρα perhaps means concretely execution (Michaelis, TDNT, IV, 526). The citation from Ps 43:23 LXX was commonly used by the rabbis with reference to the martyrdom of the pious, sometimes in a transferred sense (Billerbeck). It is not adduced merely for emphasis. Scripture as well as apocalyptic documents the fact that violent death is the lot of the believer on earth and that it corresponds to the will and declaration of God. The undoubtedly christological introduction ἕνεκεν σοῦ (Zahn; Kühl; Lagrange; Althaus, et al.) tells us that the very love of Christ which separates us from the world is the basis of persecution by the powers even to the point of martyrdom. ὅλην τὴν ἡμέραν, which in good Semitic fashion describes the whole day from morning to evening (Michel), is also emphatic. The whole of life is involved. Reconciliation with God necessarily means enmity with the world according to the law of apocalyptic. If this is not understood, it is hard to see that vv. 19-27 belong with this passage as its reverse side. The solidarity of believers with the world is more than a mere understanding of fellow human beings and readiness for them, for it is always linked to the cross. Here as there the contrast is simultaneously manifest and removed. All fraternization is excluded as a levelling down of the difference which always continues on earth. In the confrontation the new and old world do not lose their character. The bridge is not built by human beings. The ἀποκαραδοκία of unredeemed creation is a most ambivalent phenomenon. The cry for freedom can simultaneously be a cry for blood, just as the ἐλπίς of Christians is not merely assurance but also the patient endurance of martyrs and as such the criterion of the standing of a Christian.

Obedience and rebellion confront one another on a cosmic scale. What previously is rhetorically depicted as a process presupposes real struggle with eschatological severity. Only the death of Christ and the resultant intercession of the exalted Lord are our protection against an earthly superpower. But these do not spare us dying in discipleship of the Crucified. Like all that God does, the love of Christ also manifests itself in time under its opposite. Apocalyptic alone can express this and preserve us from the usual edifying interpretation of the text.

In face of the scripture passage understood as a call for suffering and death, and in face of a reality far different from ideology and enthusiasm, Paul returns to the summary of vv. 31b-34. He surpasses it with an ἀλλ' ἐν τούτοις πᾶσιν, which takes up v. 28 and the πολλῷ μᾶλλον of 5:15ff., and with the singular ὑπερνικᾶν, which points to the triumphant victory. As in v. 11, in keeping with later Greek, the readings have linked διά with the accusative of author (Lietzmann). The ἀγαπήσας is undoubtedly Christ (Eichholz, *Paulus*, 169f.), and the participle embraces both his saving act on the cross and his intercession as the exalted Lord. The basis of the world's enmity is simultaneously the cause both of earthly attestation and of eschatological victory, which now emerges as the keyword of the passage.

One again has to be clear how far the apostle parts company here with the message of autarchy and emancipation in popular philosophy. The premise of his anthropology may be seen once more. A person is defined by his particular lord. This gives rise to the dialectic of the chapter. Appearances, which depict the rejected of the world (1 Cor 4:13) in struggle and earthly hopelessness, stand in paradoxical relation to the truth. The cross and glory are dialectically connected where the Spirit rules. Standing beneath the cross marks the position of the conquerors. Their Lord sustains them through the messianic woes. He alone is their salvation, hope, and victory, just as following him is the presupposition of their tribulation.

Like v. 37, what follows is not Paul's expansion of an existing baptismal hymn (*contra* Schille, "Liebe," 237ff.). Artistic prose is used, as in 1 Cor 3:21f. and in antitheses enumerated in diatribes, e.g., life and death, height and depth, along with stereotyped combinations, e.g., angels and principalities, in order to characterize a universe at odds with its Creator. The οὔτε–οὔτε has its source in this context and can thus be employed hymnically to denote the antithetical ar⁻¹ polar forces of the cosmos. As in 14:14; 15:14, πέπεισμαι γάρ does not merely mean the apostle's own persuasion (*contra* Schille, "Liebe," 236f.) but manifests complete certainty. This introduction speaks against a hymn, as does the ὅτι clause which follows, the apostle's contrasting of ἐνεστῶτα and μέλλοντα, which embraces the dimensions of the time of the old aeon, the echoing δυνάμεις, which one would expect after ἀρχαί, the comprehensive formula οὔτε τις κτίσις ἑτέρα, and the taking up of v. 35 in the conclusion. Nevertheless, one can see how close Paul's prose can come to hymnic style.

As in the Stoic tradition the cosmos here is the σύστημα of gods and men and what is created for their sake; it is not just the world of mankind, as normally. Typically, however, it is so as the present aeon, which is ruled by many mutually warring powers and has thus sunk into chaos. In distinction from other parts of the NT, the angelic powers, which are set in a hierarchy as in Jewish texts (for the development cf. Grundmann, *Kraft*, 39-55; Hengel, *Judaism*, I, 231f.), belong to the fallen creation and are thus hostile to Christians as elsewhere (*contra* Sanday and Headlam; Schlatter; Murray; H. W. Schmidt; right here are Kittel, *TDNT*, I, 86; Michel). As star spirits (cf. BAGD, 112) they can be called στοιχεῖα τοῦ κόσμου in Gal 4:3, 8f., which does not characterize them as keepers of the law. As such they influence human destiny and have special spheres of power (Schlier, *TDNT*, I, 515).

It is hardly incidental that ὕψωμα and βάθος are mentioned in this context. These are astrological terms denoting a star's greatest nearness to, or distance from, its zenith (Lietzmann, *et al.*, though cf. Ridderbos). Personified sidereal powers are meant. We have already found personification of the powers in sin, death, spirit, and flesh. In the history-of-religions environment of the apostle, the divine and the demonic were constitutively defined in terms of the exercise of power, with a material equation of the sphere and the power. If the conclusion speaks of any other creature, this shows the tendency towards personifying distinction. In context, however, the motif of the powers is in the foreground, and ἐνεστῶτα and μέλλοντα at least point to the extension of these powers in time and space. In no circumstances should one expound ἄγγελοι, ἀρχαί, and δυνάμεις abstractly and speak in a transferred sense of the privilege, expression, and dignity of power (*contra* K. L. Schmidt, "Natur- und Geisteskräfte," 135). Nor should one demythologize them as time and space (Lagrange).

To this demonic circle belong also the forces and spheres which people call life and death and which isolate them from God. Present and future belong too as dimensions in which fate is experienced or imagined in an illusionary way to effect salvation or ruin. The tenfold listing suggests older groupings of which Paul might not have been aware. No systematic structuring may be discerned. What is furthest apart is associated. The universe detached from God, with all its historical dimensions and outworkings, is depicted as impenetrable and as everywhere limiting people (Schlier, "Mächte," 291; *Mächte*, 14-32). The situations in the list in v. 35 are now replaced by the world-rulers which cause them, so that chaos is changed into an inferno.

Only the apocalyptic world view can describe reality thus, just as this outlook alone can catch in it the cry of an enslaved creation and see the messianic woes taking place therein. In Paul apocalyptic does not lead to enthusiasm but to a somber experience of the world. It is against this background that he profiles the confession of the predestined cosmocrator Christ and Christian freedom as an anticipation of the resurrection and of the joy of conquerors. Even when inferno threatens the Christian on all sides, he is marked by the Lord, who is present for him and set in παρρησία. In a manner which differs from that of Philo his pilgrimage as a pathway in the peace of God is a ὁδὸς βασιλική, and in a manner which differs from that of the Stoics he finds even in the midst of painful experience that the claim of the powers to dominion is illusory. Precisely afflicted faith trusts in the love of Christ against all appearances. It refuses to let its discipleship be hindered. It thus represents the earthly rule of the truth which is demonically repressed according to 1:18ff., and it represents the eschatological future. In the community it may be seen that God's righteousness reveals itself in the midst of its enemies and creates a new world in the old aeon. Thus the conclusion, which emphatically at the end of v. 39 again refers to true salvation in liturgical predication of Christ, provides us not only with a summary of the preceding chapter but also with the sum of Paul's theology.

V. The Righteousness of God and the Problem of Israel (9:1–11:36)

Apart from ch. 16, no part of the epistle is so self-contained as this. Hence none may be detached so easily or, as it seems, at so little risk. It has thus been regarded as an independent section to be separated from chs. 1–8 (e.g., Feuillet, "Citation," 67), perhaps as the interpolation of an earlier Pauline treatise (Dodd). Probably no larger portion of Paul's writings can be said to have had a history of exposition which is more a suffering course of misunderstanding, acts of violence, and experimentation with shifting methods and themes (cf. Weber, *Problem*, 10ff.; C. Müller, *Gottes Volk*, 5ff.).

If it had been customary since the Reformation to read the epistle as a compendium of Pauline theology, and consequently to give undue prominence in these chapters to the question of predestination, F. C. Baur pioneered the way to a historical understanding. He made this section of the letter the hermeneutical center of the whole epistle, which as he saw it was oriented to the debate with Jewish-Christians. Christian universalism is championed here against Jewish particularism. Baur thus initiated a process which has not yet ended. By resolutely raising the question of the *Sitz im Leben* of the primitive Christianity of our letter, he also set it in the relativity of all things historical. By way of exposition of chs. 9–11 Paul, the chief witness of the Protestant churches, became first the catalyst in a radical tendency criticism of the NT, then a Janus-headed figure in the history of religions, who on the one side has been viewed in terms of eschatology as an apocalyptic, while on the other side he has been viewed in terms of the cult-piety of Hellenism as a mystic.

The failure of the Reformation to integrate chs. 9–11 into their message of justification was thus avenged. Baur recognized the weakest spot in the traditional understanding. By giving Romans a historical setting in the life of primitive Christianity, he also removed from its hinges, as the subsequent period showed, the traditional Protestant doctrine of justification, at least in the German sphere. The dogmatic statement became part of the historical development of dogma. What had hitherto been the criterion of Pauline theology lost its direct and universal authority, was caught up in the vortex of historicism, became a more or less important part of the whole, and two generations later was categorized as a polemical position in the Jewish conflict (Wrede; A. Schweitzer). In the future theology would have to go behind or beyond the doctrine of justification if it was not to reduce this to the hidden inner core of the Pauline proclamation.

It belongs to the most disturbing insights into the questionability of normal

253

exegetical work that in general the agitation produced by Baur did not immediately focus on the point indicated by him and make chs. 9–11 the center of the debate which took place. It was here that the switches were thrown. It was here that the future journey should have been determined. Openness to the message of these chapters could no longer follow the tracks of the older dogmatics. Trying to be faithful to it meant being plunged into the conflict between the theology and the practice of the apostle, and in theology having to distinguish again between what is central and what is peripheral, what is abiding and what is time-bound, personal experience and its alienation by the clothing in Hellenistic or Jewish garb. But instead exegesis leaped past this key position. This was facilitated by the irrefutable fact that Baur was mistaken when he ascribed a dominant position to Jewish-Christians in Rome. As was comprehensible in an age of historicism, the historical correction of his model made it appear that the material theological question as to the significance of chs. 9–11 for the interpretation of Paul as a whole, and the doctrine of justification in particular, was a problem of detail which could be left to apologetics or to speculation on a supposed theodicy.

This led in fact to a schizophrenia in Pauline research which is still with us, although A. Schlatter and dialectical theology strove to bridge the gap. The fronts of the previous century have shifted, of course. The religio-historical alternative has steadily lost its original fascination as the Jewish heritage of the apostle has increasingly shown itself to be the native ground, and eschatology the horizon, of Paul's theology. It has persisted in the as yet unresolved question how strongly Paul was influenced by the enthusiasm of his communities. At root, however, he can no longer be charged with a thorough syncretistic dualism, since anthropology is no longer the main issue in the debate. At least in the German-speaking world the doctrine of justification has won back in large measure the territory it had lost. As noted, however, its full reinstatement is blocked outside this sphere by the fact that it is regarded as simply an initial stage in Christian development.

In the German-speaking sphere, and increasingly in other circles too, it is paralyzed by the counter-balancing interpretation of Paul's works in terms of salvation history. This, too, has its origins in the previous century. If we are not deceived, it was again exposition of Romans 9–11 which directed exegesis of the apostle along this track with Beyschlag's *Theodicee* in 1868. In this little work an attempt is made to overcome the antithesis of predestination and indeterminism by presenting the postulate of an inner development under divine pedagogy as its reconciling bridge. The ties of this theme in terms of its world view to ideas of the time in which it arose are evident. It is the more astonishing, then, that it made little headway. This probably is connected with the fact that it sought a dogmatic or pseudo-dogmatic solution during a phase when historical positivism was determinative except in rigid confessional camps. To be sure, in a liberalistic flattening it shared some of the true concern of F. C. Baur to grasp history in its dialectical movement, but like Baur's broader intentions it was sucked into the historical wake, although its reduction in comparison with Baur's program made it more attractive and more compatible with dominant interests. Its starting point in Romans 9–11 was undoubtedly an obstacle too. No one knew how to handle these chapters, and after the earlier dogmatic controversies no one had any great desire to try. Insofar as the theme of salvation history continued to work under-

254

ground or could be adopted as a slogan, one dodged into generalities and made it a key to the interpretation of Paul's writings, the NT, and the Bible as whole. The rights and wrongs of the debate kindled need not be discussed here. Those investigations which kept the problem alive strictly in view of the exegesis of Romans 9–11 will soon be dealt with in detailed arguments. The point of the present summary is simply to show that twice in the nineteenth century the chapters achieved importance in theological history without any clear decision being reached about them or at least their importance in the interpretation of Paul as a whole being generally recognized.

The basic question today is still that of the relation between the doctrine of justification and salvation history. Exposition thus far is reduced to absurdity if an alternative is present here. However, it has produced two insights which can now be fruitful. Although Paul's message of justification undoubtedly takes concrete form in the justification of the individual, it cannot be reduced to this. Even in the individual, God's grace wants the world. If not, we end up with a Christian mystery religion. Secondly, according to the interpretation of ch. 4, to limit the problem to that, it is impossible to deny that the apostle's message of justification has the dimension of salvation history. To contest the term as such and to lose oneself thereby in further systematizing makes no sense at the present juncture. The fronts are so firmly established here that in a commentary one must be content to show as clearly as possible exegetically what is meant and why one cannot provisionally disclaim it. If one does not do that, then, as usually happens in at least one of the two camps, one should make a great curve around the exposition of chs. 9–11 or call it an impossible task.

Surely a very un-Pauline and unbiblical understanding of God's word will have to be charged against a theology which allows only existence to be described therein. If God's word is more than an idea, which for its part will become a mere figment of the mind without the kerygma, and if it fashions the reality of a new creature, without which being Christian remains merely a religious cipher, it has the function of embodying itself on earth. It does so not merely in the apostle as bearer of the gospel but also in the community as the body of Christ and in each of its members. We cannot think of God's word in isolation from its sphere of emanations in the world. It manifests itself in time and space. Salvation history, if this expression is used here, is the sphere in which God's word is perceptible as promise and gospel, awakening faith or unbelief, and setting man in the conflict between attestation and denial. This is not co-extensive with the dimension of the world and it goes beyond that of the church, although in the latter the discussion concentrates around the word. Insofar as faith or denial results from confrontation with God's word, there is no immanent continuity in salvation history. As such it can also have the opposite aspect of a history of the absence of salvation. It always reveals itself afresh over the ditches. The faithfulness of God, who never leaves creation without his address and promise, is its true continuum, to which there corresponds on earth the experience that there always has been and is a band of hearers and always the scandal of those who take offense as described in 1 Cor 1:18ff. Only when the emphasis is shifted from the operative word to the contrast of faith and unbelief, i.e., to anthropology, does it make no sense to talk of salvation history. For then the material link between the OT and the NT is necessarily snapped, the world simply becomes the theater of individual decisions, the Creator no longer reaches out for his world, and as a result there is no apocalyptic.

If salvation history is understood as suggested, God's righteousness is its center, it is the worldwide dimension of this righteousness. In place of an alternative we thus have an indissoluble material relation. In this framework, of course, the problem of Israel must be discussed and as the problem of God's faithfulness to his uttered word. It can be discussed only dialectically, for here we have an example of God's faithfulness and man's unfaithfulness in conflict. It must also be discussed in such a way that the concept of the people of God is central. Paul does not let this self-predication of the post-Easter community be constitutive for his own idea of the church nor does he simply modify it, as many think today, by the motif of the body of Christ. He consistently uses it when either polemically or typologically he has to consider the relation between the church and Israel, the old covenant and the new. He thus uses it in explicitly dialectical contexts. One might say that in it he envisions the salvation-historical aspect of the church, which stands in a special affinity to Israel as the community under promise. At the same time, however, the church has to perceive in Israel the particular threat to all recipients of the promise and the gospel, and it is preserved in such a threat only if it allows the word of God which constitutes the community to be related to Christ and interprets it in terms of the message of justification. Detailed exegesis is needed to make this more clear and precise.

Bibliography: E. Dinkler, "Prädestination bei Paulus," *Festschrift für Gunther Dehn zum 75. Geburtstag* (ed. W. Schneemelcher; 1957) 81-102 (reprint: Dinkler, *Signum Crucis* [1967] 241-269); J. Gnilka, *Die Verstockung Israels; Isaias 6, 9-10 in der Theologie der Synoptiker* (1961); E. Güttgemanns, "Heilsgeschichte bei Paulus oder Dynamik des Evangeliums," in *Studia linguistica Neotestamentica* (BEvT 60; 1971) 34-38; G. Maier, *Mensch und freier Wille nach den jüdischen Religionsparteien zwischen Ben Sira und Paulus* (1971); C. Muller-Duvernoy, "L'apôtre Paul et le problème juif," *Judaica* 15 (1959) 65-91; J. M. Oesterreicher, "Israel's Missteps and her Rise. The Dialectic of God's Design in Rom. 9–11," *Stud. Paul.Congr.*, I, 317-327; C. Plag, *Israels Wege zum Heil* (Arbeiten zur Theologie 1/40; 1969); H. Schlier, "Das Mysterium Israels," *Die Zeit der Kirche*, 232-244; Schrenk, "Missionsdokument"; C. Senft, "L'élection d'Israel et la justification," *L'Évangile, hier et aujourd'hui. Mélanges offerts au Franz-J. Leenhardt* (1968) 131-142; D. M. Stanley, "Theologia 'Promissionis' apud S. Paulum," *VD* 30 (1952) 129-142; M. Zerwick, "Drama populi Israeli secundum Rom 9–11," *VD* 46 (1968) 321-338.

A. The Apostle's Lament (9:1-5)

[1]*I speak the truth in Christ, I do not lie, and my conscience bears me witness in the Holy Spirit,* [2]*that I have deep sorrow and unceasing pain in my heart.* [3]*For I could wish that I were myself accursed and cut off from Christ for the sake of my brethren, my kinsmen according to the flesh.* [4]*They are Israelites, and to them belong the sonship and the glory and the covenants and the giving of the law and the worship and the promises; to them belong the fathers and from them (springs) the Christ according to the flesh. God who rules over all be blessed for ever. Amen.*

THE APOSTLE'S LAMENT   9:1-5

Bibliography: H. W. Bartsch, "Röm. 9, 5 und 1. Clem. 32, 4," *TZ* 21 (1965) 401-409; L. Cerfaux, "Le privilège d'Israel selon Saint Paul," *ETL* 17 (1940) 5-26; L. G. da Fonseca, "Διαθήκη—Foedus an Testamentum?" *Bib* 8 (1927) 31-50, 160-181, 290-319, 418-441; E. Kamlah, "Wie beurteilte Paulus sein Leiden?" *ZNW* 54 (1963) 217-232; O. Kuss, "Die Rolle des Apostels Paulus in der theologischen Entwicklung der Urkirche," *MTZ* 14 (1963) 1-59, 109-187; W. L. Lorimer, "Romans IX, 3-5," *NTS* 13 (1966/67) 385f.; O. Michel, "Opferbereitschaft für Israel," *In Memoriam Ernst Lohmeyer* (ed. W. Schmauch; 1951) 94-100; C. Roetzel, "Διαθῆκαι in Romans 9:4," *Bib* 51 (1970) 377-390; G. Stählin, "Zum Gebrauch von Beteuerungsformeln im NT," *NovT* 5 (1962) 115-143; C. Strömann, "Römer 9, 5," *ZNW* 8 (1907) 319f.

This section is marked by unmistakable pathos. Already on account of its rhetorical style (Michel) one should recognize in it the introductory counterpart to the conclusion in 11:33-36. If this is so, one can hardly claim that Paul did not know at the outset how his discussion would end (Senft, "L'élection," 131f.). Rather the three chapters are plainly divided into the sections 9:6-29; 9:30–10:21; and 11:1-36, and a thoroughly logical, systematic course of thought corresponds to this. In keeping with this is that here is the right place for the broached problem, after the discussion of the relation between law and Spirit in the preceding chapters. It is simply not true that the section is an excursus which is not established by the basic structure or that it does not develop the main theme (*contra* Hoppe, *Heilsgeschichte,* 138; Beare, *BHH,* III, 1612; for a correct view cf. Dupont, "Structure," 392; Goppelt, *Christentum,* 112f.; Eichholz, *Paulus,* 284ff.). The abrupt opening and change of tone in comparison with what preceded (Luz, *Geschichtsverständnis,* 19) are not convincing arguments to the contrary. They simply mark the new theme.

Even 1:9-15 and 15:14-33 do not have the same emotional emphasis. It is absurd, however, to blame the Roman readers for this (Ulonska, *Paulus,* 182; J. Knox). Paul expressly says that his sense of nationality plays a part. He never renounced his Jewishness. But this aspect should not be exaggerated (*contra* Dodd; Windisch, *Judentum,* 32ff.). There speaks here the Christian and the apostle to the Gentiles who has often been accused of hostility to Israel (Kühl; Lietzmann; Barrett). He thus bears witness with unusual solemnity, and in the style of an oath (Maurer, *TDNT,* VII, 916), to solidarity with his people (Nygren). Similar assurances (cf. BAGD, 891b) may be found in 1:9; 2 Cor 1:23; 11:31; 12:19; Gal 1:20 with reference to the apostolicity claimed in 1 Tim 2:7 (Stählin, "Beteuerungsformeln," 133).

Like the antithetical negation and the participial clause, the additions ἐν Χριστῷ and ἐν πνεύματι give emphasis, showing that the attitude is subject to divine proof. This means that "in Christ" does not have the weak sense "as a Christian determined by the salvation event" (Neugebauer, *In Christus,* 126) but the strong one "in the presence of Christ." The self-critical power of the apostle, to which the role of witness to the oath is also ascribed, is guided and justified by the Spirit (Strathmann, *TDNT,* IV, 509; Bultmann, *Theology,* I, 219).

The forensic situation indicated is maintained in v. 3. Again one should be on guard against over-interpretation. The fixed and in part conventional Jewish formula: "I will be a substitute for" (Billerbeck) forms the background although

257

not precisely the content of the statement, which speaks neither of expiation nor of a "sacrifice of annihilation" (*contra* Billerbeck; Michel, "Opferbereitschaft"). ηὐχόμην, like ἤθελον in Gal 4:20, expresses a seriously meant but unrealizable wish, not a pledge or offer. The idea of substitution is expressed in ὑπέρ, and it is tempting to follow the majority of exegetes and see a parallel to Exod 32:32. But there is no evidence that Paul had this example in mind, or that he compared himself with the Servant of the Lord (Kamlah, "Leiden," 228f.) or, as a mediator of salvation, with Christ (Windisch, *Judentum*, 32; more cautiously Muller-Duvernoy, "Problème," 68), or that he set himself alongside Moses (Munck, *Christ*, 29; *Salvation*, 306). The force of the statement lies in the ἀπὸ τοῦ Χριστοῦ. This is often not given its due in the search for OT analogies. It is not to be explained from them. Paul does not have in mind transcendent retributional suffering (Lietzmann), eschatological judgment (Michel), certainly not temporary separation (Zahn; Gaugler is right here). The *koine* form of ἀνάθημα, as often in Hellenism influenced by the LXX, has the adjectival sense "accursed," whereas originally what was meant was dedication as a taboo, and then what was banned in this way. ἀπὸ τοῦ Χριστοῦ speaks of reversing the integration into Christ accomplished in baptism. As in 1 Cor 16:22 the curse eliminates the sacramentally established fellowship by equally sacramental counterworking, which is also presupposed in 1 Cor 5:5. If God imposes it, one is definitively excluded from the body of Christ.

To be ready for this is for Christians a supreme proof of love for Israel. Hence it is no accident that the title of brethren is here extended to the Jews, which, of course, necessitates the specifying apposition (Michaelis, *TDNT*, VII, 741). The Hellenistic term συγγενεῖς denotes relatives or kinsmen. κατὰ σάρκα, as in vv. 5 [and 8, concerns the human and earthly sphere (Schweizer, *TDNT*, VII, 126f.). Remarkably Paul gives no reason for his sorrow, and the lament changes quietly into magnifying the advantages of Israel in salvation history, which were already indicated in 3:2 and which are now rhetorically enumerated.

οἵτινες is explanatory. The Jews are not just close to the apostle physically. They are and remain the people that God has chosen and set apart by his gifts (K. L. Schmidt, *Judenfrage*, 25f.). To them belongs the title of honor 'Ισραηλῖται, which now replaces the previous references to Jews (Luz, *Geschichtsverständnis*, 26f.), and which establishes a link to the πατέρες, the patriarchs as the bearers of the promise. On the basis of OT texts like Exod 4:22 their υἱοθεσία is recognized, which as an eschatological gift applies elsewhere only to Christians. The relationship of the Christian world to Abraham is now extended to all Israel in opposition to the context of ch. 4. Paul obviously understands the phenomenon of Israel no less dialectically than that of the law. If the election made it the bearer of the promise, it can fall away from the promise under the dominion of the law (cf. 1 Cor 10:1-13). On the other hand, the promise does not have only an eschatological orientation. It has also a historical sphere marked here by the people for whom special gifts of grace are characteristic according to 11:29. The plerophory in the list which follows (cf. Cerfaux, *Church*, 25ff.) stresses by its careful structuring (Luz, *Geschichtsverständnis*, 270) the fulness of the experienced blessing from complementary and overlapping points of view. ἡ δόξα, used in the absolute with no rabbinic equivalent (Billerbeck), means as in 2 Cor 3:7ff. the epiphany of the *shekinah* in the historical and cultic sphere (Schlier, "Doxa," *Stud.Paul.Congr.*, I, 45ff.; Cerfaux, *Church,* 38). διαθῆκαι, found in the plural since Sir 44:12, 18; 45:17; Wis 18:22; 2 Macc 8:15, has been assimilated to the singular context in P⁴⁶ and ensuing readings (Munck, *Christ,* 31; Bruce; *contra* Cerfaux, "Privilège," 13; possible Barrett). The reference is to the promises (Fonseca, "Foedus," 26ff.) or commands (Roetzel, "Romans 9:4") given to the fathers. νομοθεσία hardly refers to possession of the law (Gutbrod, *TDNT,* IV, 1089) but to the act of giving it (Luz, *Geschichtsverständnis,* 272). λατρεία has the cult in view, of which *m. 'Abot* 1:2 says: "The world rests on three things: the Torah, the cultus, and the exercise of good deeds." ἐπαγγελίαι probably refers particularly to the messianic promises (Lietzmann; Lagrange). The climax comes with the sharply profiled ὁ Χριστός, which clearly designates the Messiah, with a limitation to his humanity in the τὸ κατὰ σάρκα. A remembrance of the parallel in 1:3 (Michel) is doubtful, and especially so the deduction that here, as there, there must be a reference to the deity of Christ (Zahn).

The prerogatives of Israel are not limited to gifts of the primal time (*contra* Munck, *Christ,* 30) nor are they transitory (Cerfaux, "Privilège," 25). Salvation history is not immanent for Paul. Grounded in God's election and determined historically by the promise, the people whom it embraces is marked sacramentally (Schlier, "Mysterium," 235ff.). It is in this light that we are to understand the hotly debated conclusion. Interpretation should start with the fact that εὐλογητὸς εἰς τοὺς αἰῶνας, ἀμήν undoubtedly forms a double acclamation. There is no reason to detach it from what precedes, and irrespective of the details it imparts to the whole a doxological character (Ridderbos; Maier, *Israel,* 9). One cannot contest, as in an exegesis which did not yet work with stylistic criticism, its presence, but only its reference.

It can hardly be the last member in the chain, as the conjecture of a relative link ὧν ὁ seeks to assert (according to BAGD, 357a dating from the Socinian J. Schlichting; Barth; Lorrimer, "Romans IX, 3-5"; Bartsch, "Röm. 9, 5," 406ff.; cf. the discussion in Sanday and Headlam; Murray, 245ff.; Michel). We thus have the alternative debated from the days of Arianism (cf. Schelkle, *Paulus,* 331ff.; Lyonnet, *Quaestiones,* II, 21ff.): christological apposition to v. 5a or praise of God in an independent clause looking back to vv. 4-5a. The problem cannot be solved dogmatically, although this has constantly been attempted. The apostle never directly calls Christ God, let alone the emphatic ὁ ἐπὶ πάντων θεός, which would be hard to imagine in view of the subordinationism in 1 Cor 15:27f. It can hardly be accepted, then, that in an extreme paradox anticipating the later doctrine of the two natures, he is according this title to the earthly Messiah of Israel. On the other hand, like Hellenistic Christianity in general, he obviously sees in Christ the pre-existent heavenly being to whom the ἴσα θεῷ of Phil 2:6 applies. Theological interpretation will always build on either the one aspect or the other according to one's total understanding of christology, and arguments to the contrary will be rejected. Today, however, it is only along the lines of stylistic criticism that the debate can be conducted.

One must admit that the form of the doxology is unusual, for elsewhere the predicate comes first, closely related to what precedes (Zahn; Kühl; Lagrange; Prat, *Theology,* II, 126f.; Cullmann, *Christology,* 312f.; Ridderbos). Even more unusual, however, would be a Christ doxology, for which the acclamations of the Kyrios in 1 Cor 8:6; 12:3; Phil 2:11 in Paul, and the δόξα acclamations in Rev 1:6; 2 Pet 3:18, only prepare the way, no such doxology being actually found in the NT. In keeping with this is the fact that predicating Christ directly as God is also singular and that it would obscure the emphasis of the context. The main point here is that of Israel's blessings. A doxology is appropriate, since God has given the blessings and in so doing, as in blessings granted to the Christian community (Eph 4:6), he has shown himself to be ὁ ὢν ἐπὶ πάντων, namely, the one who directs history (Luz, *Geschichtsverständnis*, 27; Berger, "Abraham," 79; Cerfaux, *Christ*, 517ff.; Taylor; Jülicher; Lietzmann; Dodd; Kuss, "Rolle," 129). There is a parallel in the doxology in 11:33-36, and such a doxology impressively manifests the solidarity of the apostle to the Gentiles with his people. Insertions between the article and θεός are to be found elsewhere (Champion, "Benedictions," 124f.). The dominant christological interpretation should be rejected.

B. The Validity and Provisional Goal of Divine Election (9:6-29)

Paul now opens his essential argument. In three stages it deals with the freedom of God, the guilt of Israel, and Israel's final redemption, in such a way that the justification of the ungodly is here again the secret theme of the problem raised.

1. Who Bears the Promise? (9:6-13)

⁶*It is not as though God's word has failed. For not all who descend from Israel are really Israel.* ⁷*Not all are children because they are Abraham's seed. Instead (the rule is): "In Isaac (alone) shall your seed be called."* ⁸*This means that it is not the children of the flesh who are the children of God but (only) the children of the promise are reckoned as seed.* ⁹*For this is what the promise says: "After this time I will come and Sarah shall have a son."* ¹⁰*Nor is this all, but there is the case of Rebekah, who became pregnant by one (man), our father Isaac.* ¹¹*For when (the children) had not yet been born and had done nothing good or bad, it was said to her, in order that God's decision of election might stand,* ¹²*not in accordance with works but in accordance with him who calls: "The elder shall serve the younger."* ¹³*As it is written: "Jacob have I loved, but Esau have I hated."*

Bibliography: A. Dietzel, "Beten im Geist," *TZ* 13 (1957) 12-32; E. von Dobschütz, "Prädestination," *ThStKr* 106 (1934) 9-19; J. Jeremias, "Zur Gedankenführung in den Paulinischen Briefen," *Studia Paulina*, 146-154; S. Lyonnet, "De doctrina praedestinationis et reprobationis in Rom 9," *VD* 34 (1956) 193-201, 257-271; K. Stendahl, "The Apostle Paul and the Introspective Conscience of the West," *HTR* 56 (1963) 199-215.

The heavy observations of the lively debate clearly contrast with the elegant style of the introductory verses. In spite of the many OT quotations, however, this is not a dialogue with the Jews (Dodd; Jeremias, "Gedankenführung," 149) nor an attempt to ward off incipient anti-semitism in Gentile Christianity (Muller-Duvernoy, "Problème," 65ff.). If missionary experiences have influenced what is said (Jeremias, 148; Cerfaux, *Church,* 55), Paul himself shows no sign of it. We cannot speak either of apologetics or of controversy with specific opponents. What we have is theological reflection, which, in the style of the diatribe, is broken up by fictitious objections and the answers to them. If the break in style already shows that vv. 1-13 do not form a unity (*contra* Dupont, "Structure," 388), even less do we have in vv. 6-29 a preliminary question imposed by misunderstandings (*contra* Hoppe, *Heilsgeschichte,* 128f.). Instead, the problem of this whole part of the epistle is formulated in v. 6a (Luz, *Geschichtsverständnis,* 28; Berger, "Abraham," 79; Goppelt, *Christentum,* 113; Kühl). The present section offers a provisional solution to this.

The subsections vv. 6b-9 and vv. 10-13 are parallel and are then brought to a sharp climax in vv. 14-23. In them the issue is the fact and validity of the divine ἐκλογή, while vv. 24-29 speak of the goal of this election of Israel. Thus the different approaches have a clear orientation.

Verse 6a answers a difficulty and mentions indirectly the basis of the complaint in vv. 1f. Israel, the bearer of the promise, has rejected in unbelief the message of Christ which is the fulfilment of the promise. Has not, then, the promise as such become meaningless? The theological depth of the problem was already disclosed in 3:5: Does not God himself fail if his promises remain empty? There the objection was indignantly dismissed, but the problem remains open. The theology and the historical situation of the apostle do not allow him to be satisfied with the solution of later Gentile Christianity that the promise is fulfilled spiritually, namely, in the church (correctly Maier, *Israel,* 17; Munck, *Christ,* 34ff.; Gaugler). This statement is not renounced. Yet it is not enough, because for Paul the church does not simply replace Israel. It is not a new thing with no dimension of depth historically, which then becomes merely a historic entity. The dialectical relation of promise and gospel would thereby lose its seriousness (cf. Ulonska, *Paulus;* Conzelmann, *Outline,* 167ff.). The problem of Israel after the flesh cannot be shoved aside if one is not to end up with Marcion.

For this reason three questions interact and overlap inseparably in what follows: the meaning of Israel's history, the validity of the promise, and the faithfulness and truth of God. It is crucial that the middle one be kept in the center. If not, a survey of the history of exposition will show that there is danger of losing oneself in a theology of history, in a theodicy, or existentialistically in a discussion of the relation of word and faith. Thus detailed questions become independent of the basic problem and come falsely into view. It is not just a matter of the belief in creation (*contra* Müller, *Gottes Volk,* 100), nor of the people (Huby), nor of the confrontation of faith and reality (Luz, *Geschichtsverständnis,* 21). God, people, and faith are at issue and are inseparable, inasmuch as God's electing and differentiating word has gone out to this people in a specific way. Only thus, namely concretely, does the question of predestination have meaning at all; otherwise one would have to speak abstractly of the divine faithfulness and mercy in face of man's refusal. If the promise to the Jews has lost its validity, the gospel can no longer give final assurance (Vischer, "Geheimnis," 82) and everything will depend on a personal faith which no longer has any previously given basis. An ostensible theology of history (Kühl; Jülicher; Weber, *Problem;* Hoppe, *Heilsgeschichte,* 163; Schoeps, *Paul,* 235) unveils itself here most deeply as a theology of the word (Vischer, "Geheimnis," 91f.), and it has a place in the epistle for this reason.

οὐχ οἷον δὲ ὅτι fuses οὐχ οἷον and οὐχ ὅτι (BAGD, 562b; BDF, §304). ὁ λόγος τοῦ θεοῦ should not be related generally to the purpose and will of God (*contra* Zahn; Michel) as the principle of his rule (Cerfaux, *Church,* 59; Güttgemanns, "Heilsgeschichte," 38: the word of the cross!). In context it involves the specific promises to Israel, as in the λόγιαι τοῦ θεοῦ in 3:2. ἐκπίπτειν, used elsewhere only outside the Bible (cf. Michaelis, *TDNT,* VI, 169), means "to fail," "to lose force or validity."

With v. 6b we have the beginning of an answer to the question concealed in v. 6a (*contra* Sanday and Headlam). A reason is given why it cannot be said that God's word has failed. The concept of Israel, like that of the Jew in 2:28f., is used dialectically and its meaning in the second half of the sentence differs from that in the first. For this reason later MSS clarify it by using Ἰσραηλῖται the second time. οἱ ἐξ Ἰσραήλ concerns Israel (Kühl), not the patriarch (Schlatter). Paul is contesting the dominant view that descent determines nature. He does not do this by raising the legal question of legitimacy (*contra* Michel), for this is introduced into the argument only in the quotations in vv. 7b, 9b. He does it in terms of the dualistic antithesis of spirit (or promise) and flesh. This allows him to introduce the idea of the true Israel and correspondingly to vary the motif of the seed of Abraham, as in 4:11ff.

οὐδ' ὅτι means *neque quia* ("nor because") (Lagrange *contra* Jülicher). Paradoxically those who descend from Abraham are not necessarily children of Abraham. This statement is backed up by Gen 21:12, where the promise is linked only with Isaac. Paul, however, divides something that the OT keeps together, since the legitimacy is at stake there to which the Jews can appeal. The point of the argument of Paul is the legitimacy does not guarantee the fulfilment of the promise.

Verse 8 offers a dualistic antithesis in elucidation. The occurrence of ἐπαγγελία is in no way strange or unanticipated (*contra* Lietzmann; cf. Stanley, "Theologia," 130ff.). Materially v. 6a and the citation in v. 7b have it in view, and the whole argument demands it no less than Gal 4:21ff. For Paul only the children of God count as the real children of Abraham. Physical descent and legal legitimacy cannot guarantee this. It applies only to recipients of the promise according to v. 8b. The statement is aimed polemically against dominant views in Judaism (Oepke, *Gottesvolk,* 144). It goes beyond the rabbinic claim that divine sonship is linked to fulfilment of the law, which itself could not prevail against the popular opinion (Billerbeck). For this claim had a hortatory intent; it did not have in view Paul's dualism of flesh and promise, which now replaces that of flesh and spirit. We also should not speak of a spiritualizing of the idea of the covenant (*contra* Schoeps, *Paul,* 238; Peterson, *Kirche,* 18ff.; correctly C. Müller, *Gottes Volk,* 90). The apostle's concern is that the promise is not handed down immanently nor continued physically. It must be spoken and confirmed time and time again (Müller, *Gottes Volk,* 97ff.). In this regard Paul poses a problem which had concerned the OT prophets, Jewish apocalyptic, and then the Qumran community (Dietzel, "Beten," 27; Gnilka, *Verstockung,* 155ff. with many examples; Zeller, *Juden,* 116ff.). The people and the true community had long since ceased to be identical. The question as to the true Israel had been put with increasing urgency. In Qumran a radical answer had been given when Qumran regarded itself as the community of the new covenant. In adopting the problem, however, Paul does not adopt the Jewish answer, which could consist only in the demand for closer keeping of the Torah.

One has to realize that the predestinarian statements of the section arise out of opposition to this demand. The apostle already relates the κληθήσεται of v. 7b to calling by the word of the Creator (Maier, *Israel*, 21; C. Müller, *Gottes Volk*, 28; Luz, *Geschichtsverständnis*, 65; Berger, "Abraham"). In v. 8b he returns to the verb λογίζειν, which in non-Greek fashion stresses God's freedom (Barrett) and means acceptance in his judgment (Heidland, *Anrechnung*, 81). This is more pointed in v. 9: Isaac's birth was only in virtue of divine promise. The quotation is a conflation of Gen 18:10, 14.

Surveying the argument thus far, one sees two difficulties. Verse 8 spoke of a qualitative difference between physical descendants and the children of promise. The consequence ought to be that it is not a matter of physical descent even in the sphere of Israel (Kühl; Lagrange; C. Müller, *Gottes Volk*, 29; Dinkler, "Prädestination," 88). In conflict with that, in vv. 6b-7 Paul emphatically says "not all," thus maintaining for some the continuity between historical Israel and real Israel. It must be emphasized that such a tension (*contra* H. Müller, "Auslegung," 142; Ulonska, *Paulus*, 188) is not resolved by the concept of the holy remnant, which as distinct from contemporary Judaism the apostle uses very rarely, namely, only in the quotation at 9:29 and in ch. 11. The context forces us to attribute the presence of a true Israel within Judaism (cf. 4:11ff.; Gal 4:21ff.) purely to God's electing (C. Müller, *Gottes Volk*, 95). But then the second problem becomes even more pressing. From this perspective in vv. 4f. precisely what meaning does it have that Israel according to the flesh is designated the bearer of the promise and the recipient of sonship? For this asserts continuity in the earthly sphere (Asmussen), which is partially contested in vv. 6b-7 and radically so in v. 8. Any attempt at harmonizing blocks an adequate solution of the basic problem, which in view of the contradiction can only be dialectical and paradoxical. Hasty statements are of no use at this point. There can be no question of "ideal Israel" (Jülicher). If the people as the bearer of the promise is differentiated from the totality of its members (Gutbrod, *TDNT*, III, 386f.), one has to ask where and how this people appears. Is there in fact a continuity of the promise in earthly Israel which, however, is not sustained or guaranteed by the people as such but solely by the acting God? If so, then God is in truth this continuity and Israel is simply the earthly sphere chosen by him. This does fullest justice to the tensions in the text. But first the exegesis must be carried further.

Even more sharply than vv. 6b-9 the second round of proofs in vv. 10-13 grounds the blessing in God's work and word. The elliptical οὐ μόνον δέ, ἀλλά is familiar from 5:3, 11; 8:23. Unlike Isaac and Ishmael both Jacob and Esau are legitimate sons. Moreover, as twins there is no reason to treat them differently. The riddle of the divine election is even more difficult against such a background. Thereby even the sentence structure gets entangled. Verse 10 remains an anacoluthon, followed by a parenthesis in vv. 11-12a. Only v. 12b takes up the subject of v. 10 again, this time in the dative. κοίτην ἔχειν is a euphemism for sexual intercourse, perhaps as in Lev 18:20, 23; Num 5:20 the seminal discharge (Zahn;

Lietzmann; Lagrange; Billerbeck). ἐξ ἑνός points to the apposition, which in Jewish-Christian style calls Isaac "our father." As often in Paul, the anacoluthon indicates a statement of great theological importance. The true point lies in the parenthesis. υἱῶν should be supplied as the subject of the absolute genitive.

At least in fact, if not intentionally, the apostle rejects the haggadic tradition which projects the enmity between the two sons into the time before their birth (cf. Billerbeck). God already dealt with both when they were incapable of either good or bad. In so doing he wishes both to declare the πρόθεσις, i.e., his saving counsel as in 8:28, and to give it permanent validity (Maier, *Israel*, 27). The apposition κατ' ἐκλογήν shows us that this takes concrete shape in choice and election. As in 11:21 a determination of quality is present (Maier, *Israel*, 26). In the context this would have been enough. But the parenthesis is extended by the addition: not of works but of him who calls. The apostle is not dragging in the schemata of his doctrine of justification in a stilted and unnecessary way (*contra* Dodd; Sanday and Headlam). The divine predicate ὁ καλῶν, familiar to us from 4:17, stresses again the motif of the promise. As in creation, so in history God is he who calls and appoints people. The antithesis makes it clear that in this he acts alone when it is a matter of salvation. If the schemata of the doctrine of justification are forcibly introduced into the context, this proves how little Paul wants the theme of chs. 9–11 to be isolated from the epistle as a whole. The problem of Israel and therefore that of salvation history stand under the criteria of the doctrine of justification (Luz, *Geschichtsverständnis*, 29; Bornkamm, *Paul*, 151f.; Eichholz, *Paulus*, 297f., though cf. Zeller, *Juden*, 112). Always and everywhere God is the same in his acts. For the apostle salvation history is obviously not an immanent process of development into which justification can be fitted at the proper place (*contra* Stendahl, "Conscience," 205ff.). Rather justification retains its dominance even in face of and within the scheme of salvation history. This leads in the next verses to statements about divine election which far exceed all others in their harshness.

Verses 12b-13 offer a basis for the parenthesis with two quotations from the OT, Gen 25:23 and Mal 1:2f. As in the rabbinic tradition (Michel, *Bibel*, 83) we thus have a combination of the law and the prophets. The quotations are taken out of their context and its sense is disregarded. For Paul is no longer concerned with two peoples and their destiny (Maier, *Israel*, 28; Michel, *Bibel*, 83; Lietzmann), but timelessly (*contra* Gaugler) with the election and rejection of two persons who are elevated as types (though cf. Huby; Lagrange; Asmussen). In non-Greek fashion the elder and younger sons are distinguished by speaking of the greater and the less (Barrett, though cf. Michel, *TDNT*, IV, 649). 4 Ezra 3:16 also quotes Mal 1:2f.: "Thou didst set apart Israel for thyself, but Esau thou didst reject." The reference, however, is to the relation between Judaism and Rome, so that it does not support Paul's interpretation (cf. Odeberg, *TDNT*, II, 954), whose typology again presupposes correspondence between primal time and end-time. The same applies later to the example of Pharaoh. An eschatological approach uses the examples to illuminate the eschatological problem of Israel and in so doing prepares the way for the eschatological proclamation of vv. 22ff.

But first the motif of predestination must be explained. Expositors have tried to avoid or to soften this question, as though it presented only a hypothesis (e.g.,

264

Kirk, 123ff.). Thus one may not already here explain reprobation as historically limited in the light of ch. 11 (Schrenk, *TDNT*, IV, 209f., cf. 175ff.; Kühl; Munck, *Christ*, 60; Dobschütz, "Prädestination," 15, but cf. Weber, *Problem*, 29ff.; Hoppe, *Heilsgeschichte*, 122f.). This is true in fact. But it does not mean that the present verse has only a propaedeutic task (*contra* Weber, *Problem*, 36ff.). We have here a basic statement. Verses 10-13 are intensified in v. 14. Otherwise the typology present is not understood. It is a softening as well when a person, following the cited text in its original meaning, sees it speaking of nations, not of individuals (Sanday and Headlam; Lagrange; Lyonnet, "Doctrina"; Munck, *Christ*, 41f.; Peterson, "Kirche," 252; Leenhardt; but cf. Murray). In reality this makes the statement only worse, not better, and the typology, which does not replace historical reality (*contra* C. Müller, *Gottes Volk*, 75), becomes allegory. The use of the example of Pharaoh in the Greek gloss at Sir 16:15f. in no way supports this understanding (Kühl; Dobschütz, "Prädestination," 12; Dinkler, "Prädestination," 88). The text also refutes (Weber, *Problem*, 17ff.; Murray) the postulate that election is not counterbalanced by rejection and that the antithesis "love–hate," which is common and serious in Qumran, simply reproduces the wording of the text quoted, whereas the apostle himself expresses no more than mercy and hardening thereby (cf. v. 18) (Sanday and Headlam; Huby; Zerwick, "Drama," 235ff.). Clearly the aim of expositors who proceed along such lines is to save human responsibility, and the same is true when they relate vv. 12b-13 simply to leadership in relation to human enterprises (Huby; Schrenk, *TDNT*, IV, 175f., 179). Then a simple protest against the view presented here and a charge of inconsistency in view of Pauline practice would be far more to the point (Jülicher). Finally, it is true, of course, that this section treats the freedom and omnipotence of the Creator (C. Müller, *Gottes Volk*, 27ff.; Ridderbos). Yet one should not be satisfied with that because more happens here.

The presence of a strong concept of predestination cannot be denied (Dobschütz, "Prädestination," 9; Oepke, *Gottesvolk*, 214), although only here does Paul present double ·predestination (Dinkler, "Prädestination," 92). Not until this is admitted without reserve can one see its necessary delimitations and ask about its significance within the framework of the apostle's theology. Certainly Paul has no speculative interest in pre-temporal predestination (Ridderbos). Over against dogmatic prejudice it should be noted that here and elsewhere the predestinarian statements are not set, as in Sir 33:7ff., in the doctrine of God as such (*contra* Nygren; Weber, *Problem*, 105ff.; Maier, *Israel*, 13). Since the theme is Israel, the issue is soteriology (Asmussen). From v. 12a it follows even more precisely that the doctrine of the justification of the ungodly (*iustificatio impiorum*) is anchored in the sovereign freedom of the Creator. One would do well to remember texts like 4:17ff.; 1 Cor 1:18ff., 26ff.; 2 Cor 2:15f. They show that in Paul predestination is connnected with the word of God and manifests its efficacy. The call of God constitutes acceptance and rejection in history, whether of the promise or of the gospel. In it God shows himself to be Creator (C. Müller, *Gottes Volk*, 78f.) and Judge. This is why the apostle conversely can give examples and make deductions from biblical history as hedges here.

For Paul predestination does not have the function of displaying the prescience of God and his determination of the world. An eternal order is not program-

265

matically established thereby. God's word comes on the scene as a stigmatizing address with which salvation or perdition takes place for human beings. The category of the "before us" of this word unfolds itself in the "for us" and "against us." The result is to show that the doctrine of justification cannot be restricted to the individual or to the present situation, true though it is that it comes to concrete historical shape in anthropology. In 1:18–3:20; 5:12ff.; 8:18ff. it is not for nothing set in a cosmic framework, and it is not accidental that it is taken up into the doctrine of baptism as incorporation into the worldwide body of Christ. Soteriology and salvation history as defined earlier are inseparable. Obviously then, as Paul sees it, the problem of Israel can and must be understood in this context.

In justification it is not primarily a matter of the conscience (cf. Stendahl, "Conscience") but of God's rule over the world and concretely over the individual. God's right to the world is necessarily also his right to Israel if his election of this people and promise to it are not to be meaningless. This right is contested, however, so long as man still tries, as the example of Israel shows. to set his own rights and privileges over against God. Not only as a Jew, but also as a theologian and as the apostle to the Gentiles, Paul recognizes the fulness of the promise to Israel. If on this ground it is claimed that the seed of Abraham possesses continuity of salvation, Paul opposes to this the dialectic of the true Israel and the purely fleshly Israel. Then he advances the statement about predestination, which protects the freedom and sole efficacy of God. Both are held together under the rubric of the word of God, which alone grants continuity. The word establishes salvation history. For this reason, this constantly breaks off and even in the sphere [. of Israel (as of the church in 1 Cor 10:1-13!), which is legitimate from an earthly standpoint and has its origin in the promise, can turn into a history of ruin. Paul's doctrine of salvation history is a variation on his doctrine of the justification of the ungodly. The human and the earthly can never ensure their continuation. Received salvation is not as such a pledge of its permanence, which depends instead on the call constantly being received and accepted anew. Of course, the apostle is not satisfied-with such an assertion. Seeing the breadth and depth of the event of justification, he is forced to affirm rejection as well as election, and to derive this too from the word which moves before us. This carries with it, of course, the danger that the message of justification by faith will become meaningless and that determination by the unfathomable will of God will replace it. What follows shows at least that Paul recognized the danger.

2. God's Free Power (9:14-23)

[14]*What shall we say then? Is there injustice with God? Not at all!* [15]*For he says to Moses, "I will have mercy on whom I have mercy, and I will have compassion on whom I have compassion."* [16]*So it does not lie with him who strives and runs but with God who shows mercy.* [17]*For Scripture says to Pharaoh, "I have raised you up precisely to show my power in you and that my name should be proclaimed in all the earth."* [18]*Thus he has mercy on whom he wills and he hardens whom he wills.* [19]*You will then say to me, "Why does he still find fault (then)? For who can resist his will?"* [20]*But who are you, O*

man, to dare to answer God back? Can the work say to him who made it,
"Why have you made me thus?" [21]*Does not the potter have free control over*
the clay, to make of the same lump one vessel for an ornament and another
for lowly use? [22]*God is (thus) within his rights if he wished to display his wrath*
and make known his power (and therefore) with great patience endured the
vessels of wrath fashioned for destruction [23]*and (if he planned) to manifest the*
rich fulness of his majesty on the vessels of mercy which he had foreordained
to glory.

Bibliography: G. Bornkamm, "Paulinische Anakoluthe," *Ende des Gesetzes,* 76-92; R. Bultmann, "Gnade und Freiheit," *Glaube und Geschichte. Festschrift für Friedrich Gorgarten*
(ed. H. Runte; 1948) 7-20; V. C. Pfitzner, *Paul and the Agon Motif* (NovTSup 16; 1967). See
also the bibliography for 9:6-13. For H. Braun, "Selbstverständnis," see the bibliography
for 7:7-13.

The style of the diatribe is particularly evident in this section. There is no trace
of concrete opponents or missionary experiences. Theological problems hold the
stage and the statements made are sharpened, not softened. As the answer shows,
the question in v. 14 refers to God's acts, not his attributes (C. Müller, *Gottes*
Volk, 31). ἀδικία means judicial injustice, not deviation from a norm (*contra* Kühl)
or the wrong done to God by what has been said (*contra* Ridderbos). It is understandable that commentators have found theodicy here. But they make this abstract and discuss a concept of God, whereas for Paul everything comes down to
the justice of God in his concrete acts (Müller, *Gottes Volk,* 83ff.). The quotation
from Exod 33:19 does not speak of Moses as the mediator of revelation (*contra*
Kühl; Jülicher; Gaugler, cf. Michel; Lagrange; Schrenk, *TDNT,* II, 56 for a correct
view) but the opponent of Pharaoh. The antitheses Isaac–Ishmael and Jacob–
Esau thus continue and characterize Paul's view of salvation history, which is
always determined by the conflict between the elected and the rejected. Scripture
bears witness to this on both sides. Hence vv. 15f. and 17f. form an antithetical
parallelism in which the same basic insight follows the quotations in the form of
a dogmatic judgment.

Paul then does not actually establish the rejection of the question he has
raised. He rather reads from Scripture that God's line of action does not change
(Althaus; G. Maier, *Mensch,* 367). In content God's justice is incomparable. It
consists in the fact that he remains the Creator (Schlatter; Michel). His saving
work is thus bound to his free will. This contrasts with the Pharisaic exposition,
summed up in *Pss. Sol.* 9:4f., which demands the meriting of pity (Billerbeck).
All human cooperation in salvation is ruled out when a person truly is bound to
the power and will of the Creator.

τρέχειν, taken over from the diatribe as in 1 Cor 9:24, 26; Gal 2:2; 5:7; Phil 2:16,
means the contest in the arena (Pfitzner, *Agon,* 135f.). θέλειν means striving after
a goal. ὁ ἐλεῶν is probably already a fixed Jewish predicate for God (Billerbeck).
The statement about predestination is again linked with the doctrine of justification when God's freedom presents the essence of grace (C. Müller, *Gottes Volk,*
31; Barrett) and mercy has precedence over hardening. On the other hand, the

message of justification would not be what it is without the depth of the predestinarian statement, since it does not merely concern the debate with Judaism.
Since it destroys any autonomy of the human will and therefore also pious achievement, the right of the Creator to his creature is established in it, and God's deity
grounds and discloses man's humanity. The example of Pharaoh shows that this
is true even if one does not put his faith in God.

In v. 17 ἡ γραφή is the personified voice of God received by the later reader.
The quotation from Exod 9:16 does not follow the LXX (Michel, *Bibel*, 76). Following a text closer to the original Paul has ἐξεγείρειν, "set up, allow to appear"
for διατηρεῖσθαι, "allow to exist." The meaning is not, then, "call into being"
(Oepke, *TDNT*, II, 338) or "establish in patience" (Ridderbos, cf. the survey in
Sanday and Headlam). The first person active, substituted for the LXX second
person passive, adds emphasis to the predestinating will of God, and εἰς αὐτὸ
τοῦτο underscores that. δύναμις here is the power of the Creator in judgment.
The final clauses are coordinated as in the LXX. The second indicates materially
the result and goal of the first. διαγγέλλειν has the sense "to proclaim" (Schniewind, *TDNT*, I, 68). δύναμις and ὄνομα almost overlap, since the power manifested makes known the one who exerts it (Bietenhard, *TDNT*, V, 277). Pharaoh's
defiance serves the worldwide glorifying of the one who smites him and is thus
willed by God.

As a parallel to v. 16, but looking back again to v. 15, v. 18 draws the conclusion from that, whose point lies in the double ὃν θέλει. σκληρύνειν, "to harden,"
is to be explained from the tradition of Exod 4:21, etc., since elsewhere in the NT
it has the other meaning "to resist the word" (Michel). The verb is no less strong
than "to reject" (*contra* Kühl; Gutjahr). It should not be thought that thereby   [25
wickedness is already presupposed (Zahn; Lagrange; Leenhardt; Bardenhewer;
Munck, *Christ*, 43ff.; correctly Weber, *Problem*, 18f.). The context and antithesis
show that hardening to judgment is meant. To that extent Paul's view of salvation
history presupposes constitutively a double predestination (*gemina praedestina-
tio*), since it is oriented to the event of justification (*contra* Brunner). This links
our text with those statements according to which (cf. 1:24ff.) God's wrath hands
over the sinner to himself, the misunderstood law (cf. 3:19; 5:20; 7:8ff.) brings
universal guilt, and Adam's sin (cf. 5:12ff.) affects all humanity (Schlatter). In the
same way the fact that baptism points to prevenient grace (*gratia praeveniens*)
and the justification of the ungodly (*iustificatio impii*) belongs in such a context.
If the apostle's doctrine of predestination is denied or weakened, this affects not
only the radical nature of his doctrine of justification. A person also misunderstands the distinctiveness of his view of salvation history, which takes on the
character of a process of development with distinguishable moral stages (crassly
stated in Dodd). Even Paul's "ethics" is misinterpreted, since the grounding of
the imperative in the irreversible indicative has to be explained as the co-existence
of a moral and religious approach (Dobschütz, "Prädestination," 19) and the new
obedience no longer appears as the work of the Spirit.

Only then can one finally orient Pauline theology to the individual in such a
way that salvation history is reduced to the sum of situations of decision, and
historicity made its determinative aspect (Bultmann, *Theology*, I, 329f.; "Gnade
und Freiheit," 15). The idea that election takes place in faith, not behind or before

it (Bultmann, *loc. cit.*), undoubtedly runs counter to the apostle's view (C. Müller, *Gottes Volk*, 80f.; Maier, *Mensch*, 356f.). Here as elsewhere there is emphasis on the "prior," and for this reason election is coordinated with rejection. Election certainly manifests itself in faith and predestination is not in general described as a pre-temporal event. If, however, rejection is said to be transitory, so, too, election must be classified as transitory. Since the apostle usually relates predestination to proclamation, it takes on a decidedly historical character. God's word predestines to salvation or perdition. For this reason the doctrine of justification does not simply coincide with a doctrine of faith, and historical existence is transcended in a distinctive way (Dinkler, "Prädestination," 97). Expositors almost unanimously agree that this situation cannot be reduced to the denominator of determinism. Logically, then, it should not be linked with a view of free will and free decision (*contra* Sickenberger; Müller, *Gottes Volk*, 79ff. is right here). In either case a specific and probably outdated anthropology would become the norm of interpretation. This will call mythological and speculative the statement that God in his righteousness maintains his right to his creation, and justification will have to be illegitimately individualized and detached from salvation history.

The argument in vv. 15-18 does not take us beyond v. 13. Hence v. 19 repeats the question of v. 14 in the name of mankind's diminished responsibility (Lagrange; Nygren; Brunner; Barrett). If the counterquestion is a favorite stylistic device in the diatribe, its formulation may be connected to OT tradition as in Job 9:12b, 19b and more closely Wis 12:12; 11:21, which continues in 1QS 11:22 (Lietzmann; C. Müller, *Gottes Volk*, 30). βούλημα, "pleasure, discretion, humor" (Schrenk, *TDNT*, I, 637) and ἀνθιστάναι probably derive from the language of the LXX and point to a forensic situation. There is no reason to see in μέμφεσθαι a particularly mild expression which looks to the story of Pharaoh (Zahn). Nor is a Jew speaking here (*contra* Peterson, "Kirche," 259; Maier, *Mensch*, 372f.), since what is said applies to all people in their limits. ἀνθέστηκεν is a gnomic perfect. μενοῦν γε adds force to μὲν οὖν, "strictly," "properly" (BAGD, 503b); in contrast to classical usage (BDF, §450[4]) it stands at the beginning of the sentence (cf. 10:19; Luke 11:28; Phil 3:18). ἀνταποκρίνεθαι means "to argue with." The Greek, too, can say that a human being should not argue with God (cf. BAGD, 73a). Paul strikes down the objection. A human being cannot become God's accuser, for right is not a neutral norm for the creature but is given only by the Creator, whose own right is coincident with his creative freedom (Schlatter; Michel; Vischer, "Geheimnis," 97).

Verses 20b-21 underscore the statement with a double illustration. This must not be allegorized. It comes from a broad OT tradition (cf. Isa 29:16; 45:9; 64:7; Jer 18:3-6; Job 10:9; 33:6 and the ensuing Jewish texts) (Luz, *Geschichtsverständnis*, 238; Maier, *Mensch*, 98ff., 376 on Sir 33:7-15). Paul develops the tradition in his own way but seems to borrow from Isa 29:16 in v. 20b and comes very close to Wis 15:7 in v. 21b. The question in v. 20b reminds us of Isa 45:9 but is hardly borrowed from there. The OT texts do not have the focus in με or the οὕτως, which points not to the manner (Zahn) but the result (Kühl). πλάσσειν and ποιεῖν are already parallels in the LXX (Braun, *TDNT*, VI, 260). φύραμα means the "lump" (BAGD, 869a). τοῦ πηλοῦ goes with ἐξουσίαν. In the conclusion the reference is not to vessels of higher or lower value (Sanday and Headlam; Gutjahr;

269

Huby; Schlatter), but to the different ways they are used (Ridderbos). σκεῦος in Greek (BAGD, 754a), like the rabbinic כלי (Billerbeck), can refer to people, and in Qumran the designation as a "work of clay" is stereotypical (Braun, *Selbstverständnis*, 105ff.). Modern perception regards the subject matter and the image incommensurate: Man is not a pot (Dodd; Leenhardt; Huby; cf. Gale, *Analogy*, 200). But Jewish self-understanding did not see any difficulties in it, so that allegory is excluded (Luz, *Geschichtsverständnis*, 239). Whereas Philo traces back creation to God's ἀγαθότης, and distinguishes ἐξουσία from this as his dominion over what is created (Foerster, *TDNT*, II, 567), for Paul (cf. 1:20; 4:17) everything depends on the omnipotence of the Creator, which can also take the form of patience. Against this there is no legal appeal or autonomy of Christian liberty.

Verses 19-21 are an "episode" (Kühl; K. Barth). They do not advance the argument but probably meet objections. Verses 22-23 draw the conclusion and prepare the ground for the concrete application. The change is marked by the transition from diatribe style and wisdom motifs to eschatological terminology and thought (Munck, *Christ*, 60ff.; Peterson, "Kirche," 260; Barrett). When vessels of wrath and mercy are mentioned they refer to specific groups, although the statement is still general. In concrete application the first reference is to unbelieving Jews, even if Gentiles are substantively included (most exegetes but cf. Munck, *Christ*, 66; Michel). σκεύη ὀργῆς are spoken of as objects, not qualifyingly as instruments of wrath (*contra* Schlatter; Maurer, *TDNT*, VII, 364), although the formula in Isa 13:5 Symm; Jer 27:25 LXX speaks of "weapons of wrath." Naturally an impersonal process of wrath, carried forward by the σκεύη (*contra* A. T. Hanson, *The Wrath of the Lamb* [1957] 90ff.), is not in view, but the power of the final Judge already manifested in the present, as in 1:18–3:20. ἐνδείξασθαι has the same meaning as the noun in 3:25f., and γνωρίζειν is also a revelatory term. The statement plainly takes up v. 17 and thereby presents in reverse order (Maier, *Israel*, 39; Lyonnet, *Quaestiones*, II, 49) the typological relationship between God's sayings to Moses and Pharaoh and the eschatological event.

The complicated problem of the sentence structure is to be approached in the light of this insight. The anacoluthon again indicates a decisive step in the thought. The omitted conclusion may be taken from v. 21: It is God's right. The close connection between wrath and patience has often been confusing, so that an outdated exegesis explained it antithetically in the sense of 2:4. In *2 Apoc. Bar.* 59:6 the greatness of patience is expressed in refraining from wrath and in 4 Ezra 7:74 the period of forbearance precedes judgment (cf. Horst, *TDNT*, IV, 376ff.). If this view is adopted εἰ θέλων has to be concessive: although he intended (Sanday and Headlam; Zahn; Gutjahr; Leenhardt; Kirk; Lyonnet, "Doctrina," 263ff.). This makes the present the final time for repentance (Brunner; Stählin, *TDNT*, V, 425f.; rejected by Weber, *Problem*, 60). We reach the same sense if v. 22 is subordinated to the ἵνα clause in v. 23 (Zahn; Schlatter), and this makes understandable the dropping of the undoubtedly original (though cf. BDF, §467) καί in v. 23 by B 69 vg Or. The whole interpretation falls to the ground, however, if in v. 22 we have an eschatological equivalent of the declaration in v. 17 (Bornkamm, "Anakoluthe," 90f.; Maier, *Israel*, 44). God's judgment is already executed on the vessels of wrath in the fact that they are left to their defiance and guilt (cf. 1:24ff.). In context τὸ δυνατὸν αὐτοῦ means God's omnipotence. This mysteriously manifests itself precisely when it faces its enemies in longsuffering. ἤνεγκεν . . . thus corresponds in meaning to ἐξήγειρά σε in v. 17 and παρέδωκεν in 1:24ff. The perspective is apocalyptic and Jewish parallels show that the same is true in the case of μακροθυμία (C. Müller, *Gottes Volk*, 32). εἰ δὲ θέλων then has to be causal (Kühl; Michel; Barrett; H. W. Schmidt; Murray) or better modal: "with the purpose" (Zahn; Bornkamm, *loc. cit.*; Maurer, *TDNT*, VII, 363; Luz, *Geschichtsverständnis*, 243f.: final). καὶ ἵνα relates elliptically to θέλων (Kühl); καί does not intensify (Maurer, *TDNT*, VII, 363) but coordinates the parallel vv. 22 and 23 (Lietzmann; Lagrange; Michel; Barrett; H. W. Schmidt; Vischer, "Geheimnis," 97ff., though cf. Plag, *Wege*, 15ff., 23).

It is not accidental that Paul ends with v. 23, reversing the order of vv. 15-18. The plerophoric and perhaps liturgical (cf. Eph 1:18; 3:16) phrase πλοῦτος τῆς δόξης (Michel) makes good sense. Salvation and perdition are not counterbalanced, as might at first appear. Chapter 11 will show explicitly that perdition serves salvation. If in v. 23a δόξα designates the divine majesty (BAGD, 203b), in v. 23b it means eschatological glorification (Zahn). The two do not stand unrelated. God's πλοῦτος is in the Pauline and deutero-Pauline corpus the fulness of his grace, not of his being. This creates σκεύη ἐλέους. Eschatological glorification takes place already now in such a way that God's claim to lordship over the world (von Rad, *TDNT*, II, 242) establishes itself over his creatures and restores the divine likeness (cf. 8:30) lost according to 3:23. This does not mean, as is later asserted in 2 Pet 1:4, that they gain a share in the divine. Rather they become the sphere of the rule of grace instead of wrath, as formerly. Thus the Pauline doctrine of justification appears anew, which not only implies individual forgiveness and redemption but also declares the establishment of God's right to his possession.

Finally, the two appositions, which take up the motif of predestination again at the conclusion, must be understood from this perspective. It is not true that only here is there clear reference to foreordination to salvation and perdition. But the two participles no longer point to historical election and rejection, but to the eternal counsel (Jülicher; Lagrange; Dobschütz, "Prädestination," 13; Maier, *Mensch*, 381). One cannot evade this by giving κατηρτισμένα the nuance "to be ripe for" (Zahn; Sanday and Headlam; Lagrange; Gutjahr; Murray; Franzmann; Leenhardt; Ridderbos; Maier, *Israel*, 47, but cf. Weber, *Problem*, 30; Stählin, *TDNT*, V, 442). προητοίμασεν, which points clearly to the plan of salvation, rules this out. Rabbinic equivalents should be noted which speak apocalyptically of salvation history (Billerbeck, I, 981f.). That Paul is following an established tradition here may be seen especially from the fact that for Qumran double predestination divided the community even from the rest of Israel (Gnilka, *Verstockung*, 181f.; Braun, *Qumran*, II, 243ff.; Larsson, *Vorbild*, 297f.; Maier, *Mensch*, 202ff., 260ff.). Thus 1QS 3:15-17 says: "All being and occurrence comes from the God of knowledge. Before they are, he has fixed their place. And when they are there as appointed, they fulfil their work according to his glorious plan, and there is no alteration. In his hand are decrees for everything." There is a point of contact for this view in Judaism (cf. Bousset-Gressmann, *Religion*, 373f.; Moore, *Judaism*, I, 455ff.). As such, however, it came from outside (Maier, *Mensch*, 98ff., 113ff.), since the Rabbinate constantly defended human responsibility and therefore also human free will (Maier, *Mensch*, 363f.).

Prepared for since Sir 33:7ff., the predestinarian statements of the apostle grow on the soil of the apocalyptic represented by Qumran (C. Müller, *Gottes Volk*, 77ff.; Luz, *Geschichtsverständnis*, 228ff.). This is especially true of the appositions in vv. 22-23, which go beyond vv. 11-13. It should be remembered, of course, that our verses see both wrath and grace manifested now and use the motif of divine forbearance with regard to the vessels of wrath. Interest focuses, then, not on eternal destiny and eschatological judgment, but on salvation history rooted in the promise (Michel; on the tension at Qumran cf. Maier, *Mensch*, 230ff., 248). προητοίμασεν comes to actualization in the καλεῖν of v. 24, which is already a keyword in vv. 7 and 11. One may thus ask whether the apostle did not understand differently the tradition given to him, just as in 2 Cor 2:14ff. κατηρτισμένα related to the double qualification of the hearers which results from the message of salvation. This would make it easier to understand the dialectic of our chapter as it leads on to ch. 11. Closely related to this question is the further one whether Paul is speaking here of individuals (Dinkler, "Prädestination," 88) or not. For the typologies in vv. 9-18 maintain that he is, and the basic consideration in v. 21 is not to be understood differently. On the other hand vv. 22f. are interpreted in terms of the antithesis of church and synagogue in vv. 24-29. This permits the conclusion that Paul has these "peoples" in view when he speaks of the vessels of wrath and of mercy (*contra* Dinkler, 88, who concedes this only from v. 30 on). [Then one could certainly no longer say (Dinkler, 97; cf. Munck, *Christ*, 70; Peterson, "Kirche," 261) that Paul is primarily concerned with the anthropological problem here. Besides, the unity of the epistle cannot be maintained under such an aspect. For the moment, however, these questions are mentioned only provisionally. The sentence breaks off abruptly. Paul leaves the field of apparently abstract possibilities and of what seem even in vv. 22f. to be merely hypothetical considerations. He returns to reality (Bornkamm, "Anakoluthe," 91). He does this in such a way that it now emerges that the possibilities were not in truth abstract nor the considerations hypothetical (Luz, *Geschichtsverständnis*, 245ff.). The justice of God has a concrete goal.

3. The Provisional Goal of Divine Election (9:24-29)

²⁴*He has also called them, (namely) us, not only from the Jews but also from the Gentiles.* ²⁵*He says this in Hosea, "I will call 'my people' what was not my people and 'beloved' those who were not beloved.* ²⁶*This will happen in the place where it was said to them, 'You are not my people.' There they will be called 'sons of the living God.' "* ²⁷*But Isaiah cries concerning Israel, "Though the number of the children of Israel be as the sand of the sea, (only) the remnant will be saved.* ²⁸*For the Lord will hold a reckoning on earth, fulfilling and curtailing."* ²⁹*As Isaiah also foretold, "If the Lord of Sabaoth had not left us a seed, we should have been like Sodom and become like Gomorrah."*

Bibliography: J. A. Fitzmyer, "The Use of Explicit OT Quotations in Qumran Literature and in the NT," *NTS* 7 (1960/61) 297-333; J. Jeremias, "Der Gedanke des Heiligen Restes im Spätjudentum und in der Verkündigung Jesu," *ZNW* 42 (1949) 184-194; see also the bibliography for 9:6-13.

Since God's deity is not just an idea for Paul, vv. 6b-23 do not (Dodd) express abstract and academic considerations, but describe what really was and continues to be (Schlatter). Unlike allegory, comparisons and typology do not erase history but clarify God's acts. Verses 24-27 state the provisionally attained goal. Verse 24 presents it thematically as the church of Jews and Gentiles. It is for the sake of this that the apostle has argued from predestination. The eschatological reality is not a historically contingent event as those must maintain who deny salvation history along with the counsel to save. Conversely predestination is not despotic caprice when it establishes salvation history. Its soteriological function is just as constitutive as its connection with the word of God which works creatively and directs it. That explains the dialectic which controls our chapter (Dinkler, "Prädestination," 98).

The promise which has been given to Israel and the goal of God's saving counsel which is perceptible at present diverge. Hence Paul has to show that the divine promise is neither calculable nor a human privilege. Salvation history is not a process of continuous development. It is the history of the word which constantly goes forth afresh and accomplishes election and rejection. In this way the Jewish belief in election is transcended (Peterson, "Kirche," 262).

To the οὐ πάντες of vv. 6ff. there now corresponds the οὐ μόνον, ἀλλὰ καί. In place of the earlier restriction we now have extension. Both have a qualitative and not merely a quantitative character (Peterson, "Kirche," 262ff.). Does the καί stress ἡμᾶς (Lietzmann and most commentators), as the attraction of the relative seems to show, or is ἐκάλεσεν emphasized in an intensifying of the preceding προητοίμασεν (Kühl; Maier, *Israel*, 50)? The fact that the relative is in general continued seems to support the latter. Then ἡμᾶς is even more surprising. Ephesians regards the union of Jewish- and Gentile-Christians in the church as the eschatological mystery as such and lets Pauline theology lead to that. The apostle at least builds a path toward such a view. For "not only from the Jews but also from the Gentiles" says that the church cannot be compared either to a Jewish or to a Gentile society. In continuity with God's ancient people it is the true Israel, while in antithesis to this people it is the new people of God and the new covenant. In the Jewish view still found in Paul, Jews and Gentiles characterize the world in its unity and contradiction. Hence the church, in which both are found, is more than a religious group or even a people; it is the new world. If the ἐξ can be related to ἐκάλεσεν, it is in fact called out of the peoples of the old aeon. The popular etymology of the word ἐκκλησία is philologically incorrect, but Bengel is not mistaken when he sees in this "calling from" the derivation of the church.

The quotations which follow confirm for the apostle the fact that the uniting of Jews and Gentiles is an eschatological event. Scripture predicted this reality and thus gave expression to the προητοίμασεν. That similar groups of quotations were used in missions before Paul is undoubtedly correct (Sanday and Headlam), but it cannot be proved that they were used liturgically. The combination is Paul's own (*contra* Michel). As though they went together, he gives the sayings from Hos 2:25; 2:1 LXX a common introduction. In the first he replaces ἐρῶ by καλέσω, which was so important to him and which points again to God's creative power. He also reverses the lines so as to stress the idea of God's people. ἐν τῷ 'Ωσῆε refers to the book. The prophets are seen here as mediators of God's speech, as in the rabbis (Billerbeck) and Qumran (Fitzmyer, "Use," 302). Yet inspiration does not exclude their own responsibility as in Philo (Schrenk, *TDNT*, I, 757; distorted in Ulonska, *Paulus,* 189). ὡς καί obviously does not introduce any comparison with OT history (*contra* Sanday and Headlam; Zahn). As is his custom Paul understands the sayings as eschatologically oriented oracles without considering their original sense (Kühl; Lagrange; Maier, *Israel,* 55). In chiastic contrast to the order in v. 24 the Gentiles are the recipients of the promise, which lifts them out of chaos and makes them beloved children and the eschatological people of God. The provocative nature of this statement (*contra* Sanday and Headlam; Huby; Ridderbos) is plain when one compares it with *Jub.* 2:19: "Lo, I will separate for myself a people from all peoples; they shall keep the sabbath and I will sanctify them to me as my people and will bless them . . . and they shall be my people and I shall be their God." As pious works have here a place in the promise, so it is in rabbinic exposition of the Hosea texts (Billerbeck; Schoeps, *Paul,* 240). In Paul, however, the whole stress is on the miracle of grace which transforms the ungodly.

What has been said is repeated in the words of Hos 2:1. Obviously ἐκεῖ, whether it was already in the LXX or added by Paul (cf. Munck, *Christ,* 12, 72; *Salvation,* 306), does not denote Palestine as the site where the Gentiles will   [2 gather eschatologically, and, "it is hoped, by the end of the third missionary journey" (Munck; cf. Sanday and Headlam; Michel). ἐν τῷ τόπῳ like ἐκεῖ stands emphatically for "in the place of" (Black). Paul probably has his missionary work in view (Strathmann, *TDNT,* IV, 54) and with great audacity he takes the promises to Israel and relates them to the Gentile-Christians. This stands in sharp antithesis to the statements, for example, in 4 Ezra 6:55, 59; 7:11, in which the world was created for the sake of the Jews and the Gentile nations are declared to be nothing. The fact that the apostle takes this line, even though the drift of his argument forces him to emphasize the ongoing election of Israel, points to the most prominent feature in the eschatological present, namely, that the 'Ιουδαίῳ πρῶτον of 1:16 is paradoxically reversed, a point which is usually (Sanday and Headlam; Huby; Munck, *Christ,* 73f.; Best) missed. Both occur in the same epistle and this characterizes Paul's view of salvation history, whose continuity is not logical. Place is found for the statement that the first shall be last and for the eschatological transvaluation of values of 1 Cor 1:26ff. Paul does not think in terms of a schema of development. He presents the freedom of the Creator and the incomprehensibility of his historical direction which is determined by miracles, whereby the primal history documented in Scripture points to the reality of the history of the end-time.

This is even more strongly brought out in vv. 27ff. Only now is there reference to Israel with the two quotations from Isaiah. In Greek (BAGD, 447-48), as

274

in the rabbinic equivalent (Billerbeck), κράζειν means inspired, proclamatory speech. ὑπέρ has the same sense as περί. In the conditional clause from Isa 10:22 ὁ ἀριθμὸς τῶν υἱῶν is added from the statement of Hos 2:1 just cited. If association forms the transition from what precedes, in content an antithesis is given. But one does not then hear fresh promise and consolation as might be expected from v. 24 (Weber, *Problem*, 61f.; Zerwick, "Drama," 330ff.; Lyonnet, *Quaestiones*, II, 61f.). Instead judgment is proclaimed (Kühl; Gutjahr). Only a remnant will be saved. The hyperbole of the first clause underlines this.

This helps us to understand the following quotation from Isa 10:23, although its corrupt state does not permit of sure interpretation and a mistake in copying might be conjectured (Kühl). συντελεῖν and συντέμνειν seem to have become an apocalyptic formula from the time of Dan 5:27 LXX and 9:24 Theod. This brings out the decisive point for Paul in Isa 10:23. The sense, then, must be threatening (*contra* Zeller, *Juden*, 121; cf. on the possibilities BAGD, 792b) and will not endure the supplementation from the LXX text in the *koine*. The participles should not be separated. The unarticulated λόγον does not, then, refer to God's word, to whose restriction Paul can hardly be referring (*contra* most commentators). Does it mean the event (Ridderbos) and technically an accounting (Zahn; Gutjahr; Vischer, "Geheimnis," 102)? The possible understanding of the formula "to execute and act abruptly" (BAGD, 792b; Delling, *TDNT*, VIII, 64) would permit this, with judicial liquidation in view (Nygren; Vischer, "Geheimnis," 102). But a reference to world judgment does not correspond to the context, which speaks of the eschatological present (Maier, *Israel*, 59). Above all, it is impossible to miss an allusion to the idea of the remnant, which can be found only in συντέμνων (Jülicher; Sickenberger; Michel). Hence the participle has to mean "restrictive" (Sickenberger; Maier, *Israel*, 58f.). If the selected translation has only the value of a hypothesis, it is in keeping with the quotation from Isa 1:9, whose introduction calls for a supplementary, "It has been fulfilled." As in Rev 11:8 what was in the OT a comparison has become an eschatological reality for the apostle. The apocalyptic view of the present means that the judgment that has fallen on Israel's unbelief has to be painted so darkly that as a result the force of v. 24 is almost lost (Michel). The line from vv. 6b-22 is maintained in these final verses and not replaced by promise (*contra* Maier, *Israel*, 61). In a way which surpasses all that has been said thus far the chapter ends by seeing in Sodom and Gomorrah types of the present state of Israel as a whole.

Only against this background is it stated that the promise is not invalidated and that Jews, too, are chosen and called. The latter is no less a divine miracle. But whereas in relation to Gentiles the free power of the Creator comes to expression in the fulness of glory, in relation to Israel it does so in the preservation of a remnant. An OT motif is thus adopted which already had influenced many circles in Judaism and was of supreme significance for the earliest Jewish Christianity (cf. Jeremias, "Rest," 184ff.; Herntrich, Schrenk, *TDNT*, IV, 196ff.; Munck, *Christ*, 111f. for bibliography). Along these lines primitive Christian apocalyptic understood itself as God's people of the renewed covenant with the eschatological gathering of Israel as its task (Oepke, *Gottesvolk*, 105ff., 148ff.; Becker, *Heil Gottes*, 62ff.; Dahl, *Volk Gottes*, 84). The Qumran community had the same self-understanding, but in distinction from Christianity sought actualization along the path of a sharpening of the Torah (Gnilka, *Verstockung*, 159ff.). For Jesus (cf. Jeremias, "Rest," 191f.), as for Paul, a critical attitude to this view is characteristic, since he does not want to gather a community of those who are radically faithful to the law. The church soon parted company with it in pursuance of its worldwide mission. Paul adopts the motif here and in 11:4ff. Yet he no longer uses it as a basis for his whole ecclesiology. He has in view only a part of the ecclesiological problem, namely, that of the relation of Jewish Christianity to Judaism and also to the new people of God. This problem, with which he wrestles most intensely, cannot be solved without the existing theologoumenon of the remnant. Crowning the whole chapter here, it forms the first answer to the question which occupies him (Schrenk, *TDNT*, IV, 209f.).

It may thus be said in apocalyptic terms that even in the midst of judgment and desolation salvation retains a solid place for Israel and that the salvation history traceable from the OT has not been completely torn down (*contra* Ulonska, *Paulus*, 188). In this light there can be a backward glance at what was said about the genuine seed of Abraham in vv. 7ff., and the term "seed" in the quotation is reminiscent of that (Maier, *Israel*, 60; Munck, *Christ*, 74). To be sure this will not remain the final answer, since it causes considerable exegetical difficulty (e.g., Sanday and Headlam). Nevertheless it marks the starting point for ch. 11, as 11:4ff. shows, and to that degree it occupies a key position. God's right can be set in dialectical counterpoise with God's saving will for Israel. Israel's rejection is not treated lightly and yet the promise given to it is maintained. Both the divine word and the earthly reality are thereby taken into account.

C. Israel's Guilt and Fall (9:30–10:21)

It seems as though human responsibility has been shattered in the previous chapter. But now what was brusquely dismissed in vv. 14 and 19 is taken up as a genuine problem. Israel is not just hardened in unbelief; it is also guilty (Sanday and Headlam; Huby; Ridderbos; though cf. Munck, *Christ*, 77f.; Luz, *Geschichtsverständnis*, 30). This does not mean that an ethical statement now follows the religious one (Gaugler is right here *contra* Althaus). Nothing is said about the "primal mystery of human existence" in which God's work and our responsibility are in tension and complement one another (Althaus, cf. Weber, *Problem*, 53ff., 63). The approach remains oriented salvation historically to Israel's destiny. Predestination and human freedom are not correlative (Weber, *Problem*, 44f. is right here *contra* Murray). As will be shown, Israel's guilt grows precisely out of its predestination (in modified form Maier, *Mensch*, 384f., but cf. Zeller, *Juden*, 123). In spite of the new introduction in 10:1f., 9:30-33 are not a conclusion to vv. 26-29 (Gutjahr; Bardenhewer *contra* Lagrange; Lyonnet, *Quaestiones*, II, 72). Nor are they merely transitional (Michel; Gaugler). They state the thesis developed and established in ch. 10 (J. Weiss, "Beiträge," 239; Barrett; C. Müller, *Gottes Volk*, 37). 10:1-4 speak of the end of the law, which Israel has not perceived. 10:5-13 offer scriptural proof of this. 10:14-21 depict the hardening which Israel has brought about by its own fault.

1. The Theme (9:30-33)

[30]*What are we to conclude then? Gentiles who did not strive after righteousness have attained it, namely, the righteousness of faith.* [31]*Israel, who followed the law (which promises) righteousness, did not advance to (such a) law.* [32]*Why? Because it (lived) not by faith but in a delusion by works. They fell over the stone of stumbling.* [33](*This happened) according to Scripture, "Behold, I lay in Zion a stone of stumbling and rock of offense. But he will not be put to shame that believes in him."*

Bibliography: O. Betz, "Felsenmann und Felsengemeinde," *ZNW* 48 (1957) 49-77; A. Bonhöffer, *Epiktet und das NT* (1911); J. Rendel Harris, *Testimonies,* I (1916); R. A. Kraft, "Barnabas' Isaiah Text and the 'Testimony Book' Hypothesis," *JBL* 79 (1960) 336-350; K.-H. Müller, *Anstoss und Gericht. Eine Studie zum jüdischen Hintergrund des Paulinischen Skandalonbegriffs* (1969); E. G. Selwyn, *The First Epistle of St. Peter* (2nd ed. 1947) 268-277.

As in 8:31 the new question introduces a summarizing statement (Sanday and Headlam; Lagrange). The paradox of an event which for Paul is inconceivable is underlined by the unmistakable rhetoric in vv. 30f. As in v. 16 the image of the contest underlies the motifs of διώκειν, καταλαμβάνειν in the sense of "ultimately get hold of" (Delling, *TDNT,* IV, 10), and φθάνειν, "to win through." Deut 16:20; Prov 15:9; Sir 27:8 show the OT derivation of the phrase "to pursue righteousness." The participles are not causal (*contra* Kühl) but adversative. Verses 30 and 31 form an antithetical parallelism, although in v. 31 the concept of νόμος disruptively overshadows that of δικαιοσύνη, not for rhetorical reasons (*contra* Lietzmann), but in order to characterize Jewish piety. Since it is still maintained that righteousness is the issue in this piety, the law is spoken of dialectically and we thus have the distinctive formula νόμος δικαιοσύνης. In Pauline theology the qualitative genitive cannot denote the result (*contra* Kühl). It indicates the demand (Zahn; Jülicher) or better, in context, the promise (Michel; Bläser, *Gesetz,* 173ff.; Stuhlmacher, *Gerechtigkeit,* 92; Stalder, *Werk,* 350). The law is thus viewed as the witness of righteousness, as in 3:21.

This helps us to understand the strange statement, which later readings sought to interpret, that Israel did not attain to the law. This does not mean that what is inherited must be constantly won afresh (Lagrange). The point is that the will of God which calls for righteousness cannot be reached in the law, this being misunderstood and made a summons to achievement. This produces the paradox that even as they pursue righteousness the Jews shift the goal by false interpretation and do not reach it. The idea that the law is not to be fulfilled (Muller-Duvernoy, "Problème," 75) is completely off the mark and contradicts the Jewish view. If the passage is approached from ethical idealism, contradiction inevitably arises. Thus the statement that Gentiles did not seek after righteousness evokes both the protest of classical philologists (Bonhöffer, *Epiktet,* 152f.) and theological apologetics: God would not leave honest striving unrewarded but Gentile-Christians had not previously had moral ideals (Jülicher), or had not followed them with the requisite zeal (Dodd; Althaus), or the Jews had at least religious and ethical advantages over them (Zahn; Huby; Michel). The text, however, does not speak of moral power or of righteousness as a virtue but as a gift of salvation. This was in fact unknown to the Gentiles and misunderstood by the Jews. The problem of the good deed is not discussed as in 2:13f. At issue here is the incomprehensible God who works miracles (K. Barth).

This leads on to vv. 32f. The question how the situation depicted could arise is already answered indirectly in v. 30c. God's righteousness exists only as the righteousness of faith. This is repeated in v. 32a with the common antithesis of the doctrine of justification. ὡς in the secondary clause is striking. With a brevity which demands paraphrase it expresses in good Greek style (L. Radermacher, *NT Grammatik* [2nd ed. 1925] 26f.; Sanday and Headlam) a subjective acceptance or, here, a deceptive delusion (Maier, *Israel*, 66; Bläser, *Gesetz*, 176, *et al.*). The Jews act out of an illusion. They not only deceive themselves as to the goal, but on the pathway on which they set out they come to a fall. It is evident here that the concept of the remnant in v. 27 establishes no assurance of salvation. It establishes primarily the extent of the disaster. Almost all Israel after the flesh stands under judgment, as is now emphasized. For the first time one may see clearly what lay behind the lament in 9:1ff., the theme of v. 6a, and the following argumentation. In relation to the Christ event the Jewish people has become almost totally guilty (strangely contested in Maier, *Mensch*, 383). It has thus fallen into eschatological ruin. For Israel's destiny is decided by Christ with the necessity which fulfilled prophecy has for the apostle as an expression of God's plan of salvation.

In v. 33 Isa 28:16 is quoted. The middle of the verse, which speaks of the costliness of the stone, is dropped. Instead a fragment from Isa 8:14 is introduced which characterizes the stone as one which can cause stumbling and offense. Both passages deviate considerably from the LXX and are closer to the original, which the LXX has altered. Perhaps a later translation than the LXX lies behind Paul's version (cf. Stählin, *Skandalon*, 192). We find its characteristics in the same combination of quotations also in 1 Pet 2:6f. (Stählin, *TDNT*, VI, 751f.). τίθημι replaces the LXX ἐγὼ ἐμβάλλω and ἐν Σιών replaces εἰς τὰ θεμέλια Σειών, while ἐπ' αὐτῷ is added after ὁ πιστεύων. No less striking than the translation is the combination of citations, which changes the sense of Isa 28:16a into its opposite while leaving unchanged the promise of the conclusion. This modification was possible only for a Christian who understood Isa 28:16 messianically but regarded Israel as rejected because of its lack of faith in Christ and found a confirmation of this in Isa 8:14.

The messianic interpretation of the first passage seems to be pre-Christian (Jeremias, *TDNT*, IV, 272f.; Stählin, *TDNT*, VI, 755; Michel; Cerfaux, *Church*, 54f.). 1QH 6:26f. relates the statement to the eschatological community (O. Betz, "Felsenmann," 61ff.). If neither verse is much used by the rabbis (Billerbeck), the conjecture is at least permissible that this silence is a reply to the Christian interpretation. This also took over the saying in Ps 117:22 LXX and identified its formula κεφαλὴ γωνίας with the predicate ἀκρογωνιαῖος in Isa 28:16 LXX (Selwyn, *Epistle*, 268ff.; Cullmann, *TDNT*, VI, 97f.). Thus in 1 Pet 2:6f. all these texts follow one another and in a tradition which is independent of the present version, since the verse from the Psalms comes between the two verses from Isaiah. One finds the same tradition in *Barn.* 6:2-4, where Isa 28:16 and Ps 117:22 LXX are combined. Does this mean that Christian authors are using a collection of testimonies (so Vollmer, *Zitate,* 38ff.; Harris, *Testimonies,* 18f., 26ff.; Stählin, *Skandalon,* 193; Kraft, "Barnabas," 345; Luz, *Geschichtsverständnis,* 96f.; Zeller, *Juden,* 190)? The variations tend to rule out a fixed written source at least. Nor is there any proof at all for the daring thesis (Selwyn, *Epistle,* 273ff.) that the authors mentioned use in different ways a primitive Christian hymn which combines the OT passages. On the other hand one might say that these texts were significant for primitive Christianity, that they were combined through the catchword "stone" and meditated upon, and that they were at least used stereotypically in the missionary tradition for debate with Judaism (Michel, *Bibel,* 40ff.; C. H. Dodd, *According to the Scriptures* [3rd ed., 1953] 41ff.; Stählin, *TDNT,* VII, 353). The source, then, is probably an oral tradition which could lead to collections of testimonies.

Even if it is Paul himself who in a forced and ingenious way inserts Isa 8:14 into 28:16, it is easier to explain by the assumption that he already was familiar with a combination such as is found in 1 Pet 2:6f. The christological orientation is also Paul's concern (*contra* Selwyn, *Epistle,* 272). The stress is not primarily on the death of Jesus or the historical Jesus (*contra* Munck, *Christ,* 80; Zeller, *Juden,* 192 is right here) but on the fact that Israel comes to ruin, and by God's plan must come to ruin, over the God-given Messiah, and consequently over the fulfilment of the promise. The stone was set up in Zion by God himself, who had determined in advance to bring about stumbling and offense (Stählin, *Skandalon,* 197). πρόσκομμα and σκάνδαλον are hard to distinguish materially (ibid., 95ff., 261ff.). They mean "cause of ruin." The end of the quotation has an exclusive sense. πιστεύειν ἐπί with the dative in its OT construction means "to trust in" (Jeremias, *TDNT,* IV, 275; Bultmann, *TDNT,* VI, 216). But according to the context of this central passage Paul may understand "to believe in." Naturally καταισχύνεσθαι does not express disillusionment (Jülicher) but being put to shame eschatologically, as in 5:5. In the judgment which Judaism falls under in its unbelief only he who believes in Christ stands. As in 1 Cor 1:22ff. believers are differentiated from those who take offense at the message of Christ. The former show themselves to be σῳζόμενοι, the latter ἀπολλύμενοι. Judaism must take offense at Christ to the degree that the requirement of faith enforces a break with its religious past (Maier, *Israel,* 67f.). It cannot see that precisely in this way it is summoned back to the promise it has been given. The continuity of the fleshly conceals the continuity of the divine word maintained in Scripture. It thus conceals the eschatological goal. When Christ comes on the scene, the conflict between true and false faith becomes acute. Israel's history offers an example of this, as the next chapter shows.

2. The End of the Law (10:1-4)

¹Brethren, my heart's desire and prayer to God for them is salvation. ²I must bear them witness that they are zealous for God but not with true understanding. ³Since they did not know the righteousness of God and sought to set up their own, they became disobedient to the righteousness of God. ⁴For Christ is the end of the law to righteousness for everyone who believes.

10:1-4 THE END OF THE LAW

Bibliography: R. Bring, "Die Erfüllung des Gesetzes durch Christus," *KuD* 5 (1959) 1-22; idem, "Die Gerechtigkeit Gottes und das Alttestamentliche Gesetz," *Christus und das Gesetz* (1969) 35-72; idem, "Paul and the OT," *ST* 25 (1971) 21-60; R. Bultmann and H. Schlier, "Christus, des Gesetzes Ende" (BEvT 1; *Theologische Abhandlungen,* ed. E. Wolf; 1940); F. Flückiger, "Christus, des Gesetzes Telos," *TZ* 11 (1955) 153-57; H. Hellbardt, "Christus, das Telos des Gesetzes," *EvT* 3 (1936) 331-346; M. Hengel, *Die Zeloten* (1961); G. E. Howard, "Christ the End of the Law," *JBL* 88 (1969) 331-37; K. Sullivan, "Epignosis in the Epistles of St. Paul," *Stud.Paul.Congr.,* II, 405-416.

The opening, which is characterized by an appeal and a reference back to 9:1f., does not introduce a new theme but in its terminology and motivation elucidates 9:31f. (Maier, *Israel,* 69). The solemn declaration shows how hard the judgment which follows is for the apostle, who now clearly turns to the Christian community. The three basic statements take up the conclusion of what precedes. Israel's fall is fateful but not inexplicable. The solitary μέν in v. 1 is for emphasis. εὐδοκία, which is known from the *koine* as influenced by Judaism (Schrenk, *TDNT,* II, 742ff.), means the pleasure which asserts itself graciously, or, as in Sir 18:31, the request directed toward that (Schrenk, 746); here, as in Phil 1:15, it means the inclination (Lagrange). It manifests itself in intercession, though this should not be exaggeratedly characterized as the apostolic petition of the church (Peterson, "Kirche," 266). Obviously Paul does not think the rejection of Israel is irreversible (Bengel; Maier, *Israel,* 69, though cf. Jülicher). ὑπὲρ αὐτῶν belongs to the predicate.

The apostle is also ready to testify in public. He is prepared to confirm from his own knowledge of the matter (Strathmann, *TDNT,* IV, 496) what can be said in his people's favor. Although the verb has a juridical sense, it should not be taken to imply (*contra* C. Müller, *Gottes Volk,* 69; Jüngel, *Paulus und Jesus,* 51) a legal contest. All that is at issue is the establishment of a public fact. The objective genitive ζῆλος θεοῦ uses a technical term to characterize the piety which is oriented to the model of Phinehas and Elijah among the Maccabees and Zealots, at Qumran, and in many rabbinic circles (Hengel, *Zeloten,* 152ff.). There is no psychologizing here (*contra* Lagrange; Maier, *Israel,* 72). Instead, one of the most important aspects of Jewish history is emphasized.

The assertion that this zeal leads astray is not (*contra* Hengel, *Zeloten,* 231) a repudiation of the use of force, e.g., by the Zealots, as may be seen from what follows. For v. 3 interprets οὐ κατ' ἐπίγνωσιν. ἐπίγνωσις is not a theoretical attitude but an insightful grasping of reality (Bultmann, *TDNT,* I, 707; Sullivan, "Epignosis," 407, though cf. G. Maier, *Mensch,* 388). Correspondingly, ἀγνοεῖν, related in Jewish-Christian fashion to knowledge of God, does not mean absence of knowledge (*contra* Sanday and Headlam; Jülicher; Huby; Gutjahr; Bardenhewer; Weber, *Problem,* 47f.) but rather, as the adoption of οὐχ ὑπετάγησαν indicates, deficient or, if one takes the distinction of the verb from ὑπακούειν into account, fatefully inadequate knowledge of God (Stuhlmacher, *Gerechtigkeit,* 93). It is not, then, a question of abstractly knowing that God is love and that he demands love in return (*contra* Vischer, "Geheimnis," 105f.). For Paul, to know God means accepting his right. This is why he speaks of obedience, which one owes on the basis of a relation of subordination and refusal of which means

280

rebellion. The formulation reminds us of *2 Apoc. Bar.* 54:5: "Thou makest dark things clear and revealest hidden things to those who in faith have subjected themselves to thee and thy law." The Jew, too, as in 4 Ezra 8:56, links denial of God with unrighteousness and defines its essence as repudiation, namely, as refusal to submit to God's lordship (*2 Apoc. Bar.* 54:14) (Rössler, *Gesetz*, 77ff.). Faith and obedience are equated, as here in Paul. The difference comes to light only when the common element is perceived and the Jewish background of Paul's statement has been emphasized. According to *2 Apoc. Bar.* 51:3 one acts righteously only on the basis of the law, and according to 67:6 righteousness stems from the law. Sin is despising and perverting the law (Rössler, *Gesetz*, 78ff.). It is precisely this approach which the apostle designates as "one's own righteousness," since it is oriented to works of pious achievement and in fact leads away from faith. Hence the two formulations cover very different things. Obviously Paul is not thinking here only of the Jews of the time of Jesus (*contra* Munck, *Christ*, 81ff.). He has in mind the typically Jewish offense which is grounded in ζῆλος and which is objectively present. ζητεῖν means laborious action (Maier, *Israel*, 70), not a vain attempt (Lagrange). The adding of δικαιοσύνην to ἰδίαν as early as P⁴⁶ leads to a superfluous interpretation.

To what degree, however, is the Christian obedience which Paul staunchly extols and demands different from "one's own righteousness"? The antithesis in v. 3 and the apodictic statement in v. 4 provide the answer to this question. Since we find the same antithesis in Phil 3:9, the righteousness of God has been understood here in terms of its definition there as the righteousness which is given by God (Bultmann, *Ende*, 10ff.; *Theology*, I, 285; Cambier, *L'Évangile*, 186f.; cf. the discussion of 1:17). This is not incorrect but it does not catch the nuance of the text. If "to be subject" is not viewed as merely rhetorical, God's righteousness is understood as power (C. Müller, *Gottes Volk*, 73f.; Stuhlmacher, *Gerechtigkeit*, 93; Ziesler, *Meaning*, 206). It is not this abstractly in the sense of an objective entity (*contra* Kühl) or a divine attribute in which human beings come to participate in an enigmatic event (*contra* Lietzmann). In Paul power is always the epiphany of a will which prevails within the framework of an existing relation. In the eschatological gift of justification the Giver comes on the scene as Lord and Creator. His claim to the world is a constitutive element in his blessing. For this reason the gift is not a possession at our disposal. It rescues us both from self-will and self-boasting and also from care and anxiety about ourselves. We can now act in the freedom of released love without having to create our salvation.

Faith becomes genuine obedience when in its work the issue is not ourselves but gratitude and the manifestation of achieved freedom in openness in relation to the earth. Obedience here is not the work of the law, as the Jew understood it. It does not have to attain its own righteousness. It lives by an alien righteousness (*iustitia aliena*), namely, by the presence of the Lord who gives himself and who is continually grasped afresh by faith. The righteousness of God sets us in the sole efficacy of the Creator who works salvation on us and through us without ascribing any merit to us. Understood purely as a gift, it would not be protected against becoming a buried or misused talent, namely, an instrument of our will. For this reason faith is not identical with it. Faith is its work and manifestation. As such it is not subject to our will.

281

For this reason v. 4 does not call faith, or salvation, or God's mercy, or our justification, the end of the law, although that no doubt could have been said. What we have become and obtained is subject to temptation and therefore to the dialectic of promise and admonition. Unlike the Reformation Paul had not yet developed a dialectic of law and gospel, since law for him was always related to the Torah of Moses. To the extent that this was seen as a means of perverting God's will by pious achievement, the law could later be extended to legalism and dialectic could replace the antithesis. The apostle lays the foundation for this generalizing in his interpretation of *nomos,* but as a Jewish-Christian he does not yet undertake it. He sees law and gospel non-dialectically as mutually exclusive antitheses. Unlike the attestation of grace by believers, the victory of grace is unambivalent. He asserts the change in lordship and for this reason argues primarily in terms of christology, not anthropology or ecclesiology. In Christ we are encountered by the previously given victorious power of the righteousness of God which is not brought to realization by our attesting it but which makes this possible. Christ according to 2 Cor 1:19 is God's Yes to us. This Yes is unequivocal and irrevocable. It cannot be brought into the interplay of Yes and No, as might happen with a justified existence or with the church as a mixed body, and as must happen from the standpoint of a fellowship engaged in the instruction of its members.

Later Gentile Christianity was no longer in the same situation as the apostle. It did not grasp the importance his debate with Judaism had for him and replaced it with an internal debate within the church. Hence the conflict concerning the Mosaic Torah was ethicized, and survived only in this truncated form. Exhortation thus came to be seen as the hidden word of the law (Asmussen), and ethicizing in the direction of a general moral law was necessarily accompanied by individualizing. The problems of Christian existence and fellowship pressed to the fore in such a way that sight was lost of the profoundly apocalyptic argument of the text which sets Christ and the law (like Christ and Adam in 5:12ff.) in the contrast and contradiction of the old and new aeons. This shift of view finds typical expression in the apparently endless debate about the meaning of τέλος in this verse, which has always been a focus of exegetical discussion and which in our day can at least be approached without the former confessional prejudices.

The "pedagogical" understanding of Gal 3:24, which was already refuted at 7:6, had a disastrous effect. The παιδαγωγός is not, of course, a teacher in our sense; he is a taskmaster. Again εἰς Χριστόν has there a plainly temporal and not a final sense (*contra* Cerfaux, *Christ,* 225ff., *et al.*). When maturity is reached, the overseer is no longer needed. Whereas modern exegesis in general translates τέλος by "end" (though cf. Howard, "The End," 336f.), systematic theology of every stripe argues that "goal" (cf. Cranfield, "Law," 152ff.) or "meaning, fulfilment" can be meant (Gutjahr; Bardenhewer; Lyonnet, *Quaestiones,* II, 74f.; Asmussen; Baulès; Bring, "Gerechtigkeit," 35; Bläser, *Gesetz,* 177; for a middle position cf. Luz, *Geschichtsverständnis,* 139ff., 157). Lexically all these meanings are possible (Stalder, *Werk,* 351ff.). Yet the message of the NT soon would no longer be recognizable if exegesis were allowed to exploit every linguistic possibility, and Paul does not leave the least room for attempts of this kind. This is proved by the immediate context of 9:31ff. and 10:5ff., by the epistle in 3:21; 5:20;

7:1ff.; 8:2f., and by the theology of the apostle in Galatians, 2 Corinthians 3, and Philippians 3 (Gaugler). Arguments to the contrary (Hellbardt, "Christus," 345; Bring, "Gerechtigkeit," 10; Joest, *Gesetz und Freiheit,* 138; esp. Flückiger, "Christus," 154ff.) are based on the modern question as to the relation of the OT and the NT (Bring, "Paul," 63ff.) and an un-Pauline view of salvation history. It is ridiculous to stress the logical connection with the metaphor of the race in 9:31f. and in so doing to overlook 9:32f. (*contra* Flückiger, "Christus," 154; Joest, *loc. cit.*). εἰς δικαιοσύνην in v. 4 does not go with τέλος but like ἐκ πίστεως . . . in 1:17 with all that precedes, and grammatically it belongs to the participle that follows (*contra* Flückiger, "Christus," 155). The statement is naturally recognized only by believers. But the christological basis of its proclamation gives it universal validity. In principle there is righteousness only in the sphere of faith and not of the law (cf. on this Schoeps, *Paul,* 171ff.; Bring, "Paul," 50 speaks instead of "full righteousness"). Israel, which regarded even faith as a work of the law, could not reach the goal because only Christ enables us to recognize the true will of God and only the Spirit enables us to fulfil it. The Mosaic Torah comes to an end with Christ because man now renounces his own right in order to grant God his right (3:4). In the eschatological change the creature who wants to possess his own right is replaced by the Creator who has the right and who is acknowledged in the ὑποταγή of faith. Even for Israel no other possibility of salvation exists. Failing to understand the law, it falls into illusion and is overthrown. Christ exposes the illusion. When a person accepts him and his work he does not harden himself, as the next sections show.

3. The Word That is Near (10:5-13)

[5]*For Moses writes, "The man who does the righteousness which is of the law shall live by it."* [6]*But the righteousness of faith says, "Do not think in your heart, 'Who will ascend into heaven?'—that is, to bring Christ down—*[7]*or, 'Who will descend into the abyss?'—that is, to bring Christ up from the dead."* [8]*But what does it say? "The word is near you, on your lips and in your heart— that is, the word of faith which we preach."* [9]*For if you confess the Lord Jesus with your lips and believe with your heart that God has raised him from the dead, you will be saved.* [10]*For man believes with his heart and is justified, and confesses with his lips and is saved.* [11]*The Scripture says, "Everyone who believes in him will not be put to shame."* [12]*Thus there is no distinction between Jew and Greek. The same Lord is Lord of all and he makes all who call on him righteous.* [13]*For "everyone who calls upon the name of the Lord will be saved."*

Bibliography: W. Bieder, *Die Vorstellung von der Höllenfahrt Jesu Christi* (ATANT 19; 1949); M. Black, "The Christological Use of the OT in the NT," *NTS* 18 (1971/72) 1-14; G. Bornkamm, "Das Bekenntnis im Hebräerbrief," *ThBl* 20 (1941) 56-66; H. Conzelmann, "Paulus und die Weisheit," *NTS* 12 (1965/66) 231-244; P. Démann, "Moïse et la loi dans la pensée de saint Paul," in H. Cazelles *et al., Moïse: l'homme de l'alliance* (1955) 189-242; A. M. Goldberg, "Torah aus der Unterwelt," *BZ*, N.F. 14 (1970) 127-131; E. Kamlah, "Buchstabe und Geist," *EvT* 14 (1954) 276-282; E. Käsemann, "The Spirit and the Letter,"

10:5-13   THE WORD THAT IS NEAR

Perspectives, 138-166; G. E. Ladd, "Paul and the Law," *Soli Deo Gloria: NT Studies in Honor of William Childs Robinson* (ed. J. M. Richards; 1968) 50-67; E. Schweizer, "Zur Herkunft der Präexistenzvorstellung bei Paulus," *EvT* 19 (1959) 65-70; M. J. Suggs, "The Word is Near You: Romans 10:6-10 within the Purpose of the Letter," *Christian History and Interpretation: Studies Presented to John Knox* (ed. W. Farmer *et al.;* 1967) 289-312; P. Vielhauer, "Paulus und das AT," *Studien zur Geschichte und Theologie der Reformation* (Festschrift für Ernst Bizer; ed. L. Abramowski and J. F. Gerhard Goeters; 1969) 33-62. For Flückiger, "Christus" and Bring, "Gerechtigkeit" see the bibliography for 10:1-4.

This section is a proof from Scripture for v. 4, so that commentators have often found the opening of the argument here (H. W. Schmidt; Stalder, *Werk,* 353f.; Plag, *Wege,* 19). In vv. 5ff. two quotations from Lev 18:5 and Deut 30:11-14 are sharply contrasted, whereby the first clause of the former is left out and everything that refers to commandment and work is left out of the latter. Already Calvin was so shocked by the altering of Deuteronomy 30, to which also three interpretations belong, that he would no longer accept it as a real quotation. Even today exegetes assert that it is a rhetorically construed paraphrase of the OT text (Zahn; Sanday and Headlam; Gutjahr; Billerbeck; Barrett; Franzmann; Ulonska, *Paulus,* 191). But the threefold interpretative τοῦτ' ἔστιν makes sense only in correct exegesis (Kühl; Lietzmann; Michel; Bläser, *Gesetz,* 179; Munck, *Christ,* 85f.; Bonsirven, *Exégèse,* 307). In this regard Paul follows the pesher form (Bruce) which is especially plain in 1QpHab 12:2ff.; CD 7:14ff. for which the often violent interpretation of Scripture in actualization of its hidden eschatological content is characteristic. Longer interpretative statements are inserted, interpretation is linked to single keywords or sentences, and it is introduced by a mere demonstrative (Black, "Use," 1). The organization of the section is governed by the fact that a biblical text rounds off each thought in vv. 8, 11, and 13. Verses 6-8 offer the promise of the word that is near, vv. 9-13 deal with the eschatological realization of the promise, which is manifested by faith and confession in vv. 9-11 and by the liturgical appeal to the Lord in v. 12.

What does such a scope say for the argumentation? We are faced by an alternative here. If τέλος in v. 4 is understood as goal, one will contest a contradiction between vv. 5 and 6, and fulfilment of the law and of its promise as in 3:21 will be seen in the obedience of faith (Bläser, *Gesetz,* 179f.; Flückiger, "Christus," 155f.; Bring, "Gerechtigkeit," 55; Cranfield, "Law," 153, 157). If, however, v. 4 refers to the end of the law, vv. 5 and 6 (*contra* Ridderbos; Luz, *Geschichtsverständnis,* 92) form a sharp antithesis extending even to details of the formulation. The lawgiver Moses stands over against the personified righteousness of faith. Whereas he demands action understood as achievement, she demands reception of the word. Whereas he characteristically writes, she speaks with the living voice of the gospel, with which there is doubtless an allusion to the relation of πνεῦμα and γράμμα in 2:27ff.; 7:6; 2 Cor 3:6ff. This clearly brings out the antithesis (Kamlah, "Buchstabe," 281) and secures the meaning "end of the law" in v. 4. It is in this light that we are to understand the personification of the righteousness of faith, for which there are interesting form-critical parallels in the diatribe (Bultmann, *Stil,* 87f.; Thyen, *Stil,* 42). The conventional stylistic device takes on theological significance here if the power of the Spirit, i.e., of the exalted

Christ and the new aeon inaugurated by him, is revealed in the righteousness of faith and if this separates one from discipleship in the sphere of Moses as in v. 3. Finally, the theme of the word that is near is brought into view insofar as the Spirit brings with him the new covenant and as in 2 Cor 3:14ff., in fulfillment of Jer 38:31ff. LXX, removes the veil between Creator and creature. Tradition, which creates distance and risks perversion, is replaced by the presence of God, the demand which kills is replaced by the freedom of the gospel and sonship, the synagogue with its servants is replaced by the church and the apostolic mission. Hence the text concerns much more than a theodicy or an answer to the objection that God did not adequately prepare Israel for the eschatological events (contra Maier, Israel, 72f.; Munck, Christ, 84). The end of the law has as its reverse side the prerogative of the church as compared with the synagogue, which closes itself to the word that is near.

How important Lev 18:5 was for Paul is shown by the correct reproduction of the LXX text in Gal 3:12 and the summarizing paraphrase in Rom 2:13. Since his theology gave the text a fixed sense, the phrase τὴν δικαιοσύνην τὴν ἐκ νόμου is put first and incorporated into the ὅτι clause. P⁴⁶ and other witnesses smooth the construction by putting ὅτι directly before the quotation (accepted by H. W. Schmidt; Stalder, Werk, 355f.). Now the phrase δικαιοσύνην . . . could be related to γράφει as an accusative of relation. In further elucidation αὐτά was added to the quotation and αὐτῇ at the end was accordingly changed into αὐτοῖς. But this spoils the irony of the text (cf. Bengel: suavissima parodia). For the sake of contrast the phrase about the righteousness of the law, which sums up the first clause of Lev 18:5, is, emphatically as the object of ὁ ποιήσας, moved forward, and to be sure this is admissible according to the rules of rabbinic hermeneutics. The legal righteousness represented by Moses (though cf. Ridderbos, Paul, 155f.) demands achievement and promises temporal and eternal life only to the doer (Billerbeck; the interpretation suggested by Bring, "Gerechtigkeit," 44f., 49f., 51ff. is untenable). According to 2:17-3:19; Gal 3:10-12 Paul is convinced that no one can or should achieve salvation in this way. Moses, to whom Torah texts are ascribed by Philo too (Thyen, Stil, 70), himself draws attention to this as the mediator of the law (cf. Maier, Israel, 75) and is thus warning us against this way.

No objection can be brought against this exegesis on Jewish grounds (contra Schoeps, Paul, 198ff., 249f.). This may be seen from the analogue to the pesher style of interpretation in vv. 6ff. What seems most violent and fantastic to our mode of thinking results logically from the basic principle that Scripture is to be interpreted eschatologically (Munck, Christ, 85.) and that it proclaims the christological events in advance. This is a Jewish principle even if the consequences drawn from it are no longer so. We should neither weaken the procedure (Nygren; Leenhardt) nor dismiss it as extravagant from a modern standpoint (Pallis; Kirk; for a right view cf. Suggs, "Word," 299ff.). In the eyes of the historical critic the violation of the literal sense of Scripture in the introduction to vv. 6ff. is scarcely to be outdone. The statement is simply taken away from Moses, who has just been quoted, so that the word of the ἐντολή now can be ascribed to the righteousness of faith. But this, too, is valid on Paul's hermeneutical presuppositions. We hear of the word that is near only from the promise, which anticipates the gospel and stands in antithesis to the γράμμα, whereas the law demands the work of achievement. Although Lev 18:5 and Deut 30:11ff. belong to the same Torah, for Paul they are to be separated in terms of the content, just as the seed of Abraham after the flesh is to be separated from the true seed in 9:6ff. The apostle is not afraid to apply to Scripture too the distinguishing of spirits demanded of the prophets in 1 Cor 12:10; 14:29ff. His criterion in doing this is the contrast between the old and new aeons under the banner of the law on the one side and of the promise and the gospel on the other. In short, it is his doctrine of justification. On this basis the dialectical distinction between the law as God's documented will and pointer to the gospel and its perversion by the demand for achievement is unavoidable. If the promise is related to Abraham as the recipient of God's direct address, while γράμμα is related to Moses as the mediator of the law which Judaism misunderstood, "Moses" can no longer speak in vv. 6ff. but only the righteousness of faith. The line of reasoning is impregnable.

It has been objected, however (Schoeps, *Paul*, 197f., 213ff.), that Paul has detached the Torah from the overarching reality of the covenant and reduced it to the ethical sphere, so that only the theologoumenon of righteousness remained for him. This assertion is incorrect. While it is true that for Paul, as already in the OT and the rabbis, the ethical demand of the law largely determines the view, Paul does not limit the Torah to this in contrast to later Christianity, as the debate about circumcision shows. Also the covenant and the law are not torn asunder by him (not stated quite strongly enough in Ladd, "Law," 54f., 63ff.). Otherwise he could not have confronted the old and the new covenants with one another and taken God's ancient people as the type of the new, as in 1 Corinthians 10. To be sure, he no longer speaks, as Jewish Christianity before him did, about the renewed covenant and people of God (C. Müller, *Gottes Volk,* 101f.), for he understands the old covenant primarily in terms of the law and not, primarily at least, the law in terms of the covenant. Nevertheless, he does this precisely because he is conscious of the reciprocal character of the covenant relation in the OT (cf. Schoeps, *Paul,* 214). In the OT the human partner must also keep the covenant with his works. Even when faith is seen as the basis and sustaining unity of all works, it has to be dutifully demonstrated in good works as in Jas 2:14ff. From the Jewish angle faith and works cannot be an alternative (Schoeps, *Paul,* 200ff., 204) even if faith is emphasized and the defects of merit are granted. "By faith alone" is Christian and in its theological reflection Pauline. To want to derive it from eschatologico-christological dogmatism (Schoeps, 171ff.) is absurd and attempts to replace the meaning of the formula with a history-of-religions explanation of its background. What is not noticed then is that justification without the works of the law constitutively means the justification of the ungodly. That happens finally in order to bind our salvation to God alone and therewith to grasp grace radically.

When Paul perceives salvation in the crucified Christ and proclaims justification to the Gentiles, he does not abstract from the idea of the covenant. Rather he shatters it to the extent that he contests its exclusive tie to Israel. He also grasps it anew to the extent that he derives its truth and validity from creation. He removes from the concept the character of privilege, since the omnipotence of the Creator is not restricted even by promise and grace but precisely therein remains free from restriction (9:6ff.). For the apostle, however, the omnipotence of the Creator must be maintained soteriologically, for with the crucified Christ he proclaims the justification of the ungodly, the resurrection of the dead, and creation out of nothing, that is, grace for the needy who do not merit it. The God who is bound by his covenant partnership cannot be the God of the cross and of the ungodly. He can be only the God of the pious and of the law, which summons the pious to dutiful keeping of the covenant on the basis of good works. Against this theological background does Paul really misunderstand the law? This certainly cannot be said in the light of the sharpening of the law in rabbinic Judaism, Pharisaism, and the Qumran community, and in view of the ethics of Philo. The concept of the covenant cannot on its own protect us against pious achievement any more than confession of sins can. Privileges are shattered only by interpreting grace alone as faith alone and appealing to the omnipotence of the Creator in his unceasing activity. This is the issue in the predestinarian statements of the apostle, which radicalize his doctrine of justification (C. Müller, *Gottes Volk,* 87). Here works no longer serve one's own salvation. The piety of the devout yields to the eschatological aspect of the resurrection of the dead which is tied to the name of Jesus. Justice is thus done both to the deity of God and to the humanity of man.

If, then, the contrast between the righteousness under the law and in faith is meaningful and necessary, it still has to be explained to what extent the contrast between γράφει and λέγει can be concretely linked to this. For the quotation from Deut 30:11ff. is no less "written" than that from Lev 18. If Paul is making a distinction here, he is revealing thereby a dialectical understanding of Scripture. Something is "letter" not because it is fixed in writing but only when it raises a demand for achievement. On the other hand, what is set in writing can "speak" when it is the promise of grace. This means that γραφή and γράμμα must be differentiated. Scripture can be witness of both γράμμα and πνεῦμα but it necessarily becomes "letter" when it is not expounded by the Spirit, i.e., oriented eschatologically to the righteousness of faith. Thus the contrast between Spirit and letter does not coincide with that of Spirit and tradition; it overlaps it. Tradition, which serves the law as the demand for achievement, has been ended by Christ with the law. This explains why great portions of the OT are not mentioned by Paul. On the other hand, the Spirit constantly takes up tradition again, as the apostle's proof from Scripture very clearly shows. Then Scripture begins to "speak" and it is plain that the Spirit is not something new and unheard-of as the enthusiasts suppose, but that he possesses a field in salvation history from the very beginning, a field which becomes perceptible in the light of the gospel.

We stand here at the commencement of a theologically reflected Christian hermeneutics. Its mark is that it is not satisfied with the "It is written." It demands critical exposition, with the message of justification as the decisive criterion. Only when this message is brought to light does Scripture become a word that is near (not perceived by Luz, *Geschichtsverständnis,* 92, 110, 133ff.). The eschatological perspective shows that this is not a matter of spiritualizing Scripture after the manner of Philo. What enables one to take up Deut 30:11ff. is not greater "inwardness" (Dodd) but the article by which the church stands or falls, which determines the whole theology of the apostle and by which all proclamation is measured by him. Since what is at issue in this article is not just the salvation

287

of the individual but the lordship of God over the world, Israel's history is also seen from this standpoint.

The introduction in v. 6b seems to be taken from Deut 9:4 in order to characterize the perplexity which stands behind the questions which follow. λέγειν ἐν τῇ καρδίᾳ means "to think for oneself" (BAGD, 403b). The rabbis often dealt with Deut 30:11ff. and deduced from it that it is easy to perceive the divine word in the Torah, in Israel, among the rabbis, and in the houses of instruction (Billerbeck). This motif prepares the way for Paul's understanding, though there is no trace of any attack by Paul on the rabbinic view or of the rabbis on Christian preaching (contra Michel). The quotation is not addressed to the Jew who hopes for the Messiah but rejects Christianity (contra Zahn). The righteousness of faith speaks to the whole world, including the Jew. It is identical with the righteousness of God of v. 3 but it also characterizes its field of activity (though cf. C. Müller, Gottes Volk, 71; Stuhlmacher, Gerechtigkeit, 94), just as power and the sphere of power are repeatedly connected in the apostle and his environment. In v. 7 the text of Deut 30:13, which involves a futile voyage across the sea and which could not be applied christologically, is replaced by a reminiscence of Ps 106:26 LXX, where rising up to heaven is followed by descending into the ἄβυσσος. According to Prov 30:4; 4 Ezra 4:8; Philo De virtutibus 183, these last phrases seem to be used proverbially to designate superhuman exertions which are supposed to actualize something impossible (cf. Billerbeck; Lietzmann; Maier, Israel, 76; Jeremias, TDNT, I, 10; Schneider, TDNT, I, 521; Michel). Paul interprets it in the sense of the statements of Ps 70:20 LXX and Wis 16:13, and orients this tradition to the christological confession. For the first time in the NT the message of Christ's ascension is linked here with the descent into Hades, thus with the descent into the realm of the dead (Sanday and Headlam; Pallis; Gutjahr; Michel; Bieder, Höllenfahrt, 72f.). For the interpretation at the end of v. 7 does not allow us (contra Nygren; Barrett) to see a reference to the incarnation (Traub, TDNT, V, 526; Schweizer, "Präexistenzvorstellung," 67f.). Thus the questions in the quotation take on a sense which only a Christian can understand. They no longer characterize flights of perplexity but rhetorically name Christ as our only help in every need. Heaven is for the apostle the place of the exalted Lord. For him the question says that one wishes to bring Christ back to earth. Correspondingly, with regard to the descent into Hades he has in mind that Christ died and then entered into the realm of the dead until the resurrection. But we do not have to drag him back to earth from there. For he is no longer among the dead and no longer needs to return to earth. The argument climaxes with the question Paul now poses as to the reason for this statement. Why are the previously considered attempts foolish and unnecessary? The fragment taken from Deut 30:14 provides the answer in the name of the righteousness of faith: The word is near. In the tendency of the context this can mean only that after his exaltation Christ must be sought and found in the word. To put it pointedly, the incarnation does not need to be prolonged or repeated, since the presence of the risen Lord takes place now in the word of Christian preaching. The Farewell Discourses in John answer the same question in exactly the same way and thus reject a theology which is oriented primarily to the "historical" Jesus. Paul does not differ in this regard, as 2 Cor 5:16 shows.

288

According to 1 Cor 1:18ff.; 2 Cor 2:14ff.; 4:5f., the gospel, which is called in 1:16f. the power that reveals the righteousness of God, is the manifestation of the exalted Christ on earth. This principle of Pauline theology arises here, however, out of a problem and in an antithesis which surprisingly anticipate the theme of John's Farewell Discourses. There too it is asked: How can the disciples abide with the Lord after he has gone away? Where and how can those who are left behind obtain salvation, help, and comfort? Where and how is he present? John, too, rejects any idea of the bond with the person known on earth through historical recollection and stresses instead the presence and constantly new event of the word in Christian proclamation. In the present text, then, we come across one of the hidden roots of the Fourth Gospel.

In terms of the history of religions, however, we can come still further. Contact between our passage and Phil 2:8ff. has been asserted (Munck, *Christ*, 68f.). In an exact comparison this applies only to the schema of the humiliation and exaltation of the Redeemer and to the confession of the Kyrios. Yet this reference is important to the extent that Paul does not speak generally of humiliation and exaltation but of the crucifixion and resurrection of Christ, whereas hymnic and liturgical texts preserve the first schema. Such an observation raises the question whether Paul is not interpreting the Deuteronomy quotation from the perspective of a tradition that he received. The combination of the terms ἀναβαίνειν and καταβαίνειν also supports this, since we find it christologically in John 1:51; 3:13; (implied) 6:62. This hypothesis receives further support through the antithesis of the journeys to heaven and Hades, otherwise foreign to Paul, which is expressly stated only in 1 Pet 3:19, although it is reflected in Eph 4:8 as well. Both motifs are connected in the last passage, as here, and to be sure in a midrashic exposition of an OT passage, and there also it provides a basis for the cosmic lordship of Christ and the institution of a charismatic proclamation of the word in the community. The parallelism is so strong that a commonly present Jewish-Christian view is to be assumed. A Jewish tradition makes this even more likely. Bar 3:29f. has often been adduced as a parallel to the present passage (Lietzmann; Lagrange; Barrett; Maier, *Israel*, 76; Luz, *Geschichtsverständnis*, 92): "Who rose up to heaven and fetched and brought her from the clouds? Who went over the sea and found her?" Deut 30:13 is here referred to divine wisdom, of which Bar 3:36f. then says: "He has known every way to wisdom and granted it to Jacob his servant and Israel his beloved." The motif of nearness in the original is now set in the context of an inaccessibility for all but Israel. What at first portrayed rhetorically and antithetically the absence of any need for long searching has thus become a mythological statement about the hiddenness of *sophia* which only revelation can set aside (Stuhlmacher, *Gerechtigkeit*, 94). If everything depends on keeping the commandment to which all the members are subject, then wisdom is identical with the Torah, accessible in it, and must be kept with it. The element of divine giving is unmistakably stressed. Acceptance of this gift characterizes the Jewish community. Finally, Torah-wisdom is described and personified as a mythical being, or, better, the underlying mythical approach has not been wholly discarded (Suggs, "Word," 304ff.).

If this is presented in the framework of a homily, here again is a point of contact with the present text. Hence the Jewish tradition supplies a connecting link between the OT saying and Paul's exposition which simultaneously makes understandable the connections with the tradition of the Fourth Gospel and with Eph 4:8. The apostle frequently transfers motifs from wisdom speculation to christology (cf. esp. 1 Cor 2:9). That such transferals also took place in relation to concrete redeemer figures in Judaism may be seen from the fragment of a targum which simultaneously emphasizes the motif of the depths (cf. on this Luz, *Geschichtsverständnis*, 92f.; Black, "Use," 9, who both [unlike Goldberg, "Torah," 129] trace back the fragment to the Codex Neofiti): "Could we have someone like the prophet Moses who climbs up to heaven. . . . Could we have someone like the prophet Jonah who goes down into the depths of the sea." Jewish meditation on Deut 30:11ff. (cf. Goldberg, "Torah," 130) was obviously put to anti-Jewish use by Jewish Christianity in the controversy between church and synagogue. It came to Paul in this form.

The unique contribution of the apostle in the development of this tradition lies in the fact that his previous statement that Christ, identified with *sophia,* is the real presence of God on earth, is made serviceable to his theology of the revealing Word and is thus closer again to Deut 30:14: The exalted Christ is present only in Christian proclamation (though cf. Stuhlmacher, *Gerechtigkeit,* 97). In this regard Paul diverges from the synagogue (Zeller, *Juden,* 195f., though cf. Suggs, "Word," 311) and also clashes indirectly with any theology of the so-called facts of salvation. Only the gospel, which in context coincides with the message of justification, saves. The accent in the whole passage falls on v. 8 and the interpretation of this verse which follows (Michel; Kamlah, "Buchstabe," 281). Typically there is no longer a reference to acts and hands as instruments, as in Deut 30:14. The contrast to v. 5 cannot be overlooked. Luther paraphrases: "That righteousness consists in the work done, this in the word believed . . . we weigh the work by the word, not the word by the work" (Ficker, *Scholiae,* 240, 243). But this is only half the matter. It does not take into account the antithesis of vv. 6-7a. Moses inevitably leaves his followers in the disquiet of endless seeking if they are to fulfil his commandment. The righteousness of faith not only ends the piety of achievement, but also the despair of fluctuation in which man neither knows what he wants nor seeks what he finds (Bengel). Faith does not work his salvation but it does not need to seek it either. It does not even have to discover Christ because he is always on the scene before us already in the word of preaching. This being so, the phrase ἐν τῷ στόματί σου καὶ ἐν τῇ καρδίᾳ σου is retained from the otherwise shortened quotation, although its original meaning is completely changed. What is involved is not that we are ready for service with our total person and all our members. It is rather that there is preaching and confession. It is in this light that we are to explain the interpretative τὸ ῥῆμα τῆς πίστεως. This is not the word which is bound up with faith (Kühl) or which finds its essence in faith (Schniewind, *Wort,* 48f.). The interpretation in v. 9 shows that the reference is to the faith which is believed (*fides quae creditur*), i.e., the gospel which is always previously given to us in the form of ὁμολογία (Bultmann, *TDNT,* VI, 209; *Theology,* I, 317f.; Michel; Luz, *Geschichtsverständnis,* 93). This is true even though ὁμολογεῖν and πιστεύειν seem to be distinguished in v. 9. Both verbs relate to the content of faith fixed in the confession and consequently they cannot be materially separated. As a juridical term ὁμολογεῖν designates the binding public declaration which definitively orders a relation with the legal power. This sense is retained in religious "homology" as the response to the epiphany of the deity (Bornkamm, "Bekenntnis," 58f.; C. Müller, *Gottes Volk*, 69). Here it can be translated directly with "to proclaim" (Barrett; Kramer, *Christ*, 71ff., 78f.). There is nothing to indicate (Lagrange) that confession before the authorities is in view (Pallis; Munck, *Christ*, 89). κύριος 'Ιησοῦς was not coined as an antithesis of κύριος καῖσαρ nor did it gradually take on this polemical secondary sense (*contra* O. Cullmann, *The Earliest Christian Confessions* [1949] 27f.; Lietzmann; possible Michel; rejected Kühl; Barrett; Kramer, *Christ*, 65f.). Primarily the phrase is not confession but acclamation (Wengst, *Formeln*, 28), which naturally includes a confessional element. Its setting in life (*Sitz im Leben*) is worship.

The statement becomes a true confession only as the reference to the resurrection of Christ formally parallels and materially establishes the acclamation. Only the risen one is the Lord of the community which, on the way to the resurrection of the dead, represents the new eschatological world. The Lord of the community is also the Lord of the world which has received both its goal and judgment through the event of the resurrection. The verse has the structure of a doctrinal statement with the characteristics of sacral law. The conditional clauses describe the presupposition of salvation, which is promised by a single future verb in a pithy conclusion. It seems natural to take the ὅτι recitatively. In this case a pre-Pauline formula is adopted (Dinkler, "Prädestination," 89; Kramer, *Christ*, 20f., 65f.), into which the apostle imports the allusions to Deut 30:14. Then we can better understand why ὁμολογεῖν is remarkably put before πιστεύειν. It does not simply follow the quotation, while v. 10 restores the natural order (the majority view), and πιστεύειν in v. 9 does not mean, as is assumed without exception, the faith of the heart but adherence to the confession, which for its part is not just an expression of faith (Bultmann, *Theology*, I, 319) but a summary of the gospel which can be taught and learned, as in 1 Cor 15:3-5. Hence the order of the verbs is materially justified.

This comes out even more clearly if the acclamation is placed in a baptismal setting (Dodd; Michel), which, of course, only the threefold acclamation in Eph 4:5 can attest, or if the whole statement (cf. Mark 16:16) is understood as a summary of baptismal instruction (Bultmann, *Theology*, I, 81, 312; C. Müller, *Gottes Volk*, 70). The apostle then repeats in v. 10 the statement previosly given to him, which, like 1 Cor 15:3f., regards the resurrection of Christ as the eschatological event pure and simple. He now puts it in his own terms and in the suitable sequence of faith and confession, which is now the summary of the faith. The conceptual pair καρδία and στόμα lead to a syntactic parallelism in which v. 10a and v. 10b make identical statements. The prepositional definitions present the intended goal (though cf. Plag, *Wege*, 28). Eschatological salvation consists in justification. Here again faith should not be interpreted merely as inner understanding. For the heart as the center of personality means existence in its totality. It is as such defined by faith and manifests that in the confession.

Problems arise if one emphasizes that individual faith is at issue (Dinkler, "Prädestination," 89, 92ff.). The statements are so general and so obviously serve the antithesis of church and synagogue that the accent should be put on the ecclesiological aspect. Verse 11 confirms this. The quotation from Isa 28:16, which confirms vv. 9-10 and refers back to 9:33b, is introduced by πᾶς in the sense of "anyone" (BDF, §275[3], [6]). Universality rather than individuality is the point for Paul (Lagrange; Michel; C. Müller, *Gottes Volk,* 35). Everywhere under the lordship of the word only faith is important.

The universality of the statement is made possible by the exclusiveness underlined in vv. 11-13, which takes up 3:22 under another sign. To the universality of guilt and doom there now corresponds that of grace. Eph 2:14 establishes that also in the sense of our text when it says that the wall of partition has been torn down. Here the apostle does not have merely a single event of salvation in view but the existing lordship of Christ. If this is characterized by the unusual predicate κύριος πάντων, which however is also used in Acts 10:36, in the context this means his power over believers. Yet one must ask whether the Hellenistic predication of God as cosmocrator, which the Jews adopted (cf. BAGD, 445b), is not thereby modified and made concrete, which also comes into view in Phil 2:11 (Peterson, "Kirche," 270). The participial clause makes this even more likely.

Paul often speaks of riches as the fulness of eschatological grace (C. Müller, *Gottes Volk,* 35; Hauck, Kasch, *TDNT,* VI, 329; Murray). The community which is growing in all the world has been set in this fulness which points beyond itself. If the community is characterized with Israel's title as the host of ἐπι-καλούμενοι, as in 1 Cor 1:2 (Bultmann, *Theology,* I, 125f.; Dahl, *Volk Gottes,* 206), this is not to be limited to prayer. We are certainly not to infer from our passage that to call on Jesus in prayer had been self-evident already in earliest Christianity (*contra* Zahn; Althaus; Maier, *Israel,* 85). In fact prayer was always made "in the name" of Jesus. But there is nothing in the NT to suggest when prayer was made directly to Christ. In the first instance ἐπικαλεῖσθαι means acclamation, and then invocation of him who makes heavenly intercession for his people with the Father, thus undergirding prayer as the Mediator. Calling on the name here goes with preaching in v. 8 and homology in vv. 9f. and must therefore be related to worship. The word that is near is manifest when the community gathers, and it is so in many variations.

Thus the voice of the righteousness of faith speaks through the church in distinction from the synagogue. The word is also near in the fact that it has a fixed place on earth and a concrete bearer. The promise of Joel 3:5 LXX is thus filfilled. The quotations in vv. 11 and 13 mutually interpret one another. Salvation is found in the Christian community. As the host of believers it confesses the word which according to 2 Cor 3:6ff. was concealed and closed up in the synagogue and which is now linked to the presence of the exalted one in the church as his sphere of lordship. The OT predicted this. It is the leading witness for the replacement of the synagogue by the host which is gathered from Jew and Gentile under the word of faith that is near.

4. Israel's Guilt (10:14-21)

[14]*How can one call on him in whom he has not believed? And how can one believe in him of whom he has not heard? And how can one hear without a preacher?* [15]*And how can one preach unless he is sent? For it is written, "How timely are the feet of those who bring good news."* [16]*But they have not all*

292

become obedient to the gospel. Isaiah says (already), "Lord, who has believed our message?" [17]*So faith comes from the message heard, and the message (comes) in the power of the word of Christ.* [18]*But I ask, have they not heard? On the contrary. "Their voice has gone out into all the world and their words to the ends of the inhabited earth."* [19]*(Again) I ask, did Israel not understand? Moses answers first, "I will make you jealous of what is not a people. With a people who do not understand I will make you become angry."* [20]*Isaiah is then very bold and says, "I have been found by those who did not seek me; I will be revealed to those who did not ask after me."* [21]*But to Israel he says, "All day long I have stretched out my hands to a disobedient and obstinate people."*

Bibliography: C. Butler, "The Object of Faith according to St. Paul's Epistles," *Stud.Paul.Congr.*, I, 15-30; F. Müller, "Zwei Marginalien im Brief des Paulus an die Römer," *ZNW* 40 (1941) 249-254; F. Rehkopf, "Grammatisches zum Griechischen des NT," *Der Ruf Jesu und die Antwort der Gemeinde* (Festschrift J. Jeremias; 1970) 213-225; Roloff, *Apostolat*. For F. Müller, "Marginalien" see the bibliography for 7:14-25.

The current view that ch. 10 deals with the guilt of Israel has sometimes come in for severe criticism and been replaced by the other view that the chapter portrays God's unsuccessful concern for Judaism (Weber, *Problem,* 43ff.; Maier, *Israel,* 99f.; Munck, *Christ,* 79ff.; H. W. Schmidt; Maier, *Mensch,* 382ff.). The two are not mutually exclusive. According to vv. 18ff. the guilt consists precisely in refusal of grace. Hence it is more a matter of the correct emphasis than of serious contradiction. Is ch. 10 to be seen as a preparation for ch. 11 or as its paradoxical antithesis? This is an important question to the degree that in the first the process of salvation history is the key to interpretation whereas in the second this role is played by the doctrine of justification. The controversy over what is fundamental is reflected in detailed exegesis and already determines the structure of the present section. In any case vv. 14f. do not go with what precedes (*contra* Lietzmann; Dodd) but form the indirect basis of v. 16 by mentioning the presuppositions for receiving salvation. Faith and unbelief are not arbitrary human decisions. As obedience or disobedience they are a response to God's prevenient grace. The word that has come near simultaneously establishes the possibility of perdition.

The artistic form of the chain-syllogism in which each question retraces part of the previous one is an index of the importance of these verses. For Paul rhetoric is not a matter of verbal adornment. It is a means of substantive argument. Here it is not a matter (*contra* Munck, *Salvation,* 277, 300; *Christ,* 12) of balancing up the worldwide (v. 18) mission to the Jews which has now ended, and just as little of showing that God has done everything whereas Israel has failed at the decisive point, namely, that of faith (Dodd; Barrett). This has been said already in 9:31ff. and in the antithesis of 10:5f. Repeating this idea for emphasis would be tedious (Dodd). The parallel questions all demand the answer: It is not possible. They necessarily say, if vv. 14f. concern Israel, that Israel could not call, believe, hear, or preach because it had not been sent. But such a statement contradicts the quotation, which is neither ornamental praise of the calling of the evangelist (Lietzmann), nor a digression (H. W. Schmidt), nor a gloss (Pallis). It states rather the eschatological sending as an event. The questions replace apodictic sayings (BDF, §130[2]) in which the third person plural describes the subject "one," and no change of subject occurs (*contra* Maier, *Israel*, 88). Fundamentally the coming near of the word is traced back from the community assembled for worship, through the beginning of the state of being Christian, to the apostolic mission.

The point of the whole lies in the last rather than the first member in the chain (Weber, *Problem*, 64; Leenhardt; Murray). The quotation which follows shows that the sending on which all else depends has taken place and does take place. Only with v. 16 is there reference to Israel (Weber, *Problem*, 45), which in general has rejected the sending. If vv. 6-13 asserted the nearness of the word, and did this from the presence of a confessing, believing, and calling community, now the path is indicated along which this came about. Thereby faith is clearly described as acceptance of the kerygma (Bultmann, *TDNT*, VI, 208f.) and to that extent—only to that extent!—it is characterized as obedience (Schlatter). οὖ in v. 14 is not as often meant in a spatial sense, nor does it replace a περὶ οὖ, but it relates to the one who proclaims. In the general context this cannot possibly be the historical Jesus (*contra* Maier, *Israel*, 88f.; Munck, *Christ*, 92; Ridderbos). Obviously no distinction is made between κηρύσσειν and εὐαγγελίζεσθαι (Friedrich, *TDNT*, III, 711f.). Both verbs mean Christian preaching, which includes the element of proclamation. The authorization of sending presented by ἀποστέλλειν thus belongs to it (Friedrich, *loc. cit.*). The interpretation of the quotation will show that the apostolic commission is specifically meant (Sass, *Apostelamt*, 28f.; Bultmann, *Theology*, I, 307; Butler, "Object," 18ff.). This is developed more precisely in 2 Cor 5:18-20.

The rabbis almost always related Isa 52:7 to the messianic age (Billerbeck; Roloff, *Apostolat*, 83). In its shortened form and plural statement it deviates from both the MT and the LXX (Smits, *Citaten*, 493f.). In the *koine* and Western texts it has been amplified from the LXX (Lietzmann). The plural was perhaps suggested by the OT context and occurs also in the midrash on Ps 147:1. It becomes meaningful through the reference to the messengers of the gospel (Schniewind, Friedrich, *TDNT*, II, 715ff.; Stuhlmacher, *Gerechtigkeit*, 77; Roloff, *Apostolat*, 83, 142). The message is brought in an unusual sending (Maier, *Israel*, 89). Thus it speaks oracularly of πόδες ὡραῖοι, which is generally taken to mean "beautiful feet" after the parallel in Sir 26:18. Yet the adjective may mean "timely" in this instance (BAGD, 896b; Bultmann, "Glossen," 199). What is in view is the moment of the eschatological actualization of the promise (Lagrange), which the participle also stresses. Substantiation, not merely comparison, is denoted by καθάπερ. Scripture shows with the statement that eschatological mission is necessary. Its call to salvation is fulfilled in the present. It is not accidental that the reference to Zion is left out. The cosmic dimension of the event envisaged comes out in v. 18 (Sass, *Apostelamt*, 28f.). The heralds proclaim the entry of the world ruler. Against the background of this reality attention is directed to Israel in v. 16.

Israel also participated in the mission. As a people, however, it has not accepted either it or the gospel, so that the entire chain in vv. 14f. does not apply to it (Plag, *Wege*, 30). The place claimed for the righteousness of faith was already possessed by the tradition of the law. Faith is again characterized as obedient acceptance of the word. οὐ πάντες emphatically takes up 9:6 and the motif of the remnant in 9:27ff., whereby it means "only very few" (Rehkopf, "Grammatisches," 224). The quotation from Isa 53:1 takes on the character of a lament through the χύριε, which is not in the original text but is adopted from the LXX (Maier, *Israel*, 90f.). In it the destiny of Israel is prophetically foreseen. ἀκοή does not mean hearing (*contra* Schlatter; Brunner; Ridderbos) but what is heard, i.e., the message of the preaching, as in the LXX and 1 Thess 2:13 (Billerbeck). The goal of the argument from v. 5 on is thus reached. 9:23f. and 10:3 are confirmed (Hoppe, *Heilsgeschichte*, 125). Israel has become guilty in relation to the gospel.

The summing up of vv. 14f. in v. 17 seems curious. It seems to be an unnecessary repetition (F. Müller, "Marginalien," 253; Bultmann, "Glossen," 199; Michel; Luz, *Geschichtsverständnis*, 32). It has thus been regarded as a reader's marginal gloss. It should be noted, however, that in reality, while the result of v. 14 is summarized, we have a variation on v. 15, and the catchword ἀκοή connects vv. 16b and 18a. Hence the sentence has a transitional function (H. W. Schmidt), and it could hardly be placed after v. 15.

Initially the remarkable formula ῥῆμα Χριστοῦ must be discussed. ῥῆμα originally designated an individual saying. Hence John and Acts always use it in the plural when speaking of the message as a whole. Initially Eph 6:17; Heb 6:5; 11:3; 1 Pet 1:25 speak of the ῥῆμα θεοῦ in an obviously solemn way. The christological variation occurs in Heb 1:3 as well as here. Since Heb 1:3 relates to the word of the pre-existent mediator of creation, the use of the formula in the present verse is singular unless v. 8c be taken into account. However, precisely v. 8c is important for the interpretation here, since there is nothing in the context to recall the command of the historical Jesus in his sending out of the disciples (*contra* Maier, *Israel*, 89ff.; Munck, *Christ*, 91ff.; Kittel, *TDNT*, IV, 109; Michel). All that remains is the interpretation with reference to the word of the exalted Lord (Schniewind, *Wort*, 15) which manifests itself in the apostolic preaching and conversely makes this a means of Christ's self-revelation. There is no thought of the authority of the eye-witnesses (Butler, "Object," 19f.). Thus the genitive cannot be resolved in such a way that one finds an objective genitive or a genitive of author. The ambivalence, which is perhaps already manifested by the choice of διά instead of ἐκ, yields the theological nuance. If the expression, however, is to be explained solely from the Pauline context and regarded as a more precise variation on v. 15, one can no longer accept a gloss. Verse 17 is added precisely for the sake of this formula. Mission is now traced back to the exalted Lord, which was not possible prior to the quotation (Maier, *Israel*, 93; Plag, *Wege*, 29).

Two parallel questions in vv. 18 and 19 rob Israel of every basis for excuse. It has received Christian preaching. ἀκούειν means here "be cognizant of information." In distinction from 9:30 μενοῦν γε is used adversatively (BDF, §450[4]): Quite the contrary. Commentators have often found difficulty in the fact that the worldwide dimension of Christian preaching is attested by Ps 18:5 LXX and have thus contested that Paul understands the saying as prophecy, especially as there is no introductory formula. But saying that the words simply cover what the apostle can see is strange (Zahn; Lagrange). The exegetical difficulty then would have to be admitted for all Paul's quotations, which almost always lose their historical meaning (*contra* Lyonnet, *Quaestiones*, II, 91ff.). Furthermore, Paul is not just referring to missionary successes (*contra* Pallis; Gutjahr; Leenhardt; Munck, *Sal-*

vation, 277, 300; *Christ,* 12, 94ff.). This would not do justice to the universal and cosmic aspect (H. W. Schmidt) nor to the element of hyperbole in the use of the saying from the Psalms, where the stress is on the first words of the lines. The point is that Scripture, eschatologically interpreted, prophesies the worldwide success of Christian preaching. This is used as an argument against the Jews. They can neither ignore prophecy nor fail to see what is shaking the whole world.

The apocalyptic self-understanding of the apostle comes out most clearly in his adducing of this Psalm (cf. Schoeps, *Paul,* 230f.). In fact, he already sees the whole world filled with Christian proclamation. He undoubtedly thinks above all of his own work (Asmussen), although he speaks of the apostolic activity in general. Thus he sees himself close to the goal envisioned in Mark 13:10, and with it to the parousia.

Of all the problems which he poses for us, this is probably the most difficult: How could he be so mistaken about the endless nature of the task he had begun? The further he pressed into Asia and Europe, the more starkly he must have been confronted by the rift between his apocalyptic hope and earthly reality. The problem not only has a psychological side. Here if anywhere one can see that the apostle's thought and work do not circle around anthropology but around the conquest of the world. Anthropology is an important aspect of his theology, but it is not its controlling center. The doctrine of justification does not finally exhaust itself in the anthropological sphere. It proclaims God's right, which establishes salvation, over the whole world. If this is so, the apostle's self-deception also touches his proclamation and understandably those who come after no longer can simply adopt his theology. For him it was possible to make his doctrine of justification, which has an ecumenical (Asmussen) and not just a forensic and individualistic orientation, the central theme of a salvation history. However, he does not allow this conception to remain a theological postulate. He thinks its fulfilment can be verified from history even though it cannot stand up to the reality of history. The apostle's salvation history is the most vulnerable part of his theology. It is not governed by the idea of a gradual process of development. Normative for it is the understanding of the gospel as the attestation and anticipation of the resurrection of the dead. In its power God takes possession of the world already before the parousia in such a way that the new creation and the old creation which is falling back into chaos separate. In the following period the salvation-historical aspect, which is modified by the idea of development, and the message of justification, which is increasingly oriented to anthropology, break away from each other. This is by no means accidental once apocalyptic no longer binds them together. Paul has left us a theological concept which cannot be maintained as a unity but whose parts, even when they have fallen apart, have again and again had an impact on world history.

Only here in a quotation do we find the word οἰκουμένη. It designates the order of the inhabited world. Verse 19 sharpens the question of v. 18. γινώσκειν has the unusual sense (*contra* Bultmann, *TDNT,* I, 705; Lagrange) of *intelligere* (Kühl; Munck, *Christ,* 99f.). The name Israel is now used emphatically (Maier, *Israel,* 97). The excuse does not avail that they have heard but did not correctly grasp the sense of the message. Moses and the prophets, again represented by Isaiah, appear as witnesses against such an evasion. They prophesied the conversion of the Gentiles, so that Israel could have recognized the dawn of the eschatological age by the fulfilment of the prophecy. For it is on this that the accent is put in the two quotations which follow. The characteristic of the Gentiles as a people who do not understand, who prior to their calling do not deserve the name of people, and as a host of those who did not seek God nor ask after him, takes up the depiction in 9:25, 30. This is, however, a secondary motif here (contra Lagrange; Althaus; Maier, Israel, 99; Munck, Christ, 103). Paradoxically those whom Scripture has not prepared in advance have recognized the eschatological hour which Israel has missed. The final quotation explicitly says this.

An answer is thus given to the question of v. 19, which was rhetorically formulated with a negation in view. Israel should have been able to perceive but did not. The answer no longer involves, like the question, merely understanding the message. γινώσκειν again has the sense "to acknowledge." As in the thesis of 9:30ff. and 10:2f., guilt is established, and with this the circle of argumentation is closed. πρῶτος in v. 19 naturally does not go with the question (contra Zahn; Plag, Wege, 31) but anticipates the following quotations: first Moses. A change in Deut 32:21 is that the demonstrative pronoun is replaced by the personal pronoun denoting the speaker. In 11:11ff. Paul will return to the motif of our passage. In the light of it he understands the task of his apostleship and sees himself as one who fulfils the eschatological promise. In the end-time God reverses the situation. Those who stand in ζῆλος θεοῦ (v. 2) have to perceive God's zeal for them in the fact that he seeks to make them jealous of the Gentiles (though cf. Senft, "L'election," 137).

The intensifying of what has been said in v. 20 is indicated by ἀποτολμᾶν. The statement of Isa 65:1 should already arouse such jealousy. The opening words of the MT are reversed and they are thus referred, in contradiction to the original, to the Gentile mission (Billerbeck; though cf. Lagrange). ἐμφανὴς ἐγενόμην means the revelation which stands under the catchword ἐγγύς in v. 8. The parallelism of Isa 65:1f., being sharply emphasized by the introduction to v. 21, is changed by the apostle into an antithesis. ὅλην τὴν ἡμέραν is put first for emphasis. The phrase is a semitism and means (Michel) "daily" (cf. 8:36). ἀπείθεια, the basic sin according to Pauline theology, expresses itself in contradiction. Even eschatologically, i.e, in relation to the gospel, Israel has fallen prey to this even though God, like the father in Luke 15:11ff., stretches out his arms to it every day.

As in 9:25ff., Paul uses Scripture to sum up his argument. The selection and interpretation of the quotations, which are not taken from an existing collection [38] (Michel, Bibel, 48f.), take place in a way which primitive Christianity ascribed to the prophetic charisma and therefore with an inspiration which does not rule out the person or reason (Michel, Bibel, 69). The forceful conclusion does not say that with God there is only grace and not hardening (contra Ulonska, Paulus, 194). The predestinarian statements in ch. 9 are not revoked in our entire chapter. They are unflinchingly adopted in the appeal to Scripture. For Paul Scripture is not a documentation of God's foreknowledge of coming history. It ushers in this history and sets it in motion. The preached word invokes it by awakening obedience and resistance. In this way (cf. 2 Cor 2:15f.) it shows itself to be that which distinguishes and qualifies the lost and the saved. Hence the destruction and reconstruction of the people of God are derived from the proclamation in this chapter (C. Müller, *Gottes Volk,* 37). Israel's guilt is not merely a refusal of the word that is near. It is a rejection of it. In this context predestination characterizes, not the nature and attributes of God, but his dealings with his creation, which mean for mankind either salvation or perdition. These are not possibilities which we can realize in and of ourselves. They arise only in encounter with the word.

D. The Mystery of Salvation History (11:1-36)

The presentation of God's right and Israel's guilt seems to exclude hope for God's ancient people, except for the remnant converted to Christ. But this appearance is deceptive. God's right and Israel's guilt have been spoken about in precisely the same way as happened relative to humanity in 1:18–3:20. This says that only the premises of the argument have been established, not its goal. In what follows, then, the previous dialectic is not set aside (*contra* Maier, *Israel,* 102). Rather, it reaches its climax. This cannot be otherwise if the justification of the ungodly, as creation out of nothing and the resurrection of the dead, forms the perspective of salvation history too. The disillusioning is the presupposition of the declaration of salvation which the apostle makes, not as a theology of history (*contra* Leenhardt; H. W. Schmidt), but prophetically (Maier, *Israel,* 102) as one who proclaims the righteousness of God to "all Israel" as well as to the world. The chapter has three sections. 11:1-10 explains that Israel's hardening is not total. 11:11-24 shows that Israel's hardening made possible the salvation of the Gentiles. 11:25-32 proclaims Israel's redemption. The chapter as a whole makes it clear that the history of the promise to Israel has not been broken off.

1. Israel's Hardening is Not Total (11:1-10)

¹*I ask, then, Has God rejected his people? Impossible! For I, too, am an Israelite, of the seed of Abraham, of the tribe of Benjamin.* ²*God has not rejected his people whom he previously chose. Do you not know what Scripture records in (the history of) Elijah when he complained to God about Israel,* ³*"Lord, they have killed thy prophets, thrown down thine altars, and I alone am left, and they seek my life"?* ⁴*But what is God's reply to him? "I have kept* [2᭢ *for myself seven thousand men who have not bowed the knee to Baal."* ⁵*So, too, there is at the present moment a remnant effected by the election of grace.* ⁶*If (this is) by grace, however, it is not by works, since otherwise grace would no longer remain grace.* ⁷*What (does this mean) then? Israel did not obtain what it sought. The elect obtained it, but the rest were hardened.* ⁸*Thus it is written, "God gave them a spirit of stupor, eyes that they might not see and ears that they might not hear, to this very day."* ⁹*And David says, "Let their altar become to them a snare and a net and a trap and an occasion of retribution.* ¹⁰*May their eyes become dark so that they cannot see, and may they bend their backs for ever."*

Bibliography: C. E. B. Cranfield, "The Significance of διὰ παντός in Romans 10,11," *SE,* II (1964) 546-550; A. Dillmann, "Über Baal mit dem weiblichen Artikel," *Monatsbericht* der königlichen preussischen Akademie der Wissenschaft, 1881, 601-620; E. von Dobschütz, "Zum paulinischen Schriftbeweis," ZNW 24 (1925) 306f.; A. T. Hanson, "The Oracle in Romans xi. 4," NTS 19 (1972/73) 300-302; K. H. Rengstorf, "Paulus und die älteste römische Christenheit," SE, II (1964) 447-464; K. L. Schmidt, "Die Verstockung des Menschen durch Gott," TZ 1 (1945) 1-17.

Rhetorical questions in vv. 1, 2b, and 7 divide the section. The opening looks back to chs. 9–10, not just to the conclusion of ch. 10. It simultaneously formulates the theme of ch. 11 with the words of 1 Kgs 12:22; Ps 93:14. For this purpose the future of the verb is changed into a past form. 9:6a is thus taken up, answered from Scripture, and made concrete by the reference to Israel. Naturally Paul is not speaking of an ideal Israel (Kühl contra Zahn) but of the Jewish people, which is later called πᾶς 'Ισραήλ. The definitive repudiation of Israel is contested, as the question and exclamation in v. 1 and the explicit assurance in v. 2a already show. It has been rightly maintained that the argument, along with the formulation in v. 1, points to readers who are predominantly Gentile-Christians.

At the commencement of the new dialogue Paul declares his solidarity with his people as in chs. 9 and 10. Also here he does not do it out of patriotism (Jülicher). He does it to prove his thesis. He himself as an Israelite of the seed of Abraham is a living example of God's will to save. As in 2 Cor 11:22; Phil 3:5 there is pride in this self-predication and in the mention of his tribe. According to rabbinic tradition Benjamin went into the Red Sea first (Billerbeck). Hope of the reunification of God's people was connected with this tribe (Vischer, "Geheimnis," 112) to which Saul and Jeremiah belonged. Paul is thus a qualified Jew and a representative of his people up to his former persecution of Christians. With his conversion a sign was set up that all Israel is not by any means rejected.

The last link in the syllogistic chain in v. 2a establishes this as impossible (Maier, Israel, 107). Even unbelieving Israel stands under the once-for-all choice of God. For this is what is meant by προέγνω here, as in 8:29; there is no reason to think in terms of God's pre-temporal decree (Munck, Christ, 107). Election and rejection take place in like manner in the historical sphere and come together here (Asmussen). Hence one can and must ask what is the relation between them, and Paul's answer is that at least the latter does not undo the former. God's action, which happens to us once, stigmatizes us forever. It does not establish human claims, but it allows no escape from the divine claim which is raised with it.

This statement seems to be extremely bold. Can one really deduce the destiny of the people from that of the individual? The quotation from 1 Kgs 19:10, 18 provides the answer. Here again the LXX text has not been greatly altered. God's address is to be understood from the context. Killing the prophets is a common theme in anti-Jewish polemic (C. Müller, Gottes Volk, 45) and it is placed first because of the danger threatening the apostle. Apart from minor omissions the remarkable feature in v. 4 is the changing of the verb from a future to an aorist and from the second person singular to the first, with ἐμαυτῷ added for emphasis. Whether another LXX version had some influence here or whether Paul made the changes himself is a moot question (cf. Michel, Bibel, 77). In diatribe style ἢ οὐκ οἴδατε is a reminder of what is already known. In rabbinic fashion ἐν 'Ηλίᾳ designates the OT pericope in the Elijah narrative (Billerbeck). ἐντυγχάνειν τινὶ κατά means technically the accusation before the court (Lietzmann), the counterpart being intercession as in 8:26f., 34. χρηματισμός means the oracle, the divine saying (Hanson, "Oracle," 300-302). The feminine article before Baal is to be explained by the fact that pious Jews would not speak the name of the false god and substituted בשׁת or αἰσχύνη (Dillmann, "Artikel"; Billerbeck; BAGD, 129a). To bend the knee is a cultic gesture (Schlier, TDNT, I, 738f.).

The passage is obviously understood typologically and v. 5 draws the consequence for the present, which is characterized eschatologically by ἐν τῷ νῦν καιρῷ, as in 3:26. The point of comparison is the existence of a remnant, and this motif becomes at once the theme. Originally the number was simply meant to show the size of the group which remained faithful. In Paul, it still stands in contrast with the prophet who thinks that he alone is left. But the quotation carries us a stage further than v. 1b by already opening our view to Israel as a people. At the same time the dialectic of the remnant motif in the next verses should not be overlooked, for in these verses the remnant in sharp antithesis to the people as a whole indicates merely what remains over. There is at any rate no gradual or continuous development which leads from the remnant to the people even though there is perceived in the remnant the beginning of an encompassing eschatological event which finally embraces "all Israel." For Paul the idea of the remnant is inseparably related to that of judgment and therefore to new creation (Schrenk, Weissagung, 29; C. Müller, Gottes Volk, 46; but cf. Maier, Mensch, 395). Just for that reason the remnant can be set in contrast to the whole people (unlike, e.g., 4 Ezra 13:48ff.), although, as here, it has the whole people in view.

In content the remnant is nothing other than Jewish Christianity. Hence the motif is set in the context of Paul's doctrine of justification, and to be sure initially with the phrase λεῖμμα κατ᾿ ἐκλογὴν χάριτος and then with v. 6. The formula corresponds to ἡ κατ᾿ ἐκλογὴν πρόθεσις in 9:11. The remnant is created by the election of grace. ἐκλογή designates here the active work of the power of grace (Luz, Geschichtsverständnis, 82), whereas in v. 7 it designates its result, that is, the elect. Since this phrase relates to God's reply in v. 4 the reference is not to a pre-temporal decree but to the decree of salvation revealed in Scripture. The catchword ἐκλογή was given to Paul already by Judaism (Schrenk, TDNT, IV, 184; Fascher, RAC, VI, 415f.), which speaks in stereotyped fashion of the community of the elect, as in 1 Enoch 37-71. The Qumran writings are already controlled by the eschatological and polemical contrast between the elect remnant and the Jewish people. In these works, however, the remnant is qualified by strict [2ʰ observance of the law. In Paul, however, it is characterized by justification (v. 6). The first οὐκέτι in v. 6 logically means "not therefore" (Lietzmann), as in 7:17, 20; 14:15; Gal 3:18. ἐπεί with the meaning "otherwise" is used causally with an adversative thrust, as in 3:6; 11:22 (BDF, §456[3]). In the general corruption sovereign grace creates an eschatological remnant, and this is preserved only if it does not rely on its own works but solely on the faithfulness of the Creator to his creature.

Paul proves his thesis that Israel is not definitively rejected by arguing from the example of his own existence and that of Jewish Christianity. Why does he use typology when a simple reference might have sufficed? He could have presented the fact that he considers Jewish Christianity to be the eschatological remnant without the quotation. At a first glance, then, the typology seems to be unnecessary, for the same result could have been achieved in less oracular fashion. If it also has material sense, that cannot lie in its goal but in its cause, namely, in the situation of the apostle (cf. Leenhardt; for a different view Luz, *Geschichtsverständnis*, 81). Paul's situation can be compared with that of Elijah, and he thus finds consolation in the promise given to the latter. Elijah is not thereby a second witness (*contra* Rengstorf, "Römische Christenheit," 460), a martyr (Munck, *Salvation*, 307), a preacher of repentance and an accuser of Israel (C. Müller, *Gottes Volk*, 45). Nor is it that his zeal is reminiscent of Paul's pre-Christian past (*contra* Rengstorf, "Römische Christenheit," 461). The point of comparison to the apostle is rather that he seemed to be alone among his people and had to bewail the unbelief of Israel as Paul does in 9:30–10:3. This is what gives the typology its special significance. It does not just allow Paul to speak of the remnant. It integrates Paul's situation, prefigured in Elijah's history, into the salvation event. As will be confirmed later, Paul saw his mission as having salvation-historical character and he could thus see in himself the Elijah of the end-time (Zeller, *Juden*, 273 is sceptical).

In this context what is the function of vv. 7-10, which refer back to 9:30ff., and which thus impede the argument rather than furthering it? The quotation of Elijah reminds Paul of the reality of unbelieving Israel. The typology is also fulfilled in the fact that Elijah's contemporaries find an eschatological counterpart. The doctrine of justification, taken up in v. 6, shows why this is so. By the pathway of works which it has entered upon Israel could not reach its goal, unlike Jewish Christianity, which has abandoned this way. Now ἐκλογή and λεῖμμα are synonymous. οἱ λοιποί are Jews who do not believe in Christ. This conceals the fact that the reference is to the overwhelming majority of the people. However, Paul frequently speaks in the same way of his opponents as τινές. An eschatological view always finds the main stream where the promise is, so that there is a transvaluation of values here too. The catchword πωροῦσθαι takes up the σκληρύνειν of 9:18 and in the tradition fuses indistinguishably with πηροῦσθαι, since the result of withering, as of ossifying, is hardening, or, in a transferred sense, obduracy (Zahn, Excursus III; K. L. Schmidt, "Verstockung," 9f.; *TDNT*, V, 1023). παχύνειν joins this group as a synonym. The following quotation from Deut 29:3, which is quite freely cited, is given its point by the interpolation of the phrase πνεῦμα κατανύξεως from Isa 29:10 (Dobschütz, "Schriftbeweis," 306f.). If the genitive of the infinitive has a consecutive sense (BDF, §400[2]), the context still shows that the goal of God's will is simultaneously expressed therewith. A feature of the chapter is the combining of quotations from the Torah and the Writings or Prophets (Vollmer, *Zitate*, 37). Thus David the psalmist supports Moses in v. 9. The basic passage Ps 68:23f. LXX is influenced by θήρα from Ps 34:8 as a parallel of παγίς. The original meaning of σκάνδαλον, namely, trap or snare, is still noticeable here, and it forms the bridge to the first two expressions, which are almost synonymous (Stählin, *Skandalon*, 175ff.). The LXX seems to be quoted in a special tradition and the combination of scriptural texts under the catchword "not to see" suggests the use of a Christian collection of testimonies, as in 9:33 (Michel, *Bibel*, 86f.; L. Cerfaux, " 'L'aveuglement d'esprit' dans l'Evangile de saint Marc," *Recueil Lucien Cerfaux* [1954] II, 3ff.; Luz, *Geschichtsverständnis*, 98). Mark 4:12 par. John 12:40 and Acts 28:26f. testify to the widespread use of the first quotation and point to anti-Jewish polemic as a firm setting in life (*Sitz im Leben*).

ἀνταπόδομα in v. 9c means specifically the occasion of retribution. The whole saying is a curse (Lagrange; Michel) and there is no hint that it is directed merely against the leaders of Israel (*contra* Zahn; Muller-Duvernoy, "Problème," 80). The true difficulty of the text derives from the fact that one does not really see what the subject and predicate have to do with each other. Does τράπεζα mean the merry feast at which one is suddenly frightened (Maier, *Israel*, 113 following Gunkel's interpretation of the original; Zahn), or table fellowship (BAGD, 824b; Barrett; Michel), or in a transferred sense all that one does and all that by which one lives (Althaus; Ridderbos; Schneider, *TDNT*, V, 595; Goppelt, *TDNT*, VIII, 212)? Should one take note of rabbinic exegesis which speaks cultically of "table" (Billerbeck; Black; Lyonnet, *Quaestiones*, II, 100) and has the Passover specifically in view (Stählin, *Skandalon*, 178; Michel, *Bibel*, 354)? That cannot be derived from the context. But 1 Cor 10:21 shows that Paul could understand τράπεζα in a cultic sense, and this alone seems to make good sense here. Precisely the cultus which represents Jewish piety causes the blinding and fall of Israel, and keeps its back under the yoke from which it cannot escape.

This also helps us to understand the antithesis in v. 6 better. Not sins, but pious works prevent Judaism from obtaining the salvation held out to it, and keep it in bondage. It also explains the addition of the words "spirit of stupor" to the quotation. Israel's inability to see salvation has a demonic depth which resists the Spirit of God who expresses himself in the Christian message. In the righteousness of works there comes into effect the power which according to 1:24ff. entangles people in both guilt and doom and indicates God's wrath. One even then falls victim to the immanent power of the cosmos which comes to a peak in religiosity unless a person submits to the power of grace. Human existence stands deep in the conflict of powers when it manifests its piety. According to 1 Cor 10:21 the Lord and demons are most sharply opposed at this point. It is here that blindness and deafness arise most easily. Unbelieving Israel offers an example of this.

ἕως τῆς σήμερον ἡμέρας at the end of v. 8 points to the eschatological moment when this is revealed and the change can come. For Paul only the Judge gives grace and that through the judgment. Only the grasped judgment and the acknowledged Judge mean salvation. Therefore God can never attain his right with the pious because they think they can escape the Judge. He manifests his deity by not seeing the person of the pious. He declares himself to be in the right [2] by unveiling to us our reality and at the same time showing us his help in the righteousness he gives, which glorifies his power as Creator. Persisting in our own righteousness says on the other side that we fail to see our reality, despise the proffered help, and are obstinately unprepared to join the ungodly.

Thus the verses unfold once again, before Paul proclaims salvation for Israel, the presuppositions of this proclamation in the doctrine of justification. Israel is not saved in a different way from the Gentiles. There is only one possibility of access to the real God, namely, the righteousness of faith on which church and synagogue divide. The predestinarian statements which protect the doctrine of justification also here from every type of synergism, do not fix different conditions but point to the strange path of salvation history. In it salvation arises only for the lost and condemned. Grace replaces wrath. The new aeon which comes occupies a place precisely in the old aeon which passes. God's sovereignty triumphs over the obstinate.

There is confirmed in Israel what 1:18–3:20 established about the whole world. Just for that reason the turning can come to Israel which is announced in 3:21. Paul's doctrine of justification stands beyond religion and morality, just as the categories of determinism and indeterminism, of autonomy and heteronomy fail before it. The soteriologically oriented statements about predestination make this clear no less than the apostle's "ethics." Paul does not think in terms of anthropology but in terms of the woes of the Messiah in which the reality of the world and the power of God come into eschatological collision and salvation no longer arises by good works but by acceptance of the word of judging grace. God's freedom penetrates the fallenness of the world, even the religious world which is called Israel, and frees all those who submit to it instead of remaining isolated. There is hope always only for those who have no more hope in and of themselves. The saving God reveals himself when people have no way out. Israel is no exception here. Verses 7-10 have the function of showing that the promise of salvation in vv. 1-6 does not leap across the deliberations of chs. 9–10 but presupposes them and is possible only in the framework of Paul's doctrine of justification. Verse 6 is developed in such a way that the justification of the ungodly in this case means the justification of the obdurate. Thereby v. 32 is anticipated.

2. Israel and Gentile-Christians (11:11-24)

[11]*So I ask, Have they stumbled so as to fall? Not at all! Through their fall salvation (came) to the Gentiles so as to provoke them to jealousy.* [12]*If, however, their fall means (heavenly) riches for the world and their failure means riches for the Gentiles, how much more certainly (will) their full acceptance (mean this).* [13]*To you Gentiles I thus say, Inasmuch as I am an apostle to the Gentiles I magnify my ministry* [14]*so as to make my flesh jealous and save some of them.* [15]*For if their rejection (meant) reconciliation for the world, what (will) their acceptance (be) but life from the dead?* [16]*If the beginning is holy, so (is) the dough; if the root is holy, so (are) the branches.* [17]*But if some of the branches were broken off, while you from a wild olive tree were grafted in among them and acquired a share in the nourishing root of the (good) olive tree,* [18]*do not look scornfully on the branches. If you must vaunt yourselves, (remember), you do not support the root, but the root (supports) you.* [19]*You might argue, "Branches were broken off so that I might be grafted in."* [20]*You are right. They were broken off because of unbelief and you stand fast in faith. Do not be proud but stand in fear.* [21]*For if God has not spared the natural branches, he does not have to spare you.* [22]*Consider then the goodness and severity of God, severity to the fallen, but God's goodness to you if you continue in his goodness. Otherwise you too will be cut off.* [23]*Similarly they too will be grafted in (again) if they do not continue in unbelief. For God has the power to graft them in again.* [24]*For if you have been broken off from what is*

303

by nature a wild olive tree and grafted, contrary to nature, into a good olive tree, how much more certainly shall these (who belong to it) naturally be grafted into their own olive tree.

Bibliography: H. W. Bartsch, "Die antisemitischen Gegner des Paulus im Römerbrief," in *Antijudaismus im NT?* (ed. W. P. Eckert *et al.;* 1967) 27-43; M. M. Bourke, *A Study of the Metaphor of the Olive Tree in Romans XI* (1947).

Readers are kept in suspense because this section also does not provide the solution to the problem posed in v. 1a, although vv. 11a, 12b, 15b, and 23f. take it up. Israel's deliverance is proclaimed but not established. What is now asserted is that its unbelief has a reverse side. Through it the Gentile-Christian community has come to be formed. This thesis, stated in vv. 11f., allows the apostle to maintain that God's way with his people has not yet reached its end. According to vv. 13-15 this has consequences for his own task, and according to vv. 16-24 it has consequences for Gentile-Christians, since they have no claim to superiority.

The argument again moves according to the model of the diatribe in the form of a conversation. Verse 11a repeats the question of v. 1a more precisely and in a way which looks back to 9:32. προσκόπτειν is now divided into the two acts of πταίειν ("stumbling") and πίπτειν ("remaining down") (Michaelis, *TDNT,* VI, 164f.). According to v. 1a and the context ἵνα refers to the divine purpose (*contra* Sanday and Headlam; Lagrange). Verse 11b gives the reason for the decisive rejection of the question. παράπτωμα in connection with πίπτειν means the verifiable fall, not the transgression. The argument has two premises. Obviously only a Christian can see things in this way, and secondly a salvation-historical aspect is present. Israel's conduct has eschatological significance even when it rejects Christ. The Gentile mission arises out of this. Paul concludes from this that the instrument of God's grace against its own will continues to be the object of this grace (Zeller, *Juden,* 209ff., 239f.). Surprisingly he adduces no scripture to back this up, as one might have expected in view of the many preceding quotations (Michel). There speaks here and in what follows the prophet who can shed light on the problems of the eschatological present.

Behind v. 11b stands unspoken the apocalyptic idea that the first shall be last and the last first. The infinitive clause also has an apocalyptic sense. The reversal of earthly relations is for its part simply a stage on the divinely planned path whose end remains bound up in a special way, and against all appearances, with the destiny of Israel. The catchword παραζηλῶσαι is taken from 10:19 to elucidate [2 this matter, which is almost fantastic to us. Paul seriously counts on it that the Gentile mission will make Israel jealous and lead to its conversion. This hope can be imagined only if the conversion itself stands beyond any doubt and only the way to it obscure. The theology and practice of the apostle cannot be adequately understood unless attention is paid to this conviction. The fact that it seems absurd to us should underscore rather than reduce its importance for Paul and his interpretation. Verse 12 states more clearly the background of his thinking and hopes here. In so doing it anticipates the conclusion (Maier, *Israel,* 119).

The first clause repeats v. 11b in fine parallelism. πλοῦτος is the fulness of eschatological blessing, as in 9:23; 10:12. κόσμος means in Jewish fashion the Gentile world, precision immediately being given by ἔθνη (Sasse, *TDNT,* III, 892). The phrase sounds just as much like a formula as the statement in v. 15, and Paul is probably pointing to a tradition no longer discernible to us. The meaning of ἥττημα is the subject of lively debate. However, according to the general view it arises from the antithesis to πλήρωμα and is parallel to v. 15. A rare word, associated in false etymology with ἥττων, it cannot mean overthrow (Sanday and Headlam; Gaugler; Murray) or loss (Bardenhewer) but failure to meet demands posed, as in 1 Cor 6:7 (Maier, *Israel,* 120), or deficit (Lietzmann). It is tempting to think that πλήρωμα is equivalent to πλήρωσις in 13:10 as the fulfilling of the demand (Lietzmann; Althaus; Plag, *Wege,* 33f., 42f.). But this is ruled out by the parallel πρόσλημψις in v. 15 as well as by the phrase πλήρωμα τῶν ἐθνῶν in 11:25. The word is used in view of the fact that the remnant was mentioned earlier, and it means the filling up of this remnant as a new whole (Delling, *TDNT,* VI, 305). The motif of πᾶς Ἰσραήλ in v. 26 is thus anticipated in its eschatological modification. Whether the reference is to the act of filling up or to its result, i.e., the "full number," remains undecided. This also applies to ἥττημα, which is to be translated either by "failure" or by "deficit."

The conclusion *a minori ad majus* which is introduced by the characteristic πόσῳ μᾶλλον ends without predicate; one must infer this from the previous clause. As compared with the preceding chapters the approach is fundamentally different. Israel is the bearer of the blessing both in the present and in the future. The point is that there will no longer be a distinction between the true and the false seed, the remnant and the people. In virtue of the promise given to it Judaism is an eschatological entity as πᾶς Ἰσραήλ, and it remains so even in judgment and against its own will. Its full conversion is undoubtedly expected (Maier, *Israel,* 122), but it is bound up with the fact that salvation has come first to the Gentiles. The train of thought is fully apocalyptic.

Paul's own apostolate is involved, as vv. 13-15 show. These verses are directed to the Gentiles, without exclusively addressing the Roman readers (cf. 1:6) (*contra* Zahn). One may gather from them that there were disagreements in the community and in fact arrogance on the part of Gentile-Christians (*contra* Maier, *Israel,* 123, 130; Oesterreicher, "Rise," 322; Michel; Jülicher; Dodd; Lütgert, *Römerbrief,* 85), but hardly anti-Semitism (Munck, *Christ,* 117f.; Muller-Duvernoy, "Problème," 65f.). These might well be the reason for the epistle (Lütgert, *Römerbrief,* 83ff.; cf. Eichholz, *Paulus,* 124). Ephesians, too, shows that in a particular area of Paul's missionary work Jewish Christianity was very soon pushed out onto the margin. But this is not yet clearly visible. The admonitions of vv. 16-24 arise naturally out of the problem of the chapter and give evidence of the apostle's foresight, but tell us little about the situation in Rome (C. Müller, *Gottes Volk,* 104ff.). If the recipients of the epistle are in the first instance the Roman majority, the warning still applies to all non-Jewish Christians. They are told that precisely Paul's apostolate involves an expectation of salvation for Israel. ἐφ' ὅσον does not mean "then" in a temporal sense (Ridderbos) but modally "to the extent." ἐθνῶν ἀπόστολος is a title which summarizes 1:5, 13 (Munck, *Christ,* 122). διακονία does not imply modesty (Zahn) or humility. According to 1 Cor 12:4 it is an equivalent of charisma. In view of the eschatological background it should not be rendered "office." In context δοξάζειν can hardly be thanksgiving (Michel). Paul rather magnifies his ministry when, as in v. 12, he speaks of the fulness for the world which is connected with it. There were before and alongside him other missionaries to the Gentiles who also called themselves apostles (2 Cor 11:13). But their commission did not have the universal scope of the task in virtue of which Paul calls himself the "apostle to the Gentiles." He neither can nor will refrain from boasting of this commission because he has to do it, not on his own account, but in view of the Giver of the commission and for the sake of the fruit of the grace conferred on him. The thought is closer to 2 Cor 10:13f. than 1 Cor 9:22f., since it concerns the cosmic range of the mission. The ability to meet different people in different ways is simply the interior view and the consequence of ecumenicity.

In a distinctive way, which is at the same time unusually characteristic of the dialectic normally bound up with Paul's pride in his work, δοξάζειν is subordinated to a more far-reaching purpose in v. 14. No less typical is the mode of expression which flounders similarly to what was already observed in 1:10ff. εἴ πως suggests neither modesty nor doubt (*contra* Zahn). It is more appropriate to speak of diplomatic caution which does not yet lay the cards on the table. τινὲς ἐξ αὐτῶν is also indefinite (Munck, *Christ,* 124; *Salvation,* 45), although this does not stand in any relation to the real hope of the apostle. σώζειν is a missionary term. "My flesh" has the OT sense of "my people." The stress is on the verb, which takes up v. 11c and is supposed to show that Paul is unmistakably the instrument of God's saving will for Israel. This sounds more harmless than it is.

It must be considered that Israel is supposed to be made jealous when it sees the "fulness of the Gentiles" accepted (Murray) and that the apostle is trying with almost impossible speed to traverse the whole world in order to spread the "riches of the Gentiles." The fulness of the Gentiles will come only through Paul's universal ministry. Yet the whole world is not set in motion merely for the salvation of some Jews (*contra* Zeller, *Juden,* 274ff.). The object of the παραζηλῶσαι according to 10:19; 11:11 is rather the whole people. What is more implicit than explicit in v. 14 is in this context the expectation that Paul's ministry will realize the divine purpose and give Israel the push to the conversion depicted in vv. 25ff. This is so immense a thought that intentionally it can only be suggested. Nowhere is the apostle's unbounded sense of mission more apparent and nowhere is it more evident that apocalyptic is the driving force in Paul's theology and practice. [2 Such a mission has an inner limit only in the unlimited awareness that he is nothing more than a servant and instrument. Paul is not content to be merely an apostle to the Gentile world. He has obviously learned from Deut 32:21 that God will convert his people by provoking it to jealousy of Gentile-Christians. Christ, reigning as cosmocrator over the nations and confessed by them, will be to the Jews the sign of the end that has dawned and of the promises that have been fulfilled. He will thus be the object of their hope too. According to 2 Cor 10:4f. Paul as a captain of this Lord takes the whole world captive to his obedience. Necessarily, then, he is also an instrument in the conversion of Israel (Maier, *Israel,* 126).

If modern exegetes grasp this view at all, they dismiss it as a whim of optimism (Dodd) or question the validity of an argument which they find theologically alien and which seems to have its source in a psychologizing dialectic of history (Dinkler, "Prädestination," 96). It is, however, the apocalyptic dream of a man who tried to do in a decade what two thousand years have not managed to do. This dream had its root in two premises. For Paul the conversion of Israel is an integral part of the end of history. He himself, however, as directly the apostle to the Gentiles and indirectly, precisely in virtue of the Gentile mission, a minister in the eschatological conversion of Judaism, is nothing other than a precursor of the parousia (Sass, *Apostelamt*, 48; Munck, *Salvation*, 42-49). As both the beginning and the end of the drama of salvation are determined by the destiny of Israel (Lietzmann; Maier, *Israel*, 123), so the apostle regards himself as one who brings about the divinely willed conclusion of salvation history. If due significance is not given to these two factors, the text is not expounded but instead we have a view of Paul which is derived from his epistles by elimination and reduction. Chapters 9–11 have a diacritical function in relation to the history of Pauline exegesis, distasteful as this statement may be today.

Verse 15 takes up v. 12 and establishes vv. 13f. (Kühl; Maier, *Israel*, 126). The point is in the second clause, which goes beyond vv. 12f. and declares the apostle's work to be necessary. The antithesis of ἀποβολή ("rejection") and πρόσλημψις ("acceptance") is also found in the gloss to Sir 10:20: "Fear of the Lord is the beginning of acceptance, but the beginning of rejection is obstinacy and arrogance." Like these terms the phrases καταλλαγὴ κόσμου and ζωὴ ἐκ νεκρῶν seem to be traditional formulae. According to Johanan ben Zakkai (*b. Baba Qamma* 7:6) the sons of the Torah are a reconciliation for the world (Dahl, *Volk Gottes*, 78). When 2 Cor 5:19 speaks, in a style of hymnic tradition, of the reconciliation of the world this does not mean the ending of inner cosmic enmity, as in Col 1:20; Eph 2:16, but the reconciliation to himself which God grants his creatures. The phrase "life from the dead," which reminds us of the tradition in, e.g., John 5:24 (Munck, *Christ*, 126), is not to be given a transferred sense. It designates (*contra* Schlatter; Gaugler; Bardenhewer; Huby; Leenhardt; Murray) what Paul elsewhere calls ἀνάστασις νεκρῶν and thus refers to the parousia (the majority view today). Thus the conversion of Israel is for the apostle also the last act of salvation history (Zeller, *Juden*, 241ff.). The apocalyptic hope of Judaism that the Gentiles will come when Zion triumphs is reversed in our verses. This can hardly be unintentional, since Paul related his own work to it (Luz, *Geschichtsverständnis*, 393f.). Gentile-Christians, too, must take into account the eschatological significance of Israel. This is made clear in what follows, which is not parenthetical (*contra* Dahl, *Volk Gottes*, 245).

There is no ground in the least for boasting over Israel. Verse 16 precedes the new section thematically. It does not express a strong sense of Jewishness (Kühl) but is an apostolic statement. Two images establish the point. They need not be understood allegorically. The first refers to the cultic practice, enjoined in Num 15:20f., of consecrating a cake to God. The rabbis, too, made metaphorical use of this when they called Adam the meal offering of the world (Billerbeck). In distinction from 8:23 ἀπαρχή has, then, a technical sense here and is the LXX rendering of חלה. Being consecrated to God, it is sanctified and it also sanctifies the whole lump according to Philo *De specialibus legibus* i.131-144 (Berger, "Abraham," 83f.). Since this metaphor is not serviceable in the line of argument

307

that follows, it is replaced by a second one, the word "holy" being carried forward as a connecting link.

Paul gives no impulse to reflection on the inheriting of religious qualities (*contra* Dodd), nor does he speak of natural holiness (*contra* Jülicher). Although he does not speak of the root and the tree along the lines of the first image, but of the root and the branches, his concern is not with a process of growth (*contra* Kühl; J. Schneider, *TDNT*, III, 720f.). The issue is the relation between beginning and result, as earlier that between the part and the whole. The two cannot be separated as though they had nothing to do with each other. The first metaphor from cultic practice provides the aspect from which the second is seen: Holy means consecrated to God.

Like *Jub.* 1:16; *1 Enoch* 10:16; 93:2ff., Paul seems to presuppose the metaphor of the "plant of righteousness," or, like 1QH 8:4ff., 10ff., that of the "holy shoot" which produces the eternal plant of truth. This designates eschatological Israel. In *1 Enoch* 93:5 Abraham is the root. Thus the apostle, who is concerned with the acceptance of unbelieving Israel, is probably thinking of the patriarchs (the common view; cf. Schrenk, *TDNT*, IV, 211; Maurer, *TDNT*, VI, 989; Luz, *Geschichtsverständnis*, 275f.; Plag, *Wege*, 35), not Jewish-Christians (Kühl; Lietzmann; Barrett). The metaphors are not to be stretched beyond what is absolutely necessary (Minear, *Images*, 45ff.). Without going into details, Paul is stressing the continuity of God's hidden faithfulness in Israel's history. It is important to recognize that the approach has changed as compared with 9:6ff. Previously the emphasis was on the selection which breaks earthly continuity again and again. Now, conversely, the faithfulness which makes earthly continuity possible is underscored (Dahl, *Volk Gottes*, 242). Paul's dialectic brings the two sides together and both determine his view of salvation history, which cannot be resolved existentially or calculated rationally. The historical connection is that the Creator remains the subject and sustainer of this history. This also prevents interpretation along the lines of an immanent process of development.

The reasoning in vv. 17f. is parallel to that in vv. 19-22. There is no reason to speak of strophes (J. Weiss, "Beiträge," 241; Maier, *Israel*, 130). Metaphorical style is retained but there is no true allegorizing (*contra* Michel). As almost always in Paul, the imagery is shaped by the intended subject matter, so that statements are made which it is best not to check out from the standpoint of agriculture. There are occasional references to the practice of renewing an unfruitful olive tree by grafting in wild shoots (Billerbeck; Bruce; J. Schnieder, *TDNT*, III, 721) but it may not have been common. Paul does not refer to it, and it would coincide only in part with what he wants to say (*contra* Schoeps, *Paul*, 242, who, like others, cites Philo *De praemiis et poenis* ii.433). On the other hand, there is nothing to prove that Paul was aware that his image was contrary to nature and from that standpoint wanted to point out the miraculous character of the event portrayed (Munck, *Christ*, 128, following Zahn; Vischer, "Geheimnis," 126; Gaugler). To be sure, the process described is a miracle. But this is not being given special literary expression.

As regards κατά and παρὰ φύσιν, compare 1:26f. ἐγκεντρίζειν is a technical term. ἀγριέλαιος is perhaps an adjective in v. 17, unlike v. 24 (BAGD, 13a). ἐν αὐτοῖς means "among them," not "in place of them." ῥίζα τῆς πιότητος is the root which provides nourishment for the fruits (Sanday and Headlam; cf. Maier, *Israel,* 132), while those of the oleaster only spout water.

It is best not to characterize Paul as a child of the city (*contra* Lietzmann; Dodd). He portrays the eschatological reality in order to ward off possible arrogance on the part of the Gentile-Christians, the κατακαυχᾶσθαι, i.e., those who boastfully place themselves above others (Bultmann, *TDNT,* III, 653f.). Verse 18b sums it up. Gentile Christianity has its root in the OT people of God. Hence Gentile-Christians belong to the proselytes (C. Müller, *Gottes Volk,* 93). This idea is broadly developed in Eph 2:1ff. But it is already presented typologically in 1 Cor 10:1-13, which takes up a thought which Jewish-Christian missionaries had represented already before Paul (*contra* Munck, *Christ,* 130f. n. 203). Anti-Semitism need not thereby be postulated (*contra* Leenhardt; H. W. Schmidt).

It is a long way from the self-understanding of the earliest Palestinian community that it was the holy remnant of the eschatologically reunited Israel to the extended concept of the church as the people of God in 1 Pet 2:9. Jewish-Christians, with whom the Gentile mission began, are integrated into it. If they did not make proselytes of the Gentiles, they could no longer continue holding the Palestinian view that they were the eschatological people of twelve tribes assembled from Jews. On the other hand their ecclesiology did not yet permit them to renounce the concept of the people of God or to understand it in a purely figurative and extended sense. For them the church grew out of both Jews and Gentiles. This can be connected with the concept of the people of God only if the prophetic promise is taken seriously that at the end of the times the Gentiles will come and be fused with the holy remnant of Israel to form the eschatological people of possession.

In this modified form Paul adopts the idea of the new people and squares it dialectically with his ecclesiology, in which the new covenant stands over against the old covenant and yet is typologically prefigured by the old. This is not, of course, the main theme of his ecclesiology, which is defined by the motif of the body of Christ. On the other hand the traditional conception is indispensable to him, since the OT and the doctrine of creation force him to link the people of the promise with that of the end-time. This necessity arises as well when he has to warn his community of danger with the help of OT paradigms. One sees it also when, as here, he has to defend Israel as the bearer of the promise on the basis of Scripture. For him the concept of the people of God characterizes the eschatological phenomenon of the church in terms of its historical context. Otherwise it would no longer be traced back to the will of the Creator, and it would become a mystery group instead of God's new world.

For Paul there can be no church of Gentile-Christians alone. Such a church would be a world alongside a world and an extract from the world, not the goal of God's plan of salvation for the world. It would be abstracted from pre-Easter history. God's claim to the whole world, established with and from creation, would be renounced, and the church would be reduced to a religious society. History would be sacrificed for the sake of spirit and a counter-world set up. The concept of the people of God growing out of the root of Israel has, therefore, an indispensable function in Paul's ecclesiology, even though it is only one of its aspects and not even the center. For the apostle there is no salvation apart from the history of Israel. For salvation is for him the righteousness in which the Creator establishes his claim to the world by fulfilling the promise. 9:25ff. show that Paul even goes to the point of self-contradiction in this regard. He could do this because he allows God to take his right to a guilty, refractory, and rejected world, and grace both reveals the hitherto hidden wrath of God and ends it. Out of this there develops the dialectic of Paul's theology as a whole, which also shapes his concept of the people of God. Historically elected in the form of Israel, this people is upheld only thanks to the faithfulness of God to his promise. If it tries to assert itself over against this faithfulness, it becomes the people of unbelief, but does not thereby escape the claim of God. As there is no church without Israel, so Israel alone remains the people of God when it becomes the church.

Verses 19-22 repeat the argument of vv. 17f. in such a way that what has so far been a mere possibility now takes form in the contradiction posed by the Gentiles. Thereby the relation to unbelieving Israel is understood as a result and a historical supersession (Peterson, "Kirche," 282). The apostle's reply is not ironical (*contra* Zahn; Kühl; Lagrange; Michel; H. W. Schmidt). It establishes that the Gentile-Christian objection is right only if it is not meant historically. It must be related to, and limited by, faith and unbelief. The datives in v. 20 are causal (BDF, §196; Maier, *Israel*, 133). The missionary formula "standing in faith" is used (cf. also 1 Cor 16:13). Since the argument seems to be similar to that of Philo when in *De exsecrationibus* 152 he speaks of the ignoble shoot upon a good stump, the basis might be an item in Jewish propaganda (Michel). At any rate we do not possess faith or unbelief as qualities which cannot be lost (Luz, *Geschichtsverständnis*, 278). Precisely the believer is under threat. He must therefore be warned against pride with the semitizing phrase, as in 12:16, and in spite of the apparent contradiction to 8:15 he has to be told to fear, as in Phil 2:12. Freed from fear (*desperatio*) we can easily fall prey to a false sense of security (*securitas*), and therefore we have to fear if we are to remain free from fear of the enslaving world (Bultmann, *Theology*, I, 321f.; C. Müller, *Gottes Volk*, 95 misses the point here).

The recipient of blessing still stands before judgment and therefore before the Judge, as is worked out more fully in 1 Cor 10:1-13. The engrafted shoot learns from the example of the natural branches that there are no privileges with God, and that the goodness and severity of God cannot be separated. ἀποτομία is a common Hellenistic term for judicial severity. The expression and the style betray the influence of Jewish wisdom speech (Michel; Köster, *TDNT*, VIII, 108), which is also reflected in the rabbinic distinction between the measure of mercy and that of legal strictness (Billerbeck; Ridderbos). Since faith is a gift, one has constantly to receive it afresh from God's goodness. He who himself is constantly dependent on that will not deny it to others. The objection of the Gentile-Christians is thus rejected.

Verse 23f. can now express the apostle's hope for unbelieving Israel, which certainly also here remains tied to grace and faith. Even in his apocalyptic dreams Paul insists that there is only one way of salvation (Zeller, *Juden*, 245). One might reverse this. The application of the doctrine of justification to Israel forces Paul to these dreams. In face of the reality of Judaism this is the only way open. The bridge between the two statements is that the apostle views justification as an eschatological event. It thus takes place against the backdrop of the resurrection of the dead and the creation of a new world. Israel cannot be excluded from this. Particularly plain in all this is the fact that grace is understood as a power which overcomes unbelief and brings to faith. Miracle is therefore the presupposition of faith. God as Creator is δυνατός. This is the basis of all hope, as in 4:17f. It is also, as again in 4:17f., the end of persistence in unbelief and therefore of obduracy portrayed as a destiny. Gentile-Christians have also experienced this miracle, as the term παρὰ φύσιν shows. Paul again adds πόσῳ μᾶλλον, which brings out the supremacy of grace. The Creator wills and makes a new creation out of rejection, since only thus can he hold fast his creation. If he has done this with those who were not his people, he will do it no less with his people. Israel's guilt and doom consisted in not trusting its Creator. In this it represents all human conduct. Since Paul has experienced who God really is, in relation to Israel too he can count on him who calls what is not into being and who justifies the ungodly. If this applies to Gentiles, it applies no less where pious humanity appears representatively.

3. Israel's Redemption (11:25-32)

[25]*For I will not hide this mystery from you, brethren, so that you do not build on your own insight: Israel has experienced partial hardening until the fulness of the Gentiles comes (under God's lordship).* [26]*So, then, all Israel will be saved. For it is written, "The Redeemer will come from Zion. He will turn ungodliness from Jacob,* [27]*and this will be my covenant for them when I take away their sins."* [28]*As regards the gospel they are indeed enemies for your sake but as regards election they are beloved for the fathers' sake.* [29]*For the gifts and call of God are irrevocable.* [30]*Just as you were once disobedient to God but have now found mercy because of their disobedience,* [31]*so they have become disobedient because of the mercy (granted) to you, in order that they may find mercy.* [32]*For God has shut up all men in disobedience in order that he may have mercy on all.*

Bibliography: R. Batey, " 'So all Israel will be saved,' " *Interpretation* 20 (1966) 218-228; R. E. Brown, "The Semitic Background of the NT Mysterion, I, II," *Bib* 39 (1958) 426-448 and 40 (1959) 70-87; N. A. Dahl, "Der Name Israel," *Judaica* 6 (1950) 161-170; idem, "Die Messianität Jesu bei Paulus," *Studia Paulina*, 83-95; F. J. Leenhardt, " '. . . et sic omnis Israel salvus fieret': Rom 11, 26," *Stud.Paul.Congr.*, I, 329-340; B. Reicke, "Um der Väter willen, Röm 11, 28," *Judaica* 14 (1958) 106-114; P. Richardson, *Israel in the Apostolic Church* (1969); C. Spicq, "ἀμεταμέλητος dans Rom XI 29," *RB* 67 (1960) 210-19; P. Stuhl-macher, "Zur Interpretation von Römer 11, 25-32," *Probleme biblischer Theologie* (Festschrift für G. von Rad; 1971) 555-570; E. Vogt, " 'Mysteria' in Textibus Qumrân," *Bib* 37 (1956) 247-257; H. Windisch, "Die Sprüche vom Eingehen in das Reich Gottes," *ZNW* 27 (1928) 163-192.

The apostle is now at the goal which he has been approaching by an unusually difficult route but purposefully and with skilful dialectic. It has been plain from 11:1 onward. On the basis of Deut 32:21 vv. 11-15 have indissolubly linked salvation history, Paul's apostolate, and Israel's redemption. After the removal of the last objection in vv. 16-24 he now comes back to this in strongly argumentative fashion. The concluding thesis is stated in vv. 25-26a. Scripture proof is adduced in vv. 26b-27. Verses 28-32 both interpret (Luz, *Geschichtsverständnis,* 286) and establish the thesis through its connection with the doctrine of justification.

Verses 25-27 are by no means to be regarded as an interpolation (*contra* Plag, *Wege,* 41ff., 60, 65f.). The form of instructing Gentile-Christians is retained from v. 13 in order to suppress arrogance as in v. 20. This applies, however, only to the introduction and not to the whole section (*contra* Luz, *Geschichtsverständnis,* 292f.). As in 12:16 Prov 3:7 provides the catchword. The polemic is akin to that used against the pneumatics in 1 Cor 4:10; 2 Cor 11:19 (Michel). Those who are wise on their own are those who trust in themselves and boast. To the extent that they will not allow salvation to remain alien righteousness, they simply offer a religious variation on the attitude of the world and the ungodly.

The reading παρ' ἑαυτοῖς is probably assimilated to Prov 3:7, and ἐν ἑαυτοῖς facilitates understanding of the original dative of advantage ἑαυτοῖς (Zahn; Pallis; Lagrange; BAGD, 211-12, *contra* Lietzmann; Michel; H. W. Schmidt).

The criterion of true intelligence is the inspired insight into what is developed in vv. 28-32. The introductory formula, used as in 1:13, derives its particular meaning from the object. The ὅτι clause shows that μυστήριον, as in 1 Cor 15:51, is not knowledge of the hidden counsel to save (*contra* Lietzmann; H. W. Schmidt; C. Müller, *Gottes Volk,* 38), nor the plan of salvation (*contra* Brown, "Mysterion, I," 446), nor a doctrinal statement about this (Michel). What is in view, as in the fine parallels in 1Q 27 (J. D. Barthelemy and J. T. Milik, eds., *Discoveries in the Judaean Desert,* I [1955], 103) is the salvation event as such, which is concealed and awaits its disclosure (Bornkamm, *TDNT,* IV, 816, 822f.; Luz, *Geschichtsverständnis,* 287f.). Paul does not appeal explicitly to a special revelation of the future event nor does he see himself (*contra* Zahn) as an expositor of the words of Jesus. But this does not permit us to speak in terms of speculative fantasy (Bultmann, *Theology,* I, 484 [II, 132]). What we have here is a particularly instructive example of a violent reshaping of Jewish and Jewish-Christian tradition, which is indeed changed into its opposite (though cf. Senft, "L'élection," 140; Batey, "Israel," 222f.).

The basis is the apocalyptic expectation of the restitution of Israel and the associated pilgrimage of the nations to Zion. Perhaps we should remember also Rev 11:13 and its connection with 11:1-3, which seem to preserve the motif of the Gentile attack on Jerusalem (cf. Dan 9:24-27; Zech 12:3f. LXX; *T. Zeb.* 9:6ff.). For one finds in this the schema of the delivering up of Israel which is limited by the grace of God and finally revoked in restoration (C. Müller, *Gottes Volk,* 38ff.). Nevertheless, to say that Paul has spiritualized and christianized this schema by making the Gentile attack into the coming of converted Gentiles, and hence reinterpreting the handing over of Israel as well as its restoration (C. Müller, *Gottes Volk,* 42), is a fantastic reconstruction seductively suggested by the parallel in Rev 11:13. Probably the tradition in Mark 13:10 throws light on the background of the passage with its statement that the gospel must be preached to the whole world before the parousia (Stuhlmacher, "Interpretation," 565f.). That the restitution and the conversion of the people belong together derives from *Jub.* 1:15,

23; 23:26ff.; *Pss. Sol.* 18:4f.; *As. Mos.* 1:10 (Behm, *TDNT,* IV, 992; cf. the analysis in Zeller, *Juden,* 246ff.).

Elements of Paul's statement are in fact to be found in Jewish and Christian tradition. This shows that the statement is as such anything but superfluous for the apostle (Michel). It governs both his apocalyptic expectation and his self-understanding. The reshaping of the tradition characterizes him as a prophet (Schlatter; Jülicher; Gaugler; Michel; Ridderbos; Franzmann; Zeller, *Juden,* 253), who passes on the revelation which has been imparted to him and which distinguishes him (cf. Col 1:25ff.) (Sass, *Apostelamt,* 48; Goppelt, *Christentum,* 119, *contra* Zahn; C. Müller, *Gottes Volk,* 38; Dinkler, "Prädestination," 96).

All that has gone before leads to the conclusion that Israel's obduracy leaves room for the conversion of the Gentiles. But the completion of the latter also carries with it Israel's salvation. The position of ἀπὸ μέρους and its antithesis to πᾶς Ἰσραήλ speak against an adverbial (Michel) or even a temporal sense (Plag, *Wege,* 37). In distinction from v. 7 the limits of πώρωσις are set (H. W. Schmidt). They do not affect Jewish Christianity. ἄχρι οὖ now restricts temporally. πᾶς Ἰσραήλ is a fixed Jewish formula. It does not designate the sum of individuals (Kühl; Jülicher; Michaelis, *Versöhnung,* 125ff.) but the people which establishes the individuality of its members (Zahn; Lagrange; Munck, *Christ,* 136, following Sanday and Headlam; Dahl, "Name," 162; Gutbrod, *TDNT,* III, 387) as the fellowship of the elect (Minear, *Images,* 61, 81f.; Schoeps, *Paul,* 119). Thus the parallel *m. Sanh.* 10:1: "All Israel has a share in the future world" (Billerbeck, IV, 2, pp. 1016ff.; Plag, *Wege,* 46f.) can in context enumerate notable exceptions (Barrett). Paul modifies the formula by including in it the remnant and the λοιποί. As a similar summary he contrasts it with the phrase πλήρωμα τῶν ἐθνῶν (Oepke, *Gottesvolk,* 216; C. Müller, *Gottes Volk,* 107). The two do not imply an apokatastasis (*contra* Zahn; Lagrange) nor do they mean the plurality of peoples. In 4 Ezra 4:35f.; 2 *Apoc. Bar.* 23:4; 30:2 apocalyptic speaks of the full number of the elect and Rev 6:11; 7:4; 14:1 relate this to Christianity, so that one may see already the transition from Jewish Christianity to an expanded understanding of the whole church (P. Volz, *Eschatologie* [1934] 117, though cf. Munck, *Christ,* 132ff.). This is the only time the term is applied to Gentile-Christians alone, although we cannot say for certain that this is Pauline.

The formulary character of the phrase and absolute use of εἰσέρχεσθαι for entry into God's kingdom (Windisch, "Sprüche," 165, 171; Sanday and Headlam; Ridderbos; ecclesiologically Huby; related to the Gentile pilgrimage Plag, *Wege,* 37, 43ff., 56ff.; critical Zeller, *Juden,* 254ff.) suggest pre-Pauline tradition. καὶ οὕτως is commonly but incorrectly taken to point forward to καθώς (C. Müller, *Gottes Volk,* 43; Gutjahr; Luz, *Geschichtsverständnis,* 294; Stuhlmacher, "Interpretation," 559f.; Franzmann). As in Acts 17:33; 20:11 it has a temporal sense (Zahn; Jülicher; Althaus; Michel; Barrett; not clear Lagrange) and only thus does it mention the point of a statement which has been contested from early times (cf. Iturbe, "Omnis Israel"; Goppelt, *Christentum,* 120ff.; Zeller, *Juden,* 251).

The end of v. 25 states the precondition of the parousia and the related conversion of all Israel to which the apostle is contributing by fulfilling his own commission and which he probably hopes to see in his own lifetime (Maier, *Israel,* 142; Stuhlmacher, "Interpretation," 560). In this respect Jewish expectation is characteristically changed. Israel's redemption follows the acceptance of the Gentile world. This goes further than the scriptural proof advanced, characterizes the heart of the mystery disclosed by Paul, and marks the specific element in the revelation received by him (cf. Deut 32:21).

The quotation has Isa 59:20 in the first three lines and Isa 27:9 in the fourth. The two passages are connected by the motif of the forgiveness which results from the covenant (though cf. Zeller, *Juden*, 261f.), and this constitutes the essential content of the eschatological covenant for Paul (*contra* Zahn). As ὁ ῥυόμενος is a fixed divine predicate in the LXX, the rabbinically attested messianic interpretation of Isa 59:20 (Sanday and Headlam; Lietzmann; Michel) makes possible the Christian understanding (though cf. Ridderbos). It is also responsible for altering the text to ἐκ Σιών instead of ἕνεκεν Σιών and to the plural τὰς ἁμαρτίας. Obviously the reference is neither to the historical Jesus (Kühl; Gutjahr; Lagrange), nor to the christological event as a whole (H. W. Schmidt; Luz, *Geschichtsverständnis*, 294), nor indeed to the parousia in Jerusalem (*contra* Dahl, "Messianität," 94f.; Huby), but to the return of the exalted Christ from the heavenly Jerusalem of Gal 4:26 (Stuhlmacher, "Interpretation," 561; *contra* Zeller, *Juden*, 260f.). Whereas Christianity is already living in the new covenant, Israel will begin to do so only at the parousia, and it will do it through the same Giver, Christ, and with the related gift (cf. *Jub.* 22:14f.) of the forgiveness of sins. Only the time, not the salvation, is different. Scripture confirms this hope of the apostle.

The dialectic and the unusually careful construction of vv. 28-32 show how important this section is for Paul (Barrett). But seldom is attention paid to its function. The superscription "exegetical implications" characterizes it merely formally, but the establishment of an interpretation remains too general (*contra* Michel; Luz, *Geschichtsverständnis*, 295). Again and for the last time we find Paul's doctrine of justification (C. Müller, *Gottes Volk*, 107). This determines equally both the course and the end of salvation history. It links the destiny of Israel to that of the Gentiles. As the center of the message of the epistle it is also the criterion of faith and hope.

The statement in vv. 25f. should not be dismissed too easily as speculative fantasy. If it were this, it is hard to see why it should not have been put immediately after 9:6. The argument in chs. 9–10 would be just as superfluous as that of 11:7-10, 16-24. If we are to understand the scope of the apostle, we have to understand the long detour to the statement as both meaningful and necessary. The two long chapters are not just a preparation and basis. In them he also tries to protect the statement against the suspicion that it is mere speculation.

This means that one must leave it in the horizon which determines it. We do not have here the personal hope of a Jewish patriot or an apocalyptic. Even the scriptural proof is integrated into a broader theological nexus. The justification of the ungodly, which is announced in various places in our chapters, emerges now as the dominant theme of the whole portion. One may think that its application to Israel as a people is inadmissible, even though the way is prepared for it already in Jewish apocalyptic (Rössler, *Gesetz*, 64f.). But one has to realize that the material unity of the epistle depends on this perspective and that if this is not recognized numerous accents have to be established and an abundance of isolated kerygmatic fragments have to be isolated from one another. Paul read

Scripture in the light of his doctrine of justification. In the light of the same doctrine he assigned their places to promise, gospel, and law. All his statements are meant to be measured by justification.

That says conversely that without its apparently mythological, mystical, and apocalyptic garb this doctrine does not remain what it is and what it is meant to be, namely, the message of new creation under the right of divine grace. To give it an individual orientation is to subject it to intolerable reduction (Asmussen). The apostle cannot pass Israel by because his theology concerns the salvation of the world. On the other hand, this salvation is not to be separated from that of the rest of the world. In its presuppositions this approach is thoroughly Jewish, since Israel itself sees its history constantly defining that of the nations and therefore sets eschatology against a universal horizon. The non-Jewish factor is that in Paul the measure of the Gentile world is also that of Judaism, since the justification of the ungodly declares that Israel and its law are no longer the measure of the Gentile world (Rössler, *Gesetz,* 64ff.).

Verse 28 offers a hard paradox in which the two lines correspond antithetically in their individual members. Israel has always understood itself to be the company of the elect and beloved (Billerbeck). Apocalyptic in particular uses this title constantly. ἐκλογή here means God's action and in the context of vv. 28b-29 the epoch of salvation history determined thereby. Similarly κατὰ τὸ εὐαγγέλιον refers not merely to the release, but to the sphere of the proclamation of salvation. A debatable point is whether ἐχθροί is active: "opponents" (Zahn; Kühl; Lagrange; H. W. Schmidt; Maier, *Israel,* 145; C. Müller, *Gottes Volk,* 48; Oepke, *TNDT,* II, 70) or passive: "hated" (Lietzmann; Jülicher; Huby; Michel; Murray; Foerster, *TDNT,* II, 815). The antithetical ἀγαπητοί supports the second sense without ruling out the first. The final δι' ὑμᾶς takes up in abbreviated form the statement of v. 11b, while the causal διὰ τοὺς πατέρας does not refer to the merit of the patriarchs but according to v. 29 to their blessings and promises. The parallelism here is rhetorical as in 4:25 (Michel; Reicke, "Um der Väter willen"; Oepke, *TDNT,* II, 70). Israel's situation is distinguished from that of others by ambivalence.

Here at least it should be clear that one cannot interpret predestination in Paul with the categories of determinism or indeterminism, nor can one refer it back to God's pre-temporal decree (*contra* Maier, *Israel,* 145). Instead it is the qualification by the history of God's word which makes people what they are in truth, namely, creatures, bearers of the promise, and believers or rebels, bearers of the curse, and reprobates. For a person stands before God and under the word. He is temporally and eternally defined by the way in which he does so. Israel is simultaneously loved and rejected because it received the promise and did not accept the gospel. But it has the possibility of conversion so long as the word goes out to it (Schrenk, *Weissagung,* 32f.).

The sentence in v. 29 supports v. 28b and describes what is called God's ἀλήθεια in 3:4ff. (C. Müller, *Gottes Volk,* 112). ἀμεταμέλητος is used juridically as in 2 Cor 7:10 but without maintaining that God is bound (*contra* Schoeps, *Paul,* 241f.; Luz, *Geschichtsverständnis,* 296 correctly speaks of God's faithfulness). The meaning (BAGD, 45b) is "irrevocable" and the reference is not to love (*con-*

315

tra Spicq, "ἀμεταμέλητος," 216) but to the specific forms of grace mentioned in 9:4f. κλῆσις (*contra* Bardenhewer; H. W. Schmidt) is not to be given a specialized sense. It is the power of God's address and claim which takes place with every charisma. The term is interchangeable with charisma as in 1 Cor 7:15ff., for in his gifts the saving will of God comes on the scene as task or mission. God does not give gifts without calling and *vice versa*. The person is indelibly marked by this no matter how he responds. There is no escaping the grasp of God even when one denies him or attempts to flee from him.

The extremely skilful chiasmus in vv. 30f. does not offer a basis for what has gone before (*contra* Kühl) but expands it salvation historically. The experience of Gentile-Christians is like that of Israel. The antithesis of ποτέ, which looks to the time before baptism, and νῦν as the time of salvation which has come, is taken from the vocabulary of mission. ἀπείθεια is the manifestation and result of ἀπιστία. Mercy represents the equivalent of justification in salvation history (Bultmann, *TDNT*, II, 483f.; *Theology*, I, 282).

The end of v. 30 takes up the thought of v. 11b. τῷ ὑμετέρῳ ἐλέει in v. 31 should not be put in the final clause (Zeller, *Juden*, 213, *contra* Sanday and Headlam; Zahn; Gutjahr; Murray; Ridderbos; Munck, *Christ*, 140; Tachau, *Einst*, 111). Everything depends on the fact that Jewish disobedience made the salvation of the Gentiles possible. Hence these are most closely related in sharp antithesis. Verse 31 repeats v. 30b chiastically. But the dative no longer has a causal sense as in v. 30b (*contra* BDF, §196; BAGD, 836a; Huby). It is a dative of advantage (Dibelius, "Vier Worte," 16) and means "in favor of." The second and apparently inadequate νῦν in v. 31b has always caused trouble, and for this reason it is already left out in P⁴⁶ (cf. Zahn; Plag, *Wege*, 40) and replaced by ὕστερον in other MSS. But it is understandable in the light of the apocalyptic view of the context. The end-time is so far advanced that the πλήρωμα τῶν ἐθνῶν will soon be completed and the parousia is at hand (rejected by Luz, *Geschichtsverständnis*, 298f.; Zeller, *Juden*, 263; rightly seen by Stuhlmacher, "Interpretation," 566ff.). A τότε would not be appropriate for this reason (Stählin, *TDNT*, IV, 1112; Dibelius, "Vier Worte," 15; Michel). Paul expects the parousia, probably in his own lifetime. In the context this is, of course, only a noteworthy secondary motif, for what really counts is the law of vv. 30f. as this is formulated in v. 32.

συγκλείειν is used metaphorically as in Gal 3:23. οἱ πάντες means not only unbelieving Israel (*contra* Zahn) but the whole world (C. Müller, *Gottes Volk*, 68), namely, the Jews and the Gentiles, who are designated as κόσμος in v. 12. Again there is no thought of apocatastasis as it relates to individuals (*contra* Dodd; more cautious here is Dahl, *Volk Gottes*, 253). The goal of salvation history is that the new world should emerge from the old and that Adam's disobedience should be replaced by Adam's eschatological antitype Christ (5:19; Phil 2:8). The scope of the saying has been grasped with astonishing infrequency (cf., e.g., Tachau, *Einst*, 110ff.). We do not have here a clash of optimistic and pessimistic world views (Jülicher), nor is a process of historical development described (*contra* Hoppe, *Heilsgeschichte*, 169) under whose promise all religions stand (Dodd). The fundamental divine law of all history is incontestably proclaimed in the verse (Weber, *Problem*, 73; Maier, *Israel*, 146, 149f.). But everything is wrong when one views this from the standpoint of development (Sanday and Headlam) instead of paradox and then speaks of the cheerful and comforting result of solid assurance (Lietzmann). Vacillating between a psychological and a general historical view (Maier, *Israel*, 146), exegetes overlooked the fact that we have here the "grim unsettling axiom" which is the key and sum of the epistle (K. Barth), the concentrated expression of the Pauline doctrine of justification in its deepest paradox (Barrett; Stuhlmacher, "Interpretation," 558, 567f.).

Chapters 9–11 now repeat the transition from 1:18–3:20 to 3:21. It is no accident that there already the structure is often understood pedagogically and in terms of a process rather than a paradox, the point being missed that the apostle is not speculating but arguing in a reminiscence of his own experience and that of all Christians. It is also no accident that the law which applied there is only now formulated. Apart from the fact that Paul has reached the end of this part of the epistle, and that he can lead up to a climax as no other NT author can, the nature of the justification of the ungodly is most clearly visible when it is set forth with reference to the pious. These are represented by Israel (Zeller, *Juden*, 265f.).

The whole epistle stands under the banner of no person being justified by works and even the pious not entering the kingdom of God on the basis of their piety. What is generally called salvation history usually serves only to rob Paul's basic principle of its severity and to obscure the doctrine of justification. But Paul's theology and proclamation stand or fall with this polemic as the inseparable reverse side of his doctrine of grace. The God who acts soteriologically is always the Creator out of nothing. He always accomplishes the resurrection of the dead. He always works with what is by human judgment unserviceable material (1 Cor 1:18-31; 2 Cor 3:5f.), namely, the ungodly.

For Paul real human beings, whether Jews or Gentiles, are ungodly, and are so also as pious persons. More than any other, Paul reflected deeply in his theology on what determined the words and deeds of Jesus according to Mark 2:17. Grace breaks into the sphere of wrath and the power of the gospel is shown in the disobedient. The deity of God displays itself in the fact that it uncovers the reality of human beings and thus opens the way to the humanity of man. Paul cannot let this be restricted to individuals, since God is for him the Creator of the world and not just the one who stands over against individuals. Hence salvation history in its universal breadth is linked to the doctrine of justification. It is not its superstructure but its horizon, as anthropology marks its depth in everyday life. Paul is bold enough to view both each individual and world history from the standpoint of the doctrine of justification. The end of the old world and the beginning of the new world can be thought of only as the justification of the ungodly. Logically, then, the problem of Israel can be solved only under the same theme.

This last might be regarded as a postulate (Güttgemanns, "Heilsgeschichte," 55), but then one should not deny in advance the character of a postulate also to the rest of the apostle's message. What distinguishes the present text from the rest of the epistle is in truth the prophetic element, which requires testing and in this case criticism. The validity of the message as such is not affected by that. Above all it has to be recognized that only apocalyptic could offer the history-of-religions possibility of extending the doctrine of justification beyond the individual sphere and dealing with the salvation-historical problem of Israel under the banner of this doctrine. This is the function of the doctrine in its characteristic distinctiveness.

4. Hymn of Praise (11:33-36)

³³*O the depths of the riches, wisdom, and knowledge of God! How unsearchable are his judgments and how unfathomable his ways!* ³⁴*"For who has known the mind of the Lord, or who has been his counsellor,* ³⁵*or who has given him something first that it should be repaid him?"* ³⁶*Thus everything is from him and through him and to him. His is the glory for ever. Amen.*

Bibliography: G. Bornkamm, "The Praise of God (Romans 11. 33-36)," *Early Christian Experience*, 105-111; W. Eltester, "Schöpfungsoffenbarung und Natürliche Theologie im frühen Christentum," *NTS* 3 (1956/57) 93-114; J. Jeremias, "Chiasmus in den Paulusbriefen," *ZNW* 49 (1958) 145-156; K. Schwarzwäller, *Das Gotteslob der angefochtenen Gemeinde* (1970); E. Vogt, " 'Mysteria' in Textibus Qumrän," *Bib* 37 (1956) 247-257.

The doxology of 1:25 distinguishes the glory of the Creator from the shame of his creature. That of 9:5 gives thanks for the plenitude of the gifts of divine faithfulness which have been received. Now a doxology ends the prophetic survey of Israel's history up to its consummation, with the strongest emphasis on the disclosure of the mystery in vv. 25-32 (Zeller, *Juden*, 267f.). Irrespective of this last observation, however, the verses form an appendix to 9:1-5 and along with the unity and logic of the chapters they display the rhetorical skill of the apostle even to points of detail.

Analysis of the section has been done so thoroughly (from the time of Norden, *Agnostos Theos*, 240ff.) that only the results need be given here. We have in it a Pauline hymn in nine ascending lines. The use of triple structuring is especially striking. Two astonished exclamations are followed by three synonymous questions from Isa 40:13 LXX. An introductory γάρ is inserted in the text, and in the second question καί is replaced by ἤ. Then, in a form which is closer to the original than the LXX (Lietzmann thinks another translation is used), Job 41:3 is quoted (par. in Billerbeck). An important formula from the Stoic tradition forms the conclusion. Like the final Amen this is best understood as acclamation.

Paul uses here a technique developed in model form in Ephesians. He weaves pieces of very different origin into a united whole. There are many Jewish precedents for the questions (Billerbeck). The whole is closest to *2 Apoc. Bar.* 14:8ff.: "But who, O Lord my God, understands your judgment, or who searches out the depth of your way, or who considers the heavy burden of your path, or who can reflect on your incomprehensible decree, or who of those ever born has found the beginning and end of your wisdom?" It should be noted already here, however, that these questions, being based on human transitoriness, express resignation and differ in this regard from the scope of Paul's doxology (cf. Wilckens, *TDNT*, VII, 518).

The verbal adjectives in v. 33 with the alpha-privative are typically Hellenistic and were perhaps mediated through the dispersion synagogue. While the introduction with ὦ and the personifying address to βάθος may be Hellenistic, for the questioning exclamations with ὡς there are many OT examples (Deichgräber, *Gotteshymnus*, 62). The triple formula in v. 36 is, finally, typical of the Stoic view which identifies God and nature and regards the origin, course, and goal of the universe as divinely ordained (though cf. Lagrange). The finest example of this much varied schema is in Marcus Aurelius: περὶ ἑαυτοῦ, iv.23; ἐκ σοῦ πάντα, ἐν σοὶ πάντα, εἰς σὲ πάντα. This formula, too, was taken up by Hellenistic Judaism. It is understandable that Paul should carefully substitute a phrase with διά for that with ἐν, since there is no place in his theology for pantheism or the corresponding mysticism. As regards the structure and history-of-religions background of the verses there is essential unity to this point (Norden, *Agnostos Theos*, 240ff.; Bornkamm, "Praise," 105f.; Harder, *Gebet*, 51ff.; Vögtle, *Zukunft*, 167ff.; Michel). Differences arise only when it comes to detailed interpretation.

The genitives in v. 33a are all dependent on βάθος and thus go together (Wilckens, *TDNT*, VII, 518). To this triple formula there corresponds in reverse order the triple question of vv. 34f. (Bornkamm, "Praise," 107; Deichgräber, *Gotteshymnus*, 62) so that this interprets what the concern is in the wording of the formula. A common view, which appeals to the adjectives of v. 33b, must be resisted. The doxology is not speaking of the basically unknowable God, his attributes (Lietzmann; Jeremias, "Chiasmus," 151), and especially his absolute omnipotence, against which even Israel has no safeguards (*contra* Eltester, "Schöpfungsoffenbarung," 99). This would be in contradiction with both 1:20 and the whole kerygma of the apostle. The early church's exegesis, concerned about the essence and trinity of God, switched to the wrong track (Schelkle, *Paulus*, 408ff.). Only with the greatest caution, however, should one speak of a "theology of history" (Bultmann, *Theology*, I, 229; Vögtle, *Zukunft*, 169), although Paul was concerned with God's historical dealings. For what is in view is neither the history of the peoples (Bultmann, *Theology*, I, 229) nor world development (Beyschlag, *Theodicee*, 78) but exclusively the relation of Israel, even if this has exemplary significance. No less important is the insight that we do not have an *aporia* here (Beyschlag, *Theodicee*, 47), nor is it adequate to speak of the glorifying of and blind trust in God (*contra* Schwarzwäller, *Gotteslob*, 213, 217). This would be simply another form of the resignation of *2 Apoc. Bar.* 14:8, whereas Paul is crowning his assurance of salvation with doxology like that in Dan 2:20ff. For him Israel is not (Schwarzwäller, *Gotteslob*, 219) "indefinable" but a model of the paradox of v. 32.

As in 1 Cor 1:19 it is the God who acts under the opposite who is unsearchable and inscrutable. This God puts to shame the wisdom of the world by effecting the righteousness of the ungodly instead of the pious. This breaks all perception of a historical continuity and rationally conceivable development. Rather it is the *ad nihilum redisi* of the way of the promise of the freedom of the children of God. Precisely where that limit is established which brings an end to man's will to transcend himself there is revealed, according to a favorite theme of Paul, the πλοῦτος of God, the eschatological fulness which calls and uses every person, which gives what is needed for life and service, and which establishes joy. This is not brought about in part by human cooperation and hence it cannot be in any sense repayment of what is earned. Since omnipotence effects it, the only possible response is faith. Simultaneously divine wisdom comes on the scene, as in 1 Cor 1:21, and it needs no counsellor. Where on earth chaos rules and human beings are perverted and go about their perverting work, only that *sophia* can help which is in Christ alone (1 Cor 1:30). Finally, there also is manifested the knowledge which according to 8:29f.; 1 Cor 8 means divine electing and which is not dependent on our comprehending but on laying hold of the salvation which is by grace alone.

Paul regards the cause of all this to be the unfathomable depth of deity. Does not this stand opposed to the definitions given above, so that one has to regard the statements present (Delling, *TDNT,* I, 357) as an attempt to give an answer which has no absolute validity? At this point the total interpretation of the verse is decided. One must recall 1 Cor 2:16, where the precise question of v. 34 is raised and the apostle's answer is that we must have the νοῦς Χριστοῦ, namely, the pneuma who according to 1 Cor 2:10 searches out the depth of deity. This is probably also what the false teachers of Rev 2:24 claim for themselves, although in polemical reversal there is ascribed to them instead a knowledge of the deep things of Satan. Finally we may also adduce the many Qumran passages (cf. Vogt, "Mysteria," 247ff.; Hengel, *Judaism,* I, 222ff.) which say that God unveils to his servants the mysteries of past, present, and future. Materially as well as linguistically Paul stands here in an apocalyptic-enthusiast tradition (Michel; Leenhardt; Wilckens, *TDNT,* VII, 504f., 518; but cf. J. Knox; critical evaluation Deichgräber, *Gotteshymnus,* 63). The doxology has the same sense as 1 Cor 2:16c and later Eph 3:5ff. Pneumatics know about what is hidden from the world because God has revealed his will and way to them. They know about that which according to 1 Cor 2:9ff. no eye has seen nor ear heard nor has it entered any human heart, for they know about what God has prepared for those who love him and what his grace has given us. As the apostle sees it, there has been this kind of disclosure in chs. 9–11 and especially the conclusion. The mystery of Israel is not concealed from him. He responds to that with astonished praise.

This interpretation alone gives the preceding argument the triumphant conclusion which corresponds to 8:31ff. and which does justice both to the prophetic speech in vv. 25ff. and to the summary in v. 32. It also explains the development of v. 33a in the exclamations of v. 33b. The κρίματα are mentioned first, just as chs. 9–10 deal with judgment on Israel. The justification of the ungodly can come only from the Judge who also unmasks the ungodliness of the pious. Along the same lines the forensic situation in which the Gentiles found themselves is set forth in 1:18ff.; 2:14ff. The righteousness of God and not, as commonly assumed, his love, is the central concept in Paul's theology. To be sure, this righteousness as the covenant faithfulness of the Creator manifests itself in a saving way in God's love for the creature. But it does that in the judgment which has already come and which anticipates the last day, shatters illusions, and identifies the creature in the reality of the fall, in order thereby to hold God's deity intact. Only the judged who have been set in their proper place are saved. Only the needy who can make no boast of themselves nor insist on privileges or merits are saved. The way to salvation simply cannot be isolated from that for anyone.

Since all theology is defined by the distinction between the gracious God and the fallen creature, and thus as soteriology, christology, and ecclesiology, the divine ways and saving counsels cannot be grasped by the reason and might of the world as it seeks to transcend itself. The doxology recognizes this. In distinction from the Stoic sage, Paul is not concerned with a sympathy between the heavenly and the earthly. For this reason the τὰ πάντα formula is corrected and δι' αὐτοῦ replaces ἐν σοί. Verse 36 reminds us of 1 Cor 8:6 and the deutero-Pauline statement of Col 1:15f. where τὰ πάντα is related to the community as the new world and the play of prepositions is related to Christ's lordship in both world and church (Norden, *Agnostos Theos,* 241; Eltester, *Eikon,* 146). The tendency there is also present here, since chs. 9–11 deal with the union of Jews and Gentiles into the one people of God and the new creation. Yet Paul does not develop the thought here. His argument is not explicitly christological, and the τὰ πάντα is left undefined. Although there is no specific reflection on it, God's work is at issue. As in 1:18ff.; 5:12ff.; 8:19ff., universal redemption is in view, with christology as the center. Finally the acclamation, as in Revelation and Phil 2:11, takes up the cosmic veneration. In the praise of the community there is already uttered that which one day the whole world will have to confess and will have to confirm with its Amen.

VI. The Righteousness of God in Daily Christian Life (12:1-15:13)

At 6:11ff. it became plain that Pauline exhortation cannot be regarded as "ethics" in distinction from a preceding "dogmatics." In it justification is manifested as the grasping of our lives by Christ's lordship. Our salvation is grounded in the Creator's claim on us and this is apparent in exhortation as the reverse side of our salvation. Chapters 6 and 8 fundamentally developed this dialectic under the heading of "the obedience of the liberated." In the next portion, which, corresponding to the character of the letter, not accidentally contains the apostle's most detailed exhortation, this is concretely applied to daily Christian life. Precisely when the salvation of the world is at issue, Paul's realism can exclude neither the problem of Israel nor the dimension of the everyday. For it is in daily life that the world has its depth and specificity. What is not realized in this remains pious speculation. The standing of the Christian as faith is not controllable. But as it was not established without signs and wonders, it also does not continue without signs and wonders. Christian freedom and the new obedience manifest themselves only as the message of the gospel that God has reached out to the world and wills to have this confirmed and symbolically represented by the earthly conduct of the community. The arguments of this part of the epistle comprise general exhortation in chs. 12–13 and a clearly separate set of teaching directed to the Christians at Rome in 14:1–15:13. For the moment we may leave open the question whether the special exhortation relates to misunderstandings at Rome or is trying to head off possibilities already manifested, for example, at Corinth in a manner representative of the whole sphere of Gentile mission. The distinction, however, must surely relate to the situation and purpose of the epistle, since there is no other example of it.

A. General Exhortation: Various Dimensions of Daily Christian Life (12:1–13:14)

This portion is firmly structured too. The introduction in 12:1-2 also serves as the main theme of the instruction which follows and frames this along with the retrospective summary in 13:8-14. 12:3-21 deal with Christian responsibility, vv. 3-8 from the standpoint of accentuated community functions, vv. 9-21 in relation to brothers and opponents. 13:1-7 discuss thoroughly the relation to pagan authorities. Even though Paul allows ample play for temperament, associations, and

323

adopted traditions, his train of thought is by no means so unsystematic as many suppose today (Furnish, *Ethics*, 100f.). Viewed as a whole, the Epistle to the Romans reveals a closely knit argumentation which is hidden only to those who do not exert enough effort over it.

This is not the place to trace the development of primitive Christian exhortation. But the stage reached with Paul may at least be noted. There is not the slightest doubt that the community has maintained the legacy of its Lord out of an essential catechetical concern also in collections of sayings. As in the case of the narratives, these replace the original oral traditions in the course of time. Prophetic proclamation in the name of the exalted Christ was integrated into the history of the earthly Jesus just as Jewish sayings or those current among Gentile-Christians were adapted. Even more strongly than the rest of the message, Christian exhortation was exposed to the influences of syncretism (Furnish, *Ethics*, 43ff.). Its distinctiveness poses a problem even when it is not absolutely contested. It finds expression less in the material as such than in selection, orientation, and emphasis (Furnish, *Ethics*, 81ff., 91), to the extent that it does not grow out of specific primitive Christian situations such as persecution. On the other hand, it should be considered whether the syncretistic character of NT exhortation may be explained solely or chiefly in terms of the indisputable tendency of this type of tradition to take over related material. At this point one may perhaps see that the primitive Christian community was basically at least something other than an esoteric society. It was not just the need for concrete measures in ever-changing relations that permitted and demanded this syncretism. It was also grounded in the conviction that God's will was not completely unknown to anybody, that Christian obedience is constitutively the freedom to adapt existing moral insights, and that to that extent it is the fulfilment of authentic humanity.

Obviously the material of tradition was originally a collection of most diverse instructions which took into account the many typical situations in Christian life. Their unity did not lie in a principle from which they might be inferred or derived but in the fact that the Spirit demands the resolute and specific consecration of our lives (Schrage, *Einzelgebote*, 63ff.; Furnish, *Ethics*, 75ff.). He does not leave individual believers to their own opinions but summons them instead to conduct which is "worthy" of their Lord and his earthly community (Schrage, *Einzelgebote*, 71ff.). Two points call for emphasis. The Spirit lays demands upon each individual completely and concretely in his particular relationships and makes him capable of a new manner of life. He does this at the same time in such a way that the individual shows himself thereby to be a member of the community (ibid., 174f.). Hence primitive Christian exhortation is almost always addressed to the community and thus far it relates the individual to the community whose character should also be presented by him.

On the other side, this exhortation is not a system of casuistry embracing all possible aspects of the life of the community and its members. Surprisingly the motif of order plays a very subordinate role. The problems of worship are dealt with only at a later stage as circumstances demand. Fundamentally this is true also in relation to the settling of legal disputes, or rules of conduct for the Christian family, or worthiness for special ministry in the community, or especially dealings with Jews and pagans. Naturally conflicts soon arise in these areas. But only at a more advanced stage does the occasion arise for comprehensive discussion. Thus initially, where such matters are concerned, one reaches back to models in the world around, like the lists of virtues and vices, the household tables, penitential practice, and community rules. Both individual and community have a remarkable freedom to fashion their own relations and to vary them according to circumstances, as may be seen from the divergent formularies of the eucharist or the Lord's Prayer. There was confidence that the Spirit would show each and all what was right and necessary. Instructions are restricted to "basic motifs" of moral action (Schrage, *Einzelgebote*, 122). They are set by the context against a christological, eschatological, and sacramental background and from this they receive their distinctively Christian obligation (ibid., 187f.). Sharp reduction to essentials is at any rate characteristic. If the avoidance of both principles and casuistry is noted, one may establish that primitive Christian exhortation deals with what is required only by way of example (ibid., 127).

In time there necessarily arises a casuistical regulation of commonly debated questions. The tradition, which originally was coordinated simply by catchwords, is gradually extended systematically under certain aspects. This stage is reflected in the written exhortation in, e.g., Matthew 5–7; 18, in the lists of virtues and vices, in the household tables, and finally in the church orders in the Pastorals. So far as one can see, Paul is the first to have considered exhortation theologically even though he transmits its details in loose coordination with one another. Perhaps he is stimulated to do this by inquiries from the churches, as in 1 Corinthians. The exhortations of the Epistle to the Romans prove, however, that systematization also here derives from his theology. As the problems of 14:1–15:13 are solved in terms of the catchword of mutual acceptance on a christological foundation, it is no accident that the general exhortation is in 12:1-2 put under a general heading corresponding to the summary in 13:8-14. How strong the influence of his theology is may be seen when the individual admonition in 12:3-4 is placed in front of the motifs of the body of Christ and the charismata. There is no need to deny the existence already of a catechetical tradition. Whatever is adopted in detail and whether it is coordinated poorly or well, the whole is a logically developed projection. In it Paul gives something like an image of Christian conduct and mentions certain points of difficulty, which stand in a material sequence. The fact that the exhortation comes at the end of the epistle fits in with this understanding. The apostle here draws the consequences of his message in the daily life of the community, and in this regard he emerges yet again as the theologian who now develops his theme under a final aspect.

1. Introduction: Worship in the World (12:1-2)

¹*I thus admonish you, brethren, by the mercies of God, to present your bodies as a sacrifice which is living, holy, and acceptable to God. This is your spiritual worship.* ²*Do not be conformed to this world but be transformed in renewed thinking so that you may be able to prove what is the will of God, what is (therefore) good and acceptable and perfect.*

Bibliography: O. Casel, "Die λογικὴ λατρεία der antiken Mystik in christlich-liturgischer

Umdeutung," *Jahrbuch für Liturgiewissenschaft* 4 (1924) 37-47; C. H. Dodd, "The Primitive Catechism," *NT Essays, Manson,* 106-108; E. Käsemann, "Worship in Everyday Life: a note on Romans 12," *New Testament Questions,* 188-195; T. Y. Mullins, "Petition as a Literary Form," *NovT* 5 (1962) 46-54; P. Rossano, "L'Ideale del Bello (καλός) nell'Etica di S. Paolo," *Stud.Paul.Congr.,* II, 373-382; H. Schlier, "Vom Wesen der apostolischen Ermahnung nach Röm. 12, 1-2," *Die Zeit der Kirche,* 74-89; idem, "Die Eigenart der christlichen Mahnung nach dem Apostel Paulus," *Besinnung auf das Neue Testament. Exegetische Aufsätze und Verträge II* (1964) 340-357; H. Wenschkewitz, *Die Spiritualisierung der Kultusbegriffe; Tempel, Priester und Opfer im NT* ("Αγγελος Beiheft 4; 1932).

From our basic discussion it follows that chs. 12–13 do not allow us to construct a schema of primitive Christian catechetics dealing with the sanctity of one's calling, repudiation of pagan vices, Christian duties under the commandment of love, eschatological hope, and finally the order and discipline of the church (*contra* Dodd, "Catechism," 108f.; in criticism cf. Schrage, *Einzelgebote,* 134ff.). On this view it would be incomprehensible why Paul should very arbitrarily alter the sequence of the schema. The point of the introduction and the concluding summary would not at all be recognized by this thesis.

The catchword παρακαλεῖν, which announces the content of the chapter which follows, has a multiple sense for Paul as otherwise in Greek and the Diaspora synagogue (Schmitz, Stählin, *TDNT,* V, 773ff.; Bjerkelund, *Parakalô,* 89ff.). The context, however, clearly suggests a simple admonition, so that it is only speculative to infer from the breadth of usage of the verb the peculiarity of Christian admonition in the triad of earnest appeal, moving petition, and encouraging or consoling address (*contra* Schlier, "Eigenart," 340f.; "Wesen," 75ff.; Eichholz, *Paulus,* 265). Nor is any special emphasis, reminding us of the motif of the family of God, to be found in the address which, as often, opens the new section (*contra* Schlier, "Eigenart," 342; "Wesen," 77) or in the transitional particle οὖν, which is not to be taken causally (*contra* Cranfield, *Commentary,* 4).

In contrast, the following prepositional phrase is not to be denied, which does not in Latin fashion (Zahn; BDF, §223[4]; Furnish, *Ethics,* 102; Cranfield, *Commentary,* 5) indicate the motivating force (*contra* Oepke, *TDNT,* II, 68). As in 15:30 and a liturgical practice preserved even to this day (Schlier, "Wesen," 78ff.) it means "with appeal to" or, better, "in the name of" (Pallis). The plural οἰκτιρμοί, found elsewhere in Paul, does not refer to individual instances of mercy (*contra* Schlier, "Wesen," 78ff.; Barth; Barrett) but takes up the LXX translation of רחמים (Bjerkelund, *Parakalô,* 168); it is also Hellenistic usage to have the plural sometimes for abstract nouns (Sanday and Headlam; Lietzmann). The OT term, which is equivalent to χάρις, has in view the whole of salvation history as God's self-revelation (Bjerkelund, *Parakalô,* 163f.). Christian exhortation makes claims because it can bear witness to enacted mercy and seeks to extend it. Only when this scope is set forth is there significance in showing that *parakalo* statements are common in ancient letters, occur especially in official documents, and correspond to introductory thanksgivings (Sanday and Headlam; Bjerkelund, *Parakalô,* 17ff., 34ff., 108f.). Against this background the element of apostolic authority comes out more plainly, while the link with incantations (Bjerkelund, 164ff.) or even petitions (Mullins, "Petition," 53f.) is misleading. The prepositional phrase distinguishes Paul's statement from its literary milieu, carries the accent, and characterizes the difference in its theological relevance. Salvation activates a person and thus manifests itself as a power over our lives and the community.

The resultant demand is restricted to a single theme, as in 6:11ff. Verb and context undoubtedly use cultic language so that παριστάνειν means concretely the bringing of a sacrifice (Sanday and Headlam; Ridderbos). Presenting the body is a central demand of God resulting from the message of justification. Having made us members of Christ's kingdom, God wants us to give visible confirmation of this. Already in 6:11ff. the corporal nature of our service is decisive since what is at issue is not just our private existence but the earthly ability of this to communicate with all its possibilities with the Creator who does not renounce his claim to the world. Hence σῶμα should not be flattened to a cipher for the person (*contra* Pallis; Taylor *et al.*; for a correct view cf. Schlatter; Gaugler *et al.*). Nor is it merely the organ of moral self-confirmation (Bardenhewer; Gutjahr, cf. also Huby) or the object of asceticism (Sickenberger). It is our being in relation to the world (K. A. Bauer, *Leiblichkeit*, 179f.). Verse 2a follows logically.

With the body, the world which we are gives to God the space defined by us. In distinction from other sacrifices presented, this merits predicates which are originally cultic but which are now transposed into eschatological. In contrast to the bloody sacrifices of animals this is a living sacrifice and it is manifest in daily life (though cf. Schlier, "Wesen," 83). It is called holy, not in an ethical sense (*contra* Cranfield, *Commentary,* 10), but as open to God's present time and manifesting this. Hence the secret polemic of the first statement is strengthened. Precisely that which does not cultically take place, and which is otherwise regarded as profane, is paradoxically willed by God, manifests his rule, and, as the third predicate adds almost superfluously, is well pleasing to God.

It is probable from the context in v. 2, and from Phil 4:18; 1 Pet 2:2, 5, that baptismal exhortation is employed here in which levitical demands are simultaneously adopted and adapted. What was previously cultic is now extended to the secularity of our earthly life as a whole. Basically this means the replacement of any cultic thinking, although there have been vigorous protests against such an observation, especially from Roman Catholics (Schlier, "Eigenart," 348; "Wesen," 85; more cautiously Seidensticker, *Opfer,* 220, 325ff.). Naturally this does not mean any disparagement of worship and the sacraments. Nevertheless, these events are no longer, as in cultic thinking, fundamentally separated from everyday Christian life in such a way as to mean something other than the promise for this and the summons to it. 1 Cor 10:1-13 accentuates most sharply that what begins in those acts must be extended into the secular sphere if it is not to be cause for judgment instead of promise. Either the whole of Christian life is worship, and the gatherings and sacramental acts of the community provide equipment and instruction for this, or these gatherings and acts lead in fact to absurdity. It is not the cultus which sustains life, although the latter needs the strengthening, comforting, and ever-new anchoring in the specific event of worship. This Pauline theme was already indicated in the discussion of circumcision in 2:25ff.; 4:9ff. Its sharpness is missed if one seeks to understand it in terms of a spiritualizing of cultic motifs and terms, which in fact was a powerful factor in the pagan and Jewish environment of the apostle and probably was on the way to his understanding (*contra* Casel, "Mystik," 40ff.; Wenschkewitz, *Spiritualisierung*, 57f.; Grundmann, *TDNT*, II, 59; Kittel, *TDNT*, IV, 142; Cerfaux, *Church*, 149f., 153f.; on the process as such cf. Behm, *TDNT*, III, 187ff., 253; Seidensticker, *Opfer*, 111ff.).

Where the offering of bodily existence constitutively establishes worship, we have more than a mollifying or intensifying interiorizing of the ritual. At issue is a fundamentally different understanding of true worship. Here the *temenos* of antiquity is shattered, and while ritual in a drastically reduced form is retained it loses its threatened isolation and no longer works *ex opere operato*. The formula λογικὴ λατρεία, which is important both in the history of religions and theologically, tells us what the point is for Paul.

To understand it aright one must know its tradition, which has its origin in the Stoic and popular philosophical polemic against the superstitions of the ancient sacrificial system (Behm, *TDNT*, III, 186ff.); it is against reason and makes a mockery of the deity which permeates the world as (rational) spirit if his veneration takes place irrationally. The use of bloody animal sacrifices is thereby abhorrent (cf. Lietzmann; Wenschkewitz, *Spiritualisierung*, 55; Cranfield, *Commentary*, 11ff.). True worship means agreement with God's will to his praise in thought, will, and act. The citizen of the world has to give moral expression to authentic piety (cf. Strathmann, *TDNT*, IV, 65). Hellenistic mysticism offers a significant variation (cf. Casel, "Mystik," 38f.) on this motif of Stoicism and popular philosophy by relating it to the *oratio infusa* (heavenly praise). The finest examples of this are in the *Corpus Hermeticum*, where I:31 reads: δέξαι λογικὰς θυσίας ἁγνὰς ἀπὸ ψυχῆς καὶ καρδίας πρὸς σὲ ἀνατεταμένης, ἀνεκλάλητε, ἄρρητε, σιωπῇ φωνούμενε ("receive pure spiritual sacrifices from a soul and heart offered to you, the inexpressible, the ineffable, called in silence"), while in XII:23 we find: θρησκεία δὲ τοῦ θεοῦ μία ἐστί, μὴ εἶναι κακόν ("worship of God is one thing, not to be evil"), and the great hymn in XIII:17ff. is expressly designated as λογική and δεκτὴ θυσία in XIII:18f., 21. Even here we should not speak merely of spiritualizing, although this is certainly present. In the context the divine Spirit acts in such a way as to make the one who prays his instrument and spokesman. As God's power he extols himself through his inspired organ on earth.

Hellenistic Judaism also appropriated the motif. In Philo *De specialibus legibus* i.209 the soul, which is summoned by God's power to honor the Creator, is said to act μὴ ἀλόγως μηδ' ἀνεπιστημόνως ἀλλὰ σὺν ἐπιστήμῃ καὶ λόγῳ. If popular philosophy and the mystical view meet here, the angel in *T. Levi* 3:6 says of worship: προσφέροντες τῷ κυρίῳ ὀσμὴν εὐωδίας λογικὴν καὶ ἀναίμακτον θυσίαν. *Sib. Or.* 8:408 speaks afresh of moral action as the living sacrifice, but *Odes Sol.* 20:1ff. is completely dominated by mysticism: "I am a priest of the Lord and serve him in priestly fashion. I offer him his spiritual sacrifice. For his spirit is not as the world and the flesh nor like those who serve him carnally." The idea of divinely effected praise which both continues and replaces the cultic sacrifice governs the *Hodayoth* of Qumran (Becker, *Heil Gottes*, 129ff.), but it sheds less light on Paul's view than on its Jewish presuppositions. Paul follows the Diaspora synagogue more closely here, as may be seen from variants of the primitive Christian tradition which are closest to him. Note has been taken already of the baptismal exhortation in 1 Pet 2:2, 5. As newborn babes Christians are with the message of salvation to drink τὸ λογικὸν ἄδολον γάλα and they are now able ἀνενέγκαι πνευματικὰς θυσίας εὐπροσδέκτους θεῷ. According to 2:9 praise of Christ's mighty acts through a Christian life is to be regarded as the response to the message which calls us thereto. Linguistically this is presented as an official task and a binding office. Here it is apparent that from the time of the mystical variation of the motif λογικός and πνευματικός are interchangeable (Casel, "Mystik," 40). The main feature of the passage, however, is the transferring of what is said about *oratio infusa* or heavenly praise to Christian conduct of life as a whole. At least to that extent one is again closer to the original intention of popular philosophy. 1 Peter 2 might be understood as an echo of Paul's thought. An argument to the contrary, however, is that obviously an independent baptismal exhortation is present here, as may be seen from the motifs of spiritual milk and royal priesthood and the aretalogical catchword in 2:9. Thus the same view also appears in John 4:23ff. There adoration in spirit and in truth is the eschatological worship (Casel, "Mystik," 40), which is no longer tied to gathering at special cultic sites. Paul thus stands in a Christian tradition which is marked by fixed terms and motifs, which is mediated by Hellenistic Judaism, and which is adopted in baptismal exhortation.

We may now establish how he uses and modifies it. From it he takes the guiding theme of spiritual worship (Michel; Barrett). As may be seen from what is said about the living and well-pleasing sacrifice, the idea is not that of reasonable (*contra* Kühl; Jülicher; Lietzmann; Lagrange; Sanday and Headlam; H. W. Schmidt). Yet Paul also parts company with mysticism by incorporating all life and stressing corporeality as the characteristic sphere of this worship. This makes clear the polemical edge implied in the infinitive. Paradoxically the cultic vocabulary which he uses here serves a decidedly anti-cultic thrust (Bultmann, *Theology*, I, 114ff.). Christian worship does not consist of what is practiced at sacred sites, at sacred times, and with sacred acts (Schlatter). It is the offering of bodily existence in the otherwise profane sphere. As something constantly demanded this takes place in daily life, whereby every Christian is simultaneously sacrifice and priest. Here the universal priesthood of all believers is proclaimed of which 1 Pet 2:8 can even speak in terminology taken from sacral law.

Verse 2 is to be understood in this perspective. It does not relate only to Gentile-Christians in distinction from v. 1 (*contra* Zahn). An important point is that in the *koine* the words μορφή and σχῆμα lose the classical sense of shape or form (though cf. Zahn; Jülicher; Huby; Althaus; Brunner; Cranfield, *Commentary*, 15). This is shown, for example, by 1 Cor 7:31; 2 Cor 3:18; Phil 2:6f.; 3:21. They now designate the total nature of existence. Hence the corresponding verbs do not refer to purely external alteration (Behm, *TDNT*, IV, 755ff.). συσχηματίζεσθαι is the adaptation while μεταμορφοῦσθαι, which is more common than μετασχηματίζεσθαι, is the transformation, which in the context of the baptismal exhortation characterizes the change from the old to the new aeon. That the catchwords really come from baptismal exhortation (Michel; Furnish, *Ethics*, 105f.) is shown by the use of the phrase stemming from the apocalyptic αἰὼν οὗτος, the reference to ἀνακαίνωσις as rebirth, and the specifying of God's will as the norm of conduct. Paul sets these traditionally given motifs within his own teaching. Since he is concerned with service in daily life and the secular world, he is unable to see in Christian existence a private matter. It has a public or eschatological character which is important for the world. When God claims our bodies, in and with them he reaches after his creation. Only an existence oriented to the world does justice to his will to rule. If this will is denied, of course, this life is one of conformity to the cosmos which according to 1 Cor 7:31 is destined to perish. Christian existence, publicly offered to God corporeally as a sacrifice,   [3 is in all circumstances a pointer to the new world which has come in Christ, to the kingdom of Christ. It will be, in fact, taking form according to the particular situation, a demonstration against the present world.

The Corinthian enthusiasts thoroughly understood this, but made the wrong inferences. For this reason v. 2b states positively what is put negatively in v. 2a. Living in terms of the new birth and with a new orientation is demanded under the catchword of the renewed νοῦς, thus in antithesis to 1:28 (Furnish, Ethics, 103f.). This sounds as though the apostle is falling back either into popular philosophy, which summons man as a rational being to rational worship, or into mysticism, which thinks of νοῦς, not as man's mental ability, but as the divinely conferred and hidden spiritual mode of life. Both possibilities have been frequently championed. But when Paul speaks of νοῦς, if he is not speaking of the "mind of Christ," he always means as in the context the power of critical judgment which can keep its distance for examination or accept something as fitting (Bultmann, Theology, I, 211ff., 341; Furnish, Ethics, 104; but cf. J. Knox). Its function, then, is δοκιμάζειν, the ability to test and differentiate. As much as this is necessary in the moral field, it cannot be restricted to this field (contra Zahn; Dodd; Gutjahr; Leenhardt; Cranfield, Commentary, 18).

Practical reason needs the norm and object which is solemnly described with three appositions as θέλημα τοῦ θεοῦ (will of God). This sounds more precise than in fact it is. What God's will requires of us in a given situation cannot be established once for all, since it may be known and done only in a concrete decision in a given situation. Two things are important here. In opposition to enthusiasm Paul follows popular philosophy in speaking of what is good, well pleasing, and perfect in order to describe in the broadest sense what is required (Schrage, Einzelgebote, 117ff.; Rossano, "L'Ideale," 377ff.). Yet he does not mean (contra Jülicher; correct here are Schrage, 170f.; Delling, TDNT, VIII, 76f.) what people find good and beautiful and can justify before their own consciences. Only God's will is called good and acceptable and perfect. In a concrete case this may coincide with human ideals, but it neither merges into these nor is it to be equated with them without further ado. As in 1:19f.; 2:14ff. the apostle recognizes that everyone has guidelines and concrete responsibilities. The Christian respects and endorses these and as far as possible tries to fulfil them since he lives in and for the world and for this reason cannot disregard the phenomenon of ethics. Reason is given him so that he may perceive the demands of ethics and assess how obligatory they are. Faith does not rule out such reason, as is stressed most clearly in 1 Corinthians 14.

On the other hand, there is no missing the fact that according to baptismal exhortation there is demanded not only the eschatological renewing of the whole person, but also of the νοῦς. This does not refer merely to character (contra Bultmann, Theology, I, 211ff., 338) or disposition (contra Behm, TDNT, IV, 858) insofar as this apprehends moral duties as the demand of the *nomos* (Bultmann, *Theology*, I, 262, 327; cf. Behm, *TDNT*, IV, 756ff.) and finds their criterion (Duchrow, *Weltverantwortung*, 116f.) in love. Paul is more radical than his expositors. For him service of creation and conformity to the world are not the same thing. Eschatological decision does not coincide with ethical decision. Christian reason is not self-evidently oriented to the standards which apply elsewhere. To ask what pleases God may concretely again and again agree with what mankind and the world regard as necessary and desirable. But it may also deviate from this, since it stands dialectically opposed both to the idolizing of the world and to its despising, both to seeking the world and fleeing it (Schrage, *Einzelgebote*, 211). Christian judgment in a specific situation never excludes the "great leap" (K. Barth) and radical nonconformity (Schlier, "Wesen," 87; "Eigenart," 353; Franzmann) as the possibility and command of the hour. The emphasis in the context is undoubtedly on the critical faculty as the sign of ἀνακαίνωσις and the gift of the Spirit (Furnish, *Ethics*, 230ff.). Thus the claim is made that in the light of the new aeon Christians can do a better job with reason than the world in general does. Paradoxically they do this precisely at the point where, corresponding to God's will, they oppose the trend of this world and do what seems to be irrational, as God himself did in sending his Son to the cross.

2. Advice for Charismatics Who Stand Out (12:3-8)

³In virtue of the grace given to me I direct everyone among you not to think of himself more highly than he ought to think, but to think with soberness, each according to the measure of faith which God has allotted to him. ⁴For as we in one body have many members, and all members do not fulfil the same function, ⁵so we, the many, are one body in Christ, but individually are members in our mutual relationship. ⁶We have charismata that differ according to the grace given to us. If prophecy (let it remain) in agreement with the faith, ⁷if service (let it be truly) in service, he who teaches in teaching, ⁸he who has the cure of souls in assistance, he who gives alms impartially, he who leads the community with zealous concern, he who cares for others cheerfully.

Bibliography: F. Benoit, "L'Église Corps du Christ," *Communio* 11 (1969) 971-1028; J. Brosch, *Charismen und Ämter in der Urkirche* (1951); C. E. B. Cranfield, "μέτρον πίστεως in Romans xiii 3," *NTS* 8 (1961/62) 345-351; A. M. Dubarle, "L'Origine dans l'ancien Testament de la notion paulinienne de l'église Corps du Christ," *Stud.Paul.Congr.*, I, 231-240; E. E. Ellis, " 'Spiritual' Gifts in the Pauline Community," *NTS* 20 (1973/74) 128-144; G. Friedrich, "Geist und Amt, Wort und Dienst," *Jahrbuch der Theologische Schule Bethel*, 1952, 61-85; F. Grau, "Der neutestamentliche Begriff χάρισμα, seine Geschichte und seine Theologie" (Diss., Tübingen, 1946); H. Greeven, "Propheten, Lehrer, Vorsteher bei Paulus. Zur Frage der 'Ämter' im Urchristentum," *ZNW* 44 (1952/53) 1-43; H. Hegermann, "Zur Ableitung der Leib-Christi-Vorstellung," *TLZ* 85 (1960) 839-842; B. Hennes, "Ordines sacri," *TQ* 119 (1938) 427-469; E. Käsemann, "Ministry and Community in the NT," *Essays*, 63-94; idem, "Geist und Geistesgaben im NT," *RGG*, II, 1272-79; idem, "The Theological Problem presented by the Motif of the Body of Christ," *Perspectives*, 102-121; P. H. Menoud, *L'Église et les ministères selon le NT* (1949); H. Schlier, "Corpus Christi," *RAC*, III, 437-453; "Vom Wesen der apostolischen Ermahnung nach Röm. 12, 1-2," *Die Zeit der Kirche*, 74-89; H. Schürmann, "Die geistlichen Gnadengaben in den paulinischen Gemeinden," *Ursprung und Gestalt* (1970) 236-267; E. Schweizer, "Die Kirche als Leib Christi in den paulinischen

12:3-8 ADVICE FOR CHARISMATICS WHO STAND OUT

Homologoumena," *Neotestamentica*, 272-292; idem, "The Church as the Body of Christ," *Neotestamentica*, 317-329.

The new section involves an unusually sharp break from vv. 1-2. λέγειν here means more than "think" or "suggest" and has an imperative ring (H. W. Schmidt; Ridderbos). It is underscored by an appeal to apostolic authority in the stereotyped formula which in 1:5; 15:15; 1 Cor 3:10; Gal 2:9; Eph 3:2, 7f. designates Paul's charisma. It is not in order, then, to replace the idea of exhortation with the in many respects different one of *paraklesis* (*contra* Grabner-Haider, *Paraklese*, 4ff.). Here if anywhere direction is being given in respect to church order. In keeping is the categorical παντὶ τῷ ὄντι ἐν ὑμῖν, which demands a general hearing. Finally a theme is advanced in v. 3 which can be derived only indirectly from vv. 1-2 and which with a common Hellenistic play on words (BDF, §488[1]; BAGD, 802a, 842a; Dupont, *Gnosis*, 70f.) places the section which follows under the keyword σωφρονεῖν.

Thereby he falls back surprisingly on Greek ethics. For Aristotle σωφροσύνη is in the *Nicomachaean Ethics* 1117b.13 one of the four cardinal virtues. For Paul this borrowing was mediated by popular philosophy through the Diaspora synagogue. He christianizes it not merely by the play on words, which cannot be reproduced, but also by the loosely appended final clause, which can hardly hark back to παντί. By attraction ἑκάστῳ is thereby dependent on ἐμέρισεν.

The strangeness of this whole approach comes out even more clearly when one considers that the exhortation is not oriented, as one would expect, to baptismal instruction, eschatological expectation, or, concretely, the commandment of love. To speak of an admonition to humility (Pallis) is also not precise. What is at issue is the soberness (Bauernfeind, *TDNT,* IV, 937ff.) which keeps to the right measure (Luck, *TDNT,* VII, 1102). With justification a polemic against enthusiasm has often been perceived. Elsewhere Paul uses the slogans of popular philosophy against this and we are reminded of the apostle's experiences in Corinth. One might sharpen this to say that the entire exhortation of this chapter is decisively directed against enthusiasm and that the chapter may be explained in detail from that perspective.

On this view it is understandable that at the very outset there is a warning against arrogance, apparently also dissatisfaction with one's own gift, and why the themes of the charismata and the body of Christ which unites them are taken up, as in 1 Corinthians 12. This corresponds conversely to the fact that the ecstatic expressions of primitive Christian life, which are already chided in 1 Corinthians 12–14 and measured in 2 Corinthians 10–13 by the criteria of benefit for the community and serving and suffering discipleship of the Crucified, completely recede. Prominence is given instead to the functions which no community can be without and which obviously already enjoy special prestige. Their importance differentiates them already from the other charismata. For this reason they involve greater dangers and have to be set under the test of soberness. If all this is true, we have here more than a community ethics (Nygren; Schrage, *Einzelgebote*, 181). We have the start of a first community order, a more advanced stage being offered in the Pastorals in relation to public functions in the community.

This shows once again that only in a very limited sense can Paul's exhortation be described as "ethics." When the kinship to 1 Corinthians 12–14 is taken into account, it would be more appropriate to speak of a doctrine of charisma.

The concept of charisma is important in all Paul's theology. We have met it already in 1:11; 5:15; 6:23; 11:29. What has been said in relation to these verses must now be expanded thematically. It is by no means certain that there is any pre-Christian use of the word. The two examples in Philo at *Legum allegoriae* iii.78 mean nothing more than a "demonstration of favor," for which χάρις would normally be used, and one might ask at least whether in view of the rareness of the term there has not been later emendation. The variants of Ps 30:22; Sir 7:33; 38:30 are textually heavily suspect and have the same sense of "favor." Apart from this the term is late (Conzelmann, *TDNT*, IX, 402). Even if there were earlier and stronger attestation, Paul would still be the first to employ it technically and to give it theological weight (Cerfaux, *Christian*, 250). This can hardly be said with the same certainty of any other word or formula.

There must be some reason for this, especially in view of the fact that the apostle had an equivalent (though cf. Ellis, "Gifts," 129f.) in πνευματικά, which was given in the language of his churches, and that he did in fact make fairly common if strongly polemical use of this. According to 1 Cor 12:1, 4ff. the community had asked him, under this catchword, what its attitude should be to ecstatic manifestations at worship. Obviously he is not basically opposed to these gifts, which obviously characterize primitive Christianity. On the contrary he claims them for himself. He cannot think of the manifestation of the Spirit apart from miraculous ἐνεργήματα with which the eschatological heavenly being finds for itself a place in the earthly. Yet he does not want to see in them demonstrations of the new aeon which already as such give proof of Christian life and can claim precedence in the community, for they can also occur under demonic influence, according to 1 Cor 12:2f. For this reason he integrates them into a broader nexus, first by accepting them only as φανέρωσις and διαιρέσεις of the Spirit, thus as his differentiated effects, then secondly by assessing them according to their benefit for the whole, then by identifying them as διακονίαι and presenting ἀγάπη as their supreme goal, and finally by using χαρίσματα for them instead of πνευματικά.

The anti-enthusiastic thrust, which manifests itself in placing ecstatic ministries in parallel with administrative ministries (Ridderbos, 321ff.), is clear. Justice is still done to the main concern of his adversaries. Ecstasy and miracles are recognized as possible signs of the Spirit. But it is stressed that they remain ambivalent, since demons may produce them too. Their validity is guaranteed only by their use in the service of the community. Not their presence but only their proper use is the criterion of their Christian nature. This is what gives them their place in the list of gifts of the Spirit on which 1 Cor 12:8ff., 28ff. speak quite naturally. The replacement of χάρισμα by πνευματικόν in this context makes the point most sharply.

It does so because the power of grace is limited christologically. This rules out in advance non-Christian modes of behavior. χάρισμα is the πνευματικόν taken into the service of Christ. It is the concretion and individuation of grace (Ridderbos, *Paul*, 441f.). It thus reaches far beyond the sphere of the merely ecstatic and miraculous. It is the merit of the study of the history of religions (beginning with Gunkel, *Wirkungen*) to have brought this situation to light, although they have misconstrued what Paul does as an "ethicizing" and described it abstrusely as a "transcending of nature religion" (Lietzmann). They have not seen clearly enough the eschatological background and christological bond of the view of Paul, whose concern is not extension to the moral field but the integration of the ecstatic into the sphere of the operations of grace, and therewith its relativization.

Along the same lines, on the other hand, the aptitudes and gifts present in the individual, insofar as they are taken into the service of Christ and developed as functions of community life against religious individualism, may be described without reserve as charismata (Menoud, *L'Église*, 36f.). Against the background of the reign of Christ they are the effects of grace (Conzelmann, *TDNT*, IX, 404f.). Paul, then, does not eliminate the supernatural element which the enthusiasts emphasize. But he will not let it be isolated from the common service of the Christian and the community. Here again the distance between the cultic and the profane is broken down and precisely in this way the path is opened for an extraordinary differentiation.

In baptism every Christian receives the Spirit and his personal κλῆσις. He is thus a charismatic. The problem is that for Paul, unlike the enthusiasts, the heavenly gifts do not explode into the earthly sphere and produce radical disorder in the community. Paul wards off this danger by bringing all charismata under *agape* in 1 Corinthians 13 or by naming grace in 5:15 or eternal life in 6:23 as a synonym of the lordship of God *the* charisma, in which all others receive their origin and goal. The same end is served here when with the aid of popular philosophy Paul characterizes that soberness as the criterion which resists over-evaluating oneself and the search after the highest gifts familiar to us from Corinth.

The pneumatic is given earthly responsibility. While the charisma is a divinely given distinction for the individual it is also the limit which he cannot pass (Asmussen). He is thus put under the principle of 1 Cor 7:20 that he should remain in the state assigned to him. This seems to be conservative only when its point and implicit breadth are not perceived. For in keeping with the message of justification it is directed against all striving after autonomy, and like this message it makes possible the freedom in self-offering which uses every opportunity offered in the place in which one is. The person who feels he is autarchous shuts himself off from genuine freedom. There is that room for play of the overflowing richness of grace for each one who is not unfaithful to his κλῆσις in malicious self-righteousness and presumption.

Crossing the limit is indicated by παρ' ὃ δεῖ φρονεῖν. As in 1:25, παρά has here the sense of "in comparison with," with a tendency toward breaking loose. Christian σωφροσύνη seizes its opportunities but it does so prudently, having respect for the limits which are set by one's own existence, that of others, and the given situation. This is why there is in v. 2 the call for a renewed and critical reason which will also, and especially (1 Cor 14:14ff.), have to stand the test in relation to the gifts of the Spirit. Verse 3d expresses this with a terminology and motivation which stereotypically recur in the context of teaching on charismata. That God has made the distribution is also described in 1 Cor 7:17; 12:7, synonymously with calling, as the essence of a charisma. If this is said with reference to the individual, in this respect Paul is probably following the Jewish principle that God does not give the Spirit totally to anyone (cf. Billerbeck on John 3:34). ἑκάστῳ ὡς, which is common in such contexts, guarantees to each his own gift, but also enjoins modesty with respect to what is received, since a non-interchangeable κλῆσις finds expression therein. No one goes away empty-handed and none may disregard the supplementation and limitation through the others. To God's grace corresponds the richness with which he makes all believers charismatics according to 1 Cor 7:7 (incomprehensibly called in question in Grau, "Charisma," 197ff.), and, to be sure, does so constantly (*contra* Schrage, *Einzelgebote*, 141ff.; Barrett is right here). This has to be so if the charisma is really the concretion and individuation of the Spirit (Bultmann, *Theology*, I, 325) and the mode of personal calling.

In this way Paul establishes the universal priesthood of all believers and ascribes to all, publicly and not just privately, authority by divine right both in and over the community. Although for good enough reasons charisma and office later drifted apart, they are not to be separated from each other here any more than Spirit and office (Michel; Friedrich, "Geist," 81f.; Conzelmann, *TDNT*, IX, 406). In the position allotted to him by the divine gift each Christian cannot be replaced and he thus possesses an authority which is to be recognized by the community. It may not be reduced so long as he remains in this place as the possibility of service assigned to him. On the other hand, to the extent that his gift sets him in a concrete place, and equips him for a specific service, each has his μέτρον πίστεως, which by the gift of the Spirit he is to recognize in his renewed reason. To reach beyond that is both abandonment of reason and disdain of the sovereignty of God who gives concretely. The formula "measure of faith" used here has given rise to lively debate (survey in Cranfield, "Romans xiii 3"). Whereas some on the basis of the usual sense of faith arrive at the nuance "saving faith" (Kühl), others think of the charismatic faith which performs miracles (Bardenhewer; H. W. Schmidt), while others plead for a state of faith (Bultmann, *TDNT*, VI, 212, 219; Leenhardt). The question as to whether a genitive of apposition or a partitive genitive is present is to be decided in terms of the similar phrase in v. 6 in favor of the second possibility. According to the context Paul could speak equally well of the measure of the Spirit or of grace (Michel). The Spirit and faith are reverse sides of the same thing, seen from the standpoint of the giver on the one hand and the recipient on the other. Faith is the pneuma given to the individual and received by him. It is objective to the degree that none can establish or take it for himself and subjective because each must receive it for himself without being represented. Otherwise it would not be a gift and could not be a limit—both being connected in μέτρον. The meaning "confession" (Grabner-Haider, *Paraklese*, 16) overshoots the mark.

The statement corresponds exactly to that in 1 Cor 12:4ff., which is interpreted in Eph 4:7. It is not surprising, then, that as in 1 Cor 12:12ff. and with the same tendency as there, the apostle continues with the motif of the body of Christ which is characteristic for his ecclesiology. The distinction between the two passages is that the christological concern in the theme, and therefore the distinctive feature of Paul's ecclesiology, does not emerge so clearly here. But it is not completely absent, as is shown by the transition from the comparison in v. 4 to the theological statement in v. 5 with its predicate which denotes the reality and with the adverbial definition ἐν Χριστῷ. As in 1 Cor 12:12ff., the customary Pauline motif of the so-called mystical body of Christ is what makes the comparison possible. This rules out in advance the view that we have only a metaphor here (Minear, *Images*, 173ff.; Meuzelaar, *Leib*, 42, 149ff., etc.). A distinction must be made between the metaphorical explanation of the motif and the underlying conception of the worldwide body of the Redeemer which is most strongly worked out in the deutero-Pauline epistles. The fact that both here and in 1 Corinthians Paul has the local church in view (Schlier, "Corpus," 437f.) in no way alters the situation, since for him the local church always represents the whole church. We thus cannot avoid the question of the origin and mediation of the motif even though there is no more difficult riddle in the whole literature of mysticism (A. Schweitzer, *Mysticism*, 116), as is shown by the widely divergent attempts to solve it.

At root three possibilities for the history-of-religions explanation have been espoused and variations on these overlap. Most obvious is the idea of the gigantic [body of the cosmos, which is found before Plato, and in which, according to Middle Stoicism, the divine διοίκησις is reflected, shaping the whole by sympathy into a tension-laden unity. To this there corresponds already in oriental mythology the understanding of mankind as a microcosm in the unity of his various parts and elements (cf. Dupont, *Gnosis*, 431ff.; Schlier, "Corpus," 439f.; Hegermann, "Ableitung," 841; idem, *Schöpfungsmittler*, 138ff. with a reference to the idea of the aeons). A variant of this notion is the extension of the body motif to political and social relations. This takes place in popular philosophy and is especially known from the famous fable of Menenius in Agrippa *Liv. Hist.* ii.32, although there are many other instances. The central concern is the conception that in the polis as an organism all the members are dependent on one another. A passage like Epictetus *Discourses* ii.10.4-5 makes it plain that this is regarded as much more than an attractive picture. It can hardly be contested today that even if Paul does not borrow directly from this last idea, he does at least share with it the thought of the community as an organism (Dodd, *Gospel*, 32ff.; Robinson, *Body*, 60ff.; Bruce; Best; Cerfaux, *Church*, 182f.; Meuzelaar, *Leib*, 11f., 143, 149ff.; less strongly Bultmann, *Theology*, I, 310f.). The qualification is needed, of course, that for the apostle the members do not constitute the body but the body sets forth its members. Again (*contra* the basic thesis of Meuzelaar) the body does not just belong to the Messiah but is his earthly projection and manifestation on a worldwide scale. In contrast, no illuminating link can be traced (*contra* Hegermann) from the gigantic body of the deity or the aeon to the Pauline view, for, although the idea of the mediator of creation can be transferred to Christ, Paul's christology is determined by soteriology, not protology. The community, then, is not the body of deity—even though it is the temple of God—but the body of the exalted Christ as his earthly sphere of power. It is this even in the form of the local church. To refute these objections one would have to begin with the deutero-Pauline epistles and read their ecclesiology back into the Pauline ones in a most questionable way.

The second attempt at solution calls to mind the Semitic idea of corporate personality, which has been discussed already in relation to Adam-Christ typology. This can be done with such daring ease that one can trace direct lines of connection with the OT and to Gen 2:24 as the key text (Dubarle, "L'Origine"). It is at least presupposed if one speaks of the "body of the Messiah" (Meuzelaar, *Leib*, 124ff.), or regards the Pauline motif as a new version of the idea of the people of God, which goes back to the apostle (Oepke, *Gottesvolk*, 224; Dahl, *Volk Gottes*, 226f.), or stresses the concept of the primal ancestor (E. Schweizer, "Kirche," 276ff., 284), extending it in such a way that the idea of the body of the cosmos is transferred to humanity. Now this hypothesis cannot be ruled out completely as the background of Paul's thinking, but it is a shaky one. The NT offers for it no single incontestable instance, and one completely misses the question of the extent to which the asserted view was still alive in primitive Christianity. In any case, for Paul Christ is not the eschatological patriarch to whom the idea of the primal ancestor can be applied (*contra* Schweizer, "Kirche," 284). The antithesis between the old and the new aeons, with Adam and Christ as their representatives, is overplayed with a history-of-religions category. No real account is taken of the incomparable character of the body of Christ as a new creation. Finally, it has been discussed already at 11:17ff. that while the apostle took the idea of the people of God from primitive Christianity, he uses it only in apologetic or polemical contexts when he has to counter the claims of Israel. The concept of the body of Christ competes with it, but can hardly be derived from it in an illuminating way. The real problem in this explanation, as in the first one, is the question how the motif of the body came to be used for the church when Paul does not speak of the corporeality of the church but of the earthly sphere of power of the exalted Christ, the central problem thus being that of his christology (K. L. Schmidt, *TDNT*, III, 512).

It is the merit of the third solution that the last point at least is clearly perceived. The postulate, then, is that Christ's body in the church can be no other than that of the crucified and risen Lord (Schweizer, "Kirche," 286f.; Benoit, "L'Église," 984ff. with a large bibliography). The link between the two is made sacramentally. As baptism and the eucharist incorporate us into the community as Christ's body, we are in truth incorporated already into Christ on Golgotha. The church is (R. Schnackenburg, *The Church in the New Testament* [Eng. tr. 1965] 174f.) an extension of the crucified body (cf. Robinson, *Body*, 55ff.; Sickenberger; Benoit, "L'Église," 972ff.; Cerfaux, *Church*, 262ff.), or, when mysticism is detached from the idea of development, it is the sphere in which this Christ event takes effect (Neugebauer, *In Christus*, 104; Schweizer, "Kirche," 286f.). The body of Christ is thus the reality, or the description in imagery, of the "in Christ." This explanation has the advantage of avoiding history-of-religions explanations and interpreting the motif from inner-Christian premises, to the extent that it does not even assume a Pauline creation (e.g., Schweizer, "Kirche," 289). But the price, of course, is high. The church becomes a prolongation of Christ (Robinson, *Body*, 49ff.; T. W. Manson, *On Paul and John* [1963] 67) and believers are brought into the event of redemption itself and not just into service. Only a monograph could deal somewhat fully with the literature. All that we can do here is to compare as clearly as possible the advantages and disadvantages of the basic models of interpretation. The points where they overlap, of course, are the most interesting, since they show that one explanation is rarely found to be satisfactory and that obscurity surrounds the entire question. The history-of-religions problem can be answered with just as little satisfaction as the other problem of the Adam-Christ typology, and both most probably must be connected (Schlier, "Corpus," 445ff.; Kümmel, *Theology*, 209). The deutero-Pauline epistles speak clearly for the last assumption as the first interpretation of the Pauline passages, but so does the baptismal terminology which in 6:6 alludes to Adam with the statement about the old man. He is contrasted in Col 3:10 with the one renewed in the image of Christ. In Gal 3:27f. the unity of the community derives from putting on Christ, obviously as the new man, and this is taken up in the exhortation at 13:14. Finally 5:12ff. incontestably contrasts the spheres of dominion of Adam and Christ. As incorporation into Christ is related to baptism in 1 Cor 12:13, so it is related to celebration of the eucharist in 1 Cor 10:16. In terms of the history of religions it remains unclear how the sphere of Christ's lordship came to be called his body and also on what presuppositions Adam and Christ could be contrasted under the common denominator of *anthropos* in 1 Cor 15:45ff., so that the church could be called the body of the eschatological Adam. Such a fixation of the problem dams up the flood of hypotheses, shows where they have their origin, and enables us to criticize the related attempts at construction.

Material interpretation of our passage need not suffer under these historical difficulties. Paul is not thematically developing his ecclesiology (K. L. Schmidt, *TDNT*, III, 508f.). Naturally this is significant in every NT document but it is not to be made the central object of the epistle (*contra* Leenhardt, 13f.). Surprisingly the motif of Christ's body arises here, as in 1 Cor 12:12ff., only in the context of exhortation (Schweizer, "Kirche," 287f., 291). This shows on the one side that the apostle has already adopted it and presupposes its familiarity. It establishes on the other side that the theologoumenon as such is only the basis of a comparison and brings to the fore the concept of organism. One may not turn things around. The issue is the body of Christ as that of the eschatological Adam, not of a collective such as the church as the messianic community. Since, however, the earthly reign of Christ differentiates itself corporally from the world, and since it incorporates Christians as members while not being constituted by them, the relations between these members can be discussed under the aspect of a body (*contra* Schweizer, "Kirche," 287ff.). This is the more obvious in virtue of the fact that for Paul corporeality is the presupposition of communication and service, to which he issues a summons here in defense against enthusiastic arrogance.

The decisive point is not that the same thing happens with all Christians (*contra* Neugebauer, *In Christus*, 97f.) and that harmony reigns between them (*contra* Bruce; Best; Schürmann, *Ursprung*, 248). It is rather that in the community, which again as in 5:12ff. is related in Semitic fashion to all individuals (Jeremias, *TDNT*, VI, 541), the many confront one another and all embody a special charisma. This is not an empirical conclusion. It corresponds to the will of God and the nature of the universal priesthood. The apostle is far removed from speaking the word of any kind of uniformity. This would lead to a religious society in and alongside the world, a mystery fellowship with Christ as the cultic god. The pluriformity of the church is vitally important for its function. The multiplicity of its members, groups, and gifts gives it the character of permeability to the world around it and makes clear what is involved in the Christ who is present in his earthly reign (Benoit, "L'Église," 982ff.). Christ takes possession of every status, every present capacity and weakness of his members. He uses the most divergent forms of discipleship symbolically to penetrate the world instead of withdrawing from it. A Christianity which is supremely conscious of participation in the glory of its Lord flees from the lowliness in which it is set on earth and in which alone it can be of benefit to the exalted one. If it no longer perceives the multiplicity of its charismata and their living manifestations in thought, action, and will, if it is not also aware, as emphasized in 1 Cor 12:14ff., of their limitations, defects, and fragmentary character, it becomes stunted both inwardly and as Christ's body. It then wastes its chances of coming to each person in concrete situations and in an adequate way in order to confirm the brotherhood of Christ. Precisely from this perspective the idea of the body of Christ became the ecclesiological formula with which Hellenistic Christianity set about world mission (cf. Conzelmann, *Outline*, 262f.).

This situation, however, also has its dangers. When it is stressed that the members vary and are irreplaceable, tensions inevitably arise. The members become autonomous, encroach on one another, and try to dominate one another. Then the church again ceases to be Christ's body and changes (Dodd) into an organization of religious individuals, as the example of Corinth shows. Then an appeal to harmony, which is hidden behind the idea of organism or corporate personality, is of little avail. Pneumatic totality and unity with Christ as the life principle (Hegermann, "Ableitung," 841) are easier to banish than to achieve. Here everything depends on the fact that Christ as Creator and Judge of his community with the charismata simultaneously sets their limits, and the members remain a body "in Christ," which has the sense of "through Christ" and his Spirit. When this is so, it becomes apparent that as his earthly members they are mutually related to one another in bodily communication and tension and that their charismata are concrete forms of *charis*.

καθ' εἷς underscores this with the indeclinable (BDF, §305) εἷς. This is parallel to ἑκάστῳ ὡς in v. 3. The gift is a charisma only as service to the brother. If no one goes away empty-handed it is in order that he may pass on to others. Each has his Lord's authority behind him to the extent that he sees himself obliged by the Lord to recognize other charismata too. Union with the Lord means solidarity with others, who are also Christ's servants, in a unity which presupposes tension and never finally ends it. This being so, no ecclesiastical hierarchy can be deduced as constitutive from the motif of Christ's body even when we take into account the deutero-Pauline epistles which speak of the head of the body. Charismata are not extraordinary gifts alongside or beneath the so-called offices which in the Pastorals are linked with ordination, reconstituting a fictional apostolic succession. They are not even subject to the apostolate (*contra* Schlier, "Wesen," 81; Menoud, *L'Église*, 32, 59f.; Hennes, "Ordines," 444, and many others). To be sure, a ranking is not excluded. What follows shows this. But practical needs determine this, and these may change with the particular circumstances.

Verses 3-5 are the foundation, whose decisive content is set forth again in v. 6a, which is not dependent on v. 4 (rightly perceived by Bultmann, *Stil*, 75; Michel; Lagrange *contra* Zahn; Kühl; H. W. Schmidt). Paul can now turn to

339

specifics. In this regard εἴτε–εἴτε serves to string together as a model the various charismata. As in 1 Cor 12:8ff., 28 note is taken of what is most important for the upbuilding and unity of the community. Since the situation is not the same in Rome as in Corinth, ecstatic charismata are ignored. Instead, the kerygmatic gifts, which are almost solely mentioned in Eph 4:11, and the broadly conceived diaconal gifts are to the fore. It is no accident that the various activities are described by general nouns and participles (Michel). There are not yet fixed offices (contra Menoud, L'Église, 38f.), and it seems almost ridiculous to try to read out of the list the stages of the priestly office of Rome (contra Hennes, "Ordines," 435ff.).   [3 In the missionary world of Paul presbyteries and ordination arose initially in defense against the ecstatics and in recourse to Jewish-Christian relations. Paul does not refer to them in his genuine epistles. Otherwise it would be inconceivable that in the manifold conflicts with and in the churches the existing institutional organs should not have been given responsibility. Organization is still in its infancy. In spite of every difficulty already apparent, there is still confidence in the unifying and directing power of the Spirit, out of which also the apostle gives concrete instructions. So then his view here again does not reach beyond the local church.

For this reason there is no need to speak of the apostolate, which Paul counts among the charismata according to the stereotyped formula of v. 3, but which he understands in terms of the worldwide task of the Gentile mission. Prophecy, mentioned first, is not related to the itinerant missionaries of the Didache, and, unlike the reminiscence of relationships which already no longer existed in Eph 3:5, it is not the foundation of the church along with the apostles. Nevertheless 1 Corinthians 14 shows that the most important function in congregational life is ascribed to the prophets. The common view (e.g., Schlatter; Bardenhewer) which sees in them people who interpret the future is no more apt here than it is in relation to the OT prophets. In Gentile Christianity and in the framework of the local churches prophets seem to have been viewed essentially after the Greek model as those who declare the will of God for the present (Fascher, "προφήτης," 170ff.; Greeven, "Propheten," 10; Pallis). As Paul himself makes clear, interpretation of the sacred writings was included in this task without being constitutive for it. Preserving the tradition, which included dominical sayings, gospel stories (Schlatter; Greeven, "Propheten," 16ff.; Schrage, Einzelgebote, 135ff.; Cranfield, Commentary, 32), liturgical and catechetical materials, and mediating the OT as in Barnabas (Rengstorf, TDNT, II, 147; Schürmann, Ursprung, 257f.), was the job of teachers. If prophets are set over against those who speak in tongues in 1 Corinthians 14, they share inspiration with the latter, but in their case this is expressed by means of reason and intelligible speech, and it can thus be tested in reciprocal διάκρισις πνευμάτων. Therefore the prophets should not be distinguished from pneumatics. For in Paul's eyes all service in the community is a Spirit-given charisma and is thus pneumatic. The specific feature of prophecy is application of the message in a specific situation (as in the letters of Revelation), whether in admonition, warning, judgment, consolation, or direction. Nowhere do Paul's epistles say that a community had only one prophet or teacher. Nevertheless, the momentary inspiration of an individual can hardly have been the rule even though all charismata belong to the whole community. According to 1 Cor

14:29ff. the members of a fixed circle (Greeven, "Propheten," 34f.) succeed one another in προφητεία and διάκρισις. Since they had acknowledged authority as such, prophets could achieve importance over a wider area, become wandering preachers, and write works which have been preserved in part. We thus have the beginnings of the formation of fixed offices although the Spirit was not yet tied to churchly rites and there was not a congregational order as its confirmation.

Such an insight is important for the charismata mentioned from v. 7 on. In these we may see archetypes of later ecclesiastical institutions. What is at first done freely under the impulse of the Spirit and proves itself in the work gradually becomes indispensable. Again one may assume that a fixed circle of people was the bearer of these ministries in the local church (Schrage, *Einzelgebote*, 182). Individually and corporately they enjoyed authority and (*contra* Best) provided a model for future community leadership. Many features may pass away with time or may be lacking in specific churches. Many others may attain concrete contours. In either case functions are present which can lead to fixed offices in a definite sequence and then even are recognized by the community in solemn rites through ordination or a vow.

One phase in the transition may be discerned. Characteristically even in comparable institutions the Jewish congregational order does not seem to have been adopted either for the designation or for the installation and evaluation (Greeven, "Propheten," 40ff.), to say nothing of the fact that the ministries, as in the Pastorals, center around a presbytery or the monarchical bishop. On the other hand, the activities mentioned are no longer undertaken by random members of the community as the situation demands even though the members experience their support and their bearers complement and follow one another freely. Concrete necessities create suitable organs, from which definite modes of behavior are expected. We are certainly not to adopt the liberal tradition of separating the apostles, prophets, and teachers from the other ministers (Greeven, "Propheten," 1f.) and contesting the charismatic character of the latter (*contra* Michel; cf. Greeven, "Propheten," 37f.). An interesting point is that already possible abuses have arisen. Prophecy is obviously the most vulnerable, probably less through apocalyptic fantasy (*contra* Greeven, "Propheten," 10) than through enthusiasm, which can disrupt order with its preaching of freedom as well as favoring ascetic tendencies. For this reason it is called to the ἀναλογία πίστεως.

The meaning of this phrase is hotly debated. ἀναλογία plainly means a right relation, in the sense of correspondence. It makes no sense at all to suggest that the prophet must judge himself by his own faith (Kittel, *TDNT*, I, 347f.; Althaus; Huby; Taylor; Bruce; Murray; Cranfield, *Commentary*, 25). This would open the gates to every abuse and even false teaching. Nor can the phrase be simply equated with the μέτρον πίστεως of v. 3 (*contra* Michel), although it has something to do with this. πίστις, there regarded as the reverse side of the pneuma, must also here have an objective sense. In Paul's day, in which confessions agreed in their core but otherwise were quite variable, there is as yet no rule of faith (*contra* Baulès). Nevertheless, liturgical and, as in 1 Cor 15:1ff., catechetical instruction about the truth of the gospel with decisive christological statements and basic observations about conduct were present. Such a *fides quae creditur* in the form of Christian teaching, concretely where possible the recapitulation of the baptis-

mal confession and certainly of apostolic preaching, must be involved here (Bultmann, *TDNT*, VI, 213; Schweizer, *TDNT*, VI, 427; Schrage, *Einzelgebote*, 185). Notwithstanding his inspiration the prophet is subject to testing in this light by his associates and the assembled community, in which the appropriateness of his message has to be demonstrated. The teacher, who is not radically distinguished from the prophet (R. Meyer, *TDNT*, VI; cf. on the Rabbinate Hengel, *Judaism*, I, 206f.), provisionally does not yet need to be brought under a norm of this kind, since he is bound by the tradition entrusted to him. If there are false teachers, they come from outside the community. Since the churches are not yet organized on more than a regional level, pluriformity in teaching is not immediately recog- [
nizable. Hence the teacher is simply admonished to submit to his tradition, as all Christians are summoned to do in 6:17.

Even if prophets, teachers, and leaders, by exercising essential ministries, form the center of the church activity presupposed here, it is worth nothing that second place is given to the diaconate. This can hardly be an abstract description of what occurs in assistance of every possible kind (*contra* Huby). The deacons of Phil 1:1 and Phoebe as deaconess in 16:1 support the view that in Pauline circles initially something like a definite "office" has emerged at this point (Lietzmann; H. W. Schmidt; Cranfield, *Commentary*, 32, though cf. Jülicher; Schlatter). Naturally an obligation rests here, as elsewhere, on all Christians. But the composition of communities like those at Rome and Corinth, with many neglected widows and orphans, with the proletariat of the world harbor and a constant flow of newcomers, not to speak of the poor and the sick, demands laborers who can completely devote themselves to the tasks which grow therewith and in them recognize something like a calling. Like teachers, "servants" are exhorted to remain in their service.

The charismata mentioned in v. 8 are perhaps less closely tied to fixed bearers, although endowment and opportunities at hand also bring them forth (*contra* Leenhardt; Huby). The functions are not sharply delineated and may overlap with those already mentioned. If the παρακαλῶν exercises primarily the cure of souls, the task of the μεταδιδούς is to distribute community alms (cf. Lietzmann's examples). Faithfulness is again demanded of the former, while the latter is warned against self-interest or partiality. The simplicity which is linked with almsgiving, as in 2 Cor 9:11ff., concentrates on need alone with no eye for advantage or reward.

Completely characteristic for the envisioned phase is the fact that only now do we come to the προιστάμενος. The reference here can hardly be to the family, nor (*contra* Lagrange; Michel; Reicke, *TDNT*, VI, 701; Cranfield, *Commentary*, 35, etc.) to care and acts of love. As in 1 Thess 5:12 it may be to various organizational tasks including the founding of house-churches and (Greeven, "Propheten," 36ff.) the settlement of disputes. Since this is a thankless task, they are called to σπουδή, or total dedication (Harder, *TDNT*, VII, 566). The ἐλεῶν has the task of aiding the sick and abandoned, and he is to do this with cheerfulness, which is commended in many other places as well (Billerbeck; Bultmann, *TDNT*, III, 298f.; BAGD, 249b).

3. The Charismatic Community (12:9-21)

⁹*Let love be without hypocrisy. Hate evil, cling to the good,* ¹⁰*devote yourselves cheerfully to one another in brotherly love, rate one another more highly in esteem.* ¹¹*Do not slacken in zeal, but be fervent in the Spirit and ready at any moment for service.* ¹²*Rejoice in hope, stand fast in affliction, persevere in prayer.* ¹³*Contribute to the needs of the saints, and see where you can practice hospitality.* ¹⁴*Bless persecutors, bless and do not curse.* ¹⁵*Rejoice with those who rejoice and weep with those who weep.* ¹⁶*Be of one mind. Do not aim at high things but stoop to the lowly.* ¹⁷*Do not be conceited. Never repay anyone evil for evil but take thought for what is good in relation to all men.* ¹⁸*If possible, and so far as it depends on you, be at peace with all men.* ¹⁹*Beloved, do not avenge yourselves but make way for (God's) wrath. For it is written: "Vengeance is mine, I will repay, says the Lord."* ²⁰*Instead, if your enemy is hungry, feed him; if he is thirsty, give him something to drink. For when you do this, you heap coals of fire on his head.* ²¹*Do not let yourselves be overcome by evil, but overcome evil with good.*

Bibliography: F. Dabeck, "Der Text Röm 12:1–13:10 als Symbol des Pneuma," *Stud.Paul.Congr.*, II, 585-590; D. Daube, "Jewish Missionary Maxims in Paul," *ST* 1 (1947) 158-169; idem, "Appended Note: Participle and Imperative in 1 Peter" in E. G. Selwyn, *The First Epistle of St. Peter* (2nd ed. 1947) 467-488; W. Klassen, "Coals of Fire: Sign of Repentance or Revenge," *NTS* 9 (1962/63) 337-350; R. Leivestad, "Ταπεινός–Ταπεινόφρων," *NovT* 8 (1966) 36-47; S. Morenz, "Feurige Kohlen auf dem Haupte," *TLZ* 78 (1953) 187-192: L. Ramaroson, "Charbons ardents: 'sur la tête' ou 'pour le feu' (Pr 25:22a–Rm 12:20b)," *Bib* 51 (1970) 230-34; C. H. Ratschow, "Agape, Nächstenliebe und Bruderliebe," *ZST* 21 (1950/52) 160-182; A. P. Salom, "The Imperatival Use of the Participle in the NT," *Australian Biblical Review* 11 (1963) 41-49; C. Spicq, "Φιλόστοργος (A Propos de Rom., XII, 10)," *RB* 62 (1955) 497-510; K. Stendahl, "Non-Retaliation and Love," *HTR* 55 (1962) 343-355; C. H. Talbert, "Tradition and Redaction in Rom xii 9-21," *NTS* 16 (1969/70) 83-93. For Greeven, "Propheten," see the bibliography for 12:3-8.

Almost self-evidently, and understandably in view of the beginning in v. 9, what follows is almost always put under the theme of love (Ratschow, "Agape," 163; Dabeck, "Text," 587f., even to 13:10). On this view vv. 9-13 (Jülicher and most others) or vv. 9-16 (Lagrange) are then supposed to deal with relations to Christians, and the remaining verses discuss those to non-Christians. But the thesis is most problematic, even when it is not given stichometric support (Dabeck, "Text," 587ff.). At least not all the instructions revolve around this supposed center (Michel). At most one could say that they repeatedly turn back to its possibilities. *Agape* in v. 9a is not then clearly presented as a heading, as it is in 1 Corinthians 13. It is simply one mode of behavior among others, not the criterion and true modality of all the rest.

One also cannot counter that with the objection that parenetic tradition leaves the details without order or simply strings them together by catchwords and associations. This would mean that one can seek no common denominator. Hopelessly the traditional Luther Bible describes the whole chapter as "Rules of Christian Life." This certainly does not fit vv. 3-8, and it would require that vv. 9-21 be a list of virtues, although Paul studiously avoids this concept and its intention. We have thus to seek some other connection between this passage and vv. 3-8.

In this regard it should be noted that neither stylistically nor materially does v. 9 mark a new section. Conversely, vv. 3-6a form an introduction to all that follows. This suggests that the manifold charismatic ministry of Christians is also described in vv. 9-21. Serious account is taken thereby of the fact that every Christian is a charismatic and that the gift received by him must be verified in daily life, as the end of v. 3 demands (curiously contested in Merk, *Handeln*, 159f.). This enables us to avoid the more than dubious statements that there is now a movement from gifts to dispositions (Zahn; Jülicher; H. W. Schmidt) or to general Christian capacities (Leenhardt), or from liturgical actions to normal life (A. B. Macdonald, *Christian Worship in the Primitive Church* [1935] 18), or that we can now see that charismata and offices were not at issue earlier (Lagrange). The only difference from vv. 3-8 is that prominent and more risky charismata were mentioned first, but now the whole community and all its members are directed in exemplary fashion to what is possible and commanded for them. The only way to refute this is to separate office and community in a way that Paul would never do, to ascribe no more importance to ἑκάστῳ ὡς ὁ θεὸς ἐμέρισεν as a stereotyped description of charisma than to its equivalents κλῆσις and διακονία, to part company with 8:9 by not calling every Christian a bearer of the Spirit, thus to deny the constitutive significance of the priesthood of all believers in daily life and to reject the center of Paul's ecclesiology.

What is enumerated in vv. 9-21 is also not self-evident throughout, even though much of it will find approval among Jews and pagans. Only superficially does it seem that the title "The Great Disruption" (K. Barth) is inappropriate for this exhortation. If the weighty tradition of the OT and the teaching of Jesus come to expression thereby more and more strongly, this offers support rather than rebuttal for that view. If ministries are mentioned which are more or less possible for any Christian, it should not be forgotten that according to 1 Corinthians 14 speaking in tongues and even prophecy are widespread in the community and that in principle at least the capabilities of vv. 6b-8 are open to everyone. It is a common error to understand charisma, which certainly is an individuation of *charis*, as a possession of the individual rather than an effect of grace in the community which is represented in the individual gifts. That everyone is not suited for everything and precisely for this reason should not reach beyond what is given is completely compatible with that and is also true of the following section, at least according to intensity and outcome. Many things are harder for some than for others. If none makes the others superfluous or goes away empty-handed, none is to be violated in what is possible for him. The differences between the weak and the strong are not erased. Each must set up the sign of common calling representatively for others, and all must do it in face of the world. The exhortation is interpreted idealistically and legalistically if it is not perceived that for Paul grace gives each person a calling which he can accomplish in the realm of his ability. A charisma is always a specific share of *charis* with a specific orientation and with specific deficiencies. According to 1 Cor 13:13 even what is charismatic is revealed as provisional by the eschatological age. If the Christian does not stand privately but publicly before his Lord, he is an earthly sign of his Lord's triumph,

344

but only as a fragile vessel and in the justification of the ungodly. By his obedience he reflects the image of Jesus and the glory of the exalted one in the secularity of the world and the limitation of his own existence. In what follows, then, navigation lights are set up. The full range of situations and Christian reactions is indicated, although it cannot be presented completely. Thus no clear-cut subdivisions can be proposed, although it seems that the community stands in the foreground in vv. 9-13 and relations to non-Christians and opponents in vv. 14-21 (Jülicher; Dodd). Yet it is not just the relation to brothers that is set forth in the first section, while the converse happens in vv. 15f. One has to take account of the possibility that the apostle is using distinct traditions.

It is highly questionable whether or to what extent these strands of tradition can be reconstructed or differentiated from one another. The participles, which are to be interpreted as imperatives, have been seen as an indication that primitive Christian exhortation here follows a Hebrew or rather an Aramaic model (Daube, "Participle," 467ff.; criticized by Salom, "Use," 45ff.). The argument is basically acknowledged in relation to vv. 9-13, however in a variation if Paul is supposed to be paying tribute to Semitic practice (Cranfield, *Commentary*, 40; critically Furnish, *Ethics*, 39ff.; cf. BDF, §§468[2], 389). Against this view it may be objected that the apostle seldom does this, and it is not very obvious that v. 9b is to be seen as an allusion to the Jewish teaching of the two ways (Talbert, "Tradition," 86ff.). For vv. 14-21 the thesis is for the most part contested, for here we find both regular imperatives and LXX quotations. A traditional core of six rules and two strophes in vv. 16a, 16b, 17a, 18, 19a, and 21 is supposed to have undergone Christian redaction (Talbert, "Tradition," 88f., 90f.). But scepticism is in place all along the line to the extent that more is asserted than the imperative understanding of the participles and undeniable Jewish and Jewish-Christian influence. Detailed exegesis has the last word here.

In no case after the exegesis presented can v. 9a be related to vv. 3-8 as the conclusion (*contra* Talbert, "Tradition"), even if one recognizes that v. 9b is not directly connected with v. 9a (Cranfield, *Commentary*, 39). *Agape*, which is distinguished from brotherly love in v. 10, is, according to the earlier definition, more than feeling; it is being for others. As such it stands in danger of a confusion of motives. By means of the common Hellenistic (Wilckens, *TDNT*, VIII, 570f.) ἀνυπόκριτος it is summoned to absolute realism, which is already at issue in vv. 6b-8 and which renders wholehearted and disinterested service. If stress is laid in this way on the unconditional nature of this devotedness, the connection with v. 9b can be perceived. According to 1 Cor 13:6 *agape* has to do with truth. It is not, then, without direction. As in *T. Benj.* 8:1; *T. Dan* 6:10; *T. Gad* 5:2 (Harder, *TDNT*, VI, 562), it is, without illusions and ready for demonstrative action, involved in the good which is perceived as necessary and beneficial, and it abhors the evil. Compromising neutrality is excluded. Without fear of the reaction the Christian must take sides on behalf of his Lord and his cause.

This applies especially in relation to his brothers. The adjective φιλόστοργος, which is used only here in the NT, means first tenderness toward family and friends (Sanday and Headlam; H. W. Schmidt). Extended in the *koine* to the political and religious sphere, it then denotes respectful and sacrificial conduct (Spicq, "Φιλόστοργος," 507ff.). The redundant εἰς ἀλλήλους underscores the

345

noun. Brotherliness is to be continually sought and preserved, no simple matter in reality. The family of God (Murray) needs the constant initiative of each of its members if the claiming of privileges is to be avoided and there is to be restraint in the interests of others. προηγεῖσθαι does not mean (contra Luther; Spicq, Agape, II, 201) "beat one to it" but, as in Phil 2:3, "esteem more highly" (Büchsel, TDNT, II, 908f., with a reference to 2 Macc 10:12: "prefer"). 14:3f. will indicate that in the brother we encounter the Lord who summons and accepts, and for this reason he is to be granted recognition and even outward respect.

According to v. 11a we are always set in movement when challenged as Christians. The statement would be tautological if σπουδή did not already have the technical sense of zealous activity in the service of the Spirit (Greeven, "Propheten," 32f.; Harder, TDNT, VII, 566). This does not let us be spectators but demands hands, feet, and imagination too. In v. 11b πνεῦμα might be taken as an equivalent of ψυχή, i.e., the inner life. But the emphatic participle allows only a reference to the divine Spirit who is given us, as in Acts 18:25. The story of Pentecost illustrates it, and according to Rev 3:15 lukewarmness is the worst offense. If nothing burns, there can be no light.

Verse 11c is a bone of contention among expositors, since important variants of the Western text have καιρῷ for κυρίῳ. Poor attestation is against this. Further the related phrase outside the NT denotes opportunism (Lietzmann; BAGD, 395a). On the other hand the admonition to serve the Lord, not being interpreted in v. 12, seems unusually flat. Possibly we have a scribal error both times. καιρῷ is often preferred because of its surprising scope (Zahn; Kühl; Leenhardt; K. Barth; J. Weiss, "Beiträge," 244, although the majority is against it). It could be that because it did not sound too good it invited correction. No definitive conclusion can be reached. However, the transition to v. 12 favors καιρῷ, and what is meant is then the decisive moment when sides must be taken in a way which only the situation justifies and which is thus open to misunderstanding.

In v. 12 the datives are in rhetorical parallelism (Zahn). Hope, trial, and prayer describe in exemplary fashion the Christian life. τῇ ἐλπίδι, like the dative which follows, seems to be local (Conzelmann, TDNT, IX, 369 n. 91), although an instrumental sense is possible. At any rate hope does not have here the Greek sense of expectation of better circumstances or the OT sense of trust. It is confident reaching out for the eschatological future (Bultmann, Theology, I, 339) and is thus the basis of joy even in adversity. Verse 12b speaks of this with the eschatological term θλίψεις. Trials are not to be suffered passively. They must be carried like a burden on firm shoulders. This can be done if one perseveres in prayer as a demonstration of open access to God and of sonship.

The Western witnesses referred to in relation to v. 11 also have for the most part μνείαις for χρείαις at v. 13a. This can hardly be a slip (contra Lietzmann). It rather shows the practice of intercession for the dead if not the beginning of a cult of the saints. That the needs of saints is to be understood in terms of the collection for Jerusalem (Zahn; opposed in Cranfield, Commentary, 47) is included, but this can hardly be the meaning of the passage. ἅγιοι occurs earlier as a term which the primitive Christians used for themselves. What is in mind above all is assistance to widows, orphans, prisoners, and the needy. Verse 13b follows naturally. Good lodgings were hard to come by in antiquity, especially in the capital and ports, so that φιλοξενία was urgently needed for Christians coming from elsewhere (Spicq, *Agape*, II, 203).

The structuring of the section is skilful, although one should not speak of pairs (*contra* Michel; Leenhardt; Ridderbos; Cranfield, *Commentary*, 45). The antithesis in v. 9b is followed by synthetic parallelism in v. 10, taken up again in v. 13, while we have three-membered sayings in vv. 11 and 12. The admonitions vary materially in such a way that there can be no question of a unified tradition. Primitive Christian exhortation predominates.

Verses 14-21 are connected to v. 13 by the catchword διώκειν, which now, of course, denotes persecution. There is not now a transition to individual admonition since what is said continues to apply to the whole community (*contra* Daube, *Rabbinic Judaism*, 342). Nor can one easily defend the adoption of Jewish missionary practice after the manner of Hillel (*contra* Daube, "Maxims," 158ff.). For what is at issue here is not just adaptation to different situations but the manifestation of brotherly fellowship, as is typical for specifically primitive Christian exhortation. Verses 14 and 21 carry reminiscences of sayings of Jesus. Oddly this is not stated as such. The Synoptists, however, also show that catechetical tradition integrated dominical sayings and established their authority in the Spirit. Collections of dominical sayings went hand in hand with parenetic tradition, and the two could merge, although this involved the overlapping of two basically different concerns. It was obviously important for catechetics to assemble all teaching that might be serviceable for the Christian life, so that the OT and Jewish heritage was used too. If it is assumed that Paul is following a collection of this kind, the history of traditions, too, suggests that a new section begins with v. 14 (Michel; Barrett; Talbert, "Tradition," 86; Daube, "Maxims," 162f.). The tradition of Matt 5:44 par. sets mankind in the antithesis of blessing and cursing and thus makes it impossible for him to be neutral. For the Christian, of whom Paul is speaking, there is hatred of evil but not cursing. If he blesses his persecutors, he follows the model of his Lord and maintains solidarity with the creature of God beyond the abyss of human enmity. This is even more true when there is no such abyss. Then the second beatitude is actualized in the way in which it was already commanded of Jews (Billerbeck; Michel; Daube, "Maxims," 163f.); cf. especially Sir 7:34. Not just the exceptional situation but everyday life with its alternation of laughter and tears summons us away from the Stoic ideal of *ataraxia* not merely to participation but beyond that to demonstrated brotherhood with all (Conzelmann, *TDNT*, IX, 369). For this reason Bengel can call true rejoicing a Christian office.

Solidarity reaches its climax when v. 16a, in a very common phrase, requires the members of the community to be of one mind. This does not mean that they must think the same thoughts, which is only seldom realized and not even desirable. It is rather a matter of orientation to the single goal of the community united in grace, which, as in Phil 2:5, enables us to be of one spirit in spite of tensions, and which comes to expression in unanimity. This would be immediately broken, of course, if the high things seduced us into the ὑπερφρονεῖν of v. 3 (Luck, *TDNT*, VII, 1102). Self-assertion must then turn against the others.

In v. 16c it is not clear whether ταπεινοῖς is neuter, corresponding to ὑψηλά, or whether it is masculine. The almost universal use elsewhere in the NT favors

347

the latter (Lagrange; Best; Bruce; Cranfield, *Commentary*, 53; but cf. Gutjahr; Sickenberger; Taylor; Ridderbos). There seems to be no reason why Paul could not switch from the neuter to the masculine, and it seems unlikely that he would command Christians to stay in lowly circumstances. However, fellowship with the lowly and oppressed must be maintained, as that corresponds once again with the prototype of Jesus. The participle agrees with this. In contrast to its use in Gal 2:13; 2 Pet 3:17, or to that of ἀπάγεσθαι in 1 Cor 12:2, this does not mean "to be carried away" (*contra* Grundmann, *TDNT*, VIII, 19f.), but "to be drawn down" (Lietzmann; BAGD, 804a; H. W. Schmidt), middle "to stoop," In no case is ταπεινός to be understood as "humble" (Leivestad, "Ταπεινός," 36ff.). It means external need. Jews and Greeks oppose in the same way the idea of ταπεινοφροσύνη, the former because they can see in it only the earthly compulsion, the latter because servility seems to be unworthy of the free person (cf. Prat, *Theology*, II, 337; Dihle, *RAC*, III, 737f.; Grundmann, *TDNT*, VIII, 2ff.). In the NT, in contrast, it is a sign of the end-time which has dawned with the crucified Christ. What is now called fellow-humanity is unalterably connected with the fact that the community of Jesus is able to stand on the side of the lowly and also socially to break through the class ghetto. It would not be present if it were not there, and it would violate the law of its God who always associates with the lowly and who demonstrates this eschatologically. Entrance into the *basileia* is denied to those who do not perceptibly take their place here.

As a unit vv. 17-21 deal with the theme of retribution, which became particularly acute in times of persecution. Possibly v. 16c may be seen as a transition to this. Prov 3:7 is quoted in plural form. When God directs us to the side of the lowly, the understanding of the wise is shattered (1 Cor 1:19f.), since there what is foolish happens in contrast to the wisdom of the world. Christians cannot themselves escape this shattering. They cannot be left to their own cleverness nor use it as a weapon in the battle for existence. Otherwise they will seek to take vengeance on opponents.

Prov 3:4, which is applied in targum fashion, spoke originally of the Lord and human beings, as in 2 Cor 8:21. Paul drops the first member in v. 17 and adds an "all" instead. The compound verb is emphatic. Doing good to all is something to be planned and not just willed (Asmussen; Spicq, *Agape*, II, 206). Intention alone does not suffice. It must be considered how the aim can be effectively achieved and with proper tact. Just as v. 17a can be understood as a heading, v. 18 makes it specific. Good finds expression in the avoidance of strife and the service of peace, although significantly this has to be doubly limited by εἰ δυνατόν and τὸ ἐξ ὑμῶν. The will of others and one's own Christianity can both be limits of peace. This should not be postulated too hastily, however, nor should experience lead to resignation. In any case it does not involve heroism (*contra* Baulès; Foerster, *TDNT*, II, 444: rabbinic). In the same way Epictetus *Discourses* iv.5.24 admonishes: εἰρήνην ἄγεις πρὸς πάντας ἀνθρώπους.

The address underscores that the Christian is never to seek retribution. If serious wrong is done him, he must leave this to ὀργή, which also here means the judgment of God. τόπον διδόναι is a stereotyped Jewish phrase which is also used this way elsewhere (BAGD, 823a). The prohibition is urged through Deut 32:35. As in Heb 10:30 this deviates strikingly from the LXX and is close to the original and to *T. Onqelos,* so that one has to take account of a variant translation here (Schrenk, *TDNT,* II, 112; Michel). It is surprising that after the usual quotation formula λέγει κύριος is added. The question about the reason for this (Kittel, *TDNT,* IV, 112) has been answered by the suggestion that primitive Christian prophecy displays here an anti-Jewish tendency (Ellis, *Use,* 107ff.). Comparison with 1QS 10:17-20; CD 9:2-5 (Cranfield, *Commentary,* 56; Stendahl, "Non-Retaliation") is off the point, since the concern there is with relations with members of the sect, not with a universally valid statement (Klassen, "Coals," 346). Christians do not anticipate the last judgment but leave things in God's hands because the wrath of God (not just a principle of a moral world order as in Dodd) and retribution are at hand. They do not just defer the satisfaction of their own desires but overcome self-seeking in love.

This is the key to the quotation of Prov 25:21f. which is added in v. 20 and which apart from the initial ἀλλά corresponds exactly to the LXX. The person who feeds his hungry enemy and gives drink to his thirsty enemy heaps coals of fire on his head. Whatever may be the meaning of the original text (cf. Klassen, "Coals," 341ff.; Ramaroson, "Charbons," 233), the statement seems to point to an Egyptian penitential ritual involving a forced change of mind (Morenz, "Kohlen," 187ff.). This supports the opinion that the saying is not related to a divine penalty (Michel; Spicq, *Agape,* II, 207f.) but to the remorse and humiliation of the adversary (the majority view), although it is best not to speak of the remarkable optimism of the apostle in this regard (Kühl; Jülicher).

Verse 21 takes up again the heading in v. 17a and rounds off the section. Only love overcomes evil by the doing of good. This raises again the question whether love is not the guiding idea of the verses. If this is denied, one must grant that in any case it determines both the beginning and the end and repeatedly comes into view. Even so, the tasks mentioned here can largely be regarded as virtues which also are valid for Jews and Gentiles. All the same it is out of place to speak of ethical idealism. When a person burns in the Spirit and simultaneously associates with the lowly, this involves eschatological conduct, and the other requirements are also to be seen against this background. The heavenly nature is not to be represented as enthusiasts thought (Michel), but earthly opportunities are to be grasped. The exhortation primarily applies to the whole community, but it treats neither its structure, for example in terms of the order in the Christian family, nor the proper conduct in the assemblies, but the regulation of everyday conflicts. The individual is left unusual room to maneuver within the framework of his abilities and weaknesses. A church order can develop out of all this, as in the Pastorals. But it is not yet present here. Practice is not subjected to any theory. It arises out of the relation to the actual neighbor and out of what is necessary in a given situation. It is controlled by an intensity of demand which corresponds to the fulness of grace and which may be expected of charismatics. Verses 3-8 and 9-21 are related by the fact that both speak of charismatic service in earthly and daily reality, although the charismatic community stands in the foreground in the second section.

4. The Relation to Political Powers (13:1-7)

¹Everyone should be subject to the ruling authorities. For there is no authority except from God, and existing authorities have been set up by God. ²Thus he who resists the authorities resists what God has ordained, and those who resist will bring judgment on themselves. ³For rulers are not a terror to good works but to bad. Would you like not to have to fear the authorities? Then do what is good and you will be rewarded by them. ⁴For they are God's servant to you for good. But if you do wrong, then fear, for they do not bear the sword in vain. They are God's servant to execute wrath on those who do wrong. ⁵Therefore one must be subject, not only because of wrath, but also for the sake of conscience. ⁶For the same reason pay taxes too. For they are God's officers constantly attending to this. ⁷Pay all their dues: taxes to whom taxes (are due), customs to whom customs, fear to whom fear, honor to whom honor.

Bibliography: E. Barnikol, "Römer 13," *Studien zum NT und zur Patristik. Erich Kloster-mann zum 90. Geburtstag dargebracht* (1961) 65-133; W. Böld, *Obrigkeit von Gott? Studien zum staatstheologischen Aspekt des NT* (1962); M. Borg, "A New Context for Romans xiii," *NTS* 19 (1972/73) 205-218; H. von Campenhausen, "Zur Auslegung von Röm 13," *Aus der Frühzeit des Christentums* (1963) 81-101; O. Cullmann, *The State in the NT* (1956); 2nd German ed., *Der Staat im NT* (1961); G. Delling, *Römer 13, 1-7 innerhalb der Briefe des NT* (1963); J. Kallas, "Romans xiii 1-7: An Interpolation," *NTS* 11 (1964/65) 365-374; E. Kä-semann, "Römer 13, 1-7 in unserer Generation," *ZTK* 56 (1959) 316-376; idem, "Principles of the Interpretation of Romans 13," *New Testament Questions,* 196-216; J. Kosnetter, "Röm 13, 1-7: Zeitbedingte Vorsichtsmassregel oder grundsätzliche Einstellung," *Stud.Paul.Congr.,* I, 347-355; C. Morrison, *The Powers That Be* (SBT 29; 1960); K. H. Neufeld, "Das Ge-wissen. Ein Deutungsversuch im Anschluss an Röm 13, 1-7," *Bibel und Leben* 12 (1971) 32-45; F. Neugebauer, "Zur Auslegung von Röm 13, 1-7," *KuD* 8 (1962) 151-172; W. Schrage, *Die Christen und der Staat nach dem NT* (1971); A. Strobel, "Zum Verständnis von Röm 13," *ZNW* 47 (1956) 67-93; idem, "Furcht, wem Furcht gebührt. Zum profangriechischen Hintergrund von Röm 13, 7," *ZNW* 55 (1964) 58-62; R. Walker, *Studie zu Römer 13, 1-7* (Theologische Existenz heute, N.F. 132; 1966).

This section has given rise to particularly lively debate during the past generation in the German-speaking areas (cf. my survey). In many respects it is unique in Paul. Already the theme of relations to political powers, although touched on elsewhere, is surprising in the basic exhortation, since Christian contacts with authority were relatively few and for the most part only passive (though cf. J. Knox). If the apostle enters into the question in detail here, it must be connected with the fact that he is addressing the church in the capital city of the empire. The possibility should not be summarily dismissed that according to the Corin-thian experiences and the introduction in 12:3, Paul is calling enthusiasts back within the limits of earthly order. However, it is unlikely that among Jewish-Christians in Rome, unlike the Palestinian Zealots, there were any rebellious tendencies, even if the Diaspora synagogue was not wholly unaffected by the events prior to the Jewish War. For the most part Jews enjoyed and protected the privileges of a recognized religion. The expulsion of the Jews under Claudius was for reasons we know little about and may have had only local causes and consequences. It is doubtful whether many Christians were involved (Kosnetter, "Röm 13," 354). More probable is the suggestion that Paul is resisting the attitude which in virtue of heavenly citizenship views earthly authorities with indifference or contempt (Ridderbos, *Paul*, 323; Schrage, *Christen*, 52; Bornkamm, *Paul*, 213). The argument is no less distinctive than the theme. We do not find in it any sign of any specifically eschatological or christological motivation of the section, although attempts have been made to find this at least implicitly. Instead reference is made to the will of the Creator. This is of course common in the propaganda of Jewish and Jewish-Christian mission, but in Paul it is rare and for support for his main line of thought, and thus it is generally not thematically treated. This demands all the stronger emphasis because throughout the church's history exposition of our text has almost always been regarded as a bridge to an understanding with the political world. Emerging conflicts have mostly moved only Christian groups and they have usually been solved in such a way that one contrasted the obligation to God with the obligation required by earthly rulers. In general the verses have led to approval, at times enthusiastic (e.g., Jülicher), of the apostolic understanding of order, authority, and civil loyalty in the service of God. A basic change has taken place today, however, as the worldwide abuse of power has been so terrifyingly demonstrated. Offense now is taken at a metaphysical undergirding of political power. One feels provoked to take offense through the characterization of obedience to be produced with the formula "being subject," because it seems to contradict human dignity. The fierceness of the debate and the immense amount of literature make it advisable to mention a few basic observations prior to detailed exegesis. We should especially take into account those aspects on which a measure of consensus has been attained.

There is no reason to dispute the authenticity of the text (*contra* Pallis; Barnikol, "Römer 13"; Kallas, "Interpolation") on either external or internal grounds. The fact that Irenaeus quotes it first (*Adv. haer.* v.24.1) in opposition to the Gnostic misinterpretation of the authorities as angelic powers means nothing in face of the fact that the same tradition, which is obviously Jewish-Christian, is used already in 1 Pet 2:13-17. Possibly this passage might even be regarded as the first commentary on our text, although that remains problematic. At any rate, the great antiquity of the tradition is secured by its appearance in the framework of the household table in 1 Peter 2.

It should not be overlooked that derivatives of the stem ταγ- provide the leading idea in these verses (Delling, *Römer 13*, 39ff.; Cranfield, *Commentary*, 69f.). Their unmistakable anti-enthusiastic function may also be seen elsewhere in the Pauline epistles. Whereas ὑπαχούειν usually designates free obedience ὑποτάσσεσθαι emphasizes more strongly the fact that a divine order rules in the divinely established world and that this entails super- and sub-ordination (Delling, *Römer 13*, 49ff.; *TDNT*, VIII, 36), disregard for which is destructive of life in society. Thus the verb can be directed meaningfully against emancipatory tendencies on the part of, e.g., Christian slaves and women who demand equality, and it can be used as a superscription in household tables such as that in 1 Peter 2. For the apostle the obedience owed to God demonstrates itself in earthly form in not leaving the state of subordination but in taking account of ταπεινοφροσύνη as the mark of a Christian life (Delling, *TDNT*, VIII, 45). Otherwise one falls into anarchy, which will destroy love and peace in the community and discredit Christianity in the eyes of the world.

The matter addressed here has, then, a Pauline context which theories of interpolation do not take seriously. On the other hand, contrary to a widespread view (e.g., Delling, *Römer 13*, 12ff.; Cranfield, *Commentary*, 78f.), it cannot be proven that either consciously or by way of oral tradition Paul is referring to the saying of Jesus in Mark 12:13-17 (in criticism cf., e.g., Gaugler; Schrage, *Christen*, 51f.). Quite apart from whether the *Gattung* controversy-dialogue identifies the Synoptic pericope as a formation of the community, so that we cannot be sure whether or not the original version of the point in Mark 12:17 goes back to Jesus, Paul does not quote either the dominical saying or its tradition and he does not need to draw attention to either. If his exhortation needs additional support, it is enough to mention the undisputed practice of paying taxes and customs, for which the verb ἀποδιδόναι is the usual expression. Otherwise it would have been easy to provide the christological motivation which is so surprisingly absent.

The connection with the immediate context is debated. Two different approaches intersect or combine in this regard. On the one hand the "eschatological reservation" missing in the passage is found in vv. 11ff. (Schrage, *Christen*, 54; Merk, *Handeln*, 167; in criticism, Delling, *Römer 13*, 65ff.). On the other hand it is argued from the relation to 12:9ff. and 13:8ff., and especially the adoption of ὀφειλή from v. 7 in v. 8, that what we have here is a special instance of love (e.g., Weiss, *TDNT*, IX, 82f.). In both cases one obtains a characteristically Christian understanding of the passage.

Now there can be no denying that the entire general exhortation is bracketed by 12:1f. and 13:8ff., so that it does in fact receive a Christian impress (Merk, *Handeln*, 164ff.; *et al.*). It is obvious, then, that obedience to political powers happens only in earthly provisionality, though this element need not be pressed. [On the other hand, it is obvious that in the text itself we do not find either christological or eschatological motivation or indeed any connection with *agape*. Apart from the question whether one can love the authorities at all or demand love from them, 12:9ff. cannot be set under the theme of *agape*. One cannot take advantage materially of the slogan in v. 8, and we have in vv. 8-14 a self-contained summary corresponding to 12:1f. It follows the entire exhortation and cannot be brought into direct connection with what immediately precedes (*contra* Cranfield, *Commentary*, 62, 71; Duchrow, *Weltverantwortung*, 173; Delling, *Römer 13*, 67f.; Merk, *Handeln*, 165; Schrage, *Einzelgebote*, 262ff. in modified form).

Our section is an independent block. In view of its singular scope it can be pointedly called an alien body in Paul's exhortation, although the catchword of subordination connects it to other admonitions. In the first instance it has to be expounded in terms of itself, and only subsequently, in the light of 12:1f., can be understood as an instruction on the theme of Christian worship in the everyday world (Ridderbos, *Paul*, 321).

A variant of the attempt to bring Paul's eschatology into the text derives from recalling that for the apostle ἐξουσίαι can also mean angelic powers. The implication is drawn from that that Paul is demanding obedience to political authorities in view of the heavenly powers which are embodied in them or which stand behind them. This thesis was developed in order to emphasize the demonic nature of earthly power and to characterize the political service of the Christian as a practice to be exercised in a highly critical way. However, it is discussed seriously and in a multifaceted way only when it has been underscored by indicating the divine institution of the political powers as mediated and represented by angels (principally represented by Cullmann, *State*, 93ff., though seen only as a hypothesis in the 2nd German ed., 68ff.).

Although the assessment cannot be refuted from Paul's use of the word, the vast majority of exegetes have rejected it (cf. the objections in von Campenhausen, "Auslegung"; Delling, *Römer 13*, 24ff.; Schrage, *Einzelgebote*, 223ff.). Already the possibility of an interpretation with a different intention does not help it. The Jewish idea of national angels (cf. Morrison, *Powers*, 19f.) may not be brought into the debate, since the talk is not about them and the parenesis in general concerns obedience to rulers, not observance of regional or national laws. Even more important is the fact that in the authentic Pauline letters, unlike Heb 1:14, angelic powers are not spoken of as servants in the work of the divine creation but as forces which are hostile, or at least dangerous, to the community and the faith. One cannot object that Paul here presupposes the triumph of the exalted Christ over all heavenly and demonic powers and the angels are therewith now placed in his service. This does not emerge from the text and it contradicts the reality depicted in 8:37ff.; 1 Cor 15:24, according to which Christ's final victory over his enemies is expected only at the parousia. If it is for the most part already closely connected with the exaltation, it relates to that glory of the Kyrios which gives believers a certain hope in their earthly tribulation. A heavenly rule with the help of angelic powers is unthinkable in Paul. The worship of angels, like that of the false teachers of the Epistle to the Colossians, is ruled out for him. From this perspective the observation should be given force that in a number of NT texts ἐξουσία and ἐξουσίαι are used without any metaphysical background.

This linguistic argument may now be extended. One of the surest and most fruitful results of the discussion is the insight that in this section the apostle is using the vocabulary of Hellenistic administration (Strobel, "Verständnis," 79ff.; Delling, *TDNT*, VIII, 29f.). The phrase ἐξουσίαι τεταγμέναι describes prominent Roman officials (Strobel, 85). λειτουργός carries the wholly secular sense of the authorized representative of an administrative body, while ἀρχή designates the municipal authority (86f.). τοῦ θεοῦ διαταγή as a characteristic of the power of state comes from the legal and political sphere (Deissmann, *Light*, 86f.; Strobel, "Verständnis," 86). When the imperial authority issues orders, it is given this task by God, so that it becomes itself a divine διαταγή. This does not mean an abstract order as such, but concrete "regulation." The relation of subjects to it is often described as ὑποτάσσεσθαι in correspondence with ὑπερέχοντες, and it is defined in terms of "obligation" (Strobel, "Verständnis," 87f.; Delling, *TDNT*, VIII, 43f.). Correlative to the power of the sword, which at least in part was transferred to Caesar's deputies (Strobel, "Verständnis," 89), is the practice of commending and honoring worthy citizens and communities in official correspondence (Strobel, "Verständnis," 80f.). In this connection καλός and ἀγαθός are not moral qualities but characterize political good conduct. It fits in such a context to remind people to fulfil duties and pay taxes and customs without constraint, which seems displaced in the usual exegesis freighted with metaphysics.

In the same connection it is also easy to understand the admonition to demonstrate due fear and honor (Strobel, "Verständnis," 82f.; "Furcht," 59ff.).

Finally, it is particularly noteworthy that the puzzling phrase ἔκδικος εἰς ὀργήν can have a specific sense in such a context. While one usually thinks of the avenger, ἔκδικος can be the "agent" who acts intermediately as a representative of the governor in a community (Strobel, "Verständnis," 89f.). The extraordinary significance of this evidence comes out fully only when it is connected with the basic insight, which by no means was stressed sufficiently earlier, that the text is hortatory and that the chief accent is not on the theological or metaphysical basis but on the injunction to be subordinate to the political authorities.

Throughout church history our passage has been regarded as the classic statement of the Pauline and indeed the NT and Christian doctrine of the state, and has been made binding. Almost inevitably, then, the exhortation has stood in the shadow of a metaphysic of the state or an interrelating of church and state in salvation history. The doors have thus been opened in Christianity not only to conservative but also to reactionary views even to the point of political fanaticism. In opposition to this it must be stated emphatically that Paul is not advancing any theoretical considerations. He is certainly not making exhaustive statements about the relation to authorities. Thus he is silent about possible conflicts and the limits of earthly authority. The basis of what he demands is reduced to a minimum, while exegesis usually seeks to take from it a maximum. Over against the dominant traditional interest in our text, he does not in fact say anything about the state as such or about the Roman empire. The personal form of address is not accidental. As the apostle's terminology shows, he has in view very different local and regional authorities and he is not so much thinking of institutions as of organs and functions, ranging from the tax collector to the police, magistrates, and Roman officials. It deals with that circle of bearers of power with whom the common man may come in contact and behind which he sees the regional or central administration. The relationships of the Hellenistic period determine the field of view. Even if one does not want to relativize the demand that every existing political authority be recognized as established by the will of God, one does not evade the problem of how it is to be translated into the present situation and how it can be put into practice there.

From these premises the history-of-religions question must finally be raised. What tradition forms the basis of Paul's demand? Now there can be no contesting that in the time of the emperor-cult the empire was invested with a religious halo which could also come to expression in relation to its organs (Morrison, *Powers*, 79ff., 98ff.). Nevertheless, the statements of Paul, in spite of every reservation or distinction in detail, unmistakably derive from the tradition of Judaism and especially of the Diaspora synagogue (Billerbeck; Michel; Delling, *Römer 13*, 8ff.; Duchrow, *Weltverantwortung*, 153ff.; Schrage, *Christen*, 14ff.). For all the revolutionary utterances which are voiced, for example, in Revelation, and for all the tendency, in distinction from Paul, to stress the duties of rulers more than the obedience of subjects (Zahn; Strobel, "Verständnis," 92), a long chain of tradition is dominated by the idea of divinely established authorities. The saying in Josephus *B.J.* ii.8.7 §140: "Rule does not come to anyone apart from God," may relate only to the order in the Essene community (Neugebauer, "Auslegung,"

159; Duchrow, *Weltverantwortung*, 155). The Hebrew of Sir 4:27 commands categorically: "Do not resist rulers." To be sure, it must now be more precisely shown how Paul appropriates this tradition. In answer the structure of the section should first be considered (cf. Duchrow, *Weltverantwortung*, 139f.).

Verse 1a is obviously the superscription. As such it is introduced with some solemnity by the OT phrase πᾶσα ψυχή and the decretal jussive. Obviously no one is excluded from the rule, although already the phrase and especially the context point to the members of the community. However, if the matter is turned around in such a way as to make the sentence an apostolic decree for all mankind and all ages (Walker, *Studie*, 8ff., 11ff.), the exhortation is changed into the proclamation of a law for the whole world and the apostle becomes a new Moses who takes up the OT law and extends it universally, making absolute obedience to the political authorities part of the central content of his message. This thesis is, of course, absurd, as one may see most clearly when it attempts to combine the theology of the cross with submission to the authorities (ibid., 58). But unfortunately we are not dealing with mere ghosts at this point (for a similar thrust cf. Böld, *Obrigkeit*, 58ff., 73). After all, this shows how much the text has been misused for a millennium in the interests of political theory.

The superscription is established fundamentally in v. 1b and practically in v. 3a. Furthermore, v. 2b draws a fundamental consequence and v. 3b a practical one. Verse 4 repeats the basis of v. 1b in personal address, which was prepared for in v. 3b, and that is connected with a personal warning in v. 4b, which is again given a general application in v. 4c with the use of the same catchword "God's servant." Verse 5, summarizing, returns with one sentence to v. 1a. Verse 6a adds a supporting argument from practice, through which the arguments of vv. 1b and 4a are confirmed again in v. 6b. Verse 7 draws the concrete application of all that has been said for the total political attitude of members of the community.

One cannot maintain (*contra* Duchrow, *Weltverantwortung*) that the train of thought is followed with systematic strictness or that it falls (Neufeld, "Gewissen," 33) into a twofold teaching about the origin and task of public power and the obligations toward it. Instead (J. Weiss, "Beiträge," 244) we must speak of an argumentation which repeats itself in spirals and which is partly basic and partly practical. The argument has a view toward universally valid realities. It is not possible then to agree with systematicians when they try to infer the general world-responsibility of Christians from the passage. Naturally, obedience to the authorities forms a part of such responsibilities. Paul's concern here is exclusively with this segment, not with the world in its totality or its structures and institutions (*contra* Duchrow, *Weltverantwortung*, 171ff.). If his concern is extended, then not only is there departure from the present text but proof is given that there is less interest in the specific exhortation than in the order of creation (152) and its validation, in the wake of the ecclesiastical and dogmatic tradition. Then it comes to a view derived from Philo about a background for our passage in natural law (171ff.) and the secret theme again becomes, not the admonition itself, but its basis, now given the form of a principle.

The characterization of the powers as ὑπερέχουσαι in v. 1a seems to be superfluous. It makes sense, however, in the light of the negation in v. 1b, which with its αἱ οὖσαι refers explicitly to existing bearers of power who have and claim concrete earthly authority, just as the king receives this predicate in 1 Pet 2:13. Any principle of legitimacy is ruled out in favor of the empirical relations. It is enough that political power can assert itself. Again and again the idea of the constitutional state has been projected into the text. But there is no ground whatever for speaking about the institutions of justice and the protection of justice by their organs (*contra* Duchrow, *Weltverantwortung*, 166f.). Every sentence can apply also in a police state and it simply should not be overlooked that the apostle is in fact writing under a dictatorship with largely corrupt and capricious representatives, not to speak of the petty despotism of departments and officials. The much-favored conclusion of earlier exegesis that the epistle breathes the optimism of the first years of Nero's reign when he was influenced by Seneca is hardly represented. Insofar as Paul really takes up an aspect of justice and accords a measure of trust to the authorities, this may be explained quite naturally by the fear of anarchy, in the light of which it is easy to understand the heaping up of derivatives of the stem ταγ-.

διαταγή means structure (Zahn; Schlatter; Walker, *Studie*, 22ff.; Delling, *TDNT*, VIII, 36). διάκονος and λειτουργοί are not to be taken sacrally but mean civil servants and officials, although in their dignity as office bearers (Lietzmann; Delling, *Römer 13*, 58; Schrage, *Christen*, 57; Strathmann, *TDNT*, IV, 231, though cf. Böld, *Obrigkeit*, 62). The phrase attested as original, ἔκδικος εἰς ὀργήν, as noted already, is best translated "representative agent for wrath" (Bornkamm, *Paul*, 211). The prepositional phrase already speaks against the usual reference to the avenger (Strobel, "Verständnis," 89f. *contra*, e.g., Kühl; Leenhardt; Barrett; Morrison, *Powers*, 108; cf. on the problem Stählin, *TDNT*, V, 440).

When all this is added up, the result is that by God's will even the fallen world can point to manifestations and instruments of the order which God has set up, and that in this the Creator demonstrates his further dealings with it. There can be no question, however, of justice being regarded here as the foundation of government (*contra* Kosnetter, "Röm 13," 355), and only in a very restricted way can one speak of an "order of creation." Paul does not forget that the world is fallen creation and the text deals only with the sovereign action of God by which he makes arrangements, sets up instruments, and in place of earthly equality sanctions super- and sub-ordination (Delling, *Römer 13*, 21).

To this conclusion it cannot be seriously objected (*contra* Duchrow, *Weltverantwortung*, 142ff.) that the apostle uses arguments from natural law elsewhere and that the order of creation thereby plays a large role for him. The passages adduced do not bear the burden of proof. 1:20f. are not dealing with the visible order and purposefulness of the world but with the limitation of mankind by the majesty of the Creator. 2:14f. do not document the unwritten moral law but the demands of a higher court which a person accepts but which he does not give himself. The only instance of an argument from natural law in Paul is in 1 Cor 11:6ff., thus very characteristically in the question of hair-styles in worship. But on this one can hardly erect a systematic structure which will encompass Romans 13 except by arbitrarily developing and interpreting occasional remarks from the beginning in the sense of later church dogmatics. The ἄρχοντες, in which the powers find personal concretion according to the current manner of speech (Strobel, "Verständnis," 81), are not the representatives of cosmic harmony or a moral ideal. They are disciplinarians in relation to individual and group emancipation, which presupposes human autonomy or religiously based equality. For this reason the function of those who have power to punish moves to the foreground, and the community is assured that it has nothing to fear if it behaves properly. As it has few members in the higher strata of the population, let alone in administration and government, there is in it no emancipation which can be carried over into the secular sphere.

This being the situation both religiously and sociologically, political opposition is not allowed. Surprisingly Paul does not mention the exception that the community obviously must not let itself be forced to offend against the will of God and its own Christianity. He is plainly battling one-sidedly against the peril of enthusiasm. The problem of Revelation does not arise yet, and for this reason it is hard to reconcile with our text. Conversely, precisely the weakness of the argument is shown in that fact. Instructive in this regard is a comparison with the decreed prohibition of the active participation of women in worship in 1 Cor 14:33ff., under the same catchword ὑποταγή, where apostolic authority is supported by a reference to the universal practice of the church and conventional propriety, and in the same breath with an appeal to the νόμος and λόγος τοῦ θεοῦ. If, finally, 1 Cor 14:37f. invokes the spiritual insight of the community, this shows clearly that the exhortation is decisive, that the underlying arguments are largely taken from tradition, and that their very multiplicity is a source of weakness rather than of strength.

It cannot be denied that Paul's intention is to set up a valid order. He does it, however, in a way which is thoroughly tied to time and situation. The front against the enthusiasts is recognizable as the essential theological concern and is legitimated by the will of God, whereas the proof adduced, as in 1 Cor 11:3ff., seems to be forced in part and does not have the same persuasiveness. In such a context note should also be taken of 1 Cor 6:1ff. From an apocalyptic standpoint secular courts, thus political authorities, are disparaged and rejected when it is a matter of settling disputes within the community. At root Paul's exhortation is not theoretically derived. In Romans 13 it is not the result of a solid systematic doctrine of the order of creation. If the theological basis is not hereby set aside, it receives its proper place. In all the passages quoted it serves more or less instructively and cogently the demand which arises from the situation. It uninhibitedly makes existing tradition its own, as it does with a patriarchal view here. It is not oriented to the detailed proof, which may at times be antiquated, but to its central concern. Religious history offers the materials with which the apostle works but does not guarantee that their intention controls even the apostle himself, let alone has permanent validity. In view of democratic relationships the admonition must necessarily develop a dialectic which here does not yet come into view.

Verse 2b threatens rebels with κρίμα, which according to v. 2a and with an eschatologically understood future refers to God's judgment, but with a logical future and in the light of the motif of φόβος in vv. 3f. earthly punishment as well may be in view. The warning is followed by an attempt to awaken confidence in civil justice (Schrage, *Christen,* 57). The global statement, which takes account neither of the complicated relationships nor of the apostle's personal experiences, betrays clearly the adoption of a traditional view. The mark of rulers is the presence of power which unavoidably as such causes terror and anxiety. But the good, here undoubtedly upright citizens, need not feel affected by this (Balz, *TDNT,* IX, 214f.). According to the better readings the modes of conduct represent the doers. The personal address gives added emphasis, corresponding to the rhetoric of the diatribe, and makes the application. Wish and intention are combined in the verb θέλειν. Again the good does not refer to the relation to God (*contra* Walker, *Studie,* 33; Duchrow, *Weltverantwortung,* 158ff.; Cranfield, *Commentary,* 74) but to ordinary uprightness. Furthermore, the ἔπαινος which is daringly promised (without even a "perhaps") is not God's praise (*contra* Walker, *Studie,* 37) but the honoring which the public authorities mentioned customarily grant. The eliminating of σοί simplifies matters but weakens the element of encouragement, although this should not be taken in such a way (*contra* Lietzmann; Michel) that the authorities are ascribed the task of giving training in the good. The good in v. 4 is simply earthly well-being, in fact scarcely more than security against attacks.

Verse 4b repeats the warning of vv. 2b and 3a with a personal reference and an appeal to the power of the sword of the higher authorities. Even in its punishments the political authority is God's instrument and an agent of wrath, as established earlier. Whether ὀργή is divine or earthly wrath it is impossible to say with certainty. Other instances in Paul support the former (Leenhardt; Barrett; Morrison, *Powers,* 108; Duchrow, *Weltverantwortung,* 155) but the context of vv. 3f. and 5 favors the latter (Lagrange). In any case there is no need to recall either the divine sword (*contra* Walker, *Studie,* 40ff.) or eschatological wrath (*contra* Duchrow, 162). Earthly punishment carries out God's judgment.

While v. 5 both summarizes and strengthens, it is not the central motif (*contra* Neufeld, "Gewissen," 32). There is no serious reason to regard the sentence as an interpolation (*contra* Bultmann, "Glossen," 200), since conscience does not have to be seen here as a prescriptive court (*contra* Bultmann, *Theology,* I, 217f.; Walker, *Studie,* 47) in which the Platonic tradition of the inner man continues (Duchrow, *Weltverantwortung,* 164f.). The translation "persuasion" (Lietzmann) is too weak, while "sense of responsibility" (Schrage, *Christen,* 60) and "unimpaired conscience" (Pallis) take us too far afield. In distinction from 2:15 there is here no reflection on whether the power of critical distinction between good and evil reflects a transcendental norm, especially as good and evil do not have an ethical orientation. To say that we have addition rather than contrast in v. 5 (Walker, *Studie,* 7) is to miss the tenor of the statement. It concerns the fact that a Christian's political conduct should not be motivated by fear alone. A critical judgment may be made between uprightness and its opposite, and the political obedience demanded may be rendered accordingly. If all this stands under the catchword ἀνάγκη, this simply means necessity and not lawfulness and the divine order of the world (*contra* Grundmann, *TDNT,* I, 347) or acceptance of the divine task of the authorities (Kühl; Cranfield, *Commentary,* 347; Duchrow, *Weltverantwortung,* 139; Maurer, *TDNT,* VII, 915; Walker, *Studie,* 46f.; correctly Schrage, *Einzelgebote,* 96, 112; Ridderbos). One does not even need to be anxious about the rational faculty of the Christian as enlightened by the Spirit (Hanson, *Unity,* 95; cf. Lagrange; Michel; Neufeld, "Gewissen," 44f.), even though this does not have to be excluded. At issue is what is evident to everybody and what has binding force for this reason.

By way of example (*contra* Walker, *Studie*, 49f.) v. 6 points to the practice of paying φόρος (taxes) and τέλος (customs) (Weiss, *TDNT*, IX, 80f.). The verb (*contra* Zahn) has an indicative sense. The authority of rulers is in fact recognized. The meaning of the final phrase is not clear. The idea that the authorities constantly seek to be God's servants is obviously exaggerated if not wholly incredible. On the other hand they are not occupied solely with taxes (cf. Cranfield, *Commentary*, 77f.; Duchrow, *Weltverantwortung*, 140, 168). If (with BAGD, 715b) we take the verb to denote active concern with something, the meaning might be that as rulers discharge their functions they remain within their divine commission (Sanday and Headlam; J. Knox; Weiss, *TDNT*, IX, 83).

Verse 7 offers a plerophoric summary. Each must render what he owes. There is nothing to indicate that the last two predications relate to God (*contra* Schrage, *Christen*, 61; felt to be a problem in Cranfield, *Commentary*, 78ff.; rejected by Murray; Delling, *Römer 13*, 62; Strobel, "Furcht," 59ff.). The Christian does not render sham obedience in his external conduct. He, too, has obligations which must be met. This applies even in the political realm. Paul neither demonizes rulers nor glorifies them. The vocabulary of Hellenistic administration, the motifs borrowed from Jewish tradition, and the emphasis on exhortation must correspond to a sober exposition. The problem of political force does not come into view. This is the real problem of the passage. It can be explained only out of the one-sided front against a feared enthusiasm which emerges in 12:3 and 1 Cor 7:24, where each is directed to remain in the state in which God has placed him. As elsewhere the apostle uses themes from popular philosophy to call the enthusiasts to order, he does it here by adopting the Hellenistic ideal of the state and the citizen (Strobel, "Furcht," 59). We cannot escape daily life. We meet the will of God there. The political sphere is certainly provisional. But only enthusiasts fail to see that our worship is to be accomplished in provisional things by doing what has to be done in the given situation (Bornkamm, *Paul*, 212; Schrage, *Christen*, 51ff.).

The true charismatic community sees the demand of God precisely at this point. It verifies itself as such in the midst of earthly affliction and lowliness. If church history brings to light the danger in Paul's call for ὑποταγή, this is because it makes a theory out of his call in a particular situation, develops a system out of exhortation, and sacrifices the Spirit for the sake of the law. When a new situation is set up, for example, by a democratic system, Paul's true concern, namely, that God be served in the political sphere as well, is not invalidated. But it does not tolerate holding fast to antiquated slogans, nor is it fostered by an outdated metaphysics. The old demand must be grasped in terms of the new reality and its problems, and applied to these. Paul is confident that the charismatic community can do this.

5. Summary of the General Exhortation (13:8-14)

⁸*Owe no one anything except this (one thing): to love one another. For he who loves the other has fulfilled the law.* ⁹*If it is written: "You shall not commit*

adultery, you shall not kill, you shall not steal, you shall not covet," and any other commandment—they are all summed up in the saying: "You shall love your neighbor as yourself." [10]*Love does no wrong to a neighbor. Thus love is the fulfilling of the law.* [11]*Finally, you know what time it is. The hour already (summons) you to awake out of sleep. For our salvation (is) now nearer than when we first believed.* [12]*The night is far spent, the day is at hand. Let us then cast off the works of darkness and put on the armor of light.* [13]*Let us act as is fitting in the day, not in reveling and drunkenness, not in debauchery and lasciviousness, not in contention and strife.* [14]*But put on the Lord Jesus Christ and do not fulfil the inclination of the flesh to all kinds of desires.*

Bibliography: G. Bornkamm, "Wandlungen im alt- und neutestamentlichen Gesetzesverständnis," *Geschichte und Glaube,* II, 73-119; A. Feuillet, "Loi ancienne et Morale chrétienne d'après l'Épître aux Romains," *NRT* 92 (1970) 785-805; A. Fridrichsen, "Exegetisches zu den Paulusbriefen," *ThStKr* 102 (1930) 291-301; E. Lövestam, *Spiritual Wakefulness in the New Testament* (Eng. tr. 1963); W. Marxsen, "Der ἕτερος νόμος Röm. 13, 8," *TZ* 11 (1955) 230-37.

Surprisingly vv. 11-14 are almost universally accepted as a summary of the general exhortation, but the whole section is seldom seen as parallel to 12:1f. (though cf. K. Barth; Asmussen). Verses 8-10 are not an excursus on the theme of the law (Michel), let alone a transferring of legal obligations into the moral sphere (Sanday and Headlam; Jülicher; Lagrange; Schlatter; Althaus; Nygren; E. Brunner). The connection by the catchwords with the play on the words ὀφειλάς and ὀφείλετε (Fridrichsen, "Exegetisches," 295ff.), which is reinforced by the secondary reading ὀφείλοντες, provides a skilful transition to the summary.

Verses 8-10 and 11-14 both refer to the decisive factor in spiritual worship, whether in the dealings of Christians with one another or in their public conduct before the end of the world. The first direction links up with the specific admonitions in 12:9ff., 20f. In hindsight love emerges as the basic condition of all charismatic activity (Bengel: to love is freedom), as in 1 Cor 13:1ff. By no means accidentally it is here limited to acts toward the neighbor and essentially then to ch. 12. The connection with 13:1-7 is designated by the catchword, which can mean simultaneously "duty" and "debt."

Paul can perfectly well distinguish between the different relations, and in spite of customary assertions to the contrary he does not represent an "ethics of love." As the reference in v. 8b is not to the order of the Creator but to the sum of the law, two thoughts overlap in v. 8a. Love does not remain in debt to anyone and yet is itself an "immortal debt" (Bengel) which unlike legal debts can never be repaid. The two are so intertwined that an exception seems to be indicated by εἰ μή instead of that which has absolute validity (*contra* Cranfield, *Commentary,* 83), whereas in fact it has the same sense as ἀλλά in 1 Cor 7:17.

In v. 9 the verb ἀνακεφαλαιοῦσθαι is used in its original sense "to sum up" (cf. Schlier, *TDNT,* III, 681f.). Hence it does not mean "to complete" (*contra* Feuillet, "Morale," 796f.). Many expositions of the expression "sum of the law" reflect the difficulties in Paul's understanding of the law. It should never have been contested that the reference really is to the Torah (*contra* Spicq, *Agape,* II,

56ff.; Sanday and Headlam; cf. H. W. Schmidt). Paul is not speaking of the spiritual law (van Dülmen, *Theologie*, 173) nor of Christ as law (Bläser, *Gesetz*, 236, 239). The following examples from the second table of the Decalogue contradict an interpretation directed toward the general moral law. Hence ἕτερος, which is taken up by ὁ πλησίον in vv. 9c and 10 (cf. 2:1; 1 Cor 4:6; 14:17), is not connected with νόμος (*contra* Marxsen's thesis; Merk, *Handeln*, 165; Leenhardt; right here are Cranfield, *Commentary*, 83f.; Bornkamm, "Wandlungen," 112; cf. the surveys in Michel and Gutbrod, *TDNT*, IV, 1071ff.). The reference is neither to the rest of the law (Zahn) nor to the antithesis to the Roman law, of which the context does not speak. Verses 1-7 can be understood in this light only if there lurks in the background the Lutheran doctrine of the two kingdoms and the third use of the law in which civil righteousness is set over against the new Christian law. ἀγαπᾶν also demands an object even if here this is designated only by ἕτερος.

The real problem of the text is that there is no polemicizing against the *nomos*, let alone against another law. If love is the sum of the law, there are tendencies in this direction among the rabbis from the time of Hillel (Billerbeck, I, 357ff.; III, 306), although alongside this the demand for blind obedience always remained (cf. B. Gerhardsson, *Memory and Manuscript: Oral Tradition and Written Transmission in Rabbinic Judaism and Early Christianity* [Eng. tr. 1961] 136ff.).

[349] Beyond question Paul is following here a catechetical tradition of Jewish Christianity (cf. Matt 5:17ff.) (Michel, *Bibel*, 88f.; Feuillet, "Morale," 798). This may be seen from the use of πληροῦν, which is surprising for Paul in spite of 8:4; Gal 5:14, but which is familiar from Matt 5:17, the perfect of which is gnomic (BDF, §344). The sentence in v. 10b supports this, since in the context and *koine* usage, which no longer necessarily make strict differentiation, πλήρωμα is the equivalent of πλήρωσις (Delling, *TDNT*, VI, 305 *contra* Kühl; Murray; Feuillet, "Morale," 796f.). ἀνακεφαλαιοῦσθαι, which is a mathematical term and very unusual, presupposes the rabbinic question as to a common denominator for the numerous individual commands of the Torah. Finally, the second table of the Decalogue, as in the B variant of Deut 5:17-21 LXX with the omission of v. 20, follows the order of the Jewish Diaspora (Schlatter; Michel; Black), which is also true in part of Luke 18:20; Jas 2:11. To radicalize the statement καὶ εἴ τις ἑτέρα ἐντολή is then added. As in Gal 5:14 the Jesus tradition may be seen in the quotation from Lev 19:18. In the Christian sense this means loving one's neighbor as one would generally love oneself but can no longer do so in extreme love of the neighbor. The introductory ἐν τῷ has been left out as superfluous in textual variants (Lietzmann). From all this it follows that here, in distinction from 12:1f., Paul does not present his own argument but simply points the community to a familiar tradition. Verse 10a is a clarifying basis for vv. 8b-9 while v. 10b is a brief repetition. When this is noted, it is more understandable that while the apostle speaks globally of the fulfilling of the law he is in fact referring only to the ethical portions of the Torah (Bultmann, *Theology*, I, 341; Jülicher; Leenhardt; Bläser, *Gesetz*, 42f.; Cranfield, *Commentary*, 85; Bornkamm, "Wandlungen," 96). This differs from his usual view of the indivisibility of the Torah (cf. Ridderbos, *Paul*, 278-288) but may be explained if here, as already in part in the Synoptics and definitely in later Gentile Christianity, a tradition emerges which regards only the moral law of the OT as binding in the community. Paul could adopt this for the

sake of exhortation, not in order to proclaim an ideal (contra Lietzmann). According to 8:4 the original will of God is known and accepted by pneumatics (Nygren) in the fact that a person is removed from splendid isolation and is set in a life for others in which he is subject to disinterested obedience.

Verses 11-14 are also determined by a fixed tradition. More specifically, eschatology now gives greater intensity to the exhortation, so that one occasionally speaks of a watchman's cry (J. Weiss, "Beiträge," 245; Michel; Grabner-Haider, Paraklese, 84; Balz, TDNT, VIII, 554). Certainly it is apparent here that imminent expectation was originally the basis of Christian admonition (Grabner-Haider, Paraklese, 108ff., though cf. J. Knox), whereas in Paul baptism and pneuma have this function. The reference to the brevity of the time still remaining to the world serves to emphasize the urgency and the radical nature of the worship in daily life.

The individual motifs are already given and no longer need to be developed. It is enough simply to recall them in the framework of a summary. καὶ τοῦτο is used for intensification. καιρός again designates the moment of destiny (though cf. Kühl). The readers know that they stand in the end-time. Today many expositors try to maintain that there is development in Paul's eschatology with a tendency to soften the sharper apocalyptic element (Dodd; Cranfield, Commentary, 91ff., et al.). But these are the wishful dreams of modern exegetes. As in 1 Thess 4:13 fervent expectation is presupposed in the community, and this cannot be demythologized by referring it to eternity (Dodd; K. Barth; Althaus) or death (Sanday and Headlam; Ridderbos). The reference to the ὥρα, familiar from John, the statement of the Synoptic parables about the Lord's return at night, and the call to awake out of sleep, which occurs impressively in the small baptismal song in Eph 5:14, belong stereotypically to apocalyptic exhortation. Also judged by the content, the apostle resorts to current tradition as in vv. 8-10. In so doing he gives the section an incontestable unity.

Some distinctively Pauline emphases need not be missed by stating this. As widespread as the motif of the present as the time of decision is, it is shaped in a characteristic way by ἤδη in v. 11b and the almost chronological definition in v. 11c. There is no reason to think in terms of an apocryphon (Conzelmann, TDNT, VII, 442; IX, 345f.). προκόπτειν is taken from everyday language, but we have here an eschatological variation (Stählin, TDNT, VI, 712, 716). The time of first believing is obviously baptism, so that the parallel between sacrament and faith emerges more clearly than usual. The verses are to be regarded as typical baptismal exhortation. Day and night, contrasted also in 1 Thess 5:4ff., stand in contrast like light and darkness, and in a long dualistic tradition (cf. H. Braun, Qumran, I, 185f.; Conzelmann, TDNT, IX, 346), in which the OT concept of the day of Yahweh is only one point of contact, they characterize the antithesis of the time of this world and the dawn of the heavenly nature. Every period of time after baptism is a step toward the ultimate σωτηρία in its cosmic breadth. The night is well advanced. Its end has begun. Full day has not yet come but its light is already shining. We stand on the threshold (contra Lövestam, Wakefulness, 29ff.), which in 8:19ff. is characterized as the stage of the messianic woes. From this inferences are to be drawn for the present moment.

In a rigorous anti-enthusiasm which adopts originally enthusiastic terms and motifs (cf. Lövestam, *Wakefulness*, 26f.), importance is allotted to the earthly day precisely in view of the coming heavenly day, instead of devaluing it (Schrage, *Einzelgebote*, 24). As in 6:11ff. the present is the time of conflict.

Also part of the fixed baptismal vocabulary is the demand for the donning of spiritual armor. To relate this to the putting off of night clothes and the putting on of clothes for the day (Zahn; Kühl; Lagrange; Schlatter; Althaus; Cranfield, *Commentary*, 94) sounds almost laughable today. Originally connected mythologically with participation in the battle between light and darkness (cf. K. G. Kuhn, *TDNT*, V, 298ff.; Lövestam, *Wakefulness*, 42f.), it is applied eschatologically in 1 Thess 5:8; 2 Cor 6:7; 10:4, and in greater detail in Eph 6:13ff. The motif of weapons exchanges with that of ἔργα (cf. 1QM 15:19: "All their works are in darkness"). This controls the exhortation in Gal 5:19ff. but it remains an expression of existential commitment, not just moral conduct (*contra* Jülicher; Lagrange), as the governing genitive shows. As in v. 11 ὑμᾶς is by assimilation replaced by ἡμᾶς. The poorly attested reading ἀποβαλώμεθα in v. 12b is to be explained by the Latin translation *abiiciamus*. Assimilation to v. 12b accounts for the interchanging of ὅπλα and ἔργα in v. 12c. What is meant materially is described, as in Gal 3:27; Col 3:9ff., by the formula about putting on the Lord Jesus Christ, and, to be sure, as the new Adam. Incorporation into the body of Christ is characterized as an ongoing task (Lietzmann; Lövestam, *Wakefulness*, 39, 41). Baptismal exhortation is again the basis. Every Christian represents his Lord on earth as a member of his body, and his whole life is a constant return to baptism. As Luther rightly says, standing on God's way is moving back and forth; it is always beginning afresh. Whereas enthusiasts proclaim a metaphysical change of nature, Paul is concerned about the lordship of Christ which must be confirmed and passed on by every Christian and which stands in sharp opposition to the powers that rule the world.

Not without reason, then, the section closes in vv. 13f. with a short list of vices which is skilfully arranged in three parallel pairs in v. 13b and which closes with a rhetorically effective antithesis in v. 14. In v. 13a ὡς ἐν ἡμέρᾳ is not to be taken hypothetically (*contra* K. Barth; Barrett; correctly Ridderbos). ὡς means "as is actually the case"; you do in fact stand under the sign of the new day. εὐσχημόνως, which is a call for bourgeois rectitude and which is also used in 1 Thess 4:12, sounds quite prosaic in such a context. But it corresponds to the vices listed. Reveling and drunkenness, wild sexuality and debauchery, quarreling and strife, put in the plural for assimilation in older readings, are marks of the passing and unstable world. Christ's lordship means not only earthly stability but also the renewing of the mind (12:1f.), which resists conformity to the present aeon and opposes the power of the flesh and its urge to satisfy the desires. The phrase πρόνοιαν ποιεῖν, which is singular in the NT, has misled people to take v. 14b as limiting (BAGD, 708-709), but this is not so (*contra* the Luther Bible; Zahn; Schlatter; Althaus; Brunner; H. W. Schmidt; Behm, *TDNT*, IV, 1012). It is not a question of caring for the body without yielding to its desires. No rights must be accorded at all to the flesh and its tendencies.

The conclusion shows yet again that Paul demands a consistently anti-enthusiastic attitude from the charismatic community. Baptism means that we become Christian soldiers in the corporeal sphere and in daily life in the world. It does not bring separation from the secular world. God's reign over the world wants to manifest itself in almost trivial fashion in secular life. In the midst of cosmic chaos, frenzied possession, and secret and open filthiness, Christ demonstrates his power in and with his disciples. No matter what signs and wonders may accompany the church's mission, the extraordinary is not its mission but the fulfilment of God's will in love and the ending of earthly obsession in the cultivation of the new obedience. That means the justification of the ungodly when carried over into exhortation. Traditional material is splendidly suited to close the two chapters with a summary.

B. Special Exhortation: The Strong and the Weak in the Community (14:1–15:13)

Only in this epistle does special exhortation follow general exhortation. The uniqueness of the procedure calls for explanation. It is very possible that the apostle's earlier experiences come to expression here. If the two preceding chapters are correctly interpreted in terms of an anti-enthusiastic stance, then the supposition is at hand that he fears that what happened at Corinth might happen at Rome too, or at least that he wants to warn them against it. This is all the more so when the problem of the "strong" and the "weak" dominates 1 Corinthians 8–10 too, and when the answer is also provided there by Paul's distinctive understanding of charismata. In Corinth again the question of asceticism plays an important part. A certain connection exists at least in the background (Sanday and Headlam; Taylor; Dupont, "Appel" [see bibliography for 14:1-12] 357ff.), namely, the apostle's memory of earlier struggles. Indeed, it might even be that the Roman church knew or could expect similar conflicts. [35

This observation alone, however, is not enough. The present section does not mention abstention from meat offered to idols nor does it speak of liberation movements on the part of women or slaves. Corinthian asceticism is directed essentially to the problem of sexuality. The strong and the weak concretely represent different concerns in each case, even though the tensions permit comparisons and evoke similar arguments on Paul's part. Unless this is so, it is hard to see why the theme of this whole portion of the epistle should not stand in relation to ch. 12 and what is the point of the obvious break created by the summary in 13:8-14. The new problem may adopt and adapt experiences attained elsewhere and follow the same charismatic approach. At the same time, as in 13:1-7, it must be oriented concretely to the situation in Rome (*contra* J. Knox). Or, to put it more cautiously, it must be of significance in relation to the occasion and structure of the epistle (Schumacher, *Letzte Kapitel*, 29).

Paul obviously does not know the congregation. This does not mean, however, that he has no information about it. On the contrary, it would be quite incredible to want to contest that. From this center of communication reports must have reached Christians everywhere in the world at that time. We can initially leave open how far a full picture can be gained from the following discussion or how far we can recognize Paul's purposes for the whole of the epistle. As a postulate we might venture the thesis that Paul presupposes or suspects the existence of contending groups at Rome and that this is important for his concerns in writing.

The structure of the subdivision is as follows. Respect for the bond of brothers to the common Lord is stressed in 14:1-12, a warning against mutual judging is given in 14:13-23, Christ is set forth as a model in 15:1-6, and the unity of Jewish- and Gentile-Christians is the theme in 15:7-13 (Marxsen, *Introduction,* 96f.). We thus have a logical and purposeful train of thought.

1. The Extent and Limit of Christian Solidarity (14:1-12)

[1]*Accept the weak in faith but not for judgments about debatable opinions.* [2]*One believes he may eat everything. Another, being weak, eats only vegetables.* [3]*Let not him who eats despise him who does not. Let not him who does not eat judge him who does. For God has accepted him (too).* [4]*Who are you that you dare pass judgment on another's servant? He stands or falls to his own master. And he will stand. For the master is able to hold him up.* [5]*One regards some days as better than others, while another regards all days as good. Let each one live joyfully with his own opinion.* [6]*He who observes the [particular] day has the Lord in mind and he who eats eats with his view on the Lord, since he thanks God in prayer. Again, he who does not eat abstains in the Lord's honor, and he too thanks God in prayer.* [7]*None of us lives to himself and none of us dies to himself.* [8]*For if we live, we live to the Lord, and if we die, we die to the Lord. Hence, whether we live or die, we are the Lord's.* [9]*For Christ died and came to life again in order that he might reign over both the dead and the living.* [10]*Why, then, do you judge your brother and why do you on the other side despise your brother? For we shall all be set before the judgment seat of God.* [11]*For it is written, "I live, says the Lord. Every knee shall bow before me and every tongue shall give honor to God."* [12]*Each of us, then, shall give account of himself to God.*

Bibliography: J. Becker, "Quid πληροφορεῖσθαι in Rom 14, 5 significet," *VD* 45 (1967) 11-18; M. Black, "The Christological Use of the OT in the NT," *NTS* 18 (1971/72) 1-14; J. Dupont, "Syneidesis," *Studia Hellenistica* 5 (1948) 119-153; idem, "Appel aux faibles et aux forts dans la communauté romaine (Rom 14,1–15,13)," *Stud.Paul.Congr.,* I, 357-366; E. Riggenbach, "Die Starken und die Schwachen in der römischen Gemeinde," *ThStKr* 66 (1893) 649-678; P. Schubert, *Form and Function of the Pauline Thanksgivings* (BZNW 20; 1939).

The broad distribution of religious asceticism in antiquity is so well documented (cf. Lietzmann; Behm, *TDNT,* II, 687ff.; IV, 926ff.; Strathmann, *RAC,* I, 749ff.) that we may proceed at once to the more detailed question as to the possible motifs which might have defined the community at Rome. The difficulties of the problem have been adequately noted. In any case one may not rule out from the beginning that Paul may simply be giving illustrations to underscore his demand for mutual acceptance. For exhortation is undoubtedly again the main concern, not discussion of the situation in the church, and mutual acceptance is the catchword in this whole portion of the epistle. If, however, it is felt necessary to draw from the text references to specific groups in the community and the conflicts between them, it is not yet self-evident that it involves only two groups, for example, Jewish- and Gentile-Christians, or that we can know their positions, or even the decisive features of a single party. Interpretation must exercise the same caution which governs Paul's own argument and which leads him to express himself initially in allusions.

Against the view that Paul's concern is only the unity of the church (Leenhardt) and that in the last resort the disputes are only illustrations, it can, of course, be objected that this could motivate neither the length of the section, nor its surprising position just before the end of the epistle and not, for example, after ch. 12, nor indeed the strangely detailed treatment. In 1 Corinthians there are much deeper problems than vegetarianism, with which the apostle begins, or abstinence from wine, which he deals with in v. 21. In particular the honoring of days in vv. 5f. can hardly be regarded as hypothetical since it is related to astral worship in Gal 4:10 and is abhorred as incompatible with faith. Even if the tolerance espoused here in relation to that is surprising, one can hardly believe that we have here no more than a fictional example. It is a more likely assumption that real practices in the Roman community are indicated.

If that happens under the contrasting titles "strong" and "weak," this does not necessarily prove that only two groups were at odds. These might well be general designations which bring out the fundamental difference between circles which do not agree in every respect. Yet in the light of 1 Corinthians this is possible only if the strong are enthusiasts who practice the motto of 1 Cor 6:12: "All things are lawful," whereas the weak (cf. Rom 14:14ff. and 1 Cor 8:10) are those who are concerned about questions of clean and unclean. Finally it should not be overlooked that the discussion in 15:7ff. leads on to the theme of the unity of Christians as composed of both Jews and Gentiles. These are the components of a reality which may with great caution be postulated as that of the Roman community. In this combination the modes of behavior of the disputants are described by the catchwords "to judge" and "to despise." Furthermore, the composition of the community, in distinction from the first days of the Jewish-Christians in Rome, is determined by a Gentile-Christian majority.

These are the presuppositions of detailed exegesis. Verse 1 offers us the two catchwords of this part of the epistle. The "weak in faith" form the problem. These are people whose Christianity does not relieve them of doubts in the exercise of Christian liberty. They are a problem both because of their attitude to the strong and also because of the reaction of the latter to their anxiety. προσλαμβάνεσθαι is the apostle's constantly repeated answer to both sides of the problem. The singular is generic; it characterizes a group.

Paul addresses the strong first, since they as a majority are provoking the minority. While the conflicts are disturbing worship, and are perhaps especially acute there, the demand is not just that in worship they should accept and tolerate one another (Rauer, *Schwachen*, 82). The theory that the verb refers to baptism is completely erroneous (*contra* Schlatter; Kirk). Nor does it have a juridical sense (*contra* Michel; correctly Leenhardt; Nababan, "Bekenntnis," 35). What is meant is everyday recognition of brotherhood, in the broad sense solidarity

(Rauer, *Schwachen*, 80, 157). In all circumstances διακρίσεις διαλογισμῶν are to be avoided. In spite of its use elsewhere the compressed phrase does not simply mean doubtful thoughts (H. W. Schmidt) or harbored doubts (Michel; Schrenk, *TDNT*, II, 97; Büchsel, *TDNT*, III, 949f.). It involves the disputed views, described in v. 2 with theological importance, which lead to mutual judgments and feuding parties (Zahn; Lagrange; Ridderbos) and not just to doubts on the one side (*contra* Kühl).

Paul himself obviously sees no reason to condemn from the outset those who feel that they are strong and whom he describes as such, thereby according them at least some limited recognition. At root he is always on the side of freedom, and he does not even censure the presumption manifested in the jargon of the title the strong use for themselves but only its consequences. For him faith does not make all persons and things equal. It is also his opinion that there is a faith which does not adequately fill its place. This may manifest itself morally (Sanday and Headlam; Gaugler) or intellectually (Lagrange; Leenhardt). The problem is that of the restricted place with which one is satisfied, and the demand of the apostle is that things should not be rushed by separation or force. Acceptance in this case means leaving space for growth and communication.

In v. 2 πιστεύειν is ambivalent. It concerns opinion (Lietzmann; Asmussen) and conviction (Nababan, "Bekenntnis," 37) which emerge from Christian self-understanding. The ironical exaggeration which has the weak eating only vegetables shows that it is not a matter of meat offered to idols, as in 1 Corinthians 8–10 (*contra* Riggenbach, "Starken," 668ff.; Asmussen; H. W. Schmidt; correctly Gaugler; Nababan, "Bekenntnis," 19, 38; Merk, *Handeln,* 167). It is a matter of fundamental vegetarianism, with which abstinence relative to wine appears to be linked in v. 21 (Rauer, *Schwachen*, 97ff.). The most important factor, however, is undoubtedly the reference to the selection of days or their rejection in v. 5, even if this practice relates to a different group of people. Paul at least sees this problem against the same background as the others, and he thus mentions them together. At this point the history-of-religions definition of the position of the "weak" is both necessary and possible.

Jewish orthodoxy can be ruled out as a source (*contra* Minear, *Obedience,* 8ff.). General abstinence from meat and wine is not found there (Zahn; Kümmel, *Introduction,* 310; Rauer, *Schwachen,* 129ff. *contra* Lütgert, *Römerbrief,* 91). Individuals adopted this after the fall of Jerusalem as a sign of mourning (Billerbeck), but it did not prevail among the people as a whole. Thus Paul does not give a national motivation. Whether the Essenes abstained from meat and wine at particular fast periods is doubtful already for the reason that they could not dispense with wine, on the sabbaths at least, and members who worked agriculturally could hardly do without meat. In any case there is no reference to fasts (*contra* Behm, *TDNT,* IV, 933; Gutjahr; Rauer, *Schwachen,* 180f.). As regards the observance of days things are a little different. The religious calendar of Judaism enjoins the keeping not only of the sabbath but also of the feasts and fasts (Zahn; Riggenbach, "Starken," 653f.; Murray, 257ff.). Superstition and fear of demons also had a wide hold (Billerbeck). All the same, the apostle does not seem to have either the one or the other in mind (Schlatter; Nababan, "Bekenntnis," 48 *contra* Kühl; Sickenberger; Althaus; H. W. Schmidt), to say nothing of the fact that he should have attacked the fear of demons and a community order under the sign of the ritual law (Rauer, *Schwachen*, 133ff.).

An alternative is to see the practices of the weak as a relic of pagan religion (Rauer, *Schwachen*, 164ff., 185ff.), in which the weak must be a group of Gentile-Christians. It complicates the relationships unnecessarily, and without foundation if that term is sharpened by the unhappy label "proselyte Christians" (Marxsen, *Introduction*, 98). In favor of this alternative is the fact that there was among Hellenistic Gentiles religiously based vegetarianism and abstinence from wine, as well as astrology connected with fear of demons (Hengel, *Judaism*, I, 234ff.) which makes a distinction between lucky and unlucky days (cf. *RAC*, I, 817-831). Against it is the fact that Paul would have strenuously resisted the last of these views; thus a special group of Gentile-Christians is quite unlikely. Also this explanation causes a rift with 15:8ff. which makes it hard to incorporate the later text into the portion as a whole and which also makes it hard to understand the key theme of mutual acceptance.

When the difficulties in both views are made clear in this way the mistake lies in the alternative. Gal 4:9f.; Col 2:16ff. show that a type of Judaism which was under syncretistic influence had gained entry into the community and apparently became a danger through the adherents it had won there. The most natural theory, then, is that the Jewish-Christian minority in Rome was exposed to propaganda of this kind, which could have been constantly fed both by the pagan environment and by the group of god-fearers surrounding the Diaspora synagogue (Jülicher; Lagrange; Barrett; Althaus; Best; Bornkamm, *TDNT*, IV, 66). The relatively mild reaction of the apostle distinguishes this passage from Gal 4:9f. and Col 2:16ff. Perhaps he did not have enough information to make him fear a serious threat (*contra* Minear, *Obedience*, 10ff.). The ascetic movement might not have been linked with a rigorous Judaism as it was in Galatians. Thus the demand for circumcision played no role, nor did a developed world view embracing angelology and demonology as in Colossians. Naturally the apostle argues more cautiously in dealing with a strange church than with his own churches, and he does not want to harden any incipient distrust on the part of the Jewish-Christians. So long as he could assume that the conflicts concerned only different life-styles on the basis of different traditions he could call for mutual toleration according to the principle of 1 Cor 7:7b, 24.

The text permits only a hypothesis. If it is correct, those whom the majority call weak are rigorists who attack the strong as the strong attack them. Their faith convictions obviously lead them to charge their opponents with defective fulfilment or even violation of the divine order and requirement. Their singling out of days might seem from a modern point of view like intellectual weakness and superstition. When measured against the customs of their environment, they pay tribute to their time, just as Paul himself was persuaded of the existence of demons and their power in the everyday life of earth. From the beginnings of church history there has been a struggle between the slogans of total obedience and Christian freedom. This leads to a genuine theological conflict, which in different forms caused trouble for every Christian generation and constantly led to the formation of groups within Christianity. Thus what takes place at Rome serves as an example and it is no accident that it occurs where Jewish- and Gentile-Christians meet.

By religious descent Jewish-Christians are committed to observance of a fixed tradition which is related ultimately to the law of holiness. As an increasing sharpening of the Torah was taking place in the homeland, the same tendency also existed in the Diaspora and consequently in the daily confrontation with the Gentile environment. Religious asceticism for the sake of maintaining purity could go hand in hand here with enthusiasm which deduced from reception of the Spirit the demand that the heavenly nature should already be proclaimed ascetically on earth. In Gentile Christianity the drift of the age was expressed in the opposite direction, namely, in fanatical contempt for worldly commitments out of an unrestrained sense of freedom which set aside any concern for the brother.

In practice the theological problem of the relation between complete obedience and genuine freedom becomes the problem of the relation between faith and world view. Only theoretically can the two be soberly differentiated. In reality they constantly overlap. Hence the controversy at Rome is not to be viewed as one which has no more than historical or antiquarian interest (Nababan, "Bekenntnis," 25), as a superficial reading might suggest. This portion of the epistle too is dealing in an exemplary way with basic theological questions from which there must be no abstraction if the theme of the righteousness of God is to be dealt with in view of the daily life of Christians and its actualization in the secular world. For this reason there will always be conflict between those who claim to represent essential Christianity, feeling that they are strong, and their opponents whom they defame as weak (cf. Dupont, "Syneidesis," 131ff.; *Gnosis*, 272f.; "Appel," 138f.).

Paul adopts the current jargon of the community but he does not allow himself to be pressed into the role of a partisan. The unavoidable conflicts cannot be defused by mere friendliness (*contra* Zahn; Kühl) or by a recognition of good intentions (*contra* Gutjahr). Theological condemnation of others, which breaks off fellowship in either judgment or contempt, is impermissible. The fronts must remain porous and leave the brother room for maneuver.

Basically v. 3c applies to both sides. He who separates himself from someone whom God has set in the community—here there is in fact a reference to baptism—assails the grace and right of his Lord and usurps the function of the world-judge. A reference to legal relations in diatribe style (Michel) clarifies the offense in v. 4. οἰκέτης is the slave who stands under the head of the house alone and is thus independent of his fellow-slaves. ἀλλότριος instead of the expected ἕτερος seems to give added force. One can judge only that for which one is responsible, not what belongs to others. στήκειν and πίπτειν are probably expressions of the primitive Christian vocabulary of exhortation in which they denote standing in faith or falling from it. Here they have the more general sense of remaining in a given place or leaving it. The dative does not mean (*contra* Lagrange; correctly Zahn; Nababan, "Bekenntnis," 42, 49) to his Lord's profit or damage, but for his sake or for him. As often the comparison glides into the envisioned reality so that v. 4a is close to allegory. Only the Lord decides whether the place that he has assigned has been kept or left.

In v. 4c the reality invades the image even more strongly, although without completely obliterating it. As the master controls his servant's place and decides whether he has stood the test, he also has the possibility and privilege of putting him back in it if he has left it. The borders of the image are finally crossed with σταθήσεται δέ, which (*contra* Leenhardt) is passive and can hardly be in the eschatological future (*contra* Michaelis, *TDNT*, VI, 165; Grundmann, *TDNT*, VII, 648f., cf. Kühl; Ridderbos; Nababan, "Bekenntnis," 44). Paul is announcing his confidence that the Lord of the community, having once received a member, can cause him to stand again even when he falls. Grace is stronger than human frailty. Variant readings with the adjective give the passage an edifying sense (Michel; H. W. Schmidt). Unlike these, δυνατεῖ points both to the possibility and to the power of grace. The variants could not continue that (Lietzmann; Lagrange; Ridderbos; Nababan, "Bekenntnis," 45f.), but cross off the γάρ which provides a basis since their concern is only with reassurance.

In context v. 5 is an appendix. Does this mean that a hypothetical case is now added and weighed? Parallelism to v. 2 suggests not. Paul remembers that days are being observed too. κρίνειν, as the comparative παρά shows (Riesenfeld, *TDNT*, V, 734f.), has primarily the sense "to prefer." Some days are contrasted with others. The second relative clause, which is incomplete, indicates that on the other side there is indifference to this practice. Hence the verb takes on the sense "to approve" (BAGD, 451a). The adding of this issue as an echo might suggest that it is of lesser importance. This can hardly be so, however, if a religious calendar is presupposed here, as in Gal 4:9f.; Col 2:16ff., which demands the observance of fasts and feasts on the basis of a law which rules the cosmos. It appears, then, that Christians are in view who are convinced that days stand under lucky or unlucky stars (cf. Billerbeck; Lagrange). Paul neither justifies nor condemns this belief. Its effects on the community are the only things which disturb him. Verses 5b-6 sum up his concern epigrammatically; v. 6a is a typical *koine* interpolation (Lietzmann).

In all areas Christian life stands in service and according to 12:1f. only then in the good pleasure of the Lord, who in context is undoubtedly Christ. 1 Cor 3:21f. formulates the same motif: All things are lawful so long as we remain under Christ's lordship. A variation on this in 12:3 is that we live in charismatic freedom so long as we see the limits of the conferred gift and do not destroy the community as Christ's body. Not by accident, then, we find here too the characteristic ἕκαστος as an address in the apostolic decree. The principle does not make detailed discussion superfluous. But it sanctions different attitudes in the concrete situation. Casuistry has no place from the very first. An infinite breadth of possibilities is open to the church as a whole and also to the individual congregation, both corporately and in personal life. Where that does not exist, Christianity breaks up into sects. Christian life suffers distortion when uniformity is enforced and there is uncritical subjection to conventions.

On the other hand, there is an immovable limit. If our conduct no longer manifests belonging to Christ as an ultimate bond, our existence becomes godless. Personal freedom ends solely, but radically, with the Lord. Breadth and restriction, freedom and commitment, coincide.

Paul does not now speak, as one would expect, of faith or conscience, although νοῦς in our passage doubtless has something to do with both (cf. Bultmann,

Theology, I, 219f., 327). What the apostle has in view is the renewed reason of 12:2 whose critical capacity leads through the call into a circumscribed sphere to firm conviction and resolute action on the basis of insight into one's own situation, and from that perspective remains open to new situations and the assessment of the brother (Bultmann, *Theology,* I, 211f., 327; Behm, *TDNT,* IV, 959; Ridderbos). The pronoun gives added force. No one can escape responsibility or decision. The same full certainty of πληροφορεῖσθαι is not just expected but demanded of everybody. A Christian is not qualified, as is often said, by a bad conscience about his imperfection and irresolution in face of the confusion of the surrounding world, but by the clear insight, the assured and joyful life and work, which mark him off from others (J. Becker, "Röm 14:5," considers the middle meaning "take pleasure in," but prefers "be fulfilled").

The wordplay on φρονεῖν gives precision to v. 6a. At first it points back to the distinction of days but at the end it designates existential orientation to that which alone is essential. Not the name and sign, but the univocal will to remain a disciple, is the absolute criterion of being a Christian. What characterizes our limitation as "having the Lord in view" is at the same time the sphere of full and cheerful agreement with oneself which cannot be led astray by the attitude or opposition of others and which in fact leaves them no place. If we live to please the Lord, no one has any right to restrict our freedom, to establish norms for our judgment, or to set up a program for us. Where supposed love tries to stop us from making our own contribution to the general service, which no other can make for us, it shows itself to be in danger of the hypocrisy mentioned in 12:9. For God wants us, in our own possibilities, thoroughly nonconformist in cheerful spontaneity.

The second part of v. 6 illustrates this. εὐχαριστεῖν refers to the custom of grace at meals, which is also found among pagans (Schubert, *Thanksgivings,* 139f.) and which is self-evident for Jews (Harder, *Gebet,* 121; Beyer, *TDNT,* II, 760). Both ascetics and the strong confess at meals that they receive their nourishment from the hand of God and that they have to give thanks for this reason. Their difference in attitudes to foodstuffs does not affect their acknowledgment of the same Lord. Where that happens, rigid prohibitions make no sense and unbridled caprice is impossible. Thus existing conflicts are relativized profoundly by the higher fellowship.

In vv. 7-9 the example is set against a horizon which embraces the whole of the Christian life. In return this horizon establishes it as a characteristic example and gives an inner necessity to the detailed illustration. Hence it does not concern a parenthesis (Jülicher) or digression (Kirk) but the central statement of the passage from which all else naturally flows. The rhetorical art of the diatribe controls the formulation and leads to a climax at the end of v. 8 (Thyen, *Stil,* 56) and to the use of a confessional statement in v. 9 (Nababan, "Bekenntnis," 9, 55f.), although this does not mean that we are to see a hymn here (*contra* H. W. Schmidt). Thanksgiving is the starting point but it is not the guiding motif of the statement (*contra* Thüsing, *Per Christum,* 31). It simply illustrates that we belong to the Lord as those who are always recipients and are blessed by the act of salvation.

Life and death are the sharpest opposites in human existence, and as such are personally experienced by everyone. The Christian stands the test by the fact that he goes through both with seeing eyes. The breadth of possible variations of behavior is infinite, but in the fulness of possibilities it is ultimately determined by whether one lives and dies for self or for the Lord. As Bengel puts it, the art of living and dying is the same.

Antiquity offers many parallel sayings (cf. BAGD, 336a; Lagrange; Michel) which also reject living for oneself. The finest is that of Plutarch in *Vita Cleomenes* 31: αἰσχϱὸν γὰϱ ζῆν μόνοις ἑαυτοῖς καὶ ἀποθνῄσκειν. These already point beyond the primacy of freedom of conscience, in which one must answer only to oneself (*contra* Jülicher), even if humanity is unquestionably betrayed when decisions of conscience are not respected. Certainly the apostle is not speaking of man's responsibility for himself, and imperative variants in v. 8b are edifying emendations. For Paul living and dying to the Lord is the ultimate criterion of being a Christian. Even in everyday life, then, it is "the one ethical possibility" (K. Barth), which 12:6 already has in view.

Verse 9 puts it in a formula of faith which offers a free rendering of the traditional confession "died and rose again for us" of 1 Cor 15:3; 2 Cor 5:14f.; Gal 1:4 (Michel; Wengst, *Formeln*, 45f.; Nababan, "Bekenntnis," 27, 62). The introductory εἰς τοῦτο γάϱ rules out any exception with its apodictic sharpness. The ingressive aorist ἔζησεν, which denotes the definite act (BDF, §331; Nababan, "Bekenntnis," 61), was later felt not to be clear enough and was replaced by ἀνέστη, and then both were connected (Lietzmann; Lagrange). The fact that νεκϱῶν comes first in v. 9b is surprising at first glance. Rhetoric, which takes up the former statement chiastically, undoubtedly plays a part here. But it is emphasized in such a way that the exalted one claims rule over all things in cosmic universality [3] and that this is actualized in the community. The motif of Eph 4:8ff. is prepared for, according to which Christ has gone through life and death and now has power over both. The contour of the cosmocrator becomes visible, who leaves no one in a private sphere and who orients all things to himself. Belonging to him or not becomes the eschatological criterion of all humanity and thus characterizes all activity, transcending our criteria. The function of world-judge, which dominates vv. 10f., is consistently derived from this (Bultmann, *Theology*, I, 78; Thüsing, *Per Christum*, 35f.).

Paul can thereby return to the concrete question and give it a basic answer against the new background. In the style of the diatribe he introduces a question which with strong emphasis addresses the individuals as representatives of their group. How can we, under the banner of the universal lordship of him by whom God exercises world judgment, judge or despise a brother as though we were the standard by which he is to be measured? Verse 10c indirectly sharpens the question by pointing out with every word the risk involved in such an attitude. πάντες comes first. No matter what may divide us on earth, we must all come before the common Judge. παϱιστάνεσθαι with the dative, as in 2 Cor 4:14, is a technical Hellenistic term for being presented forensically, while βῆμα is the official judgment seat.

The context of the previous verse and possibly a reminiscence of 1 Cor 5:10 have misled secondary readings to speak of Christ instead of God (Lietzmann; Lagrange, *et al. contra* Zahn; Kühl). For the apostle, however, there is here no material difference. Christ discharges the function of Judge which is traditionally ascribed to God. He does so as God's representative. The decisive point, however, is that we must all come to this judgment and that we must already show this on earth in our dealings with the brethren.

This makes it clear that Paul's exhortation is motivated not merely by the act of salvation but also in traditional style by expectation of the end. Even if the eschatological change has already taken place, the final decision for individuals is still to come. He who stands on the threshold of his own judgment will orient his behavior to brothers in the light of this.

While vv. 7-9 are the center of the section, they must not be isolated from the rest (*contra* Nababan, "Bekenntnis," 22). Verse 11 continues and moves beyond its premises, as in Phil 2:10f. Isa 45:23 is quoted. By way of introduction the oath-like affirmation ζῶ ἐγώ, λέγει κύριος with a recitative ὅτι is brought in from Isa 49:18. Following the LXX version of A Q ἐξομολογήσεται is used. What relates to the nations in the original, and to the cosmic powers in Phil 2:10f., is applied here to every individual in keeping with the needs of exhortation. In this verse the verb does not mean (*contra* Michel, *TDNT,* V, 215) the eschatological confession of sins but acclamation connected with *proskynēsis.* Originally it was part of the ritual of enthronement as this takes place, transposed into eschatology, in relation to the exalted Christ (Phil 2:10f.). Here, as in the OT original, it is acknowledgment of God as Lord and Judge of the world in the praise of his subjects (Black, "Use," 8). This makes v. 10b more concrete, although this does not mean (*contra* Nababan, "Bekenntnis," 85) that Christ is to be taken as the speaker in the quotation. The end of the world and the destiny of the individual mean that right is God's alone and that the earth is given to him. This has obvious implications for our conduct in the community too. This is underlined in v. 12 in a hortatory conclusion introduced, as elsewhere, by ἄρα οὖν. Good readings omit οὖν and τῷ θεῷ and thus produce an axiom. λόγον διδόναι is a legal phrase: to give an account. He who knows that he must render his own account at the last judgment will be careful not to anticipate the judgment of others.

2. Marks of God's Rule in the Community (14:13-23)

¹³*Then let us not judge one another any more. Instead use your critical ability not to put a stumbling block or obstacle in the way of a brother.* ¹⁴*I know and am fully persuaded in the Lord Jesus Christ that nothing is unclean in itself but it is unclean only for him who regards it as unclean.* ¹⁵*For if your brother is caused inner distress by what you eat, you are no longer walking in love. Do not for the sake of what you eat bring ruin to one for whom Christ died.* ¹⁶*Do not let the good (which is conferred on you) be spoken of as evil.* ¹⁷*For the kingdom of God is not eating and drinking but righteousness, peace, and joy in the Holy Spirit.* ¹⁸*He, then, who serves Christ in this way is pleasing to God and approved by men.* ¹⁹*We thus pursue that which is in keeping with peace and mutual edification.* ²⁰*Do not, for the sake of food, destroy God's work. Everything is indeed clean. But it is harmful for the man who eats it if he takes offense at it.* ²¹*Better not to eat flesh or drink wine or (do) anything else that makes your brother stumble.* ²²*Hold fast the faith that you have for*

yourself in relation to God. Happy is he who does not need to judge himself for what he decides. ²³*But he who has scruples when he eats is condemned because he does not act out of faith. For everything that does not take place out of faith is sin.*

Bibliography: K. Aland, "Glosse, Interpretation, Redaktion und Komposition in der Sicht der neutestamentlichen Textkritik," *Apophoreta: Festschrift für Ernst Haenchen* (BZNW 30; 1964) 7-31; also in Aland, *Studien zur Überlieferung des NT und seines Textes* (1967) 35-57; H. Conzelmann, *1 Corinthians* (Hermeneia; 1975) 146-150; O. E. Evans, "What God Requires of Man, Romans XIV, 14," *ExpT* 69 (1957/58) 199-202; E. Peterson, "ἔργον in der Bedeutung 'Bau' bei Paulus," *Bib* 22 (1941) 439-441. For Dupont, "Appel" see the bibliography for 14:1-12.

Verse 13 is transitional. It draws inferences for both groups from what has been said. But as in v. 13b the tenor of the whole section is essentially an admonition to the strong. Diatribe style may be seen again in the interchanging of personal address and basic statements and also in the play on different senses of κρίνειν and its compounds. The basic meaning "to pass sentence" becomes "to condemn" in v. 13a and is modified to "to think critically" in v. 13b. The linking of πρόσκομμα and σκάνδαλον already given in 9:33 (Stählin, *Skandalon,* 171ff.), whose factual tautology (Stählin, *TDNT,* VI, 753; VII, 355) is avoided in variant readings by the elimination of the first noun, has an abstract effect here. The comparative in v. 13b is adversative. Instead of judging one another we should avoid putting stumbling blocks or obstacles in each other's way.

At a first glance the course of the argument is not transparent (Lietzmann). For this reason (Zahn; Bardenhewer; Michel) v. 14 has been viewed as a parenthesis and vv. 16-19 as a digression (Zahn; Leenhardt; a parenthesis, Baulès). In fact the leap from v. 13 to the principle in v. 14 and then back to exhortation can be understood only when one sees the parallelism with 1 Cor 8:7-13 even to the point of employment of the same catchwords. As there Paul agrees basically with the opinion of the strong (Minear, *Obedience,* 19), but for the sake of brotherly love and the upbuilding of the community he rejects its radical application.

A second insight must certainly be connected with this first one. Verse 14 unmistakably reminds us of the saying in Mark 7:15 and of Peter's revelation in Acts 10:10-16. In both these cases the problem of ritual purity in the Christian life is dealt with under the keyword κοινόν. Gal 2:1ff. and the apostolic decree of Acts 15:20, 29 show the deep conflicts this question involved in the pre-Pauline community. Jewish-Christians, who still felt obliged to keep the law of holiness, must have experienced a constant personal threat in dealing with Gentile-Christians, and must have seen in their free-thinking colleagues something like defectors. At stake were observance of the Torah on the one side and the unity of the community on the other side.

The problem of eating meat sacrificed to idols (1 Corinthians 8–10) was a particularly important one in this whole controversy. The struggle was sharpened to the breaking point, for the Gentile-Christian enthusiasts had no understanding of the concerns of Jewish-Christians and despised them as over-scrupulous. Paul believes that he has reason to link the Roman debate about vegetarianism and the observance of days with this conflict. For this reason he adopts the current term of Hellenistic Judaism, κοινόν (cf. Zahn's evidence), as well as the slogan πάντα καθαρά in v. 20. He thus turns against the strong, whom he obviously equates with the enthusiasts for freedom of 1 Cor 8:7ff. For him both the theological question and that of the practical course to be taken have already been decided.

He begins emphatically in v. 14 with the phrase οἶδα καὶ πέπεισμαι and with the mention of the name of Jesus. The phrase is singular. It almost has the form of an oath (Pallis) and goes beyond the formula πέπεισμαι ἐν κυρίῳ of Gal 5:10; Phil 2:24; 2 Thess 3:4. Absolute certainty and apostolic authority form a principle (Michel). From this standpoint it is idle to debate whether the apostle is appealing here to a saying of Jesus (Zahn; Jülicher; Lagrange; Leenhardt; H. W. Schmidt; Nababan, "Bekenntnis," 93; Michel) or not (Kühl; undecided Sanday and Headlam). The translation "in virtue of my fellowship" with the exalted Lord (Lietzmann; Ridderbos) is too colorless (Michel; Neugebauer, *In Christus*, 143). "In virtue of the authority of the Lord Jesus" would be better. But as in 1 Cor 11:23 there is reminiscence of a confessional tradition which not accidentally is linked to the name of Jesus as guarantor (cf. Dupont, *Gnosis*, 310). This tradition developed in the debate with Jewish-Christians zealous for the law, took the form of a compromise in the apostolic decree, was rightly given a basis in the conduct and message of Jesus in Mark 7:15, and then in Acts 10:10ff. found a further basis in a revelation to the chief apostle and first representative of free Jewish Christianity. Paul adopted and applied it as an inalienable part of his faith and mission. From this standpoint he could acknowledge that the strong were right in principle and yet paradoxically resist irresponsible practical deductions from this.

Like κοινόν ("profane"), καθαρός ("not unclean") is a catchword which comes from the Jewish and Jewish-Christian debate about the ritual law (Lietzmann; Michel; Hauck, *TDNT*, III, 416, 790f.; R. Meyer, *TDNT*, III, 418ff.). The lasting dogmatic significance of v. 14a lies in the fact that it does not just answer the question of clean and unclean foods but that it removes for Christians the basic distinction of all antiquity, which is still influential today, between the cultic sphere and the profane. As 12:1 proclaimed, this means that Christianity abandons in principle both the idea of a sacral area and its institutions. Only the position, however, makes the meaning of the negation clear. The past is replaced by a new insight which should not be regarded or designated as moral. Eschatologically and christologically grounded, now a no less fundamental antithesis between "clean" and "unclean" is set up. Unlike the Corinthian enthusiasts, Paul does not think that there are no longer any earthly limits for Christians. εἰ μή in the sense of ἀλλά (BDF, §428[3]; Pallis) indicates the exception. It probably belongs also to the adopted tradition and shares its impersonal style, perhaps also in taking up the participle by ἐκεῖνος (Michel). It is not even specifically Christian but validates the authority of conscience. If a person believes something to be unclean he must show this in his conduct; if not, he jeopardizes his humanity. To live with a violated conscience is dangerous. Stress lies, then, not on the limit of the decision of conscience (*contra* Schrage, *Einzelgebote*, 154) but on the duty of following it.

It is important to say expressly that Paul is not formulating a doctrine of adiaphora here (Kühl *contra* Asmussen; cf. Schrage, *Einzelgebote*, 155ff.). Wherever the debate about what is permitted and forbidden occurs, the necessary signs have to be set up in precisely the field of the so-called adiaphora, since in daily Christian life there can be no neutral ground (*contra* Lietzmann) between the lordship of Christ and that of antichrist. If the world of things is to a large degree profane, the creatures of God that move in it and use it are not. Thus the wind is taken out of the sails of the strong.

Taking up v. 13b with a continuing γάρ, vv. 15-16 mark the borders of our freedom by considering the temporal and eternal salvation of the brother. Often this has been interpreted in terms of faith formed by love (at least not clearly Leenhardt; E. Brunner). Love is not greater than faith and for this reason does not have the last word (*contra* H. W. Schmidt). There is a love which is without direction, which denies truth and freedom, which is only apparent love, and which is just as unchristian and finally inhuman as dogmatic intolerance. If *agape* is set above freedom (Michel), sanctification is set above faith as though faith grants only inner freedom but does not tell us, as love tells us, what we should do (E. Brunner). For this reason Christian freedom may be seen in the renouncing of one's own freedom (Bultmann, *Theology*, I, 341ff.) and its limit may be seen, not theoretically, but only in the sphere of reality (Conzelmann, *1 Corinthians*, 148). It is not determined by what the other wishes, wills, or thinks, but simply by his need, expressed by the passive λυπεῖται (Ridderbos). Thus *T. Benj.* 6:3 says too that the good person does not do harm to his neighbor. What is in mind is the state of the wounded conscience, not irritation that I break conventions and do not follow traditions. Provocation of the brother cannot be helped, since his supposed right does not have the last word any more than that which I presuppose. The last word is the Lord's alone.

Verse 15c makes things more precise when it speaks of "bringing ruin" to the brother. If the verb has eschatological significance (Rauer, *Schwachen*, 84; Mattern, *Gericht*, 117; Conzelmann, *1 Corinthians*, 149), it also includes the present violating of humanity. The relative clause which follows adopts the familiar and already discussed formula ἀπέθανεν ὑπέρ, which characterizes the saving significance of the death of Christ (Dupont, "Appel," 361). The aim is to show how severe the danger is. Misused freedom not only harms God's creature; it also perverts the meaning of the act of salvation. He who rejects Christ as Redeemer and Keeper of the brother himself leaves the sphere of salvation and enters anew [into that of cancelled self-assertion and thus into the revolt of the flesh against the Spirit. To that extent love is in fact both the fruit and the limit of true faith.

Verse 16 is to be understood strictly from the context, otherwise it remains unclear. τὸ ἀγαθόν is not at all meaningless (cf. Pallis) if, as in 8:28; 10:15, it means salvation, or, more precisely, the state of salvation (Kühl; Leenhardt; Michel; Ridderbos; Nababan, "Bekenntnis," 94), not the Christian ideal (Lietzmann), nor, in anticipation of v. 17, where a new line of thought begins, the *basileia* (Asmussen; H. W. Schmidt). Misunderstanding led to the Western reading ἡμῶν (Zahn), whereas ὑμῶν has the strong in view and ἀγαθόν has in view the ἐξουσία of 1 Cor 8:9, i.e., their freedom (Sanday and Headlam; Lagrange; Barrett; Murray; Althaus; Merk, *Handeln*, 170; Schlatter). The good of the faithful is liberty (Bengel). τὸ ἀγαθόν is perhaps used as a softening, since the possibility of perversion has already been raised. A final problem concerns those who do the evil speaking. Usually in the NT these are non-Christians (Nababan, "Bekenntnis," 95). The text is overworked if one relates it only to the weak (Gutjahr; Michel; Gaugler). A choice does not have to be made (H. W. Schmidt). Paul's point is that Christian freedom, which is bound to cause friction, should not be made questionable and the target of contempt by caprice or brotherly conflict. This would be a disavowal of the grace of God.

This interpolated thought throws light on the transition to v. 17. In context the verse is at first sight just as surprising as the parallel in v. 14. Most unusually (cf. 1 Cor 4:20) the apostle does not relate the concept of the βασιλεία τοῦ θεοῦ, which is rare in his works, to the coming kingdom of God (*contra* Lagrange). Yet according to 1 Cor 15:24f. the latter is the consummation of the already present lordship of Christ and has dawned with it. Paul combats the eschatology of the enthusiasts with the help of his apocalyptic but only insofar as this is christologically oriented and limited. This dialectic is missed if the statement is spiritualized (Leenhardt) and speaks in an edifying way of the kingdom of grace (Gutjahr) or the new order (J. Knox) or in secular fashion of Christianity or the Christian religion (Kühl; Bardenhewer; Sickenberger). If Christ's reign is to be seen in the community, God's kingdom has already achieved anticipatory reality there. On earth this can take place only under assault. The enthusiasts overlook this and hence a polemical definition is given as in 1 Cor 4:20. Those who boast of wisdom are told that it is not in words. Here the strong are told similarly that it is not in eating and drinking. The position is antithetically described there by "in power," while here it is by righteousness, peace, and joy in the Holy Spirit. The prepositional phrase relates (*contra* Zahn; Lagrange; Michel) to all three members, so that Gal 5:22, not 1 Thess 1:6, is the closest parallel.

Whereas traditional baptismal exhortation uses the formula "to inherit the kingdom" (cf. 1 Cor 6:10; 15:50; Gal 5:21), Paul seems here to argue in teaching style (Michel) but with his own definitions, which for that reason are intentionally polemical. A different understanding of the Spirit distinguishes him from champions of a realized eschatology. The Spirit does not take us out of the world and let this be demonstrated by asceticism or freedom in relation to the earthly order. On the other hand, he does not set up (*contra* Gutjahr; Baulès) a new scale of Christian virtues but places us rather in the realm of eschatological grace. Righteousness is not right action (*contra* Sanday and Headlam; Barrett) but divine power. Peace is openness toward everyone. Joy is standing under an open heaven. Not feelings but realities are here described as the marks of the inaugurated lordship of God and Christian fellowship.

Verse 18 gives added emphasis. It goes with v. 17 and the definition given there (*contra* Michel). Later MSS, to make it clear that the sentence is related to v. 17b as a whole, pedantically changed ἐν τούτῳ to ἐν τούτοις because of the three previous nouns (Kühl; Conzelmann, *TDNT*, IX, 369; Merk, *Handeln,* 170). "Serving Christ" sums up what has been said. It is the essence of the kingdom of God manifested in fellowship. It thus has the open door to God's approval, and, as is cautiously added, to that of people as well. For δόκιμος does not have the usual sense of authentication of faith as such. In antithesis to bad reports it denotes recognition (Grundmann, *TDNT*, II, 260) in which acts that are in keeping with faith are respected. Verse 19 draws from this the conclusion for principle and v. 20a the conclusion for practice. Since the well-attested adhortative is what one would expect, the somewhat stronger form of the indicative is probably original (Lagrange; Michel; Leenhardt; H. W. Schmidt *contra* Zahn; Kühl; Ridderbos). The OT phrase "to pursue peace," which is already traditionally used in 12:8, has to do here, as distinct from v. 17, with the relation to brothers. τὰ τῆς εἰρήνης is comprehensive, while τὰ τῆς οἰκοδομῆς, which is rhetorically parallel, elucidates materially the goal that is sought. "Edification" is again an anti-enthusiast catchword which defines the unity and growth of the community as the task of every charismatic action of individuals. Where brotherhood is practiced in a concern for peace, others can develop in their assigned place, as in 12:3f. In view of the connection with οἰκοδομή God's work does not mean the Christian state of the other (Zahn; Kühl; Lagrange), and certainly not the cross of Jesus (Michel), but, as in 15:2, 1 Cor 3:9, the community (Rauer, *Schwachen*, 85; Barrett; Ridderbos; Bertram, *TDNT*, II, 643) as the building of God (Peterson, "Bau"). To weaken this on account of questions of food would be an offense.

Verse 20b again didactically states a principle which says positively what v. 14a said negatively. It takes up the opinion of the strong and, like 1 Cor 6:12f., uses their slogans. As in v. 14b, however, the limitations must follow. No abstract decision can be made concerning what is good or bad when concrete people and the edification of the community are at stake. διὰ προσκόμματος denotes the accompanying circumstance. The statement is concise. This makes the sense of πρόσκομμα unclear (Stählin, *TDNT*, VI, 756, cf. *Skandalon*, 257). If the basic sense is to be retained, the point is that he who in eating causes another to stumble and fall does evil, namely, harm. In typical diatribe style v. 21, making the same point more sharply, moves over again into a hortatory application. The continuation of προσκόπτει by ἢ σκανδαλίζεται ἢ ἀσθενεῖ is strongly attested. Since there would be no reason to shorten this, the long form indicates a later interpretation along the lines of 1 Cor 8:11-13 (Lietzmann *contra* Zahn; Kühl; Lagrange). Similarly the remarkable relative attraction ἐν ᾧ is to be maintained, precisely on account of its difficulty, rather than conjecture μηδὲ ἕν (Zahn). καλόν has a normative or comparative sense (Ridderbos). It is right to avoid flesh or wine or anything else that might cause a brother to stumble, to the extent that the danger of v. 20b really threatens.

There has been emendation in v. 22. Instead of the quite superfluous relative clause good readings offer a question by eliminating ἥν. The simplification speaks against originality (though cf. Kühl). Paul recalls the motif of 12:3 that faith is imparted to each only in a limited horizon; the strong are thus required to observe these limits for themselves and before God. One's own standing in faith, and the freedom granted therewith, do not have to be denied on this account. The beatitude does not refer to inner happiness (*contra* H. W. Schmidt), as the antithesis κατακρίνεσθαι in v. 23 shows (Nababan, "Bekenntnis," 105). Nor does it involve a warning (*contra* Michel) but a confirmation for the free. δοκιμάζειν here means more than decision for what is demanded (*contra* Bultmann, *Theology*, I, 215; Ridderbos). It refers to the judgment which is reached from one's own faith and which is tested by it. Blessed is he who does not have to judge himself in this.

This agreement with the position of the strong, however, now serves only as a premise for the statement that follows. There are also the others who cannot eat all things without distress of conscience. What is called λυπεῖσθαι in v. 15 and συνείδησιν μολύνειν or τύπτειν in 1 Cor 8:7, 12 is now in a play on κρίνειν described as a state of doubt. διακρίνεσθαι is attested in this sense initially in Christian tradition (BAGD, 185a; Dupont, *Gnosis*, 270f.). It characterizes the divided person (Büchsel, *TDNT*, III, 948f.) who against his conscience is influenced by the faith of others and therefore no longer lives according to his own measure of πίστις (faith), as the principle demands that he should. As the beatitude spoke of present blessedness, the unusually hard κατακρίνειν based on the play of words speaks of condemnation in the judgment announced in the present. If on Paul's view blessedness depends on faith, fall from this necessarily means condemnation.

The conclusion confirms this with a theologically important sentence. As is generally recognized today, the context shows that the destiny of non-Christians is not at issue. On the other hand, in reaction against this understanding, one should not render the statement harmless by psychologizing it, by postulating the inner harmony (H. W. Schmidt) of him who acts morally (*contra* Sanday and Headlam; Baulès; in tendency Althaus). Certainly the parallel in 1 Cor 8:11ff. is to be noted, and πίστις is more or less identical with what is called conscience there (Bultmann, *Theology*, I, 220). Nevertheless, one must take seriously the fact that conscience is not mentioned and that even conscience can be embraced by superstition (*contra* Schrage, *Einzelgebote*, 152). To translate πίστις by good conscience (Gaugler; Ridderbos) or even more weakly by conviction (Sanday and Headlam; Lietzmann; Gutjahr; Bardenhewer; Best) is most questionable when the definition that follows is taken into account. Paul is warning against a violated conscience and protecting against a straying conscience in order to preserve man's humanity. For him it is undoubtedly sin to force the conscience of another. One may also grant that πίστις is very close here to the profane use of "persuasion," just as elsewhere belief or Christianity or Christendom itself may be indicated by it. Faith covers the whole conduct of life, and the truth which determines it does not change with changing situations. But this does not justify a moralizing of the statement. Paul is not just saying that a person should not act contrary to his deepest self-critical conviction (*contra* Sickenberger; E. Brunner) or that conscience has at least a relative autonomy (*contra* H. W. Schmidt). For the Gentile too has moral clarity and an inner confidence grounded in the judgment of conscience.

Sin arises, however, when one goes beyond the gift of God, instead of attending to one's own μέτρον πίστεως, and thus falls into ὑπερφρονεῖν. Faith is a concrete orientation to the lordship of Christ which grasps it, which in its breadth leaves room for the particularities of the members, which does not impose uniformity (Bultmann, *Theology*, I, 325f.; Nababan, "Bekenntnis," 103ff.). Christ remains the only measure for all. No one must make his faith a norm for others as they seek to serve Christ. The weak want uniformity by making their law binding for brothers, and the strong seek it too by forcing their insight on the weak. We thus try to make others in our own image and in so doing sin, since faith has to do always and exclusively with the image of Christ.

The emphasis of the section is not on the prohibitions (*contra* Michel) but on the marks of God's rule which are actualized through Christ and the Spirit in the community. When the distinction between cultic and profane was removed, the kingdom of righteousness, joy, and peace dawned. Hence there is freedom which lifts us beyond all the differences of worldly existence and relations. This bears a Christian stamp in the sense that it means solidarity in spite of every tension. Since it is not a personal possession, and finds its limit too in the Giver, it is the ability to make room for neighbors and grant freedom to brethren. In it there is mutual acceptance.

The text-critical and historical problem of the omission of chs. 15–16 and the later addition of 16:25-27 after our chapter need not be dealt with extensively here (cf. the surveys in Lietzmann; Kümmel, *Introduction*, 314-320; Aland, "Textkritik," 18ff.). Marcion, to whom the excision of the following chapters goes back, had good reasons for this, as will be seen, and it is thus understandable that there is no enthusiasm to follow his steps and leave the epistle without a doxological ending. Apart from textual considerations, the material relation between 15:1-13 and ch. 14, and between 15:14ff. and 1:9-15, is so obvious (e.g., Schumacher, *Letzte Kapitel*, 17, 29; J. Knox) that the original must have contained ch. 15 at least. The problem of 'ch. 16 may be left on one side for the time being.

3. The Model of Christ (15:1-6)

[1]*We who are strong are under obligation to bear with the weakness of the weak and not to please ourselves.* [2]*Let each of us please his neighbor for good, for edifying.* [3]*For Christ did not live to please himself, but, as it is written, "The reproaches of those who reproached you fell on me."* [4]*For whatever was written in former times was written for our learning, that in patience and the comfort (granted) by the Scriptures we might have hope.* [5]*May the God of patience and comfort grant you to be of one mind among yourselves, following Jesus Christ,* [6]*so that with one voice you may glorify God, the Father of our Lord Jesus Christ.*

Bibliography: J. A. Fitzmyer, "The Use of Explicit OT Quotations in Qumran Literature and the NT," *NTS* 7 (1960/61) 297-333. For Dupont, "Appel" see the bibliography for 14:1-12.

In distinction from the parallel discussions in the Corinthian conflict we now have thematic reflection on the model of Christ (Dupont, "Appel," 362). The new section, then, supports our interpretation of the concept of faith in 14:23. Usually vv. 1-13 are taken as a single unit (Lagrange; but cf. Dodd; Althaus), although naturally the insertion of the prayer in vv. 5-6 and the problem of Jewish- and Gentile-Christians in vv. 7ff. cannot be overlooked. The latter element speaks for not seeing vv. 7-13 merely as the doxological conclusion of the special exhortation. At the very least a new aspect of the previous theme is connected with it. At the same time it is natural to separate vv. 1-6 from ch. 14 and to see in these verses a reference to the pre-Christian past of those addressed (*contra* Zahn).

The exhortation is continued in a general sense with vv. 1-2 (Sanday and Headlam; Kühl; Lagrange). Verse 3 gives it the backing of a christologically interpreted quotation from Scripture whose force is underscored in v. 4 by reflection on the eschatological actuality of the OT. Verses 5-6 close with a rhetorically skilful prayerful request in liturgical form.

Like 14:13a, vv. 1-2 sum up the theme, and like 14:13b they are directed to the strong who are obviously a majority in the community. If Paul has already ranged himself with them in principle, he now does the same in an emphatically pedagogical way. In distinction from ch. 14 he no longer refers concretely to the conflicts at Rome (*contra* Minear, *Obedience*, 15f.). He thus prepares the way already for the conclusion of the whole. There are strong and weak everywhere, and the strong are under special obligation, as the predicate sharply emphasizes. With greater strength they also have greater responsibility (Leenhardt), while their partner is more in need of help (Ridderbos). According to 1 Cor 12:22ff. this is reason enough to accept them with care.

The apostle's charismatic teaching is in the background. In keeping with it, the differences in the community have been established in order to make possible mutual responsibility for one another and to characterize mutual dependence on one another as necessary. The mode of expression seems to be specifically Pauline; he is not following a given slogan. So βαστάζειν, which, although not used in the LXX, occurs in some other translations (Sanday and Headlam), means not just to tolerate (Barrett) but "to bear a burden" as in Gal 6:2, and ἀσθενήματα makes this clear. The nuance "to bear away" (Schlatter) is not in view. The motif μὴ ἑαυτοῖς ἀρέσκειν, for which the way is prepared since 12:2 and 14:18, and which finds a material basis in 14:7f., is distinctively Pauline. Even if Hellenistic Judaism provides the catchwords, the apostle gives them a Christian edge by putting them in the context of the commandment of love, which is recalled by πλησίον in v. 2. Love has sustaining power. Belonging to the Lord and following him, it does not seek its own benefit and cannot therefore live to please itself. Like the Sermon on the Mount, v. 2 says that pleasing God is incompatible with ignoring one's neighbor. 1 Cor 10:33 offers a variation on this in that Paul seeks to please all men. On the other hand, mere conformism or accommodation is ruled out explicitly in Gal 1:10; 1 Thess 2:4. The dialectic shows that a fundamental motif of Paul's is handled here, which was carefully considered. If a person is not an isolable being, he has neighbors as well as masters and must have a concern for fellowship. This gives rise to the danger that God's good pleasure is lost for the sake of human sympathy or that one neglects one's neighbor out of supposed piety. Renewed reason has to find out whom to please and in what way. The addition, which reminds us of 14:19, clarifies this question. The good again is what is beneficial in the comprehensive sense, and that is interpreted by οἰκοδομή (Lagrange; Ridderbos; Nababan, "Bekenntnis," 108). Living according to God's will, one pleases others by contributing to their edification instead of their inner or outer destruction. Like the community, the individual member must constantly grow, and as the doctrine of the charismata shows with its ἕκαστος ἡμῶν, each must bear his part. Yet the growth and ripening must not be forced.

This admonition is so important for Paul that he derives it christologically. As in Phil 2:5f. Christ is presented as a model, and it should be noted that according to 8:29 this model remains simultaneously the prototype. What goes for him must go for his disciples too, and it is necessary and possible only through him (Nababan, "Bekenntnis," 109). Expositors are often surprised that there is no direct reference to the life and passion of the earthly Jesus. The observation that the quotation from Ps 68:10 LXX confirms the necessity of the conduct of Jesus out of the divine plan of salvation (Schlatter; Dodd) is correct but inadequate. It does not explain why the saying, which is not taken messianically in Judaism as it already is in the primitive community (Billerbeck), is placed on the lips of Jesus himself (indefinite in Michel). As in the original text σέ refers to God (Lagrange; Ridderbos), not the neighbor (Kühl; Lietzmann). But there is no reason to say that the quotation is obscure and infelicitous in the context (Jülicher; Lietzmann). When the pious person of the OT confesses that the reproaches which are directed against God fall on him, he is thinking of the world which rebels against its Lord. Precisely that applies to Jesus, although with a shift of accent compared to Phil 2:5ff. It would fit well to refer here to the suffering Servant of the Lord, and to establish that with the adoption of Isa 57:4 under the catchword βαστάζειν in Matt 8:17. But the quotation itself does not allow such an association, since the issue is not the acceptance of human guilt but the bearing of rebellious blasphemings which determined the whole of the earthly history of Jesus (Nababan, "Bekenntnis," 109).

As in Phil 2:5ff. only one thing is emphasized (Lietzmann). But this is not (contra Schneider, TDNT, V, 240) the unselfish and humble mind of Jesus; it is the bearing of enmity against God (Murray). The incarnation, then, is not in view, but, as in Mark 15:36; Matt 27:34, 48; Luke 23:36; John 2:17; 15:25; 19:29, the passion (Michel; Ridderbos). This shows that Christ, here characterized by the article as the Messiah, "did not please himself." He was the most despised of men, and he had to be this for God's sake. To this extent he is the model and prototype of our behavior, in which the strong must associate with the weak and those in need of help, bearing their shame and exposing themselves to the reproaches of the world thereby. The Lord's saying commands this across the ages, demanding not imitation but conformity with the Christ who is characterized thus (Jervell, Imago, 253; Thüsing, Per Christum, 40).

Verse 4 does not offer another basis for vv. 1-2 (contra Sanday and Headlam; Kühl). Nor is it an interspersed doctrinal statement (Michel). It shows instead why the quotation, understood christologically, is being used in exhortation, and in a way similar to 4:24; 1 Cor 9:10; 10:11. ὅσα already means all Scripture. πάντα is interpolated as in 1 Cor 10:11; 2 Cor 5:17; Gal 4:26 (Lietzmann). The correct reading of the verb is undoubtedly προεγράφη, not προσεγράφη. Scripture documents in advance what takes place eschatologically in the correspondence of [3 primal time and end-time which is familiar from Pauline typology. Thus it points to its destiny to instruct Christ's community in the way it should conduct itself. The underlying hermeneutical view is shared with Judaism (Fitzmyer, "Quotations," 310). Its material justification is beyond question if Christ himself speaks in the quotation. This circumstance makes possible a pedagogical interpretation of the OT which is rare in Paul but which is already proclaimed in 2 Tim 3:16 and which takes on increasing importance later. This leads to the use of the word of Scripture in exhortation. From the lips of its Lord the community receives instruction as to its conduct.

Nevertheless eschatological interpretation is still connected with this in our text, since the quotation forms a basis for hope. This is initially a surprising motif in the context, since thus far there has been no reference to hope. Yet it makes sense if, connected with the prayerful request that follows, it points forward to vv. 7-13, namely, the eschatological uniting of the church of Jews and Gentiles. To be constantly oriented to that is an integral part of Christian hope. If this be so, one cannot accept the limitation of διδασκαλία to the traditional Jewish distinction between good and evil (Rengstorf, *TDNT,* II, 145), which is dubious anyway. More to the point is the remembrance of Hebrews, where the object of teaching is the instruction that God's people should pursue their way in patience and hope, grounded in the consolation which they are given by God. This also rules out the psychologizing observation that only those who hope can uphold the weak (*contra* Hanse, *TDNT,* II, 824).

Paul is addressing the whole community. Upholding the weak is part of building them up. It is not, however, the goal mentioned in v. 6 unless Scripture is merely an aid to moral betterment, as is often taught (cf. Sanday and Headlam). A debatable point is whether ὑπομονή and παράκλησις are both dependent on τῶν γραφῶν in v. 4b (so Zahn; Kühl; Schlatter). διὰ τῆς ὑπομονῆς is better left independent (Lagrange; Michel; H. W. Schmidt). Whereas the first διά denotes an accompanying circumstance, the second is causal, and the repetition of the preposition instead of a conjunctive καί is rhetorical. Scripture gives comfort and leads to patience. With both those who are instructed hold firm their hope. In the context, especially if both prepositional phrases are made dependent on τῶν γραφῶν, παράκλησις can also mean exhortation (Barrett). But in v. 5 the word is obviously used in the sense of "comfort." παράκλησιν ἔχοντες τὰ βιβλία τὰ ἅγια in 1 Macc 12:9 offers an excellent parallel to the phrase as thus understood.

As often, the purpose of the prayerful request in vv. 5f. is to bring the argument to a close. It is carefully constructed in liturgical style and suggests the reading of the letter at worship (Sanday and Headlam; Asmussen). Verse 5 expresses the apostle's concern and v. 6 the hoped-for result. Solemn divine predications, for which there are models in the Psalter (Harder, *Gebet,* 65), are very much in place here. The genitive does not indicate a quality of God but the gift in which he reveals himself. The optative also belongs to the language of prayer. The content of the request is what is enjoined in 12:16a. Beyond all differences the community and its members need a common direction for the sake of peace and mutual upbuilding. The nature of this is defined by κατὰ Χριστὸν Ἰησοῦν, which has in mind not so much the example (the common view) as the will of Kyrios (Michaelis, *TDNT,* IV, 669). The most important criterion of the way taught in Scripture is that it runs under Christ's lordship. This is also the only guarantee of authentic unity. This expresses itself in worship in common and single-minded praise.

ὁμοθυμαδόν, which is a fixed part of the vocabulary of edification in Acts, occurs only here in Paul. It derives originally (Heidland, *TDNT,* V, 186) from the political assembly. "With one voice" is plerophoric. Perhaps it comes from the LXX (Harder, *Gebet,* 57). It presupposes the picture of a chorus. If praise in worship no longer bears witness in this way to daily fellowship, the community cannot exist. In the solemn concluding formula the final member serves a purpose of identification. Beyond everything else that might be said about him, the God who is to be lauded thus is the Father of our Lord Jesus Christ and in that he is noninterchangeable.

4. Acceptance of the Gentiles as a Mark of Christ's Lordship (15:7-13)

7Therefore accept one another as Christ has accepted you to the glory of God. 8For I tell you that Christ became a servant of the circumcision for the sake of God's truth, namely, to confirm the promises to the fathers as valid. 9The Gentiles (may) nevertheless glorify God for his mercy, as it is written, "Therefore I will confess you among the Gentiles and sing praises to your name." 10He also says, "Rejoice, you Gentiles, with his people," 11and again, "Praise the Lord, all you Gentiles, and let all the peoples offer him praise," 12and Isaiah says further, "The shoot of Jesse shall come, he who arises to rule over the Gentiles. In him shall the Gentiles hope." 13May the God of hope fill you with all joy and all peace in believing, so that you may become ever richer in hope by the power of the Holy Spirit.

Bibliography: W. Bieder, *Die Verheissung der Taufe im NT* (1966); F. Hahn, *Das Verständnis der Mission im NT* (WMANT 13; 1963); A. Schulz, *Nachfolgen und Nachamen* (1962).

Most expositors understand the present section as a continuation and the broadest extension of the theme of mutual acceptance which dominates 14:1–15:6. It is now supposed to be applied to the unity of Jewish- and Gentile-Christians, namely, the total church. In fact v. 7a does take up the central motif again, and in v. 7b the thought of v. 3 and the content of the preceding text are repeated, with Jews and Gentiles taking the place of the weak and the strong. This suggests at least that the conflict depicted earlier has something to do with the diverse composition of the church at Rome, or, more precisely, that it involves the relationship between a Jewish-Christian minority and the Gentile-Christian majority, as the investigation of the history-of-religions problem made probable. Both the connection with what precedes and its extension are incontestable.

On the other hand, it is surprising that at this point where the climax seems to be reached the tensions and debates vanish completely from view. The text cannot be oriented to them (*contra* Minear, *Obedience,* 33; correctly Lagrange; Huby; Nababan, "Bekenntnis," 112). In keeping is the change of style from [3 exhortation, still present in v. 7, to the doxology indicated already in v. 6 (Nababan, "Bekenntnis," 7). Finally, what is proclaimed in vv. 9-12 is not the unity of the church but the acceptance of the Gentiles as an eschatological miracle, as already in 9:30; 10:18ff., and in some tension to 11:25ff. (A. Schulz, *Nachfolgen,* 281; Luz, *Geschichtsverständnis,* 390).

The problem present in this has been scarcely noted because the doctrine of justification has not been radically enough seen as the theme of the epistle so that the exhortation is sustained and surrounded by it. The fact that Christ accepts us finds its deepest expression, with cosmic breadth, in the fact that God has had mercy on the Gentiles. When, cutting across everything earthly, the ungodly become children of God, members of the community can no longer be unbridgeably separated by anything, mutual acceptance cannot be resisted, the differences between the strong and the weak are only child's play, and every distinction must contribute to the building up of the whole. Even the apostle's exhortation shows that his ecclesiology is shaped by the doctrine of justification and that this is not just one expression of his soteriology among others.

Not without reason v. 7 is thus regarded as a generalization (Sanday and Headlam). The keyword "to accept" marks the climax of the argument, rising above all else. The secondary clause, which summarizes vv. 1-6 and again adds precision in showing Christ to be the Messiah by the use of the article, speaks less of the model than of the bringer of salvation. For καθώς is not so much comparative here (Dupont, *Gnosis*, 55) as an indication of reason (Nababan, "Bekenntnis," 112). Otherwise the prepositional phrase at the end would be redundant, whereas it characterizes what follows as eschatological grace. The better-attested ὑμᾶς is to be preferred, especially as the change to ἡμᾶς can be explained by the doxological context (Leenhardt). The λέγω γάρ does not introduce an additional argument (*contra* Murray) but resumes Paul's proclamation in a solemn declaration (BAGD, 469b) and thus comes close to the sense of "confess."

The sentence construction of vv. 8-9 is rough. This is not because the style of the apostle is clumsy but because he has a double purpose, wanting to emphasize that grace has been imparted to all and at the same time to stress, as often in the epistle, the priority of the Jews (though cf. J. Knox). If v. 9a is made dependent on the verb in v. 8a (e.g., Lagrange) we have a clear parallelism, but v. 8b must then be regarded as an elucidating parenthesis (Zeller, *Juden*, 219f.). The normal procedure, then, is to relate the two infinitives in vv. 8b and 9a to εἰς τό. This emphasizes the stylistic break but also the distinction between the phrases ὑπὲρ ἀληθείας and ὑπὲρ ἐλέους, which is obviously intended in the context. Even in wording the statement in v. 8a is unusual and definitely formal. References to Mark 10:45 (Michel; Ridderbos) or 2 Cor 3:6 are forced, since the idea of sacrifice does not determine our passage, nor are Christ and the apostle comparable in this context. More natural is the idea that διάκονος refers to the earthly work of Jesus, corresponding to the context and the tradition in John 13 (H. W. Schmidt). The perfect γεγενῆσθαι is in this case more suitable than the variant aorist (*contra* Zahn). It naturally relates to the result, not the continuation of the event (Ridderbos). The explanation drawn from Gal 4:4 that Christ has fulfilled the requirements of the law is misleading (*contra* Sanday and Headlam). The abstract περιτομή stands for the concrete: the circumcised.

Everything depends on the conclusion. Jesus manifested himself on earth as the servant of the Jewish people. He had to do so for the sake of God's ἀλήθεια, i.e., his covenant faithfulness as in 3:4 (Nababan, "Bekenntnis," 113f.), which according to the explanation in the final clause could not allow the promises to fall. What was promised to the patriarchs (though cf. H. W. Schmidt) has been fulfilled in the sending of the Son. βεβαιοῦν has also here a legal sense embracing confirmation and fulfilment (BAGD, 138b; Schlier, *TDNT,* I, 602).

Not in any sense "ornamentally" (Lietzmann; *contra* Barrett) but in adoption of 11:30f. the work on the Gentiles is set in contrast to that. It has its basis in sheer mercy and is to be extolled as such, since it has taken place on those who were not a people and who did not have Israel's promises. Although it is not clearly expressed, one may infer from the antithesis to v. 8a that the reference here is to the work of the exalted Christ. The calling of the Gentiles goes with the state of exaltation (Bengel; cf. also Zeller, *Juden*, 220). From the standpoint of salvation history we again have ἔλεος for χάρις. We are not to think in terms of parallelism (*contra* Michel), as the Jewish phrase grace and truth might suggest. A surpassing of what was said is present: covenant faithfulness is cosmically extended.

The collection of quotations, which is not disruptive and merely directed pedagogically to the Gentiles (*contra* Jülicher), underlines with rhetorical skill (Leenhardt) such a distinction and the importance of v. 9. Paul mentioned his essential concern before in v. 8a almost as a premise in order to uphold the "firstborn right" of the Jews in relation to the salvation event. Nevertheless the acceptance of the Gentiles is for him the decisive eschatological event. Hence the keyword ἔθνη binds the quotations together. The correct rabbinic combining of sayings from the Torah, Writings, and Prophets might have been used in the missionary preaching of Jewish-Christians (Michel, *Bibel*, 54) and it may have played a role in florilegia. In spite of the same keyword, however, it must here be ascribed to the apostle himself (Michel, *Bibel*, 87), since obviously it intentionally draws ever wider circles.

The individual quotations are taken almost word for word from the LXX. It is no accident that Ps 17:50 or 2 Sam 22:50 leads off, although without the address κύριε. Only if the word stood in isolation could it be taken as no more than a Scripture proof for v. 9a. The quotations that follow show that the subject of the saying here is an individual. It should be mentioned if David is meant as the author of the psalm (Leenhardt) or, as the majority think, Christ is meant, to say nothing of the leader in worship (Michel; Bieder, *Verheissung*, 240). The statement probably is to be related back to λέγω γάρ. If so, the apostle to the Gentiles finds his own task delineated in Scripture and the object of exhomologesis is the exalted Christ (Nababan, "Bekenntnis," 119, 121). This, however, does not explain why the address of the psalm is omitted, although no other interpretation can offer any cogent grounds for this either.

Verse 10 quotes a line from Deut 32:43. If Gentiles are summoned thereby to unite with Israel in eschatological praise to God, the reference can be only to Gentile-Christians who, according to 11:17ff., have been grafted into the people of God and integrated with Jewish-Christians to form with them the eschatological community. εὐφραίνειν can have a cultic or eschatological sense but is in any case emphatic (cf. Bultmann, *TDNT*, II, 774), and a reference to Christian worship lies at hand here. In this the apostolic proclamation finds a joyful response. The introductory καὶ πάλιν is to be translated "furthermore" (BAGD, 606-607). An Aramaic equivalent proves its traditional character (Michel, *Bibel*, 72).

In v. 11 Ps 116:1 is slightly altered. The address is put before the object in the first line, the second line is attached by καί, and the imperative becomes a jussive. The climax in relation to what precedes emerges only when ἔθνη still means Gentile-Christians but λαοί already means the nations (Nababan, "Bekenntnis," 111). The praise of Christian worship becomes universal.

The final quotation from Isa 11:10 follows the LXX, which is here a paraphrase of the original text. For the opening indication of time Paul has no application since he is not concerned with the future but with the epiphany of the shoot of David which has already taken place and is indicated by ἔσται (cf. on this sense BAGD, 223b). ἀνιστάμενος also speaks of this. It is to be interpreted as a solemn predicate of Christ referring to him who has been raised again and exalted. The accent is on the infinitive. Christ has not just come to win the Gentiles for the community. He intends to rule over the cosmos (Nababan, "Bekenntnis," 122) and for this reason, as in 8:20, he is an object of hope for all creation, which is represented by the peoples. The point of the play on the key-word ἔθνη is that those who are ungodly in Jewish eyes, almost in contrast with the wisdom psalm from Qumran Cave 11 (Hengel, *Judaism*, I, 176f.), already share in part in the praise and otherwise are called to do so, and both are based on the universal lordship of Christ. Expressed here is Paul's message of justification by faith, which coincides with the revelation of the righteousness of God in the rule of Christ. The OT foreshadowed this message. The recipients of the epistle must recognize this agreement with Scripture. An apology could hardly have a more magnificent conclusion. Here the same self-understanding comes to light as in chs. 9–11. With his teaching the apostle fulfils eschatologically the will of God proclaimed in Scripture.

The prayerful request in v. 13 is parallel to that in vv. 5f. Yet one cannot speak of tautology (Lietzmann). To be sure, familiar themes, which have been discussed already, do recur. Salvation is again characterized as joy and peace which can come to expression in various ways, so that already for that reason it is a mistake to speak only of peace of soul (*contra* Foerster, *TDNT*, II, 412, 417). Typical in such a context are πληρῶσαι, which poor readings replace by πληρο-φορῆσαι, and the emphatically intensifying περισσεύειν. The phrase ἐν δυνάμει πνεύματος ἁγίου, which is not to be taken locally (*contra* Grundmann, *Kraft*, 112) but instrumentally, means the power which inspires doxology and shapes the course of Christian life. A variation appears in outline if in spite of Western readings, which broke the plerophory of successive infinitives, ἐν τῷ πιστεύειν be regarded as original (though cf. Pallis; Nababan, "Bekenntnis," 123). The way of the community has to be trodden in faith and cannot be bypassed by any doxology.

Even more important is the singular divine predication "the God of hope," which is reflected in περισσεύειν ἐν τῇ ἐλπίδι. In context this is not empty rhetoric if vv. 9-12 are rightly understood and everything climaxes in the final line of v. 12 to which the divine predication and the second infinitive in v. 13 for their part relate. Only hope does justice to this proclamation when we look away from liturgy to everyday life. Whereas vv. 5f. dealt with the united character of the community manifested in worship, the point now is that the cosmic goal of redemption is not to be forgotten for a single moment and that the burdens and necessities of daily life are to remain against this background. That is possible only in the power of the Spirit. As this section goes beyond the previous one, the same is true of v. 13 in relation to vv. 5f. This conclusion of the special exhortation forms a transition to the last part of the epistle.

VII. Conclusion (15:14-33)

The conclusion of the epistle forms a self-contained unity. If it is to be split into sections for the sake of clarity one may distinguish these sections: vv. 14-21 characterize Paul's work, vv. 22-29 explain motivations for the planned visit to Rome, and vv. 30-33 express the need for intercession.

A. The Apostle's Guiding Principle and the Standing of His Work (15:14-21)

[14]*As concerns my personal attitude to you, my brethren, I am convinced that you are full of good opinions, rich in all knowledge, and able to teach one another. [15]On some points, however, I have written you quite boldly as one who would remind you of what you know in virtue of the grace which God has given me. [16]For I have the task of being an authorized minister of Jesus Christ to the Gentiles by delivering the gospel of God as a priest so that they may be presented as a pleasing sacrifice sanctified in the Holy Spirit. [17]I thus have (reason) for boasting in Christ Jesus before God. [18]For I will not venture to refer to anything apart from what Christ has done through me to bring the Gentiles to obedience, in word and deed, [19]with the power of wonders and signs, in the power of the Spirit. Thus from Jerusalem in a sweep even to Illyricum I have been able to bring the gospel of Christ to completion. [20]I have sought my honor in preaching where Christ has not yet been named so as not to build on another's foundation. [21]Instead (I have done) as it is written, "They shall see who have never been told of him, and those who have not heard shall understand."*

Bibliography: P. Brunner, "Zur Lehre vom Gottesdienst," *Leiturgia*, I (ed. K. F. Müller; 1954) 83-364; A.-M. Denis, "La fonction apostolique et la liturgie nouvelle en esprit," *RSPT* 42 (1958) 401-436, 617-656; R. W. Funk, "The Apostolic Parousia: Form and Significance," *Christian History and Interpretation: Studies Presented to John Knox* (ed. W. R. Farmer *et al.*; 1967) 249-268; L. Gaugusch, "Untersuchungen zum Römerbrief. Der Epilog (15,14-16, 27)," *BZ* 24 (1938/39) 164-184, 252-266; A. S. Geyser, "Un essai d'explication de Rom XV, 19," *NTS* 6 (1959/60) 156-59; F. Hahn, *Das Verständnis der Mission im NT* (WMANT 13; 1963); M. Hengel, "Die Ursprünge der christlichen Mission," *NTS* 18 (1971/72) 15-38; J. Knox, "Romans XV, 14-33 and Paul's Conception of Apostolic Mission," *JBL* 83 (1964) 1-11; W. Pesch, "Zu Texten des NT über das Priestertum der Getauften," *Verborum Veritas. Festschrift für Gustav Stählin zum 70. Geburtstag* (ed. O. Böcher and K. Haacker; 1970)

303-315; H. Schelkle, "Der Apostel als Priester," *TQ* 136 (1956) 257-283; H. Schlier, "Die 'Liturgie' des apostolischen Evangeliums (Röm 15, 41-21)," *Martyria, Leiturgia, Diakonia. Festschrift für Hermann Volk zum 65. Geburtstag* (ed. O. Semmelroth; 1968) 247-259; F. Stolz, "Zeichen und Wunder. Die prophetische Legitimation und ihre Geschichte," *ZTK* 69 (1972) 125-144; E. Trocmé, "L'Épître aux Romains et la méthode missionaire de l'apôtre Paul," *NTS* 7 (1960/61) 148-153; C. Wiéner, "'Ιερουργεῖν (Rm 15, 16)," *Stud.Paul.Congr.,* II, 399-404; K. Weiss, "Paulus—Priester der christlichen Kultgemeinde," *TLZ* 79 (1954) 355-364.

This part of the epistle undoubtedly returns to the concern of the proem in 1:8-15 although without being a simple parallel to this (*contra* Nababan, "Bekenntnis," 125). It is much too formal to speak in terms of a literary "parenthesis" (*contra* Michel, *et al.*). Then it would be easy to detach what is contained and more than boldly allow it to be a teaching model preconceived by the apostle for young churches breaking away from the synagogue—a model furnished with a personal framework and dispatched as needed, in this case to Rome (Trocmé, "Méthode," 148 and with critical variations Funk, "Parousia," 268). The advance as compared with the obscurities, reservations, and retractions of the proem is not only expressed in the fact that Paul now sets forth his purposes much more concretely, explicitly, and definitely. An apologetic tendency now emerges undisguised, which compelled him to write what from this perspective is in some respects at least a kind of account of his preaching and which thus reflects earlier experiences and insights. Although the letter, even if under a limiting perspective and antithetical, presents an almost complete summary of Paul's theology, it remains, like the apostle's other writings, a document of a particular situation and cannot be pressed into the mold of teaching tractate. So long as the theology had not been sketched and focused, the proem could offer only relatively vague indications, but now these are replaced by precise statements and conceptions. Usually the high diplomacy which has gone into the construction of our epistle is not perceived. Paul carefully guards against falling into the house as soon as the door opens. For various reasons he needed Rome's help in his work, and he thus thought it good even without some pressing occasion to acquaint this unknown congregation with his preaching and work before giving his concern a clear contour. To that extent the whole epistle prepares the way for this "epilogue."

If this is so, however, the conclusion must not be isolated from the lengthy approach toward it, nor the apostle's theology reduced to a formula from this perspective which is not in keeping with it. With some justification it may be said that mission is the setting in life (*Sitz im Leben*) of this theology (Hengel, "Ursprünge," 18), although the fragments which have come down to us are more concerned with the problems of the young churches and the conflicts with adversaries emerging in them. Nor may it be denied that in the conclusion we see something of the specific missionary "strategy" of Paul (E. Brunner; Hengel, "Ursprünge," 171; Zeller, *Juden,* 74ff.), although the actualities of quite uncertain results and unattained and perhaps unattainable goals might cause us to ask whether such a "strategy" can be spared being characterized as largely illusionary. At any rate the epistle is neither a simple teaching tractate nor in language, argument, and theological level centrally a mission document, although it was written under the premise and with a view to world mission and presupposes concrete aims in this direction. The task of interpreting what follows consists in making the relation between the two aspects understandable without taking from one or the other its due importance.

Verses 14f. are undisguisedly wooing the readers (Barrett; Zeller, *Juden*, 65f.). There is no reason (*contra* Lagrange) to question the apostle's sincerity even if rhetoric and a certain amount of flattery are observed in v. 14 (Huby), as in 1 Cor 1:4ff. The entire exhortation would have been unnecessary if what is said were meant literally (Lietzmann). In a way that has seldom been repeated in church history, Paul recognizes the spiritual independence of the congregation, and he does this so emphatically that there can be no mistaking his intention. For this reason he uses the verb πέπεισμαι with the following address. He gives added emphasis with the phrases καὶ αὐτὸς ἐγώ ("I for my part") and καὶ αὐτοί ("you yourselves without the cooperation of others"), and finally heaps up praises. This is no mere matter of kind words (Althaus; J. Knox) or courteous pedagogics (Lietzmann; H. W. Schmidt; Schumacher, *Letzte Kapitel*, 38) or modesty, which is often, and incorrectly, attributed to Paul (Michel; Ridderbos). An essential element is missed if it is overlooked that Paul can use charm, anger, irony, or any other stylistic possibilities to win the churches. He does it here with a carefully constructed sentence which is divided up by the adjective μεστοί and the participles πεπληρωμένοι and δυνάμενοι and which culminates in the generous recognition of the presence of knowledge in all its variety.

Not even individual members of primitive Christianity were unblemished, not needing outside teaching and admonition (*contra* Schlatter; Lagrange). In a Hellenistic term taken from the LXX (Grundmann, *TDNT*, I, 18) ἀγαθωσύνη is ascribed to the community, weakened to ἀγάπη in unimportant variants (Lietzmann). This does not have the abstract sense of correct moral conduct (*contra* Zahn; Kühl), or the concrete sense of good will (Leenhardt; Ridderbos), nor does it mean kindness (the common view), but the uprightness (Michel; Schlier, "Liturgie," 247) which in contrast to malice expresses itself in mutual open-mindedness. With it is associated γνῶσις, which is not theoretical knowledge, nor merely knowledge which aims at edification (*contra* Bultmann, *TDNT*, I, 708; Ridderbos); rather it is insight into salvation history (Michel). This is the basis of admonition. For νουθετεῖν is more than pastoral influencing of the disposition and will (*contra* Behm, *TDNT*, IV, 1022). As in 1 Cor 4:14; 1 Thess 5:12, 14 it is correction or admonition (Delling, *TDNT*, VI, 291; Michel). The poorly attested reading ἄλλους weakens ἀλλήλους (*contra* Zahn).

Verse 15 is to be understood wholly against the background of these compliments. While τολμηρότερον is well attested, the adverb is to be preferred, since ἔγραψα relates to the whole epistle. The comparative (*contra* Zahn) does not have a superlative sense; it means "with some boldness." ἀπὸ μέρους adds a further restriction: not everywhere but in some places (though cf. Lagrange; Schumacher, *Letzte Kapitel*, 38; Gaugusch, "Untersuchungen," 165). There is no reason to think in terms of enthusiastic daring (*contra* Michel). In view of the situation in Rome which has aroused his praise, Paul says it is bold to have written so explicit and theological an epistle, and he again tries to avert any suspicion of attempted meddling or domineering. His apology reaches its high point when he says that he is simply reminding them of what they already know, adopting an occasionally used rhetorical *topos* (BAGD, 282b). In both the Jewish and the Greek world ἐπαναμιμνῄσκειν has almost the technical sense of repeating a tradition (Michel; H. W. Schmidt), and it is not to be limited to the exhortation (correctly Schlier, "Liturgie," 247; but cf. Zeller, *Juden,* 66; Bjerkelund, *Parakalô,* 159). Undoubtedly the apostle believed that he could take his doctrine of justification from the OT, in which it was indeed the main theme. On the other hand, it is no less incontestable that this message with its focus on faith alone apart from law was and remained in primitive Christianity in the position of a theological outsider and that it represents a provocation which has not found total acceptance even to this day. It testifies to great audacity, then, to use the word "remember" in relation to it (cautiously also Eichholz, *Paulus,* 125) and to maintain at the end of v. 14 that the community already had knowledge of the things said in the epistle (cf. F. C. Baur, *Paul,* 371ff.). There must have been material reasons why Paul carried his wooing to this outer limit of what is permissible. In fact he is preparing the ground for his visit and his further plans, although this puts him in the difficulty which may be seen already in the hedging of 1:11ff. He both wants to and must give an account of his preaching, but he would like to avoid giving offense or destroying confidence.

It is no accident that suddenly and sharply, as in 1:15, he stops excusing himself and insists on his authority. With the fixed formula of 1:15; 12:3, 6 he appeals to the specific grace that he has been given as the apostle to the Gentiles (Zahn; Kühl; Lietzmann), and he now includes Rome too in the sphere of his claim to authority (Schlier, "Liturgie," 258). διὰ τὴν χάριν does not mean purpose (*contra* Zahn; H. W. Schmidt) and it relates, not to the final clause that follows (*contra* Nababan, "Bekenntnis," 126), but to the preceding participle (BAGD, 181a). It thus means "in virtue of."

The rest of the section shows that vv. 14f. are a conciliatory introduction to the claim that is now raised. Verse 16 expresses this with a self-predication which has to be called highly unusual, although it appears in weaker form in Phil 2:17 and finds a parallel in 2 Cor 2:14-17; 10:4-6. The problem of the verse is sidelined if attention is focused primarily, as it mostly is, on the unquestionably liturgical vocabulary. Taken alone λειτουργός can also have the secular sense of an office-bearer. But ἱερουργεῖν undoubtedly has a cultic sense: to fulfil a priestly ministry (cf. Wiener's article; Lietzmann; Michel; Schlier, "Liturgie," 249ff.). This gives sacral significance to the noun too (*contra* Zahn). Whereas the apostle applies the thought of 12:1f. to himself when in Phil 2:17 he solemnly calls himself an offering on the altar of the common faith, here he is calling himself the priest of the Messiah Jesus to the whole of the Gentile world. The prepositional phrase rules out any talk of a "cultic community" (K. Weiss, "Paulus," 355ff.), which could hardly be spoken of in cosmic breadth. The singular formula is also intolerably generalized if the mission as such is seen (Nababan, "Bekenntnis," 7) as a cultic event or if one speaks of the ongoing liturgy of Christians (Denis, "Fonction," 403ff., 650ff.) as the true cultus established by the apostle in comparison with the Jewish cultus.

In reality the passage deals neither with the community nor the life of its members nor mission itself but solely with the delegated, authorized, and validated mandate of the apostle to the Gentiles (Schlier, "Liturgie," 251f.). Unlike his modern and romanticizing expositors, Paul in styling himself the priest of the Messiah is not stressing the cultic dimension as such. He does not regard the gospel (*contra* Schniewind, Friedrich, *TDNT*, II, 733; Denis, "Fonction," 656) as a cultic institution. Generally, then, he avoids a sacral understanding of his ministry (Pesch, "Priestertum," 314; Nababan, "Bekenntnis," 128; F. Hahn, *Verständnis der Mission*, 93; though cf. P. Brunner, "Gottesdienst," 103f.). As already in 12:1f. cultic terms and motifs are here used in a transferred eschatological sense (Michel; Schlier, "Liturgie," 248). The rest of the verse makes this plain. As a priest the apostle brings and administers not merely the apostolic tradition (*contra* Denis, "Fonction," 403) but the gospel of God, just as variants on 4 Macc 7:8 offer a similar transferred statement in relation to the Torah. The aim is the offering of the Gentile world as a sacrifice consecrated in the Holy Spirit and consequently as a pleasing sacrifice.

The phrase ἡ προσφορὰ τῶν ἐθνῶν does not refer to the self-offering of Christians which the apostle brings about (*contra* Denis, "Fonction," 405f.; Asmussen; Ridderbos). The genitive is epexegetical; the Gentile world itself is the offering. The notion is apocalyptic and corresponds to 11:11ff. In sharp contrast to the necessary, apologetic introduction Paul's self-understanding now interprets the grace and task which he personally has been given. In the last resort his metaphor of the priest of the Messiah is interchangeable with that of the cosmic conqueror (cf. 2 Cor 10:4ff.). Either way the reference is to the singular mandate and worldwide function of the apostle to the Gentiles who places the ungodly at the feet of his Lord and sets them in his triumphant procession.

Paul realizes how far he has gone but he does not intend to draw back (v. 17). He makes no attempt to defend himself against a charge of arrogance (Kühl). καύχησις can relate either to the act (Bultmann, *TDNT*, III, 649; Lagrange; Huby) or its object (cf. 2 Cor 1:12) (Michel). If P⁴⁶ ℵ A *et al.* leave out the article, which replaces a demonstrative referring back to v. 16, this is a simplification which can hardly be original (Lagrange *contra* Sanday and Headlam). τὰ πρὸς τὸν θεόν, as in Heb 2:17; 5:1, is adverbial (BDF, §160): valid before God. The statement is not stamped by affable pride over his successful life (Gaugusch, "Untersuchungen," 166f.). The faithful servant of the Lord can be proud to the extent that his work points to the gift which he has been allotted in Christ and the task which is performed in the strength of grace.

Verse 18 elucidates rather than adding something (H. W. Schmidt *contra* Michel). It combines two thoughts (Lietzmann; Barrett). The apostle can speak only of Christ's work through him, and apart from this he would not dare say anything. τολμᾶν does not denote here, as in 2 Cor 10:2, 12; 11:21, the envisioned presumption of the pneumatic. The future expresses greater reserve than the present (Lagrange). As Paul balances up his work (Nababan, "Bekenntnis," 125), λαλεῖν has almost the sense "to give an account" (though cf. Michel).

The dialectic of the catchword καύχησις also determines vv. 18-19. Paul looks back on extraordinary success, which with ὑπακοὴ ἐθνῶν presupposes the situation of 11:11ff. He is not just thinking of individuals who have been won but, bold as this might seem, of the Gentile world and its praise (vv. 9-12). In this world the obedience of Christ has been set up. This is identical with acceptance of the gospel and comes to expression in the exhomologesis befitting an epiphany. On the other hand, it is underscored that only Christ present in his instrument could effect his lordship among the peoples, so that the eschatological event is not due to the person of Paul. Just because this is self-evident to Paul he emphasizes the fact that he is an effective instrument in virtue of the grace which he has been given.

Rhetorically, then, two double phrases follow which are combined in the conclusion. The connection of word and work, which is found also in 2 Cor 10:11; 2 Thess 2:17, corresponds to the Greek distinction between speech and action. It is pointed here to the mighty works which accompany preaching, of which Heb 2:4 also speaks. Hence it is followed by the stereotyped Jewish phrase "wonders and signs," which cannot be differentiated and which designate the experience of the divine presence in mighty eschatological acts (for background material cf. Stolz, "Zeichen," 125ff., 144; Rengstorf, *TDNT*, VII, 208f., 216f., 221).

ἐν δυνάμει πνεύματος sums up with an epexegetical genitive, asserting almost tautologically the miraculous power of the exalted Lord (Grundmann, *TDNT*, II, 311). There is no point in recalling here that on the Jewish view miraculous power could be ascribed to rabbis (Billerbeck). The background is a Christian variation of the concept of the θεῖος ἀνήρ familiar to us from the Gospels and Acts. This allows the enthusiasts at Corinth to demand the "signs of an apostle" (2 Cor 12:12). Paul can claim such a legitimation in answer to his opponents there, but in so doing he relativizes it. Here, however, he imposes no restrictions. A different front is involved. He is not bringing enthusiasts back to earth or summoning them to discipleship. He is defending his demonstrated and confirmed authority to a strange congregation which may be partly suspicious. For this purpose the current idea of apostolic power is presented without reservation. The addition of ἁγίου or θεοῦ in important readings is easier to understand than the B text, which simply has πνεύματος (Zahn; Kühl; H. W. Schmidt; undecided Lietzmann), especially as the variants argue for secondary additions.

Verse 19b with an introductory ὥστε explains the success of the apostle's activity in terms of the gift which he has been given. What v. 16 calls God's gospel with a genitive of agent is now called Christ's gospel with an objective genitive. The rare phrase "to fulfil or complete the gospel" (cf. on this Friedrich, *TDNT*, II, 731 and the alternative interpretation by Delling in *TDNT*, VI, 297; Schlier, "Liturgie," 255) is to be explained in the light of the indication of area. Since this does not occur in Col 1:25, we have there no true parallel. As the world is permeated by the gospel, the gospel itself comes to fulfilment. It is of the essence of the gospel that it is not just proclaimed but that it fashions an earthly sphere of validity for the lordship of Christ. κύκλῳ, a dative of place used adverbially, does not, as formerly was occasionally assumed, describe broadening circles around Jerusalem but the wide arc between two specified points (BAGD, 457a and most commentators).

In spite of the indications in Acts, Galatians 1 seems to rule out any preaching by Paul in Jerusalem (Geyser, "Essai," 157). We have no information about his preaching in Illyricum on the Macedonian border. The references to places do not appear to be meant inclusively. They indicate the limits of missionary activity (though cf. Kühl; Schlatter; hypothetically Munck, *Salvation*, 52). The apostle is not thinking of individual churches but, in accordance with his apocalyptic approach (Lietzmann; Althaus), of peoples and lands (e.g., Schumacher, *Letzte Kapitel*, 41; Bornkamm, *Paul*, 53f.). The eastern part of the empire is defined by Jerusalem on the one hand as the salvation-historical center of the world and the starting point of the gospel, and by the end of the Via Aegnatia on the other hand. It has often been asked why Egypt particularly is not mentioned too. No answer can be given except with the problematic opinion that it belongs to the sphere of the Palestinian mission. Even if it is assumed that Paul himself is content to establish symbolic centers from which Christianity will develop independently, the statement is an enormous exaggeration when measured by geographical reality (Jülicher; Pallis; Eichholz, *Paulus*, 24f.; Zeller, *Juden*, 68). It is understandable only on the basic premise that the apostle views his work as preparatory for the imminent parousia (Sass, *Apostelamt*, 131; Schoeps, *Paul*, 229).

There results from this what in v. 20 he provocatively calls his ambition, or in the thematic explanation in 2 Cor 10:13ff. his "canon," namely, the law and limit of his commission. In spite of eminent witnesses the participle φιλοτιμούμενον is to be preferred as the more difficult reading. Materially it is dependent on v. 19b. The verse is not a delimitation (*contra* Sanday and Headlam; Jülicher; Lietzmann). As a transition to the plans announced in vv. 22ff. (Lagrange), it continues Paul's καύχησις from a new angle, which is not to be toned down (as in H. W. Schmidt).

No reason exists to link οὕτως δέ directly with the infinitive or to have the antithesis οὐχ ὅπου– ἀλλὰ καθώς appositionally follow this (*contra* Zahn; Kühl; Lagrange; Michel; Ridderbos). The participle has its own weight, and ἀλλὰ καθώς introduces the quotation in the independent statement in v. 21. The "point of honor" of acting in accordance with a given demand is mentioned also in 2 Cor 5:9; 1 Thess 4:11. As each Christian according to 12:3 has his own measure and ought to observe the valid criteria for it, the apostle is similarly bound.

Verse 20b establishes subjectively what v. 21 will objectively derive from Scripture, which Paul again quite concretely relates to his own commission. The solemn phrase "to name Christ with his name" means to proclaim the Kyrios and possibly comes from the vocabulary of mission. The thought is a variation of the explanation of 1 Cor 3:10ff. If there Christ is called the only foundation for all Christian work, a clear distinction is also made between the one who plants and the one who waters, and thus the one who founds a church is sharply distinguished from those who succeed him. The variation in relation to our passage, which is, of course, much sharper, is not as important as it seems at first sight. Paul is differentiating his work from that of other missionaries. He is not building on foundations laid by them. He finds his instructions for this in Isa 52:15, which the LXX already, unlike the original, relates to the Gentiles. The idea of the Servant of the Lord is not in view and there is nothing to suggest that the apostle is adopting such a role (*contra* Jeremias, *TDNT*, V, 708; Gaugler; Leenhardt). But the eschatological promise comes to fulfilment in the present proclamation of the gospel (Nababan, "Bekenntnis," 133) and constitutes the Pauline "canon" according to which his task is only to work as a missionary where others have not yet come.

Only an apocalyptic self-understanding can find the criterion of one's own action prefigured in Scripture in such a way that its prophecy is directed personally to the apostle and makes him the executor and therefore the predestined instrument of salvation history. In this regard a historicist approach will unavoidably lead to problems. These will be dealt with explicitly in the next section.

B. The Motivations for the Journey to Rome and the Detour to Jerusalem (15:22-29)

²²This is why I have been hindered so often from coming to you. ²³But now I have no longer any room for work in these regions, and for a long time I have had a desire to come to you. ²⁴I plan to journey to Spain and I hope that on the way I will see you and be helped on my way there by you when I have in some measure satisfied (my hope) of you. ²⁵At the moment, however, I am going to Jerusalem to minister to the saints. ²⁶For Macedonia and Achaia have resolved to send a contribution of solidarity to the poor among the saints in Jerusalem. ²⁷They are pleased to do this and they also owe it. For if the Gentiles have come to share in their spiritual blessings, they are under obligation in return to give support in physical things. ²⁸When I have completed this, and officially delivered this fruit to them, I can go by way of you to Spain. ²⁹And I know that when I come to you, I shall come with all the fulness of the blessing of Christ.

[3

Bibliography: E. Barnikol, *Römer 15. Letzte Reiseziele des Paulus: Jerusalem, Rom und Antiochien. Forschungen zur Entstehung des Urchristentums, des NT und der Kirche,* IV (1931); H. W. Bartsch, "Die Kollekte des Paulus," *Kirche in der Zeit* 20 (1965) 555f.; idem, "Die historische Situation des Römerbriefes," *SE,* IV (1968) 281-291; idem, "Die Empfänger des Römerbriefes," *ST* 25 (1971) 81-89; idem, ". . . wenn ich ihnen diese Frucht versiegelt habe. Röm 15, 28," *ZNW* 63 (1972) 95-107; W. Bieder, "Gebetswirklichkeit und Gebetsmöglichkeit bei Paulus," *TZ* 4 (1948) 22-40; G. Bornkamm, "The Letter to the Romans as Paul's Last Will and Testament," *Romans Debate,* 17-31; F. X. Dölger, "Zu σφραγίζεσθαι Rom 15, 28," *Antike und Christentum* 4 (1934) 280; D. Georgi, *Die Geschichte der Kollekte des Paulus für Jerusalem* (1965); F. Hahn, *Das Verständnis der Mission im NT* (WMANT 13; 1963); G. Harder, "Der konkrete Anlass des Römerbriefes," *Theologia Viatorum* 6 (1954/58) 13-24; K. Holl, "Der Kirchenbegriff des Paulus in seinem Verhältnis zu dem der Urgemeinde," *Gesammelte Aufsätze zur Kirchengeschichte,* II (1928) 44-67; J. Jervell, "The Letter to Jerusalem," *Romans Debate,* 61-74; G. V. Jourdan, "Κοινωνία in 1 Corinthians 10:16," *JBL* 67 (1948) 111-124; L. Keck, "The Poor among the Saints in the NT," *ZNW* 56 (1965) 100-129; idem, "The Poor among the Saints in Jewish Christianity and Qumran," *ZNW* 57 (1966) 54-78; G. Klein, "Paul's Purpose in Writing the Epistle to the Romans," *Romans Debate,* 32-49; T. W. Manson, "St. Paul's Letter to the Romans—and Others," *Studies,* 225-241 (= *Romans Debate,* 1-16); K. F. Nickle, *The Collection* (SBT 48; 1966); B. Noack, "Current and Backwater in the Epistle to the Romans," *ST* 19 (1965) 155-166; H. Preisker, "Das historische Problem des Römerbriefes," *Wissenschaftliche Zeitschrift der Friedrich-Schiller-Universität Jena/Thüringen* 2 (1952/53), Geisteswissenschaftliche Reihe, I, 25-30; L. Radermacher, "σφραγίζεσθαι Rom 15, 28," *ZNW* 32 (1933) 87-89; K. H. Rengstorf, "Paulus und die älteste römische Christenheit," *SE,* II (1964) 447-464; A. Roosen, "Le genre littéraire de l'Épître aux Romains," *SE,* II (1964) 465-472; H. Seesemann, *Der Begriff κοινωνία im NT* (BZNW 14; 1933); M. J. Suggs, "The Word is Near You: Romans 10:6-10 within the Purpose of the Letter," *Christian History and Interpretation: Studies Presented to John Knox* (ed. W. Farmer *et al.*; 1967) 289-312; A. Suhl, "Der konkrete

Anlass des Römerbriefes," *Kairos*, N.F. (1971) 119-130; T. M. Taylor, "The Place of Origin of Romans," *JBL* 67 (1948) 281-295; W. Wiefel, "The Jewish Community in Ancient Rome and the Origins of Roman Christianity," *Romans Debate*, 100-119. For Trocmé, "Méthode" see the bibliography for 15:14-21.

Whereas 1:13 does not explain why Paul has not yet made his journey to Rome, he now tells us this with a διό which refers back to vv. 20f. (cf. Noack, "Current," 160f.). So long as he met with obstacles in the Eastern Mediterranean he could not turn to the west, for which from the beginning he regarded Rome as the starting point. Common in Greek but singular in the NT, τὰ πολλά means "frequently" and almost "regularly." While well attested, πολλάκις is a softening emendation. ἔχω in v. 23b and the replacement of ἱκανῶν ἐτῶν by πολλῶν are assimilations to a later stylistic sensitivity. Verse 23a explains that the hindrances are now at an end. τόπον ἔχειν, used in a transferred sense, is a fixed phrase (Koester, *TDNT*, VIII, 205f.). κλίματα refers to the present field of mission. No matter how far Paul went on his journeys the statement can hardly be correct historically (*contra* Schumacher, *Letzte Kapitel*, 43), and it is psychologically impossible apart from his basic apocalyptic conception. It sets us before the riddle of a person and the task perceived by him, which we cannot integrate into our own historical picture. If exegetes skip by it lightly, or with questionable observations, they irresponsibly ignore Paul's theology as a whole and try to normalize its dark background. At any rate, what here is called a longing wish is in fact an integrating factor in the apostle's program from the very outset, even if the beginning can be dated only hypothetically.

After a first and perhaps relatively unsuccessful attempt to do missionary work on his own in Arabia, in service of the Antioch church and even at the Apostolic Council Paul still stood under the shadow of Barnabas. The conflict with Peter and the representatives of James seems to have separated him from Barnabas and Antioch too. It seems also to have been a turning point leading to a new self-understanding and to his world mission, which from the very beginning included plans for the west. Incessant crises in his churches were obstacles to this final goal, but now the time had come.

Verse 24 shows that Rome is viewed only as a stage on the way and a possible operational base. Naturally this could not be said openly in 1:11ff. One need not, as is occasionally done, state that this text is a contradiction to 1:11ff. or gives evidence of uncertainty. The diplomatic caution evident in the proem still controls the statement here. Paul must avoid the suspicion that he wants to make the world capital his own domain, and he does not want to say brusquely that he regards it merely as a bridgehead. Nevertheless, he states that Spain is the true goal of his journey, and there is not the slightest reason to see in v. 24b an interpolation, arbitrarily to alter the place name, or to call the Spanish mission a fiction (*contra* Barnikol, "Reiseziele," 13ff., 16f., 20).

The initially strange ὡς ἄν in v. 24a has the temporal sense "shortly" as in 1 Cor 11:34; Phil 2:23 (BDF, §455[2]; BAGD, 898b). That Paul does not see in Rome either a goal of conquest (Barnikol, "Reiseziele," 9) or a field of evangelization (Roosen, "Genre," 466ff., 471; right here is Munck, *Salvation*, 298f.) is proven by the verbs διαπορεύεσθαι ("to pass through") and θεάσθαι ("to get to know") and by the stipulated conclusion with its emphatic πρῶτον and ἀπὸ μέρους, which respectively state the provisional and limited character of his stay. On the other hand ἐμπλησθῶ, which is used figuratively for the stilling of a desire, shows us how ardently Paul longs to reach this transit-station of his new venture. Each word here helps to maintain the balance.

Only when this is noted can one see fully what he is after in v. 24b. προπέμπειν, a common word adopted into the missionary vocabulary of primitive Christianity (BAGD, 709; Michel), means escorted, as in 1 Cor 16:6, 11; 2 Cor 1:16; Acts 5:3; Tit 3:13; 3 John 6. It can be expressed in parting with prayers and good wishes (Sanday and Headlam) or even a brief accompaniment, as in Acts 20:38; 21:5. But the other passages show that those who are going can also be given provision for the journey (Zeller, *Juden*, 70f.). Paul seems to have expected this most of all at Rome, where he also might be given companions who would know the country. The community, then, was to give active support to his work and share its burdens. The epistle is written with this as at least one of its purposes. Spain was a common place of travel, as has often been shown. There were certainly some synagogues there. At the same time Paul is venturing into what is for him unknown territory, so that his wishes are completely understandable. That he can indicate these only in secondary clauses throws light on his position. As yet he dare not [3?] express them openly (J. Knox, 360f.). This stands in glaring contrast to his bold plans of conquest.

Verse 23 is an anacoluthon. The elucidation in v. 24 replaces the missing conclusion, which some later readings supply. Verse 25 moves on to a new theme; it is not then a digression (*contra* Lietzmann). There is still one obstacle to the Roman journey. Paul first has to take to Jerusalem the collection he has made. Hence νυνὶ δέ presupposes a different situation from that of v. 23. What was fundamentally announced there cannot be carried out at once. The prior history of the collection on both sides is emphasized by the fact that according to Gal 2:10 this was all the Jerusalem leaders asked of him. He obviously had to fulfil this obligation no matter what the circumstances. Perhaps this obligation was the only tie with the primitive community after the conflict at Antioch. More than his personal credibility was at stake. His theology did not allow him to break all connections with Jerusalem, nor could he afford this in his practical work. This explains his injunction in 1 Cor 16:1-4 to press the collection on Sundays, the two long chapters in 2 Corinthians 8–9, and here the strong emphasis on the results in vv. 26f.

In v. 25, as in 2 Cor 8:24, διακονεῖν has the specific, although hardly cultic, sense (*contra* Cerfaux, *Church*, 132) of the service rendered through the collection (Strathmann, *TDNT*, IV, 227; Nababan, "Bekenntnis," 137). The participle is not durative as though the reference were to the collection from its beginning to its delivery (*contra* Michel). It refers to the single act of handing it over. Although Paul uses οἱ ἅγιοι as a general word for Christians, in this instance, in terms of the apocalyptic self-understanding of the pious of Israel, it undoubtedly refers to the original congregation (cf. Lietzmann's excursus). This narrower sense points both to the origin of the predication and to its eschatological significance even in the wider use. Whereas 1 Cor 16:1 and indirectly also Acts 20:4 show that the collection included Asia Minor too, mention is made here, rather oddly, only of Macedonia and Achaia, as designations of the Roman provinces. In relation to the problems in what follows one might ask at least whether Paul is not intentionally concealing the fact that the collection is a project covering the whole sphere of his missionary work. For in view of the introductory statement of v. 25 it can hardly be supposed that the full contributions of the other churches had not yet come in. The common view is that the reference shows Corinth to be the place from which the epistle was written, and only a few scholars make a not very convincing plea for Philippi (T. M. Taylor, "Place," 285ff.; possible Friedrichs, *RGG*, V, 1138). As regards the date there is today a reaction against the past trend toward a later dating and the early part of A.D. 55 or 56 is favored (cf. Georgi, *Kollekte,* 91ff.).

The most serious difficulties arise with vv. 26 and 28. εὐδοκεῖν means a solemn but free resolve (Schrenk, *TDNT,* II, 741). The γάρ added in the repetition in v. 27 means here "indeed" (BDF, §452[2]; Ridderbos). It is stressed, then, that the churches act on their own responsibility. No mention is made of the ruling of the Apostolic Council, the initiative of the apostle, or his persistence in seeing the project through. There is a tendency to retouch the picture. The collection is presented as a pure love gift, and Paul says nothing about his obviously pressing personal obligations. In keeping with this the juridical terms ἁδρότης (2 Cor 8:20), λογεία (1 Cor 16:1), and λειτουργία (2 Cor 9:12; Phil 2:30) are now replaced by κοινωνία (cf. Holl, "Kirchenbegriff," 60f.; Georgi, *Kollekte,* 40f.; Keck, "Saints in the NT," 129). This word can be used commercially, as Phil 4:15 shows (Keck, "Saints in the NT," 118f.; Leenhardt), but in Paul it has a wholly religious ring (Seesemann, κοινωνία, 67, 99; Keck, "Saints in the NT," 118f.), not just in the sense of partnership but in that of sharing and participating (Seesemann, κοινωνία; Jourdan, "κοινωνία"; Leenhardt). A reminiscence of the LXX translation of Lev 6:2 (Billerbeck; Leenhardt) is to be rejected (Seesemann, κοινωνία, 29ff.). What is at issue is the manifestation of solidarity. Through τινά it is again weakened: it does not involve a fixed sum.

Verse 27 offers a very rational basis familiar to us from Gal 6:8ff. To be sure, there is twice a pointed reference to ὀφείλειν. Yet this has an unambiguously moral sense (Keck, "Saints in the NT," 129). If through the mission going forth from the primitive community the Gentiles have received a share in the heavenly gifts effected by the Spirit, it is right and reasonable that they should render their thanks with earthly support for those who have fallen into need. λειτουργεῖν may strengthen the motif of ὀφειλή and characterize official support (Michel), although the context gives it a religious nuance (*contra* Huby). The idea of a representative anticipation of the prophetically proclaimed pilgrimage of the peoples to Zion (Munck, *Salvation,* 303f.; Hahn, *Verständnis der Mission,* 93), which seems to motivate the collection in 2 Cor 9:10 (Georgi, *Kollekte,* 72f.) and which perhaps is reflected in the understanding of it by Jewish-Christians in Jerusalem (ibid., 27ff.), is completely dropped in our text (ibid., 81f.; Zeller, *Juden,* 282f.). It cannot even be maintained (*contra* Grundmann, *TDNT,* II, 59; Cerfaux, *Church,* 133) that the gifts symbolize the Gentiles' offering of themselves to God. The whole stress is on care and love for the primitive community, and it is not at all certain that this takes place according to the standpoint of 1 Cor 9:11 (Zeller, *Juden,* 230f.

contra Georgi, *Kollekte,* 83). Incontestably the view existed in Hellenistic syncretism that thanks should be paid to the pneumatics with earthly means, and in 2 Cor 11:7f.; 12:13ff. Paul has to ward off suspicions because he does not for his part make any such claims. Nevertheless, one cannot agree (*contra* Georgi, *Kollekte,* 83) that this view is now extended ecumenically, since only the primitive community is at issue here in its historical primacy. The demand of Gal 6:8ff. is now made concrete in terms of the concept of tradition.

There is nothing to suggest that the apostle is indirectly summoning Rome to have a share in the collection (Zeller, *Juden,* 72), to say nothing of the fact that their gift could no longer be received in time. The problem of the text lies less in what it says than in what it does not say. If the earlier history of the collection had been clearly set forth and everything had not been directed toward the proof of solidarity, Jewish-Christians in Rome, and with them the rest of the congregation, might have been most strongly convinced of loyalty to Jerusalem. It seems that Paul is swayed at this point by inner conflict and outer tensions (J. Knox; Zeller, *Juden,* 235f.). As much as he brings to light his concern for Jerusalem and the zeal of his churches awakened thereby, on the other hand he maintains his independence by laying stress on the moral ties and obligations. The difficulty in which he finds himself comes out, of course, when he envisions these ties and obligations precisely not as a special instance of ecumenical *caritas.* In the last [3 resort there are needy everywhere (Holl, "Kirchenbegriff," 59; Bornkamm, *Paul,* 40f.). The Gentile churches themselves also lived to some extent in distress. To limit the collection to Jerusalem as the place from which the gospel sprang (Holl, "Kirchenbegriff," 59; Leenhardt) is not to do justice to the breadth of the sentence in v. 27.

These observations force us to enter the ongoing controversy initiated by K. Holl's brilliant essay on the concept of the church. It can hardly be disputed that from the beginning the church in Jerusalem was organized in a way very different from the way Paul's churches were organized. Acts seems to give an authentic portrayal that even after the founding of the new center in Antioch the Christians of Jerusalem still thought of themselves as the headquarters of Christianity and that they were recognized to be this in the territories around Palestine (Holl, "Kirchenbegriff," 56ff., 61f.; A. Schweitzer, *Mysticism,* 156). The delegation from James in Antioch and in part at least Paul's Judaizing opponents may have represented this primacy over the whole of Christianity (Holl, "Kirchenbegriff," 64f.), and not the least concern of the apostle in his conflicts was to struggle against this claim raised on the basis of sacral law and to reject any subordination to Jerusalem (Bornkamm, *Paul,* 58). One can no longer strictly prove that the collection was interpreted differently, perhaps from the very first, by the two sides. Yet this assumption has a high degree of probability, and without doubt Paul did not at all times accord the same importance to the collection (cf. on this Georgi, *Kollekte*). If in spite of all the risks involved the apostle still delivered it personally, seeing in it the conclusion of the previous phase of his activity, and for this reason giving it precedence over the journey to Rome, it marks an event which is at any rate of unusual significance both ecclesiastically and theologically, but is played down in our text. Any idea that the collection was originally regarded as a Christian analogy to the Jewish temple tax can be completely ruled out (*contra* Holl, "Kirchenbegriff," 58; R. Asting, *Die Heiligkeit im Urchristentum* (FRLANT 46; 1930) 133ff.; Sass, *Apostelamt,* 120, 123; Schoeps, *Paul,* 68f.; Meuzelaar, *Leib,* 74; cf. in opposition Procksch, *TDNT,* I, 106; Munck, *Salvation,* 287ff.; Georgi, *Kollekte,* 29; Nickle, *Collection,* 87-93). If it had been, it would have had to have been made regularly and would have been an unambiguous sign of legal subjection, which Paul avoided at the Apostolic Council according to his own account in Galatians 2.

It is on these presuppositions that we must interpret the noteworthy formulae "the poor of the saints" in v. 26 and "sealing of the fruit" in v. 28. Is the genitive in the first phrase epexegetical, and therefore an eschatological self-predication of the primitive community (Holl, "Kirchenbegriff," 59; Lietzmann; Dahl, *Volk Gottes,* 18; Bammel, *TDNT,* VI, 909; Hahn, *Verständnis der Mission,* 93; Nababan, "Bekenntnis," 138; Cerfaux, *Church,* 130ff.; possible Nielen, *Gebet,* 112), or partitive? In Gal 2:10 (*contra* Munck, *Salvation,* 287) πτωχοί can be understood only as an honorary predicate. This proves its use in primitive Christianity (Bornkamm, *Paul,* 40f.; Georgi, *Kollekte,* 23; Karpp, *RAC,* II, 1117; fundamentally contested in Keck's essays). In this respect the primitive community adopted a term which pious Israel used for itself (Georgi, *Kollekte,* 26ff.) and which is employed emphatically in 1QM 11:8f., 13 (Grundmann, *TDNT,* VIII, 12; Bammel, *TDNT,* VI, 885-915, esp. 896ff., 911; G. Jeremias, *Lehrer,* 58f.; disputed by Keck, "Saints in Qumran," up to 4QpPs 37). Even if this is granted, however, both the phrase itself and the entire context, which stresses only the function of aid, favor a partitive genitive (K. L. Schmidt, *TDNT,* III, 508; Bultmann, *Theology,* I, 39; Munck, *Salvation,* 289; Georgi, *Kollekte,* 82; G. Jeremias, *Lehrer,* 61). The saints are naturally not the leaders (so Cerfaux, *Church,* 136) but the community.

Verse 28 refers solemnly, mysteriously, and obscurely to the sealing of the fruit. It is understandable that expositors should resort to hypotheses at this point. The orderly handing over of the money (Zahn; Kühl) should have been expressed less pretentiously. The reference is not to a guarantee of its integrity, of which one can think in the light of the suspicions in 2 Cor 8:20f.; 12:16 (*contra* Leenhardt; Ridderbos). The explanation, first advanced by A. Deissmann, that the phrase is taken from commercial interactions and meant originally the sealing of a sack of grain (cf. Lietzmann; BAGD, 796b; Hauck, *TDNT,* III, 615; materially presupposed by Richter, *RGG,* VI, 1367 and seen by Radermacher *et al.* from the standpoint of *pars pro toto*) calls forth the objection that Paul is speaking of the handing over, not the taking charge of the collection. The thesis has thus been adopted (Dölger, "Σφραγίζεσθαι"; Zeller, *Juden,* 232) that it involves a weakened mode of expression, which describes the transferring and guaranteeing of a sum (cf. also Fitzer, *TDNT,* VII, 948: in some sense handed over under seal). Speculatively the fruit has been referred to Paul's churches and the sealing to their integration into the primitive community through a representative symbol (Bartsch, "Situation," 290f.). But there is no way of avoiding either the identification of the fruit with the collection or the juridical sense of σφραγίζεσθαι. Introduced by καί *explicativum,* ἐπιτελεῖν, which is used also in 2 Cor 8:6, 11, is explained (Lagrange; Bartsch, "Frucht," 95). By completing an affair that has caused so many difficulties, with the collection the apostle gives the primitive community a confirmation of the success of his work with both letter and seal (Georgi, *Kollekte,*

86), testifying both to the gratitude of the Gentile-Christians and to the earthly fruit of the spiritual blessings received by them.

Verse 29 is as it were a sigh of relief as Paul contemplates the approaching end of his task. This is why we have a confident οἶδα at the beginning and the solemnly effusive phrase ἐν πληρώματι εὐλογίας Χριστοῦ at the end. Only in an edifying manner can one think of Jacob's wrestling in connection with the latter (*contra* H. W. Schmidt). It is also going too far to speak of (Georgi, *Kollekte*, 86) a cycle of blessing, although Paul is familiar with the motif and views all gifts as obligations for the further passing on of help. The emphasis is on the fact that the apostle, freed both inwardly and outwardly from an obviously heavy burden, believes that he can come to Rome with all the power he has been given and hence with the fulness of the gospel. The restricted statements of the proem are thereby surpassed here, as are those of v. 24. The bearer of the gospel will not deny his mandate even in the capital. That the hope was realized in an unexpected way, and that the Spanish mission may never have been carried out, since it is mentioned only in *1 Clem.* 5:6f., probably on the basis of our text, imparts a tragic element to the promise.

This is the point at which we must tackle thematically the question raised at vv. 14ff.: What was Paul's purpose in writing the epistle? The idea that it is either a theological tractate or a missionary writing has already been rejected. It was the merit of F. C. Baur to have energetically broken through the traditional dogmatic approach with his question as to the historical situation. At the same time he thereby plunged interpretation into difficulties which have not yet been mastered (cf. the fine survey in Kuss, *Paulus*, 179-204; Zeller, *Juden*, 38ff.; also Richter, *Untersuchungen*, 7-15). When Baur's systematic conception of an antithesis between Jewish-Christian particularism and Pauline universalism (cf. *Paul*, 321ff., 349ff.) broke down, it was found more and more difficult to do justice to the unity of the epistle. Help was sought in the quite dubious pretext that Paul is not as consistent in the course of his thought as was previously maintained but jumped about and tended to digress during pauses for dictation. Partial aspects were put in the forefront, the juridico-ethical components of his theology were separated from the sacramental, and the dogmatic from the hortatory. Chapters 9–11 were viewed as an originally independent piece which had been interpolated into the epistle (Dodd; Beare, *BHH*, III, 1613). 1:18–3:20 came to be regarded as propaedeutic and largely hypothetical. Echoes of missionary preaching were sought at every point, and these were thought to be strung together in a more or less fragmentary way (Kirk, 32). Hardest of all was to relate organically the intentions stated in the proem and the conclusion to the broad complex of teaching which is the bulk of the epistle. The almost grotesque characterizing of the latter as a backwater in distinction from the main current represented in chs. 9–11 proves this most clearly (Noack, "Current," 159ff.).

When the whole emphasis was laid on the dogmatic portion, it might be inferred from v. 29 and 1:5f., 11 that Paul was anticipating his task in Rome by proclaiming the gospel which is the foundation of the church. This can be united with a serious understanding of the principle in v. 20 only under an astonishing presupposition for Protestants, namely, that every community has to have an apostolic foundation and that so far the anonymous Christians in Rome have not had this (Klein, "Purpose," 45-49). On the same premise a plea can be made for a circular letter whose teaching is provided with marginal notes relating to the particular recipients (T. W. Manson, "Letter," 241; Trocmé, "Méthode," 151ff.; J. Knox, 360; in a weaker form Suggs, "Word," 297). If, conversely, an unbelievably good familiarity between Paul and Rome is taken as the basis, the epistle can be interpreted as a pastoral concretization of the apostolic kerygma (Rengstorf, "Paulus," 225ff.; Lyonnet, *Quaestiones,* I, 61; Minear, *Obedience,* 21ff.; Bartsch, "Empfänger," 88).

In face of such extravagant hypotheses it is tempting, if over-simple, to take the view that Paul in this epistle was just introducing himself to an unknown church and defending his preaching at the same time (Zahn; Dodd; Michel; Jülicher, *Introduction,* 112ff.; Kümmel, *Introduction,* 342f.; Georgi, *Kollekte,* 81). A variation of this approach is to see in the epistle the striking of a balance or rendering of an account with a view to the coming visit (Lagrange, xxxiiif.; Beare, *BHH,* III, 1611; Munck, *Salvation,* 299; Richter, *Untersuchungen,* 13ff.). The conjecture that different theological ideas were abroad in Rome might go hand in hand with this (Michaelis, *Einleitung,* 159). It is widely recognized that the apostle is evaluating previous experiences (Lütgert, *Römerbrief,* 33; T. W. Manson, "Letter," 241; esp. Bornkamm, "Testament," 24ff.; critical W. L. Knox, *Church,* 96). Nevertheless, even if one is prepared to accept this view in essential respects, it is still an open question why the writing, which ought surely to be called a theological legacy rather than an introduction, is much longer than usual, especially when the trip to Rome is to follow so soon (Jülicher; W. L. Knox, *Church,* 10; J. Knox, 359; Suggs, "Word," 291ff.).

Furthermore, the theme of the relation between Jewish- and Gentile-Christians, supported above all by 9–11; 14:1–15:13, has been left hanging in the air since the time of F. C. Baur. Paul is supposed correspondingly to be concerned about the reconciliation of these two groups (Zahn, 13; W. L. Knox, *Church,* 95; Marxsen, *Introduction,* 103; Harder, "Anlass," 23f.; Wiefel, "Community," 113; Bartsch, "Situation," 289; Minear, *Obedience,* 2f.; sharply criticized in Klein, "Purpose," 40f.). Variations on this conception see warnings against either antinomianism (Lütgert, *Römerbrief,* 96, 111) or even anti-Semitism (Bartsch, "Situation," 283f.; cf. Wiefel, "Community," 116ff.), or find an emphasis on the priority of the Jews (Noack, "Current," 163f.), or see intervention in the debate between the two groups (Eichholz, *Paulus,* 291, 296) and a statement of the arguments on both sides (Preisker, "Problem," 26ff.), or think that Paul turns in the same way against Judaism and Pneumaticism (Michel, 9ff.).

Recently there has been a movement away from this focus on the situation in Rome. The emphasis has been placed on the dangers threatening in Jerusalem according to vv. 30ff. and especially on the expected conflicts with Jewish-Christians there (Bornkamm, "Testament," 18ff.; Jervell, "Letter," 65f.; Suggs, "Word," 295f.; an approach to this Marxsen, *Introduction,* 100, 102; basic agreement in Kuss, *Paulus,* 196, 200). The delivery of the collection must have had the appearance of provocation to the primitive community and especially to unbelieving Jews (Georgi, *Kollekte,* 84f.). The work of the apostle and the unity of the church are at stake (Jervell, "Letter," 68), so that the theological situation at the Apostolic Council is likely to repeat itself (Bornkamm, "Testament," 19f.). Paul does not know how the battle will turn out for him personally, and therefore he cannot avoid the journey to Jerusalem (J. Knox), and he thus seeks the solidarity of the Roman congregation, which he must also represent as part of the Gentile world (Bornkamm, "Testament," 19; Jervell, "Letter," 64f., 72). What he will have to say in his defense at Jerusalem he prepares in the Roman epistle both for his own use and as a kind of report to the recipients (Jervell, "Letter," 70f.; Bornkamm, "Testament," 25ff. prefers the idea of a well-organized exposition of his message of salvation; cf. also Kuss, *Paulus,* 194).

This view is undoubtedly successful in deriving the didactic complex of the epistle, and its comprehensiveness, from the concrete situation, and yet also in giving to the latter the importance which has thus far been inappropriately withheld. It can also be granted that in the course of church history the epistle has unintentionally become the literary testament of Paul (Georgi, *Kollekte,* 90) even if the idea of calling Jerusalem the secret addressee (Fuchs, *Hermeneutik,* 191) can scarcely be justified and the superscription "the Epistle to Jerusalem" (Jervell, "Letter," 67) has a provocative and simultaneously forbidding effect. It will not do to play off salvation history against the doctrine of justification in such a way as to contrast Galatians and Romans (Jervell, "Letter," 68f.). The salvation-historical "the Jew first" is changed by the apostle in chs. 9–11 under an apocalyptic perspective to an "Israel finally." These chapters, like the polemical sections elsewhere, make it clear that Israel is incorporated into the message of the justification of the ungodly, which no apology can ever make palatable to strict Jewish-Christians who cling fast to the law. Materially, Paul's incontestable desire to achieve reconciliation and unity with the help of the collection is doomed to fail from the beginning. But his concern does not mean that we can simply describe the epistle as the testament of the apostle. His true testament consists in the Gentile-Christians on the one hand and his writings as a whole on the other. The titles selected here are the most vulnerable feature of theories such as these. What Paul expects in or of Rome remains obscure. In relation to v. 24 the thesis of the missionary basis is contested (Jervell, "Letter," 63f., 67) or played down (Bornkamm, "Testament," 19f.). The Spanish journey is not taken seriously. This is a simplifying approach based on partial blindness, which is not in keeping with the complexity of the factors present (Kuss, *Paulus,* 203), as useful as it is as a partial aspect.

The proper starting point is that Paul is in fact presenting himself together with his central message to the Roman congregation as yet unknown to him. One should also maintain that this message must necessarily be irritating for both Jews and Gentiles and that its offensiveness will come out with at least the same substantive precision as in Galatians or 1 Corinthians. If this epistle is constitutively distinguished from all the other Pauline epistles by its reflective character, mirroring earlier experiences and being interspersed by what are for the most part only invented objections, this is to be understood under the category of a "theological report." The fact that the apostle needs Rome as at least a springboard if not an operational base for his missionary plans in the west cannot be denied or viewed as unimportant according to our text. Otherwise one misses the apostle's apocalyptic self-understanding, which is almost always a piece of red-hot iron for exegesis. Inasmuch as Rome is seen only as a stage on the way, the visit there does not basically violate the "canon" of v. 20. Finally, Paul had worked in Ephesus, where the church could hardly have been founded by him, and the capital undoubtedly offered much unconquered territory even for the preaching of the gospel.

The real problem of the text and therewith the purpose for writing it lies in the combination of Rome, Jerusalem, and Spain, and, if the importance of the last two factors is sufficiently recognized, in the mediating function of Rome. This expression had been used deliberately. Fault is often found with Paul for speaking unclearly and, as it seems, irresolutely, when it is a matter of his visit and the expectations connected with this, apart from the Spanish journey. The desire for solidarity in relation to Jerusalem is stated. But this must be made more precise. Thereby the changeable history of Judaism (Wiefel, "Community," 101-108) and the beginnings of the Christian church in Rome (ibid., 109-114) have to be taken into account. The expulsion under Claudius at least decimated the large Jewish community, which was grouped around numerous synagogues and did not have united leadership as in Alexandria. It did the same to the Jewish-Christian congregation which had grown out of that community. When the edict was softened, and especially when it was repealed, Jewish-Christians returned or made their way to Rome, but they now found a Gentile-Christian majority. Even as a minority they played no very big part as Judaism in Rome took on new life. Paul could count on the fact that this group at least would understand the prob-lematic of his gospel, that it would be instructed about his work, and that it could give the Gentile-Christians a more or less adequate picture of both. He could expect that he would meet here with the suspicions regarding his apostolate and teaching which were widespread in the Diaspora. Finally (Moore, *Judaism*, I, 106f.; Kummel, *Introduction*, 308f. refer to the synagogue of the Libertines at Jerusalem [Acts 6:9]) it can hardly be doubted that from the time of Herod, with the many commercial links, there existed a brisk traffic between Jews in Rome and Jerusalem and that these influenced the Jewish-Christians too. If, then, Paul through his epistle could win over the Roman church and especially its Jewish-Christian minority, or at least dispel in part their existing suspicions, he would get rearguard protection in relation to Jerusalem too (Black, 23; Minear, *Obedi-ence*, 4f.).

Whether he was successful or not one cannot say. What can be said is that the apostle made an attempt in this direction. This is why he meets the objections of his Jewish-Christian adversaries. This is why he stresses the course of salvation history and the final acceptance of all Israel. This is why, in the conflict between the strong and the weak, he is so unusually mild and accommodating to Jewish-Christians even regarding the observance of days. This is why he bases his gospel so firmly on Scripture, from which, too, he derives his own worldwide mission. Materially he surrenders nothing and accepts every risk. He shows the full im-plications of the doctrine of the justification of the ungodly by faith, even in exhortation, and bases ecclesiology and his own apostleship solely upon that, but he does so against the background of fulfilled prophecy. The "true Jew" could not reject his argument and Gentile-Christians, being warned expressly against despising their brethren, could only see their own status supported. Paul could hope, then, that the Roman community would not only help him in the west but also strengthen his position in Jerusalem. Naturally, this is a reconstruction. But history is the field of reconstructions, and whether these are right or not depends on how far they overcome the problems posed. This hypothesis does so to a very high degree.

C. The Urgent Need for Intercession for the Apostle and the Concluding Blessing (15:30-33)

[30]I appeal to you, brethren, in the name of our Lord Jesus Christ and by the love of the Spirit, to strive with me in your prayers to God for me, [31]that I may be delivered from the unbelievers in Judea and that my appointed service for Jerusalem may be acceptable to the saints. [32]For only then can I come to you with joy and by the will of God find refreshment among you. [33]The God of peace be with you all. Amen.

Bibliography: V. C. Pfitzner, *Paul and the Agon Motif* (NovTSup 16; 1967); A. Schettler, *Die paulinische Formel "Durch Christus"* (1907). See also the bibliography for 15:22-29.

Whatever is to be said about ch. 16, these verses are the true ending of the epistle (Lagrange). Galatians and Ephesians show that greetings do not have to follow, and that it can remain short and, as in 2 Corinthians, Philippians, 1 and 2 Thessalonians, and Titus, not mention names. Paul observes no definite rule in this regard (Lietzmann). Hence it is not strange if in writing to an unknown congregation the apostle should not give greetings along with the blessing.

What is unusual is that the conclusion should consist of an urgent request for prayer, which is based on very strong fears. Paul obviously expects—and Acts bears him out—that he will run into serious complications in Jerusalem, and he does not even rule out danger to his life. This speaks once again against the characterizing of the collection as a mere love gift which might have been handed over relatively privately and without any participation on the apostle's part. If he   [3 has to hand it over in person, and thus from the beginning to pay the price of causing a stir among the Jews in Jerusalem, it undoubtedly involved an official delegation (Nickle, *Collection,* 140ff.).

But Paul also had doubts whether the Jewish-Christians in Jerusalem would receive this gift simply with gratitude, with which the obligation accepted in Galatians 2 would be discharged. Expositors usually state this circumstance without commentary. It can be explained, however, only if the conflict with the mother church had continued after the Antioch incident and reached the point where mutual relations might well be broken off (Nababan, "Bekenntnis," 141). If the condition of the Apostolic Council was no longer regarded as obviously valid by the Jewish-Christians in Jerusalem, and if in spite of their poverty they did not even want it to be carried out under the circumstances, the attempts at reconciliation would also seem to be pointless and Paul could no longer count on being recognized as a partner. But if Paul himself, while fully realizing how things might be, sticks to the arrangements, then the collection is regarded by him primarily, not as a love gift for the poor, but as a demonstration of church unity. While maintaining his independence, Paul does not want to be pushed into the role of a free lance.

He is afraid, however, that his conduct might seem to be provocative and will even embitter the Jews in Jerusalem. What he says in vv. 25ff. brings out one aspect of the collection, but not the decisive one. It veils the fact that the apostle's authority, the standing of his mission, and perhaps even his own life are at stake (Jervell, "Letter," 68; Georgi, *Kollekte*, 84f.). In this situation it is understandable and even necessary that Paul should seek supporters or at least mediators between himself and the primitive community and that he should thus set forth his message to Rome in a detailed way which will be acceptable even to distrustful Jewish-Christians.

Not without reason the introduction is especially solemn. It follows the schema of 12:1 (Bjerkelund, *Parakalô*, 54; Jervell, "Letter," 66), so that "ask" is too weak a rendering for παρακαλῶ (Spicq, *Agape*, II, 241) and διά in the prepositional phrases which follow means in liturgical style "in the power of" or "in the name of" (Stählin, *TDNT*, V, 793; Schettler, "*Durch Christus*," 50ff.). Omission of the appeal in weaker textual witnesses is even less comprehensible, since emphasis is given to the new beginning by the strong invocation of the Kyrios with all his dignities and by what is almost the adjuration of the love granted with the Spirit (though cf. Murray). In keeping with this is the prayer with the compound συναγωνίσασθαι, which is singular in the NT but which has a parallel in the simple form in Col 4:12 and which in view of the perilous situation of the apostle relates the motif of the *agōn* to prayer (Harder, *Gebet*, 204; Stauffer, *TDNT*, I, 139). The colorless translation "to help" (Pfitzner, *Agon*, 121ff.) does not do justice to this (von Severus, *RAC*, VIII, 1181), and to think of opposition to principalities and powers (Bieder, "Gebetswirklichkeit," 23) fails to recognize the enemies Paul has in view. Obviously the reference is to prayer at worship (Schumacher, *Letzte Kapitel*, 46), but the customary desire for intercession is given particular urgency by the expression used.

The perils are mentioned in v. 31. The verb suggests danger of death. ἀπό instead of ἐκ designates what has not yet come about (Ridderbos). As in 10:2f.; 11:30 ἀπειθοῦντες refers to Jews who oppose the gospel. The addition ἐν τῇ Ἰουδαίᾳ shows that they do not withstand Paul merely in Jerusalem or in the southern portion of Palestine (so BAGD, 379a) but in the land as a whole (Gutbrod, *TDNT*, III, 382). A second danger is that the Jewish-Christians conceivably might reject the collection. Their own term is used for these Jewish-Christians. The phrase διακονία μου ἡ εἰς Ἰερουσαλήμ presupposes that the community as a whole is to receive the collection, although the poor will profit most from it. If apostolic humility (Michel) is seen in the hope that the collection will be εὐπρόσδεκτος, the background is not recognized and is glossed over for purposes of edification.

Verse 32 is dependent on v. 31 with its second, almost consecutive ἵνα. Only when the dangers which threaten in Jerusalem are behind him can the apostle come to Rome ἐν χαρᾷ, which may have the profane sense "with a cheerful, relieved heart." The phrase διὰ θελήματος θεοῦ is to be preferred among many variants (Lietzmann; Ridderbos), especially as it gives expression to James' pro-

407

viso, unlike the christological modifications. Probably it refers to the whole sentence but it can also be related to the last clause, since the participle is already modified by ἐν χαρᾷ and συναναπαύεσθαι presents the longed-for goal. This verb, used in another sense in Isa 11:6 LXX, excludes for the moment all other plans. Paul waits longingly for the possibility of rest and, somewhat optimistically, for mutual refreshment. The idea that the spirit of history is on his side (Weinel, *Paulus,* 177) is out of place, although it is typical of the liberal picture of the apostle.

Verse 33 has the formula of blessing with the concluding Amen, which is also found, with slight differences, in 16:20; Phil 4:9; 2 Cor 13:11; 1 Thess 5:23; 2 Thess 3:16; Heb 13:20. Liturgical practice is given literary form here (Schlier, *TDNT,* I, 337), as is shown at least by the concluding Amen in Gal 6:18. The phrase "God of peace" is found also in *T. Dan* 5:2 and the rabbis (Billerbeck; Michel); it is traditionally Jewish. It makes particularly good sense here. Peace as the all-embracing power of God to salvation is the content of all that the apostle wishes for the Romans. P^{46} adds the doxology from 16:25-27. This has been taken as proof that we have the true conclusion here and that ch. 16 is a fragment from some other work (Kirk; Beare, *BHH,* III, 1611). This thesis crashes on the fact that 16:1-23 then follow in P^{46}, so that this text does not know the epistle in the asserted shortened form. Either it or the tradition behind it is simply strengthening the formula of blessing and thereby showing at least that materially the real epistle has come to its goal at this point.

VIII. Appendix: A Letter of Recommendation (16:1-27)

Three observations are in order before exegeting this historically interesting and much debated chapter. (1) Apart from the conclusion, its Pauline authenticity is not in doubt. Whether or not it was connected with Romans from the very first, it does not involve a so-called *eschatokollion* nor a fragment of another epistle. Against both possibilities is the fact that a self-contained and independent letter of recommendation is present in this chapter, as the two introductory verses show. For such a literary *Gattung* there are parallels in antiquity (cf. Deissmann, *Light*, 157ff., 182ff.), and we see from 1 Cor 16:3; 2 Cor 3:1 that it was used in primitive Christianity. (2) It may be unique (Kümmel, *Introduction*, 319) in that so many greetings are connected with it. But the situation of early missionary work explains this easily, and it simply presupposes that the apostle is writing to a larger community in which he has many friends. It is a mistake, however, to make the greetings the main content of the letter, since this is not in accord with either vv. 1-2 or 17-20. (3) As to the relationship to the main epistle the nature of the letter helps us neither one way nor the other. All that we can and should say is that the chapter has the character of an appendix. Only detailed examination can show whether the recipients are to be sought in Rome or elsewhere, or whether the attachment to the main epistle is probably original or secondary.

The structure of the chapter is obvious. The recommendation in vv. 1-2 is followed by various greetings in vv. 3-16. A warning against false teachers is given in vv. 17-19, and this ends with a blessing in v. 20. Verses 21-23 include greetings from the apostle's helpers and friends. Verse 24 is unquestionably a later interpolation from 2 Thess 3:18. The doxology in vv. 25-27, which in length and motivation is not like any other in Paul, can in no case relate merely to our chapter. It seems to have been written with a view to the whole epistle in its present form.

A. The Recommendation of Phoebe (16:1-2)

¹*I recommend to you Phoebe, our sister, a deaconess of the church at Cenchreae.* ²*Receive her in the Lord as is fitting for the saints, and stand by her in any situation in which she needs your aid. For she has been a help to many, and also to me personally.*

409

16:1-2 THE RECOMMENDATION OF PHOEBE

Bibliography: K. P. Donfried, "A Short Note on Romans 16," *JBL* 89 (1970) 441-49 (= *Romans Debate,* 50-60); K. Erbes, "Zeit und Ziel der Grüsse Röm 16, 3-15," *ZNW* 10 (1909) 128-147, 195-218; E. J. Goodspeed, "Phoebe's Letter of Introduction," *HTR* 44 (1951) 55-57; W. Michaelis, "Kenchreä (Zur Frage des Abfassungsortes des Rm)," *ZNW* 25 (1926) 144-154; H. M. Schenke, "Aporien im Römerbrief," *TLZ* 92 (1967) 881-88; W. Schrage, " 'Ekklesia' und 'Synagoge.' Zum Ursprung des urchristlichen Kirchenbegriffs," *ZTK* 60 (1963) 178-202.

The idea that vv. 1f. is to be considered a subscript to ch. 15 and that vv. 3-20 should be separated from that as a fragment (Schenke, "Aporien") is completely arbitrary on both counts, and it is further discredited when vv. 3-20 and 14:1–15:13 are combined to make an original Ephesian epistle. In antiquity travellers to strange places where they had neither friends nor acquaintances needed letters of recommendation as a protection against dangers, and this was particularly true in the case of women. συνίστημι is used technically. The δέ, which is certainly original (Michel), undoubtedly implies continuation (Ridderbos) and is thus the introduction to a new section. To explain it in terms of the sequence of pages in a secretarial copybook (Deissmann, *Light,* 236; cf. in opposition Erbes, "Zeit," 132; Michaelis, *Einleitung,* 163) is simply fantastic. So long as the debate whether ch. 16 is an independent piece or not is not settled, one may conjecture that it follows a prescript which has become detached.

The name Phoebe is also found elsewhere (BAGD, 864). Greek mythology often stood as a godfather when slaves were to be named and those who were set free did not renounce this. As to the Phoebe who is here called ἀδελφή as a [39 member of the Christian community, as in Phlm 2, we know only what we are told here. Variants do not allow us to decide with certainty whether the emphatic καί is original. Inasmuch as it underscores the special function, it makes good sense.

If one takes account of v. 23 Cenchreae must be the east port of Corinth. This was a center of trade and commerce with the Orient (in opposition to this traditional view cf. Michaelis, "Kenchreä," 148ff.). In port cities conditions were especially favorable for strongly proletarian congregations and there was thus a need, for charitable care of the poor, sick, widows, orphans, and arriving and departing fellow-Christians. It is often a matter of surprise that the word ἐκκλησία makes its first and incidental appearance in our letter only in this verse. But this shows how little concerned the apostle was to write a theological compendium and that ecclesiology was not in any case his primary systematic motif. In this place, in which no direct theological reflection is demanded, it may suffice simply to point out, in contrast to the traditional view, that this self-designation of the Christian community is not primarily taken from the LXX but grew out of Hellenistic political use in demarcation from the synagogue (Schrage, "Ekklesia"). It thus characterizes the empirical assembly, including the house church.

If our interpretation of Paul's teaching on charismata was correct, the constantly rekindled debate whether διάκονος already means an ecclesiastical office both here and in Phil 1:1 is superfluous (Zahn; Kühl; Lagrange; Michel; H. W. Schmidt; for the opposite view Michaelis, "Kenchreä," 146; Delling, *Worship,* 157f.; Kalsbach, *RAC,* III, 917; undecided Lietzmann; Althaus; Ridderbos). This

410

approach masks the Pauline view that each Christian is officially brought into the service of his Lord, entrusted with a particular ministry, and must exercise it, as no one else can, in and toward the community. Insofar as Phoebe has a permanent and recognized ministry, as is emphasized by the participle and the place name, one may at least see an early stage of what later became the ecclesiastical office (Barrett; Schumacher, *Letzte Kapitel,* 49; Oepke, *TDNT,* I, 787), especially as there are pagan parallels for this (BAGD, 184b).

The final clause gives the reason for the recommendation. προσδέχεσθαι does not have here the religiously deepened sense of προσλαμβάνειν in chs. 14f. but has the secular sense of welcoming and offering lodging and help. It is going too far to try to deduce from πρᾶγμα (Schumacher, *Letzte Kapitel,* 49) that Phoebe was involved in some kind of legal action. χρῄζειν τινός meant already classically "to need" (BAGD, 885). The almost tautological phrases ἐν κυρίῳ and ἀξίως τῶν ἁγίων support the recommendation. The saints here are all Christians. What is fitting for them is what corresponds to the gospel, according to Phil 1:27, or the will of the Lord. This is simply an emphatic way of saying "in a Christian manner." Phoebe has to take care of matters which are not more closely specified, which the community possibly can facilitate. παριστάνειν has the secular sense "to stand by," "to help" (Reicke, *TDNT,* V, 837f.).

A further motivation is advanced in v. 2c. Phoebe can expect help by reason of her own conduct. προστάτις, which occurs only here in the NT, cannot in the context have the juridical sense of the masculine form, i.e., the leader or representative of a fellowship (BAGD, 718b). There is no reference, then, to a "patroness" (Deissmann, *Paul,* 240; cf. Schumacher, *Letzte Kapitel,* 50). Women could not take on legal functions, and according to Revelation only in heretical circles do prophetesses seem to have had official ecclesiastical powers of leadership (*contra* Reicke, *TDNT,* VI, 703). The idea is that of the personal care which Paul and others have received at the hands of the deaconess. Surprisingly, in spite of the dominant view (cf. Zahn; Erbes, "Zeit," 129; Ridderbos; H. W. Schmidt), nothing is said about bringing the epistle, although this would have given added force to the introduction. Cenchreae is mentioned as the place of Phoebe's ministry and not of her departure. In any case it does not come into consideration for a journey to Rome. This section does not offer the slightest basis for speculative considerations.

B. Apostolic Greetings (16:3-16)

³*Greet Prisca and Aquila, my fellow workers in Christ Jesus, who risked their necks for my life, and to whom not only I, but all the churches of the Gentiles, owe thanks. ⁵(Greet) also the church in their house. Greet my beloved Epaenetus, the firstborn for Christ in Asia. ⁶Greet Mary, who has often toiled for you. ⁷Greet Andronicus and Junias, my kinsmen and (former) fellow prisoners, who are prominent among the apostles and who were Christians before me. ⁸Greet Ampliatus, my beloved in the Lord. ⁹Greet Urbanus, our fellow worker in Christ, and my beloved Stachys. ¹⁰Greet Apelles, who is approved in Christ. Greet those of the house of Aristobulus. ¹¹Greet my kinsman Herodion. Greet*

411

those of the house of Narcissus to the extent that they belong to the Lord.
¹²Greet Tryphaena and Tryphosa, who have toiled in the Lord. Greet the be-
loved Persis, who has labored much in the Lord. ¹³Greet Rufus, who is chosen
in the Lord, and his mother who (became) mine also. ¹⁴Greet Asyncritus,
Phlegon, Hermes, Patrobas, Hermas, and the brethren who are with them.
¹⁵Greet Philologus, Julia, Nereus and his sister, and Olympas, and all the
saints with them. ¹⁶Greet one another with a holy kiss. All the churches of
Christ greet you.

Bibliography: P. Feine, *Die Abfassung des Philipperbriefes in Ephesus, mit einer Anlage über Röm. 16, 3-20 als Epheserbrief* (BFCT 20/4; 1916); F. V. Filson, "The Significance of the Early Home Churches," *JBL* 58 (1939) 105-112; A. von Harnack, "Κόπος (κοπιᾶν, οἱ κοπιῶντες) im frühchristlichen Sprachgebrauch," *ZNW* 27 (1928) 1-10; K. M. Hofmann, *Philema Hagion* (BFCT N.S. 38; 1938); J. Jeremias, "Paarweise Sendung im NT," *Abba*, 132-39; J. I. H. McDonald, "Was Romans XVI a Separate Letter?" *NTS* 16 (1969/70) 369-372; T. Y. Mullins, "Greeting as a NT Form," *JBL* 87 (1968) 418-426; R. Schnackenburg, "Apostles Before and During Paul's Time," *Apostolic History and the Gospel: Biblical and Historical Essays Presented to F. F. Bruce* (ed. W. W. Gasque and R. P. Martin; 1970) 287-303. See also the bibliographies for 15:22-29 (Bartsch, "Situation"; Holl, "Kirchenbegriff"; Wiefel, "Community") and 16:1-2 (Donfried, "Note"; Erbes, "Zeit").

Long lists of greetings of this kind are not known before Paul and are not present in his other epistles, although we do find them to a lesser extent later (cf. Deissmann, *Light*, 235; Roller, *Formular*, 67ff.; McDonald, "Letter," 370). Even when such parallels are taken into account, this list is most unusual. There is reflected in it something of the multiplicity of missionary activity and the varied composition of the Gentile-Christian communities. That the situation in a large city of the empire is presupposed is obvious, and there is doubtless reason to think initially of Rome. It also makes good sense that the list is attached to a recommendation. [397 In this way Phoebe is commended at once to a great number of Christians. To put vv. 1f. with ch. 15 is a mistake from both a material and a literary standpoint, and on the other side the multiplying of greetings is not the main subject of the piece.

Paul is clearly concerned to underscore his personal tie with as many as possible, even if it be only by an adjective, and to present the activity of those mentioned. Particularly important and worthy people are named, each of whom will probably have a group of other Christians gathered around him. The common ἀγαπητός replaces "brother," as is confirmed by 1 Thess 2:8; Phlm 16, and the alternation in 1 Cor 10:1, 14 (Stauffer, *TDNT*, I, 51). The formulae "in Christ" and "in the Lord" are used in a much weaker sense and there is no distinction between them. The latter may be derived from the former and shows us clearly, precisely in our text, that the former is not to be understood mystically but characterizes Christian life as standing under the lordship of Christ which activates human beings (Neugebauer, *In Christus*, 129). This also comes to expression when the catchword κοπιᾶν is used. It means technically the effort associated with missionary work, although this meaning cannot with certainty be traced back to the apostle himself (cf. Harnack, "Κόπος").

It is interesting that several house churches appear here. In early days this was the common type of gathering. According to 1 Cor 16:19; Phlm 2; Col 4:15; Acts 12:12, groups also seem to have maintained limited autonomy within the community. If the chapter is addressed to Rome one could see in this a development of the organization which determined Roman Judaism (Dahl, *Volk Gottes*, 202; Wiefel, "Community," 113; Bartsch, "Situation," 283). Yet the verses which follow immediately throw doubt on this hypothesis.

As the most prominent members of the community Prisca and Aquila are emphatically put first, and they receive almost extravagant praise. Not only is Paul himself under a debt of gratitude to them—the secular term is used—but so, too, are all the Gentile-Christian communities. Doubtless this is not merely related to the fact that in a situation dangerous to the apostle's life, probably in a popular phrase (cf. Deissmann, *Light*, 119f.), they risked their necks for him. Precise details of the incident are not given. The lists of hardships in 2 Cor 6:5; 11:23 supply the general framework for this, and one can suspect that this particular affair took place in Ephesus on the basis of 1 Cor 15:32 and possibly Acts 18:2. For according to Acts 18:2 the expulsion of the Jews from Rome under Claudius brought this Jewish-Christian couple to Ephesus so that they could have given hospitality to Paul. The references to them in 1 Cor 16:19; 2 Tim 4:19, their description as fellow-workers of Paul, the mention of their house churches, and above all the conclusion of v. 4 justify us in regarding the two as among the leading early Christian missionaries in the Diaspora, who had begun their work independently of Paul and then continued it in association with him. Missionary couples, to whom we have express testimony in 1 Cor 9:5, are a Christian variation on the Jewish practice of sending out two "yoke-fellows" (cf. J. Jeremias, "Sendung"). The wife can have access to the women's areas, which would not be generally accessible to the husband. This part played by the Christian women in the formation of the first churches has rarely been paid sufficient attention, although our chapter requires that. Prisca only occupies the first place in a larger group.

The changeable fate and widespread activity of the couple permit us to assume that after the softening and repeal of the edict of Claudius they returned to Rome and again gathered a house church around them, although there can have been only very little time in which to do this (Lietzmann; Kümmel, *Introduction*, 319; but cf. Deissmann, *Light*, 278; Bornkamm, *Paul*, 247; Marxsen, *Introduction*, 108). The thesis, however, is based not on the text itself but only on the combination of the chapter with the epistle, and a reference to the return would have been quite possible in the context. As critical as one always must be relative to an argument from silence, its weight is strengthened by the following greeting.

The Gentile-Christian Epaenetus is called the ἀπαρχή of Asia. This means that he is the first convert in western Asia Minor, of which Ephesus is the center, just as in 1 Cor 16:15 Stephanas is called the firstborn of Achaia. One can naturally suppose that he, too, moved to Rome (Zahn; Sickenberger; Donfried, "Note," 446), possibly in company with Prisca and Aquila (Althaus). Yet that is pure speculation as long as it is not mentioned, and it is a poor one if one considers his significance in his homeland.

The reading Μαριάμ in P[46] ℵ etc. at v. 6 suggests that Mary is a Jewess (Zahn; but cf. Sanday and Headlam; Lagrange). It is open to question (*contra* BAGD, 492a) whether the name occurred outside the Jewish world. The note about strenuous efforts she undertook, which returns in v. 12b, finds a fine secular parallel in a preserved inscription (Deissmann, *Light,* 313). The ὑμᾶς, which has been emended to ἡμᾶς, leaves the question open as to how Paul knew this.

Verse 7 poses again the problem of the concept of an apostle in Paul's day. ἐπίσημοι in any case does not merely mean "esteemed by the apostles" (Zahn) but "prominent among them" (BAGD, 298a; Rengstorf, *TDNT,* VII, 268; Lietzmann; Schlatter; Michel; Schnackenburg, "Apostles," 293). The other attributes do not support the idea of a so-called "community apostle." For Andronicus and Junias, in spite of their non-Jewish names, can only be Jewish-Christian missionaries. Like those who are opposed in 2 Cor 11:5, 13, 22f. these may have claimed the title of apostle for themselves, and, as is added in intensification, they were Christians already before Paul himself. It is impossible to decide whether they belonged to the primitive community as such (Roloff, *Apostolat,* 60f.) or whether, more probably, they were delegates of Antioch, as Paul and Barnabas were called apostles in Acts 14:4, 14. To that extent it also remains unclear whether they meet the criterion of 1 Cor 9:1, namely, that of being eyewitnesses of the risen Lord, or whether the only standard is the function of founding and building up churches.

The concept of an apostle which we meet here has presumably been coined in Hellenistic Christianity at its earliest stage (Schnackenburg, "Apostles," 293f.). The two went out together as "yokefellows" in the sending out by twos (Jeremias, "Sendung," 136), and like Herodion in v. 11, with the usage of 9:3, they are designated as συγγενεῖς, "fellow-countrymen." They had suffered imprisonment with Paul. This is not to be taken figuratively (*contra* Kittel, *TDNT,* I, 196f.). The circumstances are not specified, and again the lists of sufferings in 2 Corinthians leave a lot of room for play regarding its date.

Apart from Epaenetus, all those mentioned thus far are Jewish-Christians. This may be true of some of the others as well. Many Jews in the Hellenistic period did not bear specifically Jewish names. On the other hand, the following verses provide only questionable basis for this, while the names, which are typical of those of slaves and freedmen, are common (cf. the excursus in Lietzmann).

Only pious speculation can identify the Rufus of v. 13 with the Rufus mentioned in Mark 15:21, although this equation is often made. When he is called ἐκλεκτὸς ἐν κυρίῳ, this is the application to a single individual of a term which primitive Christians commonly used for themselves. Like δόκιμος, used of Apelles in v. 10, it is a mark of distinction. In fact it is simply a more emphatic version of ἀγαπητός. The reference to his mother has given rise to many legends. The fact that Paul regards her as his own manifests the considerable thoughtfulness he has received from her, which, however, could have been granted to him everywhere.

Herodion in v. 11 is a Jewish-Christian, but in spite of his name he does not have to have had anything to do with the Herodians. That is also true of Aristobulus in v. 10, of whom one must even doubt whether he is a Christian. The formulation simply shows that there is a Christian group in his family, as is said, with an obviously restrictive clause, in v. 11 of the household of Narcissus. It is a mere hypothesis based on historical curiosity, which goes beyond the text, to say that he is an imperial freedman. The same applies to the view that because their names sound similar, and they are mentioned together, Tryphaena and Tryphosa are sisters. The lists in vv. 14 and 15 mention representative members of two house churches which include an unnamed number of other Christians.

In the Hellenistic period it is not surprising that Greek names easily predominate over all others. Specifically Roman ones cannot be picked out with any certainty (*contra* Lagrange; Donfried, "Note," 445f.). Jewish- and Gentile-Christians have intermingled. They belong for the most part to the lower social strata of the population. A sizable contingent is from the Orient. Women play an important role. A church composed in this way could exist in any large city in the empire. Undoubtedly Rome initially presents itself. Nevertheless, when one examines what the text says and what it does not say, the indicators to support this vanish so completely that doubt must arise regarding this thesis. If an alternative is sought, almost the only possibility is Ephesus, as has been asserted since the beginning of the last century (cf. the survey in Schumacher, *Letzte Kapitel*, 61ff.).

The proem of the epistle speaks against any close relationship between the apostle and the Roman church. One cannot escape this observation by referring to the exhortation in 14:1–15:13, since naturally Paul was not without any information about relationships in Rome and he had had dealings with warring Christian groups elsewhere. The supposition is impermissible that he did not know all of the people mentioned personally and was instructed about them only through intermediaries (*contra* Erbes, "Zeit," 141f.; Schumacher, *Letzte Kapitel*, 75; Kümmel, *Introduction*, 318f.). In this case the honoring predications would have a strongly rhetorical character and would lose all material credibility. The most powerful argument, strangely enough, has seldom been formulated with any precision. The Christians mentioned are the representatives of a community whose size must be doubled at least (Minear even presupposes several communities [*Obedience*, 27]). But if Paul has so many friends in Rome, he can count on it that these will champion his person and cause. The long justification of his particular teaching seems, then, to be unnecessary, his uncertainty in relation to the readers would seem even stranger, and he could even hope that those known to him there would on their own initiative intervene on his behalf in Jerusalem. From such premises it seems best to separate the present chapter from the rest of the letter and not to seek its readers in Rome.

If it is considered basically as a letter of recommendation for Phoebe, this is quite possible and speaks no less for Ephesus than for Rome. Perhaps one may also explain from that perspective why the common ἀσπασμός is not, as one would expect, in the first person singular but in the second person plural. A letter of recommendation could be sent either to a group or to an individual who would then pass on the greetings. The hypothetical character of these considerations is explicitly stressed. But one does not find oneself in a more favorable position with another view.

Like 1 Thess 5:26; 1 Cor 16:20; 2 Cor 13:12 and, with a slight modification, 1 Pet 5:14, v. 16 enjoins a brotherly kiss as a declaration of Christian fellowship. This is in keeping with the practice of antiquity on many occasions. Found sometimes in letters, it expresses a partly affectionate and partly solemn greeting (Thraede, *RAC*, VIII, 505ff.). These parallels, however, do not explain the expression "holy kiss," which stresses the witness of the mutual relationship in the realm of the eschatological fellowship of the saints.

415

Judged from the standpoint of the history of religions, it involves a mutual and general impartation of blessing as happens in another way in the laying on of hands at the healing of the sick or at ordination (not sufficiently noted by Thraede). Seen from such a perspective, it is no surprise that the injunction is found in the NT in the context of liturgical formulae (Hofmann, *Philema*, 4-17; Michel). At least in 1 Cor 16:20 it happens in the preparation for the eucharist (Hofmann, *Philema*, 24f.; Windisch, *TDNT*, I, 500f.; Stählin, *TDNT*, IX, 139; contested by Thraede, *RAC*, VIII, 508ff.). Thus the liturgical practice witnessed by Justin in *Apol.* i.65.2 is already presupposed by Paul, whereby it can remain open whether it is exclusively tied to the celebration of the eucharist.

From this perspective v. 16b is more understandable. Its relocation after v. 21 in Western MSS is an obvious emendation. People have wanted to find here the clear proof that the chapter is addressed to Rome, for only in relation to the capital can one understand the emphatic greeting from all the Christian churches (Holl, "Kirchenbegriff," 47; Kümmel, *Introduction,* 320). The force of this argument is not easily turned aside. On the other hand, it is not to be overlooked that v. 4 mentions in a similar way all the Gentile-Christian churches, and that without question presents an exaggeration. The apostle can claim to be speaking in the name of Christianity as a whole (Schumacher, *Letzte Kapitel,* 53f., 96), especially as he has delegates from the churches with him according to vv. 21ff. (Dodd). If, however, v. 16b goes with v. 16a, and if this connection is regarded as intentional, since in fact the sentence would follow better after v. 21, one might find in it the more specific idea that the holy kiss demonstrates the fellowship of all Christianity. In asking for this Paul can also greet the community in the name of this Christianity.

C. Apostolic Warning Against False Teachers and Blessing (16:17-20)

[4

17I admonish you, brethren, to take note of those who cause dissensions and difficulties contrary to the doctrine which you have learned. Avoid them. 18For such people do not serve our Lord Jesus Christ but their own bellies, and by dazzling and attractive words they deceive the hearts of the simple. 19The report of your obedience has come to all. I can thus rejoice over you. I want you to be wise as to what is good and to have no contact with what is evil. 20The God of peace will soon crush Satan under your feet. The grace of our Lord Jesus be with you.

Bibliography: W. Schmithals, "The False Teachers of Romans 16:17-20," *Paul and the Gnostics* (1972) 219-238; A. Strobel, *Untersuchungen zum eschatologischen Verzögerungsproblem, auf Grund der spätjüdisch-urchristlichen Geschichte von Habakuk 2,* 2ff. (NovTSup 2; 1961). See also the bibliographies for 15:22-29 (Georgi, *Kollekte*), 16:1-2 (Donfried, "Note"; Erbes, "Zeit"), and 16:3-16 (Feine, *Abfassung*; McDonald, "Letter").

This warning abruptly separates the greetings in vv. 3-16 and those in vv. 21-23, especially since there is nothing in the context or in the preceding epistle to explain its sharpness (J. Knox). Various attempts have been made to solve the problem (Schumacher, *Letzte Kapitel*, 55f.). The most extreme is the suggestion that a later fragment has been added here (Erbes, "Zeit," 146). More moderate is the assumption of a digression (Zahn), for which Paul's temperament is made responsible (Lietzmann; Schumacher, *Letzte Kapitel*, 56). The idea that the act of worship mentioned in v. 16 would be followed by an official warning in an equally cultic framework (Michel) is neither demonstrable nor probable. No more satisfactory is the suggestion that Paul is now speaking pastorally (Dodd) or that he is simply giving a vague preventative warning (Huby). The community obviously faces an acute danger and this relates, not to the controversies of chs. 14f. (*contra* Lietzmann; Minear, *Obedience*, 28f.; Donfried, "Note," 449), but to false teachers arriving from outside.

σκοπεῖν, as in Luke 11:35; Gal 6:1, means the taking note which is required in temptation. In the immediate context διχοστασίαι καὶ σκάνδαλα are more than group conflicts about suitable conduct or divergent theological opinions. They denote the rending of the community on the basis of seduction into heresy (Stählin, *Skandalon*, 184f.; Schlier, *TDNT*, I, 514; Fuchs, *TDNT*, VII, 415; Schmithals, "False Teachers," 220f.). While it may be true that Paul follows a fixed pattern in introducing the warning, it cannot be agreed (*contra* Bjerkelund, *Parakalô*, 160, 167) that the warning itself is "urbane." According to the tenor of the section the verb has almost the sense "I adjure." A reminiscence of 6:17 is rightly seen in the conclusion of the infinitive clause (Lietzmann; Fuchs, *TDNT*, VII, 415). This implies that there is no gloss. Anxious demarcation from the "concept of doctrine" in the Pastorals (Stählin, *Skandalon*, 185) is without justification. The apostle speaks of the faith which is believed and which is imparted and received in the form of fixed tradition of which important parts may be found in 1 Cor 11:23; 15:1. This can and must be learned. There are opponents who are trying to replace this tradition by another one. To that extent Paul furnished the impulse to the fact that the Pastorals can speak of "sound doctrine" and appeal to it. As noted earlier, the gospel is more than the kerygma. It is the norm of this and from this angle it becomes doctrine (Rengstorf, *TDNT*, IV, 412f.; Schmithals, "False Teachers," 228ff.).

The apostle orders avoidance of false teachers. In keeping with his polemical style the opponents remain anonymous but are scornfully designated as οἱ τοιοῦτοι (Michel). It is hard, then, for us to gain a clear picture of them. They must have been Christians since otherwise the antithesis in v. 18a would be meaningless (Schmithals, "False Teachers," 221, 230). For this reason earlier commentators, following F. C. Baur's historical depiction, thought of Judaizers. Since the context does not support this in the least, the problem nowadays is mostly left undiscussed or undecided. Yet there are unmistakable parallels to Phil 3:18f. and 2 Cor 11:13ff.

2 Cor 11:13ff. unmasks Jewish-Christian agitators as servants of Satan who use the deceitful methods of their master to lead the community astray. Phil 3:18f. speaks of the enemies of the cross of Christ whose god is their belly (cf. on this Arbesmann, *RAC*, XI, 356ff.). κοιλία represents thereby the essence of the σάρξ in its most extreme fallenness to the world to the point of the libertinistic excess scourged in 1 Cor 6:12ff. Decisive is the religious camouflage and the deception which this involves.

It would be too bold to try to explain the use of the *hapax legomenon* χρηστο-λογία in terms of a play on the word χριστολογία (Stählin, *Skandalon,* 186; cf. Black). Tautologically it forms a hendiadys with the secular word εὐλογία, which is used here in a bad sense: speech which is engaging but untrue (BAGD, 322b; Schmithals, "False Teachers," 232f.). ἄκακοι means the "unsuspecting" (BAGD, 29b) who are deceived in their hearts, i.e., at the innermost level. This reminds us of the polemic in 1 Cor 2:1ff.; 2 Cor 10:10f., in terms of which one can understand also the adoption of the catchword σοφοί in v. 19 (Schmithals, "False Teachers," 234f.).

The conclusion is natural that we have here an early battle against heresy which, as in 2 Corinthians 10–13 and Philippians 3, is directed against libertinizing and gnosticizing Jewish-Christians (Schmithals, "False Teachers," 222ff., 236f.; with reservations Kümmel, *Introduction,* 319). *As. Mos.* 7:4-7 is often adduced as a parallel (Lagrange; Michel). But the text fits in only with difficulty, and it lays the main stress on the exploitation of poor believers by sinful gluttons.

Verse 19a states that the community addressed is still intact. Hence Paul can rejoice in it. If its faith is characterized here simply as ὑπακοή, this means subjection to the received doctrine, which corresponds again to 6:17. The fact that this is generally known repeats the motif of 1:8, but it need not be more than a common Pauline compliment, although it raises again the question of the relationship of the chapter to the Epistle to the Romans. The enemy has not yet entered the community but is at the doors. Preparing for his attack, the apostle offers the solution. They are to be wise as to that which is good, under which salvation is to be understood, as in 8:28; 14:16 (H. W. Schmidt). The call for renewed reason in 12:2 is thereby taken up. It implies that one should not have dealings with evil. Whether there is in ἀκέραιος an echo of the dominical saying at Matt 10:16b is hard to determine, but it is not self-evident in view of Phil 2:15. The θέλω placed at the beginning has an authoritative ring.

The section ends dramatically in v. 20 with a promise which is both a prayer and a variation on a curse. In this regard one may (like Deissmann, *Light,* 421) cite ancient vengeance prayers or (like Jülicher; Lagrange; Michel) refer to the anathema of 1 Cor 16:22. Neither suffices, and to see a mere allusion to Gen 3:15 is much too harmless (*contra* Bertram, *TDNT,* VII, 924), as it is also to take from ἐν τάχει a comforting assurance that the specter will soon pass (Lagrange; Lietzmann; Schmithals, "False Teachers," 235). Gen 3:15 may have been the starting point for a mythical conception in which the serpent was identified with Satan (Foerster, *TDNT,* V, 581). It leads to a stream of apocalyptic tradition which emphasizes the imminence of the parousia (Strobel, *Verzögerungsproblem,* 181, 185) and which is represented in the promises of *Jub.* 23:29; *T. Levi* 18:11f.; *T. Sim.* 6:6; *As. Mos.* 10:1 and the imprecation in the 12th benediction of the [46 *Sheʿmone Esre* (Michel; Leenhardt; H. W. Schmidt). Prophecy is uttered here. If God is designated as the one who brings peace, this does not mean personal salvation as his gift but the defeat of Satan after the cosmic battle and the definitive eschatological liberation of the earth (Foerster, *TDNT,* II, 414).

God is the victor who destroys Satan as the dragon of the end-time. He does it, however, in such a way that the community shares in his triumph. According to the ancient gesture, as the host of victors it will set its feet on the vanquished and trample him, thus seizing eschatological power (Weiss, *TDNT,* VI, 629). Since the parousia is directly at hand, this will take place very soon. If one accepts this interpretation, the chapter cannot possibly be understood merely in terms of the greetings or be said to be without material content.

The chapter, to be sure, should then be separated from the preceding epistle (J. Knox, 365f.; Schmithals, "False Teachers," 236f.; Friedrich, *RGG,* V, 1138). The apostle is speaking here with an authority which he does sometimes indicate in relation to the Romans but which for the most part he carefully avoids. He does it with a kind of fury which does not appear elsewhere in the epistle and in answer to opponents who cannot be identified from the letter. The situation and the reaction are completely different, and the interest of 15:14-32 is lost from view. The hypothesis of a small independent letter to Ephesus has much in its favor (Feine, *Abfassung;* Michaelis, *Introduction,* 160ff.; Bornkamm, *Paul,* 247; Georgi, *Kollekte,* 79f.; though cf. J. Knox) and in a letter of recommendation (*contra* Lietzmann; Kümmel, *Introduction,* 319f.) one would not expect larger theological statements (McDonald, "Letter," 372). The problem of the typical concluding blessing will be dealt with after v. 23.

D. Greetings from the Apostle's Fellow-Workers (16:21-23)

[21]*My fellow-worker Timothy and my fellow-countrymen Lucius, Jason, and Sosipater greet you.* [22]*I Tertius, the writer of the letter, greet you in the Lord.* [23]*Gaius, who is host to me and to the whole church, greets you. The city treasurer Erastus and Quartus, a brother, greet you.*

Bibliography: G. J. Bahr, "The Subscriptions in the Pauline Letters," *JBL* 87 (1968) 27-41; H. J. Cadbury, "Erastus of Corinth," *JBL* 50 (1931) 42-58. See also the bibliographies for 15:22-29 (Bartsch, "Situation"; Georgi, *Kollekte*) and 16:1-2 (Erbes, "Zeit"; Michaelis, "Kenchreä").

If it is surprising that Paul broke off his greetings for a wild polemic in v. 17, it is no less so that he now returns to them on behalf of those with whom he is associated for the moment. This can be found "quite natural" only if vv. 17-20 are ascribed to an "entirely sudden impulse" which takes control of the writer's pen "for a couple of impressive sentences" and breaks through the restraint exercised up to that point (*contra* Lietzmann). Apart from the dubious psychology of this, which is in any case only the interpreter's last way of escaping a difficulty, the category of postscripts does justice to the problem of the chapter neither as a whole nor in detail. If vv. 17-20 are a postscript, the apostle simply develops theological theories in the epistle and does not speak to the specific situation of the community. Does the one who places 15 chapters under a fixed theme and logically develops it lose his breath at the end so that it now comes to a confused jumble of ideas which displace one another and avoid any order?

This question is all the more necessary since the present verses, coming after the blessing in v. 20, do in fact constitute a postscript, the greeting of Tertius breaks the connection between vv. 21 and 23, and the most important of Paul's writings is brought here to a very feeble conclusion. Only at the price of an arbitrary hypothesis does one partially evade these problems by putting vv. 21-23 after 15:33 (Georgi, *Kollekte*, 81; possible Bartsch, "Situation," 282).

Even less illuminating is the view that the chapter is a "spiritual" and typically Pauline extension of the ἔρρωσο which usually ends the ancient letter, with which greetings and postscripts were also connected (Roller, *Formular*, 70, 193ff.), and that the disorder is the secretary's fault (cf. also Bahr, "Subscriptions," 39). For in this case the recommendation of Phoebe loses its importance, the material difference between vv. 17-20 and the rest of the epistle is not perceived, and one is not disturbed by the fact that the concluding blessings in 15:33 and 16:20 clash no less than those in 16:20 and 16:24.

The epistle reached its goal with 15:33. No one would miss anything if there were no ch. 16. Why is it taken as settled that Paul could not have sent a short letter to Ephesus? At this point, obviously, a subjective judgment is unavoidable. The battle of opinions can never be ended. In a letter of recommendation there would be room for greetings to many acquaintances in a familiar community and also for an urgent warning to be expressed against threatened heresy. Paul's fellow-workers and the Corinthian Christians would also have contact with a church such as that at Ephesus, so that their greetings could be added after the blessing in v. 20. The ostensible disorder is most easily solved in this way, whereas it is intolerable at the end of the Roman epistle.

At least 2 Corinthians and Philippians prove that a compilation was made of Paul's epistles. It is ungenerous to sweep away the problems of the commentator by asking him to prove historically the fact that and the circumstances under which two different letters could be united (*contra* Lietzmann; Schumacher, *Letzte Kapitel*, 102f.; *et al.*). This is especially so when the undeniable problems can otherwise be mastered only with the help of psychological constructions. On the other hand, no one can contest the right of such a question. Since it in fact cannot be answered, one would only too gladly connect ch. 16 with the epistle if the hindrance of vv. 17-20 for the interpreter could be overcome.

If things are as we have supposed, it is highly questionable whether the persons mentioned now have anything to do with the collection (*contra* Erbes, "Zeit," 206f.; Schumacher, *Letzte Kapitel*, 100; Georgi, *Kollekte*, 20). Timothy as a constant companion and delegate of the apostle has a matchless claim to the predicate ὁ συνεργός μου. The three who follow are specifically said to be Jewish-Christians. Hence they can hardly be representatives of Gentile Christianity, and they alone might be considered as men who accompanied Paul with the collection. We know nothing at all of Lucius, who has been identified with Luke from the time of Origen. It is quite doubtful whether Jason is to be identified with the Jason mentioned in Acts 17:5ff., while Sosipater may be identical with the Sopator of Acts 20:4 (Lietzmann).

The only mention of Tertius is here. The use of a secretary even for private letters is common (Roller, *Formular*, 14ff.; Billerbeck) and is indirectly attested in Paul's case at 1 Cor 16:21; Gal 6:11. Oddly the secretary, too, sends greetings to the church (Windisch, *TDNT*, I, 501). This makes sense only if he is known to

[4

the recipients (Zahn; Lagrange; Schumacher, *Letzte Kapitel*, 102). The thesis that the chapter is addressed to Rome does not gain in probability as a result. Logically this greeting would originally come last. In this case v. 23 is another postscript in which the residents of Corinth send their greetings. For there is no reason to suppose that Gaius is either the Gaius of Macedonia of Acts 19:29 or the Gaius of Derbe of Acts 20:4 (*contra* Zahn; Michaelis, "Kenchreä," 145) if v. 1 and the context support the conclusion that the Gaius who is the apostle's host is the Gaius of Corinth mentioned in 1 Cor 1:14 (the majority view). Since he was one of the first to be converted at Corinth, many found their way to him. ὅλη ἡ ἐκκλησία has to mean the universal church, not the local congregation (Lagrange; Lietzmann), since it involves hospitality, and not providing a place for assembly.

Residence in Corinth also lets Erastus be distinguished from those who bear the same name in Acts 19:22 and 2 Tim 4:20. ὁ οἰκονόμος τῆς πόλεως is a common title for persons charged with the city accounts. Sometimes a slave could hold this not very lofty position (Cadbury, "Erastus," 49f.; BAGD, 560a). The brother Quartus is completely unknown.

Particularly readings which put the final doxology after 14:23 have v. 24. Formulated after 2 Thess 3:18, this either repeats or replaces the blessing in v. 20. Thus it is undoubtedly secondary. It was found to be a difficulty that the greetings should form the conclusion, and an attempt was thus made to achieve a materially correct order. This shows that the problem of the chapter was already perceived at an early date.

E. Inauthentic Concluding Doxology (16:25-27)

[25]Now to him who can strengthen you according to my gospel and the preaching of Jesus Christ, according to the revelation of the mystery which was kept hidden for eternal ages, [26]but is now disclosed by the prophetic writings and on the commission of the eternal God is made known to all nations, to bring about the obedience of faith—[27]to the only wise God (is due) through Jesus Christ glory for evermore. Amen.

Bibliography: W. Bartsch, "Die historische Situation des Römerbriefes," *SE*, IV (1968) 281-291; P. Corssen, "Zur Überlieferungsgeschichte des Römerbriefes," *ZNW* 10 (1909) 1-45; G. Delling, "ΜΟΝΟΣ ΘΕΟΣ," *TLZ* 77 (1952) 469-476; L. M. Dewailly, "Mystère et silence dans Rom. xvi. 25," *NTS* 14 (1967/68) 111-18; J. Dupont, "Pour l'histoire de la doxologie finale de l'épître aux Romains," *Revue Bénédictine* 63 (1948) 3-22; idem, "ΜΟΝΩΙ ΘΕΩΙ (Rom 16:27)," *ETL* 22 (1946) 362-375; K. Goldammer, "Der Kerygma-Begriff in der ältesten christlichen Literatur," *ZNW* 48 (1957) 77-101; E. Kamlah, *Traditionsgeschichtliche Untersuchungen zur Schlussdoxologie des Römerbriefes* (diss., Tübingen; 1955); J. Knox, "A Note on the Text of Romans," *NTS* 2 (1955/56) 191-93; E. Lohmeyer, *"Our Father." An Introduction to the Lord's Prayer* (Eng. tr. 1966; British ed. *The Lord's Prayer*, 1965); D. Lührmann, *Das Offenbarungsverständnis bei Paulus und in paulinischen Gemeinden* (WMANT 16; 1965); T. W. Manson, "St. Paul's Letter to the Romans—and Others," *Studies*, 225-241 (= *Romans Debate*, 1-16); W. Manson, "Notes on the Argument of Romans (Chapters

1-8)," *NT Essays, Manson,* 150-164; L. Mowry, "The Early Circulation of Paul's Letters," *JBL* 63 (1944) 73-86; W. Schmithals, "On the Composition and Earliest Collection of the Major Epistles of Paul," *Paul and the Gnostics* (1972) 239-274.

Our analysis suggests an editing of the epistle which manifests itself in the adding [4 of ch. 16. This also raises the problem of the authenticity, purpose, and original position of the final doxology, as the history of the text makes plain. The complex of questions can in itself and as a whole be left to NT introductions (cf. Lietzmann and Kümmel, *Introduction,* 314ff. for short surveys). Our interpretation, however, needs to be differentiated from a number of hypotheses which have been put forward.

That 16:25ff. cannot originally have torn the connection between 14:23 and 15:1-13 is evident. This version presupposes the Old Latin in which 15:1–16:23 is left out, and the epistle thus loses both the climax of the special exhortation in 15:1-13 and its concrete occasion, marked by 15:14ff. In this case the doxology is a solemn but arbitrary and undoubtedly secondary ending to the letter.

If its position became a difficulty for later copyists, the difficulty could be manifested either by leaving it out entirely as in F G etc. or by putting it after 14:23 as in A P etc., and repeating it after 16:23. An elegant solution is that of P⁴⁶, which recognizes the problem but eliminates it by placing the doxology with some material relevance after ch. 15 and treating 16:1-23 as a postscript. A genuine alternative, however, is posed only by the question whether the doxology came originally after 14:23 or 16:23, i.e., whether it was from the first linked to a shortening of the epistle or whether it was thereby moved forward. A decision on this matter depends on our understanding of the contents.

In any case one is to reject the view, presented in variations, that the epistle was originally written as a definite teaching for several churches and that with a personal postscript it could then be sent to each one in particular (Kamlah, "Untersuchungen," 2, who says that this view was already held by E. Renan, *St. Paul* [1869] 63ff.). The abbreviation of the letter came about by a later intervention in the text. The same thesis is still held today in the form that ch. 16 is an accompanying letter by means of which Romans was brought to the attention of the church in Ephesus (cf. Mowry, "Circulation," 73ff.; J. Knox, "Note," 191f.; T. W. Manson, *Studies,* 237ff. [= *Romans Debate,* 12ff.]; W. Manson, "Notes," 151f.; Best; Bruce). Even if ch. 16 is regarded as a short letter to Ephesus, Phoebe is not called the carrier of the main epistle, not to speak of a further journey to Rome as a product of the imagination. Materially it is incomprehensible why only Ephesus should be informed apart from Rome, and in the circumstances one cannot understand why Paul, who was in a hurry, should agree to a detour of this kind. It is plain from 15:14ff. that only Christians in Rome are being addressed there.

The only purpose of the thesis is in fact to explain how an independent ch. 16 came to be connected with the Epistle to the Romans. If the solution cannot be sustained and is probably even unacceptable, it confronts us at least with the problem of the rise of the Pauline corpus, at the beginning of which one must assume that various epistles were compiled and combined. Even here at the beginnings, of course, we do not get beyond vague and very questionable conjectures if, for example, Ephesus (the scholars mentioned above) or Corinth (Schmithals, "Composition," 263, 266) is named as the place of collection in the earliest stages, and therefore of the uniting of ch. 16 with the Epistle to the Romans.

This perspective, however, has the value of putting sharply the question of the purpose of the concluding doxology. Both in its position and in its many motifs this is unique in the genuine Pauline epistles, and if the independence of ch. 16 is maintained, it cannot be integrated with a small writing but can only be ascribed to the process of its combination with Romans. This means that it is not Pauline (*contra* Sanday and Headlam; Zahn; Lagrange; Sickenberger; Schumacher, *Letzte Kapitel*, 105ff.; Murray, Excursus, 262ff.; Minear, *Obedience*, 30ff.; possible Michaelis, *Einleitung*, 163; criticism from the early years of the last century, especially in F. C. Baur, *Paul*, 369f., 379ff.; cf. the survey in Kamlah, "Untersuchungen," 1ff.; Dupont, "Doxologie," 3ff.). We can leave out of consideration here the question whether it formed the conclusion of a first Pauline corpus (Schmithals, "Composition," 258f.; Bartsch, "Situation," 282). It is not improbable that it is connected with the elimination of the destination in 1:7, 15 and thus presents the "catholic" significance of the epistle as a whole (Corsson, "Überlieferungsgeschichte," 18ff.; Mowry, "Circulation," 78f.; Dupont, "Doxologie," 7f.). Its liturgical *Sitz im Leben* can hardly be disputed (Lietzmann; Jülicher, *Introduction*, 107; Champion, "Benedictions," 123; Michel; H. W. Schmidt; Ridderbos).

As in 11:36b; Gal 1:5; Phil 4:20 the normal form of a doxology is present. The designation of God comes first in the dative, then a nominative of praise, an indication of time, and finally the confirmatory Amen (Lohmeyer, *"Our Father,"* 233f.). As a concluding formula this is first found in Hellenistic Judaism (Deichgräber, *Gotteshymnus*, 39). The taking up of the predication of God by ᾧ, which is undoubtedly original (Lietzmann *contra* Zahn; BDF, §467) but which a few textual variants omit for simplification, makes the whole an anacoluthon. The offense this might cause is mitigated when one recognizes that from a literary point of view the relative clause in v. 27 uses the schema of the community's response in worship, so that the relative has the sense of a demonstrative (Kamlah, "Untersuchungen," 72, 86).

Verse 25a offers the divine predication in the traditional paraphrase through a participle with a dependent infinitive and is introduced by τῷ δυναμένῳ (cf. Eph 3:20; Jude 24f.). The nature of God is not abstractly characterized by his attributes but by the miraculous power which creates and maintains eschatological salvation (Kamlah, "Untersuchungen," 80ff.). In relation to the present community this manifests itself in στηρίζειν, which already belongs to the NT vocabulary of edification and which means preservation in the trials of the end-time (ibid., 33f.). With vv. 25a and 27 we have the schema of the original doxology, which in this text forms the framework for quite unusual extensions, but from which precisely for that reason one must proceed as the foundation (ibid., 77).

δέ at the beginning has both an introductory and a summary sense, as in Phil 4:19f.; Heb 13:20; 1 Pet 5:10. εἰς τοὺς αἰῶνας τῶν αἰώνων takes up plerophorically a former acclamation εἰς τοὺς αἰῶνας, and modifies it doxologically. As 4 Macc

18:24 shows, it stems from Greek Judaism and makes it clear that eternity is viewed here as the course of endless times. Elimination of the genitive in P[46] B C L is secondary. The statement is probably to be supplemented indicatively rather than optatively (H. W. Beyer, *TDNT,* II, 80; Kittel, *TDNT,* II, 248; Kamlah, "Untersuchungen," 86f.). Even in the latter case, however, it simply confirms what God has and what is due him (Deichgräber, *Gotteshymnus,* 32; Stuiber, *RAC,* IV, 215). The underlying schema has been christianized by the addition of διὰ 'Ιησοῦ Χριστοῦ. The not very felicitous placing of this has been ascribed to the carelessness of Tertius (Sanday and Headlam). Materially at any rate it does not go with the preceding divine predication, where it would be meaningless, but is an emphatic anticipation of what follows (Kamlah, "Untersuchungen," 84f.; uncertain Stuiber, *RAC,* IV, 214).

The fundamental dividing of the rest of the text into Pauline phrases and a hymn about the divine mystery (Kamlah's thesis) cannot be sustained, for the two flow into one another in vv. 25b-26. But it draws attention to a fact which must be the methodological starting point for the interpretation. The author is concerned to set forth the significance of Paul's apostolate, and he connects this interest with another, namely, to characterize the apostle's gospel as a mystery by adopting a traditional revelation schema which is in fact profiled in liturgical pieces. The whole is clearly structured, to the extent that three prepositional phrases depend on the introductory infinitive and the central concept which follows is defined by three participial statements before the solemn divine predication in v. 27a discloses to whom the doxology is ascribed. From the time of Origen the addition "and by the epiphany of our Lord Jesus Christ" has been attested in v. 26. This serves both interpretive and dogmatic purposes. It is unquestionably secondary (*contra* Zahn) and could be derived from 2 Tim 1:10.

κατά indicates, not the means (Schlatter) but the norm. Only in accordance with this does genuine Christian strengthening take place. An indirect polemic against false teachers is imaginable but unnecessary. The formula "according to my gospel" occurs already in 2:16. In neither case is the gospel restricted to the apostle's message. But here there is a greater concern to show that this message is a legitimate expression of the gospel. The two are indissolubly connected (Molland, *Euangelion,* 95f.). This gives the apostle his authority (Kamlah, "Untersuchungen," 42f.) and establishes that one can neither ignore his proclamation nor get behind it (Roloff, *Apostolat,* 93).

It is probably in this light that we are to understand the remarkable combination with "the kerygma of Jesus Christ." It is very tempting to take this to mean that Christ is the author of the gospel (Molland, *Euangelion,* 100) and that he is so already as the earthly Jesus (Schniewind, Friedrich, *TDNT,* II, 730; Friedrich, *TDNT,* III, 716; Zahn; Schlatter; H. W. Schmidt; Goldammer, "Kerygma-Begriff," 82; cf. the survey in Kamlah, "Untersuchungen," 61f.). In this case, according to this passage, the apostolic tradition would continue that of Jesus. If the doxology is dated late, such an interpretation is not impossible. On the basis of 10:17 one might defend a genitive of agent in such a way that the exalted Christ gives effect to the apostolic gospel. Against this interpretation, however, is the fact that the kerygma at least primarily means preaching activity (Goldammer, "Kerygma-Begriff," 80ff.) and the related genitive has to be an objective genitive. This also fits the context better, for then the specific Pauline gospel is adjoined to every genuine message of Christ. καί is explicative (Schumacher, *Letzte Kapitel*, 106f.; Kamlah, "Untersuchungen," 62).

Here at least it is apparent that (*contra* Goldammer's basic thesis with some reservations regarding the present text) κήρυγμα as a process relates to a specific content and only the accent shifts from one thing to another (Kamlah, "Untersuchungen," 63; Friedrich, *TDNT*, III, 716). The prepositional phrase in v. 25c defines this content more narrowly, and it does this with such fulness that the true theme of the doxology is already disclosed. The mode of expression seems at a first glance to be thoroughly Pauline. As 1:17; Gal 1:16 trace back the reception of the message of salvation in verb form to the divine ἀποκάλυψις (revelation), Gal 1:12 does the same in noun form. But the nearest parallel is Eph 3:3ff., and this raises already the question whether the statement is still meant apocalyptically here or does not simply designate the divine *revelatio*. This question is made more acute by the genitive which follows.

According to 1 Cor 4:1 Paul understood himself as the steward of the divine mysteries and, as 11:25ff. shows, his gospel climaxes in the preaching of a mystery. Apart from the disputed passage 1 Cor 2:1, however, Paul himself never specifically calls the gospel as such the mystery, as happens in the deutero-Pauline epistles. For Paul, according to 2 Cor 4:3f., the gospel is hidden only to unbelievers, and this is due to demonic blinding. Unlike 11:25, the present text does not speak of the event of salvation but the counsel of salvation, as is characteristic of Jewish apocalyptic (Bornkamm, *TDNT*, IV, 816) and especially Qumran (Kamlah, "Untersuchungen," 112ff.; Michel; Braun, *Qumran*, I, 187f.). This is adopted in Col 1:26f.; Eph 1:9; 3:3f., 9.

Of this mystery it is said, in the familiar antithesis of "then" and "now," that it was wrapped in silence for eternal times but has now been made known by the prophetic Scriptures. Obviously this is a somewhat individual modification of the schema of revelation which, easily changed according to the context, opposes past concealment to present disclosure in 1 Cor 2:7ff.; Col 1:26f.; Eph 3:5, 9f.; 2 Tim 1:9f.; Tit 1:2f.; 1 Pet 1:20 (Kamlah, "Untersuchungen," 89ff.). This schema is, of course, transcended by the use of a different vocabulary in the first member.

The motif of concealment lasting for many aeons is a set part of the tradition (cf. Col 1:26; Eph 3:9), and the combination χρόνοις αἰωνίοις, which seems to be absurd to us (Sasse, *TDNT*, I, 199) but which precisely reflects the Semitic concept of eternity, has the same meaning. But it stresses more sharply the temporal aspect under which it is related to election in 2 Tim 1:9 and the promise in Tit 1:2. Yet the expression and the approach are unique in the NT inasmuch as the reference is not to the hiddenness of the mystery but the silence which enwraps it in the past. The edifying observation that God's mystery is never wholly unveiled (Schumacher, *Letzte Kapitel*, 109) is of as little use as the reference to the fact that in Jewish apocalyptic, e.g., 4 Ezra 14:26, a distinction is made between doctrines which are already to be proclaimed and those which are still to be kept secret (Kamlah, "Untersuchungen," 109ff.). More important are 4 Ezra 6:38f.; 7:30; *2 Apoc. Bar.* 3:7 to the extent that they refer to the original silence before creation. Out of this there can develop the kind of speculation we have in the present verse. Whether Wis 18:14 takes a further step in this direction, indicating a tradition transposed from protology into eschatology, is doubtful (*contra* Kamlah, "Untersuchungen," 123). Our text is not talking of the divine word which leaps into the silence of the world but of the word which follows the divine silence, but even then remains a mystery (Dewailly, "Mystère," 115ff.). The closest parallels are in Ign. *Magn.* 8:2; *Eph.* 19:1, although there the speculation already goes beyond the original revelation schema with its antithesis indicating the change of aeons. It is not surprising that in this light the beginnings of Gnostic σιγή speculation have been found in our text (Corssen, "Überlieferungsgeschichte," 32ff.; Lührmann, *Offenbarungsverständnis*, 122ff.). The direction which this takes is at least shown here.

In contrast v. 26a speaks of present salvation. It is, of course, to be asked whether νῦν and φανεϱοῦν have a strict eschatological character as in 3:21 or whether they already weaken this along the lines of salvation history. For, emphasized by τε, revelation through the prophetic writings is what stands in antithesis here to the silence in eternal times. This phrase also causes difficulty. That Paul read the OT as prophecy has been shown and needs no support from Qumran parallels. But to what degree does the revelation of the eschatological mystery take place through OT prophecy? One cannot maintain that a reference to 1:2 is to be seen in our phrase, since there unlike here the writings of the prophets present the promise of the gospel. Nor can one assume that the phrase was already contained in a postulated hymn (Kamlah, "Untersuchungen," 28ff., 48f., 124). The supposed hymn in these verses is a product of the imagination. It cannot be justified on the basis of the lofty prose or the use of traditions. Stylistically it would be a monstrosity. Moreover, the material problem is not clarified by adding, without the slightest support in the text, that in apostolic exposition the OT writings are divested of their mystery-character and thus become a means of divine revelation in Christian preaching (Kamlah, "Untersuchungen," 52; Schumacher, *Letzte Kapitel,* 111). Conversely, it seems equally impossible to think in terms of NT prophecy (*contra* Jülicher; Lührmann, *Offenbarungsverständnis*, 123f.), appealing in support to Eph 3:5. There the apostles precede the prophets, and the point in our verses would be to make the apostolic message the means of present revelation.

The problem is to be approached in terms of the antithesis between silence in the past and the existence of revelatory Scriptures in the present. It can be cleared up if one presupposes the typically Greek concept of prophecy, which designates the proclamation in the name of a god (cf. Fascher, Προφήτης, 52f.). On this view writings are prophetic when they bring revelation. The doxology is composed in a community which, like that of 2 Pet 3:16, already has a collection of writings accepted as canonical, and which finds revelation only in these writings. Whether and how far the OT belongs to the collection must remain open. Unless they were Marcionites, we cannot rule out the possibility in principle. The Pauline epistles must have been included, and possibly the gospels too. The central point is that "prophetic" here is to be understood as synonymous with "bearing witness to revelation." Paul, of course, does not himself stand as a sponsor for this view. But there is a further reminiscence of him in v. 26b.

In the first instance, however, one must consider that we meet new difficulties here. The revelation schema is characterized by a temporal and material antithesis. For the surplus third member there is fundamentally neither necessity nor place. The indication of time is thus replaced by the formulated definition of circumstance κατ᾽ ἐπιταγήν ("by the command") (BAGD, 302a) which occurs already in 1 Cor 7:6; 2 Cor 8:8 and then again in 1 Tim 1:1; Tit 1:3. γνωρίζειν does, of course, occur in the traditional schema at Eph 1:9; 3:3ff., 10; Col 1:27, but in general it is synonymous with φανεροῦν, so that the thought seems to be intensified only by the prepositional phrase, which expresses the universal significance of the mystery, obviously in allusion to 1:5 (Kamlah, "Untersuchungen," 53). "Obedience of faith" is to be taken here as an objective genitive. τὰ ἔθνη means the nations. The final goal of the mystery is to bring the world under subjection to Christian teaching. This takes up a motif which comes out most strongly in lines 4-5 of the hymn in 1 Tim 3:16 (Norden, *Agnostos Theos*, 255, 5) and which there designates Christ's entry upon cosmic dominion, which, proclaimed on earth, has universal submission in faith as its result.

If this interpretation is correct, it is clear that in this part of the verse another revelation schema both combines and clashes with the preceding one. The emphasis falls now, not on the disclosure of the mystery in the scriptural canon available to the community, but on the universal proclamation, and γνωρίζεσθαι means precisely this proclamation which cannot be evaded, so that it is not as otherwise synonymous with φανεροῦσθαι (cf. Bultmann, *TDNT*, I, 718). The phrase is obviously modelled after Paul (Bultmann, *TDNT*, VI, 206).

The predications of God, which are taken from Hellenistic Judaism, are in keeping with this. αἰώνιος θεός occurs only here in the NT. It is designed to underscore the lasting and universal claim and authority of the divine ἐπιταγή. μόνος σοφὸς θεός is stereotypical in Philo (Kamlah, "Untersuchungen," 83f.). Naturally there is not expressed in it a philosophical concept of God (cf. Dupont, "Doxologie") but an OT-Jewish confession which was taken over by primitive Christianity, as in 3:30 (Delling, "ΜΟΝΟΣ ΘΕΟΣ," 474ff.). Yet one should no longer assign our verse to the liturgy (*contra* Delling, 476). The liturgical doxology is put to literary use and refashioned to give the epistle a suitable close. Different traditions are combined for the purpose, although it is not possible to discern even the core of a hymn. The description of God as "only wise" both characterizes the general thrust and defines the place of the strongly Hellenized concept of the divine mystery (cf. Lührmann, *Offenbarungsverständnis*, 126). God's wisdom sets the times under the saving counsel which is planned by it, which is already fixed in a canon, and which is made known universally by apostolic proclamation. The epistle documents this.

Whereas the excision of chs. 15–16 is attested by Marcion, the content of the doxology itself in the phrase about the divine silence does not necessarily speak for a Marcionite origin. This means that it must ultimately remain open whether a possibly Marcionite doxology was accepted by the church and put at the end of ch. 16 or whether a church composition was put by Marcionites at the end of ch. 14. In any case it cannot be ascribed to Paul himself. At most its central theme is close to ideas which are adopted and worked out in Colossians, Ephesians, and 1 Tim 3:16. But it goes beyond this stage with its speculation concerning the

427

divine silence. It is highly questionable to assert a connection with the Pastorals (*contra* Kamlah, "Untersuchungen," 128ff.), whose dating, too, is uncertain. We have to be satisfied to think in terms of a community at the beginning of the second century which was under Pauline influence. Even a later date cannot be ruled out. A stage is marked hereby in the process of collecting Paul's epistles.